STUDENT'S SOLUTIONS MANUAL

DANIEL S. MILLER
Niagara County Community College

THINKING MATHEMATICALLY

SIXTH EDITION

Robert Blitzer
Miami Dade College

PEARSON

Boston Columbus Indianapolis New York San Francisco Upper Saddle River
Amsterdam Cape Town Dubai London Madrid Milan Munich Paris Montreal Toronto
Delhi Mexico City São Paulo Sydney Hong Kong Seoul Singapore Taipei Tokyo

The author and publisher of this book have used their best efforts in preparing this book. These efforts include the development, research, and testing of the theories and programs to determine their effectiveness. The author and publisher make no warranty of any kind, expressed or implied, with regard to these programs or the documentation contained in this book. The author and publisher shall not be liable in any event for incidental or consequential damages in connection with, or arising out of, the furnishing, performance, or use of these programs.

Reproduced by Pearson from electronic files supplied by the author.

Publishing as Pearson, 75 Arlington Street, Boston, MA 02116.

ISBN-13: 978-0-321-86733-9
ISBN-10: 0-321-86733-5

2 3 4 5 6 CRK 17 16 15 14

www.pearsonhighered.com

TABLE OF CONTENTS for STUDENT SOLUTIONS

THINKING MATHEMATICALLY 6E

Chapter 1
Problem Solving and Critical Thinking

Check Points 1.1

1. Counterexamples will vary. Example: $40 \times 40 = 1600$

2. a. Add 6 each time.
$3 + 6 = 9$
$9 + 6 = 15$
$15 + 6 = 21$
$21 + 6 = 27$
$27 + 6 = 33$
3, 9, 15, 21, 27, <u>33</u>

b. Multiply by 5 each time.
$2 \times 5 = 10$
$10 \times 5 = 50$
$50 \times 5 = 250$
$250 \times 5 = 1250$
2, 10, 50, 250, <u>1250</u>

c. Cycle multiplying by 2, 3, 4.
$3 \times 2 = 6$
$6 \times 3 = 18$
$18 \times 4 = 72$
$72 \times 2 = 144$
$144 \times 3 = 432$
$432 \times 4 = 1728$
$1728 \times 2 = 3456$
6, 18, 72, 144, 432, 1728, <u>3456</u>

d. Cycle adding 8, adding 8, subtracting 14.
$1 + 8 = 9$
$9 + 8 = 17$
$17 - 14 = 3$
$3 + 8 = 11$
$11 + 8 = 19$
$19 - 14 = 5$
$5 + 8 = 13$
$13 + 8 = 21$
$21 - 14 = 7$
9, 17, 3, 11, 19, 5, 13, 21, <u>7</u>

3. a. Starting with the third number, each number is the sum of the previous two numbers, $29 + 47 = 76$

b. Starting with the second number, each number one less than twice the previous number, $2(129) - 1 = 257$

4. The shapes alternate between rectangle and triangle.
The number of little legs cycles from 1 to 2 to 3 and then back to 1.
Therefore the next figure will be a rectangle with 2 little legs.

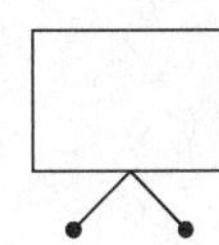

5. a. Conjecture based on results: The original number is doubled.

Select a number.	4	10	0	3
Multiply the number by 4.	$4\times4=16$	$10\times4=40$	$0\times4=0$	$3\times4=12$
Add 6 to the product.	$16+6=22$	$40+6=46$	$0+6=6$	$12+6=18$
Divide this sum by 2.	$22\div2=11$	$46\div2=23$	$6\div2=3$	$18\div2=9$
Subtract 3 from the quotient.	$11-3=8$	$23-3=20$	$3-3=0$	$9-3=6$
Summary of results:	$4 \rightarrow 8$	$10 \rightarrow 20$	$0 \rightarrow 0$	$3 \rightarrow 6$

b. Select a number: n
Multiply the number by 4: $4n$
Add 6 to the product: $4n+6$
Divide this sum by 2: $\frac{4n+6}{2} = \frac{4n}{2} + \frac{6}{2} = 2n+3$
Subtract 3 from the quotient: $2n+3-3=2n$

Concept and Vocabulary Check 1.1

1. counterexample
2. deductive
3. inductive
4. true

Exercise Set 1.1

1. Counterexamples will vary. Example: President Obama was younger than 65 at the time of his inauguration.

3. Counterexamples will vary. Example: 3 multiplied by itself is 9, which is not even.

5. Counterexamples will vary. Example: Adding 1 to the numerator and denominator of $\frac{1}{2}$ results in $\frac{2}{3}$ which is not equal to $\frac{1}{2}$.

7. Counterexamples will vary. Example: When −1 is added to itself, the result is −2, which is less than −1.

9. Pattern: Add 4
   $24 + 4 = 28$
   8, 12, 16, 20, 24, <u>28</u>

11. Pattern: Subtract 5
    $17 - 5 = 12$
    37, 32, 27, 22, 17, <u>12</u>

13. Pattern: Multiply by 3
    $243 \times 3 = 729$
    3, 9, 27, 81, 243, <u>729</u>

15. Pattern: Multiply by 2
    $16 \times 2 = 32$
    1, 2, 4, 8, 16, <u>32</u>

17. Pattern: 1 alternates with numbers that are multiplied by 2
    $16 \times 2 = 32$
    1, 4, 1, 8, 1, 16, 1, <u>32</u>

19. Pattern: Subtract 2
    $-4 - 2 = -6$
    4, 2, 0, −2, −4, <u>−6</u>

21. Pattern: Add 4 to the denominator
    $\frac{1}{18+4} = \frac{1}{22}$
    $\frac{1}{2}, \frac{1}{6}, \frac{1}{10}, \frac{1}{14}, \frac{1}{18}, \underline{\frac{1}{22}}$

23. Pattern: Multiply the denominator by 3
    $\frac{1}{27 \times 3} = \frac{1}{81}$
    $1, \frac{1}{3}, \frac{1}{9}, \frac{1}{27}, \underline{\frac{1}{81}}$

25. Pattern: The second number is obtained by adding 4 to the first number. The third number is obtained by adding 5 to the second number. The number being added to the previous number increases by 1 each time. $33+9=\underline{42}$

27. Pattern: The second number is obtained by adding 3 to the first number. The third number is obtained by adding 5 to the second number. The number being added to the previous number increases by 2 each time. $38+13=\underline{51}$

29. Pattern: Starting with the third number, each number is the sum of the previous two numbers.
    $27+44=\underline{71}$

31. Pattern: Cycle by adding 5, adding 5, then subtracting 7. $13+5=\underline{18}$

33. Pattern: The second number is obtained by multiplying the first number by 2. The third number is obtained by subtracting 1 from the second number. Then multiply by 2 and then subtract 1, repeatedly. $34-1=\underline{33}$

35. Pattern: Divide by −4
    $-1 \div (-4) = \frac{1}{4}$
    $64, -16, 4, -1, \underline{\frac{1}{4}}$

37. Pattern: The second value of each pair is 4 less than the first.
    $3 - 4 = -1$
    $(6,2), (0,-4), (7\frac{1}{2}, 3\frac{1}{2}), (2,-2), (3,\underline{-1})$

39. The figure cycles from square to triangle to circle and then repeats. So the next figure is

41. The pattern is to add one more letter to the previous figure and use the next consecutive letter in the alphabet. The next figure is shown at right.

d	d	d
d	d	

43. a. Conjecture based on results: The original number is doubled.

Select a number.	4	10	0	3
Multiply the number by 4.	$4\times4=16$	$10\times4=40$	$0\times4=0$	$3\times4=12$
Add 8 to the product.	$16+8=24$	$40+8=48$	$0+8=8$	$12+8=20$
Divide this sum by 2.	$24\div2=12$	$48\div2=24$	$8\div2=4$	$20\div2=10$
Subtract 4 from the quotient.	$12-4=8$	$24-4=20$	$4-4=0$	$10-4=6$
Summary of results:	$4\rightarrow8$	$10\rightarrow20$	$0\rightarrow0$	$3\rightarrow6$

b. $4n$

$4n+8$

$$\frac{4n+8}{2}=\frac{4n}{2}+\frac{8}{2}=2n+4$$

$2n+4-4=2n$

45. a. Conjecture based on results: The result is always 3.

Select a number.	4	10	0	3
Add 5 to the number.	$4+5=9$	$10+5=15$	$0+5=5$	$3+5=8$
Double the result.	$9\times2=18$	$15\times2=30$	$5\times2=10$	$8\times2=16$
Subtract 4.	$18-4=14$	$30-4=26$	$10-4=6$	$16-4=12$
Divide the result by 2.	$14\div2=7$	$26\div2=13$	$6\div2=3$	$12\div2=6$
Subtract the original number.	$7-4=3$	$13-10=3$	$3-0=3$	$6-3=3$
Summary of results:	$4\rightarrow3$	$10\rightarrow3$	$0\rightarrow3$	$3\rightarrow3$

b. $n+5$

$2(n+5)=2n+10$

$2n+10-4=2n+6$

$$\frac{2n+6}{2}=\frac{2n}{2}+\frac{6}{2}=n+3$$

$n+3-n=3$

47. Using inductive reasoning we predict $1+2+3+4+5+6=\frac{6\times7}{2}$.
Arithmetic verifies this result: 21 = 21

49. Using inductive reasoning we predict $1+3+5+7+9+11=6\times6$.
Arithmetic verifies this result: 36 = 36

51. Using inductive reasoning we predict $98765\times9+3=888{,}888$.
Arithmetic verifies this result:

$98765\times9+3=888{,}888$

$888{,}885+3=888{,}888$

$888{,}888=888{,}888$

53. The first multiplier increases by 33.
132 + 33 = 165
The second multiplier is 3367.
The product increases by 111,111.
165 × 3367 = 555,555 is correct.

55. b; The resulting exponent is always the first exponent added to twice the second exponent.

57. deductive; The specific value was based on a general formula.

59. inductive; The general conclusion for all full-time four-year colleges was based on specific observations.

61. a. 1, 3, 6, 10, 15, and 21 are followed by
$21 + 7 = 28$
$28 + 8 = 36$
$36 + 9 = 45$
$45 + 10 = 55$
$55 + 11 = 66$
1, 3, 6, 10, 15, 21, 28, 36, 45, 55, and 66.

b. $4 - 1 = 3$
$9 - 4 = 5$
$16 - 9 = 7$
$25 - 16 = 9$
The successive differences increase by 2.
$25 + 11 = 36$
$36 + 13 = 49$
$49 + 15 = 64$
$64 + 17 = 81$
$81 + 19 = 100$

c. The successive differences are 4, 7, and 10. Since these differences are increasing by 3 each time. The next five numbers will be found by using differences of 13, 16, 19, 22, and 25.
$22 + 13 = 35$
$35 + 16 = 51$
$51 + 19 = 70$
$70 + 22 = 92$
$92 + 25 = 117$

d. If a triangular number is multiplied by 8 and then 1 is added to the product, a square number is obtained.

67. makes sense

69. makes sense

71. a. The sums are all 30:

16	3	11
5	10	15
9	17	4

b. The sums are all 36:

17	5	14
9	12	15
10	19	7

c. For any values of a, b, and c, the sums of all rows, all columns, and both diagonals are the same.

d. The sums of the expressions in each row, each column, and each diagonal is $3a$.

e. Finding each sum verifies the conjecture that they are all $3a$.
First row: $(a+b)+(a-b-c)+(a+c)=3a$
Second row: $(a-b+c)+(a)+(a+b-c)=3a$
Third row: $(a-c)+(a+b+c)+(a-b)=3a$
First Column: $(a+b)+(a-b+c)+(a-c)=3a$
Second Column:
$(a-b-c)+(a)+(a+b+c)=3a$
Third Column:
$(a+c)+(a+b-c)+(a-b)=3a$
First Diagonal: $(a+b)+(a)+(a-b)=3a$
Second Diagonal: $(a-c)+(a)+(a+c)=3a$

73. a. The result is a three- or four- digit number in which the thousands and hundreds places represent the month of the birthday and the tens and ones places represent the day of the birthday.

b. $5[4(5M+6)+9]+D-165$
$=5[20M+24+9]+D-165$
$=5[20M+33]+D-165$
$=100M+165+D-165$
$=100M+D$

75. a. $3367 \times 3 = 10101$
$3367 \times 6 = 20202$
$3367 \times 9 = 30303$
$3367 \times 12 = 40404$

b. The first multiplier is always 3367. The second multipliers are successive multiples of 3. The product increases by 10101.

c. $3367 \times 15 = 50505$
$3367 \times 18 = 60606$

d. Inductive reasoning; it uses an observed pattern and draws conclusions from that pattern.

Check Points 1.2

1. a. The digit to the right of the billions digit is less than 5. Thus, , replace all the digits to the right with zeroes. 7,058,746,857 rounded to the nearest billion is 7,000,000,000.

b. The digit to the right of the ten thousands digit is greater than 5. Thus, add 1 to the digit to be rounded and replace all the digits to the right with zeroes. 7,058,746,857 rounded to the nearest hundred thousand is 7,058,750,000.

2. a. The digit to the right of the tenths digit is less than 5. Thus, 3.141593 rounded to the nearest tenth is 3.1.

b. The digit to the right of the ten-thousandths digit is greater than 5. Thus, 3.141593 rounded to the nearest ten-thousandth is 3.1416.

3. a. $\$3.40+\$2.25+\$5.60+\$5.40+\$3.40+\$2.85+3.95$
$\approx \$3+\$2+\$6+\$5+\$3+\$3+4$
$\approx \$26$

b. The given bill is not reasonable. It is too high.

4. a. Round \$52 per hour to \$50 per hour and assume 40 hours per week.
$\frac{40\text{ hours}}{\text{week}} \times \frac{\$50}{\text{hour}} = \frac{\$2000}{\text{week}}$
The architect's salary is $\approx \$2000$ per week.

b. Round 52 weeks per year to 50 weeks per year.
$\frac{\$2000}{\text{week}} \times \frac{50\text{ weeks}}{\text{year}} = \frac{\$100,000}{\text{year}}$
The architect's salary is $\approx \$100,000$ per year.

5. a. 0.48×2148.72

b. $0.5 \times 2100 = 1050$
Your family spent approximately \$1050 on heating and cooling last year.

6. a. The yearly increase in life expectancy can be approximated by dividing the change in life expectancy by the change in time from 1950 to 2010. $\frac{81.1-71.1}{2010-1950} = \frac{10}{60} \approx 0.17\text{ yr}$ for each subsequent birth year.

b. $\underbrace{71.1}_{\text{life expectancy in 1950}} + \underbrace{0.17}_{\text{yearly increase}}\underbrace{(2050-1950)}_{\text{number of years from 1960 to 2050}}$
$=71.1+0.17(100)$
$=71.1+17$
$=88.1\text{ yr}$

7. a. about 22%

b. The greatest rate of increase in the percentage of college students who smoked cigarettes can be found by identifying the portion of the graph with the largest upward slope. This occurs between 1994 and 1998.

c. Approximately 24% of college students smoked cigarettes in 1982 and 1994.

8. a. The yearly increase in tuition and fees can be approximated by dividing the change in tuition and fees by the change in time from 2000 to 2010. $\frac{\$26,273-\$15,518}{2010-2000}=\frac{\$10,755}{10}\approx\$1076$

b. $T=\underbrace{15,518}_{\text{Cost in 2000}}+\underbrace{1076}_{\text{yearly increase}}x$

c. 2014 is 14 years after 2000. Thus,
$$\begin{aligned}T&=15,518+1076x\\&=15,518+1076(14)\\&=\$30,582\end{aligned}$$

Concept and Vocabulary Check 1.2

1. estimation
2. circle graph
3. mathematical model
4. true
5. true
6. false

Exercise Set 1.2

1. a. 19,465,200

   b. 19,465,000

   c. 19,470,000

   d. 19,500,000

   e. 19,000,000

   f. 20,000,000

3. 2.718

5. 2.71828

7. 2.718281828

9. $350+600=950$
Actual answer of 955 compares reasonably well

11. $9+1+19=29$
Actual answer of 29.23 compares quite well

13. $32-11=21$
Actual answer of 20.911 compares quite well

15. $40\times6=240$
Actual answer of 218.185 compares not so well

17. $0.8\times400=320$
Actual answer of 327.06 compares reasonably well

19. $48\div3=16$
Actual answer of 16.49 compares quite well

21. 30% of 200,000 is 60,000
Actual answer of 59,920.96 compares quite well

23. $$\begin{aligned}&\$3.47+\$5.89+\$19.98+\$2.03+\$11.85+\$0.23\\&\approx\$3+\$6+\$20+\$2+\$12+\$0\\&\approx\$43\end{aligned}$$

25. Round \$19.50 to \$20 per hour.
40 hours per week
(40 × \$20) per week = \$800/week
Round 52 weeks to 50 weeks per year.
50 weeks per year
(50 × \$800) per year = \$40,000
\$19.50 per hour ≈ \$40,000 per year

27. Round the \$605 monthly payment to \$600.
3 years is 36 months.
Round the 36 months to 40 months.
\$600 × 40 months = \$24,000 total cost.
\$605 monthly payment for 3 years ≈ \$24,000 total cost.

29. Round the raise of \$310,000 to \$300,000.
Round the 294 professors to 300.
\$300,000 ÷ 300 professors = \$1000 per professor.
\$310,000 raise ≈ \$1000 per professor.

31. Round \$61,500 to \$60,000 per year.
Round 52 weeks per year to 50 weeks per year.
50 weeks × 40 hours per week = 2000 hours
\$60,000 ÷ 2000 hours = \$30 per hour
\$61,500 per year ≈ \$30 per hour

33. $80\times365\times24=700,800$ hr

35. $\frac{0.2\times100}{0.5}=\frac{20}{0.5}=40$
Actual answer of 42.03 compares quite reasonable.

37. The given information suggests \$30 would be a good estimate per calculator.
$\$30\times10=\$300$ which is closest to choice b.

39. The given information suggests 65 mph would be a good rate estimate and 3.5 would be a good time estimate.
$65 \times 3.5 = 227.5$ which is closest to choice c.

41. The given information suggests you can count 1 number per second.
$\frac{10000}{60 \times 60} \approx 2.77$ or 3 hours

43. $\approx 0.10 \times 16,000,000 = 1,600,000$
10% of 16,000,000 is 1,600,000 high school teenagers.

45. a. about 85 people per 100

b. $(85 - 23) \times 87 \approx 5400$

47. a. $\frac{25.1 - 9.7}{2010 - 1980} = \frac{15.4}{30} \approx 0.5$
The annual increase is about 0.5%.

b. $9.7 + 0.5(2020 - 1980) = 9.7 + 0.5(40)$
$= 29.7$
In 2020 the percentage will be approximately 29.7%.

49. a. The percentage of Americans who considered Iraq their country's greatest enemy in 2001 was about 38%.

b. The greatest rate of decrease was from 2008 to 2009.

c. 2003

51. a. $\frac{390 - 310}{2010 - 1950} = \frac{80}{60} \approx 1.33$ ppm per year

b. $C = 310 + 1.33x$

c. 2050 is 100 years after 1950.
$C = 310 + 1.33(100) = 443$ ppm

67. does not make sense; Explanations will vary. Sample explanation: Very large numbers and very small numbers often must be estimated when using a calculator.

69. does not make sense; Explanations will vary. Sample explanation: Some mathematical models can break down over time.

71. a

73. b

75. $20 \times 16 \times 50 = 16,000$ hours .
$\frac{16,000}{24} \approx 667$ days
$\frac{667}{365} \approx 1.8$ yr

Check Points 1.3

1. The amount of money given to the cashier is unknown.

2. Step 1: Understand the problem.
Bottles: 128 ounces costs $5.39
Boxes: a 9-pack of 6.75 ounce boxes costs $3.15
We must determine whether bottles or boxes are the better value.
Step 2: Devise a plan.
Dividing the cost by the number of ounces will give us the cost per ounce. We will need to multiply 9 by 6.75 to determine the total number of ounces the boxes contain. The lower cost per ounce is the best value.
Step 3: Carry out the plan and solve the problem.
Unit price for the bottles:
$\frac{\$5.39}{128 \text{ ounces}} \approx \$0.042$ per ounce
Unit price for the boxes:
$\frac{\$3.15}{9 \times 6.75 \text{ ounces}} = \frac{\$3.15}{60.75 \text{ ounces}} \approx \$0.052$ per ounce
Bottles have a lower price per ounce and are the better value.
Step 4: Look back and check the answer.
This answer satisfies the conditions of the problem.

3. Step 1: Understand the problem.
We are given the cost of the computer, the amount of cash paid up front, and the amount paid each month. We must determine the number of months it will take to finish paying for the computer.
Step 2: Devise a plan.
Subtract the amount paid in cash from the cost of the computer. This results in the amount still to be paid. Because the monthly payments are $45, divide the amount still to be paid by 45. This will give the number of months required to pay for the computer.
Step 3: Carry out the plan and solve the problem.
The balance is $\$980 - \$350 = \$630$. Now divide the $630 balance by $45, the monthly payment.

$$\$630 \div \frac{\$45}{\text{month}} = \$630 \times \frac{\text{month}}{\$45}$$
$$= \frac{630 \text{ months}}{45} = 14 \text{ months.}$$

Step 4: Look back and check the answer.
This answer satisfies the conditions of the problem. 14 monthly payments at $45 each gives $14\times\$45=\$630$. Adding in the up front cash payment of $350 gives us $\$630+\$350=\$980$. $980 is the cost of the computer.

4. Step 1: Understand the problem.
The total change must always be 30 cents. One possible coin combination is six nickels. Another is three dimes. We need to count all such combinations.
Step 2: Devise a plan.
Make a list of all possible coin combinations. Begin with the coins of larger value and work toward the coins of smaller value.
Step 3: Carry out the plan and solve the problem.

Quarters	Dimes	Nickels
1	0	1
0	3	0
0	2	2
0	1	4
0	0	6

There are 5 combinations.
Step 4: Look back and check the answer.
Check to see that no combinations are omitted, and that those given total 30 cents. Also double-check the count.

5. Step 1: Understand the problem.
We must determine the number of jeans/T-shirt combinations that we can make.
For example, one such combination would be to wear the blue jeans with the beige shirt.
Step 2: Devise a plan.
Each pair of jeans could be matched with any of the three shirts. We will make a tree diagram to show all combinations.
Step 3: Carry out the plan and solve the problem.

JEANS	T-SHIRT	COMBINATIONS
Blue jeans	Beige shirt	Blue jeans-Beige shirt
	Yellow shirt	Blue jeans-Yellow shirt
	Blue shirt	Blue jeans-Blue shirt
Black jeans	Beige shirt	Black jeans-Beige shirt
	Yellow shirt	Black jeans-Yellow shirt
	Blue shirt	Black jeans-Blue shirt

There are 6 different outfits possible.
Step 4: Look back and check the answer.
Check to see that no combinations are omitted, and double-check the count.

6. Step 1: Understand the problem.
There are many possible ways to visit each city once and then return home. We must find a route that costs less than $1460.
Step 2: Devise a plan.
From city *A* fly to the city with the cheapest available flight. Repeat this until all cities have been visited and then fly home. If this cost is above $1460 then use trial and error to find other alternative routes.
Step 3: Carry out the plan and solve the problem.
A to *D* costs $185, *D* to *E* costs $302, *E* to *C* costs $165, *C* to *B* costs $305, *B* back to *A* costs $500
$\$185+\$302+\$165+\$305+\$500=\$1457$
The route *A*, *D*, *E*, *C*, *B*, *A* costs less than $1460
Step 4: Look back and check the answer.
This answer satisfies the conditions of the problem.

Trick Questions 1.3

1. The farmer has 12 sheep left since all but 12 sheep died.

2. All 12 months have [at least] 28 days.

3. The doctor and brother are brother and sister.

4. You should light the match first.

Concept and Vocabulary Check 1.3

1. understand

2. devise a plan

3. false

4. false

Exercise Set 1.3

1. The price of the computer is needed.

3. The number of words per page is needed.

5. Weekly salary is unnecessary information.
$212-200=12$ items sold in excess of 200
$12\times\$15=\$180$ extra is received.

7. How much the attendant was given is not necessary.
There were 5 hours of parking.
1st hour is $2.50
4 hours at $0.50/hr
$$\$2.50+(4\times\$0.50)=\$2.50+\$2.00 = \$4.50$$
$4.50 was charged.

9. a. Step 1: Understand the problem.
Box #1: 15.3 ounces costs \$3.37
Box #2: 24 ounces costs \$4.59
We must determine whether Box #1 or Box #2 is the better value.
Step 2: Devise a plan.
Dividing the cost by the number of ounces will give us the cost per ounce. The lower cost per ounce is the best value.
Step 3: Carry out the plan and solve the problem.
Unit price for Box #1:
$$\frac{\$3.37}{15.3 \text{ ounces}} \approx \$0.22 \text{ per ounce}$$
Unit price for Box #2:
$$\frac{\$4.59}{24 \text{ ounces}} \approx \$0.19 \text{ per ounce}$$
The cereal that is 24 ounces for \$4.59 is the better value.
Step 4: Look back and check the answer.
This answer satisfies the conditions of the problem.

b. Unit price for Box #1: \$0.22 per ounce
Unit price for Box #2:
$$\frac{\$4.59}{24 \text{ ounces}} \times \frac{16 \text{ ounces}}{\text{pound}} \approx \$3.06 \text{ per pound}$$

c. No, explanations will vary.

11. Step 1: Comparing two yearly salaries
Step 2:
Convert the second person's wages to yearly salary.
Step 3:
The person that earns \$3750/month earns $12 \times \$3750 = \$45,000$/year. The person that earns \$48,000/year gets \$3000 more per year.
Step 4:
It appears to satisfy the conditions of the problem.

13. Step 1:
Find the difference between two methods of payment.
Step 2:
Compute total costs and compare two figures.
Step 3:
By spreading purchase out, the total comes to:
$\$100 + 14(\$50) = \$100 + \$700 = \$800$
$\$800 - \$750 = \$50$ saved by paying all at once
Step 4:
It satisfies the conditions of problem.

15. Step 1:
Determine profit on goods sold.
Step 2:
Find total cost of buying product and comparing with gross sales.
Step 3:
Purchased: (\$65 per dozen)(6 dozen) = \$390
Sold: 6 dozen = 72 calculators
$\frac{72}{3} = 24$ groups of 3 at \$20 per group.
$24 \times \$20 = \$480$
$\$480 - \$390 = \$90$ profit
Step 4:
It satisfies the conditions of the problem.

17. Step 1: Determine profit for ten-day period.
Step 2: Compare totals.
Step 3:
(200 slices)(\$1.50) = \$300 for pizza
(85 sandwiches)(\$2.50) = \$212.50 for sandwiches
For 10 day period:
$$\text{Gross: } 10(\$300)+10(\$212.50) = \$3000+\$2125.00 = \$5125.00$$
Expenses: 10(\$60) = \$600
Profit: \$5125.00 – \$600 = \$4525
Step 4:
It satisfies the conditions of the problem.

19. Step 1:
Compute total rental cost.
Step 2:
Add rental cost and mileage cost to get total cost.
Step 3:
Rental costs:
(2 weeks)(\$220 per week) = \$440
Mileage: (500 miles)(\$0.25) = \$125
Total: \$440 + \$125 = \$565
Step 4:
It satisfies the conditions of problem.

21. Step 1:
A round trip was made; we need to determine how much was walked or ridden.
Step 2:
Add up the totals walked and ridden and compare.
Step 3:
It is 5 miles between the homes or a 10 mile round trip. The first 3 were covered with the bicycle, leaving 7 miles covered by walking.
7 miles – 3 miles = 4 miles more that was walked.
Step 4:
It satisfies the conditions of the problem.

23. Step 1:
Determine profit by comparing expenses with gross sales.
Step 2:
Calculate expenses and gross sales and compare.
Step 3:
Expense:
(25 calculators)(\$30) = \$750

Gross Sales:
(22 calculators)($35.00) = $770
The storeowner receives $30 – $2 = $28 for each returned calculator.
(3 calculators)($28) = $84

Total Income:
$770 + $84 = $854
Profit=Income–Expenses
=$854–$750
=$104
Step 4:
It satisfies the conditions of the problem.

25. The car depreciates at
$\frac{23,000-2700}{7} = \$2900$ per year.
$23,000-3(2900) = \$14,300$

27. Use a list.

2 Quarters	3 Dimes	5 Nickels
1	2	0
1	1	2
1	0	4
0	3	3
0	2	5

There are 5 ways.

29. Make a list of all possible selections:
Depp/Foxx, Depp/Stewart, Depp/Hilary, Foxx/Stewart, Foxx/Hilary, Stewart/Hilary
There are 6 ways.

31. Use a list.

Pennies	Nickels	Dimes
21	0	0
16	1	0
11	2	0
11	0	1
6	3	0
6	1	1
1	4	0
1	2	1
1	0	2

There are 9 ways.

33. Use a list.

1 pt	5 pt	10-pt	Total
3	0	0	3
2	1	0	7
1	2	0	11
2	0	1	12
0	3	0	15
1	1	1	16
0	2	1	20
1	0	2	21
0	1	2	25
0	0	3	30

There are 10 different totals.

35. The average expense is $\frac{42+10+26+32+30}{5} = \$28$
Thus, B owes $18 and C owes $2, A is owed $14, D is owed $4, and E is owed $2.
To resolve these discrepancies, B should give A $14 and give D $4, while C should give E $2.

37. Make a list of all possible orders:
TFFF, FTFF, FFTF, FFFT
The "True" could be written 1st, 2nd, 3rd, or 4th.
There are 4 ways.

39. The order the racers finished was; Andy, Darnell, Caleb, Beth, Ella.

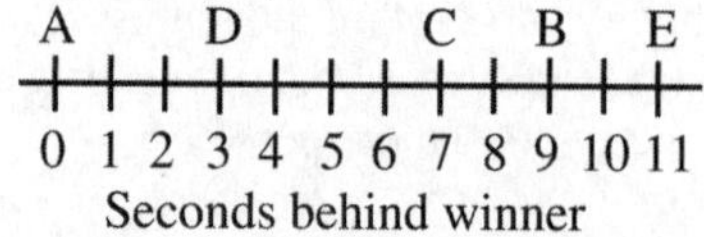

41. Home→Bank→Post Office→Dry Cleaners→Home will take 11.5 miles.

43. CO→WY→UT→AZ→NM→CO→UT

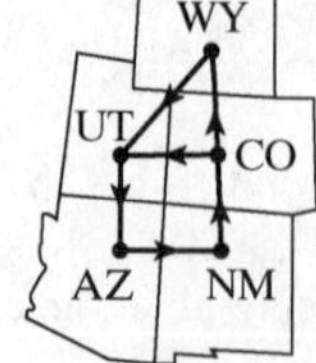

45. The problem states that the psychology major knocks on Jose's wall, and Jose's dorm is adjacent to Bob's dorm but not Tony's. Therefore Bob is the psychology major.

47. a.

5	22	18
28	15	2
12	8	25

b.

4	9	8
11	7	3
6	5	10

49.

9	6	7
8	1	4
3	2	5

51.

$$\begin{array}{r} 156 \\ 28\overline{)4368} \\ \underline{28} \\ 156 \\ \underline{140} \\ 168 \\ \underline{168} \\ 0 \end{array}$$

57. makes sense

59. does not make sense; Explanations will vary. Sample explanation: When you are bogged down with a problem, it can often be helpful to stop working on it and return to it later.

61. You should choose the dentist whose teeth show the effects of poor dental work because he took good care of the other dentist's teeth.

63. It is Friday. The first person is lying (as expected) because he told the truth on Thursday. The second is truthfully admitting that he lied the previous day.

65. Answers will vary.

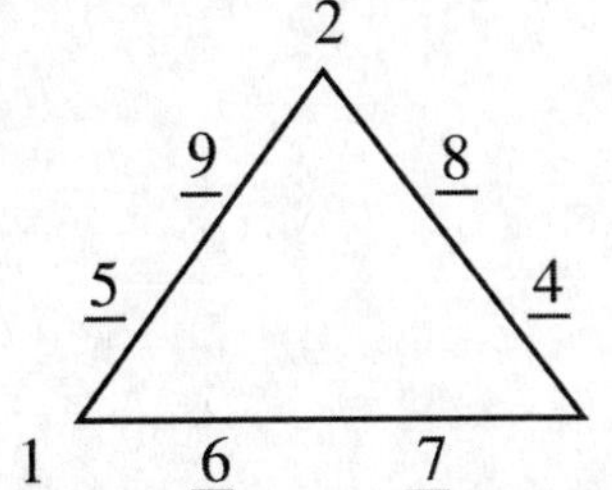

67. There is no missing dollar; in the end the customers paid a total of \$27 of which \$25 went to the restaurant and \$2 was stolen by the waiter.

69. Answers will vary. One method is to start by multiplying 30 by each state's fraction of the population.

State A: $30\times\frac{275}{1890}\approx 4.365$ or 4

State B: $30\times\frac{383}{1890}\approx 6.079$ or 6

State C: $30\times\frac{465}{1890}\approx 7.381$ or 7

State D: $30\times\frac{767}{1890}\approx 12.175$ or 12

Notice that 4, 6, 7, and 12 add to 29, so there is 1 more representative to be allocated. We could give this extra representative to state C because it had the largest decimal part (0.381). This leads to an allocation of state A: 4, state B: 6, state C: 8, and state D: 12.

Chapter 1 Review Exercises

1. Deductive; the specific conclusion about *Carrie* was based on a general statement about all Stephen King books.

2. Inductive; the general conclusion for this next book was based on past specific observations.

3. Pattern: Add 5
$19 + 5 = 24$
4, 9, 14, 19, $\underline{24}$

4. Pattern: Multiply by 2
$56 \times 2 = 112$
7, 14, 28, 56, $\underline{112}$

5. Pattern: Numbers added increase by 1
$1 + 2 = 3$
$3 + 3 = 6$
$6 + 4 = 10$
$10 + 5 = 15$
$15 + 6 = 21$
1, 3, 6, 10, 15, $\underline{21}$

6. Notice that $\frac{1}{2} = \frac{3}{6}$
Pattern: Add 1 to the denominator
$\frac{3}{7+1} = \frac{3}{8}$
$\frac{3}{4}, \frac{3}{5}, \frac{3}{6}, \frac{3}{7}, \underline{\frac{3}{8}}$ or
$\frac{3}{4}, \frac{3}{5}, \frac{1}{2}, \frac{3}{7}, \underline{\frac{3}{8}}$

7. Pattern: Divide by −2

$-5 \div (-2) = \frac{-5}{-2} = \frac{5}{2}$ or $2\frac{1}{2}$

$40, -20, 10, -5, \underline{\frac{5}{2}}$

8. Pattern: Subtract 60

$-140 - 60 = -200$

$40, -20, -80, -140, \underline{-200}$

9. Each number beginning with the third number is the sum of the previous two numbers. $16 + 26 = \underline{42}$

10. To get the second number, multiply the first number by 3. Then multiply the second number by 2 to get the third number. Then multiply by 3 and then by 2, repeatedly. $216 \times 2 = \underline{432}$

11. The pattern is alternating between square and circle while the line rotates 90° clockwise. The next figure is shown at right.

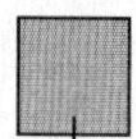

12. Using inductive reasoning we predict $2+4+8+16+32 = 64-2$.
Arithmetic verifies this result:

$$2+4+8+16+32 = 64-2$$
$$62 = 62$$

13. Using inductive reasoning we predict $444 \div 12 = 37$.
Arithmetic verifies this result: $444 \div 12 = 37$

$$37 = 37$$

14. a. Conjecture based on results: The result is the original number.

Select a number.	4	10	0	3
Double the number.	$4 \times 2 = 8$	$10 \times 2 = 20$	$0 \times 2 = 0$	$3 \times 2 = 6$
Add 4 to the product.	$8+4=12$	$20+4=24$	$0+4=4$	$6+4=10$
Divide this sum by 2.	$12 \div 2 = 6$	$24 \div 2 = 12$	$4 \div 2 = 2$	$10 \div 2 = 5$
Subtract 2 from the quotient.	$6-2=4$	$12-2=10$	$2-2=0$	$5-2=3$
Summary of results:	4 → 4	10 → 10	0 → 0	3 → 3

b. $2n$

$2n+4$

$\frac{2n+4}{2} = \frac{2n}{2} + \frac{4}{2} = n+2$

$n+2-2 = n$

15. a. 923,187,500

b. 923,187,000

c. 923,200,000

d. 923,000,000

e. 900,000,000

16. **a.** 1.5

b. 1.51

c. 1.507

d. 1.5065917

17. $2+4+10=16$
Actual answer: 15.71
quite reasonable

18. $9\times 50=450$
Actual answer: 432.67
quite reasonable

19. $20\div 4=5$
Actual answer: 4.79
quite reasonable

20. $0.60\times 4000=2400$
Actual answer: 2397.0548
quite reasonable

21. \$8.47 + \$0.89 + \$2.79 + \$0.14 + \$1.19 + \$4.76
≈ \$8 + \$1 + \$3 + \$0 + \$1 + \$5
≈ \$18

22. Round 78 hours to 80, round \$6.85 to \$7.00. 78 × \$6.85 ≈ 80 × \$7.00 ≈ \$560

23. Round book price to \$1.00 each.
Round chair price to \$12.00 each.
Round plate price to \$15.00.
(21 × \$0.85) + (2 × \$11.95) + \$14.65
≈ (21 × \$1) + (2 × \$12) + \$15
≈ \$21 + \$24 + \$15
≈ \$60

24. 28% of 17,487,475 can be estimated as 30% of 17,000,000.
$0.3\times 1{,}700{,}000=5{,}100{,}000$ students

25. The given information suggests \$900 would be a good estimate for weekly salary.
$\$900\times 10\times 4=\$36{,}000$ which is choice b.

26. $60\times 60\times 24=86{,}400$ which is closest to choice c.

27. **a.** The Asian group exceeds 100. They have a population of about 122.

b. 30×33 million $=990$ million

28. **a.** $\dfrac{28.0-6.0}{2006-1950}=\dfrac{22.0}{56}=0.4$
average increase: 0.4% per year

b. $6.0+0.4(2020-1950)=6.0+0.4(70)=34$
About 34% of people 25 years of age and older will be college graduates in 2020.

29. **a.** The woman's maximum heart rate was about 115 beats per minute. This occurred after about 10 minutes.

b. The woman's minimum heart rate was about 64 beats per minute. This occurred after about 8 minutes.

c. between 9 and 10 minutes

d. 9 minutes

30. **a.** $\dfrac{309.3-203.3}{2010-1970}=\dfrac{106}{40}\approx 2.65$ million per year

b. $p=203.3+2.65x$

c. $p=203.3+2.65(2020-1970)=335.8$ million

31. The weight of the child is needed.

32. The unnecessary information is the customer giving the driver a \$20 bill.
For a 6 mile trip, the first mile is \$3.00, and the next 5 miles are \$0.50/half-mile or \$1.00/mile. The cost is
\$3.00 + (5 × \$1.00) = \$3.00 + \$5.00
= \$8.00.

33. Total of 28 × 2 = 56 frankfurters would be needed.
$\dfrac{56}{7}=8$. Therefore, 8 pounds would be needed.

34. Rental for 3 weeks at \$175 per week is 3 × \$175 = \$525. Mileage for 1200 miles at \$0.30 per mile is 1200 × \$0.30 = \$360. Total cost is \$525 + \$360 = \$885.

35.. Plan A is \$90 better.
Cost under Plan A: $100+0.80(1500)=\$1300$
Cost under Plan B: $40+0.90(1500)=\$1390$

36. The flight leaves Miami at 7:00 A.M. Pacific Standard Time. With a lay-over of 45 minutes, it arrives in San Francisco at 1:30 P.M. Pacific Standard Time, 6 hrs 30 min. – 45 min = 5 hours 45 minutes.

37. At steady decrease in value: $\dfrac{\$37{,}000-\$2600}{8\text{ years}}=\dfrac{\$34{,}400}{8\text{ years}}=\$4300/\text{year}$

After 5 years: $\$4300\times 5=\$21{,}500$ decrease in value
Value of car: \$37,000 – \$21,500 = \$15,500

38. The machine will accept nickels, dimes, quarters.

nickels	dimes	quarters
7	0	0
5	1	0
3	2	0
2	0	1
1	3	0
0	1	1

There are 6 combinations.

Chapter 1 Test

1. deductive

2. inductive

3. $0+5=5$
$5+5=10$
$10+5=15$
$15+5=20$
0, 5, 10, 15, <u>20</u>

4. $\dfrac{1}{6\times 2}=\dfrac{1}{12}$

$\dfrac{1}{12\times 2}=\dfrac{1}{24}$

$\dfrac{1}{24\times 2}=\dfrac{1}{48}$

$\dfrac{1}{48\times 2}=\dfrac{1}{96}$

$\dfrac{1}{6},\dfrac{1}{12},\dfrac{1}{24},\dfrac{1}{48},\underline{\dfrac{1}{96}}$

5. $3367\times 15=50{,}505$

6. The outer figure is always a square. The inner figure appears to cycle from triangle to circle to square. The line segments at the bottom alternate from two to one. The next shape is shown at right.

7. a. Conjecture based on results: The original number is doubled.

Select a number.	4	10	3
Multiply the number by 4.	$4\times4=16$	$10\times4=40$	$3\times4=12$
Add 8 to the product.	$16+8=24$	$40+8=48$	$12+8=20$
Divide this sum by 2.	$24\div2=12$	$48\div2=24$	$20\div2=10$
Subtract 4 from the quotient.	$12-4=8$	$24-4=20$	$10-4=6$
Summary of results:	4 → 8	10 → 20	3 → 6

b. $4n$

$4n+8$

$\frac{4n+8}{2}=\frac{4n}{2}+\frac{8}{2}=2n+4$

$2n+4-4=2n$

8. 3,300,000

9. 706.38

10. Round $47.00 to $50.00.
Round $311.00 to $310.00.
Round $405.00 to $410.00.
Round $681.79 to $680.00.
Total needed for expenses:
$47.00 + $311.00 + $405.00
≈ $50.00 + $310.00 + $410.00
≈ $770.00
Additional money needed:
$770.00 – $681.79 ≈ $770.00 – $680.00
≈ $90

11. Round $485,000 to $500,000.
Round number of people to 20.

$\frac{\$485{,}000}{19\text{ people}}\approx\frac{\$500{,}000}{20\text{ people}}$

$\approx \$25{,}000$ per person

12. $0.48992 \times 120 \approx 0.5 \times 120 \approx 60$

13. 11% of 512 billion can be estimated by 10% of 500 billion.
0.10×500 billion = 50 billion

14. $72{,}000\div30=2400$ which is choice a.

15. a. 2001; about 1275 discharges

b. 2010; about 275 discharges

c. They decreased at the greatest rate where the graph has the steepest downward slope. This occurred between 2001 and 2002

d. There were about 1000 discharges in 1997 under this policy.

16. **a.** $\dfrac{48.4-17.6}{2010-1968}=\dfrac{30.8}{42}\approx 0.7\%$ per year

b. $p=17.6+0.7x$

c. $p=17.6+0.7(2020-1968)=54\%$

17. For 3 hours:

Estes: \$9 per $\frac{1}{4}$ hour

$3 \times 4 = 12$ quarter-hours $\rightarrow 12 \times \$9 = \$108$

Ship and Shore: \$20 per $\frac{1}{2}$ hour

$3 \times 2 = 6$ half-hours $\rightarrow 6 \times \$20 = \$120$
Estes is a better deal by
$\$120 - \$108 = \$12.00$.

18. 20 round trips mean 40 one-way trips at \$11/trip.
(40 trips)(32 passengers)(\$11)
= \$14,080 in one day

19. $\$960-\$50=\$910$ remaining to pay

$\dfrac{\$910}{\$35 \text{ per week}}=26$ weeks

20. Belgium will have 160,000 more.
Greece: $10{,}600{,}000-28{,}000(35)=9{,}620{,}000$
Belgium: $10{,}200{,}000-12{,}000(35)=9{,}780{,}000$

Chapter 2
Set Theory

Check Points 2.1

1. Set L is the set of the first six lowercase letters in the English alphabet.

2. $M = \{\text{April, August}\}$

3. $O = \{1, 3, 5, 7, 9\}$

4. **a.** not the empty set; Many numbers meet the criteria to belong to this set.

   b. the empty set; No numbers meet the criteria, thus this set is empty

   c. not the empty set; "nothing" is not a set.

   d. not the empty set; This is a set that contains one element, that element is a set.

5. **a.** true; 8 is an element of the given set.

   b. true; r is not an element of the given set.

   c. false; {Monday} is a set and the set {Monday} is not an element of the given set.

6. **a.** $A = \{1, 2, 3\}$

   b. $B = \{15, 16, 17, \ldots\}$

   c. $O = \{1, 3, 5, \ldots\}$

7. **a.** {1, 2, 3, 4, ..., 199}

   b. {51, 52, 53, 54, ..., 200}

8. **a.** $n(A) = 5$; the set has 5 elements

   b. $n(B) = 1$; the set has only 1 element

   c. $n(C) = 8$; Though this set lists only five elements, the three dots indicate 12, 13, and 14 are also elements.

   d. $n(D) = 0$ because the set has no elements.

9. No, the sets are not equivalent. Set A has 5 elements yet set B has only 4 elements.

10. **a.** true; {O, L, D} = {D, O, L} because the sets contain exactly the same elements.

    b. false; The two sets do not contain exactly the same elements.

Concept and Vocabulary Check 2.1

1. roster; set builder

2. empty; $\varnothing$

3. is an element

4. natural numbers

5. cardinal; $n(A)$

6. equivalent

7. equal

Exercise Set 2.1

1. This is well defined and therefore it is a set.

3. This is a matter of opinion and not well defined, thus it is not a set.

5. This is well defined and therefore it is a set.

7. The set of known planets in our Solar System. Note to student: This exercise did not forget Pluto. In 2006, based on the requirement that a planet must dominate its own orbit, the International Astronomical Union removed Pluto from the list of planets.

9. The set of months that begin with J.

11. The set of natural numbers greater than 5.

13. The set of natural numbers between 6 and 20, inclusive.

15. {winter, spring, summer, fall}

17. {September, October, November, December}

19. $\{1, 2, 3\}$

21. $\{1, 3, 5, 7, 9, 11\}$

23. {1, 2, 3, 4, 5}

25. {6, 7, 8, 9, ...}

27. {7, 8, 9, 10}

29. {10, 11, 12, 13, ..., 79}

31. {2}

33. not the empty set

35. empty set

37. not the empty set
Note that the number of women who served as U.S. president before 2016 is 0. Thus the number 0 is an element of the set.

39. empty set

41. empty set

43. not the empty set

45. not the empty set

47. true
3 is a member of the set.

49. true
12 is a member of the set.

51. false
5 is *not* a member of the set.

53. true
11 is *not* a member of the set.

55. false
37 is a member of the set.

57. false
4 is a member of the set.

59. true
13 is *not* a member of the set.

61. false
16 is a member of the set.

63. false
The set {3} is *not* a member of the set.

65. true
–1 is *not* a natural number.

67. $n(A) = 5$; There are 5 elements in the set.

69. $n(B) = 15$; There are 15 elements in the set.

71. $n(C) = 0$; There are *no* days of the week beginning with A.

73. $n(D) = 1$; There is 1 element in the set.

75. $n(A) = 4$; There is 4 elements in the set.

77. $n(B) = 5$; There is 5 elements in the set.

79. $n(C) = 0$; There are no elements in the set.

81. **a.** Not equivalent
The number of elements is not the same.

b. Not equal
The two sets contain different elements.

83. **a.** Equivalent
The number of elements is the same.

b. Not equal
The elements are not exactly the same.

85. **a.** Equivalent
The number of elements is the same.

b. Equal
The elements are exactly the same.

87. **a.** Equivalent
Number of elements is the same.

b. Not equal
The two sets contain different elements.

89. **a.** Equivalent
Number of elements is the same.

b. Equal
The elements are exactly the same.

91. infinite

93. finite

95. finite

97. $\{x|x \in \mathbb{N} \text{ and } x \geq 61\}$

99. $\{x|x \in \mathbb{N} \text{ and } 61 \leq x \leq 89\}$

101. Answers will vary; an example is: $\{0, 1, 2, 3\}$ and $\{1, 2, 3, 4\}$.

103. Impossible. Equal sets have exactly the same elements. This would require that there also must be the same number of elements.

105. {New Zealand, Australia, United States}

107. {Australia, United States, United Kingdom, Switzerland, Ireland}

109. {United Kingdom, Switzerland, Ireland}

111. { }

113. {12, 19}

115. {20, 21}

117. There is not a one-to-one correspondence. These sets are not equivalent.

125. does not make sense; Explanations will vary. Sample explanation: The natural numbers do not include negative numbers. Since the temperature will be below zero, a set that includes negative numbers would be necessary.

127. makes sense

129. false; Changes to make the statement true will vary. A sample change is: If a roster set contains three dots, it is finite if there is an ending value after the three dots.

131. true

133. false; Changes to make the statement true will vary. A sample change is: Though that set has many values, it is still a finite set.

135. false; Changes to make the statement true will vary. A sample change is: If 0 is removed from a set, it will lower the cardinality of that set by one.

Check Points 2.2

1. a. $\not\subseteq$; because 6, 9, and 11 are not in set *B*.

b. $\subseteq$; because all elements in set *A* are also in set *B*.

c. $\subseteq$; because all elements in set *A* are also in set *B*.

2. a. Both $\subseteq$ and $\subset$ are correct.

b. Both $\subseteq$ and $\subset$ are correct.

3. Yes, the empty set is a subset of any set.

4. a. 16 subsets, 15 proper subsets
There are 4 elements, which means there are 2^4 or 16 subsets. There are $2^4 - 1$ proper subsets or 15.

b. 64 subsets, 63 proper subsets
There are 6 elements, which means there are 2^6 or 64 subsets. There are $2^6 - 1$ proper subsets or 63.

Concept and Vocabulary Check 2.2

1. $A \subseteq B$; every element in set *A* is also an element in set *B*

2. $A \subset B$; sets *A* and *B* are not equal

3. the empty; subset

4. 2^n

5. $2^n - 1$

Exercise Set 2.2

1. $\subseteq$

3. $\not\subseteq$

5. $\not\subseteq$

7. $\not\subseteq$
Subset cannot be larger than the set.

9. $\subseteq$

11. $\not\subseteq$

13. $\subseteq$

15. $\not\subseteq$

17. $\subseteq$

19. $\subseteq$ or $\subset$

21. $\subseteq$

23. neither

25. both

27. $\subseteq$

29. $\subseteq$

31. both

33. both

35. both

37. neither

39. $\subseteq$

41. true

43. false
{Ralph} is a subset, not Ralph.

45. true

47. false
The symbol "$\varnothing$" is not a member of the set.

49. true

51. false
All elements of {1, 4} are members of {4, 1}

53. true

55. { } {Border Collie} {Poodle} {Border Collie, Poodle}

57. { } {t} {a} {b} {t, a} {t, b} {a, b} {t, a, b}

59. { } {0}

61. 16 subsets, 15 proper subsets
There are 4 elements, which means there are 2^4 or 16 subsets. There are $2^4 - 1$ proper subsets or 15.

63. 64 subsets, 63 proper subsets
There are 6 elements, which means there are 2^6 or 64 subsets. There are $2^6 - 1$ proper subsets or 63.

65. 128 subsets, 127 proper subsets
There are 7 elements, which means there are 2^7 or 128 subsets. There are $2^7 - 1$ proper subsets or 127.

67. 8 subsets, 7 proper subsets
There are 3 elements, which means there are 2^3 or 8 subsets. There are $2^3 - 1$ proper subsets or 7.

69. false; The set $\{1, 2, 3, ..., 1000\}$ has $2^{1000} - 1$ proper subsets.

71. true

73. false; $\varnothing \subseteq \{\varnothing, \{\varnothing\}\}$

75. true

77. true

79. true

81. false; The set of subsets of {a, e, i, o, u} contains 2^5 or 32 elements.

83. false; $D \subseteq T$

85. true

87. false; If $x \in W$, then $x \in D$.

89. true

91. true

93. $2^5 = 32$ option combinations

95. $2^6 = 64$ viewing combinations

97. $2^8 = 256$ city combinations

105. does not make sense; Explanations will vary. Sample explanation: The set's elements are not members of the other set.

107. does not make sense; Explanations will vary. Sample explanation: The same formulas are used for each of the mentioned problems.

109. false; Changes to make the statement true will vary. A sample change is: The set has one element and has $2^1 = 2$ subsets.

111. false; Changes to make the statement true will vary. A sample change is: The empty set does not have a proper subset.

113. 0, 5¢, 10¢, 25¢, 40¢, 15¢, 30¢, 35¢
Since there are 3 elements or coins, there are 2^3 or 8 different coin combinations.

Check Points 2.3

1. a. $\{1, 5, 6, 7, 9\}$

   b. $\{1, 5, 6\}$

   c. $\{7, 9\}$

2. a. $\{a, b, c, d\}$

   b. $\{e\}$

   c. $\{e, f, g\}$

   d. $\{f, g\}$

3. $A' = \{b, c, e\}$; those are the elements in U but not in A.

4. a. $\{1, 3, 5, \underline{7}, \underline{10}\} \cap \{6, \underline{7}, \underline{10}, 11\} = \{7, 10\}$

   b. $\{1, 2, 3\} \cap \{4, 5, 6, 7\} = \varnothing$

   c. $\{1, 2, 3\} \cap \varnothing = \varnothing$

5. a. $\{1, 3, 5, 7, 10\} \cup \{6, 7, 10, 11\}$
   $= \{1, 3, 5, 6, 7, 10, 11\}$

   b. $\{1, 2, 3\} \cup \{4, 5, 6, 7\} = \{1, 2, 3, 4, 5, 6, 7\}$

   c. $\{1, 2, 3\} \cup \varnothing = \{1, 2, 3\}$

6. a. $A \cup B = \{b, c, e\}$
   $(A \cup B)' = \{a, d\}$

   b. $A' = \{a, d, e\}$
   $B' = \{a, d\}$
   $A' \cap B' = \{a, d\}$

7. a. $\{5\}$; region II

   b. $\{2, 3, 7, 11, 13, 17, 19\}$; the complement of region II

   c. $\{2, 3, 5, 7, 11, 13\}$; regions I, II, and III

   d. $\{17, 19\}$; the complement of regions I, II, and III

   e. $\{5, 7, 11, 13, 17, 19\}$; the complement of A united with B

   f. $\{2, 3\}$; A intersected with the complement of B

8. $n(A \cup B) = n(A) + n(B) - n(A \cap B)$
   $= 26 + 11 - 9$
   $= 28$

Concept and Vocabulary Check 2.3

1. Venn diagrams
2. complement; A'
3. intersection; $A \cap B$
4. union; $A \cup B$
5. $n(A) + n(B) - n(A \cap B)$
6. true
7. false
8. true
9. false

Exercise Set 2.3

1. U is the set of all composers.

3. U is the set of all brands of soft drinks.

5. $A' = \{c, d, e\}$

7. $C' = \{b, c, d, e, f\}$

9. $A' = \{6, 7, 8, \ldots, 20\}$

11. $C' = \{2, 4, 6, 8, \ldots, 20\}$

13. $A' = \{21, 22, 23, 24, \ldots\}$

15. $C' = \{1, 3, 5, 7, \ldots\}$

17. $A = \{1, 3, 5, 7\}$
    $B = \{1, 2, 3\}$
    $A \cap B = \{1, 3\}$

19. $A = \{1, 3, 5, 7\}$
    $B = \{1, 2, 3\}$
    $A \cup B = \{1, 2, 3, 5, 7\}$

21. $A = \{1, 3, 5, 7\}$
    $U = \{1, 2, 3, 4, 5, 6, 7\}$
    $A' = \{2, 4, 6\}$

23. $A' = \{2, 4, 6\}$
    $B' = \{4, 5, 6, 7\}$
    $A' \cap B' = \{4, 6\}$

25. $A = \{1, 3, 5, 7\}$
$C' = \{1, 7\}$
$A \cup C' = \{1, 3, 5, 7\}$

27. $A = \{1, 3, 5, 7\}$
$C = \{2, 3, 4, 5, 6\}$
$A \cap C = \{3, 5\}$
$(A \cap C)' = \{1, 2, 4, 6, 7\}$

29. $A = \{1, 3, 5, 7\}$ $C = \{2, 3, 4, 5, 6\}$
$A' = \{2, 4, 6\}$ $C' = \{1, 7\}$
$A' \cup C' = \{1, 2, 4, 6, 7\}$

31. $A = \{1, 3, 5, 7\}$ $B = \{1, 2, 3\}$
$(A \cup B) = \{1, 2, 3, 5, 7\}$
$(A \cup B)' = \{4, 6\}$

33. $A = \{1, 3, 5, 7\}$
$A \cup \varnothing = \{1, 3, 5, 7\}$

35. $A \cap \varnothing = \varnothing$

37. $A \cup U = U$
$U = \{1, 2, 3, 4, 5, 6, 7\}$

39. $A \cap U = A$
$A = \{1, 3, 5, 7\}$

41. $A = \{a, g, h\}$
$B = \{b, g, h\}$
$A \cap B = \{g, h\}$

43. $A = \{a, g, h\}$
$B = \{b, g, h\}$
$A \cup B = \{a, b, g, h\}$

45. $A = \{a, g, h\}$
$U = \{a, b, c, d, e, f, g, h\}$
$A' = \{b, c, d, e, f\}$

47. $A' = \{b, c, d, e, f\}$
$B' = \{a, c, d, e, f\}$
$A' \cap B' = \{c, d, e, f\}$

49. $A = \{a, g, h\}$
$C' = \{a, g, h\}$
$A \cup C' = \{a, g, h\}$

51. $A = \{a, g, h\}$
$C = \{b, c, d, e, f\}$
$A \cap C = \varnothing$
$(A \cap C)' = \{a, b, c, d, e, f, g, h\}$

53. $A' = \{b, c, d, e, f\}$
$C' = \{a, g, h\}$
$A' \cup C' = \{a, b, c, d, e, f, g, h\}$

55. $A = \{a, g, h\}$
$B = \{b, g, h\}$
$A \cup B = \{a, b, g, h\}$
$(A \cup B)' = \{c, d, e, f\}$

57. $A \cup \varnothing = A$
$A = \{a, g, h\}$

59. $A \cap \varnothing = \varnothing$

61. $A = \{a, g, h\}$
$U = \{a, b, c, d, e, f, g, h\}$
$A \cup U = \{a, b, c, d, e, f, g, h\}$

63. $A = \{a, g, h\}$
$U = \{a, b, c, d, e, f, g, h\}$
$A \cap U = \{a, g, h\}$

65. $A = \{a, g, h\}$
$B = \{b, g, h\}$
$B' = \{a, c, d, e, f\}$
$A \cap B = \{g, h\}$
$(A \cap B) \cup B' = \{a, c, d, e, f, g, h\}$

67. $A = \{1, 3, 4, 7\}$

69. $U = \{1, 2, 3, 4, 5, 6, 7, 8, 9\}$

71. $A \cap B = \{3, 7\}$

73. $B' = \{1, 4, 8, 9\}$

75. $(A \cup B)' = \{8, 9\}$

77. $A = \{1, 3, 4, 7\}$
$B' = \{1, 4, 8, 9\}$
$A \cap B' = \{1, 4\}$

79. $B = \{\triangle$, two, four, six$\}$

81. $A \cup B = \{\triangle$, #, \$, two, four, six$\}$

83. $n(A \cup B) = n(\{\triangle, \#, \$, \text{two, four, six}\}) = 6$

85. $n(A') = 5$

87. $(A \cap B)' = \{\#, \$, \text{two, four, six, 10, 01}\}$

89. $A' \cap B = \{\text{two, four, six}\}$

91. $n(U) - n(B) = 8 - 4 = 4$

93. $n(A \cup B) = n(A) + n(B) - n(A \cap B)$
$= 17 \quad + 20 \quad - 6$
$= 31$

95. $n(A \cup B) = n(A) + n(B) - n(A \cap B)$
$= 17 \quad + 17 \quad - 7$
$= 27$

97. $A = \{1, 3, 5, 7\}$
$B = \{2, 4, 6, 8\}$
$A \cup B = \{1, 2, 3, 4, 5, 6, 7, 8\}$

99. $U = \{1, 2, 3, 4, 5, 6, 7, 8\}$
$A = \{1, 3, 5, 7\}$
$A \cap U = \{1, 3, 5, 7\}$

101. $A = \{1, 3, 5, 7\}$
$C' = \{1, 6, 7, 8\}$
$A \cap C' = \{1, 7\}$

103. $U = \{1, 2, 3, 4, 5, 6, 7, 8\}$
$B = \{2, 4, 6, 8\}$
$C = \{2, 3, 4, 5\}$
$B \cap C = \{2, 4\}$

$(B \cap C)' = \{1, 3, 5, 6, 7, 8\}$

105. $A \cup (A \cup B)'$
$= \{23, 29, 31, 37, 41, 43, 53, 59, 61, 67, 71\}$

107. $n(U)\left[n(A \cup B) - n(A \cap B)\right] = 12[7 - 2]$
$= 12(5) = 60$

109. {Ashley, Mike, Josh}

111. {Ashley, Mike, Josh, Emily, Hannah, Ethan}

113. {Ashley}

115. {Jacob}

117. Region III, *elementary school teacher* is in set *B* but not set *A*.

119. Region I, *surgeon* is in set *A* but not set *B*.

121. Region II, *family doctor* is in set *A* and set *B*.

123. Region I, 11 is in set *A* but not set *B*.

125. Region IV, 15 is in neither set *A* nor set *B*.

127. Region II, 454 is in set *A* and set *B*.

129. Region III, 9558 is in set *B* but not set *A*.

131. Region I, 9559 is in set *A* but not set *B*.

133. {1980, 1990} ∩ {1980, 1990, 2000}
= {1980, 1990}

135. {1980, 1990} ∪ {1980, 1990, 2000}
= {1980, 1990, 2000}

137. {1990, 2000, 2010} ∩ {1980} = ∅

139. $n(A \cup B) = n(A) + n(B) - n(A \cap B)$
$= 178 \quad + 154 \quad - 49$
$= 283$ people

153. makes sense

155. makes sense

157. true

159. false; Changes to make the statement true will vary. A sample change is: If $A \subseteq B$, then $A \cup B = B$.

161. false; Changes to make the statement true will vary. A sample change is: $A \cap \varnothing = \varnothing$

163. true

165.

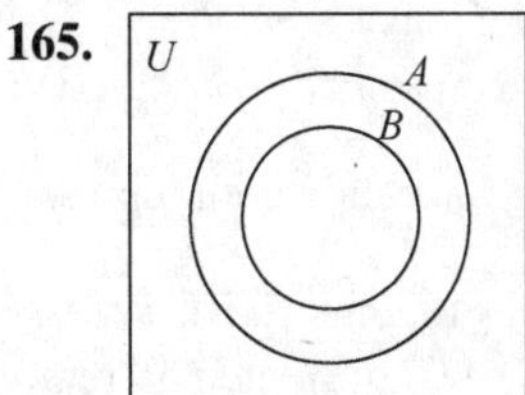

167.

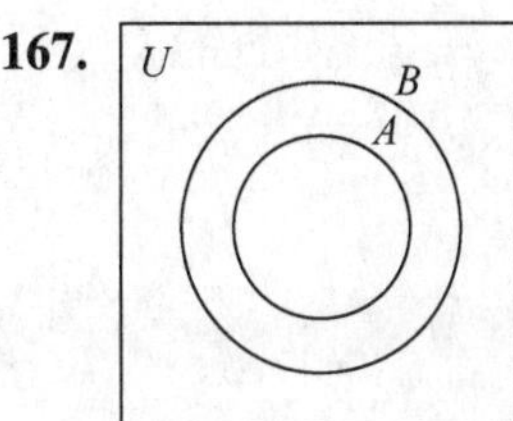

Check Points 2.4

1. **a.** $A \cup (B \cap C) = \{a, b, c, d\} \cup \{b, f\}$
$= \{a, b, c, d, f\}$

b. $(A \cup B) \cap (A \cup C) = \{a, b, c, d, f\} \cap \{a, b, c, d, f\}$
$= \{a, b, c, d, f\}$

c. $A \cap (B \cup C') = \{a, b, c, d\} \cap (\{a, b, d, f\} \cup \{a, d, e\})$
$= \{a, b, c, d\} \cap \{a, b, d, e, f\}$
$= \{a, b, d\}$

2. **a.** C is represented by regions IV, V, VI, and VII.
Thus, $C = \{5, 6, 7, 8, 9\}$

b. $B \cup C$ is represented by regions II, III, IV, V, VI, and VII.
Thus, $B \cup C = \{1, 2, 5, 6, 7, 8, 9, 10, 12\}$

c. $A \cap C$ is represented by regions IV and V.
Thus, $A \cap C = \{5, 6, 7\}$

d. B' is represented by regions I, IV, VII, and VIII.
Thus, $B' = \{3, 4, 6, 8, 11\}$

e. $A \cup B \cup C$ is represented by regions I, II, III, IV, V, VI, and VII.
Thus, $A \cup B \cup C = \{1, 2, 3, 5, 6, 7, 8, 9, 10, 11, 12\}$

3. 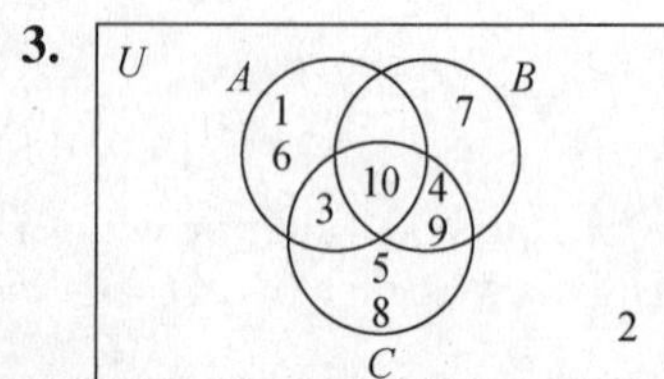

4. **a.** $A \cup B$ is represented by regions I, II, and III.
Therefore $(A \cup B)'$ is represented by region IV.

b. A' is represented by regions III and IV.
B' is represented by regions I and IV.
Therefore $A' \cap B'$ is represented by region IV.

c. $(A \cup B)' = A' \cap B'$ because they both represent region IV.

5. **a.** $B \cup C$ is represented by regions II, III, IV, V, VI, and VII.
Therefore $A \cap (B \cup C)$ is represented by regions II, IV, and V.

b. $A \cap B$ is represented by regions II and V.
$A \cap C$ is represented by regions IV and V.
Therefore $(A \cap B) \cup (A \cap C)$ is represented by regions II, IV, and V.

c. $A \cap (B \cup C) = (A \cap B) \cup (A \cap C)$ because they both represent region IV.

Concept and Vocabulary Check 2.4

1. inside parentheses
2. eight
3. false
4. true

Exercises 2.4

1. $B \cap C = \{2, 3\}$
$A \cup (B \cap C) = \{1, 2, 3, 5, 7\}$

3. $A \cup B = \{1, 2, 3, 5, 7\}$
$A \cup C = \{1, 2, 3, 4, 5, 6, 7\}$
$(A \cup B) \cap (A \cup C) = \{1, 2, 3, 5, 7\}$

5. $A' = \{2, 4, 6\}$ $C' = \{1, 7\}$
$B \cup C' = \{1, 2, 3, 7\}$
$A' \cap (B \cup C') = \{2\}$

7. $A' = \{2, 4, 6\}$ $C' = \{1, 7\}$
$A' \cap B = \{2\}$
$A' \cap C' = \varnothing$
$(A' \cap B) \cup (A' \cap C') = \{2\}$

9. $A = \{1, 3, 5, 7\}$
$B = \{1, 2, 3\}$
$C = \{2, 3, 4, 5, 6\}$
$A \cup B \cup C = \{1, 2, 3, 4, 5, 6, 7\}$
$(A \cup B \cup C)' = \varnothing$

11. $A = \{1, 3, 5, 7\}$
$B = \{1, 2, 3\}$
$A \cup B = \{1, 2, 3, 5, 7\}$
$(A \cup B)' = \{4, 6\}$
$C = \{2, 3, 4, 5, 6\}$
$(A \cup B)' \cap C = \{4, 6\}$

13. $B \cap C = \{b\}$
$A \cup (B \cap C) = \{a, b, g, h\}$

15. $A \cup B = \{a, b, g, h\}$
$A \cup C = \{a, b, c, d, e, f, g, h\}$
$(A \cup B) \cap (A \cup C) = \{a, b, g, h\}$

17. $A' = \{b, c, d, e, f\}$
$C' = \{a, g, h\}$
$B \cup C' = \{a, b, g, h\}$
$A' \cap (B \cup C') = \{b\}$

19. $A' = \{b, c, d, e, f\}$
$A' \cap B = \{b\}$
$C' = \{a, g, h\}$
$A' \cap C' = \varnothing$
$(A' \cap B) \cup (A' \cap C') = \{b\}$

21. $A \cup B \cup C = \{a, b, c, d, e, f, g, h\}$
$(A \cup B \cup C)' = \varnothing$

23. $A \cup B = \{a, b, g, h\}$
$(A \cup B)' = \{c, d, e, f\}$
$(A \cup B)' \cap C = \{c, d, e, f\}$

25. II, III, V, VI

27. I, II, IV, V, VI, VII

29. II, V

31. I, IV, VII, VIII

33. $A = \{1, 2, 3, 4, 5, 6, 7, 8\}$

35. $A \cup B = \{1, 2, 3, 4, 5, 6, 7, 8, 9, 10, 11\}$

37. $A = \{1, 2, 3, 4, 5, 6, 7, 8\}$
$B = \{4, 5, 6, 9, 10, 11\}$
$A \cup B = \{1, 2, 3, 4, 5, 6, 7, 8, 9, 10, 11\}$
$(A \cup B)' = \{12, 13\}$

39. The set contains the elements in the two regions where the circles representing sets *A* and *B* overlap.
$A \cap B = \{4, 5, 6\}$

41. The set contains the element in the center region where the circles representing sets *A*, *B*, and *C* overlap.
$A \cap B \cap C = \{6\}$

43. $A \cap B \cap C = \{6\}$
$(A \cap B \cap C)' = \{1, 2, 3, 4, 5, 7, 8, 9, 10, 11, 12, 13\}$

45. 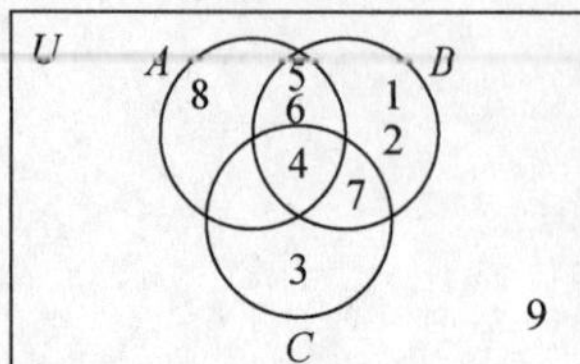

47. 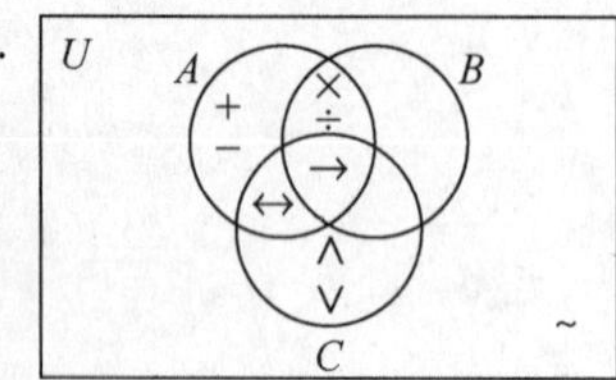

49. a. II

b. II

c. $A \cap B = B \cap A$

51. a. I, III, IV

b. IV

c. No, $(A \cap B)' \neq A' \cap B'$

53. Set A is represented by regions I and II.
Set A' is represented by regions III and IV.
Set B is represented by regions II and III.
Set B' is represented by regions I and IV.
$A' \cup B$ is represented by regions II, III, and IV.
$A \cap B'$ is represented by region I.
Thus, $A' \cup B$ and $A \cap B'$ are not equal for all sets A and B.

55. Set A is represented by regions I and II.
Set B is represented by regions II and III.
$(A \cup B)'$ is represented by region IV.
$(A \cap B)'$ is represented by regions I, III, and IV.
Thus, $(A \cup B)'$ and $(A \cap B)'$ are not equal for all sets A and B.

57. Set A is represented by regions I and II.
Set A' is represented by regions III and IV.
Set B is represented by regions II and III.
Set B' is represented by regions I and IV.
$(A' \cap B)'$ is represented by regions I, II, and IV.
$A \cup B'$ is represented by regions I, II, and IV.
Thus, $A' \cap B$ and $A \cup B'$ are equal for all sets A and B.

59. a. II, IV, V, VI, VII

b. II, IV, V, VI, VII

c. $(A \cap B) \cup C = (A \cup C) \cap (B \cup C)$

61. a. II, IV, V

b. I, II, IV, V, VI

c. No
The results in **a** and **b** show $A \cap (B \cup C) \neq A \cup (B \cap C)$ because of the different regions represented.

63. The left expression is represented by regions II, IV, and V. The right expression is represented by regions II, IV, V, VI, and VII. Thus this statement is not true.

65. Both expressions are represented by regions II, III, IV, V, and VI. Thus this statement is true and is a theorem.

67. Both expressions are represented by region I. Thus this statement is true and is a theorem.

69. a. $A \cup (B' \cap C') = \{\text{c, e, f}\}$
$(A \cup B') \cap (A \cup C') = \{\text{c, e, f}\}$

b. $A \cup (B' \cap C') = \{1, 3, 5, 7, 8\}$
$(A \cup B') \cap (A \cup C') = \{1, 3, 5, 7, 8\}$

c. $A \cup (B' \cap C') = (A \cup B') \cap (A \cup C')$

d. $A \cup (B' \cap C')$ and $(A \cup B') \cap (A \cup C')$ are both represented by regions I, II, IV, V, and VIII. Thus, the conjecture in part c is a theorem.

71. $(A \cap B') \cap (A \cup B)$

73. $A' \cup B$

75. $(A \cap B) \cup C$

77. $A' \cap (B \cup C)$

79. {Ann, Jose, Al, Gavin, Amy, Ron, Grace}

81. {Jose}

83. {Lily, Emma}

85. {Lily, Emma, Ann, Jose, Lee, Maria, Fred, Ben, Sheila, Ellen, Gary}

87. {Lily, Emma, Al, Gavin, Amy, Lee, Maria}

89. {Al, Gavin, Amy}

91. The set of students who scored 90% or above on exam 1 and exam 3 but not on exam 2 is the empty set.

93. Region I

95. Region V

97. Region VI

99. Region III

101. Region IV

103. Region VI

105. Venn diagram:

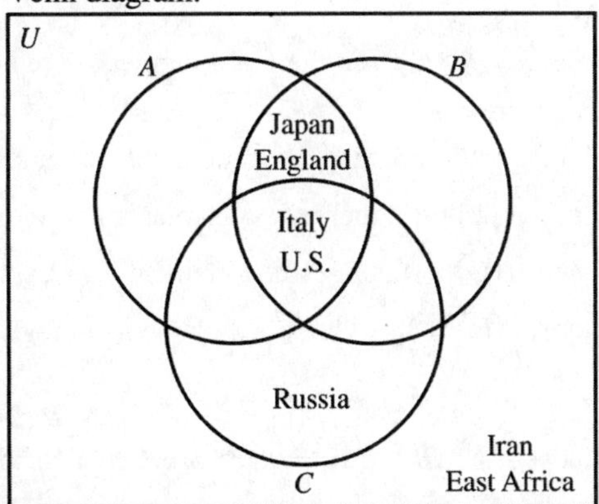

109. does not make sense; Explanations will vary. Sample explanation: You should begin by placing elements in the innermost region.

111. makes sense

113. AB^+

115. no

Check Points 2.5

1. **a.** $55 + 20 = 75$

b. $20 + 70 = 90$

c. 20

d. $55 + 20 + 70 = 145$

e. 55

f. 70

g. 30

h. $55 + 20 + 70 + 30 = 175$

2. Start by placing 700 in region II.
Next place $1190 - 700$ or 490 in region III.
Since half of those surveyed were women, place $1000 - 700$ or 300 in region I.
Finally, place $2000 - 300 - 700 - 490$ or 510 in region IV.

a. 490 men agreed with the statement and are represented by region III.

b. 510 men disagreed with the statement and are represented by region IV.

3. Since 2 people collect all three items, begin by placing a 2 in region V.
Since 29 people collect baseball cards and comic books, 29 – 2 or 27 should be placed in region II.
Since 5 people collect baseball cards and stamps, 5 – 2 or 3 should be placed in region IV.
Since 2 people collect comic books and stamps, 2 – 2 or 0 should be placed in region VI.
Since 108 people collect baseball cards, 108 – 27 – 3 – 2 or 76 should be placed in region I.
Since 92 people collect comic books, 92 – 27 – 2 – 0 or 63 should be placed in region III.
Since 62 people collect stamps, 62 – 3 – 2 – 0 or 57 should be placed in region VII.
Since there were 250 people surveyed, place $250 - 76 - 27 - 63 - 3 - 2 - 0 - 57 = 22$ in region VIII.

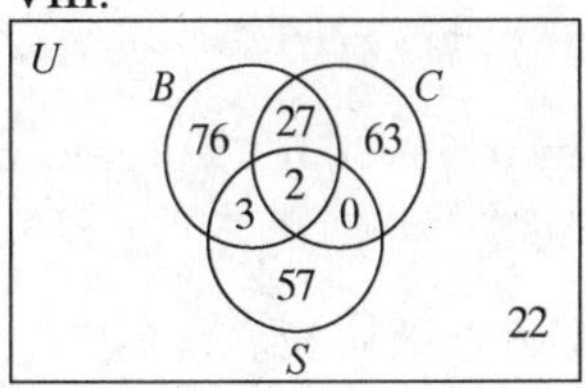

4. a. 63 as represented by region III.

   b. 3 as represented by region IV.

   c. 136 as represented by regions I, IV, and VII.

   d. 30 as represented by regions II, IV, and VI.

   e. 228 as represented by regions I through VII.

   f. 22 as represented by region VIII.

Concept and Vocabulary Check 2.5

1. and/but
2. or
3. not
4. innermost; subtraction
5. true
6. true
7. false
8. true

Exercise Set 2.5

1. 26

3. 17

5. 37

7. 7

9. Region I has 21 – 7 or 14 elements.
   Region III has 29 – 7 or 22 elements.
   Region IV has 48 – 14 – 7– 22 or 5 elements.

11. 17 as represented by regions II, III, V, and VI.

13. 6 as represented by regions I and II.

15. 28 as represented by regions I, II, IV, V, VI, and VII.

17. 9 as represented by regions IV and V.

19. 3 as represented by region VI.

21. 19 as represented by regions III, VI, and VII.

23. 21 as represented by regions I, III, and VII.

25. 34 as represented by regions I through VII.

27. Since $n(A \cap B) = 3$, there is 1 element in region II.
    Since $n(A \cap C) = 5$, there are 3 elements in region IV.
    Since $n(B \cap C) = 3$, there is 1 element in region VI.
    Since $n(A) = 11$, there are 5 elements in region I.
    Since $n(B) = 8$, there are 4 elements in region III.
    Since $n(C) = 14$, there are 8 elements in region VII.
    Since $n(U) = 30$, there are 6 elements in region VIII.

29. Since $n(A \cap B \cap C) = 7$, there are 7 elements in region V.
    Since $n(A \cap B) = 17$, there are 10 elements in region II.
    Since $n(A \cap C) = 11$, there are 4 elements in region IV.
    Since $n(B \cap C) = 8$, there is 1 element in region VI.
    Since $n(A) = 26$, there are 5 elements in region I.
    Since $n(B) = 21$, there are 3 elements in region III.
    Since $n(C) = 18$, there are 6 elements in region VII.
    Since $n(U) = 38$, there are 2 elements in region VIII.

31. Since $n(A \cap B \cap C) = 2$, there are 2 elements in region V.
    Since $n(A \cap B) = 6$, there are 4 elements in region II.
    Since $n(A \cap C) = 9$, there are 7 elements in region IV.
    Regions II, IV, and V contain a total of 13 elements, yet set *A* is stated to contain a total of only 10 elements. That is impossible.

33. $4+5+2+7=18$ respondents agreed with the statement.

35. $2+7=9$ women agreed with the statement.

37. 9 women who are not African American disagreed with the statement.

39. Parts b, c, and d are labeled.

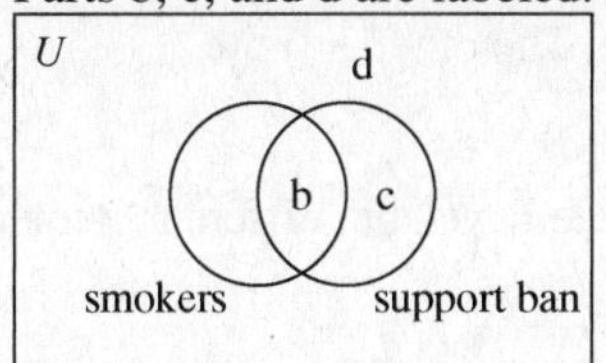

41. Parts b, c, and d are labeled.

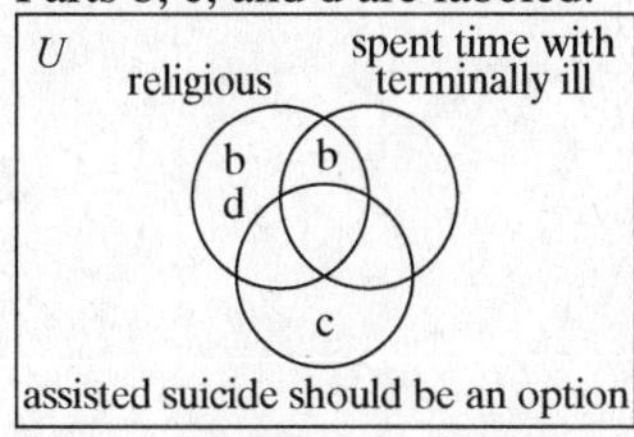

Answers for part e will vary.

43. Begin by placing 7 in the region that represents both newspapers and television.

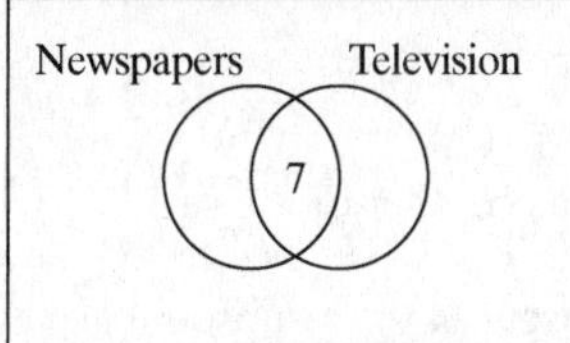

a. Since 29 students got news from newspapers, $29 - 7 = 22$ got news from only newspapers.

b. Since 43 students got news from television, $43 - 7 = 36$ got news from only television.

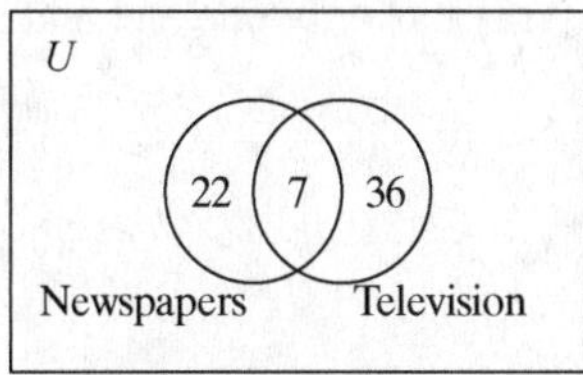

c. $22 + 7 + 36 = 65$ students who got news from newspapers or television.

d. Since 75 students were surveyed, $75 - 65 = 10$ students who did not get news from either.

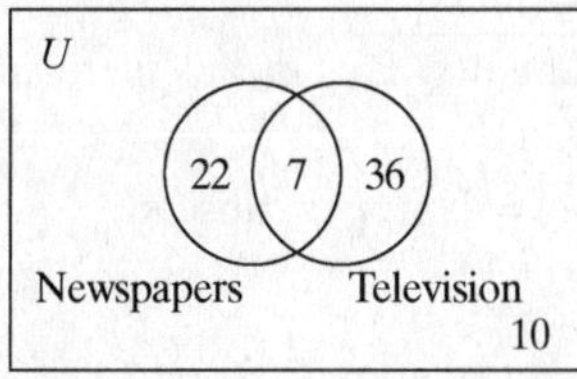

45. Construct a Venn diagram.

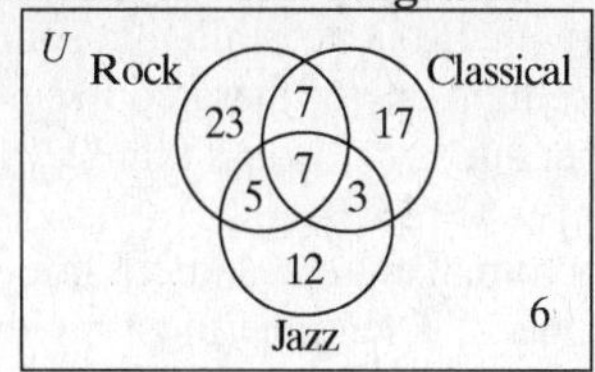

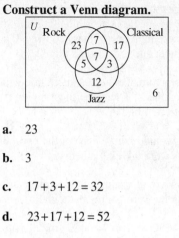

a. 23

b. 3

c. $17 + 3 + 12 = 32$

d. $23 + 17 + 12 = 52$

e. $7 + 3 + 5 + 7 = 22$

f. 6

47. Construct a Venn diagram.

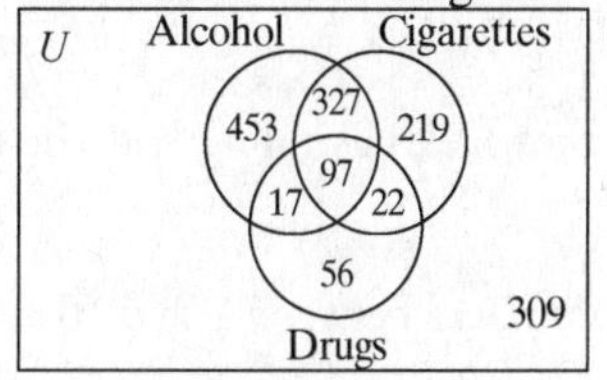

a. 1500 (all eight regions)

b. 1135 (the six regions of sets *A* and *C*)

c. 56 (region VII)

d. 327 (region II)

e. 526 (regions I, IV, and VII)

f. 366 (regions II, IV, and VI)

g. 1191 (regions I through VII)

51. does not make sense; Explanations will vary. Sample explanation: A survey problem could present the information in any order.

53. does not make sense; Explanations will vary. Sample explanation: Since there is a circle to represent smokers, then nonsmokers are represented by being placed outside that circle, not in a separate circle.

55. false; Changes to make the statement true will vary. A sample change is: It is possible that some students are taking more than one of these courses. If so, then the number surveyed is less than 220.

57. false; Changes to make the statement true will vary. A sample change is: Then innermost region is the first region to be filled in.

59. **a.** 0; This would assume none of the psychology students were taking mathematics.

b. 30; This would assume all 30 students taking psychology were taking mathematics.

c. 60; $U = 150$ so with 90 taking mathematics, if we assume all the psychology students are taking mathematics courses, $U - 90 = 60$.

Chapter 2 Review Exercises

1. the set of days of the week beginning with the letter T

2. the set of natural numbers between 1 and 10, inclusive

3. {m, i, s}

4. {8, 9, 10, 11, 12}

5. {1, 2, 3, …, 30}

6. not empty

7. empty set

8. $\in$
93 is an element of the set.

9. $\notin$
{d} is a subset, not a member; "d" would be a member.

10. 12
12 months in the year.

11. 15

12. $\neq$
The two sets do not contain exactly the same elements.

13. $\neq$
One set is infinite. The other is finite.

14. Equivalent
Same number of elements, but different elements.

15. Equal and equivalent
The two sets have exactly the same elements.

16. finite

17. infinite

18. $\subseteq$

19. $\not\subseteq$

20. $\subseteq$

21. $\subseteq$

22. both

23. false; Texas is not a member of the set.

24. false; 4 is not a subset. {4} is a subset.

25. true

26. false; It is a subset but not a proper subset.

27. true

28. false; The set {six} has only one element so it has $2^1 = 2$ subsets.

29. true

30. $\varnothing$ {1} {5} {1, 5}
{1, 5} is not a proper subset.

31. There are 5 elements. This means there are $2^5 = 32$ subsets.
There are $2^5 - 1 = 31$ proper subsets.

32. {January, June, July}
There are 3 elements. This means there are $2^3 = 8$ subsets.
There are $2^3 - 1 = 7$ proper subsets.

33. $A \cap B = \{1, 2, 4\}$

34. $A \cup B' = \{1, 2, 3, 4, 6, 7, 8\}$

35. $A' \cap B = \{5\}$

36. $(A \cup B)' = \{6, 7, 8\}$

37. $A' \cap B' = \{6, 7, 8\}$

38. $\{4, 5, 6\}$

39. $\{2, 3, 6, 7\}$

40. $\{1, 4, 5, 6, 8, 9\}$

41. $\{4, 5\}$

42. $\{1, 2, 3, 6, 7, 8, 9\}$

43. $\{2, 3, 7\}$

44. $\{6\}$

45. $\{1, 2, 3, 4, 5, 6, 7, 8, 9\}$

46. $$\begin{aligned} n(A \cup B) &= n(A) + n(B) - n(A \cap B) \\ &= 25 + 17 - 9 \\ &= 33 \end{aligned}$$

47. $B \cap C = \{1, 5\}$
$A \cup (B \cap C) = \{1, 2, 3, 4, 5\}$

48. $A \cap C = \{1\}$
$(A \cap C)' = (2, 3, 4, 5, 6, 7, 8\}$
$(A \cap C)' \cup B = \{1, 2, 3, 4, 5, 6, 7, 8\}$

49. $\{c, d, e, f, k, p, r\}$

50. $\{f, p\}$

51. $\{c, d, f, k, p, r\}$

52. $\{c, d, e\}$

53. $\{a, b, c, d, e, g, h, p, r\}$

54. $\{f\}$

55.

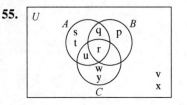

56. The shaded regions are the same for $(A \cup B)'$ and $A' \cap B'$. Therefore $(A \cup B)' = A' \cap B'$

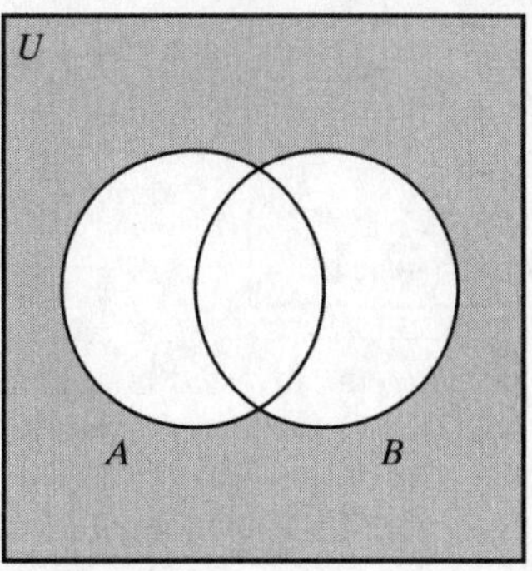

57. The statement is false because the shaded regions are different.

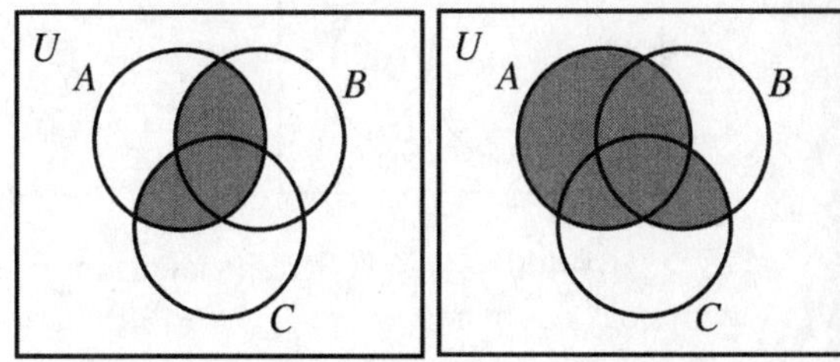

58. United States is in V; Italy is in IV; Turkey is in VIII; Norway is in V; Pakistan is in VIII; Iceland is in V; Mexico is in I

59. a. Parts b and c are labeled.

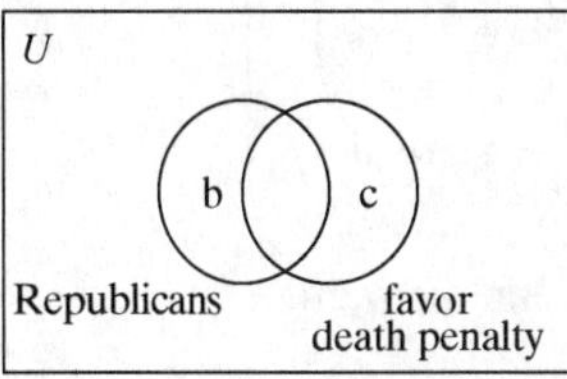

60. Begin by placing 400 in the region that represents both stocks and bonds.

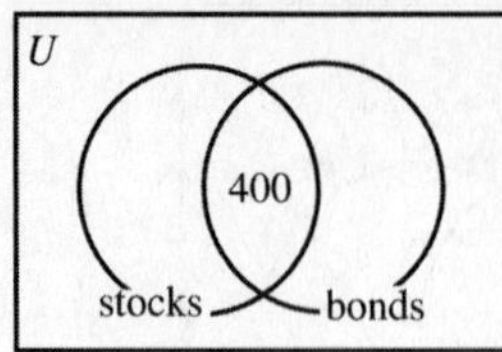

a. Since 650 respondents invested in stocks, $650-400=250$ invested in only stocks.

Furthermore, since 550 respondents invested in bonds, $550-400=150$ invested in only bonds. Place this data in the Venn diagram.

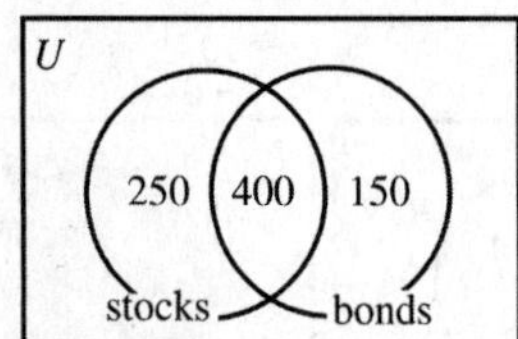

b. $250+400+150=800$ respondents invested in stocks or bonds.

c. Since 1000 people were surveyed, $1000-800=200$ respondents who did not invest in either.

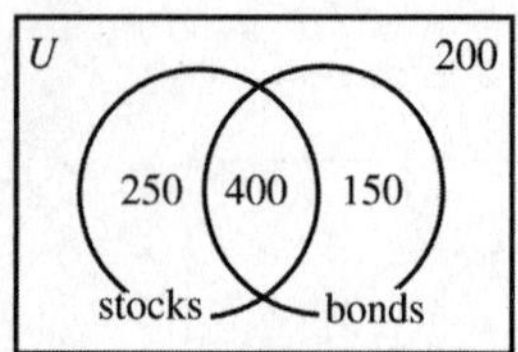

61. Construct a Venn diagram.

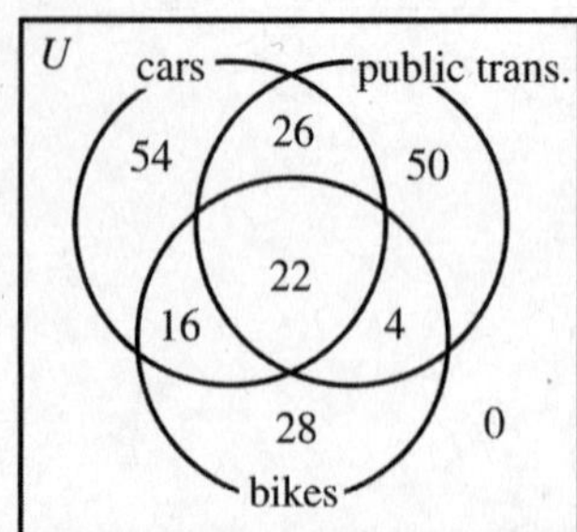

a. 50

b. 26

c. $54+26+50=130$

d. $26+16+4=46$

e. 0

Chapter 2 Test

1. {18, 19, 20, 21, 22, 23, 24}

2. false, {6} is not an element of the set, but 6 is an element.

3. true, both sets have seven elements.

4. true

5. false, *g* is not an element in the larger set.

6. true

7. false, 14 is an element of the set.

8. false, Number of subsets: 2^N where *N* is the number of elements. There are 5 elements. $2^5=32$ subsets

9. false, $\varnothing$ is *not* a proper subset of itself.

10. $\varnothing$ {6} {9} {6, 9}
{6, 9} is not a proper subset.

11. {a, b, c, d, e, f}

12. $B \cap C = \{\text{e}\}$
$(B \cap C)' = \{\text{a, b, c, d, f, g}\}$

13. $C' = \{\text{b, c, d, f}\}$
$A \cap C' = \{\text{b, c, d}\}$

14. $A \cup B = \{\text{a, b, c, d, e, f}\}$
$(A \cup B) \cap C = \{\text{a, e}\}$

15. $B' = \{\text{a, b, g}\}$
$A \cup B' = \{\text{a, b, c, d, g}\}$
$n(A \cup B') = 5$

16. {b, c, d, i, j, k}

17. {a}

18. {a, f, h}

19.

U
A
B
4
1
5
6
7
2
3

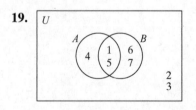

20. Both expressions are represented by regions III, VI, and VII. Thus this statement is true and is a theorem.

21. a. region V

b. region VII

c. region IV

d. region I

e. region VI

22. a.

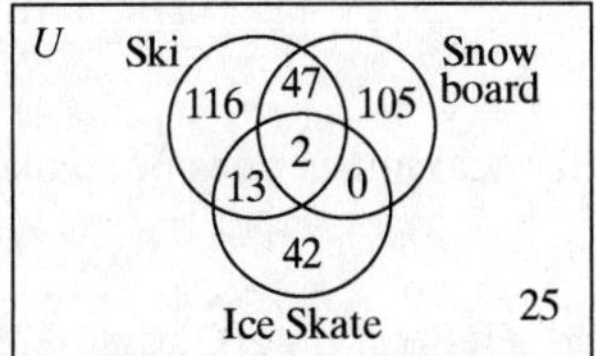

b. 263 (regions I, III, and VII)

c. 25 (region VIII)

d. 62 (regions II, IV, V, and VI)

e. 0 (region VI)

f. 147 (regions III, VI, and VII)

g. 116 (region I)

Chapter 3
Logic

Check Points 3.1

1. a. Paris is not the capital of Spain.

   b. July is a month.

2. a. ~p

   b. ~q

3. Chicago O'Hare is not the world's busiest airport.

4. Some new tax dollars will not be used to improve education.
   At least one new tax dollar will not be used to improve education.

Concept and Vocabulary Check 3.1

1. true; false
2. false; true
3. $\sim p$; not p
4. quantified
5. There are no *A* that are not *B*
6. There exists at least one *A* that is a *B*
7. All *A* are not *B*.
8. Not all *A* are *B*.
9. Some *A* are not *B*.
10. No *A* are *B*.

Exercise Set 3.1

1. statement

3. statement

5. not a statement

7. statement

9. not a statement

11. statement

13. statement

15. It is not raining.

17. Facts cease to exist when they are ignored.

19. Chocolate in moderation is good for the heart.

21. ~p

23. ~r

25. Listening to classical music does not make infants smarter.

27. Sigmund Freud's father was 20 years older than his mother.

29. a. There are no whales that are not mammals.

    b. Some whales are not mammals.

31. a. At least one student is a business major.

    b. No students are business majors.

33. a. At least one thief is not a criminal.

    b. All thieves are criminals.

35. a. All Democratic presidents have not been impeached.

    b. Some Democratic presidents have been impeached.

37. a. All seniors graduated.

    b. Some seniors did not graduate.

39. a. Some parrots are not pets.

    b. All parrots are pets.

41. a. No atheist is a churchgoer.

    b. Some atheists are churchgoers.

43. Some Africans have Jewish ancestry.

45. Some rap is not hip-hop.

47. a. All birds are parrots.

b. false; Some birds are not parrots.

49. a. No college students are business majors.

b. false; Some college students are business majors.

51. a. All people like Sara Lee.

b. Some people don't like Sara Lee.

53. a. No safe thing is exciting.

b. Some safe things are exciting.

55. a. Some great actors are not Tom Hanks.

b. All great actors are Tom Hanks.

57. b

59. true

61. false; Some college students in the United States are willing to marry without romantic love.

63. true

65. false; The sentence "5% of college students in Australia are willing to marry without romantic love" is a statement.

75. does not make sense; Explanations will vary. Sample explanation: Statements that have opposite truth values are not necessarily negations of each other.

77. does not make sense; Explanations will vary. Sample explanation: The correctness of the spelling is not relevant.

79. Answers will vary. Possible answer: Some mammals are not cats (true). Some cats are not mammals (false).

Check Points 3.2

1. a. $q \wedge p$ **b.** $\sim p \wedge q$

2. a. $p \vee q$ **b.** $q \vee \sim p$

3. a. $\sim p \to \sim q$ **b.** $q \to \sim p$

4. $\sim q \to p$

5. a. $q \leftrightarrow p$ **b.** $\sim p \leftrightarrow \sim q$

6. a. It is not true that he earns $105,000 yearly and that he is often happy.

b. He is not often happy and he earns $105,000 yearly.

c. It is not true that if he is often happy then he earns $105,000 yearly.

7. a. If the plant is fertilized and watered, then the plant does not wilt.

b. The plant is fertilized, and if the plant is watered then it does not wilt.

8. p: There is too much homework.; q: A teacher is boring.; r: I take the class.

a. $(p \vee q) \to \sim r$ **b.** $p \vee (q \to \sim r)$

Concept and Vocabulary Check 3.2

1. $p \wedge q$; conjunction

2. $p \vee q$; disjunction

3. $p \to q$; conditional

4. $p \leftrightarrow q$; biconditional

5. true

6. false

7. true

8. false

9. true

10. true

11. true

12. true

13. false

Exercise Set 3.2

1. $p \wedge q$

3. $q \wedge \sim p$

5. $\sim q \wedge p$

7. $p \vee q$; I study (p) or (∨) I pass the course. (q)

9. $p \vee \sim q$; I study (p) or (∨) I do not pass the course. (~q)

11. $p \rightarrow q$;
If (→) this is an alligator, (p) then this is a reptile. (q)

13. $\sim p \rightarrow \sim q$;
If this is not an alligator, (~p) then (→)
this is not a reptile. (~q)

15. $\sim q \rightarrow \sim p$
Note that the original sentence...
This is not an alligator if it's not a reptile.
... is equivalent to the sentence...
If it's not a reptile, then it is not an alligator.

17. $p \rightarrow q$
Note that "*q* is necessary for *p*" is shown symbolically as $p \rightarrow q$.

19. $p \rightarrow \sim q$
Note that the original sentence...
You do not have feathers if you are human.
... is equivalent to the sentence...
If you are human, then you do not have feathers.

21. $q \rightarrow \sim p$
Note that the original sentence...
Not being human is necessary for having feathers.
... is equivalent to the sentence...
If you have feathers, then you are not human.

23. $p \rightarrow \sim q$
Note that the original sentence...
Being human is sufficient for not having feathers.
... is equivalent to the sentence...
If you are human, then you do not have feathers.

25. $q \rightarrow \sim p$
Note that the original sentence...
You have feathers only if you're not human.
... is equivalent to the sentence...
If you have feathers, then you are not human.

27. $p \leftrightarrow q$;
The campus is closed (p) if and only if (↔) it is Sunday. (q)

29. $\sim q \leftrightarrow \sim p$;
It is not Sunday (~q) if and only if (↔)
the campus is not closed. (~p)

31. $q \leftrightarrow p$

33. The heater is not working and the house is cold.

35. The heater is working or the house is not cold.

37. If the heater is working then the house is not cold.

39. The heater is working if and only if the house is not cold.

41. It is July 4th and we are not having a barbeque.

43. It is not July 4th or we are having a barbeque.

45. If we are having a barbeque, then it is not July 4th.

47. It is not July 4th if and only if we are having a barbeque.

49. It is not true that Romeo loves Juliet and Juliet loves Romeo.

51. Romeo does not love Juliet and Juliet loves Romeo.

53. Neither Juliet loves Romeo nor Romeo loves Juliet.

55. Juliet does not love Romeo or Romeo loves Juliet.

57. Romeo does not love Juliet and Juliet does not love Romeo.

59. $(p \wedge q) \vee r$; $\left(\underset{p}{\underline{\text{The temperature outside is freezing}}}\ \underset{\wedge}{\underline{\text{and}}}\ \underset{q}{\underline{\text{the heater is working,}}}\right)\ \underset{\vee}{\underline{\text{or}}}\ \underset{r}{\underline{\text{the house is cold.}}}$

61. $(p \vee {\sim}q) \rightarrow r$; $\left(\underset{}{\underline{\text{If}}}\ \underset{p}{\underline{\text{the temperature outside is freezing}}}\ \underset{\vee}{\underline{\text{or}}}\ \underset{\sim q}{\underline{\text{the heater is not working,}}}\right)\ \underset{\rightarrow}{\underline{\text{then}}}\ \underset{r}{\underline{\text{the house is cold.}}}$

63. $r \leftrightarrow (p \wedge {\sim}q)$; $\underset{r}{\underline{\text{The house is cold}}}\ \underset{\leftrightarrow}{\underline{\text{if and only if}}}\ \left(\underset{p}{\underline{\text{the temperature outside is freezing}}}\ \underset{\wedge}{\underline{\text{and}}}\ \underset{\sim q}{\underline{\text{the heater isn't working.}}}\right)$

65. $(p \wedge {\sim} q) \rightarrow r$;
$\left(\underset{p}{\underline{\text{The temperature outside is freezing}}}\ \underset{\wedge}{\underline{\text{and}}}\ \underset{\sim q}{\underline{\text{the heater isn't working}}}\right)\ \underset{\rightarrow}{\underline{\text{is a sufficient condition for}}}\ \underset{r}{\underline{\text{the house being cold.}}}$

67. If the temperature is above 85° and we have finished studying, then we go to the beach.

69. The temperature is above 85°, and if we finished studying then we go to the beach.

71. ${\sim} r \rightarrow ({\sim} p \vee {\sim} q)$; If we do not go to the beach, then the temperature is not above 85° or we have not finished studying.

73. If we do not go to the beach then we have not finished studying, or the temperature is above 85°.

75. $r \leftrightarrow (p \wedge q)$; We will go to the beach if and only if the temperature is above 85° and we have finished studying.

77. The temperature is above 85° if and only if we have finished studying, and we go to the beach.

79. If we do not go to the beach, then it is not true that both the temperature is above 85° and we have finished studying.

81. p: I like the teacher.; q: The course is interesting.; r: I miss class.; $(p \vee q) \rightarrow {\sim} r$

83. p: I like the teacher.; q: The course is interesting.; r: I miss class.; $p \vee (q \rightarrow {\sim} r)$

85. p: I like the teacher.; q: The course is interesting.; r: I miss class.; $r \leftrightarrow {\sim} (p \wedge q)$

87. p: I like the teacher.; q: The course is interesting.; r: I miss class.; $(p \rightarrow {\sim} r) \leftrightarrow q$

89. p: I like the teacher.; q: The course is interesting.; r: I miss class.; s: I spend extra time reading the book.;
$({\sim} p \wedge r) \rightarrow ({\sim} q \vee s)$

91. p: Being French is necessary for being a Parisian.; q: Being German is necessary for being a Berliner.; ${\sim} p \rightarrow {\sim} q$

93. p: You file an income tax report.; q: You file a complete statement of earnings.; r: You are a taxpayer.; s: You are an authorized tax preparer.; $(r \vee s) \rightarrow (p \wedge q)$

95. p: You are wealthy.; q: You are happy.; r: You live contentedly.; ${\sim} (p \rightarrow (q \wedge r))$

97. $[p \rightarrow (q \vee r)] \leftrightarrow (p \wedge r)$

99. $(p \rightarrow p) \leftrightarrow [(p \wedge p) \rightarrow {\sim} p]$

101. p: You can get rid of the family skeleton.
q: You may as well make it dance.
${\sim}p \rightarrow q$

103. p: You know what you believe.
q: I can answer your questions.
$(p \to q) \wedge \sim q$

105. p: I am an intellectual.
q: I would be pessimistic about America.
$((p \to q) \wedge \sim p) \to \sim q$

115. makes sense

117. does not make sense; Explanations will vary. Sample explanation: Wearing red is necessary (not sufficient) for being a Chinese bride.

119. $\Big(\Big(\underbrace{\text{Shooting unarmed civilians is morally justifiable}}_{p}\ \underbrace{\text{if and only if}}_{\leftrightarrow}\ \underbrace{\text{bombing unarmed civilians is morally justifiable,}}_{q}\Big)$

$\underbrace{\text{and}}_{\wedge}\ \underbrace{\text{as the former is not morally justifiable,}}_{\sim p}\Big) \to \Big(\underbrace{\text{neither is the latter.}}_{\sim q}\Big)$

Check Points 3.3

1. p: $3+5=8$ is true
q: $2\times 7=20$ is false

a. $p \wedge q$
$T \wedge F$
F

b. $p \wedge \sim q$
$T \wedge \sim F$
$T \wedge T$
T

c. $\sim p \vee q$
$\sim T \vee F$
$F \vee F$
F

d. $\sim p \vee \sim q$
$\sim T \vee \sim F$
$F \vee T$
T

2. $\sim(p \vee q)$

p	q	$p \vee q$	$\sim(p \vee q)$
T	T	T	F
T	F	T	F
F	T	T	F
F	F	F	T

3. $\sim p \wedge \sim q$

p	q	$\sim p$	$\sim q$	$\sim p \wedge \sim q$
T	T	F	F	F
T	F	F	T	F
F	T	T	F	F
F	F	T	T	T

4. $(p \wedge \sim q) \vee \sim p$

p	q	$\sim p$	$\sim q$	$p \wedge \sim q$	$(p \wedge \sim q) \vee \sim p$
T	T	F	F	F	F
T	F	F	T	T	T
F	T	T	F	F	T
F	F	T	T	F	T

5. $p \wedge \sim p$ is false in all cases.

p	$\sim p$	$p \wedge \sim p$
T	F	F
F	T	F

6. p: I study hard.; q: I ace the final.; r: I fail the course.

a.

p	q	r	$q \vee r$	$p \wedge (q \vee r)$
T	T	T	T	T
T	T	F	T	T
T	F	T	T	T
T	F	F	F	F
F	T	T	T	F
F	T	F	T	F
F	F	T	T	F
F	F	F	F	F

b. false

7. p: Two percent of American women are homely.
q: More than half of American women are good looking
r: 5% of American men are strikingly attractive.
p is true, q is false, r is false

$(p \vee q) \wedge \sim r$

$(\text{T} \vee \text{F}) \wedge \sim \text{F}$

$\text{T} \wedge \text{T}$

T

Concept and Vocabulary Check 3.3

1. opposite
2. both p and q are true
3. both p and q are false
4. true
5. true
6. true
7. false
8. true

Exercise Set 3.3

1. $\sim q$

$\sim \text{F}$

T

3. $p \wedge q$

$\text{T} \wedge \text{F}$

F

5. $\sim p \wedge q$

$\sim \text{T} \wedge \text{F}$

$\text{F} \wedge \text{F}$

F

7. $\sim p \wedge \sim q$

$\sim \text{T} \wedge \sim \text{F}$

$\text{F} \wedge \text{T}$

F

9. $q \vee p$

$\text{F} \vee \text{T}$

T

11. $p \vee \sim q$

$\text{T} \vee \sim \text{F}$

$\text{T} \vee \text{T}$

T

13. $p \vee \sim p$

$\text{T} \vee \sim \text{T}$

$\text{T} \vee \text{F}$

T

15. $\sim p \vee \sim q$

$\sim \text{T} \vee \sim \text{F}$

$\text{F} \vee \text{T}$

T

17. $\sim p \wedge p$

p	$\sim p$	$\sim p \wedge p$
T	F	F
F	T	F

19. $\sim p \wedge q$

p	q	$\sim p$	$\sim p \wedge q$
T	T	F	F
T	F	F	F
F	T	T	T
F	F	T	F

21. $\sim(p \vee q)$

p	q	$p \vee q$	$\sim(p \vee q)$
T	T	T	F
T	F	T	F
F	T	T	F
F	F	F	T

23. $\sim p \wedge \sim q$

p	q	$\sim p$	$\sim q$	$\sim p \wedge \sim q$
T	T	F	F	F
T	F	F	T	F
F	T	T	F	F
F	F	T	T	T

25. $p \vee \sim q$

p	q	$\sim q$	$p \vee \sim q$
T	T	F	T
T	F	T	T
F	T	F	F
F	F	T	T

27. $\sim(\sim p \vee q)$

p	q	$\sim p$	$\sim p \vee q$	$\sim(\sim p \vee q)$
T	T	F	T	F
T	F	F	F	T
F	T	T	T	F
F	F	T	T	F

29. $(p \vee q) \wedge \sim p$

p	q	$\sim p$	$p \vee q$	$(p \vee q) \wedge \sim p$
T	T	F	T	F
T	F	F	T	F
F	T	T	T	T
F	F	T	F	F

31. $\sim p \vee (p \wedge \sim q)$

p	q	$\sim p$	$\sim q$	$p \wedge \sim q$	$\sim p \vee (p \wedge \sim q)$
T	T	F	F	F	F
T	F	F	T	T	T
F	T	T	F	F	T
F	F	T	T	F	T

33. $(p \vee q) \wedge (\sim p \vee \sim q)$

p	q	$\sim p$	$\sim q$	$p \vee q$	$\sim p \vee \sim q$	$(p \vee q) \wedge (\sim p \vee \sim q)$
T	T	F	F	T	F	F
T	F	F	T	T	T	T
F	T	T	F	T	T	T
F	F	T	T	F	T	F

35. $(p \wedge \sim q) \vee (p \wedge q)$

p	q	$\sim q$	$p \wedge \sim q$	$p \wedge q$	$(p \wedge \sim q) \vee (p \wedge q)$
T	T	F	F	T	T
T	F	T	T	F	T
F	T	F	F	F	F
F	F	T	F	F	F

37. $p \wedge (\sim q \vee r)$

p	q	r	$\sim q$	$\sim q \vee r$	$p \wedge (\sim q \vee r)$
T	T	T	F	T	T
T	T	F	F	F	F
T	F	T	T	T	T
T	F	F	T	T	T
F	T	T	F	T	F
F	T	F	F	F	F
F	F	T	T	T	F
F	F	F	T	T	F

39. $(r \wedge \sim p) \vee \sim q$

p	q	r	$\sim p$	$\sim q$	$r \wedge \sim p$	$(r \wedge \sim p) \vee \sim q$
T	T	T	F	F	F	F
T	T	F	F	F	F	F
T	F	T	F	T	F	T
T	F	F	F	T	F	T
F	T	T	T	F	T	T
F	T	F	T	F	F	F
F	F	T	T	T	T	T
F	F	F	T	T	F	T

41. $\sim (p \vee q) \wedge \sim r$

p	q	r	$p \vee q$	$\sim (p \vee q)$	$\sim r$	$\sim (p \vee q) \wedge \sim r$
T	T	T	T	F	F	F
T	T	F	T	F	T	F
T	F	T	T	F	F	F
T	F	F	T	F	T	F
F	T	T	T	F	F	F
F	T	F	T	F	T	F
F	F	T	F	T	F	F
F	F	F	F	T	T	T

43. **a.** p: You did the dishes.; q: You left the room a mess.; $\sim p \wedge q$

b. See truth table for Exercise 19.

c. The statement is true when p is false and q is true.

45. a. p: I bought a meal ticket.; q: I used it.; $\sim(p \wedge \sim q)$

b. $\sim(p \wedge \sim q)$

p	q	$\sim q$	$p \wedge \sim q$	$\sim(p \wedge \sim q)$
T	T	F	F	T
T	F	T	T	F
F	T	F	F	T
F	F	T	F	T

c. Answers will vary; an example is: The statement is true when p and q are true.

47. a. p: The student is intelligent.; q: The student is an overachiever.; $(p \vee q) \wedge \sim q$

b.

p	q	$\sim q$	$p \vee q$	$(p \vee q) \wedge \sim q$
T	T	F	T	F
T	F	T	T	T
F	T	F	T	F
F	F	T	F	F

c. The statement is true when p is true and q is false.

49. a. p: Married people are healthier than single people.; q: Married people are more economically stable than single people.; r: Children of married people do better on a variety of indicators.; $(p \wedge q) \wedge r$

b.

p	q	r	$p \wedge q$	$(p \wedge q) \wedge r$
T	T	T	T	T
T	T	F	T	F
T	F	T	F	F
T	F	F	F	F
F	T	T	F	F
F	T	F	F	F
F	F	T	F	F
F	F	F	F	F

c. The statement is true when p, q, and r are all true.

51. a. p: I go to office hours.; q: I ask questions.; r: My professor remembers me.; $(p \wedge q) \vee \sim r$

b.

p	q	r	$\sim r$	$p \wedge q$	$(p \wedge q) \vee \sim r$
T	T	T	F	T	T
T	T	F	T	T	T
T	F	T	F	F	F
T	F	F	T	F	T
F	T	T	F	F	F
F	T	F	T	F	T
F	F	T	F	F	F
F	F	F	T	F	T

c. Answers will vary; an example is: The statement is true when p, q, and r are all true.

53. $p \wedge (q \vee r)$

$F \wedge (T \vee F)$

$F \wedge T$

F

55. $\sim p \vee (q \wedge \sim r)$

$\sim F \vee (T \wedge \sim F)$

$T \vee (T \wedge T)$

$T \vee T$

T

57. $\sim(p \wedge q) \vee r$

$\sim(F \wedge T) \vee F$

$\sim(F) \vee F$

$T \vee F$

T

59. $\sim(p \vee q) \wedge \sim(p \wedge r)$

$\sim(F \vee T) \wedge \sim(F \wedge F)$

$\sim(T) \wedge \sim(F)$

$F \wedge T$

F

61. $(\sim p \wedge q) \vee (\sim r \wedge p)$

$(\sim F \wedge T) \vee (\sim F \wedge F)$

$(T \wedge T) \vee (T \wedge F)$

$T \vee F$

T

63. $\sim[\sim(p \wedge \sim q) \vee \sim(\sim p \vee q)]$

p	q	$\sim[\sim(p \wedge \sim q) \vee \sim(\sim p \vee q)]$
T	T	F
T	F	F
F	T	F
F	F	F

65. $[(p \wedge \sim r) \vee (q \wedge \sim r)] \wedge \sim(\sim p \vee r)$

p	q	r	$[(p \wedge \sim r) \vee (q \wedge \sim r)] \wedge \sim(\sim p \vee r)$
T	T	T	F
T	T	F	T
T	F	T	F
T	F	F	T
F	T	T	F
F	T	F	F
F	F	T	F
F	F	F	F

67. *p*: You notice this notice.; *q*: You notice this notice is not worth noticing.; $(p \vee \sim p) \wedge q$

p	q	$\sim p$	$p \vee \sim p$	$(p \vee \sim p) \wedge q$
T	T	F	T	T
T	F	F	T	F
F	T	T	T	T
F	F	T	T	F

The statement is true when q is true.

69. *p*: $x \leq 3$; *q*: $x \geq 7$; $\sim(p \vee q) \wedge (\sim p \wedge \sim q)$

p	q	$\sim p$	$\sim q$	$p \vee q$	$\sim(p \vee q)$	$\sim p \wedge \sim q$	$\sim(p \vee q) \wedge (\sim p \wedge \sim q)$
T	T	F	F	T	F	F	F
T	F	F	T	T	F	F	F
F	T	T	F	T	F	F	F
F	F	T	T	F	T	T	T

The statement is true when both p and q are false.

71. The percent body fat in women peaks at age 55 and the percent body fat in men does not peak at age 65 . This statement is false.

73. The percent body fat in women does not peak at age 55 and men have more than 24% body fat at age 25. This statement is false.

75. The percent body fat in women peaks at age 55 or the percent body fat in men does not peak at age 65. This statement is true.

77. The percent body fat in women does not peak at age 55 or men have more than 24% body fat at age 25. This statement is false.

79. The percent body fat in women peaks at age 55 and the percent body fat in men peaks at age 65, or men have more than 24% body fat at age 25. This statement is true.

81. *p*: More than 10% named business.; *q*: 9% named engineering.; $p \vee \sim q$; true

83. *p*: 7.5% named teaching.; *q*: 6.9% named nursing.; *r*: 12% named business. $(p \vee q) \wedge \sim r$; true

85. **a.** Hora Gershwin

b. Bolera Mozart does not have a master's degree in music. Cha-Cha Bach does not either play three instruments or have five years experience playing with a symphony orchestra.

95. does not make sense; Explanations will vary. Sample explanation: When filling in the truth values for a column of a truth table, only one or two previous columns are necessary.

97. does not make sense; Explanations will vary. Sample explanation: Since there is only one simple statement, there are only two possible truth values.

101. $p \veebar q$

p	q	$p \veebar q$
T	T	F
T	F	T
F	T	T
F	F	F

Check Points 3.4

1. $\sim p \to \sim q$

p	q	$\sim p$	$\sim q$	$\sim p \to \sim q$
T	T	F	F	T
T	F	F	T	T
F	T	T	F	F
F	F	T	T	T

The rightmost column shows that the statement is false when p is false and q is true; otherwise the statement is true.

2. $[(p \to q) \wedge \sim q] \to \sim p$ is a tautology because the final column is always true.

p	q	$\sim p$	$\sim q$	$p \to q$	$(p \to q) \wedge \sim q$	$[(p \to q) \wedge \sim q] \to \sim p$
T	T	F	F	T	F	T
T	F	F	T	F	F	T
F	T	T	F	T	F	T
F	F	T	T	T	T	T

3. **a.** p: You use Hair Grow.; q: You apply it daily.; r: You go bald.

p	q	r	$\sim r$	$p \wedge q$	$(p \wedge q) \to \sim r$
T	T	T	F	T	F
T	T	F	T	T	T
T	F	T	F	F	T
T	F	F	T	F	T
F	T	T	F	F	T
F	T	F	T	F	T
F	F	T	F	F	T
F	F	F	T	F	T

b. No, the claim is not false under these conditions as shown by the third row resulting in a T.

4. $(p \vee q) \leftrightarrow (\sim p \to q)$ is a tautology because all cases are true.

p	q	$\sim p$	$p \vee q$	$\sim p \to q$	$(p \vee q) \leftrightarrow (\sim p \to q)$
T	T	F	T	T	T
T	F	F	T	T	T
F	T	T	T	T	T
F	F	T	F	F	T

5. $(p \wedge q) \to r$

$(\text{T} \wedge \text{F}) \to \text{F}$

$\text{F} \to \text{F}$

T

Under these conditions, the claim is true.

Concept and Vocabulary Check 3.4

1. p is true and q is false
2. tautology; implications; self-contradiction
3. p and q have the same truth value
4. false

5. false

6. true

7. true

Exercise Set 3.4

1. $p \to {\sim}q$

p	q	$\sim q$	$p \to {\sim}q$
T	T	F	F
T	F	T	T
F	T	F	T
F	F	T	T

3. $\sim(q \to p)$

p	q	$q \to p$	$\sim(q \to p)$
T	T	T	F
T	F	T	F
F	T	F	T
F	F	T	F

5. $(p \wedge q) \to (p \vee q)$

p	q	$p \wedge q$	$p \vee q$	$(p \wedge q) \to (p \vee q)$
T	T	T	T	T
T	F	F	T	T
F	T	F	T	T
F	F	F	F	T

7. $(p \to q) \wedge {\sim}q$

p	q	$p \to q$	$\sim q$	$(p \to q) \wedge {\sim}q$
T	T	T	F	F
T	F	F	T	F
F	T	T	F	F
F	F	T	T	T

9. $(p \vee q) \to r$

p	q	r	$p \vee q$	$(p \vee q) \to r$
T	T	T	T	T
T	T	F	T	F
T	F	T	T	T
T	F	F	T	F
F	T	T	T	T
F	T	F	T	F
F	F	T	F	T
F	F	F	F	T

11. $r \to (p \wedge q)$

p	q	r	$p \wedge q$	$r \to (p \wedge q)$
T	T	T	T	T
T	T	F	T	T
T	F	T	F	F
T	F	F	F	T
F	T	T	F	F
F	T	F	F	T
F	F	T	F	F
F	F	F	F	T

13. $\sim r \wedge (\sim q \to p)$

p	q	r	$\sim q$	$\sim r$	$\sim q \to p$	$\sim r \wedge (\sim q \to p)$
T	T	T	F	F	T	F
T	T	F	F	T	T	T
T	F	T	T	F	T	F
T	F	F	T	T	T	T
F	T	T	F	F	T	F
F	T	F	F	T	T	T
F	F	T	T	F	F	F
F	F	F	T	T	F	T

15. $\sim(p \wedge r) \to (\sim q \vee r)$

p	q	r	$\sim q$	$p \wedge r$	$\sim (p \wedge r)$	$\sim q \vee r$	$\sim(p \wedge r) \to (\sim q \vee r)$
T	T	T	F	T	F	T	T
T	T	F	F	F	T	F	F
T	F	T	T	T	F	T	T
T	F	F	T	F	T	T	T
F	T	T	F	F	T	T	T
F	T	F	F	F	T	F	F
F	F	T	T	F	T	T	T
F	F	F	T	F	T	T	T

17. $p \leftrightarrow \sim q$

p	q	$\sim q$	$p \leftrightarrow \sim q$
T	T	F	F
T	F	T	T
F	T	F	T
F	F	T	F

19. $\sim(p \leftrightarrow q)$

p	q	$p \leftrightarrow q$	$\sim(p \leftrightarrow q)$
T	T	T	F
T	F	F	T
F	T	F	T
F	F	T	F

21. $(p \leftrightarrow q) \rightarrow p$

p	q	$p \leftrightarrow q$	$(p \leftrightarrow q) \rightarrow p$
T	T	T	T
T	F	F	T
F	T	F	T
F	F	T	F

23. $(\sim p \leftrightarrow q) \rightarrow (\sim p \rightarrow q)$

p	q	$\sim p$	$\sim p \leftrightarrow q$	$\sim p \rightarrow q$	$(\sim p \leftrightarrow q) \rightarrow (\sim p \rightarrow q)$
T	T	F	F	T	T
T	F	F	T	T	T
F	T	T	T	T	T
F	F	T	F	F	T

25. $[(p \wedge q) \wedge (q \rightarrow p)] \leftrightarrow (p \wedge q)$

p	q	$p \wedge q$	$q \rightarrow p$	$(p \wedge q) \wedge (q \rightarrow p)$	$[(p \wedge q) \wedge (q \rightarrow p)] \leftrightarrow (p \wedge q)$
T	T	T	T	T	T
T	F	F	T	F	T
F	T	F	F	F	T
F	F	F	T	F	T

27. $(p \leftrightarrow q) \rightarrow \sim r$

p	q	r	$\sim r$	$p \leftrightarrow q$	$(p \leftrightarrow q) \rightarrow \sim r$
T	T	T	F	T	F
T	T	F	T	T	T
T	F	T	F	F	T
T	F	F	T	F	T
F	T	T	F	F	T
F	T	F	T	F	T
F	F	T	F	T	F
F	F	F	T	T	T

29. $(p \wedge r) \leftrightarrow \sim (q \vee r)$

p	q	r	$p \wedge r$	$q \vee r$	$\sim (q \vee r)$	$(p \wedge r) \leftrightarrow \sim (q \vee r)$
T	T	T	T	T	F	F
T	T	F	F	T	F	T
T	F	T	T	T	F	F
T	F	F	F	F	T	F
F	T	T	F	T	F	T
F	T	F	F	T	F	T
F	F	T	F	T	F	T
F	F	F	F	F	T	F

31. $[r \vee (\sim q \wedge p)] \leftrightarrow \sim p$

p	q	r	$\sim q$	$\sim q \wedge p$	$r \vee (\sim q \wedge p)$	$\sim p$	$[r \vee (\sim q \wedge p)] \leftrightarrow \sim p$
T	T	T	F	F	T	F	F
T	T	F	F	F	F	F	T
T	F	T	T	T	T	F	F
T	F	F	T	T	T	F	F
F	T	T	F	F	T	T	T
F	T	F	F	F	F	T	F
F	F	T	F	F	T	T	T
F	F	F	F	F	F	T	F

33. $[(p \rightarrow q) \wedge q] \rightarrow p$ is neither.

p	q	$p \rightarrow q$	$(p \rightarrow q) \wedge q$	$[(p \rightarrow q) \wedge q] \rightarrow p$
T	T	T	T	T
T	F	F	F	T
F	T	T	T	F
F	F	T	F	T

35. $[(p \rightarrow q) \wedge \sim q] \rightarrow \sim p$ is a tautology.

p	q	$\sim p$	$\sim q$	$p \rightarrow q$	$(p \rightarrow q) \wedge \sim q$	$[(p \rightarrow q) \wedge \sim q] \rightarrow \sim p$
T	T	F	F	T	F	T
T	F	F	T	F	F	T
F	T	T	F	T	F	T
F	F	T	T	T	T	T

37. $[(p \vee q) \wedge p] \rightarrow \sim q$ is neither.

p	q	$\sim q$	$p \vee q$	$(p \vee q) \wedge p$	$[(p \vee q) \wedge p] \rightarrow \sim q$
T	T	F	T	T	F
T	F	T	T	T	T
F	T	F	T	F	T
F	F	T	F	F	T

39. $(p \rightarrow q) \rightarrow (\sim p \vee q)$ is a tautology.

p	q	$\sim p$	$p \rightarrow q$	$\sim p \vee q$	$(p \rightarrow q) \rightarrow (\sim p \vee q)$
T	T	F	T	T	T
T	F	F	F	F	T
F	T	T	T	T	T
F	F	T	T	T	T

41. $(p \wedge q) \wedge (\sim p \vee \sim q)$ is a self-contradiction.

p	q	$\sim p$	$\sim q$	$p \wedge q$	$\sim p \vee \sim q$	$(p \wedge q) \wedge (\sim p \vee \sim q)$
T	T	F	F	T	F	F
T	F	F	T	F	T	F
F	T	T	F	F	T	F
F	F	T	T	F	T	F

43. $\sim(p \wedge q) \leftrightarrow (\sim p \wedge \sim q)$ is neither.

p	q	$\sim p$	$\sim q$	$p \wedge q$	$\sim(p \wedge q)$	$\sim p \wedge \sim q$	$\sim(p \wedge q) \leftrightarrow (\sim p \wedge \sim q)$
T	T	F	F	T	F	F	T
T	F	F	T	F	T	F	F
F	T	T	F	F	T	F	F
F	F	T	T	F	T	T	T

45. $(p \to q) \leftrightarrow (q \to p)$ is neither.

p	q	$p \to q$	$q \to p$	$(p \to q) \leftrightarrow (q \to p)$
T	T	T	T	T
T	F	F	T	F
F	T	T	F	F
F	F	T	T	T

47. $(p \to q) \leftrightarrow (\sim p \vee q)$ is a tautology.

p	q	$\sim p$	$p \to q$	$\sim p \vee q$	$(p \to q) \leftrightarrow (\sim p \vee q)$
T	T	F	T	T	T
T	F	F	F	F	T
F	T	T	T	T	T
F	F	T	T	T	T

49. $(p \leftrightarrow q) \leftrightarrow [(q \to p) \wedge (p \to q)]$ is a tautology.

p	q	$q \to p$	$p \to q$	$p \leftrightarrow q$	$(q \to p) \wedge (p \to q)$	$(p \leftrightarrow q) \leftrightarrow [(q \to p) \wedge (p \to q)]$
T	T	T	T	T	T	T
T	F	T	F	F	F	T
F	T	F	T	F	F	T
F	F	T	T	T	T	T

51. $(p \wedge q) \leftrightarrow (\sim p \vee r)$ is neither

p	q	r	$\sim p$	$p \wedge q$	$\sim p \vee r$	$(p \wedge q) \leftrightarrow (\sim p \vee r)$
T	T	T	F	T	T	T
T	T	F	F	T	F	F
T	F	T	F	F	T	F
T	F	F	F	F	F	T
F	T	T	T	F	T	F
F	T	F	T	F	T	F
F	F	T	T	F	T	F
F	F	F	T	F	T	F

53. $[(p \to q) \wedge (q \to r)] \to (p \to r)$ is a tautology.

p	q	r	$p \to q$	$q \to r$	$(p \to q) \wedge (q \to r)$	$p \to r$	$[(p \to q) \wedge (q \to r)] \to (p \to r)$
T	T	T	T	T	T	T	T
T	T	F	T	F	F	F	T
T	F	T	F	T	F	T	T
T	F	F	F	T	F	F	T
F	T	T	T	T	T	T	T
F	T	F	T	F	F	T	T
F	F	T	T	T	T	T	T
F	F	F	T	T	T	T	T

55. $[(q \to r) \wedge (r \to \sim p)] \leftrightarrow (q \wedge p)$ is neither.

p	q	r	$[(q \to r) \wedge (r \to \sim p)] \leftrightarrow (q \wedge p)$
T	T	T	F
T	T	F	F
T	F	T	T
T	F	F	F
F	T	T	F
F	T	F	T
F	F	T	F
F	F	F	F

57. a. p: You do homework right after class.; q: You fall behind.; $(p \to \sim q) \wedge (\sim p \to q)$

b.

p	q	$\sim p$	$\sim q$	$p \to \sim q$	$\sim p \to q$	$(p \to \sim q) \wedge (\sim p \to q)$
T	T	F	F	F	T	F
T	F	F	T	T	T	T
F	T	T	F	T	T	T
F	F	T	T	T	F	F

c. Answers will vary; an example is: The statement is true when p and q have opposite truth values.

59. a. p: You cut and paste from the Internet.; q: You cite the source.; r: You are charged with plagiarism.; $(p \wedge \sim q) \to r$

b.

p	q	r	$\sim q$	$p \wedge \sim q$	$(p \wedge \sim q) \to r$
T	T	T	F	F	T
T	T	F	F	F	T
T	F	T	T	T	T
T	F	F	T	T	F
F	T	T	F	F	T
F	T	F	F	F	T
F	F	T	T	F	T
F	F	F	T	F	T

c. Answers will vary; an example is: The statement is true when p, q, and r are all true.

61. a. p: You are comfortable in your room.; q: You are honest with your roommate.; r: You enjoy the college experience.; $(p \leftrightarrow q) \vee \sim r$

b.

p	q	r	$\sim r$	$p \leftrightarrow q$	$(p \leftrightarrow q) \vee \sim r)$
T	T	T	F	T	T
T	T	F	T	T	T
T	F	T	F	F	F
T	F	F	T	F	T
F	T	T	F	F	F
F	T	F	T	F	T
F	F	T	F	T	T
F	F	F	T	T	T

c. Answers will vary; an example is: The statement is true when p, q, and r are all true.

63. a. p: I enjoy the course.; q: I choose the class based on the professor.; r: I choose the class based on the course description.; $p \leftrightarrow (q \wedge \sim r)$

b.

p	q	r	$\sim r$	$q \wedge \sim r$	$p \leftrightarrow (q \wedge \sim r)$
T	T	T	F	F	F
T	T	F	T	T	T
T	F	T	F	F	F
T	F	F	T	F	F
F	T	T	F	F	T
F	T	F	T	T	F
F	F	T	F	F	T
F	F	F	T	F	T

c. Answers will vary; an example is: The statement is true when p, q, and r are all false.

65. $\sim(p \to q)$

$\sim(\text{F} \to \text{T})$

$\sim\text{T}$

F

67. $\sim p \leftrightarrow q$

$\sim\text{F} \leftrightarrow \text{T}$

$\text{T} \leftrightarrow \text{T}$

T

69. $q \to (p \wedge r)$

$\text{T} \to (\text{F} \wedge \text{F})$

$\text{T} \to \text{F}$

F

71. $(\sim p \wedge q) \leftrightarrow \sim r$

$(\sim\text{F} \wedge \text{T}) \leftrightarrow \sim\text{F}$

$(\text{T} \wedge \text{T}) \leftrightarrow \text{T}$

$\text{T} \leftrightarrow \text{T}$

T

73. $\sim[(p \to \sim r) \leftrightarrow (r \wedge \sim p)]$

$\sim[(\text{F} \to \sim\text{F}) \leftrightarrow (\text{F} \wedge \sim\text{F})]$

$\sim[(\text{F} \to \text{T}) \leftrightarrow (\text{F} \wedge \text{T})]$

$\sim[\text{T} \leftrightarrow \text{F}]$

$\sim\text{F}$

T

75. $(p \to q) \leftrightarrow [(p \wedge q) \to \sim p]$

p	q	$(p \to q) \leftrightarrow [(p \wedge q) \to \sim p]$
T	T	F
T	F	F
F	T	T
F	F	T

77. $[p \to (\sim q \vee r)] \leftrightarrow (p \wedge r)$

p	q	r	$[p \to (\sim q \vee r)] \leftrightarrow (p \wedge r)$
T	T	T	T
T	T	F	T
T	F	T	T
T	F	F	F
F	T	T	F
F	T	F	F
F	F	T	F
F	F	F	F

79. p: You love a person.; q: You marry that person.; $(q \to p) \wedge (\sim p \to \sim q)$

p	q	$\sim p$	$\sim q$	$q \to p$	$\sim p \to \sim q$	$(q \to p) \wedge (\sim p \to \sim q)$
T	T	F	F	T	T	T
T	F	F	T	T	T	T
F	T	T	F	F	F	F
F	F	T	T	T	T	T

Answers will vary; an example is: The statement is true when both p and q are true.

81. p: You are happy.; q: You live contentedly.; r: You are wealthy.; $\sim [r \to (p \wedge q)]$

p	q	r	$p \wedge q$	$r \to (p \wedge q)$	$\sim [r \to (p \wedge q)]$
T	T	T	T	T	F
T	T	F	T	T	F
T	F	T	F	F	T
T	F	F	F	T	F
F	T	T	F	F	T
F	T	F	F	T	F
F	F	T	F	F	T
F	F	F	F	T	F

Answers will vary; an example is: The statement is true when p is false and both q and r are true.

83. p: There was an increase in the percentage who believed in God.; q: There was a decrease in the percentage who believed in Heaven.; r: There was an increase in the percentage who believed in the devil.; The statement is of the form $(p \wedge q) \to r$ with p false, q true, and r false.

$(p \wedge q) \to r$

$(\text{F} \wedge \text{T}) \to \text{F}$

$\text{F} \to \text{F}$

T

Therefore the statement is true.

85. p: There was a decrease in the percentage who believed in God.; q: There was an increase in the percentage who believed in Heaven.; r: The percentage believing in the devil decreased.; The statement is of the form $(p \leftrightarrow q) \vee r$ with p true, q false, and r true.

$(p \leftrightarrow q) \vee r$

$(\text{T} \leftrightarrow \text{F}) \vee \text{T}$

$\text{F} \vee \text{T}$

T

Therefore the statement is true.

87. p: Fifteen percent are capitalists.; q: Thirty-four percent are members of the upper middle class.; r: The number of working poor exceeds the number belonging to the working class.; The statement is of the form $(p \vee \sim q) \leftrightarrow r$ with p false, q false, and r false.

$(p \vee \sim q) \leftrightarrow r$

$(\text{F} \vee \sim \text{F}) \leftrightarrow \text{F}$

$(\text{F} \vee \text{T}) \leftrightarrow \text{F}$

$\text{T} \leftrightarrow \text{F}$

F

89. p: There are more people in the lower-middle class than in the capitalist and upper-middle classes combined.; q: One percent are capitalists.; r: Thirty-four percent belong to the upper-middle class.; The statement is of the form $p \rightarrow (q \wedge r)$ with p true, q true, and r false.

$p \rightarrow (q \wedge r)$

$\text{T} \rightarrow (\text{T} \wedge \text{F})$

$\text{T} \rightarrow \text{F}$

F

Therefore the statement is false.

97. makes sense

99. does not make sense; Explanations will vary. Sample explanation: The compound statement is false if "each man has a definite set of rules" and "men are machines" are opposite truth values of each other.

101. Answers will vary. Possible column headings:

p	q	$p \rightarrow q$	$\sim p$	$(p \rightarrow q) \vee \sim p$	$\sim p \rightarrow [(p \rightarrow q) \vee \sim p]$

Check Points 3.5

1. a. $p \vee q$ and $\sim q \rightarrow p$ are equivalent.

p	q	$\sim q$	$p \vee q$	$\sim q \rightarrow p$
T	T	F	T	T
T	F	T	T	T
F	T	F	T	T
F	F	T	F	F

The statements are equivalent since their truth values are the same.

b. $p \vee q$: I attend classes or I lose my scholarship.

…is equivalent to… $\sim q \rightarrow p$: If I do not lose my scholarship, then I attend classes.

2. $\sim p$ and $\sim[\sim(\sim p)]$ are equivalent.

p	$\sim p$	$\sim(\sim p)$	$\sim[\sim(\sim p)]$
T	F	T	F
F	T	F	T

The statements are equivalent since their truth values are the same.

3. Given: If it's raining, then I need a jacket.
p: It's raining.
q: I need a jacket.
a: It's not raining or I need a jacket.
b: I need a jacket or it's not raining.
c: If I need a jacket, then it's raining.
d: If I do not need a jacket, then it's not raining.

The given is *not* equivalent to statement **(c)**

				Given	**a**	**b**	**c**	**d**
p	q	$\sim p$	$\sim q$	$p \rightarrow q$	$\sim p \vee q$	$q \vee \sim p$	$q \rightarrow p$	$\sim q \rightarrow \sim p$
T	T	F	F	T	T	T	T	T
T	F	F	T	F	F	F	T	F
F	T	T	F	T	T	T	F	T
F	F	T	T	T	T	T	T	T

4. a. If you're not driving too closely, then you can't read this.

b. If it's not time to do the laundry, then you have clean underwear.

c. If supervision during exams is required, then some students are not honest.

d. $q \rightarrow (p \vee r)$

5. Converse: If you don't see a Club Med, then you are in Iran.; Inverse: If you are not in Iran, then you see a Club Med.; Contrapositive: If you see a Club Med, then you are not in Iran.

Concept and Vocabulary Check 3.5

1. equivalent; $\equiv$

2. $\sim q \rightarrow \sim p$

3. $q \to p$

4. $\sim p \to \sim q$

5. equivalent; converse; inverse

6. false

7. false

Exercise Set 3.5

1. a. $\sim p \to q$ and $p \vee q$ are equivalent.

p	q	$\sim p$	$\sim p \to q$	$p \vee q$
T	T	F	T	T
T	F	F	T	T
F	T	T	T	T
F	F	T	F	F

b. The United States supports the development of solar-powered cars or it will suffer increasing atmospheric pollution.

3. not equivalent

5. equivalent

7. equivalent

9. not equivalent

11. not equivalent

13. equivalent

15. Given: I saw the original *King Kong* or the 2005 version.
p: I saw the original *King Kong*.
q: I saw the 2005 version.
a: If I did not see the original King Kong, I saw the 2005 version.
b: I saw both the original *King Kong* and the 2005 version.
c: If I saw the original *King Kong*, I did not see the 2005 version
d: If I saw the 2005 version, I did not see the original *King Kong*.

The given is equivalent to statement **(a)**

		Given	**a**	**b**	**c**	**d**
p	q	$p \vee q$	$\sim p \to q$	$p \wedge q$	$p \to \sim q$	$q \to \sim p$
T	T	T	T	T	F	F
T	F	T	T	F	T	T
F	T	T	T	F	T	T
F	F	F	F	F	T	T

17. Given: It is not true that Sondheim and Picasso are both musicians.
p: Sondheim is a musician.
q: Picasso is a musician.
a: Sondheim is not a musician or Picasso is not a musician.
b: If Sondheim is a musician, then Picasso is not a musician.
c: Sondheim is not a musician and Picasso is not a musician.
d: If Picasso is a musician, then Sondheim is not a musician.

The given is *not* equivalent to statement **(c)**

		Given	**a**	**b**	**c**	**d**
p	q	$\sim(p \wedge q)$	$\sim p \vee \sim q$	$p \to \sim q$	$\sim p \wedge \sim q$	$q \to \sim p$
T	T	F	F	F	F	F
T	F	T	T	T	F	T
F	T	T	T	T	F	T
F	F	T	T	T	T	T

19. Converse: If I am in Illinois, then I am in Chicago.
Inverse: If I am not in Chicago, then I am not in Illinois.
Contrapositive: If I am not in Illinois, I am not in Chicago.

21. Converse: If I cannot hear you, then the stereo is playing.
Inverse: If the stereo is not playing, then I can hear you.
Contrapositive: If I can hear you, then the stereo is not playing.

23. Converse: If you die, you don't laugh.
Inverse: If you laugh, you don't die.
Contrapositive: If you don't die, you laugh.

25. Converse: If all troops were withdrawn, then the president is telling the truth.
Inverse: If the president is not telling the truth, then some troops were not withdrawn.
Contrapositive: If some troops were not withdrawn, then the president was not telling the truth.

27. Converse: If some people suffer, then all institutions place profit above human need.
Inverse: If some institutions do not place profit above human need, then no people suffer.
Contrapositive: If no people suffer, then some institutions do not place profit above human need.

29. Converse: $\sim r \to \sim q$; Inverse: $q \to r$; Contrapositive: $r \to q$

31. If a person diets, then he or she loses weight.
Converse: If a person loses weight, then he or she is dieting.
Inverse: If a person is not dieting, then he or she is not losing weight.
Contrapositive: If a person is not losing weight, then he or she is not dieting.

33. If a vehicle has no flashing light on top, then it is not an ambulance.
Converse: If a vehicle is not an ambulance, then it has no flashing light on top.
Inverse: If a vehicle has a flashing light on top, then it is an ambulance.
Contrapositive: If a vehicle is an ambulance, then it has a flashing light on top.

35. If a person is an attorney, then he or she has passed the bar exam.
Converse: If a person has passed the bar exam, then he or she is an attorney.
Inverse: If a person is not an attorney, then he or she has not passed the bar exam.
Contrapositive: If a person has not passed the bar exam, then he or she is not an attorney.

37. If a person is a pacifist, then he or she is not a warmonger.
Converse: If a person is not a warmonger, then he or she is a pacifist.
Inverse: If a person is not a pacifist, then he or she is a warmonger.
Contrapositive: If a person is a warmonger, then he or she is not a pacifist.

39. a. The conditional statement is true.

b. Converse: If the age of sexual consent is 14, then the country is Italy.
Inverse: If the country is not Italy, then the age of sexual consent is not 14.
Contrapositive: If the age of sexual consent is not 14, then the country is not Italy.
The contrapositive is true.
The converse and inverse are not necessarily true.

47. does not make sense; Explanations will vary. Sample explanation: A conditional statement and its contrapositive always have the same truth value.

49. makes sense

Check Points 3.6

1. You do not have a fever and you have the flu.

2. Bart Simpson is not a cartoon character or Tony Soprano is not a cartoon character.

3. You do not leave by 5 P.M. and you arrive home on time.

4. **a.** Some horror movies are not scary or none are funny.

b. Your workouts are not strenuous and you get stronger.

5. p: It is windy.
q: We can swim.
r: We can sail.
The statement can be represented symbolically as $\sim p \rightarrow (q \wedge \sim r)$.
Next write the contrapositive and simplify.
$\sim(q \wedge \sim r) \rightarrow \sim(\sim p)$
$[\sim q \vee \sim(\sim r)] \rightarrow p$
$(\sim q \vee r) \rightarrow p$
Thus, $\sim p \rightarrow (q \wedge \sim r) \equiv (\sim q \vee r) \rightarrow p$.
The original statement is equivalent to "If we cannot swim or we can sail, then it is windy."

Concept and Vocabulary Check 3.6

1. $p \wedge \sim q$; antecedent; and; consequent

2. $\sim p \vee \sim q$; $\sim p \wedge \sim q$

3. or

4. and

5. false

Exercise Set 3.6

1. The negation of $p \rightarrow q$ is $p \wedge \sim q$: I am in Los Angeles and not in California.

3. The negation of $p \rightarrow q$ is $p \wedge \sim q$: It is purple and it is a carrot.

5. The negation of $p \rightarrow q$ is $p \wedge \sim q$: He doesn't, and I won't.

7. The negation of $p \rightarrow q$ is $p \wedge \sim q$: There is a blizzard, and some schools are not closed.

9. The negation of $\sim q \rightarrow \sim r$ is $\sim q \wedge r$

11. Australia is not an island or China is not an island.

13. My high school did not encourage creativity or did not encourage diversity.

15. Jewish scripture does not give a clear indication of a heaven and it does not give a clear indication of an afterlife.

17. The United States has eradicated neither poverty nor racism.

19. $\sim(\sim p \wedge q)$
$\sim(\sim p) \vee \sim q$
$p \vee \sim q$

21. p: You attend lecture.
q: You study.
r: You succeed.
The statement can be represented symbolically as $(p \wedge q) \rightarrow r$.
Next write the contrapositive and simplify.
$\sim r \rightarrow \sim(p \wedge q)$
$\sim r \rightarrow (\sim p \vee \sim q)$
Thus, $(p \wedge q) \rightarrow r \equiv \sim r \rightarrow (\sim p \vee \sim q)$.
The original statement is equivalent to "If you do not succeed, then you did not attend lecture or did not study."

23. p: He cooks.
q: His wife cooks.
r: His child cooks.
The statement can be represented symbolically as $\sim p \to (q \vee r)$.
Next write the contrapositive and simplify.
$\sim(q \vee r) \to \sim(\sim p)$
$(\sim q \wedge \sim r) \to p$
Thus, $\sim p \to (q \vee r) \equiv (\sim q \wedge \sim r) \to p$.
The original statement is equivalent to "If his wife does not cook and his child does not cook, then he does."

25. Write the contrapositive of $p \to (q \vee \sim r)$ and simplify.
$\sim(q \vee \sim r) \to \sim p$
$[\sim q \wedge \sim(\sim r)] \to \sim p$
$(\sim q \wedge r) \to \sim p$
Thus, $p \to (q \vee \sim r) \equiv (\sim q \wedge r) \to \sim p$.

27. I'm going to neither Seattle nor San Francisco.

29. I do not study and I pass.

31. I am going or he is not going.

33. A bill does not become law or it receives majority approval.

35. Write the negation of $p \vee \sim q$ and simplify.
$\sim(p \vee \sim q)$
$\sim p \wedge \sim(\sim q)$
$\sim p \wedge q$
Thus the negation of $p \vee \sim q$ is $\sim p \wedge q$.

37. Write the negation of $p \wedge (q \vee r)$ and simplify.
$\sim[p \wedge (q \vee r)]$
$\sim p \vee \sim(q \vee r)$
$\sim p \vee (\sim q \wedge \sim r)$
Thus the negation of $p \wedge (q \vee r)$ is $\sim p \vee (\sim q \wedge \sim r)$.

39. None are equivalent.

		a	b	c
p	q	$p \to \sim q$	$\sim p \vee q$	$\sim p \to q$
T	T	F	T	T
T	F	T	T	F
F	T	T	T	T
F	F	T	F	T

41. None are equivalent.

		a	b	c
p	q	$\sim(p\wedge\sim q)$	$\sim p\wedge q$	$p\vee\sim q$
T	T	T	F	T
T	F	F	F	T
F	T	T	T	F
F	F	T	F	T

43. a and b are equivalent.

			a	b	c
p	q	r	$p\rightarrow(\sim q\vee\sim r)$	$(q\wedge r)\rightarrow\sim p$	$\sim p\rightarrow(q\wedge r)$
T	T	T	F	F	T
T	T	F	T	T	T
T	F	T	T	T	T
T	F	F	T	T	T
F	T	T	T	T	T
F	T	F	T	T	F
F	F	T	T	T	F
F	F	F	T	T	F

45. a and b are equivalent.

			a	b	c
p	q	r	$p\wedge(q\vee r)$	$p\wedge\sim(\sim q\wedge\sim r)$	$p\rightarrow(q\vee r)$
T	T	T	T	T	T
T	T	F	T	T	T
T	F	T	T	T	T
T	F	F	F	F	F
F	T	T	F	F	T
F	T	F	F	F	T
F	F	T	F	F	T
F	F	F	F	F	T

47. If there is no pain, there is no gain.; Converse: If there is no gain, then there is no pain.; Inverse: If there is pain, then there is gain.; Contrapositive: If there is gain, then there is pain.; Negation: There is no pain and there is gain.

49. If you follow Buddha's "Middle Way," then you are neither hedonistic nor ascetic.; Converse: If you are neither hedonistic nor ascetic, then you follow Buddha's "Middle Way."; Inverse: If you do not follow Buddha's "Middle Way," then you are either hedonistic or ascetic.; Contrapositive: If you are either hedonistic or ascetic, then you do not follow Buddha's "Middle Way."; Negation: You follow Buddha's "Middle Way" and you are either hedonistic or ascetic.

51. $p\wedge(\sim r\vee s)$

53. $\sim p\vee(r\wedge s)$

55. **a.** false

b. Smoking does not reduce life expectancy by 2370 days or heart disease does not reduce life expectancy by 1247 days.

c. true

57. a. true

b. Homicide does not reduce life expectancy by 74 days and fire reduces life expectancy by 25 days.

c. false

59. a. true

b. Drowning reduces life expectancy by ten times the number of days as airplane accidents and drowning reduces life expectancy by 24 days.

c. false

65. makes sense

67. makes sense

69. Contrapositive: If no one is eating turkey, then it is not Thanksgiving.
Negation: It is thanksgiving and no one is eating turkey.

Check Points 3.7

1. The argument is valid. ***p*:** The U.S. must energetically support the development of solar-powered cars. ***q*:** The U.S. must suffer increasing atmospheric pollution.

$p \vee q$
$\sim q$
$\therefore p$

p	q	$\sim q$	$p \vee q$	$(p \vee q) \wedge \sim q$	$[(p \vee q) \wedge \sim p] \rightarrow p$
T	T	F	T	F	T
T	F	T	T	T	T
F	T	F	T	F	T
F	F	T	F	F	T

2. The argument is valid. ***p*:** I study for 5 hours. ***q*:** I fail.

$p \vee q$
$\sim p$
$\therefore q$

p	q	$\sim p$	$p \vee q$	$(p \vee q) \wedge \sim p$	$[(p \vee q) \wedge p] \rightarrow q$
T	T	F	T	F	T
T	F	F	T	F	T
F	T	T	T	T	T
F	F	T	F	F	T

3. The argument is invalid. ***p*:** You lower the fat in your diet. ***q*:** You lower your cholesterol. ***r*:** You reduce your risk of heart disease.

$p \rightarrow q$
$q \rightarrow r$
$\therefore \sim p \rightarrow \sim r$

p	q	r	$p \rightarrow q$	$q \rightarrow r$	$\sim p \rightarrow \sim r$	$[(p \rightarrow q) \wedge (q \rightarrow r)] \rightarrow (\sim p \rightarrow \sim r)$
T	T	T	T	T	T	T
T	T	F	T	F	T	T
T	F	T	F	T	T	T
T	F	F	F	T	T	T
F	T	T	T	T	F	F
F	T	F	T	F	T	T
F	F	T	T	T	F	F
F	F	F	T	T	T	T

4. a. $p \vee q$

$\underline{\sim q}$

$\therefore p$

This argument is valid by Disjunctive Reasoning.

b. $p \to q$

$\underline{q}$

$\therefore p$

This argument is invalid by Fallacy of the Converse.

c. $p \to q$

$\underline{q \to r}$

$\therefore p \to r$

This argument is valid by Transitive Reasoning.

5. The argument is valid. ***p*:** people are good. ***q*:** laws are needed to prevent wrongdoing. ***r*:** laws will succeed in preventing wrongdoing.

$p \to \sim q$

$\underline{\sim p \to \sim r}$

$\therefore \sim q \vee \sim r$

p	q	r	$p \to \sim q$	$\sim p \to \sim r$	$\sim q \vee \sim r$	$[(p \to \sim q) \wedge (\sim p \to \sim r)] \to (\sim q \vee \sim r)$
T	T	T	F	T	F	T
T	T	F	F	T	T	T
T	F	T	T	T	T	T
T	F	F	T	T	T	T
F	T	T	T	F	F	T
F	T	F	T	T	T	T
F	F	T	T	F	T	T
F	F	F	T	T	T	T

6. Let ***p*** be: all people lead
Let ***q*** be: no people follow
This argument of the form $p \to q$

$\underline{\sim q}$

$\therefore \sim p$

The conclusion, $\sim p$, in words would be: Some people do not lead.

Concept and Vocabulary Check 3.7

1. valid

2. q; valid; $[(p \to q) \wedge p] \to q$

3. $\sim p$; valid; $[(p \to q) \wedge \sim q] \to \sim p$

4. $p \to r$; valid; $[(p \to q) \wedge (q \to r)] \to (p \to r)$

5. q; valid; $[(p \vee q) \wedge \sim p] \to q$

6. p

7. $\sim q$

8. false

9. true

10. false

Exercise Set 3.7

1. This is an invalid argument.

p	q	$\sim p$	$\sim q$	$p \to q$	$(p \to q) \wedge \sim p$	$[(p \to q) \wedge \sim p] \to \sim q$
T	T	F	F	T	F	T
T	F	F	T	F	F	T
F	T	T	F	T	T	F
F	F	T	T	T	T	T

3. This is a valid argument.

p	q	$\sim p$	$\sim q$	$p \to \sim q$	$(p \to \sim q) \wedge q$	$[(p \to \sim q) \wedge q] \to \sim p$
T	T	F	F	F	F	T
T	F	F	T	T	F	T
F	T	T	F	T	T	T
F	F	T	T	T	F	T

5. This is a valid argument.

p	q	$\sim q$	$p \wedge \sim q$	$(p \wedge \sim q) \wedge p$	$[(p \wedge \sim q) \wedge p] \to \sim q$
T	T	F	F	F	T
T	F	T	T	T	T
F	T	F	F	F	T
F	F	T	F	F	T

7. This is an invalid argument.

p	q	$p \to q$	$q \to p$	$p \wedge q$	$[(p \to q) \wedge (q \to p)]$	$[(p \to q) \wedge (q \to p)] \to (p \wedge q)$
T	T	T	T	T	T	T
T	F	F	T	F	F	T
F	T	T	F	F	F	T
F	F	T	T	F	T	F

9. This is an invalid argument.

p	q	r	$p \to q$	$q \to r$	$r \to p$	$(p \to q) \wedge (q \to r)$	$[(p \to q) \wedge (q \to r)] \to (r \to p)$
T	T	T	T	T	T	T	T
T	T	F	T	F	T	F	T
T	F	T	F	T	T	F	T
T	F	F	F	T	T	F	T
F	T	T	T	T	F	T	F
F	T	F	T	F	T	F	T
F	F	T	T	T	F	T	F
F	F	F	T	T	T	T	T

11. This is a valid argument.

p	q	r	$p\to q$	$q\wedge r$	$p\vee r$	$(p\to q)\wedge(q\wedge r)$	$[(p\to q)\wedge(q\wedge r)]\to(p\vee r)$
T	T	T	T	T	T	T	T
T	T	F	T	F	T	F	T
T	F	T	F	F	T	F	T
T	F	F	F	F	T	F	T
F	T	T	T	T	T	T	T
F	T	F	T	F	F	F	T
F	F	T	T	F	T	F	T
F	F	F	T	F	F	F	T

13. This is a valid argument.

p	q	r	$\sim p$	$\sim r$	$p\leftrightarrow q$	$q\to r$	$\sim r\to\sim p$	$(p\leftrightarrow q)\wedge(q\to r)$	$[(p\leftrightarrow q)\wedge(q\to r)]\to(\sim r\to\sim p)$
T	T	T	F	F	T	T	T	T	T
T	T	F	F	T	T	F	F	F	T
T	F	T	F	F	F	T	T	F	T
T	F	F	F	T	F	T	F	F	T
F	T	T	T	F	F	T	T	F	T
F	T	F	T	T	F	F	T	F	T
F	F	T	T	F	T	T	T	T	T
F	F	F	T	T	T	T	T	T	T

15. This is a valid argument. ***p*:** It is cold. ***q*:** Motorcycle started.

$p\to\sim q$

q

$\therefore\sim p$

p	q	$\sim p$	$\sim q$	$p\to\sim q$	$(p\to\sim q)\wedge q$	$[(p\to\sim q)\wedge q\to\sim p]$
T	T	F	F	F	F	T
T	F	F	T	T	F	T
F	T	T	F	T	T	T
F	F	T	T	T	F	T

17. This an invalid argument. ***p*:** There is a dam. ***q*:** There is flooding.

$p\vee q$

q

$\therefore\sim p$

p	q	$\sim p$	$p\vee q$	$(p\vee q)\wedge q$	$[(p\vee q)\wedge q]\to\sim p$
T	T	F	T	T	F
T	F	F	T	F	T
F	T	T	T	T	T
F	F	T	F	F	T

19. p: We close the door.
q: There is less noise.

$p\to q$

q

$\therefore p$

Invalid, by fallacy of the converse.

21. $p\to q$

$\sim p\to q$

$\therefore q$

valid

23. p: We criminalize drugs.
q: We damage the future of young people.

$p \vee q$
$\underline{\sim q}$
$\therefore p$
Valid, by disjunctive reasoning.

25. This is an invalid argument. $\boldsymbol{p}$**:** All people obey the law. $\boldsymbol{q}$**:** No jails are needed.

$p \to q$
$\underline{\sim p}$
$\therefore \sim q$

p	q	$\sim p$	$\sim q$	$p \to q$	$(p \to q) \wedge \sim p$	$[(p \to q) \wedge \sim p] \to \sim q$
T	T	F	F	T	F	T
T	F	F	T	F	F	T
F	T	T	F	T	T	F
F	F	T	T	T	T	T

27. $p \to q$
$\underline{q \to r}$
$\therefore p \to r$
valid

29. $p \to q$
$\underline{q \to r}$
$\therefore r \to p$
invalid

31. This is a valid argument. $\boldsymbol{p}$**:** Tim plays $\boldsymbol{q}$**:** Janet plays $\boldsymbol{r}$**:** Team wins

$(p \wedge q) \to r$
$\underline{p \wedge \sim r}$
$\therefore \sim q$

p	q	r	$\sim q$	$\sim r$	$p \wedge q$	$p \wedge \sim r$	$(p \wedge q) \to r$
T	T	T	F	F	T	F	T
T	T	F	F	T	T	T	F
T	F	T	T	F	F	F	T
T	F	F	T	T	F	T	T
F	T	T	F	F	F	F	T
F	T	F	F	T	F	F	T
F	F	T	T	F	F	F	T
F	F	F	T	T	F	F	T

$[(p \wedge q) \to r] \wedge (p \wedge \sim r)$	$[[(p \wedge q) \to r] \wedge (p \wedge \sim r)] \to \sim q$
F	T
F	T
F	T
T	T
F	T
F	T
F	T
F	T

33. This is a valid argument. ***p*:** It rains ***q*:** It snows ***r*:** I read

$(p \vee q) \rightarrow r$

$\sim r$

$\therefore \sim(p \vee q)$

p	q	r	$\sim r$	$p \vee q$	$\sim(p \vee q)$	$(p \vee q) \rightarrow r$
T	T	T	F	T	F	T
T	T	F	T	T	F	F
T	F	T	F	T	F	T
T	F	F	T	T	F	F
F	T	T	F	T	F	T
F	T	F	T	T	F	F
F	F	T	F	F	T	T
F	F	F	T	F	T	T

$[(p \vee q) \rightarrow r] \wedge \sim r$	$[[(p \vee q) \rightarrow r] \wedge \sim r] \rightarrow \sim(p \vee q)$
F	T
F	T
F	T
F	T
F	T
F	T
F	T
T	T

35. This is an invalid argument. ***p*:** It rains ***q*:** It snows ***r*:** I read

$(p \vee q) \rightarrow r$

r

$\therefore p \vee q$

p	q	r	$p \vee q$	$(p \vee q) \rightarrow r$	$[(p \vee q) \rightarrow r] \wedge r$	$[[(p \vee q) \rightarrow r] \wedge r] \rightarrow (p \vee q)$
T	T	T	T	T	T	T
T	T	F	T	F	F	T
T	F	T	T	T	T	T
T	F	F	T	F	F	T
F	T	T	T	T	T	T
F	T	F	T	F	F	T
F	F	T	F	T	T	F
F	F	F	F	T	F	T

37. This is an invalid argument. ***p*:** It's hot. ***q*:** It's humid. ***r*:** I complain.

$(p \wedge q) \rightarrow r$
$\underline{\sim p \vee \sim q}$
$\therefore \sim r$

p	q	r	$\sim p$	$\sim q$	$\sim r$	$p \wedge q$	$\sim p \vee \sim q$	$(p \wedge q) \rightarrow r$
T	T	T	F	F	F	T	F	T
T	T	F	F	F	T	T	F	F
T	F	T	F	T	F	F	T	T
T	F	F	F	T	T	F	T	T
F	T	T	T	F	F	F	T	T
F	T	F	T	F	T	F	T	T
F	F	T	T	T	F	F	T	T
F	F	F	T	T	T	F	T	T

$[(p \wedge q) \rightarrow r] \wedge (\sim p \vee \sim q)$	$[[(p \wedge q) \rightarrow r] \wedge (\sim p \vee \sim q)] \rightarrow \sim r$
F	T
F	T
T	F
T	T
T	F
T	T
T	F
T	T

39. $p \rightarrow q$
$\underline{\sim p \rightarrow r}$
$\therefore q \vee r$
valid

$p \rightarrow q$
41. $q \rightarrow \sim r$
$\underline{r}$
$\therefore \sim p$
valid

43. *p*: A person is a chemist.
q: A person has a college degree.

$p \rightarrow q$
$\underline{\sim q}$
$\therefore \sim p$
My best friend is not a chemist. By contrapositive reasoning.

45. *p*: Writers improve.
q: "My Mother the Car" dropped from primetime.

$p \vee q$
$\underline{\sim p}$
$\therefore q$
"My Mother the Car" was dropped from primetime. By disjunctive reasoning.

47. p: All electricity off.
q: No lights work.

$p \to q$
$\underline{\sim q}$
$\therefore \sim p$

Some electricity is not off. By contrapositive reasoning.

49. p: I vacation in Paris.
q: I eat French pastries.
r: I gain weight.

$p \to q$
$\underline{q \to r}$
$\therefore p \to r$

If I vacation in Paris, I gain weight. By transitive reasoning.

51. This is an invalid argument.

$p \to q$
$\underline{\sim p}$
$\therefore \sim q$

p	q	$\sim p$	$\sim q$	$p \to q$	$(p \to q) \wedge \sim p$	$[(p \to q) \wedge \sim p] \to \sim q$
T	T	F	F	T	F	T
T	F	F	T	F	F	T
F	T	T	F	T	T	F
F	F	T	T	T	T	T

53. $p \vee q$
$\underline{\sim p}$
$\therefore q$
valid

55. $p \to q$
$\underline{q}$
$\therefore p$
Invalid.

57. This is a valid argument.

$p \to q$
$\underline{\sim q}$
$\therefore \sim p$

p	q	$\sim p$	$\sim q$	$p \to q$	$(p \to q) \wedge \sim q$	$[(p \to q) \wedge \sim q] \to \sim p$
T	T	F	F	T	F	T
T	F	F	T	F	F	T
F	T	T	F	T	F	T
F	F	T	T	T	T	T

59. $p \to q$
$\underline{q \to r}$
$\therefore p \to r$
valid

61. p: Poverty causes crime.
q: Crime sweeps American cities during the Great Depression.

$p \to q$
$\underline{\sim q}$
$\therefore \sim p$

Valid. By contrapositive reasoning.

63. h

65. i

67. c

69. a

71. j

73. d

83. does not make sense; Explanations will vary. Sample explanation: Conclusions must be based on logic, not based on personal feelings.

85. does not make sense; Explanations will vary. Sample explanation: The argument is valid.

87. p: You only spoke when spoken to, and
I only speak when spoken to.
q: Nobody would ever say anything.

$p \to q$
$\underline{\sim q}$
$\therefore \sim p$

People sometimes speak without being spoken to.

p	q	$\sim p$	$\sim q$	$p \to q$	$(p \to q) \wedge \sim q$	$[(p \to q) \wedge \sim q] \to \sim p$
T	T	F	F	T	F	T
T	F	F	T	F	F	T
F	T	T	F	T	F	T
F	F	T	T	T	T	T

89. The doctor either destroys the base on which the placebo rests or jeopardizes a relationship built on trust.

Check Points 3.8

1. The argument is valid.

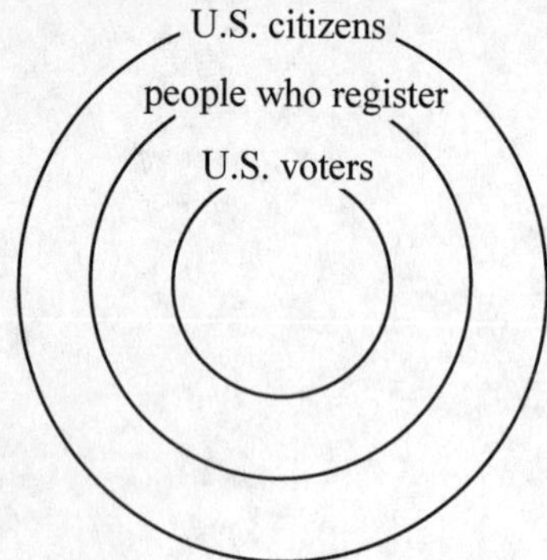

2. The argument is invalid.

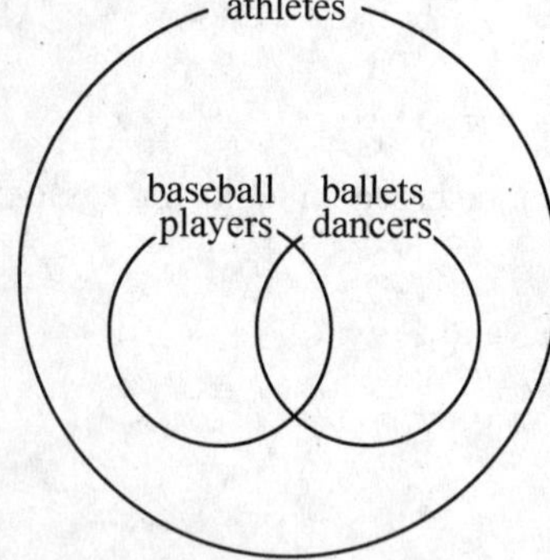

3. The argument is valid.

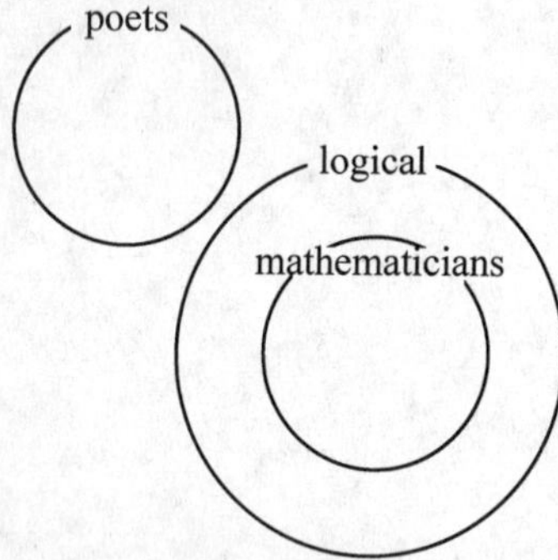

4. The argument is invalid.

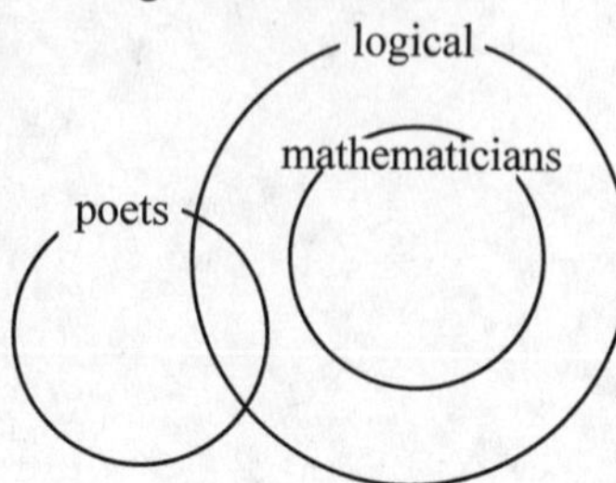

5. The argument is invalid.

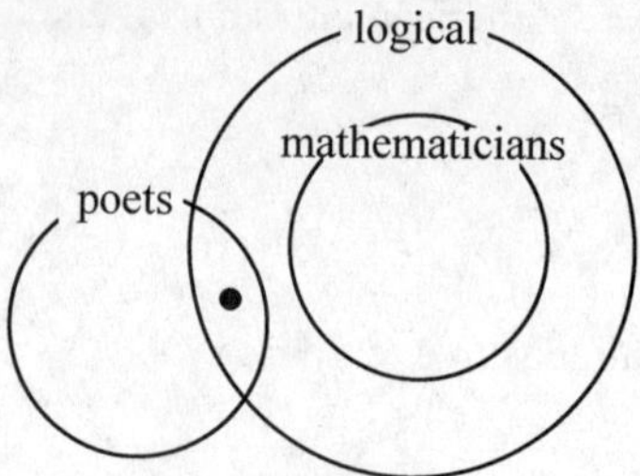

6. The argument is invalid.
The • is Euclid.

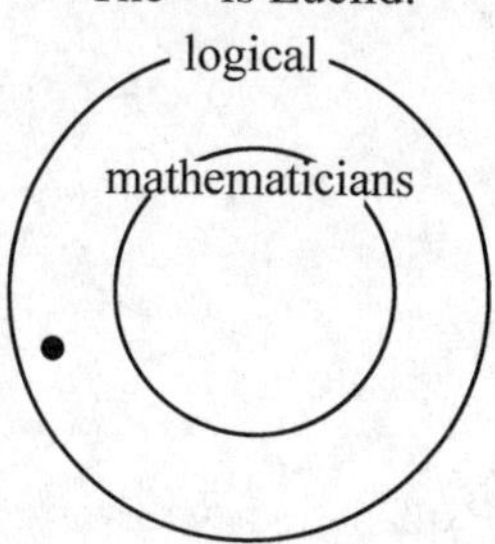

Concept and Vocabulary Check 3.8

1. All *A* are *B*

2. No *A* are *B*

3. Some *A* are *B*

4. Some *A* are not *B*

5. false

6. false

Exercise Set 3.8

1. Valid.

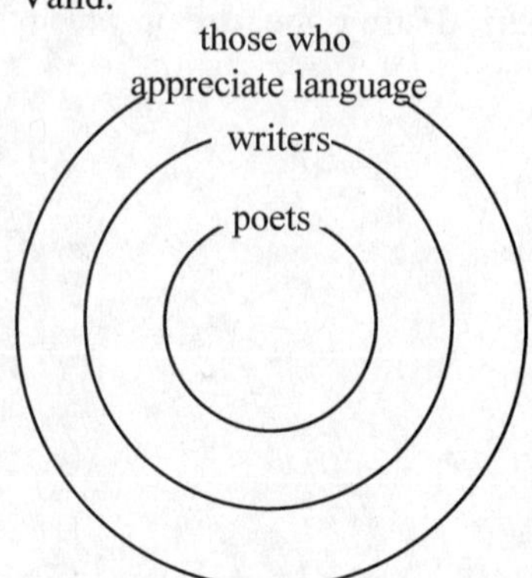

3. Invalid.

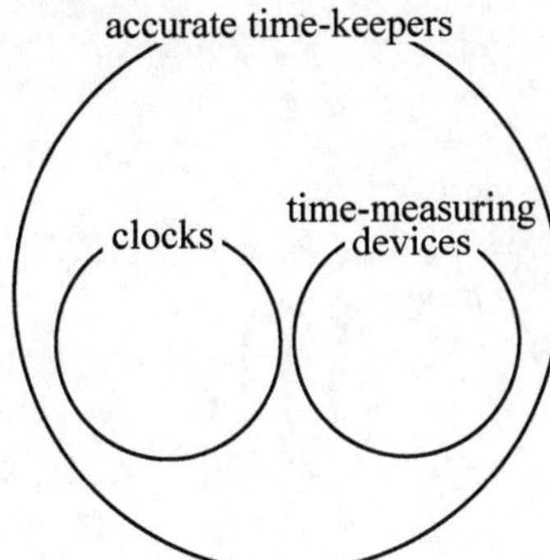

5. Valid.

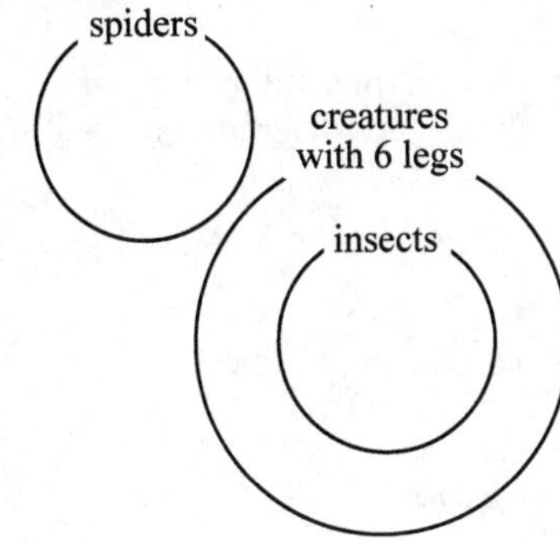

7. Invalid.

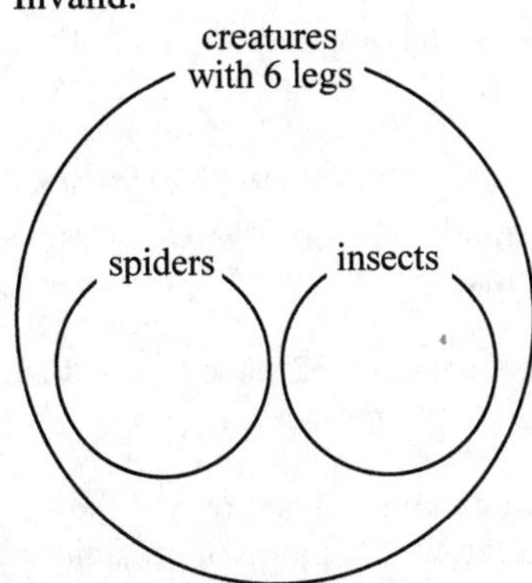

9. Invalid.

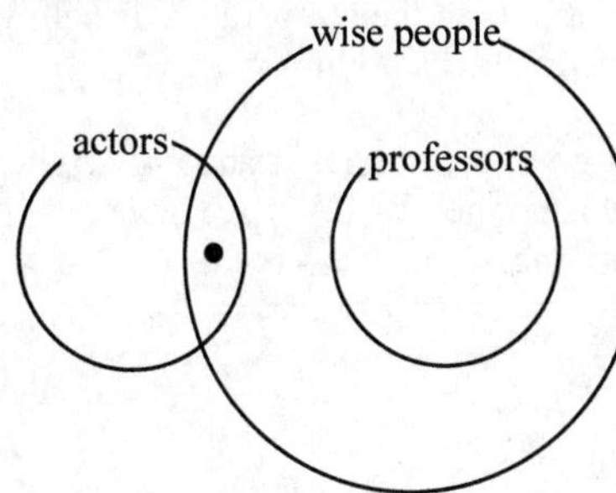

11. Valid.

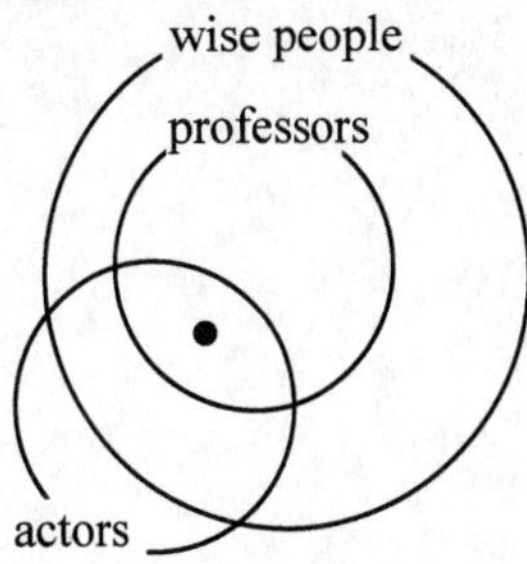

13. Valid. The • is Savion Glover.

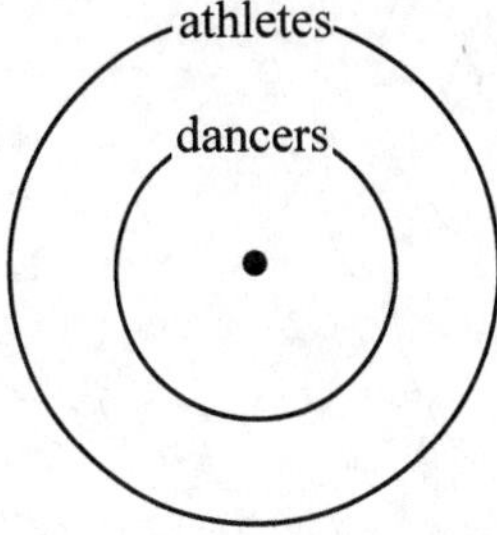

15. Invalid. The • is Savion Glover.

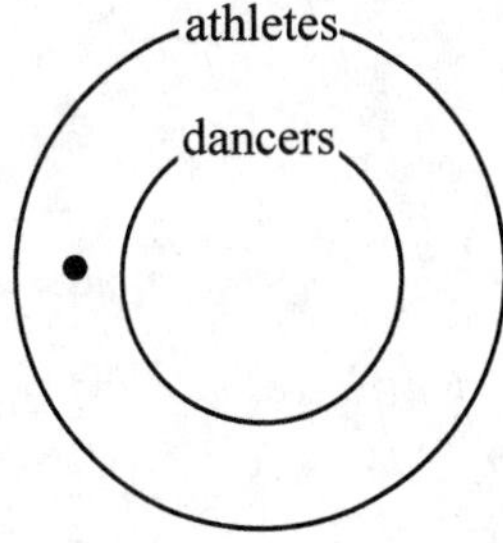

17. Invalid.

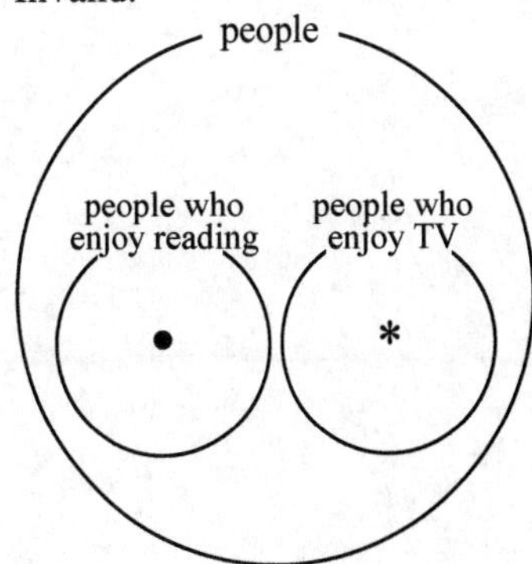

19. Valid.

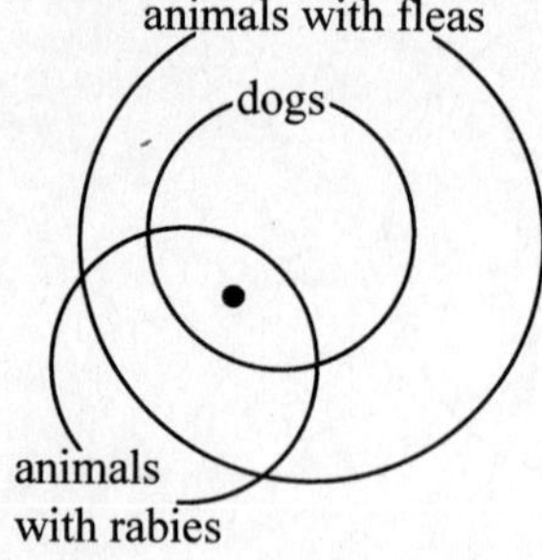

21. Valid.

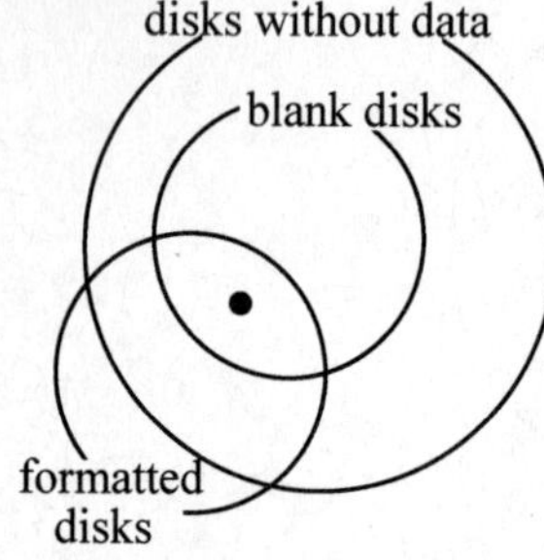

23. Valid. The • is 8.

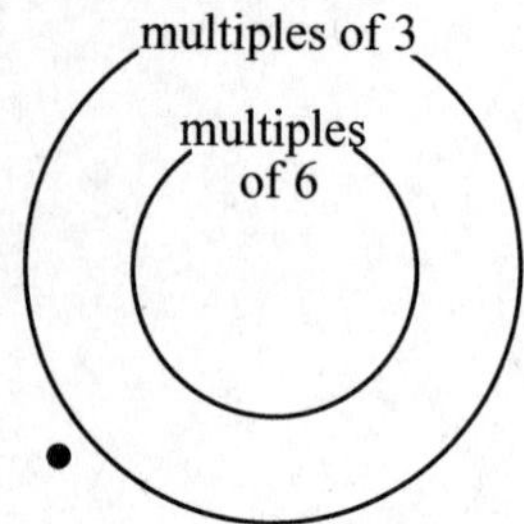

25. Invalid.

27. Invalid.

29. Valid.

31. Invalid.

33. Invalid.

35. Invalid.

37. Valid.

39. Valid.

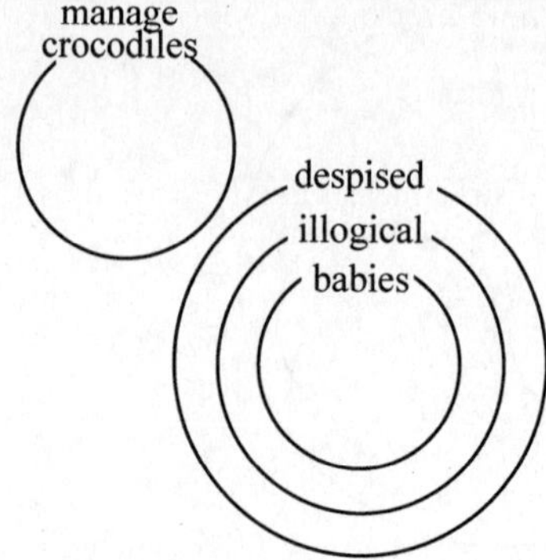

43. makes sense

45. does not make sense; Explanations will vary. Sample explanation: Euler diagrams can be used for this purpose.

47. b is true.

49. Some teachers are amusing people.

Chapter 3 Review Exercises

1. $(p \wedge q) \rightarrow r$; If the temperature is below 32° and we have finished studying, then we go to the movies.

2. $\sim r \rightarrow (\sim p \vee \sim q)$; If we do not go to the movies, then the temperature is not below 32° or we have not finished studying.

3. The temperature is below 32°, and if we finished studying, we go to the movies.

4. We will go to the movies if and only if the temperature is below 32° and we have finished studying.

5. It is not true that both the temperature is below 32° and we have finished studying.

6. We will not go to the movies if and only if the temperature is not below 32° or we have not finished studying.

7. $(p \wedge q) \vee r$

8. $(p \vee \sim q) \rightarrow r$

9. $q \rightarrow (p \leftrightarrow r)$

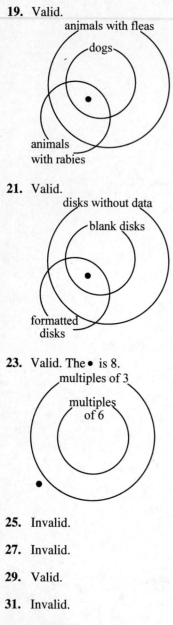

10. $r \leftrightarrow (p \wedge \sim q)$

11. $p \rightarrow r$

12. $q \rightarrow \sim r$

13. Some houses are not made with wood.

14. Some students major in business.

15. No crimes are motivated by passion.

16. All Democrats are registered voters.

17. Some new taxes will not be used for education.

18. neither

p	q	$\sim p$	$\sim p \wedge q$	$p \vee (\sim p \wedge q)$
T	T	F	F	T
T	F	F	F	T
F	T	T	T	T
F	F	T	F	F

19. neither

p	q	$\sim p$	$\sim q$	$\sim p \vee \sim q$
T	T	F	F	F
T	F	F	T	T
F	T	T	F	T
F	F	T	T	T

20. neither

p	q	$\sim p$	$\sim p \vee q$	$p \rightarrow (\sim p \vee q)$
T	T	F	T	T
T	F	F	F	F
F	T	T	T	T
F	F	T	T	T

21. neither

p	q	$\sim q$	$p \leftrightarrow \sim q$
T	T	F	F
T	F	T	T
F	T	F	T
F	F	T	F

22. tautology

p	q	$\sim p$	$\sim q$	$p \vee q$	$\sim(p \vee q)$	$\sim p \wedge \sim q$	$\sim(p \vee q) \rightarrow (\sim p \wedge \sim q)$
T	T	F	F	T	F	F	T
T	F	F	T	T	F	F	T
F	T	T	F	T	F	F	T
F	F	T	T	F	T	T	T

23. neither

p	q	r	$\sim r$	$p \vee q$	$(p \vee q) \rightarrow \sim r$
T	T	T	F	T	F
T	T	F	T	T	T
T	F	T	F	T	F
T	F	F	T	T	T
F	T	T	F	T	F
F	T	F	T	T	T
F	F	T	F	F	T
F	F	F	T	F	T

24. neither

p	q	r	$p \wedge q$	$p \wedge r$	$(p \wedge q) \leftrightarrow (p \wedge r)$
T	T	T	T	T	T
T	T	F	T	F	F
T	F	T	F	T	F
T	F	F	F	F	T
F	T	T	F	F	T
F	T	F	F	F	T
F	F	T	F	F	T
F	F	F	F	F	T

25. neither

p	q	r	$r \rightarrow p$	$q \vee (r \rightarrow p)$	$p \wedge [q \vee (r \rightarrow p)]$
T	T	T	T	T	T
T	T	F	T	T	T
T	F	T	T	T	T
T	F	F	T	T	T
F	T	T	F	T	F
F	T	F	T	T	F
F	F	T	F	F	F
F	F	F	T	T	F

26. a. p: I'm in class.; q: I'm studying.; $(p \vee q) \wedge \sim p$

b. $(p \vee q) \wedge \sim p$

p	q	$\sim p$	$p \vee q$	$(p \vee q) \wedge \sim p$
T	T	F	T	F
T	F	F	T	F
F	T	T	T	T
F	F	T	F	F

c. The statement is true when p is false and q is true.

27. a. p: You spit from a truck.; q: It's legal.; r: You spit from a car.; $(p \to q) \wedge (r \to \sim q)$

b.

p	q	r	$\sim q$	$p \to q$	$r \to \sim q$	$(p \to q) \wedge (r \to \sim q)$
T	T	T	F	T	F	F
T	T	F	F	T	T	T
T	F	T	T	F	T	F
T	F	F	T	F	T	F
F	T	T	F	T	F	F
F	T	F	F	T	T	T
F	F	T	T	T	T	T
F	F	F	T	T	T	T

c. The statement is true when p and q are both false.

28. $\sim(q \leftrightarrow r)$

$\sim(\text{F} \leftrightarrow \text{F})$

$\sim\text{T}$

F

29. $(p \wedge q) \to (p \vee r)$

$(\text{T} \wedge \text{F}) \to (\text{T} \vee \text{F})$

$\text{F} \to \text{T}$

T

30. $(\sim q \to p) \vee (r \wedge \sim p)$

$(\sim\text{F} \to \text{T}) \vee (\text{F} \wedge \sim\text{T})$

$(\text{T} \to \text{T}) \vee (\text{F} \wedge \text{F})$

$\text{T} \vee \text{F}$

T

31. $\sim[(\sim p \vee r) \to (q \wedge r)]$

$\sim[(\sim\text{T} \vee \text{F}) \to (\text{F} \wedge \text{F})]$

$\sim[(\text{F} \vee \text{F}) \to \text{F}]$

$\sim[\text{F} \to \text{F}]$

$\sim\text{T}$

F

32. p: The 2000 diversity index was 47.; q: The index increased from 2000 to 2010.
$p \wedge \sim q$ is false.

33. p: The diversity index decreased from 1980 through 2010.; q: The index was 55 in 1980.; r: The index was 34 in 2010.
$p \to (q \wedge r)$ is true.

34. p: The diversity index increased by 6 from 1980 to 1990.; q: The diversity index increased by 7 from 1990 to 2000.; r: The index was at a maximum in 2010.
$(p \leftrightarrow q) \vee \sim r$ is true.

35. a. $\sim p \vee q \equiv p \rightarrow q$

p	q	$\sim p$	$\sim p \vee q$	$p \rightarrow q$
T	T	F	T	T
T	F	F	F	F
F	T	T	T	T
F	F	T	T	T

b. If the triangle is isosceles, then it has two equal sides.

36. c
The original statement is of the form $p \wedge q$.
The original statement is equivalent to statement c which is of the form $\sim p \rightarrow q$.

37. not equivalent

p	q	$\sim(p \leftrightarrow q)$	$\sim p \vee \sim q$
T	T	F	F
T	F	T	T
F	T	T	T
F	F	F	T

38. equivalent

p	q	r	$\sim p \wedge (q \vee r)$	$(\sim p \wedge q) \vee (\sim p \wedge r)$
T	T	T	F	F
T	T	F	F	F
T	F	T	F	F
T	F	F	F	F
F	T	T	T	T
F	T	F	T	T
F	F	T	T	T
F	F	F	F	F

39. Converse: If I am in the South, then I am in Atlanta.
Inverse: If I am not in Atlanta, then I am not in the South.
Contrapositive: If I am not in the South, then I am not in Atlanta.

40. Converse: If today is not a holiday, then I am in class.
Inverse: If I am not in class, then today is a holiday.
Contrapositive: If today is a holiday, then I'm not in class.

41. Converse: If I pass all courses, then I worked hard.
Inverse: If I don't work hard, then I don't pass some courses.
Contrapositive: If I do not pass some course, then I did not work hard.

42. Converse: $\sim q \rightarrow \sim p$; Inverse: $p \rightarrow q$; Contrapositive: $q \rightarrow p$

43. An argument is sound and it is not valid.

44. I do not work hard and I succeed.

45. $\sim r \wedge \sim p$

46. Chicago is not a city or Maine is not a city.

47. Ernest Hemingway was neither a musician nor an actor.

48. p: the number is positive.
q: the number is negative.
r: the number is zero.
The statement can be represented symbolically as $(\sim p \wedge \sim q) \rightarrow r$.
Next write the contrapositive and simplify.
$\sim(r) \rightarrow \sim(\sim p \wedge \sim q)$
$\sim r \rightarrow (p \vee q)$
Thus, $(\sim p \wedge \sim q) \rightarrow r \equiv \sim r \rightarrow (p \vee q)$.
The original statement is equivalent to "If a number is not zero, then the number is positive or negative."

49. I do not work hard and I succeed.

50. She is using her car or she is not taking a bus.

51. Write the negation of $\sim p \vee q$ and simplify.
$\sim(\sim p \vee q)$
$\sim(\sim p) \wedge \sim q$
$p \wedge \sim q$

52. **a** and **c** are equivalent.

		a	b	c
p	q	$p \rightarrow q$	$\sim p \rightarrow \sim q$	$\sim p \vee q$
T	T	T	T	T
T	F	F	T	F
F	T	T	F	T
F	F	T	T	T

53. **a** and **b** are equivalent.

		a	b	c
p	q	$\sim p \rightarrow q$	$\sim q \rightarrow p$	$\sim p \wedge \sim q$
T	T	T	T	F
T	F	T	T	F
F	T	T	T	F
F	F	F	F	T

54. **a** and **c** are equivalent.

		a	b	c
p	q	$p \vee \sim q$	$\sim q \rightarrow p$	$\sim(\sim p \wedge q)$
T	T	T	T	T
T	F	T	T	T
F	T	F	T	F
F	F	T	F	T

55. none

56. The argument is invalid.

p	q	$\sim q$	$p \rightarrow q$	$(p \rightarrow q) \wedge \sim q$	$[(p \rightarrow q) \wedge \sim q] \rightarrow p$
T	T	F	T	F	T
T	F	T	F	F	T
F	T	F	T	F	T
F	F	T	T	T	F

57. The argument is valid.

p	q	r	$p \wedge q$	$q \to r$	$p \to r$	$(p \wedge q) \wedge (q \to r)$	$[(p \wedge q) \wedge (q \to r)] \to (p \to r)$
T	T	T	T	T	T	T	T
T	T	F	T	F	F	F	T
T	F	T	F	T	T	F	T
T	F	F	F	T	F	F	T
F	T	T	F	T	T	F	T
F	T	F	F	F	T	F	T
F	F	T	F	T	T	F	T
F	F	F	F	T	T	F	T

58. The argument is invalid. **p:** Tony plays. **q:** Team wins.

$p \to q$
q
$\therefore p$

p	q	$p \to q$	$(p \to q) \wedge q$	$[(p \to q) \wedge q] \to p$
T	T	T	T	T
T	F	F	F	T
F	T	T	T	F
F	F	T	F	T

59. The argument is invalid. **p:** Plant is fertilized. **q:** Plant turns yellow.

$p \vee q$
q
$\therefore \sim p$

p	q	$\sim p$	$p \vee q$	$(p \vee q) \wedge q$	$[(p \vee q) \wedge q] \to \sim p$
T	T	F	T	T	F
T	F	F	T	F	T
F	T	T	T	T	T
F	F	T	F	F	T

60. The argument is valid. **p:** A majority of legislators vote for a bill. **q:** Bill does not become law.

$p \vee q$
$\sim p$
$\therefore q$

p	q	$\sim p$	$p \vee q$	$(p \vee q) \wedge \sim p$	$[(p \vee q) \wedge \sim p] \to q$
T	T	F	T	F	T
T	F	F	T	F	T
F	T	T	T	T	T
F	F	T	F	F	T

61. The argument is valid. **p:** Good baseball player. **q:** Good hand–eye coordination.

$p \to q$
$\sim q$
$\therefore \sim p$

p	q	$\sim p$	$\sim q$	$p \to q$	$(p \to q) \wedge \sim q$	$[(p \to q) \wedge \sim q] \to \sim p$
T	T	F	F	T	F	T
T	F	F	T	F	F	T
F	T	T	F	T	F	T
F	F	T	T	T	T	T

62. The argument is valid. **p:** You love the person you marry **q:** You can fall out of love.

$p \to \sim q$
$\sim p \to q$
$\therefore p \leftrightarrow \sim q$

p	q	$\sim p$	$\sim q$	$p \to \sim q$	$\sim p \to q$	$p \leftrightarrow \sim q$	$[(p \to \sim q) \wedge (\sim p \to q)] \to (p \leftrightarrow \sim q)$
T	T	F	F	F	T	F	T
T	F	F	T	T	T	T	T
F	T	T	F	T	T	T	T
F	F	T	T	T	F	F	T

63. The argument is invalid. ***p*:** I purchase season tickets to the football games ***q*:** I attend all lectures.

$$\begin{array}{l} p \rightarrow \sim q \\ \underline{\quad r \rightarrow q} \\ \therefore \sim r \rightarrow p \end{array}$$

p	q	r	$p \rightarrow \sim q$	$r \rightarrow q$	$\sim r \rightarrow p$	$(p \rightarrow \sim q) \wedge (r \rightarrow q)$	$[(p \rightarrow \sim q) \wedge (r \rightarrow q)] \rightarrow (\sim r \rightarrow p)$
T	T	T	F	T	T	F	T
T	T	F	F	T	T	F	T
T	F	T	T	F	T	F	T
T	F	F	T	T	T	T	T
F	T	T	T	T	T	T	T
F	T	F	T	T	F	T	F
F	F	T	T	F	T	F	T
F	F	F	T	T	F	T	F

64. Invalid.

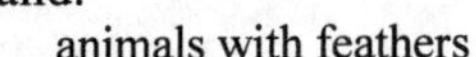

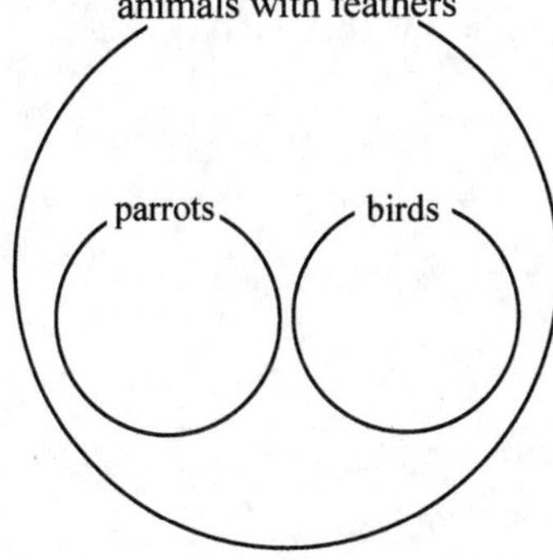

65. Valid.

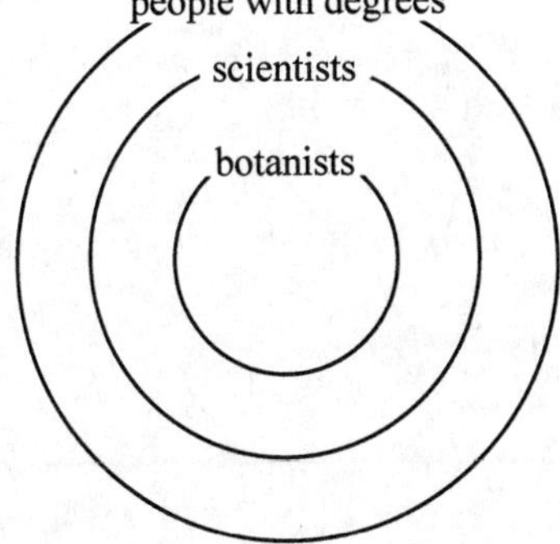

66. Valid.

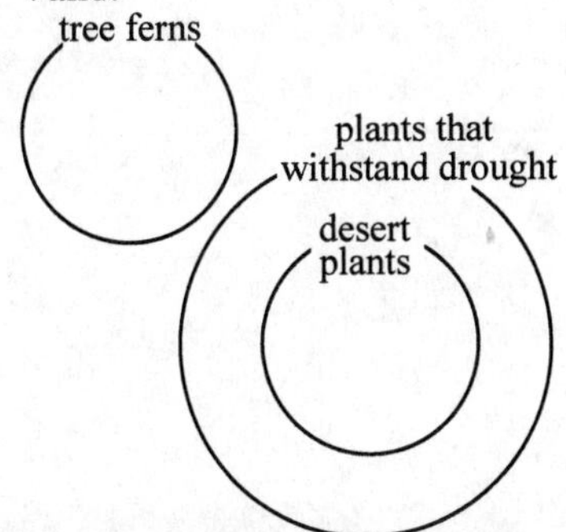

67. Invalid.

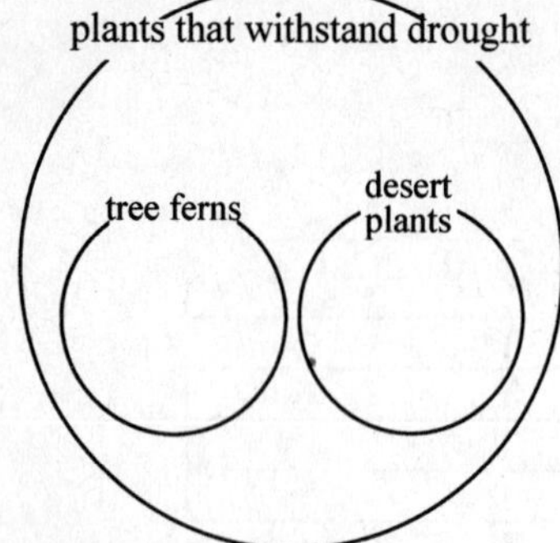

68. Invalid.

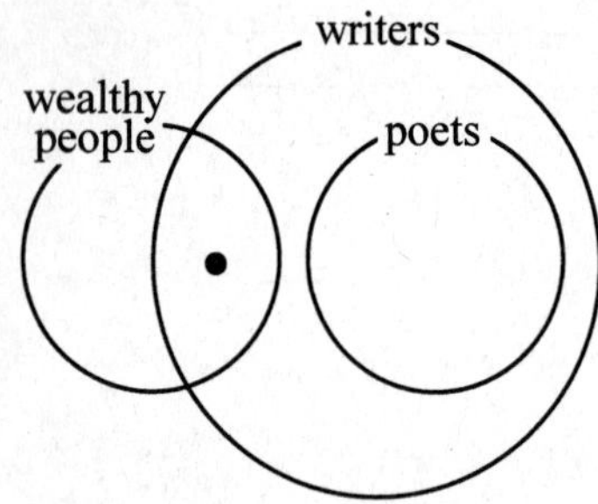

69. Valid.

Chapter 3 Test

1. If I'm registered and I'm a citizen, then I vote.

2. I don't vote if and only if I'm not registered or I'm not a citizen.

3. I'm neither registered nor a citizen.

4. $(p \wedge q) \vee {\sim}r$

5. $({\sim}p \vee {\sim}q) \rightarrow {\sim}r$

6. $r \rightarrow q$

7. Some numbers are not divisible by 5.

8. No people wear glasses.

9. $p \wedge (\sim p \vee q)$

p	q	$\sim p$	$\sim p \vee q$	$p \wedge (\sim p \vee q)$
T	T	F	T	T
T	F	F	F	F
F	T	T	T	F
F	F	T	T	F

10. $\sim(p \wedge q) \leftrightarrow (\sim p \vee \sim q)$

p	q	$\sim p$	$\sim q$	$p \wedge q$	$\sim(p \wedge q)$	$(\sim p \vee \sim q)$	$\sim(p \wedge q) \leftrightarrow (\sim p \vee \sim q)$
T	T	F	F	T	F	F	T
T	F	F	T	F	T	T	T
F	T	T	F	F	T	T	T
F	F	T	T	F	T	T	T

11. $p \leftrightarrow (q \vee r)$

p	q	r	$q \vee r$	$p \leftrightarrow (q \vee r)$
T	T	T	T	T
T	T	F	T	T
T	F	T	T	T
T	F	F	F	F
F	T	T	T	F
F	T	F	T	F
F	F	T	T	F
F	F	F	F	T

12. p: You break the law.; q: You change the law.; $(p \wedge q) \rightarrow \sim p$

p	q	$\sim p$	$p \wedge q$	$(p \wedge q) \rightarrow \sim p$
T	T	F	T	F
T	F	F	F	T
F	T	T	F	T
F	F	T	F	T

Answers will vary; an example is: The statement is true when p is false.

13. $\sim(q \rightarrow r)$

$\sim(\text{T} \rightarrow \text{F})$

$\sim\text{F}$

T

14. $(p \vee r) \leftrightarrow (\sim r \wedge p)$

$(\text{F} \vee \text{F}) \leftrightarrow (\sim\text{F} \wedge \text{F})$

$\text{F} \leftrightarrow (\text{T} \wedge \text{F})$

$\text{F} \leftrightarrow \text{F}$

T

15. **a.** p: There was an increase in the percentage spent on food..
q: There was an increase in the percentage spent on health care.
r: By 2010, the percentage spent on health care was more than triple the percentage spent on food..
$\sim p \vee (q \vee r)$

b. $\sim p \vee (q \vee r)$
$\sim F \vee (T \vee F)$
$T \vee T$
T
The statement is true.

16. b

17. If it snows, then it is not August.

18. Converse: If I cannot concentrate, then the radio is playing.
Inverse: If the radio is not playing, then I can concentrate.

19. It is cold and we use the pool.

20. The test is not today and the party is not tonight.

21. The banana is not green or it is ready to eat.

22. a and b are equivalent.

		a	b	c
p	q	$\sim p \to q$	$p \vee q$	$p \to \sim q$
T	T	T	T	F
T	F	T	T	T
F	T	T	T	T
F	F	F	F	T

23. a and c are equivalent.

		a	b	c
p	q	$\sim(p \vee q)$	$\sim p \to \sim q$	$\sim p \wedge \sim q$
T	T	F	T	F
T	F	F	T	F
F	T	F	F	F
F	F	T	T	T

24. The argument is invalid. ***p*:** Parrot talks. ***q*:** It is intelligent.

$p \to q$
$\underline{q}$
$\therefore p$

25. The argument is valid. ***p*:** I am sick. ***q*:** I am tired.

$p \vee q$
$\underline{\sim q}$
$\therefore p$

26. The argument is invalid. ***p*:** I am going. ***q*:** You are going.

$p \leftrightarrow \sim q$
$\underline{q}$
$\therefore p$

27. Invalid.

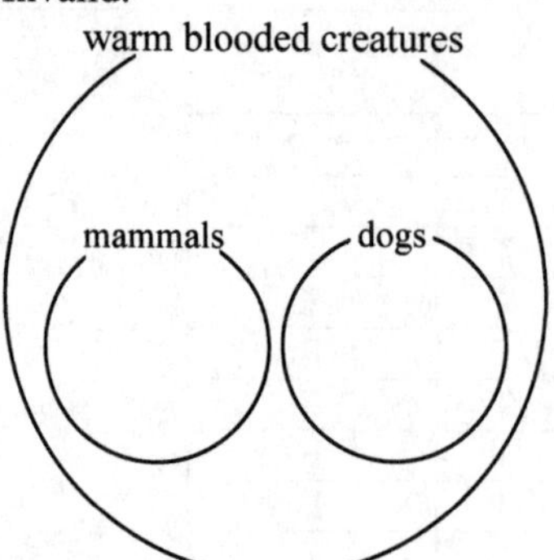

28. Valid.

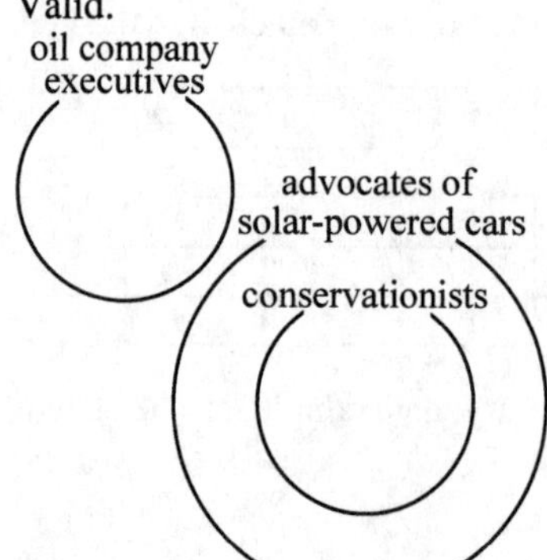

29. Invalid.

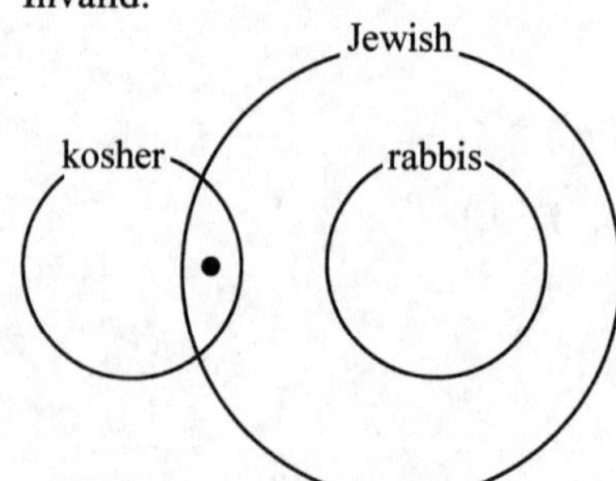

Chapter 4
Number Representation and Calculation

Check Points 4.1

1. a. $4026 = (4\times10^3)+(0\times10^2)+(2\times10^1)+(6\times1) = (4\times1000)+(0\times100)+(2\times10)+(6\times1)$

b. $24,232 = (2\times10^4)+(4\times10^3)+(2\times10^2)+(3\times10^1)+(2\times1)$
$= (2\times10,000)+(4\times1000)+(2\times100)+(3\times10)+(2\times1)$

2. a. $6000+70+3=6073$ **b.** $80,000+900=80,900$

3. a. First, represent the numeral in each place value as a Hindu-Arabic numeral. Then multiply them by their place values and find the sum.

vvv   <<   <<< v
↓   ↓   ↓

$(3\times60^2)+(20\times60)+(31\times1)$
$=(3\times3600)+(20\times60)+(31\times1)$
$=10,800+1200+31$
$=12,031$

b. First, represent the numeral in each place value as a Hindu-Arabic numeral. Then multiply them by their place values and find the sum.

vv   <   <vv   v
↓   ↓   ↓   ↓

$(2\times60^3)+(10\times60^2)+(12\times60)+(1\times1)$
$=(2\times216,000)+(10\times3600)+(12\times60)+(1\times1)$
$=432,000+36,000+720+1$
$=468,721$

4. a. First, represent the numeral in each place value as a Hindu-Arabic numeral. Then multiply them by their place values and find the sum.

$11 \times 18\times20^2 = 11 \times 7200 = 79,200$
$3 \times 18\times20^1 = 3 \times 360 = 1080$
$0 \times 20 = 0 \times 20 = 0$
$13 \times 1 = 13 \times 1 = 13$
$80,293$

b. First, represent the numeral in each place value as a Hindu-Arabic numeral. Then multiply them by their place values and find the sum.

$2 \times 18\times20^3 = 2 \times 144,000 = 288,000$
$0 \times 18\times20^2 = 0 \times 7200 = 0$
$6 \times 18\times20^1 = 6 \times 360 = 2160$
$16 \times 20 = 16 \times 20 = 320$
$10 \times 1 = 10 \times 1 = 10$
$290,490$

Concept and Vocabulary Check 4.1

1. numeral
2. Hindu-Arabic
3. 7; 10,000,000
4. expanded; positional
5. 10^4; 10^3; 10^2; 10^1; 1
6. 10; 60
7. 10; 1; 1; 1; 10; 10; 1; 1
8. 60^3; 60^2; 60^1; 11; 1
9. 18×20^4;
10. 18×20; 720; 20; 60; 1; 9; 789; 789

Exercise Set 4.1

1. $5^2 = 5 \times 5 = 25$

3. $2^3 = 2 \times 2 \times 2 = 8$

5. $3^4 = 3 \times 3 \times 3 \times 3 = 81$

7. $10^5 = 10 \times 10 \times 10 \times 10 \times 10 = 100{,}000$

9. $36 = (3 \times 10^1) + (6 \times 1) = (3 \times 10) + (6 \times 1)$

11. $249 = (2 \times 10^2) + (4 \times 10^1) + (9 \times 1) = (2 \times 100) + (4 \times 10) + (9 \times 1)$

13. $703 = (7 \times 10^2) + (0 \times 10^1) + (3 \times 1) = (7 \times 100) + (0 \times 10) + (3 \times 1)$

15. $4856 = (4 \times 10^3) + (8 \times 10^2) + (5 \times 10^1) + (6 \times 1) = (4 \times 1000) + (8 \times 100) + (5 \times 10) + (6 \times 1)$

17. $3070 = (3 \times 10^3) + (0 \times 10^2) + (7 \times 10^1) + (0 \times 1) = (3 \times 1000) + (0 \times 100) + (7 \times 10) + (0 \times 1)$

19. $34{,}569 = (3 \times 10^4) + (4 \times 10^3) + (5 \times 10^2) + (6 \times 10^1) + (9 \times 1)$
$= (3 \times 10{,}000) + (4 \times 1000) + (5 \times 100) + (6 \times 10) + (9 \times 1)$

21. $230{,}007{,}004 = (2 \times 10^8) + (3 \times 10^7) + (0 \times 10^6) + (0 \times 10^5) + (0 \times 10^4) + (7 \times 10^3) + (0 \times 10^2) + (0 \times 10^1) + (4 \times 1)$
$= (2 \times 100{,}000{,}000) + (3 \times 10{,}000{,}000) + (0 \times 1{,}000{,}000) + (0 \times 100{,}000)$
$+ (0 \times 10{,}000) + (7 \times 1000) + (0 \times 100) + (0 \times 10) + (4 \times 1)$

23. $70 + 3 = 73$

25. $300 + 80 + 5 = 385$

27. $500{,}000 + 20{,}000 + 8000 + 700 + 40 + 3 = 528{,}743$

29. $7000 + 2 = 7002$

31. $600{,}000{,}000 + 2000 + 7 = 600{,}002{,}007$

33. $(10+10+1+1+1)\times 1 = 23\times 1 = 23$

35. $(10+10+1)\times 60^1 + (1+1)\times 1 = (21\times 60) + 2 = 1260 + 2 = 1262$

37. $(10+10+10)\times 60^1 + (10+10+10+1+1+1)\times 1 = (30\times 60) + 33 = 1800 + 33 = 1833$

39. $(1+1+1)\times 60^2 + (10+1+1)\times 60^1 + (1+1+1)\times 1 = (3\times 3600) + (12\times 60) + 3 = 10{,}800 + 720 + 3 = 11{,}523$

41.
$$\begin{aligned}&(10+10+1)\times 60^2 + (1+1+1+1)\times 60^1 + (10+1)\times 1\\&= (21\times 60^2) + (4\times 60^1) + (11\times 1)\\&= (21\times 3600) + (4\times 60) + 11\\&= 75{,}600 + 240 + 11\\&= 75{,}851\end{aligned}$$

43.
$$\begin{aligned}&(10+1)\times 60^3 + (10+1)\times 60^2 + (10+1)\times 60^1 + (10+1)\times 1\\&= (11\times 60^3) + (11\times 60^2) + (11\times 60^1) + (11\times 1)\\&= (11\times 216{,}000) + (11\times 3600) + (11\times 60) + 11\\&= 2{,}376{,}000 + 39{,}600 + 660 + 11\\&= 2{,}416{,}271\end{aligned}$$

45.
$$\begin{aligned}&(1+1+1)\times 60^3 + (1+1)\times 60^2 + (1)\times 60^1 + (1)\times 1\\&= (3\times 216{,}000) + (2\times 3600) + (1\times 60) + (1\times 1)\\&= 648{,}000 + 7200 + 60 + 1\\&= 655{,}261\end{aligned}$$

47. $14\times 1 = 14$

49.
$$\begin{array}{rrrrrrr}19 & \times & 18\times 20^1 = & 19 & \times & 360 = & 6840\\0 & \times & 20 = & 0 & \times & 20 = & 0\\6 & \times & 1 = & 6 & \times & 1 = & \underline{6}\\ & & & & & & 6846\end{array}$$

51.
$$\begin{array}{rrrrrrr}8 & \times & 18\times 20^1 = & 8 & \times & 360 = & 2880\\8 & \times & 20 = & 8 & \times & 20 = & 160\\8 & \times & 1 = & 8 & \times & 1 = & \underline{8}\\ & & & & & & 3048\end{array}$$

53.
$$\begin{array}{rcrcrcrcr} 2 & \times & 18\times 20^2 = & 2 & \times & 7200 = & 14{,}400 \\ 0 & \times & 18\times 20^1 = & 0 & \times & 360 = & 0 \\ 0 & \times & 20 = & 0 & \times & 20 = & 0 \\ 11 & \times & 1 = & 11 & \times & 1 = & \underline{11} \\ & & & & & & 14{,}411 \end{array}$$

55.
$$\begin{array}{rcrcrcr} 10 & \times & 18\times 20^2 = & 10 & \times & 7200 = & 72{,}000 \\ 10 & \times & 18\times 20^1 = & 10 & \times & 360 = & 3{,}600 \\ 0 & \times & 20 = & 0 & \times & 20 = & 0 \\ 10 & \times & 1 = & 10 & \times & 1 = & \underline{10} \\ & & & & & & 75{,}610 \end{array}$$

57.
$$\begin{array}{rcrcrcr} 5 & \times & 18\times 20^4 = & 5 & \times & 2{,}880{,}000 = & 14{,}400{,}000 \\ 10 & \times & 18\times 20^3 = & 10 & \times & 144{,}000 = & 1{,}440{,}000 \\ 0 & \times & 18\times 20^2 = & 0 & \times & 7200 = & 0 \\ 6 & \times & 18\times 20^1 = & 6 & \times & 360 = & 2160 \\ 2 & \times & 20 = & 2 & \times & 20 = & 40 \\ 3 & \times & 1 = & 3 & \times & 1 = & \underline{3} \\ & & & & & & 15{,}842{,}203 \end{array}$$

59.
$$\begin{array}{rcrcrcr} 10 & \times & 18\times 20^4 = & 10 & \times & 2{,}880{,}000 = & 28{,}800{,}000 \\ 5 & \times & 18\times 20^3 = & 5 & \times & 144{,}000 = & 720{,}000 \\ 0 & \times & 18\times 20^2 = & 0 & \times & 7200 = & 0 \\ 0 & \times & 18\times 20^1 = & 0 & \times & 360 = & 0 \\ 11 & \times & 20 = & 11 & \times & 20 = & 220 \\ 4 & \times & 1 = & 4 & \times & 1 = & \underline{4} \\ & & & & & & 29{,}520{,}224 \end{array}$$

61.
$$\begin{aligned} &\left[(1)\times 60^2+(10+10)\times 60^1+(10+10+1)\times 1\right]+\left[(10+1)\times 60^2+(10+10+10)\times 60^1+(1+1+1+1)\times 1\right] \\ &=\left[(1)\times 60^2+(20)\times 60^1+(21)\times 1\right]+\left[(11)\times 60^2+(30)\times 60^1+(4)\times 1\right] \\ &=[3600+1200+21]+[39{,}600+1800+4] \\ &=4821+41{,}404 \\ &=46{,}225 \\ &=(4\times 10^4)+(6\times 10^3)+(2\times 10^2)+(2\times 10^1)+(5\times 1) \end{aligned}$$

63.
$$\begin{aligned} &[(1\times 360)+(6\times 20)+(6\times 1)]+[(5\times 360)+(0\times 20)+(13\times 1)] \\ &=[360+120+6]+[1800+0+13] \\ &=486+1813 \\ &=2299 \\ &=(2\times 10^3)+(2\times 10^2)+(9\times 10^1)+(9\times 1) \end{aligned}$$

65. 0.4759

67. 0.700203

69. 5000.03

71. 30,700.05809

73. 9734

75. 8097

77. $10^2 + 11^2 + 12^2 = 13^2 + 14^2$

$100 + 121 + 144 = 169 + 196$

$365 = 365$

365 is the number of days in a non-leap year.

87. does not make sense; Explanations will vary. Sample explanation: The numeral will need zeroes as place holders: 4,000,300.

89. makes sense

91. Change to Hindu-Arabic:

$$\begin{aligned} 7 \times 360 &= 2520 \\ 7 \times 20 &= 140 \\ 7 \times 1 &= 7 \\ \hline & \ 2667 \end{aligned}$$

Change to Babylonian:

$= 2667$

$= 2640 + 27$

$= (44 \times 60) + 27$

$= (10+10+10+10+1+1+1+1) \times 60 + (10+10+1+1+1+1+1+1+1) \times 1$

< < < < v v v v   < < v v v v v v v

Check Points 4.2

1. $3422_{\text{five}} = (3 \times 5^3) + (4 \times 5^2) + (2 \times 5^1) + (2 \times 1)$

$= (3 \times 5 \times 5 \times 5) + (4 \times 5 \times 5) + (2 \times 5) + (2 \times 1)$

$= 375 + 100 + 10 + 2$

$= 487$

2. $110011_{\text{two}} = (1 \times 2^5) + (1 \times 2^4) + (0 \times 2^3) + (0 \times 2^2) + (1 \times 2^1) + (1 \times 1)$

$= (1 \times 32) + (1 \times 16) + (0 \times 8) + (0 \times 4) + (1 \times 2) + (1 \times 1)$

$= 32 + 16 + 2 + 1$

$= 51$

3. $AD4_{\text{sixteen}} = (10 \times 16^2) + (13 \times 16^1) + (4 \times 1)$

$= (10 \times 16 \times 16) + (13 \times 16) + (4 \times 1)$

$= 2560 + 208 + 4$

$= 2772$

4. $6_{\text{ten}} = (1\times5)+(1\times1) = 11_{\text{five}}$

5. The place values in base 7 are ...7^4, 7^3, 7^2, 7^1, 1 or ...2401, 343, 49, 7, 1

$$\begin{array}{r} 1 \\ 343\overline{)365} \\ \underline{343} \\ 22 \end{array} \qquad \begin{array}{r} 0 \\ 49\overline{)22} \\ \underline{0} \\ 22 \end{array} \qquad \begin{array}{r} 3 \\ 7\overline{)22} \\ \underline{21} \\ 1 \end{array}$$

$$\begin{aligned} 365_{\text{ten}} &= (1\times343)+(0\times49)+(3\times7)+(1\times1) \\ &= (1\times7^3)+(0\times7^2)+(3\times7^1)+(1\times1) \\ &= 1031_{\text{seven}} \end{aligned}$$

6. The place values in base 2 are ...2^5, 2^4, 2^3, 2^2, 2^1, 1 or ...32, 16, 8, 4, 2, 1

$$\begin{array}{r} 1 \\ 32\overline{)51} \\ \underline{32} \\ 19 \end{array} \qquad \begin{array}{r} 1 \\ 16\overline{)19} \\ \underline{16} \\ 3 \end{array} \qquad \begin{array}{r} 0 \\ 8\overline{)3} \\ \underline{0} \\ 3 \end{array} \qquad \begin{array}{r} 0 \\ 4\overline{)3} \\ \underline{0} \\ 3 \end{array} \qquad \begin{array}{r} 1 \\ 2\overline{)3} \\ \underline{2} \\ 1 \end{array}$$

Use the five quotients and the final remainder to write the answer.
$51_{\text{ten}} = 110011_{\text{two}}$

7. The place values in base 5 are ...5^4, 5^3, 5^2, 5^1, 1 or ...3125, 625, 125, 25, 5, 1

$$\begin{array}{r} 4 \\ 625\overline{)2763} \\ \underline{2500} \\ 263 \end{array} \qquad \begin{array}{r} 2 \\ 125\overline{)263} \\ \underline{250} \\ 13 \end{array} \qquad \begin{array}{r} 0 \\ 25\overline{)13} \\ \underline{0} \\ 13 \end{array} \qquad \begin{array}{r} 2 \\ 5\overline{)13} \\ \underline{10} \\ 3 \end{array}$$

Use the four quotients and the final remainder to write the answer.

$$\begin{aligned} 2763_{\text{ten}} &= (4\times625)+(2\times125)+(0\times25)+(2\times5)+(3\times1) \\ &= (4\times5^4)+(2\times5^3)+(0\times5^2)+(2\times5^1)+(3\times1) \\ &= 42023_{\text{five}} \end{aligned}$$

Concept and Vocabulary Check 4.2

1. 5; 0, 1, 2, 3, 4

2. 5^2; 5^1; 1

3. 2; 0, 1

4. 2^3; 2^2; 2^1; 1

5. 13

6. 731

7. two; eight; sixteen

Exercise Set 4.2

1. $(4\times 5^1)+(3\times 1)$
$=20+3$
$=23$

3. $(5\times 8^1)+(2\times 1)$
$=40+2$
$=42$

5. $(1\times 4^2)+(3\times 4^1)+(2\times 1)$
$=16+12+2$
$=30$

7. $(1\times 2^3)+(0\times 2^2)+(1\times 2^1)+(1\times 1)$
$=8+0+2+1=11$

9. $(2\times 6^3)+(0\times 6^2)+(3\times 6^1)+(5\times 1)=432+0+18+5$
$=455$

11. $(7\times 8^4)+(0\times 8^3)+(3\times 8^2)+(5\times 8^1)+(5\times 1)=28{,}672+0+192+40+5$
$=28{,}909$

13. $(2\times 16^3)+(0\times 16^2)+(9\times 16^1)+(6\times 1)=8192+0+144+6$
$=8342$

15. $(1\times 2^5)+(1\times 2^4)+(0\times 2^3)+(1\times 2^2)+(0\times 2^1)+(1\times 1)=32+16+0+4+0+1$
$=53$

17. $(10\times 16^3)+(12\times 16^2)+(14\times 16^1)+(5\times 1)=40{,}960+3072+224+5$
$=44{,}261$

19. 12_{five}

21. 14_{seven}

23. 10_{two}

25. 101_{two}

27. 1000_{two}

29. 31_{four}

31. 101_{six}

33. $$\begin{array}{r} 3 \\ 25\overline{)87} \\ \underline{75} \\ 12 \end{array} \quad \begin{array}{r} 2 \\ 5\overline{)12} \\ \underline{10} \\ 2 \end{array}$$

$87 = 322_{\text{five}}$

35. $$\begin{array}{r} 1 \\ 64\overline{)108} \\ \underline{64} \\ 44 \end{array} \quad \begin{array}{r} 2 \\ 16\overline{)44} \\ \underline{32} \\ 12 \end{array} \quad \begin{array}{r} 3 \\ 4\overline{)12} \\ \underline{12} \\ 0 \end{array}$$

$108 = 1230_{\text{four}}$

37. $$\begin{array}{r} 1 \\ 16\overline{)19} \\ \underline{16} \\ 3 \end{array} \quad \begin{array}{r} 0 \\ 8\overline{)3} \\ \underline{0} \\ 3 \end{array} \quad \begin{array}{r} 0 \\ 4\overline{)3} \\ \underline{0} \\ 3 \end{array} \quad \begin{array}{r} 1 \\ 2\overline{)3} \\ \underline{2} \\ 1 \end{array}$$

$19 = 10011_{\text{two}}$

39. $$\begin{array}{r} 1 \\ 32\overline{)57} \\ \underline{32} \\ 25 \end{array} \quad \begin{array}{r} 1 \\ 16\overline{)25} \\ \underline{16} \\ 9 \end{array} \quad \begin{array}{r} 1 \\ 8\overline{)9} \\ \underline{8} \\ 1 \end{array} \quad \begin{array}{r} 0 \\ 4\overline{)1} \\ \underline{0} \\ 1 \end{array} \quad \begin{array}{r} 0 \\ 2\overline{)1} \\ \underline{0} \\ 1 \end{array}$$

$57 = 111001_{\text{two}}$

41. $$\begin{array}{r} 1 \\ 64\overline{)90} \\ \underline{64} \\ 26 \end{array} \quad \begin{array}{r} 0 \\ 32\overline{)26} \\ \underline{0} \\ 26 \end{array} \quad \begin{array}{r} 1 \\ 16\overline{)26} \\ \underline{16} \\ 10 \end{array} \quad \begin{array}{r} 1 \\ 8\overline{)10} \\ \underline{8} \\ 2 \end{array} \quad \begin{array}{r} 0 \\ 4\overline{)2} \\ \underline{0} \\ 2 \end{array} \quad \begin{array}{r} 1 \\ 2\overline{)2} \\ \underline{2} \\ 0 \end{array}$$

$90 = 1011010_{\text{two}}$

43. $$\begin{array}{r} 1 \\ 81\overline{)138} \\ \underline{81} \\ 57 \end{array} \quad \begin{array}{r} 2 \\ 27\overline{)57} \\ \underline{54} \\ 3 \end{array} \quad \begin{array}{r} 0 \\ 9\overline{)3} \\ \underline{0} \\ 3 \end{array} \quad \begin{array}{r} 1 \\ 3\overline{)3} \\ \underline{3} \\ 0 \end{array}$$

$138 = 12010_{\text{three}}$

45. $$\begin{array}{r} 1 \\ 216\overline{)386} \\ \underline{216} \\ 170 \end{array} \quad \begin{array}{r} 4 \\ 36\overline{)170} \\ \underline{144} \\ 26 \end{array} \quad \begin{array}{r} 4 \\ 6\overline{)26} \\ \underline{24} \\ 2 \end{array}$$

$386 = 1442_{\text{six}}$

47. $$\begin{array}{r} 4 \\ 343\overline{)1599} \\ \underline{1372} \\ 227 \end{array} \quad \begin{array}{r} 4 \\ 49\overline{)227} \\ \underline{196} \\ 31 \end{array} \quad \begin{array}{r} 4 \\ 7\overline{)31} \\ \underline{28} \\ 3 \end{array}$$

$1599 = 4443_{\text{seven}}$

49. $3052 = 3000 + 52$

$= (50 \times 60^1) + (52 \times 1)$

= <<<<< <<<<< vv

51. $23{,}546 = 21{,}600 + 1920 + 26$

$= (6 \times 60^2) + (32 \times 60^1) + (26 \times 1)$

= vvvvvv <<< vv << vvvvvvv

53. 9307

$= 7200 + 1800 + 300 + 7$

$= (1 \times 7200) + (5 \times 360) + (15 \times 20) + (7 \times 1)$

•
—
— — —
• •
—

55. 28,704

$= 21{,}600 + 6840 + 260 + 4$

$= (3 \times 7200) + (19 \times 360) + (13 \times 20) + (4 \times 1)$

• • •
• • • •
— — —
• • •
— —
• • • •

57. $34_{five} = (3 \times 5^1) + (4 \times 1)$

$= 15 + 4$

$= 19_{ten}$

$19_{ten} = 14 + 5$

$= (2 \times 7^1) + (5 \times 1)$

$= 25_{seven}$

59. $110010011_{two} = 403_{ten}$

$403_{ten} = 384 + 16 + 3$

$= (6 \times 8^2) + (2 \times 8^1) + (3 \times 1)$

$= 623_{eight}$

61. Since A = 65, F = 70

$70 = 64 + 0 + 0 + 0 + 4 + 2 + 0$

$= 1 \cdot 2^6 + 0 \cdot 2^5 + 0 \cdot 2^4 + 0 \cdot 2^3 + 1 \cdot 2^2 + 1 \cdot 2^1 + 0 \cdot 1$

$= 1000110_{two}$

63. Since a = 97, m = 109

$109 = 64 + 32 + 0 + 8 + 4 + 0 + 1$

$= 1 \cdot 2^6 + 1 \cdot 2^5 + 0 \cdot 2^4 + 1 \cdot 2^3 + 1 \cdot 2^2 + 0 \cdot 2^1 + 1 \cdot 1$

$= 1101101_{two}$

65. 1010000_{two} 1000001_{two} 1001100_{two}

64+16	64+1	64+8+4
80	65	76
P	A	L

The word is PAL.

67.

M	o	m
77	111	109
64+8+4+1	64+32+8+4+2+1	64+32+8+4+1
1001101_{two}	1101111_{two}	1101101_{two}

The sequence is 100110111011111101101

73. does not make sense; Explanations will vary. Sample explanation: Base *b* contains *b* digits.

75. makes sense

77. Preceding: Following:

$$\begin{array}{r} 888_{nine} \\ -\ 1_{nine} \\ \hline 887_{nine} \end{array} \qquad \begin{array}{r} 888_{nine} \\ +\ 1_{nine} \\ \hline 1000_{nine} \end{array}$$

79. 11111011_{two}

$(1\times 2^7)+(1\times 2^6)+(1\times 2^5)+(1\times 2^4)+(1\times 2^3)+(0\times 2^2)+(1\times 2^1)+(1\times 1)$

$=128+64+32+16+8+0+2+1$

$=251$

$3A6_{twelve}$

$(3\times 12^2)+(10\times 12^1)+(6\times 1)=432+120+6=558$

673_{eight}

$(6\times 8^2)+(7\times 8^1)+(3\times 1)=384+56+3=443$

11111011_{two}, 673_{eight}, $3A6_{twelve}$

Check Points 4.3

1.
$$\begin{array}{r} {}^{1}\\ 32_{five} \\ +44_{five} \\ \hline 131_{five} \end{array}$$

$2+4=6=(1\times 5^1)+(1\times 1)=11_{five}$

$1+3+4=8=(1\times 5^1)+(3\times 1)=13_{five}$

2.
$$\begin{array}{r} {}^{1\,1} \\ 111_{\text{two}} \\ +111_{\text{two}} \\ \hline 1110_{\text{two}} \end{array}$$
$$1+1=2=(1\times 2^1)+(0\times 1)=10_{\text{two}}$$
$$1+1+1=3=(1\times 2^1)+(1\times 1)=11_{\text{two}}$$

3.
$$\begin{array}{r} {}^{3\,6} \\ 41_{\text{five}} \\ -23_{\text{five}} \\ \hline 13_{\text{five}} \end{array}$$

4.
$$\begin{array}{r} {}^{4\,8\,3\,11} \\ 5144_{\text{seven}} \\ -3236_{\text{seven}} \\ \hline 1605_{\text{seven}} \end{array}$$

5.
$$\begin{array}{r} {}^{2} \\ 45_{\text{seven}} \\ \times\ 3_{\text{seven}} \\ \hline 201_{\text{seven}} \end{array}$$
$$3\times 5=15=(2\times 7^1)+(1\times 1)=21_{\text{seven}}$$
$$(3\times 4)+2=14=(2\times 7^1)+(0\times 1)=20_{\text{seven}}$$

6.
$$\begin{array}{r} 23\phantom{_{\text{four}}} \\ 2_{\text{four}}\overline{)112_{\text{four}}} \\ \underline{10}\phantom{2_{\text{four}}} \\ 12\phantom{_{\text{four}}} \\ \underline{12}\phantom{_{\text{four}}} \\ 0\phantom{_{\text{four}}} \end{array}$$
$$23_{\text{four}}$$

Concept and Vocabulary Check 4.3

1. 1; 1; 11
2. 1; 1; 11
3. 1; 5; 15; 1; 5
4. 7; 7; 10; 5; 10; 5; 3; 1; 15
5. 2; 1; 21; 1; 2; 2; 2; 0; 20; 201
6. 2; 20
7. true

Exercise Set 4.3

Note: Numbers with no base specified are base 10.

1.
$$\begin{array}{r} {}^{1} \\ 23_{\text{four}} \\ +13_{\text{four}} \\ \hline 102_{\text{four}} \end{array}$$
$$3+3=6=(1\times 4^1)+(2\times 1)=12_{\text{four}}$$
$$1+2+1=4=(1\times 4^1)+(0\times 1)=10_{\text{four}}$$

3.
$$\begin{array}{r} {}^{1} \\ 11_{\text{two}} \\ +11_{\text{two}} \\ \hline 110_{\text{two}} \end{array}$$
$$1+1+1=3=(1\times 2^1)+(1\times 1)=11_{\text{two}}$$

5.
$$\begin{array}{r} {}^{1\,1} \\ 342_{\text{five}} \\ +413_{\text{five}} \\ \hline 1310_{\text{five}} \end{array}$$
$$2+3=5=(1\times 5^1)+(0\times 1)=10_{\text{five}}$$
$$1+4+1=6=(1\times 5^1)+(1\times 1)=11_{\text{five}}$$
$$1+3+4=8=(1\times 5^1)+(3\times 1)=13_{\text{five}}$$

7.
$$\begin{array}{r} {}^{1\,1} \\ 645_{\text{seven}} \\ +324_{\text{seven}} \\ \hline 1302_{\text{seven}} \end{array}$$
$$5+4=9=(1\times 7^1)+(2\times 1)=12_{\text{seven}}$$
$$1+4+2=7=(1\times 7^1)+(0\times 1)=10_{\text{seven}}$$
$$1+6+3=10=(1\times 7^1)+(3\times 1)=13_{\text{seven}}$$

9.
$$\begin{array}{r} {}^{1\,1\,1} \\ 6784_{\text{nine}} \\ +7865_{\text{nine}} \\ \hline 15760_{\text{nine}} \end{array}$$
$$4+5=9=(1\times 9^1)+(0\times 1)=10_{\text{nine}}$$
$$1+8+6=15=(1\times 9^1)+(6\times 1)=16_{\text{nine}}$$
$$1+7+8=16=(1\times 9^1)+(7\times 1)=17_{\text{nine}}$$
$$1+6+7=14=(1\times 9^1)+(5\times 1)=15_{\text{nine}}$$

11.

$$\begin{array}{r} {}^{1\,1} \\ 14632_{\text{seven}} \\ +5604_{\text{seven}} \\ \hline 23536_{\text{seven}} \end{array}$$

$6+6=12=(1\times 7^1)+(5\times 1)=15_{\text{seven}}$

$1+4+5=10=(1\times 7^1)+(3\times 1)=13_{\text{seven}}$

13.

$$\begin{array}{r} {}^{2\,6} \\ 32_{\text{four}} \\ -13_{\text{four}} \\ \hline 13_{\text{four}} \end{array}$$

15.

$$\begin{array}{r} {}^{1\,8} \\ 23_{\text{five}} \\ -14_{\text{five}} \\ \hline 4_{\text{five}} \end{array}$$

17.

$$\begin{array}{r} {}^{6\,13} \\ 475_{\text{eight}} \\ -267_{\text{eight}} \\ \hline 206_{\text{eight}} \end{array}$$

19.

$$\begin{array}{r} {}^{4\,12\ \ 10} \\ 563_{\text{seven}} \\ -164_{\text{seven}} \\ \hline 366_{\text{seven}} \end{array}$$

21.

$$\begin{array}{r} {}^{0\,1\,2} \\ 1001_{\text{two}} \\ -111_{\text{two}} \\ \hline 10_{\text{two}} \end{array}$$

23.

$$\begin{array}{r} {}^{1\,2\,3} \\ 1200_{\text{three}} \\ -1012_{\text{three}} \\ \hline 111_{\text{three}} \end{array}$$

25.

$$\begin{array}{r} {}^{3} \\ 25_{\text{six}} \\ \times 4_{\text{six}} \\ \hline 152_{\text{six}} \end{array}$$

$(2_{\text{six}}\times 4_{\text{six}})+3_{\text{six}}=8_{\text{ten}}+3_{\text{six}}$

$=12_{\text{six}}+3_{\text{six}}$

$=15_{\text{six}}$

27.

$$\begin{array}{r} 11_{\text{two}} \\ \times\ 1_{\text{two}} \\ \hline 11_{\text{two}} \end{array}$$

29.

$$\begin{array}{r} {}^{3\,2} \\ 543_{\text{seven}} \\ \times\ \ 5_{\text{seven}} \\ \hline 4011_{\text{seven}} \end{array}$$

$3\times 5=15=(2\times 7^1)+(1\times 1)=21_{\text{seven}}$

$(4\times 5)+2=22=(3\times 7^1)+(1\times 1)=31_{\text{seven}}$

$(5\times 5)+3=28=(4\times 7^1)+(0\times 1)=40_{\text{seven}}$

31.

$$\begin{array}{r} {}^{1\,1} \\ 623_{\text{eight}} \\ \times\ \ 4_{\text{eight}} \\ \hline 3114_{\text{eight}} \end{array}$$

$(3_{\text{eight}}\times 4_{\text{eight}})=12_{\text{ten}}$

$=(1\times 8^1)+(4\times 1)$

$=14_{\text{eight}}$

$(2_{\text{eight}}\times 4_{\text{eight}})+1_{\text{eight}}=8_{\text{ten}}+1_{\text{ten}}$

$=9_{\text{ten}}$

$=(1\times 8^1)+(1\times 1)$

$=11_{\text{eight}}$

$(6_{\text{eight}}\times 4_{\text{eight}})+1_{\text{eight}}=24_{\text{ten}}+1_{\text{ten}}$

$=25_{\text{ten}}$

$=(3\times 8^1)+(1\times 1)$

$=31_{\text{eight}}$

33.

$$\begin{array}{r} 21_{\text{four}} \\ \times 12_{\text{four}} \\ \hline 102 \\ 210 \\ \hline 312_{\text{four}} \end{array}$$

$21_{\text{four}}\times 2_{\text{four}}=9_{\text{ten}}\times 2_{\text{ten}}$

$=18$

$=(1\times 4^2)+(0\times 4)+(2\times 1)$

$=102_{\text{four}}$

$21_{\text{four}}\times 1_{\text{four}}=21_{\text{four}}$

35.

$$\begin{array}{r} 20 \\ 2_{\text{four}}\overline{)100_{\text{four}}} \\ \underline{10} \\ 00 \end{array}$$

20_{four}

37. 41_{five} remainder of 1

$$\begin{array}{r} 41 \\ 3_{five}\overline{)224_{five}} \\ \underline{22} \\ 04 \\ \underline{3} \\ 1 \end{array}$$

39.

$$\begin{array}{r} {}^{1\,1} \\ 10110_{two} \\ +\ 10100_{two} \\ \hline 1000110_{two} \end{array}$$

41.

$$\begin{array}{r} {}^{1\,1\,1} \\ 11111_{two} \\ +\ 10110_{two} \\ \hline 110101_{two} \end{array}$$

$$\begin{array}{r} 110101_{two} \\ -\quad 101_{two} \\ \hline 110000_{two} \end{array}$$

43.

$$\begin{array}{r} 1011_{two} \\ \times\quad 101_{two} \\ \hline 1011_{two} \\ +\ 101100_{two} \\ \hline 110111_{two} \end{array}$$

45.

$$\begin{array}{r} D3_{sixteen} \\ \times\quad 8A_{sixteen} \\ \hline 83E_{sixteen} \\ +\ 6980_{sixteen} \\ \hline 71BE_{sixteen} \end{array}$$

47.

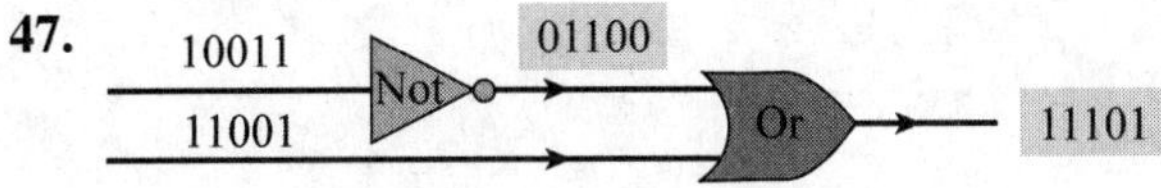

49.

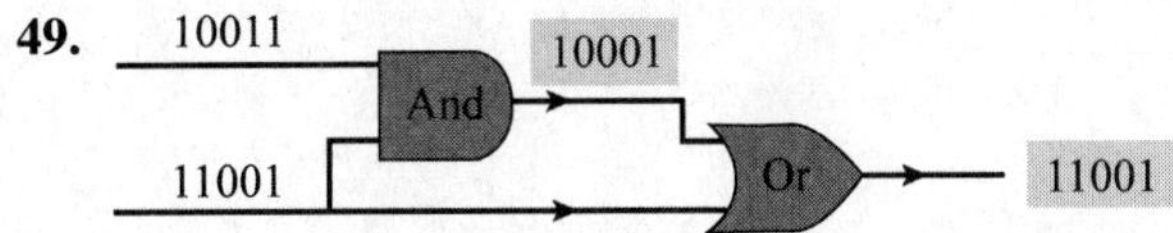

51.

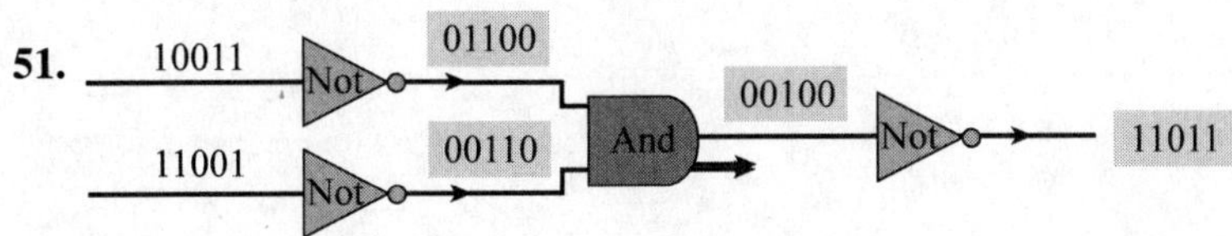

53. The circuit in Exercise 47 is a conditional gate.

57. makes sense

59. makes sense

61.

$$\begin{array}{rrr} & 4 \text{ hours}, & 26 \text{ minutes}, & 57 \text{ seconds} \\ + & 3 \text{ hours}, & 46 \text{ minutes}, & 39 \text{ seconds} \\ \hline & 7 \text{ hours}, & 72 \text{ minutes}, & 96 \text{ seconds} \\ & \downarrow & \downarrow & \downarrow \\ & 7 \text{ hours}, & 73 \text{ minutes}, & 36 \text{ seconds} \\ & \downarrow & \downarrow & \downarrow \\ & 8 \text{ hours}, & 13 \text{ minutes}, & 36 \text{ seconds} \end{array}$$

63.

$$\begin{array}{r} 56_{\text{seven}} \\ 31_{\text{seven}}\overline{)2426_{\text{seven}}} \\ \underline{215} \\ 246 \\ \underline{246} \\ 0 \end{array}$$

Check Points 4.4

1. $100,000+100,000+100,000+100+100+10+10+1+1=300,222$

2. $2563=1000+1000+100+100+100+100+100+10+10+10+10+10+10+1+1+1$
𓆼𓆼𓍢𓍢𓍢𓍢𓍢∩∩∩∩∩∩|||

3. $\text{MCCCLXI}=1000+100+100+100+50+10+1=1361$

4. $\text{MCDXLVII}=\overbrace{1000}^{\text{M}}+\overbrace{(500-100)}^{\text{CD}}+\overbrace{(50-10)}^{\text{XL}}+\overbrace{5}^{\text{V}}+\overbrace{1}^{\text{I}}+\overbrace{1}^{\text{I}}=1000+400+40+5+1+1=1447$

5. $399=100+100+100+90+9=\overbrace{100}^{\text{C}}+\overbrace{100}^{\text{C}}+\overbrace{100}^{\text{C}}+\overbrace{(100-10)}^{\text{XC}}+\overbrace{(10-1)}^{\text{IX}}=\text{CCCXCIX}$

6. $2693=2000+600+90+3$
二
千
六
百
九
十
三

7. $\omega\pi\varepsilon=800+80+5=885$

Concept and Vocabulary Check 4.4

1. 1000; 100; 100; 10; 1; 1; 1212

2. 10; 10; 1; 1; 1; dccccbbaaa

3. true

4. add; +; 110

5. subtract; $-$; 40

6. 1000; 50; 1000; 50,000

7. true

8. H; Y; D; X; F

9. true

10. VPC

11. 6000; 500; 30; 5; 36,535

12. true

Exercise Set 4.4

1. 322

3. 300,423

5. 132

7. $423 = (4 \times 100) + (2 \times 10) + (3 \times 1)$
   𓍢𓍢𓍢𓍢𓎆𓎆𓏺𓏺𓏺

9. $1846 = (1 \times 1000) + (8 \times 100) + (4 \times 10) + (6 \times 1)$
   𓆼𓍢𓍢𓍢𓍢𓍢𓍢𓍢𓍢𓎆𓎆𓎆𓎆𓏺𓏺𓏺𓏺𓏺𓏺

11. $23{,}547 = (2 \times 10{,}000) + (3 \times 1000) + (5 \times 100) + (4 \times 10) + (7 \times 1)$
   𓂭𓂭𓆼𓆼𓆼𓍢𓍢𓍢𓍢𓍢𓎆𓎆𓎆𓎆𓏺𓏺𓏺𓏺𓏺𓏺𓏺

13. XI = 11

15. XVI = 16

17. XL = 40

19. LIX = 59

21. CXLVI = 146

23. MDCXXI = 1621

25. MMDCLXXVII = 2677

27. $\overline{\text{IX}}$CDLXVI = 9466

29. 43 = XLIII

31. 129 = CXXIX

33. 1896 = MDCCCXCVI

35. 6892 = $\overline{\text{VI}}$DCCCXCII

37. $80+8=88$

$$\left.\begin{matrix}8\\10\end{matrix}\right\}80$$

$$8\}8$$

39. $500+20+7=527$

$$\left.\begin{matrix}5\\100\end{matrix}\right\}500$$

$$\left.\begin{matrix}2\\10\end{matrix}\right\}20$$

$$7\}7$$

41. $2000+700+70+6=2776$

$$\left.\begin{matrix}2\\1000\end{matrix}\right\}2000$$

$$\left.\begin{matrix}7\\100\end{matrix}\right\}700$$

$$\left.\begin{matrix}7\\10\end{matrix}\right\}70$$

$$6\}6$$

43.
四
十
三

45.
五
百
八
十
三

47.
四
千
八
百
七
十

49. $\iota\beta=12$

51. $\sigma\lambda\delta=234$

53. $43=\mu\gamma$

55. $483=\upsilon\pi\gamma$

57. The value of this numeral is 2324.
Roman numeral: MMCCCXXIV
Chinese numeral:

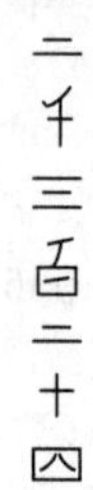

59. The value of this numeral is 1741.
Egyptian numeral: 𓆼𓍢𓍢𓍢𓍢𓍢𓍢𓍢𓎆𓎆𓎆𓎆𓏺
Chinese numeral:

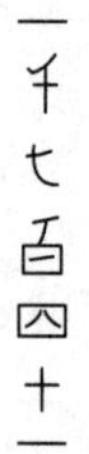

61. The value of this numeral is 404.
$404=3104_{\text{five}}$

63. The value of this numeral is 192.
$192=1232_{\text{five}}$

65. 𓎆𓎆𓎆𓎆𓎆𓎆𓎆𓎆𓎆𓏺𓏺𓏺𓏺𓏺𓏺𓏺

67. 1776 is the date the Declaration of Independence was signed.

69. Hindu-Arabic: 4,640,224

77. does not make sense; Explanations will vary. Sample explanation: The Egyptian numeration system does not use the same subtraction rule as the Roman numeral system.

79. makes sense

81. Preceding: 𓍢𓍢𓎆𓎆𓎆𓎆𓎆𓎆𓎆𓎆𓎆𓏺𓏺𓏺𓏺𓏺𓏺𓏺𓏺𓏺

Following: 𓍢𓍢𓍢

Chapter 4 Review Exercises

1. $11^2 = 11 \times 11 = 121$

2. $7^3 = 7 \times 7 \times 7 = 343$

3. $472 = (4 \times 10^2) + (7 \times 10^1) + (2 \times 1) = (4 \times 100) + (7 \times 10) + (2 \times 1)$

4. $8076 = (8 \times 10^3) + (0 \times 10^2) + (7 \times 10^1) + (6 \times 1) = (8 \times 1000) + (0 \times 100) + (7 \times 10) + (6 \times 1)$

5. $70,329 = (7 \times 10^4) + (0 \times 10^3) + (3 \times 10^2) + (2 \times 10^1) + (9 \times 1)$
$= (7 \times 10,000) + (0 \times 1000) + (3 \times 100) + (2 \times 10) + (9 \times 1)$

6. 706,953

7. 740,000,306

8. <v <vvv $= (10+1) \times 60^1 + (10+1+1+1) \times 1$
$= (11 \times 60^1) + (13 \times 1)$
$= 660 + 13$
$= 673$

9. vv << <<<
$= (1+1) \times 60^2 + (10+10) \times 60^1 + (10+10+10) \times 1$
$= (2 \times 60^2) + (20 \times 60) + (30 \times 1)$
$= (2 \times 3600) + 1200 + 30$
$= 7200 + 1230$
$= 8430$

10. $6 \times 360 = 2160$
$8 \times 20 = 160$
$11 \times 1 = 11$
2331

11. $9 \times 7200 = 64,800$
$2 \times 360 = 720$
$0 \times 20 = 0$
$16 \times 1 = 16$
65,536

12. Each position represents a particular value. The symbol in each position tells how many of that value are represented.

13. $34_{\text{five}} = (3 \times 5^1) + (4 \times 1)$
$= 15 + 4$
$= 19$

14. $110_{two} = (1\times2^2)+(1\times2^1)+(0\times1)$
$= 4+2+0$
$= 6$

15. $643_{seven} = (6\times7^2)+(4\times7^1)+(3\times1)$
$= 294+28+3$
$= 325$

16. $1084_{nine} = (1\times9^3)+(0\times9^2)+(8\times9^1)+(4\times1)$
$= 729+0+72+4$
$= 805$

17. $\text{FD3}_{sixteen} = (15\times16^2)+(13\times16^1)+(3\times1)$
$= 3840+208+3$
$= 4051$

18. $202202_{three} = (2\times3^5)+(0\times3^4)+(2\times3^3)+(2\times3^2)+(0\times3^1)+(2\times1)$
$= 486+0+54+18+0+2$
$= 560$

19. $89 = (3\times5^2)+(2\times5^1)+(4\times1)$
$= 324_{five}$

20. $21 = (1\times2^4)+(0\times2^3)+(1\times2^2)+(0\times2^1)+(1\times1)$
$= 10101_{two}$

21. $473 = (1\times3^5)+(2\times3^4)+(2\times3^3)+(1\times3^2)+(1\times3^1)+(2\times1)$
$= 243+162+54+9+3+2$
$= 122112_{three}$

22. $7093 = (2\times7^4)+(6\times7^3)+(4\times7^2)+(5\times7^1)+(2\times1)$
$= 4802+2058+196+35+2$
$= 26452_{seven}$

23. $9348 = (1\times6^5)+(1\times6^4)+(1\times6^3)+(1\times6^2)+(4\times6^1)+(0\times1)$
$= 7776+1296+216+36+24$
$= 111140_{six}$

24. $554 = (3\times12^2)+(\text{A}\times12^1)+(2\times1)$
$= \text{3A2}_{twelve}$

25.
$$\begin{array}{r} {}^{1}\\ 46_{seven} \\ +53_{seven} \\ \hline 132_{seven} \end{array}$$

26.
$$\begin{array}{r} 1\,1\phantom{4_{eight}} \\ 574_{eight} \\ +605_{eight} \\ \hline 1401_{eight} \end{array}$$

27.
$$\begin{array}{r} 1111\phantom{1_{two}} \\ 11011_{two} \\ 10101_{two} \\ \hline 110000_{two} \end{array}$$

28.
$$\begin{array}{r} 1\phantom{3C_{sixteen}} \\ 43C_{sixteen} \\ +694_{sixteen} \\ \hline AD0_{sixteen} \end{array}$$

29.
$$\begin{array}{r} 2\;10\phantom{_{six}} \\ \not{3}\not{4}_{six} \\ 25_{six} \\ \hline 5_{six} \end{array}$$

30.
$$\begin{array}{r} 5\;8\;11\phantom{_{seven}} \\ \not{6}2\not{4}_{seven} \\ -246_{seven} \\ \hline 345_{seven} \end{array}$$

31.
$$\begin{array}{r} 0\,1\,2\phantom{1_{two}} \\ 1\not{0}\not{0}1_{two} \\ -110_{two} \\ \hline 11_{two} \end{array}$$

32.
$$\begin{array}{r} 3\,6\,1\,6\phantom{_{five}} \\ \not{4}\not{1}\not{2}\not{1}_{five} \\ -1312_{five} \\ \hline 2304_{five} \end{array}$$

33.
$$\begin{array}{r} 1\phantom{2_{four}} \\ 32_{four} \\ \times\ 3_{four} \\ \hline 222_{four} \end{array}$$

34.
$$\begin{array}{r} 2\phantom{3_{seven}} \\ 43_{seven} \\ \times\ 6_{seven} \\ \hline 354_{seven} \end{array}$$

35.
$$\begin{array}{r} 2\,2\phantom{3_{five}} \\ 123_{five} \\ 4_{five} \\ \hline 1102_{five} \end{array}$$

36.
$$
\begin{array}{r}
133 \\
2_{\text{four}}\overline{)\,332_{\text{four}}} \\
\underline{2} \\
13 \\
\underline{12} \\
12 \\
\underline{12} \\
0
\end{array}
$$

133_{four}

37.
$$
\begin{array}{r}
12 \\
4_{\text{five}}\overline{)\,103_{\text{five}}} \\
\underline{4} \\
13 \\
\underline{13} \\
0
\end{array}
$$

12_{five}

38. 1246

39. 12,432

40. $2486 = (2 \times 1000) + (4 \times 100) + (8 \times 10) + (6 \times 1)$
𓆼𓆼𓍢𓍢𓍢𓍢𓎆𓎆𓎆𓎆𓎆𓎆𓎆𓎆𓏺𓏺𓏺𓏺𓏺𓏺

41. $34{,}573 = (3 \times 10{,}000) + (4 \times 1000) + (5 \times 100) + (7 \times 10) + (3 \times 1)$
𓂭𓂭𓂭𓆼𓆼𓆼𓆼𓍢𓍢𓍢𓍢𓍢𓎆𓎆𓎆𓎆𓎆𓎆𓎆𓏺𓏺𓏺

42. DDCCCBAAAA = 2314

43. 5492 = DDDDDCCCCBBBBBBBBBAA

44. Answers will vary.

45. CLXIII = 163

46. MXXXIV = 1034

47. MCMXC = 1990

48. 49 = XLIX

49. 2965 = MMCMLXV

50. If symbols increase in value from left to right, subtract the value of the symbol on the left from the symbol on the right.

51. $500+50+4=554$

$$\left.\begin{matrix}5\\100\end{matrix}\right\}500$$

$$\left.\begin{matrix}5\\10\end{matrix}\right\}50$$

$$4\}4$$

52. $8000+200+50+3=8253$

$$\left.\begin{matrix}8\\1000\end{matrix}\right\}8000$$

$$\left.\begin{matrix}2\\100\end{matrix}\right\}200$$

$$\left.\begin{matrix}5\\10\end{matrix}\right\}50$$

$$3\}3$$

53. 二
百
七
十
四

54. 三
千
五
百
八
十
七

55. 365

56. 4520

57. G
Y
I
X
C

58. F
Z
H
Y
E
X
D

59. Answers will vary.

60. $\chi\nu\gamma = 653$

61. $\chi o\eta = 678$

62. $453 = \upsilon\nu\gamma$

63. $902 = \pi\beta$

64. UNG = 357

65. mhZRD = 37,894

66. rXJH = 80,618

67. 597 = WRG

68. 25,483 = lfVQC

Chapter 4 Test

1. $9 \times 9 \times 9 = 729$

2. $567 = (5 \times 10^2) + (6 \times 10^1) + (7 \times 1)$
$= (5 \times 100) + (6 \times 10) + (7 \times 1)$

3. $63{,}028 = (6 \times 10^4) + (3 \times 10^3) + (0 \times 10^2) + (2 \times 10^1) + (8 \times 1)$
$= (6 \times 10{,}000) + (3 \times 1000) + (0 \times 100) + (2 \times 10) + (8 \times 1)$

4. 7000 + 400 + 90 + 3 = 7493

5. $400{,}000 + 200 + 6 = 400{,}206$

6. A number represents, "How many?" whereas a numeral is a symbol used to write a number.

7. A symbol for zero is needed as a place holder when there are no values for a position.

8. $<< <\vee\vee \;\; <\vee = (10+10) \times 60^2 + (10+1+1) \times 60^1 + (10+1) \times 1$
$= (20 \times 60^2) + (12 \times 60) + (11 \times 1) = 72{,}000 + 720 + 11 = 72{,}731$

9.
$$\begin{array}{r} 4 \times 360 = 1440 \\ 6 \times 20 = 120 \\ 0 \times 1 = \underline{0} \\ 1560 \end{array}$$

10. $423_{\text{five}} = (4 \times 5^2) + (2 \times 5^1) + (3 \times 1) = 4 \times 25 + 10 + 3 = 100 + 10 + 3 = 113$

11. $267_{\text{nine}} = (2 \times 9^2) + (6 \times 9^1) + (7 \times 1) = 2 \times 81 + 54 + 7 = 162 + 54 + 7 = 223$

12. $110101_{\text{two}} = (1 \times 2^5) + (1 \times 2^4) + (0 \times 2^3) + (1 \times 2^2) + (0 \times 2^1) + (1 \times 1) = 32 + 16 + 0 + 4 + 0 + 1 = 53$

13. $77=(2\times3^3)+(2\times3^2)+(1\times3^1)+(2\times1)=2212_{\text{three}}$

14. $56=(1\times2^5)+(1\times2^4)+(1\times2^3)+(0\times2^2)+(0\times2^1)+(0\times1)=111000_{\text{two}}$

15. $1844=(2\times5^4)+(4\times5^3)+(3\times5^2)+(3\times5^1)+(4\times1)=1250+500+75+15+4=24334_{\text{five}}$

16.
$$\begin{array}{r} {}^{1\,1}\\ 234_{\text{five}}\\ +423_{\text{five}}\\ \hline 1212_{\text{five}} \end{array}$$

17.
$$\begin{array}{r} {}^{5\,9}\\ 5\not{6}2_{\text{seven}}\\ -145_{\text{seven}}\\ \hline 414_{\text{seven}} \end{array}$$

18.
$$\begin{array}{r} {}^{2}\\ 54_{\text{six}}\\ \times\ 3_{\text{six}}\\ \hline 250_{\text{six}} \end{array}$$

19.
$$\begin{array}{r} 221\\ 3_{\text{five}}\overline{)\,1213_{\text{five}}}\\ \underline{11}\\ 11\\ \underline{11}\\ 03\\ \underline{3}\\ 0 \end{array}$$

221_{five}

20. 20,303

21. $32,634=(3\times10,000)+(2\times1000)+(6\times100)+(3\times10)+(4\times1)$

𓂭𓂭𓂭𓆼𓆼𓍢𓍢𓍢𓍢𓍢𓍢𓎆𓎆𓎆𓏺𓏺𓏺𓏺

22. $\text{MCMXCIV}=\overbrace{1000}^{\text{M}}+\overbrace{(1000-100)}^{\text{CM}}+\overbrace{(100-10)}^{\text{XC}}+\overbrace{(5-1)}^{\text{IV}}=1000+900+90+4=1994$

23. $459=\overbrace{(500-100)}^{\text{CD}}+\overbrace{50}^{\text{L}}+\overbrace{(10-1)}^{\text{IX}}=\text{CDLIX}$

24. Answers will vary.

Chapter 5
Number Theory and the Real Number System

Check Points 5.1

1. The statement given in part (b) is true.

   a. false, 8 does not divide 48,324 because 8 does not divide 324.

   b. true, 6 divides 48,324 because both 2 and 3 divide 48,324. 2 divides 48,324 because the last digit is 4. 3 divides 48,324 because the sum of the digits, 21, is divisible by 3.

   c. false, 4 *does* divide 48,324 because the last two digits form 24 which is divisible by 4.

2. 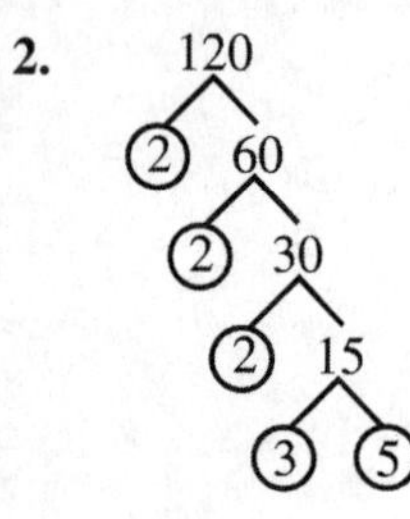

   $120 = 2^3 \cdot 3 \cdot 5$

3. $225 = 3^2 \cdot 5^2$

   $825 = 3 \cdot 5^2 \cdot 11$

   Greatest Common Divisor: $3 \cdot 5^2 = 75$

4. $192 = 2^6 \cdot 3$

   $288 = 2^5 \cdot 3^2$

   Greatest Common Divisor: $2^5 \cdot 3 = 96$
   The largest number of people that can be placed in each singing group is 96.

5. $18 = 2 \cdot 3^2$

   $30 = 2 \cdot 3 \cdot 5$

   Least common multiple is: $90 = 2 \cdot 3^2 \cdot 5$

6. $40 = 2^3 \cdot 5$

   $60 = 2^2 \cdot 3 \cdot 5$

   Least common multiple is: $120 = 2^3 \cdot 3 \cdot 5$
   It will be 120 minutes, or 2 hours, until both movies begin again at the same time.
   The time will be 5:00 PM.

Concept and Vocabulary Check 5.1

1. prime
2. composite
3. greatest common divisor
4. least common multiple
5. false
6. true
7. false
8. false

Exercise Set 5.1

1. 6944

   a. Yes. The last digit is four.

   b. No. The sum of the digits is 23, which is not divisible by 3.

   c. Yes. The last two digits form 44, which is divisible by 4.

   d. No. The number does not end in 0 or 5.

   e. No. The number is not divisible by both 2 and 3.

   f. Yes. The last three digits form 944, which is divisible by 8.

   g. No. The sum of the digits is 23, which is not divisible by 9.

   h. No. The number does not end in 0.

   i. No. The number is not divisible by both 3 and 4.

3. 21,408

   a. Yes. The last digit is eight.

   b. Yes. The sum of the digits is 15, which is divisible by 3.

   c. Yes. The last two digits form 08, which is divisible by 4.

d. No. The number does not end in 0 or 5.

e. Yes. The number is divisible by both 2 and 3.

f. Yes. The last three digits form 408, which is divisible by 8.

g. No. The sum of the digits is 15, which is not divisible by 9.

h. No. The number does not end in 0.

i. Yes. The number is divisible by both 3 and 4.

5. 26,428

a. Yes. The last digit is 8.

b. No. The sum of the digits is 22, which is not divisible by 3.

c. Yes. The last 2 digits form 28, which is divisible by 4.

d. No. The last digit is eight.

e. No. The number is not divisible by both two and three.

f. No. The last three digits form 428, which is not divisible by 8.

g. No. The sum of the digits is 22, which is not divisible by 9.

h. No. The number does not end in 0.

i. No. The number is not divisible by 3 and 4.

7. 374,832

a. Yes. The last digit is 2.

b. Yes. The sum of the digits is 27, which is divisible by 3.

c. Yes. The last two digits form 32, which is divisible by 4.

d. No. The last digit is two.

e. Yes. The number is divisible by 2 and 3.

f. Yes. The last 3 digits form 832, which is divisible by 8.

g. Yes. The sum of the digits is 27, which is divisible by 9.

h. No. The last digit is 2.

i. Yes. The number is divisible by both 3 and 4.

9. 6,126,120

a. Yes. The last digit is 0.

b. Yes. The sum of the digits is 18, which is divisible by 3.

c. Yes. The last two digits form 20, which is divisible by 4.

d. Yes. The last digit is 0.

e. Yes. The number is divisible by both 2 and 3.

f. Yes. The last 3 digits form 120, which is divisible by 8.

g. Yes. The sum of the digits is 18, which is divisible by 9.

h. Yes. The last digit is 0.

i. Yes. The number is divisible by both 3 and 4.

11. true. $5958 \div 3 = 1986$
The sum of the digits is 27, which is divisible by 3.

13. true. $10{,}612 \div 4 = 2653$
The last two digits form 12, which is divisible by 4.

15. false

17. true; $104{,}538 \div 6 = 17{,}423$
The number is divisible by both 2 and 3.

19. true; $20{,}104 \div 8 = 2513$
The last three digits form 104, which is divisible by 8.

21. false

23. true; $517{,}872 \div 12 = 43{,}156$
The number is divisible by both 3 and 4.

25.
75
(3) 25
(5) (5)
$75 = 3 \cdot 5^2$

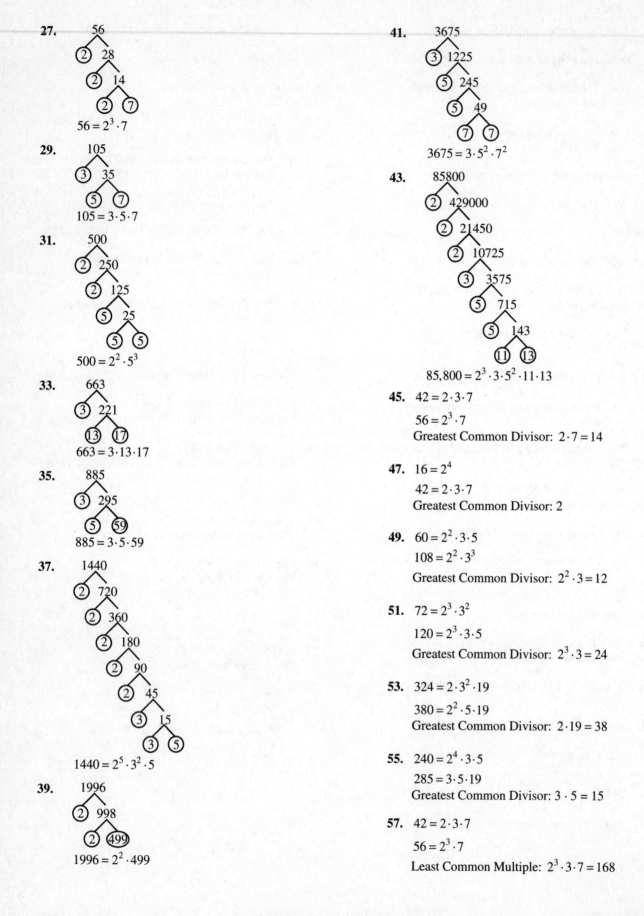

27. 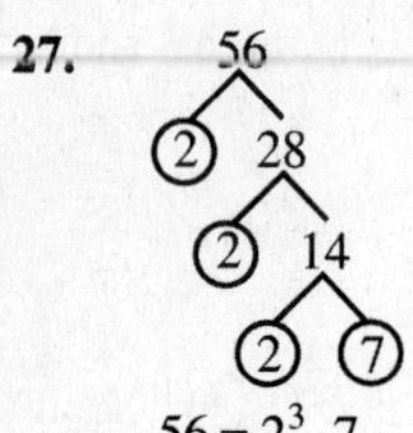

$56 = 2^3 \cdot 7$

29. 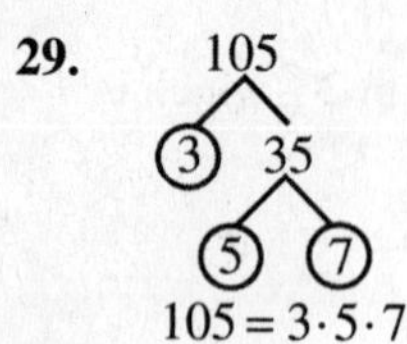

$105 = 3 \cdot 5 \cdot 7$

31. 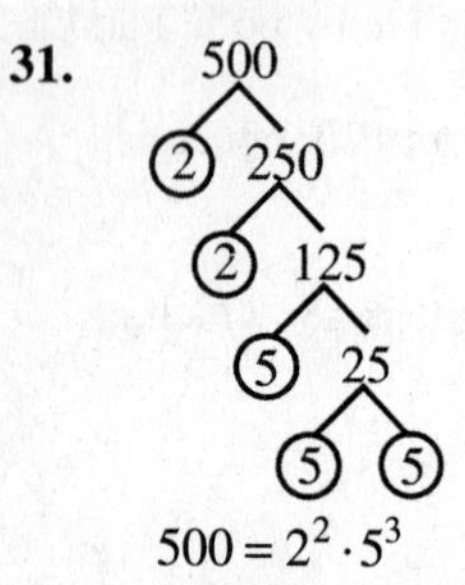

$500 = 2^2 \cdot 5^3$

33. 663

3 221

13 17

$663 = 3 \cdot 13 \cdot 17$

35. 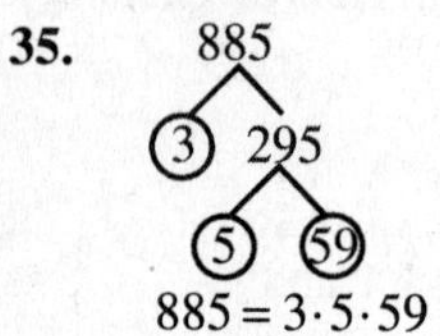

$885 = 3 \cdot 5 \cdot 59$

37. 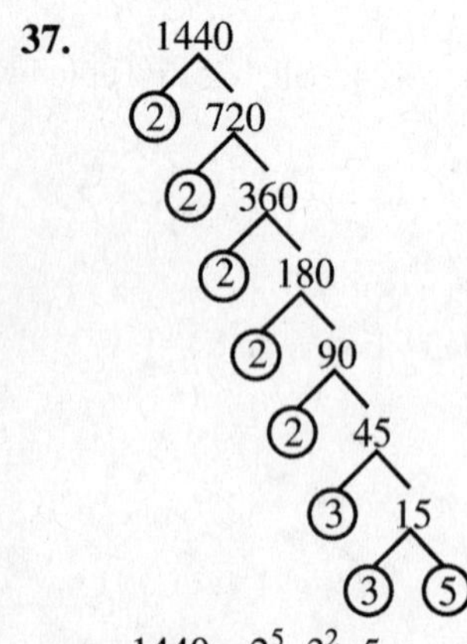

$1440 = 2^5 \cdot 3^2 \cdot 5$

39. 1996

2 998

2 499

$1996 = 2^2 \cdot 499$

41. 3675

3 1225

5 245

5 49

7 7

$3675 = 3 \cdot 5^2 \cdot 7^2$

43. 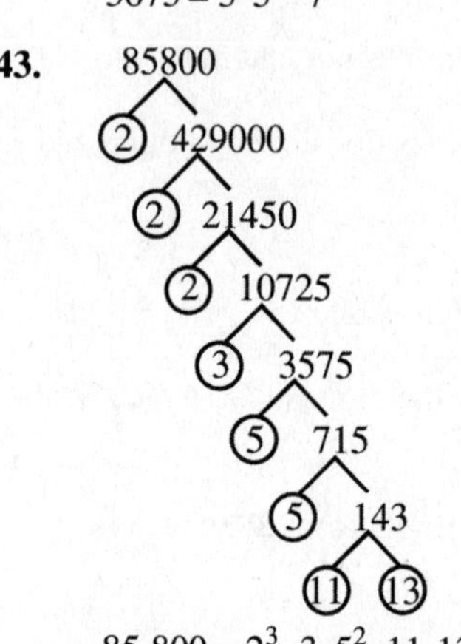

$85,800 = 2^3 \cdot 3 \cdot 5^2 \cdot 11 \cdot 13$

45. $42 = 2 \cdot 3 \cdot 7$

$56 = 2^3 \cdot 7$

Greatest Common Divisor: $2 \cdot 7 = 14$

47. $16 = 2^4$

$42 = 2 \cdot 3 \cdot 7$

Greatest Common Divisor: 2

49. $60 = 2^2 \cdot 3 \cdot 5$

$108 = 2^2 \cdot 3^3$

Greatest Common Divisor: $2^2 \cdot 3 = 12$

51. $72 = 2^3 \cdot 3^2$

$120 = 2^3 \cdot 3 \cdot 5$

Greatest Common Divisor: $2^3 \cdot 3 = 24$

53. $324 = 2 \cdot 3^2 \cdot 19$

$380 = 2^2 \cdot 5 \cdot 19$

Greatest Common Divisor: $2 \cdot 19 = 38$

55. $240 = 2^4 \cdot 3 \cdot 5$

$285 = 3 \cdot 5 \cdot 19$

Greatest Common Divisor: $3 \cdot 5 = 15$

57. $42 = 2 \cdot 3 \cdot 7$

$56 = 2^3 \cdot 7$

Least Common Multiple: $2^3 \cdot 3 \cdot 7 = 168$

59. $16 = 2^4$

$42 = 2 \cdot 3 \cdot 7$

Least Common Multiple: $2^4 \cdot 3 \cdot 7 = 336$

61. $60 = 2^2 \cdot 3 \cdot 5$

$108 = 2^2 \cdot 3^3$

Least Common Multiple: $2^2 \cdot 3^3 \cdot 5 = 540$

63. $72 = 2^3 \cdot 3^2$

$120 = 2^3 \cdot 3 \cdot 5$

Least Common Multiple: $2^3 \cdot 3^2 \cdot 5 = 360$

65. $342 = 2 \cdot 3^2 \cdot 19$

$380 = 2^2 \cdot 5 \cdot 19$

Least Common Multiple: $2^2 \cdot 3^2 \cdot 5 \cdot 19 = 3420$

67. $240 = 2^4 \cdot 3 \cdot 5$

$285 = 3 \cdot 5 \cdot 19$

Least Common Multiple

$= 2^4 \cdot 3 \cdot 5 \cdot 19$

$= 4560$

69. $d = 8$

$9 | 12,348$

71. $d = 6$

$8 | 76,523,456$

73. $d = 2,\ 6$

$4 | 963,232$ and $4 | 963,236$

75. 28 is a perfect number.
$28 = 1 + 2 + 4 + 7 + 14$

77. 20 is not a perfect number.
$20 \neq 1 + 2 + 4 + 5 + 10$

79. 41 is not an emirp because 14 is not prime.

81. 107 is an emirp because 701 is also prime.

83. 13 is not a Germain prime because $2(13) + 1 = 27$ is not prime.

85. 241 is not a Germain prime because $2(241) + 1 = 483$ is not prime.

87. The GCD of 24 and 27 is 3.
The LCM of 24 and 27 is 216.
$3 \times 216 = 648$

$24 \times 27 = 648$

The product of the greatest common divisor and least common multiple of two numbers equals the product of the two numbers.

89. The numbers are the prime numbers less than 100.

91. $300 = 2^2 \cdot 3 \cdot 5^2$

$144 = 2^4 \cdot 3^2$

Greatest Common Divisor: $2^2 \cdot 3 = 12$

There would be 25 groups with 12 bottles of water each. There would be 12 groups with 12 cans of food each.

93. $310 = 2 \cdot 5 \cdot 31$

$460 = 2^2 \cdot 5 \cdot 23$

Greatest Common Divisor: $2 \cdot 5 = 10$

There would be 31 groups of 10 five-dollar bills. There would be 46 groups of 10 ten-dollar bills.

95. $6 = 2 \cdot 3$

$10 = 2 \cdot 5$

Least Common Multiple is: $2 \cdot 3 \cdot 5 = 30$

It will be 30 more nights until both have the evening off, or July 1.

97. $15 = 3 \cdot 5$

$18 = 2 \cdot 3^2$

Least Common Multiple is: $2 \cdot 3^2 \cdot 5 = 90$

It takes 90 minutes.

111. does not make sense; Explanations will vary. Sample explanation: For the greatest common factor, select the common prime factors with the *smallest* exponent. For the least common multiple, select all prime factors with the *largest* exponent.

113. does not make sense; Explanations will vary. Sample explanation: Not all such numbers of this form are prime.

115. **a.** GCD = $2^{14} \cdot 3^{25} \cdot 5^{30}$

b. LCM = $2^{17} \cdot 3^{37} \cdot 5^{31}$

117. $85 + 15 = 100 = 2^2 \cdot 5^2$

$100 + 15 = 115 = 5 \cdot 23$

LCM = $2^2 \cdot 5 \cdot 23 = 2300$

The films will begin at the same time

2300 min $\left(= 38\frac{1}{3}\text{hr} \right)$ after noon (today), or at 2:20 A.M. on the third day.

119. Yes, since 96 is divisible by 4, then 67,234,096 is divisible by 4.

121. Yes, since 4 + 8 + 2 + 0 + 1 + 6 + 5 +1 = 27 is divisible by 9, then 48,201,651 is divisible by 9.

Check Points 5.2

1. (a) at −4, (b) at 0, (c) at 3 on the number line −5 −4 −3 −2 −1 0 1 2 3 4 5

2. a. $6 > -7$ because 6 is to the right of –2 on the number line.

b. $-8 < -1$ because –8 is to the left of –1 on the number line.

c. $-25 < -2$ because –25 is to the left of –2 on the number line.

d. $-14 < 0$ because –14 is to the left of 0 on the number line.

3. a. $|-8| = 8$ because –8 is 8 units from 0.

b. $|6| = 6$ because 6 is 6 units from 0.

c. $-|8| = -8$ because 8 is 8 units from 0 and the negative of 8 is –8.

4. a. $30-(-7)=30+7=37$

b. $-14-(-10)=-14+10=-4$

c. $-14-10=-24$

5. a. $\overbrace{3}^{\text{eats 5 servings}} - \overbrace{(-5)}^{\text{frequently stressed}} = 3+5=8$ years

b. $\overbrace{-1}^{\text{less than 6 to 8 hours of sleep}} - \overbrace{(-15)}^{\text{smokes cigarettes}} = -1+15=14$ years

6. a. $(-5)^2 = (-5)(-5) = 25$

b. $-5^2 = -(5\cdot 5) = -25$

c. $(-4)^3 = (-4)(-4)(-4) = -64$

d. $(-3)^4 = (-3)(-3)(-3)(-3) = 81$

7. $7^2 - 48 \div 4^2 \cdot 5 + 2$
$= 49 - 48 \div 16 \cdot 5 + 2$
$= 49 - 3 \cdot 5 + 2$
$= 49 - 15 + 2$
$= 34 + 2$
$= 36$

8. $(-8)^2 - (10-13)^2(-2)$
$= (-8)^2 - (-3)^2(-2)$
$= 64 - (9)(-2)$
$= 64 - (-18)$
$= 64 + (+18)$
$= 82$

Concept and Vocabulary Check 5.2

1. $\{1, \ldots, -3, -2, -1, 0, 1, 2, 3, \ldots 1\}$

2. left

3. the distance from 0 to *a*

4. additive inverses

5. false

6. true

7. true

8. false

Exercise Set 5.2

1.
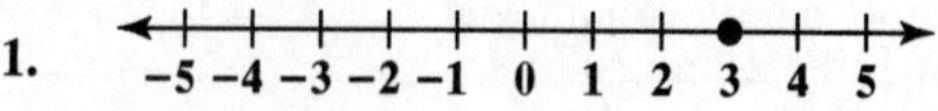

3.
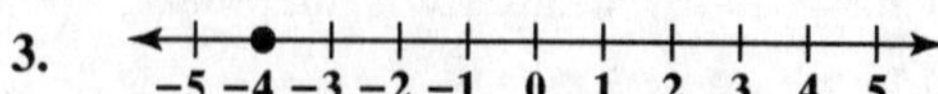

5. $-2 < 7$ because –2 is to the left of 7 on the number line.

7. $-13 < -2$ because –13 is to the left of –2 on the number line.

9. $8 > -50$ because 8 is to the right of –50 on the number line.

11. $-100 < 0$ because -100 is to the left of 0 on the number line.

13. $|-14| = 14$ because -14 is 14 units from 0.

15. $|14| = 14$ because 14 is 14 units from 0.

17. $|-300{,}000| = 300{,}000$ because $-300{,}000$ is 300,000 units from 0.

19. $-7+(-5)=-12$

21. $12+(-8)=4$

23. $6+(-9)=-3$

25. $-9+(+4)=-5$

27. $-9+(-9)=-18$

29. $9+(-9)=0$

31. $13-8=5$

33. $8-15=8+(-15)=-7$

35. $4-(-10)=4+10=14$

37. $-6-(-17)=-6+17=11$

39. $-12-(-3)=-12+3=-9$

41. $-11-17=-11+(-17)=-28$

43. $6(-9)=-54$

45. $(-7)(-3)=21$

47. $(-2)(6)=-12$

49. $(-13)(-1)=13$

51. $0(-5)=0$

53. $5^2=5\cdot 5=25$

55. $(-5)^2=(-5)\cdot(-5)=25$

57. $4^3=4\cdot 4\cdot 4=64$

59. $(-5)^3=(-5)(-5)(-5)=25(-5)=-125$

61. $(-5)^4=(-5)(-5)(-5)(-5)=625$

63. $-3^4=-[3\cdot 3\cdot 3\cdot 3]=-81$

65. $(-3)^4=(-3)(-3)(-3)(-3)=81$

67. $\frac{-12}{4}=-3$

69. $\frac{21}{-3}=-7$

71. $\frac{-90}{-3}=30$

73. $\frac{0}{-7}=0$

75. $\frac{-7}{0}$ is undefined

77. $(-480)\div 24=\frac{-480}{24}=-20$

79. $(465)\div(-15)=\frac{465}{-15}=-31$

81. $7+6\cdot 3=7+18=25$

83. $(-5)-6(-3)=-5+18=13$

85.
$$\begin{aligned}6-4(-3)-5&=6-(-12)-5\\&=6+12-5\\&=18-5\\&=13\end{aligned}$$

87.
$$\begin{aligned}3-5(-4-2)&=3-5(-6)\\&=3-(-30)\\&=3+30\\&=33\end{aligned}$$

89. $(2-6)(-3-5)=(-4)(-8)=32$

91.
$$\begin{aligned}3(-2)^2-4(-3)^2&=3(4)-4(9)\\&=12-36\\&=-24\end{aligned}$$

93.
$$\begin{aligned}(2-6)^2-(3-7)^2&=(-4)^2-(-4)^2\\&=16-16\\&=0\end{aligned}$$

95. $6(3-5)^3-2(1-3)^3=6(-2)^3-2(-2)^3$
$=6(-8)-2(-8)$
$=-48+16$
$=-32$

97. $8^2-16\div 2^2\cdot 4-3=64-16\div 4\cdot 4-3$
$=64-4\cdot 4-3$
$=64-16-3$
$=45$

99. $24\div\left[3^2\div(8-5)\right]-(-6)$
$=24\div[9\div 3]-(-6)$
$=24\div 3+6$
$=8+6$
$=14$

101. $8-3[-2(2-5)-4(8-6)]$
$=8-3[-2(-3)-4(2)]$
$=8-3[6-8]$
$=8-3[-2]$
$=8+6$
$=14$

103. $-2^2+4[16\div(3-5)]$
$=-4+4[16\div(-2)]$
$=-4+4[-8]$
$=-4-32$
$=-36$

105. $4|10-(8-20)|$
$=4|10-(-12)|$
$=4|10+12|$
$=4|22|$
$=88$

107. $\left[-5^2+(6-8)^3-(-4)\right]-\left[|-2|^3+1-3^2\right]$
$=\left[-5^2+(-2)^3-(-4)\right]-\left[2^3+1-3^2\right]$
$=[-25-8-(-4)]-[8+1-9]$
$=[-25-8+4]-[8+1-9]$
$=[-33+4]-[0]$
$=-29-0$
$=-29$

109. $\dfrac{12\div 3\cdot 5\left|2^2+3^2\right|}{7+3-6^2}$
$=\dfrac{12\div 3\cdot 5|4+9|}{7+3-36}$
$=\dfrac{12\div 3\cdot 5|13|}{10-36}$
$=\dfrac{12\div 3\cdot 5\cdot 13}{-26}$
$=\dfrac{4\cdot 5\cdot 13}{-26}$
$=\dfrac{260}{-26}$
$=-10$

111. $-10-(-2)^3=-10-(-8)=-10+8=-2$

113. $[2(7-10)]^2=[2(-3)]^2=[-6]^2=36$

115. The difference in elevation is
$20,320-(-282)$
$=20,320+282$
$=20,602$ feet

117. $12,\ 12\left(-\frac{1}{2}\right)=-6,\ -6\left(-\frac{1}{2}\right)=3,\ 3\left(-\frac{1}{2}\right)=-\frac{3}{2},$
You shrink your life span by 5 years.

119. $-5+(-6)=-11$
You shrink your life span by 11 years.

121. $5+(-5)=0$
Your life span has no change.

123. $10-(-15)=10+15=25$
25 years

125. $-5-(-6)=-5+6=1$
1 year

127. a. $1991 - 1863 = 128$
In 2001, there was a \$128 billion surplus.

b. $2304 - 3603 = -1299$
In 2011, there was a \$1299 billion deficit.

c. $128 - (-1299) = 128 + 1299 = 1427$
The difference is \$1427 billion.

129. 2007 deficit: $2568 - 2729 = -161$
2011 deficit: $2304 - 3603 = -1299$
The difference between the 2007 deficit and the 2011 deficit was
$-161 - (-1299) = -161 + 1299 = 1138$ or \$1138 billion.

131. $3^\circ - (-4^\circ) = 3^\circ + 4^\circ = 7^\circ$ F

133. $-24^\circ - (-22^\circ) = -24^\circ + 22^\circ = -2^\circ$ F

145. makes sense

147. makes sense

149. $(8 - 2) \cdot 3 - 4 = 14$

151. –36

Check Points 5.3

1. $72 = 2^3 \cdot 3^2$
$90 = 2 \cdot 5 \cdot 3^2$
Greatest Common Divisor is $2 \cdot 3^2$ or 18.
$$\frac{72}{90} = \frac{72 \div 18}{90 \div 18} = \frac{4}{5}$$

2. $2\frac{5}{8} = \frac{8 \cdot 2 + 5}{8} = \frac{16 + 5}{8} = \frac{21}{8}$

3. $\frac{5}{3} = 1\frac{2}{3}$

4. a. $\frac{3}{8} = 0.375$

$$\begin{array}{r} 0.375 \\ 8\overline{)3.000} \\ \underline{24} \\ 60 \\ \underline{56} \\ 40 \\ \underline{40} \\ 0 \end{array}$$

b. $\frac{5}{11} = 0.\overline{45}$

$$\begin{array}{r} 0.4545\ldots \\ 11\overline{)5.0000} \\ \underline{44} \\ 60 \\ \underline{55} \\ 50 \\ \underline{44} \\ 60 \\ \underline{55} \\ 5 \end{array}$$

5. a. $0.9 = \frac{9}{10}$

b. $0.86 = \frac{86}{100} = \frac{86 \div 2}{100 \div 2} = \frac{43}{50}$

c. $0.053 = \frac{53}{1000}$

6. $n = 0.\overline{2}$
$n = 0.22222\ldots$
$10n = 2.22222\ldots$

$$\begin{array}{r} 10n = 2.2222\ldots \\ -n = 0.2222\ldots \\ \hline 9n = 2.0 \end{array}$$

$n = \frac{2}{9}$

7.
$$n = 0.\overline{79}$$
$$n = 0.7979\ldots$$
$$100n = 79.7979\ldots$$

$$\begin{array}{r} 100n = 79.7979\ldots \\ -\quad n = \ 0.7979\ldots \\ \hline 99n = 79 \end{array}$$
$$n = \frac{79}{99}$$

8. a. $\frac{4}{11}\cdot\frac{2}{3}=\frac{8}{33}$

b. $\left(-\frac{3}{7}\right)\left(-\frac{14}{4}\right)=\frac{42}{28}=\frac{42\div 14}{28\div 14}=\frac{3}{2}$ or $1\frac{1}{2}$

c. $\left(3\frac{2}{5}\right)\left(1\frac{1}{2}\right)=\frac{17}{5}\cdot\frac{3}{2}=\frac{51}{10}$ or $5\frac{1}{10}$

9. a. $\frac{9}{11}\div\frac{5}{4}=\frac{9}{11}\cdot\frac{4}{5}=\frac{36}{55}$

b. $-\frac{8}{15}\div\frac{2}{5}=-\frac{8}{15}\cdot\frac{5}{2}=-\frac{40}{30}=-\frac{4}{3}$ or $-1\frac{1}{3}$

c. $3\frac{3}{8}\div 2\frac{1}{4}=\frac{27}{8}\div\frac{9}{4}=\frac{27}{8}\cdot\frac{4}{9}=\frac{108}{72}=\frac{3}{2}$ or $1\frac{1}{2}$

10. a. $\frac{5}{12}+\frac{3}{12}=\frac{5+3}{12}=\frac{8}{12}=\frac{2}{3}$

b. $\frac{7}{4}-\frac{1}{4}=\frac{7-1}{4}=\frac{6}{4}=\frac{3}{2}$ or $1\frac{1}{2}$

c.
$$-3\frac{3}{8}-\left(-1\frac{1}{8}\right)=-\frac{27}{8}-\left(-\frac{9}{8}\right)$$
$$=-\frac{27}{8}+\frac{9}{8}$$
$$=\frac{-27+9}{8}$$
$$=\frac{-18}{8}$$
$$=-\frac{9}{4}$$
or $-2\frac{1}{4}$

11. $\frac{1}{5}+\frac{3}{4}=\frac{1}{5}\cdot\frac{4}{4}+\frac{3}{4}\cdot\frac{5}{5}=\frac{4}{20}+\frac{15}{20}=\frac{19}{20}$

12. $\frac{3}{10}-\frac{7}{12}=\frac{3}{10}\cdot\frac{6}{6}-\frac{7}{12}\cdot\frac{5}{5}=\frac{18}{60}-\frac{35}{60}=-\frac{17}{60}$

13.
$$\left(-\tfrac{1}{2}\right)^2-\left(\tfrac{7}{10}-\tfrac{8}{15}\right)^2(-18)$$
$$=\left(-\tfrac{1}{2}\right)^2-\left(\tfrac{21}{30}-\tfrac{16}{30}\right)^2(-18)$$
$$=\left(-\tfrac{1}{2}\right)^2-\left(\tfrac{5}{30}\right)^2(-18)$$
$$=\left(-\tfrac{1}{2}\right)^2-\left(\tfrac{1}{6}\right)^2(-18)$$
$$=\tfrac{1}{4}-\tfrac{1}{36}(-18)$$
$$=\tfrac{1}{4}+\tfrac{18}{36}$$
$$=\tfrac{1}{4}+\tfrac{2}{4}$$
$$=\tfrac{3}{4}$$

14. First, find the sum:
$\frac{1}{3}+\frac{1}{2}=\frac{1}{3}\cdot\frac{2}{2}+\frac{1}{2}\cdot\frac{3}{3}=\frac{2}{6}+\frac{3}{6}=\frac{5}{6}$

Next, divide by 2: $\frac{5}{6}\div\frac{2}{1}=\frac{5}{6}\cdot\frac{1}{2}=\frac{5}{12}$

15. Amount of eggs needed
$$=\frac{\text{desired serving size}}{\text{recipe serving size}}\times\text{eggs in recipe}$$
$$=\frac{7\ \not{\text{dozen}}}{5\ \not{\text{dozen}}}\times 2\text{ eggs}$$
$$=\frac{14}{5}\text{ eggs}$$
$$=2\frac{4}{5}\text{ eggs}$$
$$\approx 3\text{ eggs}$$

Concept and Vocabulary Check 5.3

1. rational; integers; zero
2. improper; the numerator is greater than the denominator
3. terminate/stop; have repeating digits
4. reciprocal/multiplicative inverse
5. false
6. false
7. true
8. false

Exercise Set 5.3

1. $10 = 2 \cdot 5$

$15 = 3 \cdot 5$

Greatest Common Divisor is 5.

$\frac{10}{15} = \frac{10 \div 5}{15 \div 5} = \frac{2}{3}$

3. $15 = 3 \cdot 5$

$18 = 2 \cdot 3^2$

Greatest Common Divisor is 3.

$\frac{15}{18} = \frac{15 \div 3}{18 \div 3} = \frac{5}{6}$

5. $24 = 2^3 \cdot 3$

$42 = 2 \cdot 3 \cdot 7$

Greatest Common Divisor is $2 \cdot 3$ or 6.

$\frac{24}{42} = \frac{24 \div 6}{42 \div 6} = \frac{4}{7}$

7. $60 = 2^2 \cdot 3 \cdot 5$

$108 = 2^2 \cdot 3^3$

Greatest Common Divisor is $2^2 \cdot 3$ or 12.

$\frac{60}{108} = \frac{60 \div 12}{108 \div 12} = \frac{5}{9}$

9. $342 = 2 \cdot 3^2 \cdot 19$

$380 = 2^2 \cdot 5 \cdot 19$

Greatest Common Divisor is $2 \cdot 19$ or 38.

$\frac{342}{380} = \frac{342 \div 38}{380 \div 38} = \frac{9}{10}$

11. $308 = 2^2 \cdot 7 \cdot 11$

$418 = 2 \cdot 11 \cdot 19$

Greatest Common Divisor is $2 \cdot 11$ or 22.

$\frac{308}{418} = \frac{308 \div 22}{418 \div 22} = \frac{14}{19}$

13. $2\frac{3}{8} = \frac{8 \cdot 2 + 3}{8} = \frac{16 + 3}{8} = \frac{19}{8}$

15. $-7\frac{3}{5} = -\frac{5 \cdot 7 + 3}{5} = -\frac{35 + 3}{5} = -\frac{38}{5}$

17. $12\frac{7}{16} = \frac{16 \cdot 12 + 7}{16} = \frac{192 + 7}{16} = \frac{199}{16}$

19. $\frac{23}{5} = 4\frac{3}{5}$

21. $-\frac{76}{9} = -8\frac{4}{9}$

23. $\frac{711}{20} = 35\frac{11}{20}$

25. $\frac{3}{4} = 0.75$

$$\begin{array}{r} 0.75 \\ 4\overline{)3.00} \\ \underline{28} \\ 20 \\ \underline{20} \\ 0 \end{array}$$

27. $\frac{7}{20} = 0.35$

$$\begin{array}{r} 0.35 \\ 20\overline{)7.00} \\ \underline{60} \\ 100 \\ \underline{100} \\ 0 \end{array}$$

29. $\frac{7}{8} = 0.875$

$$\begin{array}{r} 0.875 \\ 8\overline{)7.000} \\ \underline{64} \\ 60 \\ \underline{56} \\ 40 \\ \underline{40} \\ 0 \end{array}$$

31. $\frac{9}{11} = 0.\overline{81}$

$$\begin{array}{r} 0.8181\ldots \\ 11\overline{)9.0000} \\ \underline{88} \\ 20 \\ \underline{11} \\ 90 \\ \underline{88} \\ 20 \\ \underline{11} \\ 9 \end{array}$$

33. $\frac{22}{7} = 3.142857$

$$\begin{array}{l} \quad 3.142857\ldots \\ 7\overline{)22.000000} \\ \quad \underline{21} \\ \quad\ 10 \\ \quad\ \ \underline{7} \\ \quad\ \ 30 \\ \quad\ \ \underline{28} \\ \quad\ \ \ 20 \\ \quad\ \ \ \underline{14} \\ \quad\ \ \ \ 60 \\ \quad\ \ \ \ \underline{56} \\ \quad\ \ \ \ \ 40 \\ \quad\ \ \ \ \ \underline{35} \\ \quad\ \ \ \ \ \ 50 \\ \quad\ \ \ \ \ \ \underline{49} \\ \quad\ \ \ \ \ \ \ 10 \end{array}$$

35. $\frac{2}{7} = 0.\overline{285714}$

$$\begin{array}{l} \quad 0.2857142\ldots \\ 7\overline{)\ 2.000000} \\ \quad \underline{14} \\ \quad\ 60 \\ \quad\ \underline{56} \\ \quad\ \ 40 \\ \quad\ \ \underline{35} \\ \quad\ \ \ 50 \\ \quad\ \ \ \underline{49} \\ \quad\ \ \ \ 10 \\ \quad\ \ \ \ \ \underline{7} \\ \quad\ \ \ \ \ 30 \\ \quad\ \ \ \ \ \underline{28} \\ \quad\ \ \ \ \ \ 20 \\ \quad\ \ \ \ \ \ \underline{14} \\ \quad\ \ \ \ \ \ \ 6 \end{array}$$

37. $0.3 = \frac{3}{10}$

39. $0.4 = \frac{4}{10} = \frac{4 \div 2}{10 \div 2} = \frac{2}{5}$

41. $0.39 = \frac{39}{100}$

43. $0.82 = \frac{82}{100} = \frac{82 \div 2}{100 \div 2} = \frac{41}{50}$

45. $0.725 = \frac{725}{1000}$

$725 = 5^2 \cdot 29$

$1000 = 2^3 \cdot 5^3$

Greatest Common Divisor is 5^2 or 25.

$\frac{725}{1000} = \frac{725 \div 25}{1000 \div 25} = \frac{29}{40}$

47. $0.5399 = \frac{5399}{10{,}000}$

49.

$$\begin{aligned} n &= 0.777\ldots \\ 10n &= 7.777\ldots \end{aligned}$$

$$\begin{array}{r} 10n = 7.777\ldots \\ \underline{-n = 0.777\ldots} \\ 9n = 7 \\ n = \frac{7}{9} \end{array}$$

51.

$$\begin{aligned} n &= 0.999\ldots \\ 10n &= 9.999\ldots \end{aligned}$$

$$\begin{array}{r} 10n = 9.999\ldots \\ \underline{-n = 0.999\ldots} \\ 9n = 9 \\ n = 1 \end{array}$$

53.

$$\begin{aligned} n &= 0.3636\ldots \\ 100n &= 36.3636\ldots \end{aligned}$$

$$\begin{array}{r} 100n = 36.3636\ldots \\ \underline{-n = 0.3636\ldots} \\ 99n = 36 \\ n = \frac{36}{99} \text{ or } \frac{4}{11} \end{array}$$

55.

$$\begin{aligned} n &= 0.257257\ldots \\ 1000n &= 257.257257\ldots \end{aligned}$$

$$\begin{array}{r} 1000n = 257.257257\ldots \\ \underline{-n = .257257\ldots} \\ 999n = 257 \\ n = \frac{257}{999} \end{array}$$

57. $\frac{3}{8} \cdot \frac{7}{11} = \frac{3 \cdot 7}{8 \cdot 11} = \frac{21}{88}$

59. $\left(-\frac{1}{10}\right)\left(\frac{7}{12}\right)=\frac{(-1)(7)}{10\cdot 12}=\frac{-7}{120}=-\frac{7}{120}$

61. $\left(-\frac{2}{3}\right)\left(-\frac{9}{4}\right)=\frac{(-2)(-9)}{3\cdot 4}=\frac{18}{12}=\frac{3}{2}$

63. $\left(3\frac{3}{4}\right)\left(1\frac{3}{5}\right)=\frac{15}{4}\cdot\frac{8}{5}=\frac{120}{20}=\frac{6}{1}=6$

65. $\frac{5}{4}\div\frac{3}{8}=\frac{5}{4}\cdot\frac{8}{3}=\frac{5\cdot 8}{4\cdot 3}=\frac{40}{12}=\frac{10}{3}$

67. $-\frac{7}{8}\div\frac{15}{16}=-\frac{7}{8}\cdot\frac{16}{15}$
$=\frac{(-7)(16)}{8\cdot 15}$
$=\frac{-112}{120}$
$=-\frac{14}{15}$

69. $6\frac{3}{5}\div 1\frac{1}{10}=\frac{33}{5}\div\frac{11}{10}=\frac{33}{5}\cdot\frac{10}{11}=\frac{330}{55}=\frac{6}{1}=6$

71. $\frac{2}{11}+\frac{3}{11}=\frac{2+3}{11}=\frac{5}{11}$

73. $\frac{5}{6}-\frac{1}{6}=\frac{5-1}{6}=\frac{4}{6}=\frac{2}{3}$

75. $\frac{7}{12}-\left(-\frac{1}{12}\right)=\frac{7}{12}+\frac{1}{12}=\frac{7+1}{12}=\frac{8}{12}=\frac{2}{3}$

77. $\frac{1}{2}+\frac{1}{5}=\left(\frac{1}{2}\right)\left(\frac{5}{5}\right)+\left(\frac{1}{5}\right)\left(\frac{2}{2}\right)$
$=\frac{5}{10}+\frac{2}{10}$
$=\frac{5+2}{10}$
$=\frac{7}{10}$

79. $\frac{3}{4}+\frac{3}{20}=\left(\frac{3}{4}\right)\left(\frac{5}{5}\right)+\frac{3}{20}$
$=\frac{15}{20}+\frac{3}{20}$
$=\frac{15+3}{20}$
$=\frac{18}{20}$
$=\frac{9}{10}$

81. $\frac{5}{24}+\frac{7}{30}=\left(\frac{5}{24}\right)\left(\frac{5}{5}\right)+\left(\frac{7}{30}\right)\left(\frac{4}{4}\right)$
$=\frac{25}{120}+\frac{28}{120}$
$=\frac{25+28}{120}$
$=\frac{53}{120}$

83. $\frac{13}{18}-\frac{2}{9}=\frac{13}{18}-\frac{2}{9}\left(\frac{2}{2}\right)$
$=\frac{13}{18}-\frac{4}{18}$
$=\frac{13-4}{18}$
$=\frac{9}{18}$
$=\frac{1}{2}$

85. $\frac{4}{3}-\frac{3}{4}=\frac{4}{3}\left(\frac{4}{4}\right)-\frac{3}{4}\left(\frac{3}{3}\right)$
$=\frac{16}{12}-\frac{9}{12}$
$=\frac{16-9}{12}$
$=\frac{7}{12}$

87. $\frac{1}{15}-\frac{27}{50}$

$15=3\cdot 5$

$50=2\cdot 5^2$

Least Common Multiple is $2\cdot 3\cdot 5^2=6\cdot 25=150$

$$\frac{1}{15}\left(\frac{10}{10}\right)-\frac{27}{50}\left(\frac{3}{3}\right)=\frac{10}{150}-\frac{81}{150}$$
$$=\frac{10-81}{150}$$
$$=-\frac{71}{150}$$

89. $2\frac{2}{3}+1\frac{3}{4}=2\frac{8}{12}+1\frac{9}{12}=\frac{32}{12}+\frac{21}{12}=\frac{53}{12}$ or $4\frac{5}{12}$

91. $3\frac{2}{3}-2\frac{1}{2}=3\frac{4}{6}-2\frac{3}{6}=\frac{22}{6}-\frac{15}{6}=\frac{7}{6}$ or $1\frac{1}{6}$

93. $-5\frac{2}{3}+3\frac{1}{6}=-5\frac{4}{6}+3\frac{1}{6}=\frac{-34}{6}+\frac{19}{6}=-\frac{15}{6}=-\frac{5}{2}$

or $-2\frac{1}{2}$

95. $-1\frac{4}{7}-\left(-2\frac{5}{14}\right)=-1\frac{8}{14}+2\frac{5}{14}=\frac{-22}{14}+\frac{33}{14}=\frac{11}{14}$

97. $\left(\frac{1}{2}-\frac{1}{3}\right)\div\frac{5}{8}=\left[\left(\frac{1}{2}\right)\left(\frac{3}{3}\right)-\frac{1}{3}\left(\frac{2}{2}\right)\right]\div\frac{5}{8}$

$$=\left(\frac{3}{6}-\frac{2}{6}\right)\div\frac{5}{8}$$
$$=\frac{1}{6}\div\frac{5}{8}$$
$$=\frac{1}{6}\cdot\frac{8}{5}$$
$$=\frac{1\cdot 8}{6\cdot 5}$$
$$=\frac{8}{30}$$
$$=\frac{4}{15}$$

99. $-\frac{9}{4}\left(\frac{1}{2}\right)+\frac{3}{4}\div\frac{5}{6}=-\frac{9}{8}+\frac{9}{10}$

$$=-\frac{9}{40}$$

101. $\dfrac{\frac{7}{9}-3}{\frac{5}{6}}\div\frac{3}{2}+\frac{3}{4}=\dfrac{-\frac{20}{9}}{\frac{5}{6}}\div\frac{3}{2}+\frac{3}{4}$

$$=-\frac{8}{3}\times\frac{2}{3}+\frac{3}{4}$$
$$=-\frac{16}{9}+\frac{3}{4}$$
$$=-\frac{37}{36}\text{ or }-1\frac{1}{36}$$

103. $\frac{1}{4}-6(2+8)\div\left(-\frac{1}{3}\right)\left(-\frac{1}{9}\right)$

$$=\frac{1}{4}-6(10)\div 3$$
$$=\frac{1}{4}-60\div 3$$
$$=\frac{1}{4}-20$$
$$=-19\frac{3}{4}$$

105. $\frac{1}{4}+\frac{1}{3}=\left(\frac{1}{4}\right)\left(\frac{3}{3}\right)+\left(\frac{1}{3}\right)\left(\frac{4}{4}\right)$

$$=\frac{3}{12}+\frac{4}{12}$$
$$=\frac{3+4}{12}$$
$$=\frac{7}{12}$$

$\frac{7}{12}\div 2=\frac{7}{12}\cdot\frac{1}{2}=\frac{7}{24}$

107. $\frac{1}{2}+\frac{2}{3}=\left(\frac{1}{2}\right)\left(\frac{3}{3}\right)+\left(\frac{2}{3}\right)\left(\frac{2}{2}\right)$

$$=\frac{3}{6}+\frac{4}{6}$$
$$=\frac{3+4}{6}$$
$$=\frac{7}{6}$$

$\frac{7}{6}\div 2=\frac{7}{6}\cdot\frac{1}{2}=\frac{7}{12}$

109. $-\frac{2}{3}+\left(-\frac{5}{6}\right)=\left(-\frac{2}{3}\right)\left(\frac{2}{2}\right)-\frac{5}{6}$

$=\frac{-4}{6}-\frac{5}{6}$

$=\frac{-4-5}{6}$

$=-\frac{9}{6}$

$-\frac{9}{6}\div 2=-\frac{9}{6}\cdot\frac{1}{2}=-\frac{9}{12}=-\frac{3}{4}$

111. $\frac{13}{4}+\frac{13}{9}=\frac{13\cdot 9}{4\cdot 9}+\frac{13\cdot 4}{9\cdot 4}$

$=\frac{117}{36}+\frac{52}{36}$

$=\frac{117+52}{36}$

$=\frac{169}{36}$

$\frac{13}{4}\times\frac{13}{9}=\frac{13\cdot 13}{4\cdot 9}$

$=\frac{169}{36}$

Both are equal to $\frac{169}{36}$

113. $\frac{5}{2^2\cdot 3^2}-\frac{1}{2\cdot 3^2}=\frac{5}{2^2\cdot 3^2}-\frac{2}{2}\cdot\frac{1}{2\cdot 3^2}$

$=\frac{5}{2^2\cdot 3^2}-\frac{2}{2^2\cdot 3^2}$

$=\frac{3}{2^2\cdot 3^2}$

$=\frac{1}{2^2\cdot 3}$

115. $\frac{1}{2^4\cdot 5^3\cdot 7}+\frac{1}{2\cdot 5^4}-\frac{1}{2^3\cdot 5^2}$

$=\frac{5}{5}\cdot\frac{1}{2^4\cdot 5^3\cdot 7}+\frac{2^3\cdot 7}{2^3\cdot 7}\cdot\frac{1}{2\cdot 5^4}-\frac{2\cdot 5^2\cdot 7}{2\cdot 5^2\cdot 7}\cdot\frac{1}{2^3\cdot 5^2}$

$=\frac{5}{2^4\cdot 5^4\cdot 7}+\frac{56}{2^4\cdot 5^4\cdot 7}-\frac{350}{2^4\cdot 5^4\cdot 7}$

$=-\frac{289}{2^4\cdot 5^4\cdot 7}$

117. $0.\overline{54}<0.58\overline{3}$

$\frac{6}{11}<\frac{7}{12}$

119. $-0.8\overline{3}>-0.\overline{8}$

$-\frac{5}{6}>-\frac{8}{9}$

121. **a.** $\frac{560}{1600}=\frac{7}{20}$

b. $0.35=35\%$

c. $\frac{720}{1600}=\frac{9}{20}$

d. $0.45=45\%$

e. $45\%-35\%=10\%$

123. For each ingredient in the recipe, multiply the original quantity by $\frac{8}{16}$ or $\frac{1}{2}$.

$\frac{2}{3}\cdot\frac{1}{2}=\frac{1}{3}$ cup butter

$5\cdot\frac{1}{2}=\frac{5}{2}=2\frac{1}{2}$ ounces unsweetened chocolate

$1\frac{1}{2}\cdot\frac{1}{2}=\frac{3}{2}\cdot\frac{1}{2}=\frac{3}{4}$ cup sugar

$2\cdot\frac{1}{2}=1$ teaspoon vanilla

$2\cdot\frac{1}{2}=1$ egg

$1\cdot\frac{1}{2}=\frac{1}{2}$ cup flour

125. For each ingredient in the recipe, multiply the original quantity by $\frac{20}{16}$ or $\frac{5}{4}$.

$\frac{2}{3}\cdot\frac{5}{4}=\frac{5}{6}$ cup butter

$5\cdot\frac{5}{4}=\frac{25}{4}=6\frac{1}{4}$ ounces unsweetened chocolate

$1\frac{1}{2}\cdot\frac{5}{4}=\frac{3}{2}\cdot\frac{5}{4}=\frac{15}{8}=1\frac{7}{8}$ cups sugar

$2\cdot\frac{5}{4}=\frac{5}{2}=2\frac{1}{2}$ teaspoons vanilla

$2\cdot\frac{5}{4}=\frac{5}{2}=2\frac{1}{2}$ eggs

$1\cdot\frac{5}{4}=\frac{5}{4}=1\frac{1}{4}$ cups flour

127. Begin by dividing the 1 cup of butter by the quantity of butter needed for a 16-brownie batch:

$1\div\frac{2}{3}=1\times\frac{3}{2}=\frac{3}{2}=1\frac{1}{2}$

Thus, 1 cup of butter is enough for $1\frac{1}{2}$ batches.

Since each batch makes 16 brownies, $1\frac{1}{2}$ batches will make $16\times1\frac{1}{2}=24$ brownies. Thus, 1 cup of butter is enough for 24 brownies.

129. $2\frac{2}{3}\cdot\frac{11}{8}=\frac{8}{3}\cdot\frac{11}{8}=\frac{88}{24}=\frac{11}{3}$ or $3\frac{2}{3}$ cups of water.

131. **a.** Strings D, E, G, A, and B are $\frac{8}{9}$ of the length of the previous string.

b. There are black keys to the left of the keys for the notes D, E, G, A, and B.

133. $24-\frac{1}{16}-7\frac{1}{2}=\frac{24}{1}-\frac{1}{16}-\frac{15}{2}=\frac{384}{16}-\frac{1}{16}-\frac{120}{16}=\frac{263}{16}=16\frac{7}{16}$ in.

135. $1-\frac{5}{12}-\frac{1}{4}=\frac{12}{12}-\frac{5}{12}-\frac{3}{12}=\frac{4}{12}=\frac{1}{3}$ ownership.

137. The total distance is their sum: $\frac{3}{4}+\frac{2}{5}=\frac{15}{20}+\frac{8}{20}=\frac{23}{20}$ miles.

The difference is the amount farther: $\frac{3}{4}-\frac{2}{5}=\frac{15}{20}-\frac{8}{20}=\frac{7}{20}$ mile.

139. $\frac{3}{5}$ of the total goes to relatives, so there is $\frac{2}{5}$ of the estate left. $\frac{1}{4}$ of that $\frac{2}{5}$ goes for AIDS research:

$\frac{1}{4}\cdot\frac{2}{5}=\frac{2}{20}=\frac{1}{10}$

153. makes sense

155. makes sense

157. Conjecture: The sums of $\frac{2}{3}$, $\frac{3}{4}$, and $\frac{4}{5}$ will be followed by a sum of $\frac{5}{6}$.

Verification:
$$\begin{aligned}\frac{1}{1\cdot2}+\frac{1}{2\cdot3}+\frac{1}{3\cdot4}+\frac{1}{4\cdot5}+\frac{1}{5\cdot6}&=\frac{1}{2}+\frac{1}{6}+\frac{1}{12}+\frac{1}{20}+\frac{1}{30}\\&=\frac{30}{60}+\frac{10}{60}+\frac{5}{60}+\frac{3}{60}+\frac{2}{60}\\&=\frac{50}{60}\\&=\frac{5}{6}\end{aligned}$$

Check Points 5.4

1. a. $\sqrt{12} = \sqrt{4 \cdot 3} = \sqrt{4} \cdot \sqrt{3} = 2\sqrt{3}$

b. $\sqrt{60} = \sqrt{4 \cdot 15} = \sqrt{4} \cdot \sqrt{15} = 2\sqrt{15}$

c. $\sqrt{55}$ cannot be simplified.

2. a. $\sqrt{3} \cdot \sqrt{10} = \sqrt{3 \cdot 10} = \sqrt{30}$

b. $\sqrt{10} \cdot \sqrt{10} = \sqrt{10 \cdot 10} = \sqrt{100} = 10$

c. $\sqrt{6} \cdot \sqrt{2} = \sqrt{6 \cdot 2} = \sqrt{12} = \sqrt{4} \cdot \sqrt{3} = 2\sqrt{3}$

3. a. $\dfrac{\sqrt{80}}{\sqrt{5}} = \sqrt{\dfrac{80}{5}} = \sqrt{16} = 4$

b. $\dfrac{\sqrt{48}}{\sqrt{6}} = \sqrt{\dfrac{48}{6}} = \sqrt{8} = \sqrt{4} \cdot \sqrt{2} = 2\sqrt{2}$

4. a. $8\sqrt{3} + 10\sqrt{3} = (8+10)\sqrt{3} = 18\sqrt{3}$

b. $4\sqrt{13} - 9\sqrt{13} = (4-9)\sqrt{13} = -5\sqrt{13}$

c. $7\sqrt{10} + 2\sqrt{10} - \sqrt{10} = (7+2-1)\sqrt{10} = 8\sqrt{10}$

5. a. $\sqrt{3} + \sqrt{12} = \sqrt{3} + \sqrt{4} \cdot \sqrt{3} = \sqrt{3} + 2\sqrt{3} = 3\sqrt{3}$

b. $4\sqrt{8} - 7\sqrt{18}$

$= 4\sqrt{4 \cdot 2} - 7\sqrt{9 \cdot 2}$

$= 4 \cdot 2\sqrt{2} - 7 \cdot 3\sqrt{2}$

$= 8\sqrt{2} - 21\sqrt{2}$

$= (8-21)\sqrt{2}$

$= -13\sqrt{2}$

6. a. $\dfrac{25}{\sqrt{10}} = \dfrac{25}{\sqrt{10}} \cdot \dfrac{\sqrt{10}}{\sqrt{10}} = \dfrac{25\sqrt{10}}{\sqrt{100}} = \dfrac{25\sqrt{10}}{10} = \dfrac{5\sqrt{10}}{2}$

b. $\sqrt{\dfrac{2}{7}} = \dfrac{\sqrt{2}}{\sqrt{7}} = \dfrac{\sqrt{2}}{\sqrt{7}} \cdot \dfrac{\sqrt{7}}{\sqrt{7}} = \dfrac{\sqrt{14}}{\sqrt{49}} = \dfrac{\sqrt{14}}{7}$

c. $\dfrac{5}{\sqrt{18}} = \dfrac{5}{\sqrt{18}} \cdot \dfrac{\sqrt{2}}{\sqrt{2}} = \dfrac{5\sqrt{2}}{\sqrt{36}} = \dfrac{5\sqrt{2}}{6}$

Concept and Vocabulary Check 5.4

1. terminating; repeating

2. π

3. $\sqrt{n}$; n

4. 49; 6; $7\sqrt{6}$

5. coefficient

6. 8; 10; $18\sqrt{3}$

7. 5; 4; $9\sqrt{2}$

8. rationalizing the denominator

9. $\sqrt{7}$

10. $\sqrt{3}$

Exercise Set 5.4

1. $\sqrt{9} = 3$ because $3^2 = 9$.

3. $\sqrt{25} = 5$ because $5^2 = 25$.

5. $\sqrt{64} = 8$ because $8^2 = 64$.

7. $\sqrt{121} = 11$ because $11^2 = 121$.

9. $\sqrt{169} = 13$ because $13^2 = 169$.

11. a. $\sqrt{173} \approx 13.2$

    b. $\sqrt{173} \approx 13.15$

    c. $\sqrt{173} \approx 13.153$

13. a. $\sqrt{17,761} \approx 133.3$

    b. $\sqrt{17,761} \approx 133.27$

    c. $\sqrt{17,761} \approx 133.270$

15. a. $\sqrt{\pi} \approx 1.8$

    b. $\sqrt{\pi} \approx 1.77$

    c. $\sqrt{\pi} \approx 1.772$

17. $\sqrt{20} = \sqrt{4 \cdot 5} = \sqrt{4} \cdot \sqrt{5} = 2\sqrt{5}$

19. $\sqrt{80} = \sqrt{16 \cdot 5} = \sqrt{16} \cdot \sqrt{5} = 4\sqrt{5}$

21. $\sqrt{250} = \sqrt{25 \cdot 10} = \sqrt{25} \cdot \sqrt{10} = 5\sqrt{10}$

23. $$\begin{aligned} 7\sqrt{28} &= 7\sqrt{4 \cdot 7} \\ &= 7\sqrt{4} \cdot \sqrt{7} \\ &= 7 \cdot 2 \cdot \sqrt{7} \\ &= 14\sqrt{7} \end{aligned}$$

25. $\sqrt{7} \cdot \sqrt{6} = \sqrt{7 \cdot 6} = \sqrt{42}$

27. $\sqrt{6} \cdot \sqrt{6} = \sqrt{6 \cdot 6} = \sqrt{36} = 6$

29. $$\begin{aligned} \sqrt{3} \cdot \sqrt{6} &= \sqrt{3 \cdot 6} \\ &= \sqrt{18} \\ &= \sqrt{9 \cdot 2} \\ &= \sqrt{9} \cdot \sqrt{2} \\ &= 3\sqrt{2} \end{aligned}$$

31. $$\begin{aligned} \sqrt{2} \cdot \sqrt{26} &= \sqrt{2 \cdot 26} \\ &= \sqrt{52} \\ &= \sqrt{4 \cdot 13} \\ &= \sqrt{4} \cdot \sqrt{13} \\ &= 2\sqrt{13} \end{aligned}$$

33. $\dfrac{\sqrt{54}}{\sqrt{6}} = \sqrt{\dfrac{54}{6}} = \sqrt{9} = 3$

35. $$\begin{aligned} \frac{\sqrt{90}}{\sqrt{2}} &= \sqrt{\frac{90}{2}} \\ &= \sqrt{45} \\ &= \sqrt{9 \cdot 5} \\ &= \sqrt{9} \cdot \sqrt{5} \\ &= 3\sqrt{5} \end{aligned}$$

37. $\dfrac{-\sqrt{96}}{\sqrt{2}} = -\sqrt{\dfrac{96}{2}}$
$= -\sqrt{48}$
$= -\sqrt{16\cdot 3}$
$= -\sqrt{16}\cdot\sqrt{3}$
$= -4\sqrt{3}$

39. $7\sqrt{3}+6\sqrt{3} = (7+6)\sqrt{3} = 13\sqrt{3}$

41. $4\sqrt{13}-6\sqrt{13} = (4-6)\sqrt{13} = -2\sqrt{13}$

43. $\sqrt{5}+\sqrt{5} = 1\sqrt{5}+1\sqrt{5} = (1+1)\sqrt{5} = 2\sqrt{5}$

45. $4\sqrt{2}-5\sqrt{2}+8\sqrt{2} = (4-5+8)\sqrt{2} = 7\sqrt{2}$

47. $\sqrt{5}+\sqrt{20} = 1\sqrt{5}+\sqrt{4}\cdot\sqrt{5}$
$= 1\sqrt{5}+2\sqrt{5}$
$= (1+2)\sqrt{5}$
$= 3\sqrt{5}$

49. $\sqrt{50}-\sqrt{18} = \sqrt{25}\cdot\sqrt{2}-\sqrt{9}\cdot\sqrt{2}$
$= 5\sqrt{2}-3\sqrt{2}$
$= (5-3)\sqrt{2}$
$= 2\sqrt{2}$

51. $3\sqrt{18}+5\sqrt{50} = 3\sqrt{9}\cdot\sqrt{2}+5\sqrt{25}\cdot\sqrt{2}$
$= 3\cdot 3\cdot\sqrt{2}+5\cdot 5\sqrt{2}$
$= 9\sqrt{2}+25\sqrt{2}$
$= (9+25)\sqrt{2}$
$= 34\sqrt{2}$

53. $\dfrac{1}{4}\sqrt{12}-\dfrac{1}{2}\sqrt{48} = \dfrac{1}{4}\sqrt{4}\cdot\sqrt{3}-\dfrac{1}{2}\sqrt{16}\cdot\sqrt{3}$
$= \dfrac{1}{4}\cdot 2\cdot\sqrt{3}-\dfrac{1}{2}\cdot 4\cdot\sqrt{3}$
$= \dfrac{1}{2}\sqrt{3}-\dfrac{4}{2}\sqrt{3}$
$= \left(\dfrac{1}{2}-\dfrac{4}{2}\right)\sqrt{3}$
$= -\dfrac{3}{2}\sqrt{3}$

55. $3\sqrt{75}+2\sqrt{12}-2\sqrt{48}$
$= 3\cdot\sqrt{25}\cdot\sqrt{3}+2\cdot\sqrt{4}\cdot\sqrt{3}-2\cdot\sqrt{16}\cdot\sqrt{3}$
$= 3\cdot 5\cdot\sqrt{3}+2\cdot 2\cdot\sqrt{3}-2\cdot 4\cdot\sqrt{3}$
$= 15\sqrt{3}+4\sqrt{3}-8\sqrt{3}$
$= (15+4-8)\sqrt{3}$
$= 11\sqrt{3}$

57. $\dfrac{5}{\sqrt{3}} = \dfrac{5}{\sqrt{3}}\cdot\dfrac{\sqrt{3}}{\sqrt{3}} = \dfrac{5\sqrt{3}}{\sqrt{9}} = \dfrac{5\sqrt{3}}{3}$

59. $\dfrac{21}{\sqrt{7}} = \dfrac{21}{\sqrt{7}}\cdot\dfrac{\sqrt{7}}{\sqrt{7}} = \dfrac{21\sqrt{7}}{\sqrt{49}} = \dfrac{21\sqrt{7}}{7} = 3\sqrt{7}$

61. $\dfrac{12}{\sqrt{30}} = \dfrac{12\sqrt{30}}{\sqrt{30}\sqrt{30}}$
$= \dfrac{12\sqrt{30}}{\sqrt{900}}$
$= \dfrac{12\sqrt{30}}{30}$
$= \dfrac{2\sqrt{30}}{5}$

63. $\dfrac{15}{\sqrt{12}} = \dfrac{15}{\sqrt{4\cdot 3}}$
$= \dfrac{15}{\sqrt{4}\sqrt{3}}$
$= \dfrac{15}{2\sqrt{3}}$
$= \dfrac{15\sqrt{3}}{2\sqrt{3}\sqrt{3}}$
$= \dfrac{15\sqrt{3}}{2\sqrt{9}}$
$= \dfrac{15\sqrt{3}}{2\cdot 3}$
$= \dfrac{15\sqrt{3}}{6}$
$= \dfrac{5\sqrt{3}}{2}$

65. $\sqrt{\dfrac{2}{5}} = \dfrac{\sqrt{2}}{\sqrt{5}} = \dfrac{\sqrt{2}}{\sqrt{5}}\cdot\dfrac{\sqrt{5}}{\sqrt{5}} = \dfrac{\sqrt{10}}{\sqrt{25}} = \dfrac{\sqrt{10}}{5}$

67. $3\sqrt{8}-\sqrt{32}+3\sqrt{72}-\sqrt{75}$
$=6\sqrt{2}-4\sqrt{2}+18\sqrt{2}-5\sqrt{3}$
$=20\sqrt{2}-5\sqrt{3}$

69. $3\sqrt{7}-5\sqrt{14}\cdot\sqrt{2}=3\sqrt{7}-5\sqrt{28}$
$=3\sqrt{7}-10\sqrt{7}$
$=-7\sqrt{7}$

71. $\frac{\sqrt{32}}{5}+\frac{\sqrt{18}}{7}=\frac{4\sqrt{2}}{5}+\frac{3\sqrt{2}}{7}$
$=\frac{28\sqrt{2}}{35}+\frac{15\sqrt{2}}{35}$
$=\frac{43\sqrt{2}}{35}$

73. $\frac{\sqrt{2}}{\sqrt{3}}+\frac{\sqrt{3}}{\sqrt{2}}$
$=\frac{\sqrt{2}}{\sqrt{3}}\cdot\frac{\sqrt{2}}{\sqrt{2}}+\frac{\sqrt{3}}{\sqrt{2}}\cdot\frac{\sqrt{3}}{\sqrt{3}}$
$=\frac{2}{\sqrt{6}}+\frac{3}{\sqrt{6}}$
$=\frac{5}{\sqrt{6}}$
$=\frac{5}{\sqrt{6}}\cdot\frac{\sqrt{6}}{\sqrt{6}}$
$=\frac{5\sqrt{6}}{6}$

75. $d(x)=\sqrt{\frac{3x}{2}}$
$d(72)=\sqrt{\frac{3(72)}{2}}$
$=\sqrt{3(36)}$
$=\sqrt{3}\cdot\sqrt{36}$
$=6\sqrt{3}\approx 10.4$ miles
A passenger on the pool deck can see roughly 10.4 miles.

77. $v=\sqrt{20L}; L=245$
$v=\sqrt{20\cdot 245}=\sqrt{4900}=70$
The motorist was traveling 70 miles per hour, so he was speeding.

79. a. 41 in.

b. $h=2.9\sqrt{x}+20.1$
$=2.9\sqrt{50}+20.1$
≈ 40.6 in.
The estimate from part (a) describes the median height obtained from the formula quite well.

81. a. At birth we have $x=0$.
$y=2.9\sqrt{x}+36$
$=2.9\sqrt{0}+36$
$=2.9(0)+36$
$=36$
According to the model, the head circumference at birth is 36 cm.

b. At 9 months we have $x=9$.
$y=2.9\sqrt{x}+36$
$=2.9\sqrt{9}+36$
$=2.9(3)+36$
$=44.7$
According to the model, the head circumference at 9 months is 44.7 cm.

c. At 14 months we have $x=14$.
$y=2.9\sqrt{x}+36$
$=2.9\sqrt{14}+36$
≈ 46.9
According to the model, the head circumference at 14 months is roughly 46.9 cm.

d. The model describes healthy children.

83. The message is "Paige Fox is bad at math."

85. $R_f\sqrt{1-\left(\frac{v}{c}\right)^2}=R_f\sqrt{1-\left(\frac{0.9c}{c}\right)^2}$
$=R_f\sqrt{1-(0.9)^2}$
$=R_f\sqrt{0.19}$
$=0.44R_f$
If 100 weeks have passed for your friend on Earth, then you were gone for $0.44(100)=44$ weeks.

95. does not make sense; Explanations will vary. Sample explanation: The enemy will be charged, but it will take a very long time at the rate he is counting.

97. does not make sense; Explanations will vary. Sample explanation: The radicals can not be combined into one radical.
$2\sqrt{20}+4\sqrt{75}=2\sqrt{4\cdot 5}+4\sqrt{25\cdot 3}=4\sqrt{5}+20\sqrt{3}$

99. false; Changes to make the statement true will vary. A sample change is: $\sqrt{9}+\sqrt{16}=3+4=7\neq 25$

101. false; Changes to make the statement true will vary. A sample change is: $\frac{\sqrt{64}}{2}=\frac{8}{2}=4$

103. $-\pi\approx -3.14$
$-\pi > -3.5$

105. The square root is multiplied by $\sqrt{2}$.

107. $\sqrt{2}+\sqrt{\frac{1}{2}}=\sqrt{2}+\frac{\sqrt{1}}{\sqrt{2}}=\sqrt{2}+\frac{\sqrt{1}}{\sqrt{2}}\cdot\frac{\sqrt{2}}{\sqrt{2}}$
$=\sqrt{2}+\frac{\sqrt{2}}{2}=\frac{2\sqrt{2}}{2}+\frac{\sqrt{2}}{2}$
$=\frac{2\sqrt{2}+\sqrt{2}}{2}$
$=\frac{(2+1)\sqrt{2}}{2}=\frac{3\sqrt{2}}{2}$

Check Points 5.5

1. $\left\{-9,\ -1.3,\ 0,\ 0.\bar{3},\ \frac{\pi}{2},\ \sqrt{9},\ \sqrt{10}\right\}$

a. Natural numbers: $\sqrt{9}$ because $\sqrt{9}=3$

b. Whole numbers: 0, $\sqrt{9}$

c. Integers: −9, 0, $\sqrt{9}$

d. Rational numbers: −9, −1.3, 0, $0.\bar{3}$, $\sqrt{9}$

e. Irrational numbers: $\frac{\pi}{2}$, $\sqrt{10}$

f. Real numbers: All numbers in this set.

2. a. Associative property of multiplication

b. Commutative property of addition

c. Distributive property of multiplication over addition

d. Commutative property of multiplication

e. Identity property of addition

f. Inverse property of multiplication

3. a. Yes, the natural numbers are closed with respect to multiplication.

b. No, the integers are not closed with respect to division. Example: $3\div 5=0.6$ which is not an integer.

4. a. The entries in the body of the table are all elements of the set.

b. $(2\oplus 2)\oplus 3=2\oplus(2\oplus 3)$
$0\oplus 3=2\oplus 1$
$3=3$

c. The identity element is 0, because it does not change anything.

d. The inverse of 0 is 0, the inverse of 1 is 3, the inverse of 2 is 2, and the inverse of 3 is 1.

e. $1\oplus 3=3\oplus 1$
$0=0$

$3\oplus 2=2\oplus 3$
$1=1$

Concept and Vocabulary Check 5.5

1. rational; irrational
2. closure
3. $ab=ba$
4. $(a+b)+c=a+(b+c)$
5. $a(b+c)=ab+ac$
6. identity
7. identity; 1

8. multiplicative inverse (or reciprocal); multiplicative identity

9. 0; 1; 1

10. true

Exercise Set 5.5

1. $\left\{-9, -\frac{4}{5}, 0, 0.25, \sqrt{3}, 9.2, \sqrt{100}\right\}$

a. Natural numbers: $\sqrt{100}$ because $\sqrt{100} = 10$

b. Whole numbers: 0, $\sqrt{100}$

c. Integers: –9, 0, $\sqrt{100}$

d. Rational numbers: –9, $-\frac{4}{5}$, 0, 0.25, 9.2, $\sqrt{100}$

e. Irrational numbers: $\sqrt{3}$

f. Real numbers: All numbers in this set.

3. $\left\{-11, -\frac{5}{6}, 0, 0.75, \sqrt{5}, \pi, \sqrt{64}\right\}$

a. Natural numbers: $\sqrt{64}$ because $\sqrt{64} = 8$

b. Whole numbers: 0 and $\sqrt{64}$

c. Integers: −11, 0, $\sqrt{64}$

d. Rational numbers: −11, $-\frac{5}{6}$, 0, 0.75, $\sqrt{64}$

e. Irrational numbers: $\sqrt{5}$, π

f. Real numbers: All numbers in this set.

5. 0 is the only whole number that is not a natural number.

7. Answers will vary. Possible answer: 0.5

9. Answers will vary. Possible answer: 7

11. Answers will vary. Possible answer: $\sqrt{3}$

13. $3+(4+5)=3+(5+4)$

15. $9\cdot(6+2)=9\cdot(2+6)$

17. $(4\cdot5)\cdot3=4\cdot(5\cdot3)$

19. $7\cdot(4+5)=7\cdot4+7\cdot5$

21. $5(6+\sqrt{2})=5\cdot6+5\cdot\sqrt{2}=30+5\sqrt{2}$

23. $\sqrt{7}(3+\sqrt{2})=\sqrt{7}\cdot3+\sqrt{7}\cdot\sqrt{2}=3\sqrt{7}+\sqrt{14}$

25. $\sqrt{3}(5+\sqrt{3})=\sqrt{3}\cdot5+\sqrt{3}\cdot\sqrt{3}=5\sqrt{3}+\sqrt{9}$
$=5\sqrt{3}+3$

27. $\sqrt{6}(\sqrt{2}+\sqrt{6})=\sqrt{6}\cdot\sqrt{2}+\sqrt{6}\cdot\sqrt{6}$
$=\sqrt{12}+\sqrt{36}$
$=2\sqrt{3}+6$

29. Commutative property of addition.

31. Associative property of addition.

33. Commutative property of addition.

35. Distributive property of multiplication over addition.

37. Associative property of multiplication

39. Identity property of multiplication.

41. Inverse property of addition.

43. Inverse property of multiplication.

45. Answers will vary.
Example: $1-2=-1$

47. Answers will vary.
Example: $\frac{-2}{8}=-\frac{1}{4}$

49. Answers will vary.
Example: $\sqrt{5}\sqrt{5}=\sqrt{25}=5$

51. a. The entries in the body of the table are all elements of the set.

b. $(4\oplus6)\oplus7=4\oplus(6\oplus7)$
$2\oplus7=4\oplus5$
$1=1$

c. The identity element is 0.

d. The inverse of 0 is 0, the inverse of 1 is 7, the inverse of 2 is 6, the inverse of 3 is 5, the inverse of 4 is 4, the inverse of 5 is 3, the inverse of 6 is 2, and the inverse of 7 is 1.

e. $5 \oplus 6 = 6 \oplus 5$

$3 = 3$

$4 \oplus 7 = 7 \oplus 4$

$3 = 3$

53. true

55. false

57. $5(x+4)+3x$

$=(5x+20)+3x$ distributive property

$=(20+5x)+3x$ commutative property of addition

$=20+(5x+3x)$ associative property

$=20+(5+3)x$ distributive property

$=20+8x$

$=8x+20$ commutative property of addition

59. a. $c \triangle (d \square e) = (c \triangle d) \square (c \triangle e)$

$c \triangle c = b \square d$

$e = e$

b. distributive property

61. $d \triangle [d \square (d \triangle d)] = d \triangle [d \square e]$

$= d \triangle c$

$= b$

63. $x \square d = a$ is true if $x = c$.

65. $x \triangle (e \square d) = b$

$x \triangle c = b$ is true if $x = d$.

67. vampire

69. not a vampire

71. narcissistic; $3^3 + 7^3 + 0^3 = 370$

73. not narcissistic; $3^3 + 7^3 + 2^3 = 374$, not 372

75. a. distributive property

b. $\dfrac{D(A+1)}{24} = \dfrac{200(12+1)}{24}$

$= \dfrac{200(13)}{24}$

$= \dfrac{2600}{24}$

≈ 108 mg

$\dfrac{DA+D}{24} = \dfrac{200 \cdot 12 + 200}{24}$

$= \dfrac{2400+200}{24}$

$= \dfrac{2600}{24}$

≈ 108 mg

77. Sevenfold rotational symmetry

89. makes sense

91. makes sense

93. false; Changes to make the statement true will vary. A sample change is: All whole numbers are integers.

95. false; Changes to make the statement true will vary. A sample change is: Some irrational numbers are negative.

97. false; Changes to make the statement true will vary. A sample change is: $(24 \div 6) \div 2 \neq 24 \div (6 \div 2)$

99. false; Changes to make the statement true will vary. A sample change is: $2 \cdot a + 5 \neq 5 \cdot a + 2$

Check Points 5.6

1. a. $19^0 = 1$

b. $(3\pi)^0 = 1$

c. $(-14)^0 = 1$

d. $-14^0 = -1$

2. a. $9^{-2} = \dfrac{1}{9^2} = \dfrac{1}{81}$

b. $6^{-3} = \dfrac{1}{6^3} = \dfrac{1}{216}$

c. $12^{-1} = \dfrac{1}{12}$

3. a. $7.4\times10^9 = 7{,}400{,}000{,}000$

b. $3.017\times10^{-6} = 0.000003017$

4. a. $7{,}410{,}000{,}000 = 7.41\times10^9$

b. $0.000000092 = 9.2\times10^{-8}$

5. $$\begin{aligned}410\times10^7 &= (4.1\times10^2)\times10^7\\ &= 4.1\times(10^2\times10^7)\\ &= 4.1\times10^{2+7}\\ &= 4.1\times10^9\end{aligned}$$

6. $$\begin{aligned}(1.3\times10^7)\times(4\times10^{-2}) &= (1.3\times4)\times(10^7\times10^{-2})\\ &= 5.2\times10^{7+(-2)}\\ &= 5.2\times10^5\\ &= 520{,}000\end{aligned}$$

7. $$\begin{aligned}\frac{6.9\times10^{-8}}{3\times10^{-2}} &= \left(\frac{6.9}{3}\right)\times\left(\frac{10^{-8}}{10^{-2}}\right)\\ &= 2.3\times10^{-8-(-2)}\\ &= 2.3\times10^{-6}\\ &= 0.0000023\end{aligned}$$

8. a. $$\begin{aligned}&0.0036\times5{,}200{,}000\\ &= 3.6\times10^{-3}\times5.2\times10^6\\ &= (3.6\times5.2)\times(10^{-3}\times10^6)\\ &= 18.72\times10^3\\ &= 1.872\times10\times10^3\\ &= 1.872\times10^4\end{aligned}$$

b. Based on part (a):
$$\begin{aligned}&0.0036\times5{,}200{,}000\\ &= 1.872\times10^4\\ &= 18{,}720\end{aligned}$$

9. $$\frac{2.6\times10^{12}}{3.12\times10^8} = \left(\frac{2.6}{3.12}\right)\times\left(\frac{10^{12}}{10^8}\right) \approx 0.83\times10^4 = \$8300$$

Concept and Vocabulary Check 5.6

1. add
2. multiply
3. subtract
4. one
5. a number greater than or equal to 1 and less than 10; 10 to an integer power
6. false
7. false
8. false
9. true
10. false

Exercise Set 5.6

1. $2^2\cdot2^3 = 2^{2+3} = 2^5 = 32$

3. $4\cdot4^2 = 4^1\cdot4^2 = 4^{1+2} = 4^3 = 64$

5. $(2^2)^3 = 2^{2\cdot3} = 2^6 = 64$

7. $(1^4)^5 = 1^{4\cdot5} = 1^{20} = 1$

9. $\frac{4^7}{4^5} = 4^{7-5} = 4^2 = 16$

11. $\frac{2^8}{2^4} = 2^{8-4} = 2^4 = 16$

13. $3^0 = 1$

15. $(-3)^0 = 1$

17. $-3^0 = -1$

19. $2^{-2} = \frac{1}{2^2} = \frac{1}{4}$

21. $4^{-3} = \frac{1}{4^3} = \frac{1}{64}$

23. $2^{-5}=\frac{1}{2^5}=\frac{1}{32}$

25. $3^4\cdot 3^{-2}=3^{4+(-2)}=3^2=9$

27. $3^{-3}\cdot 3=3^{-3}\cdot 3^1=3^{-3+1}=3^{-2}=\frac{1}{3^2}=\frac{1}{9}$

29. $\frac{2^3}{2^7}=2^{3-7}=2^{-4}=\frac{1}{2^4}=\frac{1}{16}$

31. $\left(x^5x^3\right)^{-2}=\left(x^8\right)^{-2}=\frac{1}{\left(x^8\right)^2}=\frac{1}{x^{16}}$

33. $\frac{\left(x^3\right)^4}{\left(x^2\right)^7}=\frac{x^{12}}{x^{14}}=\frac{1}{x^2}$

35. $\left(\frac{x^5}{x^2}\right)^{-4}=\left(x^3\right)^{-4}=x^{-12}=\frac{1}{x^{12}}$

37. $\frac{2x^5\cdot 3x}{15x^6}=\frac{6x^6}{15x^6}=\frac{6}{15}=\frac{2}{5}$

39. $\left(-2x^3y^{-4}\right)\left(3x^{-1}y\right)=-6x^2y^{-3}=-\frac{6x^2}{y^3}$

41. $\frac{30x^2y^5}{-6x^8y^{-3}}=-\frac{5y^8}{x^6}$

43. $2.7\times10^2=270$

45. $9.12\times10^5=912{,}000$

47. $8\times10^7=8.0\times10^7=80{,}000{,}000$

49. $1\times10^5=1.0\times10^5=100{,}000$

51. $7.9\times10^{-1}=0.79$

53. $2.15\times10^{-2}=0.0215$

55. $7.86\times10^{-4}=0.000786$

57. $3.18\times10^{-6}=0.00000318$

59. $370=3.7\times10^2$

61. $3600=3.6\times10^3$

63. $32{,}000=3.2\times10^4$

65. $220{,}000{,}000=2.2\times10^8$

67. $0.027=2.7\times10^{-2}$

69. $0.0037=3.7\times10^{-3}$

71. $0.00000293=2.93\times10^{-6}$

73. $820\times10^5=\left(8.2\times10^2\right)\times10^5=8.2\times10^7$

75. $0.41\times10^6=\left(4.1\times10^{-1}\right)\times10^6=4.1\times10^5$

77. $2100\times10^{-9}=\left(2.1\times10^3\right)\times10^{-9}=2.1\times10^{-6}$

79. $$\begin{aligned}(2\times10^3)(3\times10^2)&=(2\times3)\times(10^{3+2})\\&=6\times10^5\\&=600{,}000\end{aligned}$$

81. $$\begin{aligned}(2\times10^9)(3\times10^{-5})&=(2\times3)\times(10^{9-5})\\&=6\times10^4\\&=60{,}000\end{aligned}$$

83. $$\begin{aligned}(4.1\times10^2)(3\times10^{-4})&=(4.1\times3)\times(10^{2-4})\\&=12.3\times10^{-2}\\&=1.23\times10\times10^{-2}\\&=1.23\times10^{-1}\\&=0.123\end{aligned}$$

85. $$\begin{aligned}\frac{12\times10^6}{4\times10^2}&=\left(\frac{12}{4}\right)\times\left(\frac{10^6}{10^2}\right)\\&=3\times10^{6-2}\\&=3\times10^4\\&=30{,}000\end{aligned}$$

87. $$\begin{aligned}\frac{15\times10^4}{5\times10^{-2}}&=\left(\frac{15}{5}\right)\times\left(\frac{10^4}{10^{-2}}\right)\\&=3\times10^{4-(-2)}\\&=3\times10^6\\&=3{,}000{,}000\end{aligned}$$

89. $\dfrac{6\times10^3}{2\times10^5}=\left(\dfrac{6}{2}\right)\times\left(\dfrac{10^3}{10^5}\right)$
$=3\times10^{3-5}$
$=3\times10^{-2}$
$=0.03$

91. $\dfrac{6.3\times10^{-6}}{3\times10^{-3}}=\left(\dfrac{6.3}{3}\right)\times\left(\dfrac{10^{-6}}{10^{-3}}\right)$
$=2.1\times10^{-6-(-3)}$
$=2.1\times10^{-3}$
$=0.0021$

93. $(82{,}000{,}000)(3{,}000{,}000{,}000)$
$=(8.2\times10^7)(3.0\times10^9)$
$=(8.2\times3.0)\times(10^{7+9})$
$=24.6\times10^{16}$
$=2.46\times10\times10^{16}$
$=2.46\times10^{17}$

95. $(0.0005)(6{,}000{,}000)$
$=(5.0\times10^{-4})(6.0\times10^6)$
$=(5.0\times6.0)(10^{-4+6})$
$=30\times10^2$
$=3\times10\times10^2$
$=3\times10^3$

97. $\dfrac{9{,}500{,}000}{500}=\dfrac{9.5\times10^6}{5\times10^2}$
$=\left(\dfrac{9.5}{5}\right)\times(10^{6-2})$
$=1.9\times10^4$

99. $\dfrac{0.00008}{200}=\dfrac{8\times10^{-5}}{2\times10^2}$
$=\left(\dfrac{8}{2}\right)\times(10^{-5-2})$
$=4\times10^{-7}$

101. $\dfrac{480{,}000{,}000{,}000}{0.00012}=\dfrac{4.8\times10^{11}}{1.2\times10^{-4}}$
$=\left(\dfrac{4.8}{1.2}\right)\times(10^{11-(-4)})$
$=4\times10^{15}$

103. $\dfrac{2^4}{2^5}+\dfrac{3^3}{3^5}=\dfrac{1}{2}+\dfrac{1}{3^2}$
$=\dfrac{1}{2}+\dfrac{1}{9}$
$=\dfrac{11}{18}$

105. $\dfrac{2^6}{2^4}-\dfrac{5^4}{5^6}=\dfrac{2^2}{1}-\dfrac{1}{5^2}$
$=4-\dfrac{1}{25}$
$=\dfrac{99}{25}$
$=3\dfrac{24}{25}$

107. $\dfrac{(5\times10^3)(1.2\times10^{-4})}{(2.4\times10^2)}=2.5\times10^{-3}$

109. $\dfrac{(1.6\times10^4)(7.2\times10^{-3})}{(3.6\times10^8)(4\times10^{-3})}=0.8\times10^{-4}=8\times10^{-5}$

111. **a.** 2.17×10^{12}

b. 3.09×10^8

c. $\dfrac{2.17\times10^{12}}{3.09\times10^8}=\dfrac{2.17}{3.09}\times\dfrac{10^{12}}{10^8}$
$\approx0.702\times10^4$
$=7.02\times10^3$
$=7020$
\$7020 per American

113. $1340\times10^6\cdot7.90=1.34\times10^9\cdot7.9$
$=1.34\cdot7.9\times10^9$
$=10.586\times10^9$
$=1.0586\times10^{10}$
Box-office receipts were $\$1.0586\times10^{10}$ in 2010.

115. $5.3\times10^{-23}\cdot20{,}000=5.3\times10^{-23}\cdot2\times10^4$
$=5.3\cdot2\times10^{-23}\cdot10^4$
$=10.6\times10^{-19}$
$=1.06\times10^1\cdot10^{-19}$
$=1.06\times10^{-18}$
The mass is 1.06×10^{-18} gram.

117. $3.2\times10^7\cdot127=3.2\times10^7\cdot1.27\times10^2$
$=3.2\cdot1.27\times10^7\cdot10^2$
$=4.064\times10^9$
Americans eat 4.064×10^9 chickens per year.

129. makes sense

131. does not make sense; Explanations will vary. Sample explanation: Tax collections is the U.S. exceed \$1 trillion, where as this number is only about \$20 million.

133. false; Changes to make the statement true will vary. A sample change is: $4^{-2}>4^{-3}$.

135. false; Changes to make the statement true will vary. A sample change is: $(-2)^4\neq2^{-4}$ because $16\neq\frac{1}{16}$.

137. false; Changes to make the statement true will vary. A sample change is: $534.7\neq5347$.

139. false; Changes to make the statement true will vary. A sample change is: $(7\times10^5)+(2\times10^{-3})=700{,}000.002$.

141. Answers will vary. Possible answer:
$2.0\times10^0=2.0\times1=2$
There is no advantage here since $10^0=1$.

Check Points 5.7

1. 100, 100 + 20 = 120, 120 + 20 = 140, 140 + 20 = 160, 160 + 20 = 180, 180 + 20 = 200
100, 120, 140, 160, 180, and 200

2. 8, 8 – 3 = 5, 5 – 3 = 2, 2 – 3 = –1, –1 – 3 = –4, –4 – 3 = –7
8, 5, 2, –1, –4, and –7

3. $a_n=a_1+(n-1)d$
$a_9=6+(9-1)(-5)$
$=6+8(-5)$
$=6-40$
$=-34$

4. a. $a_n = a_1 + (n-1)d$

$a_n = 16 + (n-1)(0.35)$

$= 16 + 0.35n - 0.35$

$= 0.35n + 15.65$

b. $a_n = 0.35n + 15.65$

$= 0.35(21) + 15.65$

$= 23$

23% of the U.S. population is projected to be Latino in 2030.

5. $12,\ 12\left(-\frac{1}{2}\right) = -6,\ -6\left(-\frac{1}{2}\right) = 3,\ 3\left(-\frac{1}{2}\right) = -\frac{3}{2},$

$-\frac{3}{2}\left(-\frac{1}{2}\right) = \frac{3}{4},\ \frac{3}{4}\left(-\frac{1}{2}\right) = -\frac{3}{8}$

$12,\ -6,\ 3,\ -\frac{3}{2},\ \frac{3}{4},\ -\frac{3}{8}$

6. $a_n = a_1 r^{n-1}$ with $a_1 = 5,\ r = -3,$ and $n = 7$

$a_7 = 5(-3)^{7-1} = 5(-3)^6 = 5(729) = 3645$

7. $a_n = a_1 r^{n-1}$ with $a_1 = 3$ and $r = \frac{6}{3} = 2$. Thus $a_n = 3(2)^{n-1}$

$a_8 = 3(2)^{8-1} = 3(2)^7 = 3(128) = 384$

Concept and Vocabulary Check 5.7

1. arithmetic; common difference

2. $a_n = a_1 + (n-1)d$; the first term; the common difference

3. geometric; common ratio

4. $a_n = a_1 r^{n-1}$; the first term; the common ratio

Exercise Set 5.7

1. 8, 8 + 2 = 10, 10 + 2 = 12, 12 + 2 = 14, 14 + 2 = 16, 16 + 2 = 18
8, 10, 12, 14, 16, and 18

3. 200, 200 + 20 = 220, 220 + 20 = 240, 240 + 20 = 260, 260 + 20 = 280, 280 + 20 = 300
200, 220, 240, 260, 280, and 300

5. –7, –7 + 4 = –3, –3 + 4 = 1, 1 + 4 = 5, 5 + 4 = 9, 9 + 4 = 13
–7, –3, 1, 5, 9, and 13

7. –400, –400 + 300 = –100, –100 + 300 = 200, 200 + 300 = 500, 500 + 300 = 800, 800 + 300 = 1100
–400, –100, 200, 500, 800, and 1100

9. 7, 7 – 3 = 4, 4 – 3 = 1, 1 – 3 = –2, –2 – 3 = –5, –5 – 3 = –8
7, 4, 1, –2, –5, and –8

11. 200, 200 – 60 = 140, 140 – 60 = 80, 80 – 60 = 20, 20 – 60 = –40, –40 – 60 = –100
200, 140, 80, 20, –40, and –100

13. $\frac{5}{2}, \frac{5}{2}+\frac{1}{2}=\frac{6}{2}=3, \frac{6}{2}+\frac{1}{2}=\frac{7}{2}, \frac{7}{2}+\frac{1}{2}=\frac{8}{2}=4, \frac{8}{2}+\frac{1}{2}=\frac{9}{2}, \frac{9}{2}+\frac{1}{2}=\frac{10}{2}=5$
$\frac{5}{2}, 3, \frac{7}{2}, 4, \frac{9}{2}$, and 5

15. $\frac{3}{2}, \frac{6}{4}+\frac{1}{4}=\frac{7}{4}, \frac{7}{4}+\frac{1}{4}=\frac{8}{4}=2, \frac{8}{4}+\frac{1}{4}=\frac{9}{4}, \frac{9}{4}+\frac{1}{4}=\frac{10}{4}=\frac{5}{2}, \frac{10}{4}+\frac{1}{4}=\frac{11}{4}$
$\frac{3}{2}, \frac{7}{4}, 2, \frac{9}{4}, \frac{5}{2}$, and $\frac{11}{4}$

17. 4.25, 4.25 + 0.3 = 4.55, 4.55 + 0.3 = 4.85, 4.85 + 0.3 = 5.15, 5.15 + 0.3 = 5.45, 5.45 + 0.3 = 5.75
4.25, 4.55, 4.85, 5.15, 5.45, and 5.75

19. 4.5, 4.5 – 0.75 = 3.75, 3.75 – 0.75 = 3, 3 – 0.75 = 2.25, 2.25 – 0.75 = 1.5, 1.5 – 0.75 = 0.75
4.5, 3.75, 3, 2.25, 1.5, and 0.75

21. $a_1 = 13, d = 4$
$$\begin{aligned} a_6 &= 13+(6-1)(4) \\ &= 13+5(4) \\ &= 13+20 \\ &= 33 \end{aligned}$$

23. $a_1 = 7, d = 5$
$$\begin{aligned} a_{50} &= 7+(50-1)(5) \\ &= 7+49(5) \\ &= 7+245 \\ &= 252 \end{aligned}$$

25. $a_1 = -5, d = 9$
$$\begin{aligned} a_9 &= -5+(9-1)(9) \\ &= -5+8(9) \\ &= -5+72 \\ &= 67 \end{aligned}$$

27. $a_1 = -40, d = 5$
$$\begin{aligned} a_{200} &= -40+(200-1)(5) \\ &= -40+199(5) \\ &= -40+995 \\ &= 955 \end{aligned}$$

29. $a_1 = 8, d = -10$
$$\begin{aligned} a_{10} &= 8 + (10-1)(-10) \\ &= 8 + 9(-10) \\ &= 8 - 90 \\ &= -82 \end{aligned}$$

31. $a_1 = 35, d = -3$
$$\begin{aligned} a_{60} &= 35 + (60-1)(-3) \\ &= 35 + 59(-3) \\ &= 35 + (-177) \\ &= -142 \end{aligned}$$

33. $a_1 = 12, d = -5$
$$\begin{aligned} a_{12} &= 12 + (12-1)(-5) \\ &= 12 + 11(-5) \\ &= 12 + (-55) \\ &= -43 \end{aligned}$$

35. $a_1 = -70, d = -2$
$$\begin{aligned} a_{90} &= -70 + (90-1)(-2) \\ &= -70 + 89(-2) \\ &= -70 + (-178) \\ &= -248 \end{aligned}$$

37. $a_1 = 6, d = \frac{1}{2}$
$$\begin{aligned} a_{12} &= 6 + (12-1)\left(\frac{1}{2}\right) \\ &= 6 + 11\left(\frac{1}{2}\right) \\ &= \frac{12}{2} + \frac{11}{2} \\ &= \frac{23}{2} \end{aligned}$$

39. $a_1 = 14, d = -0.25$
$$\begin{aligned} a_{50} &= 14 + (50-1)(-0.25) \\ &= 14 + 49(-0.25) \\ &= 14 + (-12.25) \\ &= 1.75 \end{aligned}$$

41. $a_n = a_1 + (n-1)d$ with $a_1 = 1, d = 4$
$$\begin{aligned} a_n &= 1 + (n-1)4 \\ &= 1 + 4n - 4 \\ &= 4n - 3 \end{aligned}$$
Thus $a_{20} = 4(20) - 3 = 77$.

43. $a_n = a_1 + (n-1)d$ with $a_1 = 7, d = -4$
$$\begin{aligned} a_n &= 7 + (n-1)(-4) \\ &= 7 - 4n + 4 \\ &= -4n + 11 \end{aligned}$$
Thus $a_{20} = -4(20) + 11 = -69$.

45. $a_n = a_1 + (n-1)d$ with $a_1 = 9, d = 2$
$$\begin{aligned} a_n &= 9 + (n-1)2 \\ &= 9 + 2n - 2 \\ &= 2n + 7 \end{aligned}$$
Thus $a_{20} = 2(20) + 7 = 47$.

47. $a_n = a_1 + (n-1)d$ with $a_1 = -20, d = -4$
$$\begin{aligned} a_n &= -20 + (n-1)(-4) \\ &= -20 - 4n + 4 \\ &= -4n - 16 \end{aligned}$$
Thus $a_{20} = -4(20) - 16 = -96$.

49. $a_1 = 4, r = 2$
$4, 4 \cdot 2 = 8, 8 \cdot 2 = 16, 16 \cdot 2 = 32, 32 \cdot 2 = 64,$
$64 \cdot 2 = 128$
4, 8, 16, 32, 64, 128

51. $a_1 = 1000, r = 1$
$1000, 1000 \cdot 1 = 1000, 1000 \cdot 1 = 1000, \ldots$
1000, 1000, 1000, 1000, 1000, 1000

53. $a_1 = 3, r = -2$
3, 3(–2) = –6, –6(–2) = 12, 12(–2)
= –24, –24(–2) = 48, 48(–2) = –96
3, –6, 12, –24, 48, –96

55. $a_1 = 10, r = -4$
10, 10(–4) = –40, –40(–4) = 160,
160(–4) = –640, –640(–4) = 2560,
2560(–4) = –10,240
10, –40, 160, –640, 2560,and –10,240

57. $a_1 = 2000, r = -1$
2000, 2000(–1) = –2000,
–2000(–1) = 2000, ...
2000, –2000, 2000, –2000, 2000, –2000

59. $a_1 = -2, r = -3$
–2, –2(–3) = 6, 6(–3) = –18, –18(–3) = 54,
54(–3) = –162, –162(–3) = 486
–2, 6, –18, 54, –162, 486

61. $a_1 = -6,\ r = -5$
$-6,\ -6(-5) = 30,\ 30(-5) = -150,$
$-150(-5) = 750,\ 750(-5) = -3750,$
$-3750(-5) = 18{,}750$
$-6,\ 30,\ -150,\ 750,\ -3750,\ 18750$

63. $a_1 = \frac{1}{4},\ r = 2$
$\frac{1}{4},\ \frac{1}{4}\cdot 2 = \frac{1}{2},\ \frac{1}{2}\cdot 2 = 1,\ 1\cdot 2 = 2,\ 2\cdot 2 = 4,$
$4\cdot 2 = 8$
$\frac{1}{4},\ \frac{1}{2},\ 1,\ 2,\ 4,\ 8$

65. $a_1 = \frac{1}{4},\ r = \frac{1}{2}$
$\frac{1}{4},\ \frac{1}{4}\cdot\frac{1}{2} = \frac{1}{8},\ \frac{1}{8}\cdot\frac{1}{2} = \frac{1}{16},\ \frac{1}{16}\cdot\frac{1}{2} = \frac{1}{32},$
$\frac{1}{32}\cdot\frac{1}{2} = \frac{1}{64},\ \frac{1}{64}\cdot\frac{1}{2} = \frac{1}{128}$
$\frac{1}{4},\ \frac{1}{8},\ \frac{1}{16},\ \frac{1}{32},\ \frac{1}{64},\ \frac{1}{128}$

67. $a_1 = -\frac{1}{16},\ r = -4$
$-\frac{1}{16},\ -\frac{1}{16}\cdot(-4) = \frac{1}{4},\ \frac{1}{4}\cdot(-4) = -1,$
$-1(-4) = 4,\ 4(-4) = -16,\ -16(-4) = 64$
$-\frac{1}{16},\ \frac{1}{4},\ -1,\ 4,\ -16,\ 64$

69. $a_1 = 2,\ r = 0.1$
$2,\ 2(0.1) = 0.2,\ 0.2(0.1) = 0.02,$
$0.02(0.1) = 0.002,\ 0.002(0.1) = 0.0002,$
$0.0002(0.1) = 0.00002.$
$2,\ 0.2,\ 0.02,\ 0.002,\ 0.0002,\ 0.00002$

71. $a_1 = 4,\ r = 2$
$$\begin{aligned} a_5 &= 4(2)^{7-1} \\ &= 4(2)^6 \\ &= 4(64) \\ &= 256 \end{aligned}$$

73. $a_1 = 2,\ r = 3$
$$\begin{aligned} a_{20} &= 2(3)^{20-1} \\ &= 2(3)^{19} \\ &= 2{,}324{,}522{,}934 \\ &\approx 2.32\times 10^9 \end{aligned}$$

75. $a_1 = 50,\ r = 1$
$$\begin{aligned} a_{100} &= 50(1)^{100-1} \\ &= 50(1)^{99} \\ &= 50 \end{aligned}$$

77. $a_1 = 5,\ r = -2$
$$\begin{aligned} a_7 &= 5(-2)^{7-1} \\ &= 5(-2)^6 \\ &= 320 \end{aligned}$$

79. $a_1 = 2,\ r = -1$
$$\begin{aligned} a_{30} &= 2(-1)^{30-1} \\ &= 2(-1)^{29} \\ &= -2 \end{aligned}$$

81. $a_1 = -2,\ r = -3$
$$\begin{aligned} a_6 &= -2(-3)^{6-1} \\ &= -2(-3)^5 \\ &= 486 \end{aligned}$$

83. $a_1 = 6,\ r = \frac{1}{2}$
$$\begin{aligned} a_8 &= 6\left(\frac{1}{2}\right)^{8-1} \\ &= 6\left(\frac{1}{2}\right)^7 \\ &= \frac{6}{128} \\ &= \frac{3}{64} \end{aligned}$$

85. $a_1 = 18,\ r = -\frac{1}{3}$
$$\begin{aligned} a_6 &= 18\left(-\frac{1}{3}\right)^{6-1} \\ &= 18\left(-\frac{1}{3}\right)^5 \\ &= -\frac{18}{243} \\ &= -\frac{2}{27} \end{aligned}$$

87. $a_1 = 1000,\ r = -\dfrac{1}{2}$

$$a_{40} = 1000\left(-\frac{1}{2}\right)^{40-1}$$
$$= 1000\left(-\frac{1}{2}\right)^{39}$$
$$\approx -1.82\times 10^{-9}$$

89. $a_1 = 1{,}000{,}000,\ r = 0.1$

$$a_8 = 1{,}000{,}000(0.1)^{8-1}$$
$$= 1{,}000{,}000(0.1)^7$$
$$= 0.1$$

91. $a_n = a_1 r^{n-1}$ with $a_1 = 3$ and $r = \dfrac{12}{3} = 4$.

Thus $a_n = 3(4)^{n-1}$

$a_7 = 3(4)^{7-1} = 3(4)^6 = 3(4096) = 12{,}288$

93. $a_n = a_1 r^{n-1}$ with $a_1 = 18$ and $r = \dfrac{6}{18} = \dfrac{1}{3}$.

Thus $a_n = 18\left(\dfrac{1}{3}\right)^{n-1}$

$a_7 = 18\left(\dfrac{1}{3}\right)^{7-1} = 18\left(\dfrac{1}{3}\right)^6 = 18\left(\dfrac{1}{729}\right) = \dfrac{18}{729} = \dfrac{2}{81}$

95. $a_n = a_1 r^{n-1}$ with $a_1 = 1.5$ and $r = \dfrac{-3}{1.5} = -2$.

Thus $a_n = 1.5(-2)^{n-1}$

$a_7 = 1.5(-2)^{7-1} = 1.5(-2)^6 = 1.5(64) = 96$

97. $a_n = a_1 r^{n-1}$ with $a_1 = 0.0004$ and $r = \dfrac{-0.004}{0.0004} = -10$. Thus $a_n = 0.0004(-10)^{n-1}$

$a_7 = 0.0004(-10)^{7-1} = 0.0004(-10)^6 = 0.0004(1{,}000{,}000) = 400$

99. The common difference of the arithmetic sequence is 4.
$2 + 4 = 6,\ 6 + 4 = 10,\ 10 + 4 = 14,$
$14 + 4 = 18,\ 18 + 4 = 22$
2, 6, 10, 14, 18, 22, …

101. The common ratio of the geometric sequence is 3.
$5\cdot 3 = 15,\ 15\cdot 3 = 45,\ 45\cdot 3 = 135,$ 5, 15, 45, 135, 405, 1215, …
$135\cdot 3 = 405,\ 405\cdot 3 = 1215$

103. The common difference of the arithmetic sequence is 5.
$-7 + 5 = -2,\ -2 + 5 = 3,\ 3 + 5 = 8,$
$8 + 5 = 13,\ 13 + 5 = 18.$
−7, −2, 3, 8, 13, 18, …

105. The common ratio of the geometric sequence is $\frac{1}{2}$.

$3\cdot\frac{1}{2}=\frac{3}{2}$, $\frac{3}{2}\cdot\frac{1}{2}=\frac{3}{4}$, $\frac{3}{4}\cdot\frac{1}{2}=\frac{3}{8}$, $\frac{3}{8}\cdot\frac{1}{2}=\frac{3}{16}$

$\frac{3}{16}\cdot\frac{1}{2}=\frac{3}{32}$

$3, \frac{3}{2}, \frac{3}{4}, \frac{3}{8}, \frac{3}{16}, \frac{3}{32}, \ldots$

107. The common difference of the arithmetic sequence is $\frac{1}{2}$.

$\frac{1}{2}+\frac{1}{2}=1$, $1+\frac{1}{2}=\frac{3}{2}$, $\frac{3}{2}+\frac{1}{2}=2$, $2+\frac{1}{2}=\frac{5}{2}$,

$\frac{5}{2}+\frac{1}{2}=3$

$\frac{1}{2}, 1, \frac{3}{2}, 2, \frac{5}{2}, 3, \ldots$

109. The common ratio of the geometric sequence is –1.

$7(-1)=-7$, $-7(-1)=7$, $7(-1)=-7$,

$-7(-1)=7$, $7(-1)=-7$

$7, -7, 7, -7, 7, -7, \ldots$

111. The common difference of the arithmetic sequence is –14.

$7-14=-7$, $-7-14=-21$, $-21-14=-35$, $-35-14=-49$, $-49-14=-63$

$7, -7, -21, -35, -49, -63, \ldots$

113. The common ratio of the geometric sequence is $\sqrt{5}$.

$\sqrt{5}\cdot\sqrt{5}=5$, $5\cdot\sqrt{5}=5\sqrt{5}$, $5\sqrt{5}\cdot\sqrt{5}=25$,

$25\cdot\sqrt{5}=25\sqrt{5}$, $25\sqrt{5}\cdot\sqrt{5}=125$

$\sqrt{5}, 5, 5\sqrt{5}, 25, 25\sqrt{5}, 125, \ldots$

115. arithmetic; use $S_n=\frac{n}{2}(a_1+a_n)$

$$S_{10}=\frac{10}{2}(4+58)=310$$

117. geometric; use $S_n=\frac{a_1(1-r^n)}{1-r}$

$$S_{10}=\frac{2(1-3^{10})}{1-3}=59{,}048$$

119. geometric; use $S_n=\frac{a_1(1-r^n)}{1-r}$

$$S_{10}=\frac{3\left(1-(-2)^{10}\right)}{1-(-2)}=-1023$$

121. arithmetic; use $S_n = \frac{n}{2}(a_1 + a_n)$

$$S_{10} = \frac{10}{2}(-10+26) = 80$$

123. $1+2+3+4+\cdots+100$

$$S_{100} = \frac{100}{2}(1+100) = 5050$$

125. a.
$$\begin{aligned} a_n &= a_1 + (n-1)d \\ a_n &= 18.4 + (n-1)0.6 \\ &= 18.4 + 0.6n - 0.6 \\ &= 0.6n + 17.8 \end{aligned}$$

b.
$$\begin{aligned} a_n &= 0.6n + 17.8 \\ &= 0.6(30) + 17.8 \\ &= 35.8 \end{aligned}$$

The percentage is projected to be 35.8% in 2019.

127. Company A: $a_{10} = 24000 + (10-1)1600 = 38,400$
Company B: $b_{10} = 28000 + (10-1)1000 = 37,000$
Company A will pay $1400 more in year 10.

129. $a_1 = 1,\ r = 2$

$$\begin{aligned} a_{15} &= 1(2)^{15-1} \\ &= 2^{14} \\ &= 16,384 \end{aligned}$$

On the 15th day you will put aside $16,384.

131.
$$\begin{aligned} a_7 &= \$3,000,000(1.04)^{7-1} \\ &\approx \$3,795,957 \text{ salary in year 7.} \end{aligned}$$

133. a.
$$r_{2000 \text{ to } 2001} = \frac{34.21}{33.87} \approx 1.01$$
$$r_{2001 \text{ to } 2002} = \frac{34.55}{34.21} \approx 1.01$$
$$r_{2002 \text{ to } 2003} = \frac{34.90}{34.55} \approx 1.01$$
$$r_{2003 \text{ to } 2004} = \frac{35.25}{34.90} \approx 1.01$$
$$r_{2004 \text{ to } 2005} = \frac{35.60}{35.25} \approx 1.01$$
$$r_{2005 \text{ to } 2006} = \frac{36.00}{35.60} \approx 1.01$$
$$r_{2006 \text{ to } 2007} = \frac{36.36}{36.00} \approx 1.01$$
$$r_{2007 \text{ to } 2008} = \frac{36.72}{36.36} \approx 1.01$$
$$r_{2008 \text{ to } 2009} = \frac{37.09}{36.72} \approx 1.01$$
$$r_{2009 \text{ to } 2010} = \frac{37.25}{37.09} \approx 1.01$$

r is approximately 1.01 for all but one division.

b.
$$a_n = a_1 r^{n-1}$$
$$a_n = 33.87(1.01)^{n-1}$$

c. Since year 2020 is the 21th term, find a_{21}.

$$a_n = 33.87(1.01)^{n-1}$$
$$a_{21} = 33.87(1.01)^{21-1} \approx 41.33$$

The population of California will be approximately 41.33 million in 2020.

143. makes sense

145. makes sense

147. false; Changes to make the statement true will vary. A sample change is: The sequence does not have a common difference and is therefore not an arithmetic sequence.

149. true

151. false; Changes to make the statement true will vary. A sample change is: Adjacent terms of a geometric sequence have a common ratio.

153. true

Chapter 5 Review Exercises

1. 238,632
2: Yes; The last digit is 2.
3: Yes; The sum of the digits is 24, which is divisible by 3.
4: Yes; The last two digits form 32, which is divisible by 4.
5: No; The last number does not end in 0 or 5.
6: Yes; The number is divisible by both 2 and 3.
8: Yes; The last three digits form 632, which is divisible by 8.
9: No; The sum of the digits is 24, which is not divisible by 9.
10: No; the last digit is not 0.
12: Yes; The number is divisible by both 3 and 4.
The number is divisible by 2, 3, 4, 6, 8, 12.

2. 421,153,470
2: Yes; The last digit is 0.
3: Yes; The sum of the digits is 27, which is divisible by 3.
4: No; The last two digits form 70, which is not divisible by 4.
5: Yes; The number ends in 0.
6: Yes; The number is divisible by both 2 and 3.
8: No; The last three digits form 470, which is not divisible by 8.
9: Yes; The sum of the digits is 27, which is divisible by 9.
10: Yes; The number ends in 0.
12: No; The number is not divisible by both 3 and 4.
The number is divisible by 2, 3, 5, 6, 9, 10.

3. $705 = 3 \cdot 5 \cdot 47$

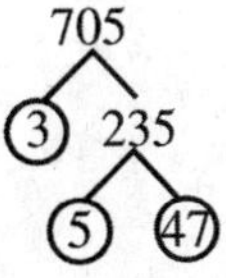

4. $960 = 2^6 \cdot 3 \cdot 5$

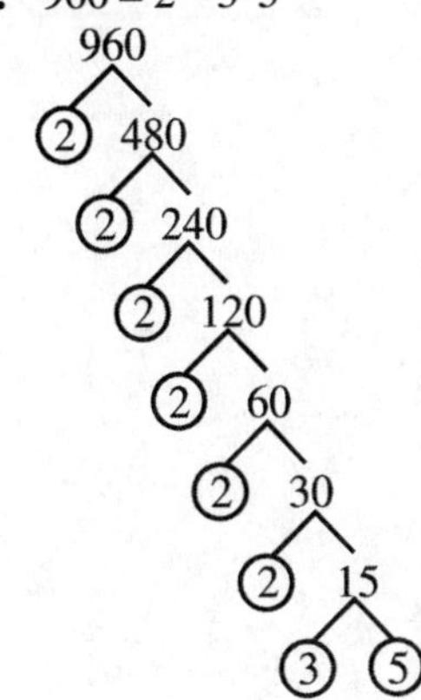

5. $6825 = 3 \cdot 5^2 \cdot 7 \cdot 13$

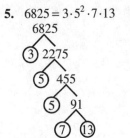

6825
3 2275
5 455
5 91
7 13

6. $30 = 2 \cdot 3 \cdot 5$

$48 = 2^4 \cdot 3$
Greatest Common Divisor = $2 \cdot 3 = 6$
Least Common Multiple = $2^4 \cdot 3 \cdot 5 = 240$

7. $36 = 2^2 \cdot 3^2$

$150 = 2 \cdot 3 \cdot 5^2$
Greatest Common Divisor = $2 \cdot 3 = 6$
Least Common Multiple = $2^2 \cdot 3^2 \cdot 5^2 = 900$

8. $216 = 2^3 \cdot 3^3$

$254 = 2 \cdot 127$
Greatest Common Divisor = 2
Least Common Multiple = $2^3 \cdot 3^3 \cdot 127$
$= 27,432$

9. $24 = 2^3 \cdot 3$

$60 = 2^2 \cdot 3 \cdot 5$

Greatest Common Divisor = $2^2 \cdot 3 = 12$
There can be 12 people placed on each team.

10. $42 = 2 \cdot 3 \cdot 7$

$56 = 2^3 \cdot 7$
Least Common Multiple = $2^3 \cdot 3 \cdot 7 = 168$
$168 \div 60 = 2.8$ or 2 hours and 48 minutes. They will begin again at 11:48 A.M.

11. $-93 < 17$ because -93 is to the left of 17 on the number line.

12. $-2 > -200$ because -2 is to the right of -200 on the number line.

13. $|-860| = 860$ because -860 is 860 units from 0 on the number line.

14. $|53| = 53$ because 53 is 53 units from 0 on the number line.

15. $|0| = 0$ because 0 is 0 units from 0 on the number line.

16. $8 + (-11) = -3$

17. $-6 + (-5) = -11$

18. $-7 - 8 = -7 + (-8) = -15$

19. $-7 - (-8) = -7 + 8 = 1$

20. $(-9)(-11) = 99$

21. $5(-3) = -15$

22. $\frac{-36}{-4} = 9$

23. $\frac{20}{-5} = -4$

24. $-40 \div 5 \cdot 2 = -8 \cdot 2 = -16$

25. $-6 + (-2) \cdot 5 = -6 + (-10) = -16$

26. $6 - 4(-3 + 2) = 6 - 4(-1) = 6 + 4 = 10$

27.
$$\begin{aligned} 28 \div (2 - 4^2) &= 28 \div (2 - 16) \\ &= 28 \div (-14) \\ &= -2 \end{aligned}$$

28.
$$\begin{aligned} 36 - 24 \div 4 \cdot 3 - 1 &= 36 - 6 \cdot 3 - 1 \\ &= 36 - 18 - 1 \\ &= 18 - 1 \\ &= 17 \end{aligned}$$

29. $-57 - (-715) = -57 + 715 = \$658$ billion

30. $40 = 2^3 \cdot 5$

$75 = 3 \cdot 5^2$

Greatest Common Divisor is 5.

$\frac{40}{75} = \frac{40 \div 5}{75 \div 5} = \frac{8}{15}$

31. $36 = 2^2 \cdot 3^2$

$150 = 2 \cdot 3 \cdot 5^2$

Greatest Common Divisor is $2 \cdot 3$ or 6.

$\frac{36}{150} = \frac{36 \div 6}{150 \div 6} = \frac{6}{25}$

32. $165 = 3 \cdot 5 \cdot 11$

$180 = 2^2 \cdot 3^2 \cdot 5$

Greatest Common Divisor is $3 \cdot 5$ or 15.

$\frac{165}{180} = \frac{165 \div 15}{180 \div 15} = \frac{11}{12}$

33. $5\frac{9}{11} = \frac{11 \cdot 5 + 9}{11} = \frac{64}{11}$

34. $-3\frac{2}{7} = -\frac{7 \cdot 3 + 2}{7} = -\frac{23}{7}$

35. $\frac{27}{5} = 5\frac{2}{5}$

36. $-\frac{17}{9} = -1\frac{8}{9}$

37. $\frac{4}{5} = 0.8$

$$\begin{array}{r} 0.8 \\ 5\overline{)4.0} \\ \underline{40} \\ 0 \end{array}$$

38. $\frac{3}{7} = 0.\overline{428571}$

$$\begin{array}{r} 0.4285714 \\ 7\overline{)3.0000000} \\ \underline{28} \\ 20 \\ \underline{14} \\ 60 \\ \underline{56} \\ 40 \\ \underline{35} \\ 50 \\ \underline{49} \\ 10 \\ \underline{7} \\ 30 \\ \underline{28} \\ 2 \end{array}$$

39. $\frac{5}{8}=0.625$

$$\begin{array}{r} 0.625 \\ 8\overline{)5.000} \\ \underline{48} \\ 20 \\ \underline{16} \\ 40 \\ \underline{40} \\ 0 \end{array}$$

40. $\frac{9}{16}=0.5625$

$$\begin{array}{r} 0.5625 \\ 16\overline{)9.0000} \\ \underline{80} \\ 100 \\ \underline{96} \\ 40 \\ \underline{32} \\ 80 \\ \underline{80} \\ 0 \end{array}$$

41. $0.6=\frac{6}{10}=\frac{6\div 2}{10\div 2}=\frac{3}{5}$

42. $0.68=\frac{68}{100}$

$68=2^2\cdot 17$

$100=2^2\cdot 5^2$

Greatest Common Divisor is 2^2 or 4.

$\frac{68\div 4}{100\div 4}=\frac{17}{25}$

43. $0.588=\frac{588}{1000}$

$588=2^2\cdot 3\cdot 7^2$

$1000=2^3\cdot 5^3$

Greatest Common Divisor is 2^2 or 4.

$\frac{588\div 4}{1000\div 4}=\frac{147}{250}$

44. $0.0084=\frac{84}{10{,}000}$

$84=2^2\cdot 3\cdot 7$

$10{,}000=2^4\cdot 5^4$

Greatest Common Divisor is 2^2 or 4.

$\frac{84\div 4}{10{,}000\div 4}=\frac{21}{2500}$

45. $n=0.555\ldots$
$10n=5.555\ldots$

$$\begin{aligned} 10n &= 5.555\ldots \\ -\quad n &= 0.555\ldots \\ \hline 9n &= 5 \\ n &= \frac{5}{9} \end{aligned}$$

46. $n=0.3434\ldots$
$100n=34.3434\ldots$

$$\begin{aligned} 100n &= 34.3434\ldots \\ -\quad n &= 0.3434\ldots \\ \hline 99n &= 34 \\ n &= \frac{34}{99} \end{aligned}$$

47. $n=0.113113\ldots$
$1000n=113.113113\ldots$

$$\begin{aligned} 1000n &= 113.113113\ldots \\ -\quad n &= 0.113113\ldots \\ \hline 999n &= 113 \\ n &= \frac{113}{999} \end{aligned}$$

48. $\frac{3}{5}\cdot\frac{7}{10}=\frac{3\cdot 7}{5\cdot 10}=\frac{21}{50}$

49. $\left(3\frac{1}{3}\right)\left(1\frac{3}{4}\right)=\frac{10}{3}\cdot\frac{7}{4}=\frac{70}{12}=\frac{35}{6}$ or $5\frac{5}{6}$

50. $\frac{4}{5}\div\frac{3}{10}=\frac{4}{5}\cdot\frac{10}{3}=\frac{4\cdot 10}{5\cdot 3}=\frac{40}{15}=\frac{8}{3}$

51. $-1\frac{2}{3}\div 6\frac{2}{3}=-\frac{5}{3}\div\frac{20}{3}=-\frac{5}{3}\cdot\frac{3}{20}=-\frac{15}{60}=-\frac{1}{4}$

52. $\frac{2}{9}+\frac{4}{9}=\frac{2+4}{9}=\frac{6}{9}=\frac{2}{3}$

53. $\frac{7}{9}+\frac{5}{12}=\frac{7}{9}\cdot\frac{4}{4}+\frac{5}{12}\cdot\frac{3}{3}$
$=\frac{28}{36}+\frac{15}{36}$
$=\frac{28+15}{36}$
$=\frac{43}{36}$

54. $\frac{3}{4}-\frac{2}{15}=\frac{3}{4}\cdot\frac{15}{15}-\frac{2}{15}\cdot\frac{4}{4}$
$=\frac{45}{60}-\frac{8}{60}$
$=\frac{45-8}{60}$
$=\frac{37}{60}$

55. $\frac{1}{3}+\frac{1}{2}\cdot\frac{4}{5}=\frac{1}{3}+\frac{1\cdot 4}{2\cdot 5}$
$=\frac{1}{3}+\frac{4}{10}$
$=\frac{1}{3}+\frac{2}{5}$
$=\frac{1}{3}\cdot\frac{5}{5}+\frac{2}{5}\cdot\frac{3}{3}$
$=\frac{5}{15}+\frac{6}{15}$
$=\frac{11}{15}$

56. $\frac{3}{8}\left(\frac{1}{2}+\frac{1}{3}\right)=\frac{3}{8}\left(\frac{1}{2}\cdot\frac{3}{3}+\frac{1}{3}\cdot\frac{2}{2}\right)$
$=\frac{3}{8}\left(\frac{3}{6}+\frac{2}{6}\right)$
$=\frac{3}{8}\left(\frac{5}{6}\right)$
$=\frac{15}{48}$
$=\frac{5}{16}$

57. $\frac{1}{2}-\frac{2}{3}\div\frac{5}{9}+\frac{3}{10}=\frac{1}{2}-\frac{2}{3}\times\frac{9}{5}+\frac{3}{10}$
$=\frac{1}{2}-\frac{6}{5}+\frac{3}{10}$
$=\frac{5}{10}-\frac{12}{10}+\frac{3}{10}$
$=-\frac{4}{10}$
$=-\frac{2}{5}$

58. $\left(\frac{1}{2}+\frac{1}{3}\right)\div\left(\frac{1}{4}-\frac{3}{8}\right)=\left(\frac{3}{6}+\frac{2}{6}\right)\div\left(\frac{2}{8}-\frac{3}{8}\right)$
$=\left(\frac{5}{6}\right)\div\left(\frac{-1}{8}\right)$
$=\frac{5}{6}\times\frac{8}{-1}$
$=-\frac{20}{3}$
$=-6\frac{2}{3}$

59. $\frac{1}{7}+\frac{1}{8}=\frac{1}{7}\cdot\frac{8}{8}+\frac{1}{8}\cdot\frac{7}{7}$
$=\frac{8}{56}+\frac{7}{56}$
$=\frac{15}{56}$
$\frac{15}{56}\div 2=\frac{15}{56}\cdot\frac{1}{2}=\frac{15}{112}$

60. $\frac{3}{4}+\frac{3}{5}=\frac{3}{4}\cdot\frac{5}{5}+\frac{3}{5}\cdot\frac{4}{4}$
$=\frac{15}{20}+\frac{12}{20}$
$=\frac{27}{20}$
$\frac{27}{20}\div 2=\frac{27}{20}\cdot\frac{1}{2}=\frac{27}{40}$

61. $4\frac{1}{2}\cdot\frac{15}{6}=\frac{9}{2}\cdot\frac{15}{6}=\frac{135}{12}=\frac{45}{4}$ or $11\frac{1}{4}$ pounds.

62. $1-\left(\frac{1}{4}+\frac{1}{3}\right)=1-\left(\frac{1}{4}\cdot\frac{3}{3}+\frac{1}{3}\cdot\frac{4}{4}\right)$
$=1-\left(\frac{3}{12}+\frac{4}{12}\right)$
$=\frac{12}{12}-\frac{7}{12}$
$=\frac{5}{12}$

At the end of the second day, $\frac{5}{12}$ of the tank is filled with gas.

63. $\sqrt{28}=\sqrt{4\cdot 7}=\sqrt{4}\cdot\sqrt{7}=2\sqrt{7}$

64. $\sqrt{72}=\sqrt{36\cdot 2}=\sqrt{36}\cdot\sqrt{2}=6\sqrt{2}$

65. $\sqrt{150}=\sqrt{25\cdot 6}=\sqrt{25}\cdot\sqrt{6}=5\sqrt{6}$

66. $\sqrt{300}=\sqrt{100\cdot 3}=\sqrt{100}\cdot\sqrt{3}=10\sqrt{3}$

67. $\sqrt{6}\cdot\sqrt{8}=\sqrt{6\cdot 8}=\sqrt{48}=\sqrt{16}\cdot\sqrt{3}=4\sqrt{3}$

68. $\sqrt{10}\cdot\sqrt{5}=\sqrt{10\cdot 5}$
$=\sqrt{50}$
$=\sqrt{25}\cdot\sqrt{2}$
$=5\sqrt{2}$

69. $\frac{\sqrt{24}}{\sqrt{2}}=\sqrt{\frac{24}{2}}=\sqrt{12}=\sqrt{4}\cdot\sqrt{3}=2\sqrt{3}$

70. $\frac{\sqrt{27}}{\sqrt{3}}=\sqrt{\frac{27}{3}}=\sqrt{9}=3$

71. $\sqrt{5}+4\sqrt{5}=1\sqrt{5}+4\sqrt{5}=(1+4)\sqrt{5}=5\sqrt{5}$

72. $7\sqrt{11}-13\sqrt{11}=(7-13)\sqrt{11}=-6\sqrt{11}$

73. $\sqrt{50}+\sqrt{8}=\sqrt{25}\cdot\sqrt{2}+\sqrt{4}\cdot\sqrt{2}$
$=5\sqrt{2}+2\sqrt{2}$
$=(5+2)\sqrt{2}$
$=7\sqrt{2}$

74. $\sqrt{3}-6\sqrt{27}=\sqrt{3}-6\sqrt{9}\cdot\sqrt{3}$
$=\sqrt{3}-6\cdot 3\sqrt{3}$
$=1\sqrt{3}-18\sqrt{3}$
$=(1-18)\sqrt{3}$
$=-17\sqrt{3}$

75. $2\sqrt{18}+3\sqrt{8}=2\sqrt{9}\cdot\sqrt{2}+3\sqrt{4}\cdot\sqrt{2}$
$=2\cdot 3\cdot\sqrt{2}+3\cdot 2\cdot\sqrt{2}$
$=6\sqrt{2}+6\sqrt{2}$
$=(6+6)\sqrt{2}$
$=12\sqrt{2}$

76. $\frac{30}{\sqrt{5}}=\frac{30}{\sqrt{5}}\cdot\frac{\sqrt{5}}{\sqrt{5}}=\frac{30\sqrt{5}}{\sqrt{25}}=\frac{30\sqrt{5}}{5}=6\sqrt{5}$

77. $\sqrt{\frac{2}{3}}=\frac{\sqrt{2}}{\sqrt{3}}=\frac{\sqrt{2}}{\sqrt{3}}\cdot\frac{\sqrt{3}}{\sqrt{3}}=\frac{\sqrt{6}}{\sqrt{9}}=\frac{\sqrt{6}}{3}$

78. $W=4\sqrt{2x}$
$=4\sqrt{2\cdot 6}$
$=4\sqrt{12}$
$=8\sqrt{3}\approx 13.9$ feet per second

79. $\left\{-17, -\frac{9}{13}, 0, 0.75, \sqrt{2}, \pi, \sqrt{81}\right\}$

a. Natural numbers:
$\sqrt{81}$ because $\sqrt{81}=9$

b. Whole numbers: 0, $\sqrt{81}$

c. Integers: –17, 0, $\sqrt{81}$

d. Rational numbers:
$-17, -\frac{9}{13}, 0, 0.75, \sqrt{81}$

e. Irrational numbers: $\sqrt{2}$, π

f. Real numbers: All numbers in this set.

80. Answers will vary. Example: –3

81. Answers will vary. Example: $\frac{1}{2}$

82. Answers will vary: Example: $\sqrt{2}$

83. Commutative property of addition

84. Associative property of multiplication

85. Distributive property of multiplication over addition.

86. Commutative property of multiplication

87. Commutative property of multiplication

88. Commutative property of addition

89. Inverse property of multiplication

90. Identity property of multiplication

91. Answers will vary. Example: $2 \div 6 = \frac{1}{3}$

92. Answers will vary. Example: $4 - 5 = -1$

93. **a.** The entries in the body of the table are all elements of the set.

b. $$\begin{aligned}(4 \oplus 2) \oplus 3 &= 4 \oplus (2 \oplus 3)\\ 1 \oplus 3 &= 4 \oplus 0\\ 4 &= 4\end{aligned}$$

c. The identity element is 0, because it does not change anything.

d. The inverse of 0 is 0, the inverse of 1 is 4, the inverse of 2 is 3, the inverse of 3 is 2, and the inverse of 4 is 1.

e. $$\begin{aligned}3 \oplus 4 &= 4 \oplus 3\\ 2 &= 2\end{aligned}$$

$$\begin{aligned}3 \oplus 2 &= 2 \oplus 3\\ 0 &= 0\end{aligned}$$

94. $6 \cdot 6^2 = 6^1 \cdot 6^2 = 6^{1+2} = 6^3 = 216$

95. $2^3 \cdot 2^3 = 2^{3+3} = 2^6 = 64$

96. $(2^2)^2 = 2^{2 \cdot 2} = 2^4 = 16$

97. $(3^3)^2 = 3^{3 \cdot 2} = 3^6 = 729$

98. $\frac{5^6}{5^4} = 5^{6-4} = 5^2 = 25$

99. $7^0 = 1$

100. $(-7)^0 = 1$

101. $6^{-3} = \frac{1}{6^3} = \frac{1}{216}$

102. $2^{-4} = \frac{1}{2^4} = \frac{1}{16}$

103. $\frac{7^4}{7^6} = 7^{4-6} = 7^{-2} = \frac{1}{7^2} = \frac{1}{49}$

104. $3^5 \cdot 3^{-2} = 3^{5-2} = 3^3 = 27$

105. $4.6 \times 10^2 = 460$

106. $3.74 \times 10^4 = 37{,}400$

107. $2.55 \times 10^{-3} = 0.00255$

108. $7.45 \times 10^{-5} = 0.0000745$

109. $7520 = 7.52 \times 10^3$

110. $3{,}590{,}000 = 3.59 \times 10^6$

111. $0.00725 = 7.25 \times 10^{-3}$

112. $0.000000409 = 4.09 \times 10^{-7}$

113. $420 \times 10^{11} = \left(4.2 \times 10^2\right) \times 10^{11} = 4.2 \times 10^{13}$

114. $0.97 \times 10^{-4} = \left(9.7 \times 10^{-1}\right) \times 10^{-4} = 9.7 \times 10^{-5}$

115. $$\begin{aligned}(3 \times 10^7)(1.3 \times 10^{-5}) &= (3 \times 1.3) \times 10^{7-5}\\ &= 3.9 \times 10^2\\ &= 390\end{aligned}$$

116. $$\begin{aligned}(5 \times 10^3)(2.3 \times 10^2) &= (5 \times 2.3) \times 10^{3+2}\\ &= 11.5 \times 10^5\\ &= 1.15 \times 10 \times 10^5\\ &= 1.15 \times 10^6\\ &= 1{,}150{,}000\end{aligned}$$

117. $\dfrac{6.9\times10^{3}}{3\times10^{5}}=\left(\dfrac{6.9}{3}\right)\times10^{3-5}$
$=2.3\times10^{-2}$
$=0.023$

118. $\dfrac{2.4\times10^{-4}}{6\times10^{-6}}=\left(\dfrac{2.4}{6}\right)\times10^{-4-(-6)}$
$=0.4\times10^{-4+6}$
$=0.4\times10^{2}$
$=40$

119. $(60,000)(540,000)=(6.0\times10^{4})(5.4\times10^{5})$
$=(6.0\times5.4)\times10^{4+5}$
$=32.4\times10^{9}$
$=3.24\times10\times10^{9}$
$=3.24\times10^{10}$

120. $(91,000)(0.0004)=(9.1\times10^{4})(4\times10^{-4})$
$=(9.1\times4)\times10^{4-4}$
$=36.4\times10^{0}$
$=3.64\times10^{1}$

121. $\dfrac{8,400,000}{4000}=\dfrac{8.4\times10^{6}}{4\times10^{3}}$
$=\left(\dfrac{8.4}{4}\right)\times10^{6-3}$
$=2.1\times10^{3}$

122. $\dfrac{0.000003}{0.00000006}=\dfrac{3\times10^{-6}}{6\times10^{-8}}$
$=\left(\dfrac{3}{6}\right)\times10^{-6-(-8)}$
$=0.5\times10^{2}$
$=5\times10^{-1}\times10^{2}$
$=5\times10^{1}$

123. 1.3×10^{12}

124. 3.2×10^{7}

125. $\dfrac{1.3\times10^{12}}{3.2\times10^{7}}\approx0.40625\times10^{5}=40,625$ years

126. $180(3.2\times10^{4})(5\times10^{6})=(180\times3.2\times5)\times(10^{4}\times10^{6})$
$=2880\times10^{10}$
$=2.88\times10^{13}$

127. $a_1=7,\ d=4$
$7,\ 7+4=11,\ 11+4=15,\ 15+4=19,\ 19+4=23,$
$23+4=27$
7, 11, 15, 19, 23, 27

128. $a_1=-4,\ d=-5$
$-4,\ -4-5=-9,\ -9-5=-14,\ -14-5=-19,$
$-19-5=-24,\ -24-5=-29$
$-4, -9, -14, -19, -24, -29$

129 $a_1=\dfrac{3}{2},\ d=-\dfrac{1}{2}$
$\dfrac{3}{2},\ \dfrac{3}{2}-\dfrac{1}{2}=\dfrac{2}{2}=1,\ \dfrac{2}{2}-\dfrac{1}{2}=\dfrac{1}{2},\ \dfrac{1}{2}-\dfrac{1}{2}=0,$
$0-\dfrac{1}{2}=-\dfrac{1}{2},\ -\dfrac{1}{2}-\dfrac{1}{2}=-1$
$\dfrac{3}{2},\ 1,\ \dfrac{1}{2},\ 0,\ -\dfrac{1}{2},\ -1$

130. $a_1=5,\ d=3$
$a_6=5+(6-1)(3)$
$=5+5(3)$
$=5+15$
$=20$

131. $a_1=-8,\ d=-2$
$a_{12}=-8+(12-1)(-2)$
$=-8+11(-2)$
$=-8+(-22)$
$=-30$

132. $a_1=14,\ d=-4$
$a_{14}=14+(14-1)(-4)$
$=14+13(-4)$
$=14+(-52)$
$=-38$

133. $a_n=a_1+(n-1)d$ with $a_1=-7,\ d=4$
$a_n=-7+(n-1)4$
$=-7+4n-4$
$=4n-11$
Thus $a_{20}=4(20)-11=69$.

134. $a_n = a_1 + (n-1)d$ with $a_1 = 200,\ d = -20$

$$\begin{aligned} a_n &= 200 + (n-1)(-20) \\ &= 200 - 20n + 20 \\ &= -20n + 220 \end{aligned}$$

Thus $a_{20} = -20(20) + 220 = -180$.

135. $a_1 = 3,\ r = 2$

$3,\ 3 \cdot 2 = 6,\ 6 \cdot 2 = 12,\ 12 \cdot 2 = 24,$
$24 \cdot 2 = 48,\ 48 \cdot 2 = 96$
$3, 6, 12, 24, 48, 96$

136. $a_1 = \frac{1}{2},\ r = \frac{1}{2}$

$\frac{1}{2},\ \frac{1}{2} \cdot \frac{1}{2} = \frac{1}{4},\ \frac{1}{4} \cdot \frac{1}{2} = \frac{1}{8},\ \frac{1}{8} \cdot \frac{1}{2} = \frac{1}{16},$
$\frac{1}{16} \cdot \frac{1}{2} = \frac{1}{32},\ \frac{1}{32} \cdot \frac{1}{2} = \frac{1}{64}$
$\frac{1}{2}, \frac{1}{4}, \frac{1}{8}, \frac{1}{16}, \frac{1}{32}, \frac{1}{64}$

137. $a_1 = 16,\ r = -\frac{1}{2}$

$16,\ 16\left(-\frac{1}{2}\right) = -8,\ -8\left(-\frac{1}{2}\right) = 4,\ 4\left(-\frac{1}{2}\right) = -2,$
$-2\left(-\frac{1}{2}\right) = 1,\ 1\left(-\frac{1}{2}\right) = -\frac{1}{2}$
$16, -8, 4, -2, 1, -\frac{1}{2}$

138. $a_1 = 2,\ r = 3$

$$\begin{aligned} a_4 &= 2(3)^{4-1} \\ &= 2(3)^3 \\ &= 2(27) \\ &= 54 \end{aligned}$$

139. $a_1 = 16,\ r = \frac{1}{2}$

$$\begin{aligned} a_6 &= 16\left(\frac{1}{2}\right)^{6-1} \\ &= 16\left(\frac{1}{2}\right)^5 \\ &= \frac{16}{32} \\ &= \frac{1}{2} \end{aligned}$$

140. $a_1 = -3,\ r = 2$

$$\begin{aligned} a_5 &= -3(2)^{5-1} \\ &= -3(2)^4 \\ &= -3(16) \\ &= -48 \end{aligned}$$

141. $a_n = a_1 r^{n-1}$ with $a_1 = 1$ and $r = \frac{2}{1} = 2$. Thus

$$\begin{aligned} a_n &= 2^{n-1} \\ a_8 &= 2^{8-1} = 2^7 = 128 \end{aligned}$$

142. $a_n = a_1 r^{n-1}$ with $a_1 = 100$ and $r = \frac{10}{100} = \frac{1}{10}$. Thus

$$\begin{aligned} a_n &= 100\left(\frac{1}{10}\right)^{n-1} \\ a_8 &= 100\left(\frac{1}{10}\right)^{8-1} \\ &= 100\left(\frac{1}{10}\right)^7 \\ &= \frac{100}{10{,}000{,}000} \\ &= \frac{1}{100{,}000} \end{aligned}$$

143. The common difference in the arithmetic sequence is 5.
$4 + 5 = 9,\ 9 + 5 = 14,\ 14 + 5 = 19,$
$19 + 5 = 24,\ 24 + 5 = 29$
$4, 9, 14, 19, 24, 29, \ldots$

144. The common ratio in the geometric sequence is 3.
$2 \cdot 3 = 6,\ 6 \cdot 3 = 18,\ 18 \cdot 3 = 54,\ 54 \cdot 3 = 162,$
$162 \cdot 3 = 486$
$2, 6, 18, 54, 162, 486, \ldots$

145. The common ratio in the geometric sequence is $\frac{1}{4}$.

$1 \cdot \frac{1}{4} = \frac{1}{4},\ \frac{1}{4} \cdot \frac{1}{4} = \frac{1}{16},\ \frac{1}{16} \cdot \frac{1}{4} = \frac{1}{64},$
$\frac{1}{64} \cdot \frac{1}{4} = \frac{1}{256},\ \frac{1}{256} \cdot \frac{1}{4} = \frac{1}{1024}$
$1, \frac{1}{4}, \frac{1}{16}, \frac{1}{64}, \frac{1}{256}, \frac{1}{1024}, \ldots$

146. The common difference in the arithmetic sequence is -7.
$0 - 7 = -7,\ -7 - 7 = -14,\ -14 - 7 = -21,\ -21 - 7 = -28,$
$-28 - 7 = -35$
$0, -7, -14, -21, -28, -35, \ldots$

147. a. $a_n = 34.5 + (n-1)(-0.3)$
$= 34.5 - 0.3n + 0.3$
$= 34.8 - 0.3n$

b. $a_n = 34.8 - 0.3n$
$a_{56} = 34.8 - 0.3(56)$
$= 18$
The model projects wives will devote 18 hours per week to housework in 2020.

148. a. Divide each value by the previous value:

$\frac{18.80}{18.44} \approx 1.02$

$\frac{18.44}{18.15} \approx 1.02$

$\frac{18.15}{17.86} \approx 1.02$

$\frac{17.86}{17.58} \approx 1.02$

$\frac{17.58}{17.30} \approx 1.02$

$\frac{17.30}{17.03} \approx 1.02$

$\frac{17.03}{16.76} \approx 1.02$

$\frac{16.76}{16.50} \approx 1.02$

$\frac{16.50}{16.24} \approx 1.02$

$\frac{16.24}{15.98} \approx 1.02$

The population is increasing geometrically with $r = 1.02$.

b. $a_n = 15.98(1.02)^n$

c. 2080 is 8 decades after 2000 so $n = 8$.
$a_n = 15.98(1.02)^{n-1}$
$a_{31} = 15.98(1.02)^{31-1}$
≈ 28.95
In 2030, the model predicts Florida's population will be 28.95 million.

Chapter 5 Test

1. 391,248

2: Yes; the last digit is 8.

3: Yes; the sum of the digits is 27, which is divisible by 3.

4: Yes; the last two digits form 48, which is divisible by 4.

5: No; the number does not end in 0 or 5.

6: Yes; the number is divisible by both 2 and 3.

8: Yes; the last three digits form 248, which is divisible by 8.

9: Yes; the sum of the digits is 27, which is divisible by 9.

10: No; the number does not end in 0.

12: Yes; the number is divisible by both 3 and 4.

391, 248 is divisible by 2, 3, 4, 6, 8, 9, 12.

2. $252 = 2^2 \cdot 3^2 \cdot 7$

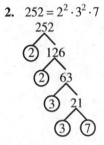

252
(2) 126
(2) 63
(3) 21
(3) (7)

3. $48 = 2^4 \cdot 3$
$72 = 2^3 \cdot 3^2$
Greatest Common Divisor $= 2^3 \cdot 3 = 24$
Least Common Multiple $= 2^4 \cdot 3^2 = 144$

4. $-6 - (5 - 12) = -6 - (-7) = -6 + 7 = 1$

5. $(-3)(-4) \div (7-10) = (-3)(-4) \div (-3)$
$= 12 \div (-3)$
$= -4$

6. $(6-8)^2(5-7)^3 = (-2)^2(-2)^3$
$= 4(-8)$
$= -32$

7. $\frac{7}{12} = 0.58\overline{3}$

$$\begin{array}{r} 0.5833\ldots \\ 12\overline{)7.0000} \\ \underline{60} \\ 100 \\ \underline{96} \\ 40 \\ \underline{36} \\ 40 \\ \underline{36} \\ 4 \end{array}$$

8. $n = 0.6464\ldots$
$100n = 64.6464\ldots$

$$\begin{array}{r} 100n = 64.6464\ldots \\ -\quad n = \ 0.6464\ldots \\ \hline 99n = 64 \end{array}$$

$n = \frac{64}{99}$

9. $\left(-\frac{3}{7}\right) \div \left(-2\frac{1}{7}\right) = \left(-\frac{3}{7}\right) \div \left(-\frac{15}{7}\right)$
$= \left(-\frac{3}{7}\right) \cdot \left(-\frac{7}{15}\right)$
$= \frac{(-3)(-7)}{7 \cdot 15}$
$= \frac{21}{105}$
$= \frac{1}{5}$

10. $\frac{19}{24} - \frac{7}{40} = \frac{19}{24} \cdot \frac{5}{5} - \frac{7}{40} \cdot \frac{3}{3}$
$= \frac{95}{120} - \frac{21}{120}$
$= \frac{95-21}{120}$
$= \frac{74}{120}$
$= \frac{37}{60}$

11. $\frac{1}{2} - 8\left(\frac{1}{4} + 1\right) = \frac{1}{2} - 8\left(\frac{5}{4}\right)$
$= \frac{1}{2} - 10$
$= \frac{1}{2} - \frac{20}{2}$
$= -\frac{19}{2}$

12. $\frac{1}{2} + \frac{2}{3} = \frac{1}{2} \cdot \frac{3}{3} + \frac{2}{3} \cdot \frac{2}{2}$
$= \frac{3}{6} + \frac{4}{6}$
$= \frac{7}{6}$

$\frac{7}{6} \div 2 = \frac{7}{6} \cdot \frac{1}{2} = \frac{7}{12}$

13. $\sqrt{10} \cdot \sqrt{5} = \sqrt{10 \cdot 5}$
$= \sqrt{50}$
$= \sqrt{25 \cdot 2}$
$= \sqrt{25} \cdot \sqrt{2}$
$= 5\sqrt{2}$

14. $\sqrt{50} + \sqrt{32} = \sqrt{25} \cdot \sqrt{2} + \sqrt{16} \cdot \sqrt{2}$
$= 5\sqrt{2} + 4\sqrt{2}$
$= (5+4)\sqrt{2}$
$= 9\sqrt{2}$

15. $\frac{6}{\sqrt{2}} = \frac{6}{\sqrt{2}} \cdot \frac{\sqrt{2}}{\sqrt{2}} = \frac{6\sqrt{2}}{\sqrt{4}} = \frac{6\sqrt{2}}{2} = 3\sqrt{2}$

16. The rational numbers are
$-7, -\frac{4}{5}, 0, 0.25, \sqrt{4}, \frac{22}{7}$.

17. Commutative property of addition

18. Distributive property of multiplication over addition

19. $3^3 \cdot 3^2 = 3^{3+2} = 3^5 = 243$

20. $\frac{4^6}{4^3} = 4^{6-3} = 4^3 = 64$

21. $8^{-2} = \frac{1}{8^2} = \frac{1}{64}$

22. $(3\times10^8)(2.5\times10^{-5}) = (3\times2.5)\times10^{8-5}$
$= 7.5\times10^3$
$= 7500$

23. $\dfrac{49{,}000}{0.007} = \dfrac{4.9\times10^4}{7\times10^{-3}}$
$= \left(\dfrac{4.9}{7}\right)\times10^{4-(-3)}$
$= 0.7\times10^7$
$= 7\times10^{-1}\times10^7$
$= 7\times10^6$

24. $\$53.6\times10^9 = (\$5.36\times10^1)\times10^9 = \$5.36\times10^{10}$

25. $307\times10^6 = (3.07\times10^2)\times10^6 = 3.07\times10^8$

26. $\dfrac{5.36\times10^{10}}{3.07\times10^8} = \left(\dfrac{5.36}{3.07}\right)\times10^2$
$\approx 1.75\times10^2$
$\approx \$175$

27. $a_1 = 1, d = -5$
$1, 1-5=-4, -4-5=-9,$
$-9-5=-14, -14-5=-19,$
$-19-5=-24$
$1, -4, -9, -14, -19, -24$

28. $a_1 = -2,\ d = 3$
$a_9 = -2+(9-1)(3)$
$= -2+8(3)$
$= -2+24$
$= 22$

29. $a_1 = 16,\ r = \dfrac{1}{2}$
$16,\ 16\cdot\dfrac{1}{2} = 8,\ 8\cdot\dfrac{1}{2} = 4,\ 4\cdot\dfrac{1}{2} = 2,\ 2\cdot\dfrac{1}{2} = 1,\ 1\cdot\dfrac{1}{2} = \dfrac{1}{2}$
$16, 8, 4, 2, 1, \dfrac{1}{2}$

30. $a_1 = 5,\ r = 2$
$a_7 = 5(2)^{7-1}$
$= 5(2)^6$
$= 5(64)$
$= 320$

Chapter 6
Algebra: Equations and Inequalities

Check Points 6.1

1. $8+6(x-3)^2 = 8+6(13-3)^2$
$= 8+6(10)^2$
$= 8+6(100)$
$= 608$

2. If $x=-5$, then $x^2+4x-7 = (-5)^2+4(-5)-7$
$= 25-20-7$
$= -2$

3. If $x=5$ and $y=-1$, then
$-3x^2+4xy-y^3 = -3(5)^2+4(5)(-1)-(-1)^3$
$= -3(25)-20-(-1)$
$= -75-20+1$
$= -94$

4. $M = -120x^2+998x+590$
$M = -120(4)^2+998(4)+590$
$= 2662$
According to the model, men between the ages of 19 and 30 with this lifestyle need 2662 calories per day. This underestimates the actual value shown in the bar graph by 38 calories.

5. $7(2x-3)-11x = 7\cdot 2x-7\cdot 3-11x$
$= 14x-21-11x$
$= 3x-21$

6. $7(4x^2+3x)+2(5x^2+x) = 28x^2+21x+10x^2+2x$
$= 38x^2+23x$

7. $6x+4[7-(x-2)] = 6x+4[7-x+2]$
$= 6x+4[9-x]$
$= 6x+36-4x$
$= 2x+36$

Concept and Vocabulary Check 6.1

1. evaluating

2. equation

3. terms

4. coefficient

5. factors

6. like terms

Exercise Set 6.1

1. $5x+7 = 5\cdot 4+7 = 20+7 = 27$

3. $-7x-5 = -7(-4)-5 = 28-5 = 23$

5. $x^2+4 = 5^2+4 = 25+4 = 29$

7. $x^2-6 = (-2)^2-6 = 4-6 = -2$

9. $-x^2+4 = -(5)^2+4 = -25+4 = -21$

11. $-x^2-6 = -(-2)^2-6 = -4-6 = -10$

13. $x^2+4x = (10)^2+4\cdot 10 = 100+40 = 140$

15. $8x^2+17 = 8(5)^2+17$
$= 8(25)+17$
$= 200+17$
$= 217$

17. $x^2-5x = (-11)^2-5(-11)$
$= 121+55$
$= 176$

19. $x^2+5x-6 = 4^2+5\cdot 4-6$
$= 16+20-6$
$= 30$

21. $4+5(x-7)^3 = 4+5(9-7)^3$
$= 4+5(2)^3$
$= 4+5(8)$
$= 44$

23. $x^2-3(x-y) = 2^2-3(2-8)$
$= 4-3(-6)$
$= 4+18$
$= 22$

25. $2x^2-5x-6=2(-3)^2-5(-3)-6$
$=2(9)-5(-3)-6$
$=18+15-6$
$=27$

27. $-5x^2-4x-11=-5(-1)^2-4(-1)-11$
$=-5(1)-4(-1)-11$
$=-5+4-11$
$=-12$

29. $3x^2+2xy+5y^2=3(2)^2+2(2)(3)+5(3)^2$
$=3(4)+2(2)(3)+5(9)$
$=12+12+45$
$=69$

31. $-x^2-4xy+3y^3=-(-1)^2-4(-1)(-2)+3(-2)^3$
$=-(1)-8+3(-8)$
$=-1-8-24$
$=-33$

33. If $x=-2$ and $y=4$ then
$$\frac{2x+3y}{x+1}=\frac{2(-2)+3(4)}{-2+1}=\frac{-4+12}{-1}=\frac{8}{-1}=-8$$

35. $C=\frac{5}{9}(50-32)=\frac{5}{9}(18)=10$
10°C is equivalent to 50°F.

37. $h=4+60t-16t^2=4+60(2)-16(2)^2$
$=4+120-16(4)=4+120-64$
$=124-64=60$
Two seconds after it is kicked, the ball's height is 60 feet.

39. $7+2(x+9)$
$=7+(2x+18)$ [distributive property]
$=7+(18+2x)$ [commutative property of addition]
$=(7+18)+2x$ [associative property of addition]
$=25+2x$
$=2x+25$ [commutative property of addition]

41. $7x+10x=17x$

43. $5x^2-8x^2=-3x^2$

45. $3(x+5)=3x+15$

47. $4(2x-3)=8x-12$

49. $5(3x+4)-4=5\cdot 3x+5\cdot 4-4$
$=15x+20-4$
$=15x+16$

51. $5(3x-2)+12x=5\cdot 3x-5\cdot 2+12x$
$=15x-10+12x$
$=27x-10$

53. $7(3y-5)+2(4y+3)$
$=7\cdot 3y-7\cdot 5+2\cdot 4y+2\cdot 3$
$=21y-35+8y+6$
$=29y-29$

55. $5(3y-2)-(7y+2)=15y-10-7y-2$
$=8y-12$

57. $3(-4x^2+5x)-(5x-4x^2)=-12x^2+15x-5x+4x^2$
$=-8x^2+10x$

59. $7-4[3-(4y-5)]=7-4[3-4y+5]$
$=7-4[8-4y]$
$=7-32+16y$
$=16y-25$

61. $8x-3[5-(7-6x)]=8x-3[5-7+6x]$
$=8x-3[-2+6x]$
$=8x+6-18x$
$=-10x+6$

63. $18x^2+4-\left[6\left(x^2-2\right)+5\right]$
$=18x^2+4-\left[6x^2-12+5\right]$
$=18x^2+4-\left[6x^2-7\right]$
$=18x^2+4-6x^2+7$
$=18x^2-6x^2+4+7$
$=(18-6)x^2+11=12x^2+11$

65. $2(3x^2-5)-[4(2x^2-1)+3]$
$=6x^2-10-[8x^2-4+3]$
$=6x^2-10-[8x^2-1]$
$=6x^2-10-8x^2+1$
$=-2x^2-9$

67. a. $H = \frac{7}{10}(220 - a)$

$H = \frac{7}{10}(220 - 20)$

$= \frac{7}{10}(200)$

$= 140$

The lower limit of the heart rate for a 20-year-old with this exercise goal is 140 beats per minute.

b. $H = \frac{4}{5}(220 - a)$

$H = \frac{4}{5}(220 - 20)$

$= \frac{4}{5}(200)$

$= 160$

The upper limit of the heart rate for a 20-year-old with this exercise goal is 160 beats per minute.

69. $F = -82x^2 + 654x + 620$

$F = -82(4)^2 + 654(4) + 620$

$= 1924$

According to the formula those in this group need 1924 calories. That underestimates the value shown in the graph by 76 calories.

71. a. 22%

b. $p = -0.01s^2 + 0.8s + 3.7$

$p = -0.01(30)^2 + 0.8(30) + 3.7$

$= 18.7$

The formula gives a value of 18.7%. This is less than the estimate from part (a).

81. makes sense

83. makes sense

85. false; Changes to make the statement true will vary. A sample change is: The coefficient of x is 1.

87. false; Changes to make the statement true will vary. A sample change is: $-x - x = -x + (-x) = -2x$

89. false; Changes to make the statement true will vary. A sample change is: $3 + 7x \neq 10x$

91. true

93. $\frac{0.5x + 5000}{x}$

a. $x = 100$

$\frac{0.5(100) + 5000}{100} = \$50.50$

$x = 1000$

$\frac{0.5(1000) + 5000}{1000} = \$5.50$

$x = 10{,}000$

$\frac{0.5(10{,}000) + 5000}{10{,}000} = \$1$

b. No; the business must produce at least 10,000 clocks each week to be competitive.

Check Points 6.2

1. $4x + 5 = 29$

$4x + 5 - 5 = 29 - 5$

$4x = 24$

$\frac{4x}{4} = \frac{24}{4}$

$x = 6$

Check:

$4x + 5 = 29$

$4(6) + 5 = 29$

$24 + 5 = 29$

$29 = 29$

The solution set is $\{6\}$.

2. $6(x - 3) - 10x = -10$

$6x - 18 - 10x = -10$

$-4x - 18 = -10$

$-4x - 18 + 18 = -10 + 18$

$-4x = 8$

$\frac{-4x}{-4} = \frac{8}{-4}$

$x = -2$

Check:

$6(-2 - 3) - 10(-2) = -10$

$6(-5) + 20 = -10$

$-30 + 20 = -10$

$-10 = -10$

The solution set is $\{-2\}$.

3.
$$2x+9=8x-3$$
$$2x+9-8x=8x-3-8x$$
$$-6x+9=-3$$
$$-6x+9-9=-3-9$$
$$-6x=-12$$
$$\frac{-6x}{-6}=\frac{-12}{-6}$$
$$x=2$$
The solution set is {2}.

4.
$$4(2x+1)-29=3(2x-5)$$
$$8x+4-29=6x-15$$
$$8x-25=6x-15$$
$$8x-25-6x=6x-15-6x$$
$$2x-25=-15$$
$$2x-25+25=-15+25$$
$$2x=10$$
$$\frac{2x}{2}=\frac{10}{2}$$
$$x=5$$
The solution set is {5}.

5.
$$\frac{2x}{3}=7-\frac{x}{2}$$
$$6\cdot\frac{2x}{3}=6\cdot\left(7-\frac{x}{2}\right)$$
$$6\cdot\frac{2x}{3}=6\cdot7-6\cdot\frac{x}{2}$$
$$2\cdot2x=42-3x$$
$$4x=42-3x$$
$$4x+3x=42-3x+3x$$
$$7x=42$$
$$\frac{7x}{7}=\frac{42}{7}$$
$$x=6$$
The solution set is {6}.

6.
$$D=\frac{10}{9}x+\frac{53}{9}$$
$$10=\frac{10}{9}x+\frac{53}{9}$$
$$9\cdot10=9\cdot\left(\frac{10}{9}x+\frac{53}{9}\right)$$
$$90=10x+53$$
$$37=10x$$
$$3.7=x$$
This is shown on the graph as the point (3.7, 10).

7. a.
$$\frac{10}{x}=\frac{2}{3}$$
$$10\cdot3=2x$$
$$30=2x$$
$$\frac{30}{2}=\frac{2x}{2}$$
$$15=x$$
The solution set is {15}.

b.
$$\frac{22}{60-x}=\frac{2}{x}$$
$$22x=2(60-x)$$
$$22x=120-2x$$
$$22x+2x=120-2x+2x$$
$$24x=120$$
$$\frac{24x}{24}=\frac{120}{24}$$
$$x=5$$
The solution set is {5}.

8. Let x = the property tax on the \$420,000 house.
$$\frac{\text{Tax on \$250,000 house}}{\text{Assessed value (\$250,000)}}=\frac{\text{Tax on \$420,000 house}}{\text{Assessed value (\$420,000)}}$$
$$\frac{\$3500}{\$250{,}000}=\frac{\$x}{\$420{,}000}$$
$$\frac{3500}{250{,}000}=\frac{x}{420{,}000}$$
$$250{,}000x=(3500)(420{,}000)$$
$$250{,}000x=1{,}470{,}000{,}000$$
$$\frac{250{,}000x}{250{,}000}=\frac{1{,}470{,}000{,}000}{250{,}000}$$
$$x=5880$$
The property tax is \$5880.

9. Let x = the number of deer in the refuge.

$$\frac{120\text{ tagged deer}}{x}=\frac{25\text{ tagged deer in sample}}{150\text{ deer in sample}}$$

$$\frac{120}{x}=\frac{25}{150}$$
$$25x=(120)(150)$$
$$25x=18{,}000$$
$$\frac{25x}{25}=\frac{18{,}000}{25}$$
$$x=720$$

There are approximately 720 deer in the refuge.

10.
$$3x+7=3(x+1)$$
$$3x+7=3x+3$$
$$3x+7-3x=3x+3-3x$$
$$7=3$$

There is no solution, $\varnothing$.

11.
$$7x+9=9(x+1)-2x$$
$$7x+9=9x+9-2x$$
$$7x+9=7x+9$$
$$9=9$$

The solution set is $\{x|x \text{ is a real number}\}$.

Concept and Vocabulary Check 6.2

1. linear
2. equivalent
3. $b+c$
4. bc
5. apply the distributive property
6. simplified; solved
7. least common denominator; 12
8. proportion
9. $ad=bc$
10. no; $\varnothing$
11. true; $\{x|x \text{ is a real number}\}$
12. false
13. false
14. false
15. false

Exercise Set 6.2

1.
$$x-7=3$$
$$x-7+7=3+7$$
$$x=10$$

The solution set is $\{10\}$.

3.
$$x+5=-12$$
$$x+5-5=-12-5$$
$$x=-17$$

The solution set is $\{-17\}$.

5.
$$\frac{x}{3}=4$$
$$3\left(\frac{x}{3}\right)=3(4)$$
$$x=12$$

The solution set is $\{12\}$.

7.
$$5x=45$$
$$\frac{5x}{5}=\frac{45}{5}$$
$$x=9$$

The solution set is $\{9\}$.

9.
$$8x=-24$$
$$\frac{8x}{8}=\frac{-24}{8}$$
$$x=-3$$

The solution set is $\{-3\}$.

11.
$$-8x=2$$
$$\frac{-8x}{-8}=\frac{2}{-8}$$
$$x=-\frac{1}{4}$$

The solution set is $\left\{-\frac{1}{4}\right\}$.

13.
$$5x+3=18$$
$$5x+3-3=18-3$$
$$5x=15$$
$$\frac{5x}{5}=\frac{15}{5}$$
$$x=3$$

The solution set is $\{3\}$.

15.
$$\begin{aligned} 6x-3&=63\\ 6x-3+3&=63+3\\ 6x&=66\\ \frac{6x}{6}&=\frac{66}{6}\\ x&=11 \end{aligned}$$
The solution set is $\{11\}$.

17.
$$\begin{aligned} 4x-14&=-82\\ 4x-14+14&=-82+14\\ 4x&=-68\\ \frac{4x}{4}&=\frac{-68}{4}\\ x&=-17 \end{aligned}$$
The solution set is $\{-17\}$.

19.
$$\begin{aligned} 14-5x&=-41\\ 14-5x-14&=-41-14\\ -5x&=-55\\ \frac{-5x}{-5}&=\frac{-55}{-5}\\ x&=11 \end{aligned}$$
The solution set is $\{11\}$.

21.
$$\begin{aligned} 9(5x-2)&=45\\ 45x-18&=45\\ 45x-18+18&=45+18\\ 45x&=63\\ \frac{45x}{45}&=\frac{63}{45}\\ x&=\frac{7}{5} \end{aligned}$$
The solution set is $\left\{\frac{7}{5}\right\}$.

23.
$$\begin{aligned} 5x-(2x-10)&=35\\ 5x-2x+10&=35\\ 3x+10&=35\\ 3x+10-10&=35-10\\ 3x&=25\\ \frac{3x}{3}&=\frac{25}{3}\\ x&=\frac{25}{3} \end{aligned}$$
The solution set is $\left\{\frac{25}{3}\right\}$.

25.
$$\begin{aligned} 3x+5&=2x+13\\ 3x+5-5&=2x+13-5\\ 3x&=2x+8\\ 3x-2x&=2x+8-2x\\ x&=8 \end{aligned}$$
The solution set is $\{8\}$.

27.
$$\begin{aligned} 8x-2&=7x-5\\ 8x-2+2&=7x-5+2\\ 8x&=7x-3\\ 8x-7x&=7x-3-7x\\ x&=-3 \end{aligned}$$
The solution set is $\{-3\}$.

29.
$$\begin{aligned} 7x+4&=x+16\\ 7x+4-4&=x+16-4\\ 7x&=x+12\\ 7x-x&=x+12-x\\ 6x&=12\\ \frac{6x}{6}&=\frac{12}{6}\\ x&=2 \end{aligned}$$
The solution set is $\{2\}$.

31.
$$\begin{aligned} 8y-3&=11y+9\\ 8y-3+3&=11y+9+3\\ 8y&=11y+12\\ 8y-11y&=11y+12-11y\\ -3y&=12\\ \frac{-3y}{-3}&=\frac{12}{-3}\\ y&=-4 \end{aligned}$$
The solution set is $\{-4\}$.

33.
$$\begin{aligned} 2(4-3x)&=2(2x+5)\\ 8-6x&=4x+10\\ 8-6x-8&=4x+10-8\\ -6x&=4x+2\\ -6x-4x&=4x+2-4x\\ -10x&=2\\ \frac{-10x}{-10}&=\frac{2}{-10}\\ x&=-\frac{1}{5} \end{aligned}$$
The solution set is $\left\{-\frac{1}{5}\right\}$.

35.
$$\begin{aligned} 8(y+2) &= 2(3y+4) \\ 8y+16 &= 6y+8 \\ 8y+16-16 &= 6y+8-16 \\ 8y &= 6y-8 \\ 8y-6y &= 6y-8-6y \\ 2y &= -8 \\ \frac{2y}{2} &= \frac{-8}{2} \\ y &= -4 \end{aligned}$$
The solution set is $\{-4\}$.

37.
$$\begin{aligned} 3(x+1) &= 7(x-2)-3 \\ 3x+3 &= 7x-14-3 \\ 3x+3 &= 7x-17 \\ 3x+3-3 &= 7x-17-3 \\ 3x &= 7x-20 \\ 3x-7x &= 7x-20-7x \\ -4x &= -20 \\ \frac{-4x}{-4} &= \frac{-20}{-4} \\ x &= 5 \end{aligned}$$
The solution set is $\{5\}$.

39.
$$\begin{aligned} 5(2x-8)-2 &= 5(x-3)+3 \\ 10x-40-2 &= 5x-15+3 \\ 10x-42 &= 5x-12 \\ 10x-42+42 &= 5x-12+42 \\ 10x &= 5x+30 \\ 10x-5x &= 5x+30-5x \\ 5x &= 30 \\ \frac{5x}{5} &= \frac{30}{5} \\ x &= 6 \end{aligned}$$
The solution set is $\{6\}$.

41.
$$\begin{aligned} 6 &= -4(1-x)+3(x+1) \\ 6 &= -4+4x+3x+3 \\ 6 &= -1+7x \\ 6+1 &= -1+7x+1 \\ 7 &= 7x \\ \frac{7}{7} &= \frac{7x}{7} \\ 1 &= x \end{aligned}$$
The solution set is $\{1\}$.

43.
$$\begin{aligned} 10(z+4)-4(z-2) &= 3(z-1)+2(z-3) \\ 10z+40-4z+8 &= 3z-3+2z-6 \\ 6z+48 &= 5z-9 \\ 6z+48-48 &= 5z-9-48 \\ 6z-5z &= 5z-57-5z \\ z &= -57 \end{aligned}$$
The solution set is $\{-57\}$.

45. $\frac{2x}{3}-5=7$

To clear the equation of fractions, multiply both sides by the least common denominator (LCD), which is 3.
$$\begin{aligned} 3\left(\tfrac{2}{3}x-5\right) &= 3(7) \\ 3\cdot\tfrac{2}{3}x-3\cdot5 &= 21 \\ 2x-15 &= 21 \\ 2x-15+15 &= 21+15 \\ 2x &= 36 \\ \frac{2x}{2} &= \frac{36}{2} \\ x &= 18 \end{aligned}$$
The solution set is $\{18\}$.

47. $\frac{x}{3}+\frac{x}{2}=\frac{5}{6}$

To clear the equation of fractions, multiply both sides by the least common denominator (LCD), which is 6.
$$\begin{aligned} 6\left(\frac{x}{3}+\frac{x}{2}\right) &= 6\left(\frac{5}{6}\right) \\ 2x+3x &= 5 \\ 5x &= 5 \\ \frac{5x}{5} &= \frac{5}{5} \\ x &= 1 \end{aligned}$$
The solution set is $\{1\}$.

49. $20-\frac{z}{3}=\frac{z}{2}$

To clear the equation of fractions, multiply both sides by the least common denominator (LCD), which is 6.

$$6\left(20-\frac{z}{3}\right)=6\left(\frac{z}{2}\right)$$
$$120-2z=3z$$
$$120-2z+2z=3z+2z$$
$$120=5z$$
$$\frac{120}{5}=\frac{5z}{5}$$
$$24=z$$

The solution set is $\{24\}$.

51. $\frac{y}{3}+\frac{2}{5}=\frac{y}{5}-\frac{2}{5}$

To clear the equation of fractions, multiply both sides by the least common denominator (LCD), which is 15.

$$15\left(\frac{y}{3}+\frac{2}{5}\right)=15\left(\frac{y}{5}+\frac{2}{5}\right)$$
$$15\left(\frac{y}{3}\right)+15\left(\frac{2}{5}\right)=15\left(\frac{y}{5}\right)+15\left(-\frac{2}{5}\right)$$
$$5y+6=3y-6$$
$$5y+6-3y=3y-6-3y$$
$$2y+6=-6$$
$$2y+6-6=-6-6$$
$$2y=-12$$
$$\frac{2y}{2}=\frac{-12}{2}$$
$$y=-6$$

The solution set is $\{-6\}$.

53. $\frac{3x}{4}-3=\frac{x}{2}+2$

To clear the equation of fractions, multiply both sides by the least common denominator (LCD), which is 8.

$$8\left(\frac{3x}{4}-3\right)=8\left(\frac{x}{2}+2\right)$$
$$8\left(\frac{3x}{4}\right)-8\cdot 3=8\left(\frac{x}{2}\right)+8\cdot 2$$
$$6x-24=4x+16$$
$$6x-24-4x=4x+16-4x$$
$$2x-24=16$$
$$2x-24+24=16+24$$
$$2x=40$$
$$\frac{2x}{2}=\frac{40}{2}$$
$$x=20$$

The solution set is $\{20\}$.

55. $\frac{3x}{5}-x=\frac{x}{10}-\frac{5}{2}$

$$10\left(\frac{3x}{5}-x\right)=10\left(\frac{x}{10}-\frac{5}{2}\right)$$
$$10\left(\frac{3x}{5}\right)-10(x)=10\left(\frac{x}{10}\right)-10\left(\frac{5}{2}\right)$$
$$6x-10x=x-25$$
$$-4x=x-25$$
$$-4x-x=x-25-x$$
$$-5x=-25$$
$$\frac{-5x}{-5}=\frac{-25}{-5}$$
$$x=5$$

The solution set is $\{5\}$.

57. $\frac{x-3}{5}-1=\frac{x-5}{4}$

To clear the equation of fractions, multiply both sides by the least common denominator (LCD), which is 20.

$$20\left(\frac{x-3}{5}-1\right)=20\left(\frac{x-5}{4}\right)$$
$$4(x-3)-20=5(x-5)$$
$$4x-12-20=5x-25$$
$$4x-5x-32=5x-5x-25$$
$$-x-32=-25$$
$$-x-32+32=-25+32$$
$$-x=7$$
$$-1(-x)=-1(7)$$
$$x=-7$$

The solution set is $\{-7\}$.

59. $\frac{24}{x}=\frac{12}{7}$

$$12x=24\cdot 7$$
$$12x=168$$
$$\frac{12x}{12}=\frac{168}{12}$$
$$x=14$$

The solution set is $\{14\}$.

61. $\frac{x}{6}=\frac{18}{4}$

$$4x=6\cdot 18$$
$$4x=108$$
$$\frac{4x}{4}=\frac{108}{4}$$
$$x=27$$

The solution set is $\{27\}$.

63. $\frac{-3}{8}=\frac{x}{40}$

$$8x=-3(40)$$
$$8x=-120$$
$$\frac{8x}{8}=\frac{-120}{8}$$
$$x=-15$$

The solution set is $\{-15\}$.

65. $\frac{x}{12}=-\frac{3}{4}$

$$4x=12(-3)$$
$$4x=-36$$
$$x=-9$$

The solution set is $\{-9\}$.

67. $\frac{x-2}{12}=\frac{8}{3}$

$$3(x-2)=12(8)$$
$$3x-6=96$$
$$3x=102$$
$$x=34$$

The solution set is $\{34\}$.

69. $\frac{x}{7}=\frac{x+14}{5}$

$$5x=7(x+14)$$
$$5x=7x+98$$
$$-2x=98$$
$$x=-49$$

The solution set is $\{-49\}$.

71. $\frac{y+10}{10}=\frac{y-2}{4}$

$$4(y+10)=10(y-2)$$
$$4y+40=10y-20$$
$$4y+40-40=10y-20-40$$
$$4y=10y-60$$
$$4y-10y=10y-60-10y$$
$$-6y=-60$$
$$\frac{-6y}{-6}=\frac{-60}{-6}$$
$$y=10$$

The solution set is $\{10\}$.

73. $3x-7=3(x+1)$

$$3x-7=3x+3$$
$$3x-7-3x=3x+3-3x$$
$$-7=3$$

The statement is false. The solution set is { }.

75. $2(x+4)=4x+5-2x+3$

$$2x+8=2x+8$$
$$2x-8-2x=2x+8-2x$$
$$8=8$$

The statement is true. The solution set is $\{x|x \text{ is a real number}\}$.

77. $7+2(3x-5)=8-3(2x+1)$

$$7+6x-10=8-6x-3$$
$$6x-3=5-6x$$
$$6x+6x-3=5-6x+6x$$
$$12x-3=5$$
$$12x-3+3=5+3$$
$$12x=8$$
$$\frac{12x}{12}=\frac{8}{12}$$
$$x=\frac{2}{3}$$

The solution set is $\left\{\frac{2}{3}\right\}$.

79. $4x+1-5x=5-(x+4)$

$$-x+1=5-x-4$$
$$-x+1=1-x$$
$$-x+1+x=1-x+x$$
$$1=1$$

The statement is true. The solution set is $\{x|x \text{ is a real number}\}$.

81. $4(x+2)+1=7x-3(x-2)$

$$4x+8+1=7x-3x+6$$
$$4x+9=4x+6$$
$$4x-4x+9=4x-4x+6$$
$$9=6$$

The statement is false. The solution set is { }.

83. $3-x=2x+3$

$$3-x+x=2x+x+3$$
$$3=3x+3$$
$$3-3=3x+3-3$$
$$0=3x$$
$$\frac{0}{3}=\frac{3x}{3}$$
$$0=x$$

The solution set is $\{0\}$.

85. $\frac{x}{3}+2=\frac{x}{3}$

$$6\left(\frac{x}{3}+2\right)=6\left(\frac{x}{3}\right)$$
$$2x+12=2x$$
$$2x+12-2x=2x-2x$$
$$12=0$$

The statement is false. The solution set is { }.

87. $\frac{x}{3}=\frac{x}{2}$

$$3x=2x$$
$$3x-2x=2x-2x$$
$$x=0$$

The solution set is $\{0\}$.

89. $\frac{x-2}{5}=\frac{3}{10}$

$$10(x-2)=3\cdot 5$$
$$10x-20=15$$
$$10x-20+20=15+20$$
$$10x=35$$
$$\frac{10x}{10}=\frac{35}{10}$$
$$x=\frac{7}{2}$$

The solution set is $\left\{\frac{7}{2}\right\}$.

91. $\frac{x}{2}-\frac{x}{4}+4=x+4$

$$4\left(\frac{x}{2}-\frac{x}{4}+4\right)=4(x+4)$$
$$4\left(\frac{x}{2}\right)-4\left(\frac{x}{4}\right)+16=4x+16$$
$$2x-x+16=4x+16$$
$$x+16=4x+16$$
$$x-x+16=4x-x+16$$
$$16=3x+16$$
$$16-16=3x+16-16$$
$$0=3x$$
$$\frac{0}{3}=\frac{3x}{3}$$
$$0=x$$

The solution set is $\{0\}$.

93. Solve: $4(x-2)+2=4x-2(2-x)$
$$4x-8+2=4x-4+2x$$
$$4x-6=6x-4$$
$$-2x-6=-4$$
$$-2x=2$$
$$x=-1$$
Now, evaluate x^2-x for $x=-1$:
$$x^2-x=(-1)^2-(-1)$$
$$=1-(-1)=1+1=2$$

95. Solve for x.
$$\frac{x}{5}-2=\frac{x}{3}$$
$$15\cdot\left(\frac{x}{5}-2\right)=15\cdot\frac{x}{3}$$
$$3x-30=5x$$
$$-2x=30$$
$$x=-15$$
Solve for y.
$$-2y-10=5y+18$$
$$-2y-5y=18+10$$
$$-7y=28$$
$$y=-4$$
Evaluate
$$x^2-(xy-y)=(-15)^2-[(-15)(-4)-(-4)]$$
$$=161$$

97. $\left[(3+6)^2\div 3\right]\cdot 4=-54x$
$$\left(9^2\div 3\right)\cdot 4=-54x$$
$$(81\div 3)\cdot 4=-54x$$
$$27\cdot 4=-54x$$
$$108=-54x$$
$$-2=x$$
The solution set is $\{-2\}$.

99. $5-12x=8-7x-\left[6\div 3\left(2+5^3\right)+5x\right]$
$$5-12x=8-7x-[6\div 3(2+125)+5x]$$
$$5-12x=8-7x-[6\div 3\cdot 127+5x]$$
$$5-12x=8-7x-[2\cdot 127+5x]$$
$$5-12x=8-7x-[254+5x]$$
$$5-12x=8-7x-254-5x$$
$$5-12x=-12x-246$$
$$5=-246$$
The final statement is a contradiction, so the equation has no solution. The solution set is $\varnothing$.

101. $0.7x+0.4(20)=0.5(x+20)$
$$0.7x+8=0.5x+10$$
$$0.2x+8=10$$
$$0.2x=2$$
$$x=10$$
The solution set is $\{10\}$.

103. $4x+13-\{2x-[4(x-3)-5]\}=2(x-6)$
$$4x+13-\{2x-[4x-12-5]\}=2x-12$$
$$4x+13-\{2x-[4x-17]\}=2x-12$$
$$4x+13-\{2x-4x+17\}=2x-12$$
$$4x+13-\{-2x+17\}=2x-12$$
$$4x+13+2x-17=2x-12$$
$$6x-4=2x-12$$
$$4x-4=-12$$
$$4x=-8$$
$$x=-2$$
The solution set is $\{-2\}$.

105.
$$\frac{W}{2} - 3H = 53$$
$$\frac{W}{2} - 3(6) = 53$$
$$\frac{W}{2} - 18 = 53$$
$$\frac{W}{2} - 18 + 18 = 53 + 18$$
$$\frac{W}{2} = 71$$
$$2 \cdot \frac{W}{2} = 2 \cdot 71$$
$$W = 142$$
According to the formula, the healthy weight of a person of height 5'6" is 142 pounds. This is 13 pounds below the upper end of the range shown in the bar graph

107. a.
$$p + \frac{x}{2} = 37$$
$$p + \frac{40}{2} = 37$$
$$p + 20 = 37$$
$$p = 17$$
According to the model, 17% of American adults smoked cigarettes in 2010. This underestimates the value shown in the bar graph by 2%.

b.
$$p + \frac{x}{2} = 37$$
$$7 + \frac{x}{2} = 37$$
$$\frac{x}{2} = 30$$
$$x = 60$$
According to the model, only 7% of American adults will smoke cigarettes 60 years after 1970, or 2030.

109. Let x = number of quarts.
$$\frac{160}{5} = \frac{200}{x}$$
$$160x = 5 \cdot 200$$
$$160x = 1000$$
$$\frac{160x}{160} = \frac{1000}{160}$$
$$x = 6.25$$
A person who weighs 200 pounds will have about 6.25 quarts of blood.

111. Let x = the tail length.
$$\frac{4}{3.6} = \frac{6}{x}$$
$$4x = 6 \cdot 3.6$$
$$4x = 21.6$$
$$\frac{4x}{4} = \frac{21.6}{4}$$
$$x = 5.4$$
The tail length is 5.4 feet.

113. Let x = the total number of fur seal pups in the rookery.
$$\frac{\text{Original \# tagged}}{\text{Total \# fur seal pups}} = \frac{\text{\# tagged in sample}}{\text{\# in sample}}$$
$$\frac{4963}{x} = \frac{218}{900}$$
$$218x = (4963)(900)$$
$$218x = 4{,}466{,}700$$
$$\frac{218x}{218} = \frac{4{,}466{,}700}{218}$$
$$x \approx 20{,}489$$
There were approximately 20,489 fur seal pups in the rookery.

125. makes sense

127. does not make sense; Explanations will vary. Sample explanation: The solution set is all real numbers.

129. Possible answers:
$$6x = 25 + x$$
$$2(x + 3) = 16$$
$$-x + 9 = x - 1$$

131. Yes: Her height is slightly over 5 feet tall.
$$f = 0.432h - 10.44$$
$$16 = 0.432h - 10.44$$
$$26.44 = 0.432h$$
$$61.2 \approx h$$

Check Points 6.3

1. Let $x =$ the median starting salary, in thousands of dollars, of education majors.
Let $x+21 =$ the median starting salary, in thousands of dollars, of computer science majors.
Let $x+14 =$ the median starting salary, in thousands of dollars, of economics majors.

$$x+(x+21)+(x+14)=140$$
$$x+x+21+x+14=140$$
$$3x+35=140$$
$$3x=105$$
$$x=35$$
$$x+21=56$$
$$x+14=49$$

The median starting salary of education majors is \$35 thousand, of computer science majors is \$56 thousand, and of economics majors is \$49 thousand.

2. Let $x =$ the number of years after 1969.

$$85-0.9x=25$$
$$-0.9x=25-85$$
$$-0.9x=-60$$
$$x=\frac{-60}{-0.9}$$
$$x\approx 67$$

25% of freshmen will respond this way 67 years after 1969, or 2036.

3. Let $x =$ the number of text messages at which the costs of the two plans are the same.

$$\overbrace{15+0.08x}^{\text{Plan A}}=\overbrace{3+0.12x}^{\text{Plan B}}$$
$$15+0.08x-15=3+0.12x-15$$
$$0.08x=0.12x-12$$
$$0.08x-0.12x=0.12x-12-0.12x$$
$$-0.04x=-12$$
$$\frac{-0.04x}{-0.04}=\frac{-12}{-0.04}$$
$$x=300$$

The two plans are the same at 300 text messages.

4. Let $x =$ the computer's price before the reduction.

$$x-0.30x=840$$
$$0.70x=840$$
$$x=\frac{840}{0.70}$$
$$x=1200$$

Before the reduction the computer's price was \$1200.

5.
$$2l+2w=P$$
$$2l+2w-2l=P-2l$$
$$2w=P-2l$$
$$\frac{2w}{2}=\frac{P-2l}{2}$$
$$w=\frac{P-2l}{2}$$

6.
$$T=D+pm$$
$$T-D=D-D+pm$$
$$T-D=pm$$
$$\frac{T-D}{p}=\frac{pm}{p}$$
$$\frac{T-D}{p}=m$$
$$m=\frac{T-D}{p}$$

Concept and Vocabulary Check 6.3

1. $x+658.6$

2. $31+2.4x$

3. $4+0.15x$

4. $x-0.15x$ or $0.85x$

5. isolated on one side

6. subtract b; divide by m

Exercise Set 6.3

1. Let $x =$ the number

$$5x-4=26$$
$$5x=30$$
$$x=6$$

The number is 6.

3. Let $x =$ the number

$$x-0.20x=20$$
$$0.80x=20$$
$$x=25$$

The number is 25.

5. Let $x =$ the number

$$0.60x+x=192$$
$$1.6x=192$$
$$x=120$$

The number is 120.

7. Let x = the number
$0.70x = 224$
$x = 320$
The number is 320.

9. Let x = the number
$x+26$ = the other number
$x+(x+26)=64$
$x+x+26=64$
$2x+26=64$
$2x=38$
$x=19$
If $x = 19$, then $x+26=45$.
The numbers are 19 and 45.

11. $x-(x+4)=x-x-4=-4$

13. $6(-5x)=-30x$

15. $5x-2x=3x$

17. $8x-(3x+6)=8x-3x-6=5x-6$

19. Let x = the number of years spent watching TV.
Let $x+19$ = the number of years spent sleeping.
$x+(x+19)=37$
$x+x+19=37$
$2x+19=37$
$2x=18$
$x=9$
$x+19=28$
Americans will spend 9 years watching TV and 28 years sleeping.

21. Let x = the average salary, in thousands, for an American whose final degree is a bachelor's.
Let $2x-49$ = the average salary, in thousands, for an American whose final degree is a master's.
$x+(2x-49)=116$
$x+2x-49=116$
$3x-49=116$
$3x=165$
$x=55$
$2x-49=61$
The average salary for an American whose final degree is a bachelor's is $55 thousand and for an American whose final degree is a master's is $61 thousand.

23. Let x = the number of years since 2000.
$31+2.4x=67$
$2.4x=67-31$
$2.4x=36$
$x=\frac{36}{2.4}$
$x=15$
67% of American adults will view college education as essential 15 years after 2000, or 2015.

25. **a.** Let x = the number of deaths, in thousands, per day.
Let $3x-84$ = the number of births, in thousands, per day.
$(3x-84)-x=228$
$3x-84-x=228$
$2x-84=228$
$2x=312$
$x=156$
$3x-84=384$
births: 384,000
deaths: 156,000

b. $228{,}000 \cdot 365 = 83{,}220{,}000$
≈ 83 million

c. $\frac{315 \text{ million}}{83 \text{ million}} \approx 4$
It will take about 4 years.

27. Let x = the number of years until the car's value reaches $9000.
$24{,}000-3000x=9000$
$-3000x=-15{,}000$
$\frac{-3000x}{-3000}=\frac{-15{,}000}{-3000}$
$x=5$
It will take 5 years until the car's value reaches $9000.

29. Let x = the number of months.
The cost for Club A: $25x+40$
The cost for Club B: $30x+15$
$25x+40=30x+15$
$-5x+40=15$
$-5x=-25$
$x=5$
The total cost for the clubs will be the same at 5 months. The cost will be
$25(5)+40=30(5)+15=\$165$

31. Let x = the number of uses.
Cost without discount pass: $1.25x$
Cost with discount pass: $15+0.75x$

$$1.25x = 15+0.75x$$
$$0.50x = 15$$
$$x = 30$$

The bus must be used 30 times in a month for the costs to be equal.

33. Let x = dollars of merchandise purchased.

$$\underbrace{100+0.80x}_{\text{Plan A}} = \underbrace{40+0.90x}_{\text{Plan B}}$$
$$0.80x - 0.90x = 40-100$$
$$-0.10x = -60$$
$$x = \$600$$

\$600 of merchandise must be purchased for the costs to be equal.
The cost of each plan would be
$100+0.80(600) = \$580$

35. Let x = the number of years (after 2010).
College A's enrollment: $13,300+1000x$
College B's enrollment: $26,800-500x$

$$13,300+1000x = 26,800-500x$$
$$13,300+1500x = 26,800$$
$$1500x = 13,500$$
$$x = 9$$

The two colleges will have the same enrollment 9 years after 2010, or 2019.
That year the enrollments will be
$13,300+1000(9)$
$= 26,800-500(9)$
$= 22,300$ students.

37. Let x = the cost of the television set.

$$x-0.20x = 336$$
$$0.80x = 336$$
$$x = 420$$

The television set's price is \$420.

39. Let x = the nightly cost

$$x+0.08x = 162$$
$$1.08x = 162$$
$$x = 150$$

The nightly cost is \$150.

41. Let c = the dealer's cost

$$584 = c+0.25c$$
$$584 = 1.25c$$
$$467.20 = c$$

The dealer's cost is \$467.20.

43. $A = LW$ for L

$$\frac{A}{W} = \frac{LW}{W}$$
$$\frac{A}{W} = L \text{ or } L = \frac{A}{W}$$

45. $A = \frac{1}{2}bh$ for b

$$2(A) = 2\left(\frac{1}{2}bh\right)$$
$$2A = bh$$
$$\frac{2A}{h} = \frac{bh}{h}$$
$$\frac{2A}{h} = b \text{ or } b = \frac{2A}{h}$$

47. $I = Prt$ for P

$$\frac{I}{rt} = \frac{Prt}{rt}$$
$$\frac{I}{rt} = P \text{ or } P = \frac{I}{rt}$$

49. $E = mc^2$ for m

$$\frac{E}{c^2} = \frac{mc^2}{c^2}$$
$$\frac{E}{c^2} = m \text{ or } m = \frac{E}{c^2}$$

51. $y = mx+b$ for m

$$y-b = mx+b-b$$
$$y-b = mx$$
$$\frac{y-b}{x} = \frac{mx}{x}$$
$$\frac{y-b}{x} = m \text{ or } m = \frac{y-b}{x}$$

53. $A = \frac{1}{2}h(a+b)$ for a

$$2\cdot A = 2\cdot\frac{1}{2}h(a+b)$$
$$2A = h(a+b)$$
$$2A = ha+hb$$
$$2A-hb = ha$$
$$\frac{2A-bh}{h} = \frac{ha}{h}$$
$$a = \frac{2A-bh}{h}$$

55. $S = P + Prt$ for r

$$S - P = P + Prt - P$$
$$S - P = Prt$$
$$\frac{S-P}{Pt} = \frac{Prt}{Pt}$$
$$\frac{S-P}{Pt} = r \text{ or } r = \frac{S-P}{Pt}$$

57. $Ax + By = C$ for x

$$Ax + By = C$$
$$Ax = C - By$$
$$x = \frac{C - By}{A}$$

59. $a_n = a_1 + (n-1)$ for n

$$a_n = a_1 + (n-1)d$$
$$a_n - a_1 = dn - d$$
$$a_n - a_1 + d = dn$$
$$\frac{a_n - a_1 + d}{d} = n$$

65. does not make sense; Explanations will vary. Sample explanation: Though mathematical models can often provide excellent estimates about future attitudes, they cannot guarantee precise predictions.

67. does not make sense; Explanations will vary. Sample explanation: Solving a formula for one of its variables does not produce a numerical value for the variable.

69. Let x = original price
$x - 0.4x = 0.6x$ = price after first reduction
$0.6x - 0.4(0.6x)$ = price after second reduction

$$0.6x - 0.24x = 72$$
$$0.36x = 72$$
$$x = 200$$

The original price was $200.

71. Let x = number of problems solved correctly, then
$26 - x$ = number of problems done incorrectly

$$0.08x = 0.05(26 - x)$$
$$0.08x = 1.30 - 0.05x$$
$$0.08x + 0.05x = 1.30 - 0.05x + 0.05x$$
$$0.13x = 1.30$$
$$\frac{0.13x}{0.13} = \frac{1.30}{0.13}$$
$$x = 10$$

There were 10 problems solved correctly.

73. Let x = the number of plants originally stolen
After passing the first security guard, the thief has:

$$x - \left(\frac{1}{2}x + 2\right) = x - \frac{1}{2}x - 2 = \frac{1}{2}x - 2$$

After passing the second security guard, the thief has: $\frac{1}{2}x - 2 - \left(\frac{\frac{1}{2}x - 2}{2} + 2\right) = \frac{1}{4}x - 3$

After passing the third security guard, the thief has:

$$\frac{1}{4}x - 3 - \left(\frac{\frac{1}{4}x - 3}{2} + 2\right) = \frac{1}{8}x - \frac{7}{2}$$

Thus, $\frac{1}{8}x - \frac{7}{2} = 1$

$$x - 28 = 8$$
$$x = 36$$

The thief stole 36 plants.

75.

$$\frac{ax-b}{b} = \frac{c-d}{d}$$
$$d(ax-b) = b(c-d)$$
$$dax - db = bc - bd$$
$$dax = bc - bd + db$$
$$dax = bc$$
$$x = \frac{bc}{ad}$$

Check Points 6.4

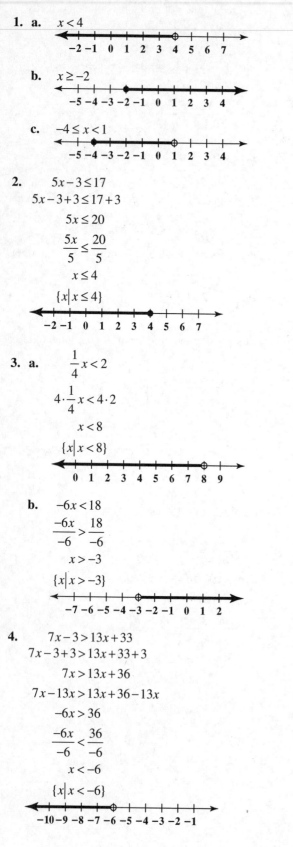

1. a. $x < 4$

b. $x \geq -2$

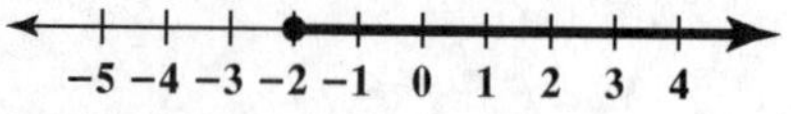

c. $-4 \leq x < 1$

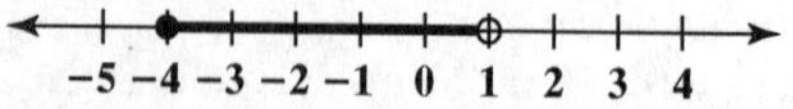

2.
$$\begin{aligned} 5x - 3 &\leq 17 \\ 5x - 3 + 3 &\leq 17 + 3 \\ 5x &\leq 20 \\ \frac{5x}{5} &\leq \frac{20}{5} \\ x &\leq 4 \end{aligned}$$
$\{x|x \leq 4\}$

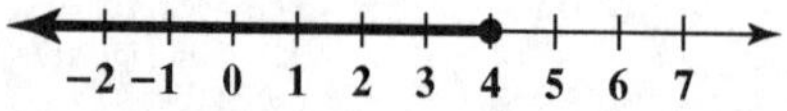

3. a.
$$\begin{aligned} \frac{1}{4}x &< 2 \\ 4 \cdot \frac{1}{4}x &< 4 \cdot 2 \\ x &< 8 \end{aligned}$$
$\{x|x < 8\}$

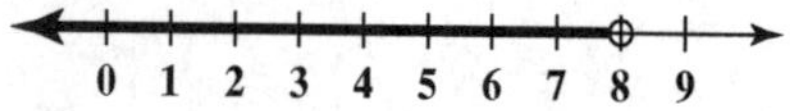

b.
$$\begin{aligned} -6x &< 18 \\ \frac{-6x}{-6} &> \frac{18}{-6} \\ x &> -3 \end{aligned}$$
$\{x|x > -3\}$

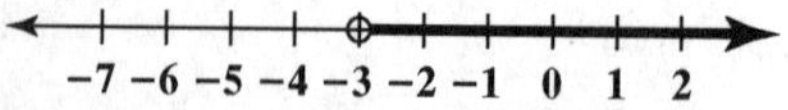

4.
$$\begin{aligned} 7x - 3 &> 13x + 33 \\ 7x - 3 + 3 &> 13x + 33 + 3 \\ 7x &> 13x + 36 \\ 7x - 13x &> 13x + 36 - 13x \\ -6x &> 36 \\ \frac{-6x}{-6} &< \frac{36}{-6} \\ x &< -6 \end{aligned}$$
$\{x|x < -6\}$

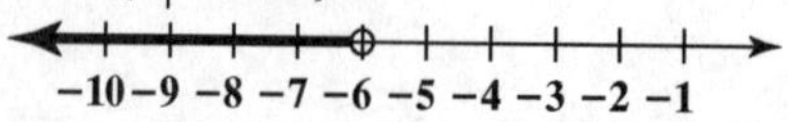

5.
$$\begin{aligned} 2(x-3) - 1 &\leq 3(x+2) - 14 \\ 2x - 6 - 1 &\leq 3x + 6 - 14 \\ 2x - 7 &\leq 3x - 8 \\ 2x - 7 + 7 &\leq 3x - 8 + 7 \\ 2x &\leq 3x - 1 \\ 2x - 3x &\leq 3x - 1 - 3x \\ -x &\leq -1 \\ \frac{-x}{-1} &\geq \frac{-1}{-1} \\ x &\geq 1 \end{aligned}$$
$\{x|x \geq 1\}$

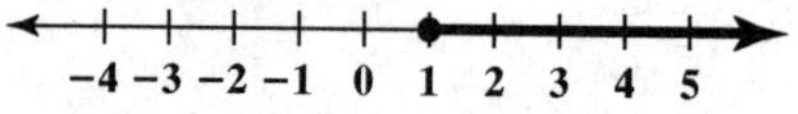

6.
$$\begin{aligned} 1 &\leq 2x + 3 < 11 \\ -2 &\leq 2x < 8 \\ -1 &\leq x < 4 \end{aligned}$$
The solution set is $\{x|-1 \leq x < 4\}$ or $[-1, 4)$.

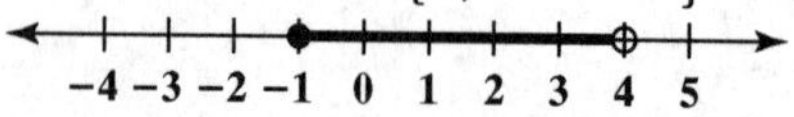

7. Let x = your grade on the final exam.
$$\begin{aligned} \frac{82 + 74 + 78 + x + x}{5} &\geq 80 \\ \frac{234 + 2x}{5} &\geq 80 \\ 5\left(\frac{234 + 2x}{5}\right) &\geq 5(80) \\ 234 + 2x &\geq 400 \\ 234 + 2x - 234 &\geq 400 - 234 \\ 2x &\geq 166 \\ \frac{2x}{2} &\geq \frac{166}{2} \\ x &\geq 83 \end{aligned}$$
You need at least an 83% on the final to get a B in the course.

Concept and Vocabulary Check 6.4

1. is not included; is included
2. $\{x|x < a\}$
3. $\{x|a < x \leq b\}$
4. negative
5. false

6. false

7. false

8. true

Exercise Set 6.4

1. $x > 6$

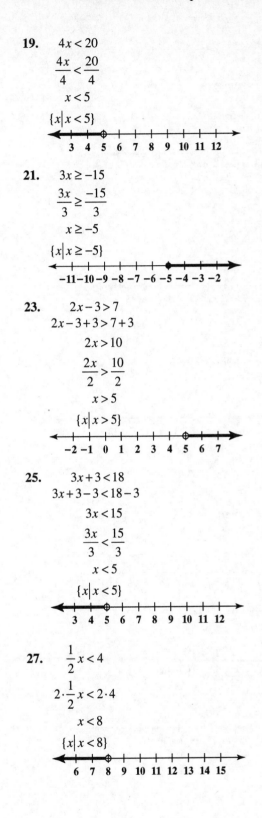

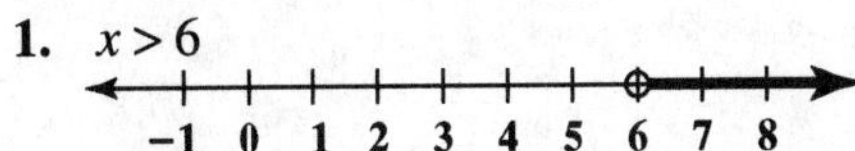

3. $x < -4$

5. $x \geq -3$

7. $x \leq 4$

9. $-2 < x \leq 5$

11. $-1 < x < 4$

13.
$$x - 3 > 2$$
$$x - 3 + 3 > 2 + 3$$
$$x > 5$$
$$\{x | x > 5\}$$

15.
$$x + 4 \leq 9$$
$$x + 4 - 4 \leq 9 - 4$$
$$x \leq 5$$
$$\{x | x \leq 5\}$$

17.
$$x - 3 < 0$$
$$x - 3 + 3 < 0 + 3$$
$$x < 3$$
$$\{x | x < 3\}$$

19.
$$4x < 20$$
$$\frac{4x}{4} < \frac{20}{4}$$
$$x < 5$$
$$\{x | x < 5\}$$

21.
$$3x \geq -15$$
$$\frac{3x}{3} \geq \frac{-15}{3}$$
$$x \geq -5$$
$$\{x | x \geq -5\}$$

23.

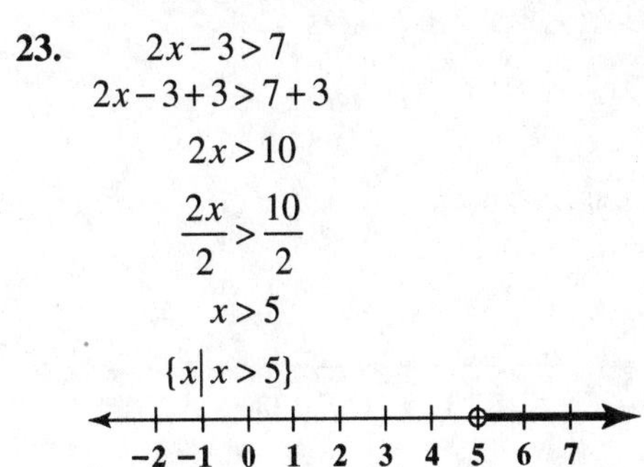

$$2x - 3 > 7$$
$$2x - 3 + 3 > 7 + 3$$
$$2x > 10$$
$$\frac{2x}{2} > \frac{10}{2}$$
$$x > 5$$
$$\{x | x > 5\}$$

25.

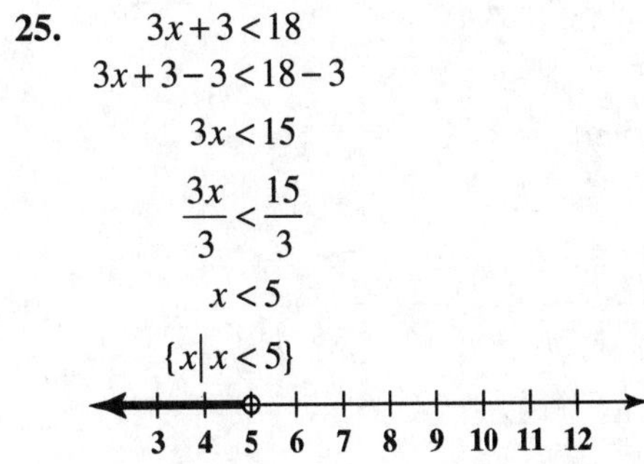

$$3x + 3 < 18$$
$$3x + 3 - 3 < 18 - 3$$
$$3x < 15$$
$$\frac{3x}{3} < \frac{15}{3}$$
$$x < 5$$
$$\{x | x < 5\}$$

27.

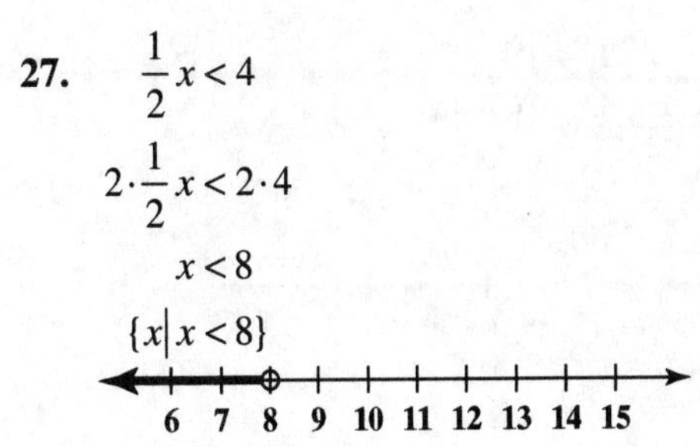

$$\frac{1}{2}x < 4$$
$$2 \cdot \frac{1}{2}x < 2 \cdot 4$$
$$x < 8$$
$$\{x | x < 8\}$$

29. $\frac{x}{3} > -2$

$3 \cdot \frac{x}{3} > 3 \cdot (-2)$

$x > -6$

$\{x | x > -6\}$

31. $-3x < 15$

$\frac{-3x}{-3} > \frac{15}{-3}$

$x > -5$

$\{x | x > -5\}$

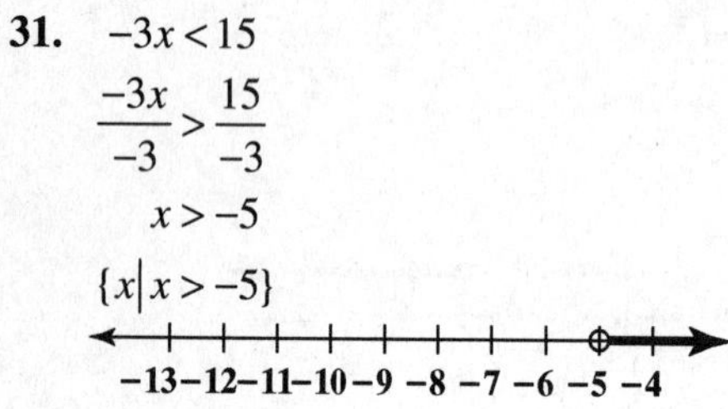

33. $-3x \geq -15$

$\frac{-3x}{-3} \leq \frac{-15}{-3}$

$x \leq 5$

$\{x | x \leq 5\}$

35. $3x + 4 \leq 2x + 7$

$3x + 4 - 4 \leq 2x + 7 - 4$

$3x \leq 2x + 3$

$3x - 2x \leq 2x + 3 - 2x$

$x \leq 3$

$\{x | x \leq 3\}$

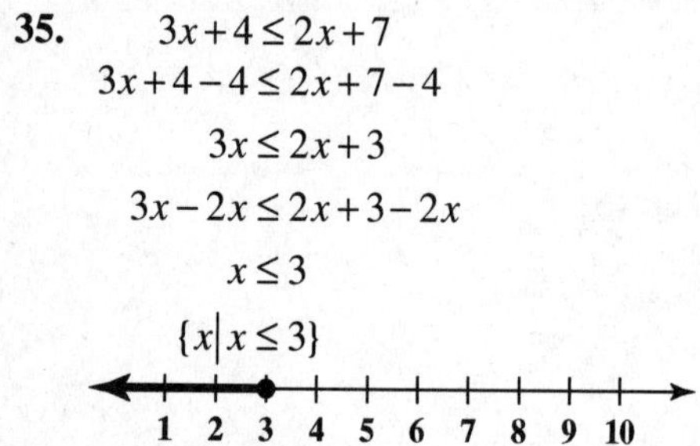

37. $5x - 9 < 4x + 7$

$5x - 9 + 9 < 4x + 7 + 9$

$5x < 4x + 16$

$5x - 4x < 4x + 16 - 4x$

$x < 16$

$\{x | x < 16\}$

39. $-2x - 3 < 3$

$-2x - 3 + 3 < 3 + 3$

$-2x < 6$

$\frac{-2x}{-2} > \frac{6}{-2}$

$x > -3$

$\{x | x > -3\}$

41. $3 - 7x \leq 17$

$3 - 7x - 3 \leq 17 - 3$

$-7x \leq 14$

$\frac{-7x}{-7} \geq \frac{14}{-7}$

$x \geq -2$

$\{x | x \geq -2\}$

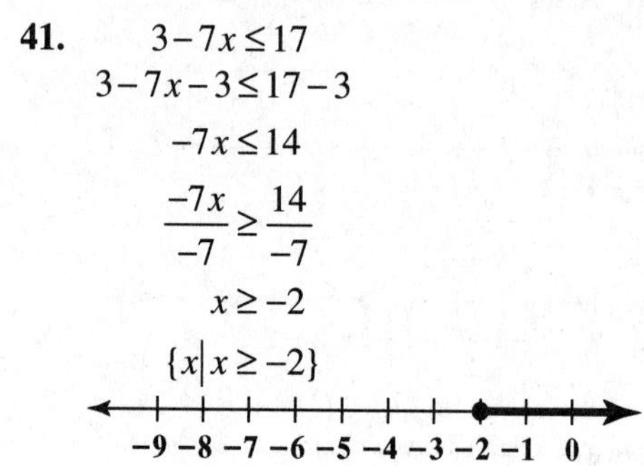

43. $-x < 4$

$\frac{-x}{-1} > \frac{4}{-1}$

$x > -4$

$\{x | x > -4\}$

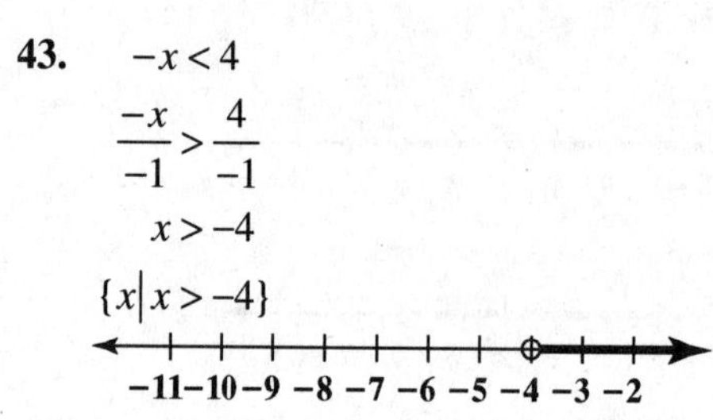

45. $5 - x \leq 1$

$5 - x - 5 \leq 1 - 5$

$-x \leq -4$

$\frac{-x}{-1} \geq \frac{-4}{-1}$

$x \geq 4$

$\{x | x \geq 4\}$

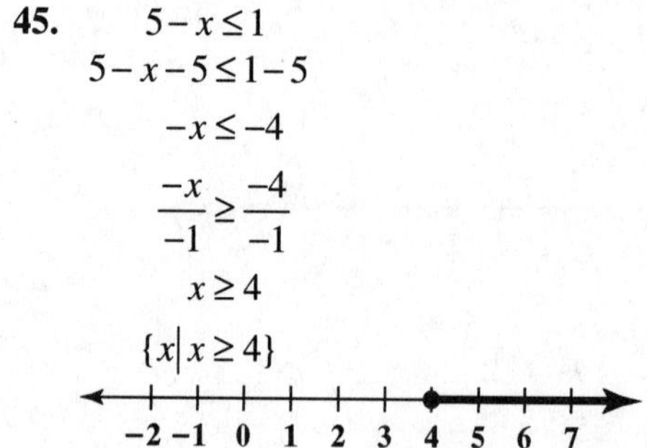

47.
$$\begin{aligned} 2x-5 &> -x+6 \\ 2x-5+5 &> -x+6+5 \\ 2x &> -x+11 \\ 2x+x &> -x+11+x \\ 3x &> 11 \\ \frac{3x}{3} &> \frac{11}{3} \\ x &> \frac{11}{3} \end{aligned}$$
$$\left\{x \middle| x > \frac{11}{3}\right\}$$

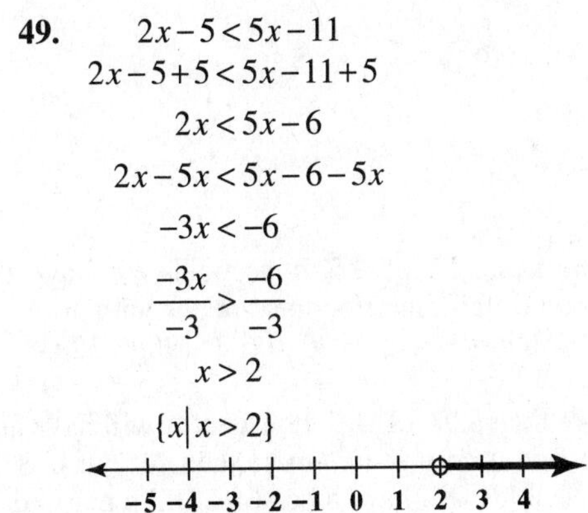

49.
$$\begin{aligned} 2x-5 &< 5x-11 \\ 2x-5+5 &< 5x-11+5 \\ 2x &< 5x-6 \\ 2x-5x &< 5x-6-5x \\ -3x &< -6 \\ \frac{-3x}{-3} &> \frac{-6}{-3} \\ x &> 2 \end{aligned}$$
$$\{x|x>2\}$$

51.
$$\begin{aligned} 3(x+1)-5 &< 2x+1 \\ 3x+3-5 &< 2x+1 \\ 3x-2 &< 2x+1 \\ 3x-2+2 &< 2x+1+2 \\ 3x &< 2x+3 \\ 3x-2x &< 2x+3-2x \\ x &< 3 \end{aligned}$$
$$\{x|x<3\}$$

53.

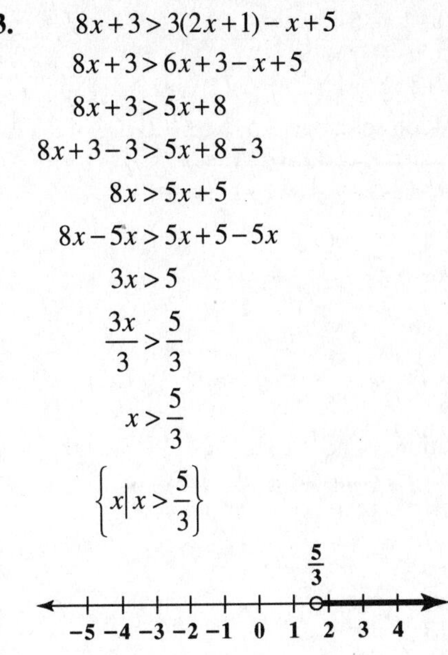

$$\begin{aligned} 8x+3 &> 3(2x+1)-x+5 \\ 8x+3 &> 6x+3-x+5 \\ 8x+3 &> 5x+8 \\ 8x+3-3 &> 5x+8-3 \\ 8x &> 5x+5 \\ 8x-5x &> 5x+5-5x \\ 3x &> 5 \\ \frac{3x}{3} &> \frac{5}{3} \\ x &> \frac{5}{3} \end{aligned}$$
$$\left\{x \middle| x > \frac{5}{3}\right\}$$

55.

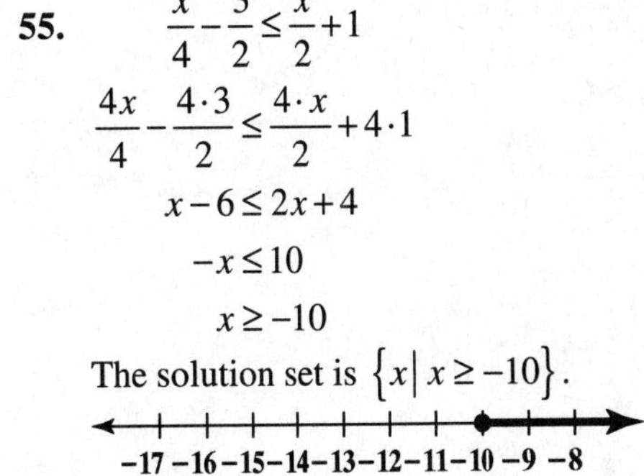

$$\begin{aligned} \frac{x}{4}-\frac{3}{2} &\le \frac{x}{2}+1 \\ \frac{4x}{4}-\frac{4\cdot 3}{2} &\le \frac{4\cdot x}{2}+4\cdot 1 \\ x-6 &\le 2x+4 \\ -x &\le 10 \\ x &\ge -10 \end{aligned}$$
The solution set is $\{x|\,x\ge -10\}$.

57.

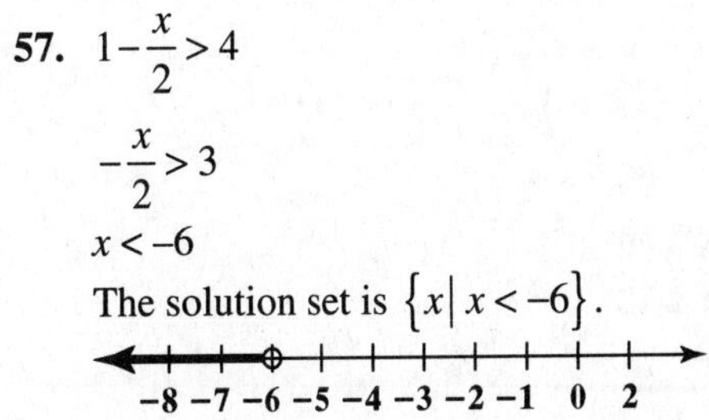

$1-\frac{x}{2}>4$

$-\frac{x}{2}>3$

$x<-6$

The solution set is $\{x|\,x<-6\}$.

59. $6<x+3<8$
$6-3<x+3-3<8-3$
$3<x<5$
The solution set is $\{x|\,3<x<5\}$.

61. $-3 \bullet x-2<1$
$-1 \bullet x<3$
The solution set is $\{x|-1\le x<3\}$.

63. $-11 < 2x - 1 \bullet -5$
$-10 < 2x \bullet -4$
$-5 < x \bullet -2$
The solution set is $\{x \mid -5 < x \le -2\}$.

−8 −7 −6 −5 −4 −3 −2 −1 0 1

65. $-3 \le \frac{2}{3}x - 5 < -1$

$2 \le \frac{2}{3}x < 4$

$3 \bullet x < 6$

The solution set is $\{x \mid 3 \le x < 6\}$.

0 1 2 3 4 5 6 7 8 9

67. $Ax + By > C$

$Ax > C - By$

$x > \frac{C - By}{A}$

69. $Ax + By > C$

$Ax > C - By$

$x < \frac{C - By}{A}$

71. $\{x \mid x + 5 \ge 2x\}$ or $\{x \mid x \le 5\}$

$x + 5 \ge 2x$

$-x \ge -5$

$x \le 5$

73. $\{x \mid 2(4 + x) \le 36\}$ or $\{x \mid x \le 14\}$

$2(4 + x) \le 36$

$8 + 2x \le 36$

$2x \le 28$

$x \le 14$

75. $\left\{x \,\middle|\, \frac{3x}{5} + 4 \le 34\right\}$ or $\{x \mid x \le 50\}$

$\frac{3x}{5} + 4 \le 34$

$\frac{3x}{5} \le 30$

$3x \le 150$

$x \le 50$

77. $\{x \mid 0 < x < 4\}$

79. intimacy ≥ passion or
passion ≤ intimacy

81. commitment > passion or
passion < commitment

83. The maximum level of intensity for passion is 9. This occurs after 3 years.

85. a. $I = \frac{1}{4}x + 26$

$\frac{1}{4}x + 26 > 33$

$\frac{1}{4}x > 7$

$x > 28$

More than 33% of U.S. households will have an interfaith marriage in years after 2016 (i.e. $1988 + 28$).

b. $N = \frac{1}{4}x + 6$

$\frac{1}{4}x + 6 > 14$

$\frac{1}{4}x > 8$

$x > 32$

More than 14% of U.S. households will have a person of faith married to someone with no religion in years after 2020 (i.e. $1988 + 32$).

c. More than 33% of U.S. households will have an interfaith marriage *and* more than 14% of U.S. households will have a person of faith married to someone with no religion in years after 2020.

87. a. $\frac{86 + 88 + x}{3} \ge 90$

$\frac{174 + x}{3} \ge 90$

$3 \cdot \frac{174 + x}{3} \ge 3 \cdot 90$

$174 + x \ge 270$

$174 + x - 174 \ge 270 - 174$

$x \ge 96$

You must get at least 96 on the final to earn an A in the course.

b. $$\frac{86+88+x}{3}<80$$
$$\frac{174+x}{3}<80$$
$$3\cdot\frac{174+x}{3}<80\cdot 3$$
$$174+x<240$$
$$174+x-174<240-174$$
$$x<66$$
If you get less than a 66 on the final you will lose your B in the course.

89. Let x = number of miles driven.
$$80+0.25x\le 400$$
$$80+0.25x-80\le 400-80$$
$$0.25x\le 320$$
$$\frac{0.25x}{0.25}\le\frac{320}{0.25}$$
$$x\le 1280$$
You can drive at most 1280 miles.

91. Let x = number of cement bags.
$$245+95x\le 3000$$
$$245+95x-245\le 3000-245$$
$$95x\le 2755$$
$$\frac{95x}{95}\le\frac{2755}{95}$$
$$x\le 29$$
At most 29 bags can be safely lifted.

93. $$28\le 20+0.40(x-60)\le 40$$
$$28\le 20+0.40x-24\le 40$$
$$28\le 0.40x-4\le 40$$
$$32\le 0.40x\le 44$$
$$80\le x\le 110$$

Between 80 and 110 ten minutes, inclusive.

99. makes sense

101. makes sense

103. Let x = number of miles driven.
Basic: 260
Continental: $80+0.25x$
$$260<80+0.25x$$
$$260-80<80+0.25x-80$$
$$180<0.25x$$
$$\frac{180}{0.25}<\frac{0.25x}{0.25}$$
$$720<x \text{ or } x>720$$
The miles driven must exceed 720 for Basic Rental to be a better deal than Continental.

Check Points 6.5

1. $$(x+5)(x+6)=x\cdot x+x\cdot 6+5\cdot x+5\cdot 6$$
$$=x^2+6x+5x+30$$
$$=x^2+11x+30$$

2. $$(7x+5)(4x-3)=7x\cdot 4x+7x(-3)+5\cdot 4x+5(-3)$$
$$=28x^2-21x+20x-15$$
$$=28x^2-x-15$$

3. $x^2+5x+6=(x+2)(x+3)$

4. $x^2+3x-10=(x+5)(x-2)$

5. $5x^2-14x+8=(5x-4)(x-2)$

6. $6y^2+19y-7=(3y-1)(2y+7)$

7. $$(x+6)(x-3)=0$$
$$x+6=0 \quad\text{or}\quad x-3=0$$
$$x=-6 \qquad\qquad x=3$$
The solution set is $\{-6, 3\}$.

8. $$x^2-6x=16$$
$$x^2-6x-16=16-16$$
$$x^2-6x-16=0$$
$$(x+2)(x-8)=0$$
$$x+2=0 \quad\text{or}\quad x-8=0$$
$$x=-2 \qquad\qquad x=8$$
The solution set is $\{-2, 8\}$.

9. $2x^2+7x-4=0$

$(2x-1)(x+4)=0$

$2x-1=0 \quad \text{or} \quad x+4=0$

$2x=1 \qquad x=-4$

$x=\frac{1}{2}$

The solution set is $\left\{-4, \frac{1}{2}\right\}$.

10. $8x^2+2x-1=0$

$$x=\frac{-b\pm\sqrt{b^2-4ac}}{2a}$$

$$x=\frac{-(2)\pm\sqrt{(2)^2-4(8)(-1)}}{2(8)}$$

$$x=\frac{-2\pm\sqrt{4+32}}{16}$$

$$x=\frac{-2\pm\sqrt{36}}{16}$$

$$x=\frac{-2\pm 6}{16}$$

$$x=\frac{-2+6}{16} \quad \text{or} \quad x=\frac{-2-6}{16}$$

$$x=\frac{4}{16} \qquad x=\frac{-8}{16}$$

$$x=\frac{1}{4} \qquad x=-\frac{1}{2}$$

The solution set is $\left\{-\frac{1}{2}, \frac{1}{4}\right\}$.

11. $2x^2=6x-1$

$2x^2-6x+1=0$

$$x=\frac{-b\pm\sqrt{b^2-4ac}}{2a}$$

$$x=\frac{-(-6)\pm\sqrt{(-6)^2-4(2)(1)}}{2(2)}$$

$$x=\frac{6\pm\sqrt{36-8}}{4}$$

$$x=\frac{6\pm\sqrt{28}}{4}$$

$$x=\frac{6\pm 2\sqrt{7}}{4}$$

$$x=\frac{2\left(3\pm\sqrt{7}\right)}{4}$$

$$x=\frac{3\pm\sqrt{7}}{2}$$

$$x=\frac{3+\sqrt{7}}{2} \quad \text{or} \quad x=\frac{3-\sqrt{7}}{2}$$

The solution set is $\left\{\frac{3+\sqrt{7}}{2}, \frac{3-\sqrt{7}}{2}\right\}$.

12. $P=0.01A^2+0.05A+107$

$115=0.01A^2+0.05A+107$

$0=0.01A^2+0.05A-8$

$a=0.01, \quad b=0.05, \quad c=-8$

$$A=\frac{-b\pm\sqrt{b^2-4ac}}{2a}$$

$$A=\frac{-(0.05)\pm\sqrt{(0.05)^2-4(0.01)(-8)}}{2(0.01)}$$

$$A=\frac{-0.05\pm\sqrt{0.3225}}{0.02}$$

$$A\approx\frac{-0.05+\sqrt{0.3225}}{0.02} \qquad A\approx\frac{-0.05-\sqrt{0.3225}}{0.02}$$

$$A\approx 26 \qquad A\approx -31$$

Age cannot be negative, reject the negative answer. Thus, a woman whose normal systolic blood pressure is 115 mm Hg is 26 years old.

Concept and Vocabulary Check 6.5

1. $2x^2$; $3x$; $10x$; 15

2. + 10

3. -6

4. $+5$

5. -7

6. -3

7. -4

8. $2x-3$

9. $3x+4$

10. quadratic

11. $A=0$ or $B=0$

12. subtracting 18

13. $x=\dfrac{-b\pm\sqrt{b^2-4ac}}{2a}$; quadratic formula

14. false

15. false

16. false

17. false

18. false

Exercise Set 6.5

1. $(x+3)(x+5)=x^2+5x+3x+15$
$=x^2+8x+15$

3. $(x-5)(x+3)=x^2+3x-5x-15$
$=x^2-2x-15$

5. $(2x-1)(x+2)=2x^2+4x-1x-2$
$=2x^2+3x-2$

7. $(3x-7)(4x-5)=12x^2-15x-28x+35$
$=12x^2-43x+35$

9. $x^2+5x+6=(x+2)(x+3)$
Check: $(x+2)(x+3)$
$=x^2+3x+2x+6$
$=x^2+5x+6$

11. $x^2-2x-15=(x-5)(x+3)$
Check: $(x-5)(x+3)$
$=x^2+3x-5x-15$
$=x^2-2x-15$

13. $x^2-8x+15=(x-3)(x-5)$
Check: $(x-3)(x-5)$
$=x^2-5x-3x+15$
$=x^2-8x+15$

15. $x^2-9x-36=(x-12)(x+3)$
Check: $(x-12)(x+3)$
$=x^2+3x-12x-36$
$=x^2-9x-36$

17. $x^2-8x+32$ is prime.

19. $x^2+17x+16=(x+16)(x+1)$
Check: $(x+16)(x+1)$
$=x^2+x+16x+16$
$=x^2+17x+16$

21. $2x^2+7x+3=(2x+1)(x+3)$
Check: $(2x+1)(x+3)$
$=2x^2+6x+x+3$
$=2x^2+7x+3$

23. $2x^2-17x+30=(2x-5)(x-6)$
Check: $(2x-5)(x-6)$
$=2x^2-12x-5x+30$
$=2x^2-17x+30$

25. $3x^2-x-2=(3x+2)(x-1)$
Check: $(3x+2)(x-1)$
$=3x^2-3x+2x-2$
$=3x^2-x-2$

27. $3x^2-25x-28=(3x-28)(x+1)$
Check: $(3x-28)(x+1)$
$=3x^2+3x-28x-28$
$=3x^2-25x-28$

29. $6x^2 - 11x + 4 = (2x-1)(3x-4)$
Check: $(2x-1)(3x-4)$
$= 6x^2 - 8x - 3x + 4$
$= 6x^2 - 11x + 4$

31. $4x^2 + 16x + 15 = (2x+5)(2x+3)$
Check: $(2x+5)(2x+3)$
$= 4x^2 + 6x + 10x + 15$
$= 4x^2 + 16x + 15$

33. $(x-8)(x+3) = 0$
$x - 8 = 0$ or $x + 3 = 0$
$x = 8$ $\quad x = -3$
The solution set is {–3, 8}.

35. $(4x+5)(x-2) = 0$
$4x + 5 = 0$ or $x-2=0$
$4x = -5$ $\quad x = 2$
$x = -\frac{5}{4}$
The solution set is $\left\{-\frac{5}{4}, 2\right\}$.

37. $x^2 + 8x + 15 = 0$
$(x+5)(x+3) = 0$
$x + 5 = 0$ or $x + 3 = 0$
$x = -5$ $\quad x = -3$
The solution set is {–5, –3}.

39. $x^2 - 2x - 15 = 0$
$(x-5)(x+3) = 0$
$x - 5 = 0$ or $x + 3 = 0$
$x = 5$ $\quad x = -3$
The solution set is {–3, 5}.

41. $x^2 - 4x = 21$
$x^2 - 4x - 21 = 0$
$(x+3)(x-7) = 0$
$x + 3 = 0$ or $x - 7 = 0$
$x = -3$ $\quad x = 7$
The solution set is {–3, 7}.

43. $x^2 + 9x = -8$
$x^2 + 9x + 8 = 0$
$(x+8)(x+1) = 0$
$x + 8 = 0$ or $x + 1 = 0$
$x = -8$ $\quad x = -1$
The solution set is {–8, –1}.

45. $x^2 - 12x = -36$
$x^2 - 12x + 36 = 0$
$(x-6)(x-6) = 0$
$x - 6 = 0$ or $x - 6 = 0$
$x = 6$ $\quad x = 6$
The solution set is {6}.

47. $2x^2 = 7x + 4$
$2x^2 - 7x - 4 = 0$
$(2x+1)(x-4) = 0$
$2x + 1 = 0$ or $x - 4 = 0$
$2x = -1$ $\quad x = 4$
$x = -\frac{1}{2}$
The solution set is $\left\{-\frac{1}{2}, 4\right\}$.

49. $5x^2 + x = 18$
$5x^2 + x - 18 = 0$
$(5x-9)(x+2) = 0$
$5x - 9 = 0$ or $x + 2 = 0$
$5x = 9$ $\quad x = -2$
$x = \frac{9}{5}$
The solution set is $\left\{-2, \frac{9}{5}\right\}$.

51. $x(6x+23) + 7 = 0$
$6x^2 + 23x + 7 = 0$
$(2x+7)(3x+1) = 0$
$2x + 7 = 0$ or $3x + 1 = 0$
$2x = -7$ $\quad 3x = -1$
$x = -\frac{7}{2}$ $\quad x = -\frac{1}{3}$
The solution set is $\left\{-\frac{7}{2}, -\frac{1}{3}\right\}$.

53. $x^2+8x+15=0$

$$x=\frac{-b\pm\sqrt{b^2-4ac}}{2a}$$
$$x=\frac{-8\pm\sqrt{8^2-4(1)(15)}}{2(1)}$$
$$x=\frac{-8\pm\sqrt{4}}{2}$$
$$x=\frac{-8\pm 2}{2}$$
$$x=\frac{-8-2}{2} \quad \text{or} \quad x=\frac{-8+2}{2}$$
$$x=-5 \qquad\qquad x=-3$$

The solution set is $\{-5, -3\}$.

55. $x^2+5x+3=0$

$$x=\frac{-b\pm\sqrt{b^2-4ac}}{2a}$$
$$x=\frac{-5\pm\sqrt{5^2-4(1)(3)}}{2(1)}$$
$$x=\frac{-5\pm\sqrt{13}}{2}$$

The solution set is $\left\{\frac{-5-\sqrt{13}}{2}, \frac{-5+\sqrt{13}}{2}\right\}$.

57. $x^2+4x=6$

$$x^2+4x-6=0$$
$$x=\frac{-b\pm\sqrt{b^2-4ac}}{2a}$$
$$x=\frac{-4\pm\sqrt{4^2-4(1)(-6)}}{2(1)}$$
$$x=\frac{-4\pm\sqrt{40}}{2}$$
$$x=\frac{-4\pm 2\sqrt{10}}{2}$$
$$x=-2\pm\sqrt{10}$$

The solution set is $\left\{-2-\sqrt{10}, -2+\sqrt{10}\right\}$.

59. $x^2+4x-7=0$

$$x=\frac{-b\pm\sqrt{b^2-4ac}}{2a}$$
$$x=\frac{-4\pm\sqrt{4^2-4(1)(-7)}}{2(1)}$$
$$x=\frac{-4\pm\sqrt{44}}{2}$$
$$x=\frac{-4\pm 2\sqrt{11}}{2}$$
$$x=-2\pm\sqrt{11}$$

The solution set is $\left\{-2-\sqrt{11}, -2+\sqrt{11}\right\}$.

61. $x^2-3x=18$

$$x^2-3x-18=0$$
$$x=\frac{-b\pm\sqrt{b^2-4ac}}{2a}$$
$$x=\frac{-(-3)\pm\sqrt{(-3)^2-4(1)(-18)}}{2(1)}$$
$$x=\frac{3\pm\sqrt{81}}{2}$$
$$x=\frac{3\pm 9}{2}$$
$$x=\frac{3-9}{2} \quad \text{or} \quad x=\frac{3+9}{2}$$
$$x=-3 \qquad\qquad x=6$$

The solution set is $\{-3, 6\}$.

63. $6x^2-5x-6=0$

$$x=\frac{-b\pm\sqrt{b^2-4ac}}{2a}$$
$$x=\frac{-(-5)\pm\sqrt{(-5)^2-4(6)(-6)}}{2(6)}$$
$$x=\frac{5\pm\sqrt{169}}{12}$$
$$x=\frac{5\pm 13}{12}$$
$$x=\frac{5+13}{12} \quad \textit{or} \quad x=\frac{5-13}{12}$$
$$x=\frac{18}{12} \qquad\qquad x=\frac{-8}{12}$$
$$x=\frac{3}{2} \qquad\qquad x=-\frac{2}{3}$$

The solution set is $\left\{\frac{3}{2}, -\frac{2}{3}\right\}$.

65. $x^2-2x-10=0$

$$x=\frac{-b\pm\sqrt{b^2-4ac}}{2a}$$
$$x=\frac{-(-2)\pm\sqrt{(-2)^2-4(1)(-10)}}{2(1)}$$
$$x=\frac{2\pm\sqrt{44}}{2}$$
$$x=\frac{2\pm2\sqrt{11}}{2}$$
$$x=1\pm\sqrt{11}$$

The solution set is $\{1-\sqrt{11},\ 1+\sqrt{11}\}$.

67. $x^2-x=14$

$$x^2-x-14=0$$
$$x=\frac{-b\pm\sqrt{b^2-4ac}}{2a}$$
$$x=\frac{-(-1)\pm\sqrt{(-1)^2-4(1)(-14)}}{2(1)}$$
$$x=\frac{1\pm\sqrt{57}}{2}$$

The solution set is $\left\{\frac{1-\sqrt{57}}{2},\ \frac{1+\sqrt{57}}{2}\right\}$.

69. $6x^2+6x+1=0$

$$x=\frac{-b\pm\sqrt{b^2-4ac}}{2a}$$
$$x=\frac{-6\pm\sqrt{6^2-4(6)(1)}}{2(6)}$$
$$x=\frac{-6\pm\sqrt{12}}{12}$$
$$x=\frac{-6\pm2\sqrt{3}}{12}$$
$$x=\frac{-3\pm\sqrt{3}}{6}$$

The solution set is $\left\{\frac{-3-\sqrt{3}}{6},\ \frac{-3+\sqrt{3}}{6}\right\}$.

71. $4x^2=12x-9$

$$4x^2-12x+9=0$$
$$x=\frac{-b\pm\sqrt{b^2-4ac}}{2a}$$
$$x=\frac{-(-12)\pm\sqrt{(-12)^2-4(4)(9)}}{2(4)}$$
$$x=\frac{12\pm\sqrt{0}}{8}$$
$$x=\frac{12}{8}=\frac{3}{2}$$

The solution set is $\left\{\frac{3}{2}\right\}$.

73. $\frac{3x^2}{4}-\frac{5x}{2}-2=0$

$$3x^2-10x-8=0$$
$$(x-4)(3x+2)=0$$
$$x-4=0 \quad\text{or}\quad 3x+2=0$$
$$x=4 \qquad x=-\frac{2}{3}$$

The solution set is $\left\{-\frac{2}{3},4\right\}$.

75. $(x-1)(3x+2)=-7(x-1)$

$$3x^2-x-2=-7x+7$$
$$3x^2+6x-9=0$$
$$x^2+2x-3=0$$
$$(x-1)(x+3)=0$$
$$x-1=0 \quad\text{or}\quad x+3=0$$
$$x=1 \qquad x=-3$$

The solution set is $\{-3,1\}$.

77. $(2x-6)(x+2)=5(x-1)-12$

$$(2x-6)(x+2)=5x-5-12$$
$$2x^2-2x-12=5x-17$$
$$2x^2-7x+5=0$$
$$(x-1)(2x-5)=0$$
$$x-1=0 \quad\text{or}\quad 2x-5=0$$
$$x=1 \qquad x=\frac{5}{2}$$

The solution set is $\left\{1,\frac{5}{2}\right\}$.

79. $2x^2 - 9x - 3 = 9 - 9x$

$2x^2 = 12$

$x^2 = 6$

$x = \pm\sqrt{6}$

The solution set is $\{\pm\sqrt{6}\}$.

81. Let x = the number.

$x^2 - (6 + 2x) = 0$

$x^2 - 2x - 6 = 0$

Apply the quadratic formula.

$a = 1 \quad b = -2 \quad c = -6$

$$x = \frac{-(-2) \pm \sqrt{(-2)^2 - 4(1)(-6)}}{2(1)}$$

$$= \frac{2 \pm \sqrt{4 - (-24)}}{2} = \frac{2 \pm \sqrt{28}}{2}$$

$$= \frac{2 \pm \sqrt{4 \cdot 7}}{2} = \frac{2 \pm 2\sqrt{7}}{2} = 1 \pm \sqrt{7}$$

We disregard $1 - \sqrt{7}$ because it is negative, and we are looking for a positive number. Thus, the number is $1 + \sqrt{7}$.

83. $N = \dfrac{t^2 - t}{2}$

$36 = \dfrac{t^2 - t}{2}$

$72 = t^2 - t$

$0 = t^2 - t - 72$

$0 = (t + 8)(t - 9)$

$t + 8 = 0 \quad \text{or} \quad t - 9 = 0$

$t = -8 \qquad t = 9$

Thus, the league has 9 teams.

85. a. $p = 0.004x^2 - 0.36x + 14$

$p = 0.004(80)^2 - 0.36(80) + 14 = 10.8$

According to the model, 10.8% of the U.S. population was foreign-born in 2000. This overestimates the actual number by 0.4%.

b. $p = 0.004x^2 - 0.36x + 14$

$18 = 0.004x^2 - 0.36x + 14$

$0 = 0.004x^2 - 0.36x - 4$

Apply the quadratic formula.

$a = 0.004 \quad b = -0.36 \quad c = -4$

$$x = \frac{-(-0.36) \pm \sqrt{(-0.36)^2 - 4(0.004)(-4)}}{2(0.004)}$$

$x \approx -10 \text{ or } x \approx 100$

We disregard -10 because it is prior to when the model applies.

18% of the U.S. population will be foreign-born 100 years after 1920, or 2020.

87. a. $\dfrac{1}{\Phi - 1}$

b. $\dfrac{\Phi}{1} = \dfrac{1}{\Phi - 1}$

$(\Phi - 1)\dfrac{\Phi}{1} = (\Phi - 1)\dfrac{1}{\Phi - 1}$

$\Phi^2 - \Phi = 1$

$\Phi^2 - \Phi - 1 = 0$

$$\Phi = \frac{-b \pm \sqrt{b^2 - 4ac}}{2a}$$

$$\Phi = \frac{-(-1) \pm \sqrt{(-1)^2 - 4(1)(-1)}}{2(1)}$$

$$\Phi = \frac{1 \pm \sqrt{1 + 4}}{2}$$

$\Phi = \dfrac{1 \pm \sqrt{5}}{2}$, reject negative

$$\Phi = \frac{1 + \sqrt{5}}{2}$$

c. The golden ratio is $\dfrac{1 + \sqrt{5}}{2}$ to 1.

93. does not make sense; Explanations will vary. Sample explanation: There are an infinite number of such pairs.

95. does not make sense; Explanations will vary. Sample explanation: The factoring method would be quicker.

97. If $b^2 - 4ac$ is negative, there are no real solutions because the square root of a negative number is not real. If $b^2 - 4ac = 0$, then there is one rational solution. If $b^2 - 4ac$ is a positive perfect square, then there are two rational solutions. If $b^2 - 4ac$ is positive, but not a perfect square, then there are two irrational solutions.

99. $x^2 + 4x + b$

$(x+3)(x+1) = x^2 + 4x + 3$

$(x+2)(x+2) = x^2 + 4x + 4$

Therefore, $b = 3, 4$.

101. $x^2 + 2\sqrt{3}x - 9 = 0$

$$x = \frac{-b \pm \sqrt{b^2 - 4ac}}{2a}$$

$$x = \frac{-2\sqrt{3} \pm \sqrt{(2\sqrt{3})^2 - 4(1)(-9)}}{2(1)}$$

$$x = \frac{-2\sqrt{3} \pm \sqrt{48}}{2}$$

$$x = \frac{-2\sqrt{3} \pm 4\sqrt{3}}{2}$$

$x = -\sqrt{3} \pm 2\sqrt{3}$

$x = -\sqrt{3} + 2\sqrt{3}$ or $x = -\sqrt{3} - 2\sqrt{3}$

$x = \sqrt{3}$ $\qquad x = -3\sqrt{3}$

The solution set is $\left\{-3\sqrt{3}, \sqrt{3}\right\}$.

Chapter 6 Review Exercises

1. $6x + 9 = 6 \cdot 4 + 9 = 24 + 9 = 33$

2.
$$\begin{aligned} 7x^2 + 4x - 5 &= 7(-2)^2 + 4(-2) - 5 \\ &= 7(4) + 4(-2) - 5 \\ &= 28 - 8 - 5 \\ &= 15 \end{aligned}$$

3.
$$\begin{aligned} 6 + 2(x-8)^3 &= 6 + 2(5-8)^3 \\ &= 6 + 2(-3)^3 \\ &= 6 + 2(-27) \\ &= 6 - 54 \\ &= -48 \end{aligned}$$

4. $D = 0.005x^2 + 0.55x + 34$

$$\begin{aligned} D &= 0.005(30)^2 + 0.55(30) + 34 \\ &= 55 \end{aligned}$$

The U.S. diversity index was 55% in 2010. This is the same as the value displayed in the bar graph.

5.
$$\begin{aligned} 5(2x-3) + 7x &= 10x - 15 + 7x \\ &= 17x - 15 \end{aligned}$$

6.
$$\begin{aligned} 3(4y-5) - (7y-2) &= 12y - 15 - 7y + 2 \\ &= 5y - 13 \end{aligned}$$

7.
$$\begin{aligned} 2(x^2 + 5x) + 3(4x^2 - 3x) &= 2x^2 + 10x + 12x^2 - 9x \\ &= 14x^2 + x \end{aligned}$$

8.
$$\begin{aligned} 4x + 9 &= 33 \\ 4x + 9 - 9 &= 33 - 9 \\ 4x &= 24 \\ \frac{4x}{4} &= \frac{24}{4} \\ x &= 6 \end{aligned}$$

The solution set is $\{6\}$.

9.
$$\begin{aligned} 5x - 3 &= x + 5 \\ 5x - 3 + 3 &= x + 5 + 3 \\ 5x &= x + 8 \\ 5x - x &= x + 8 - x \\ 4x &= 8 \\ \frac{4x}{4} &= \frac{8}{4} \\ x &= 2 \end{aligned}$$

The solution set is $\{2\}$.

10.
$$\begin{aligned} 3(x+4) &= 5x - 12 \\ 3x + 12 &= 5x - 12 \\ 3x + 12 - 12 &= 5x - 12 - 12 \\ 3x &= 5x - 24 \\ 3x - 5x &= 5x - 24 - 5x \\ -2x &= -24 \\ \frac{-2x}{-2} &= \frac{-24}{-2} \\ x &= 12 \end{aligned}$$

The solution set is $\{12\}$.

11. $2(x-2)+3(x+5)=2x-2$
$$\begin{aligned} 2x-4+3x+15&=2x-2\\ 5x+11&=2x-2\\ 5x+11-11&=2x-2-11\\ 5x&=2x-13\\ 5x-2x&=2x-13-2x\\ 3x&=-13\\ \frac{3x}{3}&=\frac{-13}{3}\\ x&=-\frac{13}{3} \end{aligned}$$
The solution set is $\left\{-\frac{13}{3}\right\}$.

12. $\frac{2x}{3}=\frac{x}{6}+1$
$$\begin{aligned} 6\left(\frac{2x}{3}\right)&=6\left(\frac{x}{6}+1\right)\\ 4x&=x+6\\ 4x-x&=x+6-x\\ 3x&=6\\ \frac{3x}{3}&=\frac{6}{3}\\ x&=2 \end{aligned}$$
The solution set is $\{2\}$.

13. $7x+5=5(x+3)+2x$
$$\begin{aligned} 7x+5&=5x+15+2x\\ 7x+5&=7x+15\\ 5&=15 \end{aligned}$$
This is a false statement. The solution set is { }.

14. $7x+13=2(2x-5)+3x+23$
$$\begin{aligned} 7x+13&=4x-10+3x+23\\ 7x+13&=7x+13\\ 13&=13 \end{aligned}$$
This is a true statement. The solution set is $\{x|x \text{ is a real number}\}$.

15. $\frac{3}{x}=\frac{15}{25}$
$$\begin{aligned} 3\cdot 25&=x\cdot 15\\ 75&=15x\\ \frac{75}{15}&=\frac{15x}{15}\\ 5&=x \end{aligned}$$
The solution set is $\{5\}$.

16. $\frac{-7}{5}=\frac{91}{x}$
$$\begin{aligned} -7\cdot x&=5\cdot 91\\ -7x&=455\\ \frac{-7x}{-7}&=\frac{455}{-7}\\ x&=-65 \end{aligned}$$
The solution set is $\{-65\}$.

17. $\frac{x+2}{3}=\frac{4}{5}$
$$\begin{aligned} 5(x+2)&=3\cdot 4\\ 5x+10&=12\\ 5x+10-10&=12-10\\ 5x&=2\\ \frac{5x}{5}&=\frac{2}{5}\\ x&=\frac{2}{5} \end{aligned}$$
The solution set is $\left\{\frac{2}{5}\right\}$.

18. $\frac{5}{x+7}=\frac{3}{x+3}$
$$\begin{aligned} 5(x+3)&=3(x+7)\\ 5x+15&=3x+21\\ 5x+15-15&=3x+21-15\\ 5x&=3x+6\\ 5x-3x&=3x+6-3x\\ 2x&=6\\ \frac{2x}{2}&=\frac{6}{2}\\ x&=3 \end{aligned}$$
The solution set is $\{3\}$.

19. Let x = number of teachers

$$\frac{3}{50}=\frac{x}{5400}$$
$$50\cdot x=3\cdot 5400$$
$$50x=16,200$$
$$\frac{50x}{50}=\frac{16,200}{50}$$
$$x=324$$

There should be 324 teachers for 5400 students.

20. Let x = number of trout in lake

$$\frac{32}{82}=\frac{112}{x}$$
$$32x=82\cdot 112$$
$$32x=9184$$
$$\frac{32x}{32}=\frac{9184}{32}$$
$$x=287$$

There are 287 trout in the lake.

21. a. In 1995, the graph indicates a value of about $15,000.

b. Model 1:

$$C=438x+10,800$$
$$C=438(10)+10,800$$
$$C=15,180$$

This value describes the estimate reasonably well.

c. Model 2:

$$C=0.3x^2+430x+10,824$$
$$C=0.3x^2+430x+10,824$$
$$C=0.3(10)^2+430(10)+10,824$$
$$C=15,154$$

This value describes the estimate reasonably well.

d.

$$C=438x+10,800$$
$$28,320=438x+10,800$$
$$17,520=438x$$
$$40=x$$

Model 1 predicts the year will be 40 years after 1985, or 2025.

22. Let $x=$ the body count in *Scream.*
Let $x+2=$ the body count in *Scream 2.*
Let $x+3=$ the body count in *Scream 3.*

$$x+(x+2)+(x+3)+10=33$$
$$x+x+2+x+3+10=33$$
$$3x+15=33$$
$$3x=18$$
$$x=6$$
$$x+2=8$$
$$x+3=9$$

The body count in *Scream*, *Scream 2*, and *Scream 3*, respectively, is 6, 8, and 9.

23. Let x = the number of years after 1980.

$$2.69+0.15x=8.69$$
$$0.15x=6$$
$$x=40$$

The average price of a movie ticket will be $8.69 40 years after 1980, or 2020.

24.

$$15+.05x=5+.07x$$
$$10=.02x$$
$$500=x$$

Both plans cost the same at 500 text messages.

25. Let x = the original price of the phone

$$48=x-0.20x$$
$$48=0.80x$$
$$60=x$$

The original price is $60.

26. Let x = the amount sold to earn $800 in one week.

$$800=300+0.05x$$
$$500=0.05x$$
$$10,000=x$$

Sales must be $10,000 in one week to earn $800.

27.

$$Ax-By=C$$
$$Ax=By+C$$
$$\frac{Ax}{A}=\frac{By+C}{A}$$
$$x=\frac{By+C}{A}$$

28.

$$A=\frac{1}{2}bh$$
$$2A=bh$$
$$\frac{2A}{b}=\frac{bh}{b}$$
$$\frac{2A}{b}=h$$
$$h=\frac{2A}{b}$$

29.
$$A = \frac{B+C}{2}$$
$$2A = B + C$$
$$2A - C = B$$
$$B = 2A - C$$

30.
$$vt + gt^2 = s$$
$$gt^2 = s - vt$$
$$\frac{gt^2}{t^2} = \frac{s - vt}{t^2}$$
$$g = \frac{s - vt}{t^2}$$

31.
$$2x - 5 < 3$$
$$2x - 5 + 5 < 3 + 5$$
$$2x < 8$$
$$\frac{2x}{2} < \frac{8}{2}$$
$$x < 4$$
$$\{x | x < 4\}$$

3 4 5 6 7 8 9 10 11 12

32.
$$\frac{x}{2} > -4$$
$$2 \cdot \frac{x}{2} > 2(-4)$$
$$x > -8$$
$$\{x | x > -8\}$$

−14 −13 −12 −11 −10 −9 −8 −7 −6 −5

33.
$$3 - 5x \le 18$$
$$3 - 5x - 3 \le 18 - 3$$
$$-5x \le 15$$
$$\frac{-5x}{-5} \ge \frac{15}{-5}$$
$$x \ge -3$$
$$\{x | x \ge -3\}$$

−10 −9 −8 −7 −6 −5 −4 −3 −2 −1

34.
$$4x + 6 < 5x$$
$$4x + 6 - 6 < 5x - 6$$
$$4x < 5x - 6$$
$$4x - 5x < 5x - 6 - 5x$$
$$-x < -6$$
$$\frac{-x}{-1} > \frac{-6}{-1}$$
$$x > 6$$
$$\{x | x > 6\}$$

−2 −1 0 1 2 3 4 5 6 7

35.

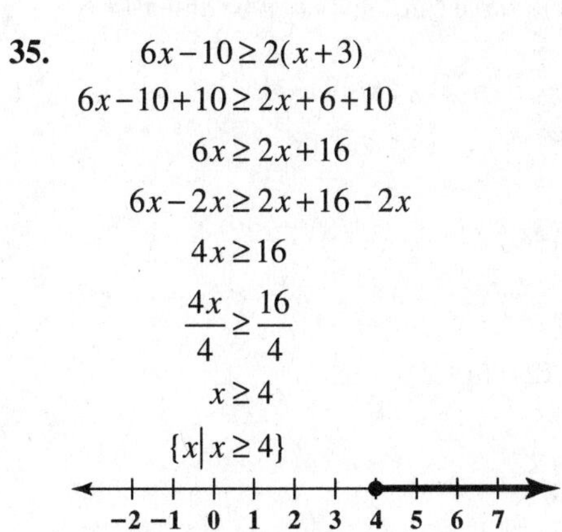

$$6x - 10 \ge 2(x+3)$$
$$6x - 10 + 10 \ge 2x + 6 + 10$$
$$6x \ge 2x + 16$$
$$6x - 2x \ge 2x + 16 - 2x$$
$$4x \ge 16$$
$$\frac{4x}{4} \ge \frac{16}{4}$$
$$x \ge 4$$
$$\{x | x \ge 4\}$$

−2 −1 0 1 2 3 4 5 6 7

36.

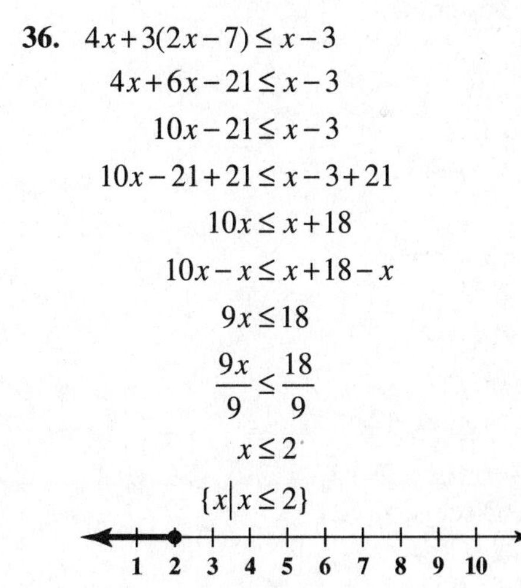

$$4x + 3(2x - 7) \le x - 3$$
$$4x + 6x - 21 \le x - 3$$
$$10x - 21 \le x - 3$$
$$10x - 21 + 21 \le x - 3 + 21$$
$$10x \le x + 18$$
$$10x - x \le x + 18 - x$$
$$9x \le 18$$
$$\frac{9x}{9} \le \frac{18}{9}$$
$$x \le 2$$
$$\{x | x \le 2\}$$

1 2 3 4 5 6 7 8 9 10

37.

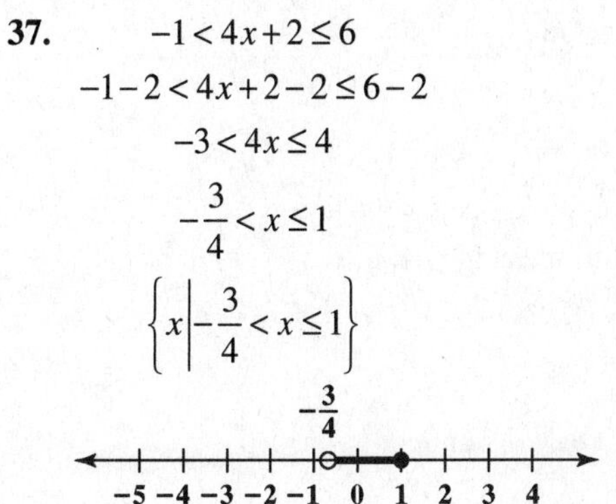

$$-1 < 4x + 2 \le 6$$
$$-1 - 2 < 4x + 2 - 2 \le 6 - 2$$
$$-3 < 4x \le 4$$
$$-\frac{3}{4} < x \le 1$$
$$\left\{x \middle| -\frac{3}{4} < x \le 1\right\}$$

$-\frac{3}{4}$

−5 −4 −3 −2 −1 0 1 2 3 4

38. Let x = score on third test.

$$\frac{42+74+x}{3} \geq 60$$
$$\frac{116+x}{3} \geq 60$$
$$3 \cdot \frac{116+x}{3} \geq 3 \cdot 60$$
$$116+x \geq 180$$
$$116+x-116 \geq 180-116$$
$$x \geq 64$$

The score on the third test must be at least 64.

39. $(x+9)(x-5) = x^2-5x+9x-45$
$= x^2+4x-45$

40. $(4x-7)(3x+2) = 12x^2+8x-21x-14$
$= 12x^2-13x-14$

41. $x^2-x-12 = (x-4)(x+3)$

42. $x^2-8x+15 = (x-5)(x-3)$

43. x^2+2x+3 is prime.

44. $3x^2-17x+10 = (3x-2)(x-5)$

45. $6x^2-11x-10 = (3x+2)(2x-5)$

46. $3x^2-6x-5$ is prime.

47. $x^2+5x-14=0$

$(x+7)(x-2)=0$

$x+7=0$ or $x-2=0$

$x=-7$ $\quad$ $x=2$

The solution set is $\{-7, 2\}$.

48. $x^2-4x=32$

$x^2-4x-32=0$

$(x-8)(x+4)=0$

$x-8=0$ or $x+4=0$

$x=8$ $\quad$ $x=-4$

The solution set is $\{-4, 8\}$.

49. $2x^2+15x-8=0$

$(2x-1)(x+8)=0$

$2x-1=0$ or $x+8=0$

$2x=1$ $\quad$ $x=-8$

$x=\frac{1}{2}$

The solution set is $\left\{-8, \frac{1}{2}\right\}$.

50. $3x^2=-21x-30$

$3x^2+21x+30=0$

$(3x+6)(x+5)=0$

$3x+6=0$ or $x+5=0$

$3x=-6$ $\quad$ $x=-5$

$x=-2$

The solution set is $\{-5, -2\}$.

51. $x^2-4x+3=0$

$$x=\frac{-b\pm\sqrt{b^2-4ac}}{2a}$$
$$x=\frac{-(-4)\pm\sqrt{(-4)^2-4(1)(3)}}{2(1)}$$
$$x=\frac{4\pm\sqrt{4}}{2}$$
$$x=\frac{4\pm2}{2}$$
$$x=\frac{4-2}{2} \quad \text{or} \quad x=\frac{4+2}{2}$$
$$x=1 \qquad x=3$$

The solution set is $\{1, 3\}$.

52. $x^2-5x=4$

$x^2-5x-4=0$

$$x=\frac{-b\pm\sqrt{b^2-4ac}}{2a}$$
$$x=\frac{-(-5)\pm\sqrt{(-5)^2-4(1)(-4)}}{2(1)}$$
$$x=\frac{5\pm\sqrt{41}}{2}$$

The solution set is $\left\{\frac{5-\sqrt{41}}{2}, \frac{5+\sqrt{41}}{2}\right\}$.

53. $2x^2 + 5x - 3 = 0$

$$x = \frac{-b \pm \sqrt{b^2 - 4ac}}{2a}$$

$$x = \frac{-5 \pm \sqrt{5^2 - 4(2)(-3)}}{2(2)}$$

$$x = \frac{-5 \pm \sqrt{49}}{4}$$

$$x = \frac{-5 \pm 7}{4}$$

$$x = \frac{-5+7}{4} \quad \text{or} \quad x = \frac{-5-7}{4}$$

$$x = \frac{1}{2} \qquad\qquad x = -3$$

The solution set is $\left\{-3, \frac{1}{2}\right\}$.

54. $3x^2 - 6x = 5$

$$3x^2 - 6x - 5 = 0$$

$$x = \frac{-b \pm \sqrt{b^2 - 4ac}}{2a}$$

$$x = \frac{-(-6) \pm \sqrt{(-6)^2 - 4(3)(-5)}}{2(3)}$$

$$x = \frac{6 \pm \sqrt{96}}{6}$$

$$x = \frac{6 \pm 4\sqrt{6}}{6}$$

$$x = \frac{3 \pm 2\sqrt{6}}{3}$$

The solution set is $\left\{\frac{3-2\sqrt{6}}{3}, \frac{3+2\sqrt{6}}{3}\right\}$.

55. a. $B = 1.7x^2 + 6x + 26$

$$B = 1.7(8)^2 + 6(8) + 26$$

$$B = 182.8$$

$$\approx 183$$

According to formula, there were 183 bicycle-friendly communities in 2011.
This overestimates the value in the graph by 3.

b. $B = 1.7x^2 + 6x + 26$

$$826 = 1.7x^2 + 6x + 26$$

$$0 = 1.7x^2 + 6x - 800$$

$$x = \frac{-b \pm \sqrt{b^2 - 4ac}}{2a}$$

$$x = \frac{-(6) \pm \sqrt{(6)^2 - 4(1.7)(-800)}}{2(1.7)}$$

$$x = 20 \quad x \approx -24$$

20 years after 2003, or 2023.

Chapter 6 Test

1. $x^3 - 4(x-1)^2 = (-2)^3 - 4(-2-1)^2$

$$= -8 - 4(-3)^2$$

$$= -8 - 4(9)$$

$$= -8 - 4(9)$$

$$= -44$$

2. $5(3x-2) - (x-6) = 15x - 10 - x + 6$

$$= 14x - 4$$

3. $12x + 4 = 7x - 21$

$$5x = -25$$

$$x = -5$$

The solution set is $\{-5\}$.

4. $3(2x-4) = 9 - 3(x+1)$

$$6x - 12 = 9 - 3x - 3$$

$$6x - 12 = 6 - 3x$$

$$6x - 12 + 12 = 6 - 3x + 12$$

$$6x = -3x + 18$$

$$6x + 3x = -3x + 18 + 3x$$

$$9x = 18$$

$$\frac{9x}{9} = \frac{18}{9}$$

$$x = 2$$

The solution set is $\{2\}$.

5. $3(x-4) + x = 2(6+2x)$

$$3x - 12 + x = 12 + 4x$$

$$4x - 12 = 4x + 12$$

$$-12 = 12$$

This is a false statement. The solution set is { }.

6. $\frac{x}{5}-2=\frac{x}{3}$

$15\left(\frac{x}{5}-2\right)=15\left(\frac{x}{3}\right)$

$3x-30=5x$

$-2x=30$

$x=-15$

The solution set is $\{-15\}$.

7. $By-Ax=A$

$By=Ax+A$

$\frac{By}{B}=\frac{Ax+A}{B}$

$y=\frac{Ax+A}{B}$

8. a. Model 1:

$p=-0.3x+30$

$p=-0.3(30)+30$

$p=21$

Model 1 predicts 21%, which overestimates the value in the graph by 0.2.

b. Model 2:

$p=-0.003x^2-0.22x+30$

$p=-0.003(30)^2-0.22(30)+30$

$p=20.7$

Model 2 predicts 20.7%, which underestimates the value in the graph by 0.1.

c. $p=-0.3x+30$

$17.7=-0.3x+30$

$0.3x=12.3$

$x=41$

Model 1 predicts the year will be 41 years after 1980, or 2021.

9. $\frac{5}{8}=\frac{x}{12}$

$8\cdot x=5\cdot 12$

$8x=60$

$\frac{8x}{8}=\frac{60}{8}$

$x=7.5$

The solution set is $\{7.5\}$.

10. $\frac{x+5}{8}=\frac{x+2}{5}$

$5(x+5)=8(x+2)$

$5x+25=8x+16$

$5x+25-25=8x+16-25$

$5x=8x-9$

$5x-8x=8x-9-8x$

$-3x=-9$

$\frac{-3x}{-3}=\frac{-9}{-3}$

$x=3$

The solution set is $\{3\}$.

11. Let x = number of elk in the park.

$\frac{5}{150}=\frac{200}{x}$

$5x=150\cdot 200$

$5x=30{,}000$

$\frac{5x}{5}=\frac{30{,}000}{5}$

$x=6000$

There are 6000 elk in the park.

12. Let x = the number of times "sorry" was used.
Let $x+419=$ the number of times "love" was used.
Let $x+32=$ the number of times "thanks" was used.

$x+(x+419)+(x+32)=1084$

$x+x+419+x+32=1084$

$3x+451=1084$

$3x=633$

$x=211$

$x+419=630$

$x+32=243$

The word "sorry" was used 211 times, the word "love" was used 630 times, and the word "thanks" was used 243 times.

13. Let x = the number of years since the car was purchased

$\text{Value}=50{,}750-5500x$

$12{,}250=50{,}750-5500x$

$-38500=-5500x$

$\frac{-38500}{-5500}=\frac{-5500x}{-5500}$

$x=7$

The car will have a value of \$12,250 after 7 years.

14. Let x = the number of text messages.
Plan A: 25
Plan B: $0.06x+13$

$$0.06x+13=25$$
$$0.06x=12$$
$$\frac{0.06x}{0.06}=\frac{12}{0.06}$$
$$x=200$$

The cost will be the same for 200 text messages.

15. Let x = the original selling price

$$20=x-0.60x$$
$$20=0.40x$$
$$50=x$$

The original price is \$50.

16.

$$6-9x\ge 33$$
$$6-9x-6\ge 33-6$$
$$-9x\ge 27$$
$$\frac{-9x}{-9}\le\frac{27}{-9}$$
$$x\le -3$$
$$\{x|x\le -3\}$$

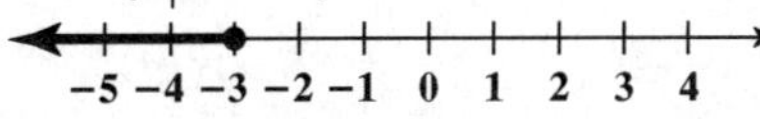

17.

$$4x-2>2(x+6)$$
$$4x-2>2x+12$$
$$4x-2+2>2x+12+2$$
$$4x>2x+14$$
$$4x-2x>2x+14-2x$$
$$2x>14$$
$$\frac{2x}{2}>\frac{14}{2}$$
$$x>7$$
$$\{x|x>7\}$$

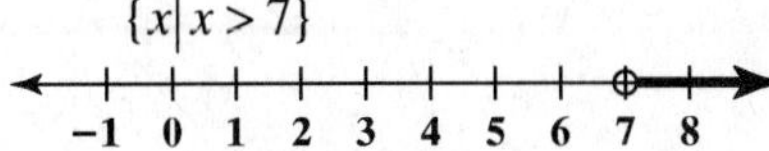

18.

$$-3\le 2x+1<6$$
$$-3-1\le 2x+1-1<6-1$$
$$-4\le 2x<5$$
$$-2\le x<\frac{5}{2}$$
$$\left\{x\middle|-2\le x<\frac{5}{2}\right\}$$

19. Let x = grade on 4th examination.

$$\frac{76+80+72+x}{4}\ge 80$$
$$\frac{228+x}{4}\ge 80$$
$$4\cdot\frac{228+x}{4}\ge 80\cdot 4$$
$$228+x\ge 320$$
$$228+x-228\ge 320-228$$
$$x\ge 92$$

The student must earn at least a 92 to receive a B.

20. $(2x-5)(3x+4)=6x^2+8x-15x-20$
$=6x^2-7x-20$

21. $2x^2-9x+10=(2x-5)(x-2)$

22.

$$x^2+5x=36$$
$$x^2+5x-36=0$$
$$(x+9)(x-4)=0$$
$$x+9=0 \quad\text{or}\quad x-4=0$$
$$x=-9 \qquad\qquad x=4$$

The solution set is $\{-9, 4\}$.

23. $2x^2+4x=-1$

$$2x^2+4x+1=0$$
$$x=\frac{-b\pm\sqrt{b^2-4ac}}{2a}$$
$$x=\frac{-4\pm\sqrt{4^2-4(2)(1)}}{2(2)}$$
$$x=\frac{-4\pm\sqrt{8}}{4}$$
$$x=\frac{-4\pm2\sqrt{2}}{4}$$
$$x=\frac{-2\pm\sqrt{2}}{2}$$

The solution set is $\left\{\frac{-2-\sqrt{2}}{2}, \frac{-2+\sqrt{2}}{2}\right\}$.

24. $43x+575=1177$

$$43x=602$$
$$x=14$$

The system's income will be \$1177 billion 14 years after 2004, or 2018.

25. $B = 0.07x^2 + 47.4x + 500$

$1177 = 0.07x^2 + 47.4x + 500$

$0 = 0.07x^2 + 47.4x - 677$

$0 = 0.07x^2 + 47.4x - 677$

$$x = \frac{-b \pm \sqrt{b^2 - 4ac}}{2a}$$

$$x = \frac{-(47.4) \pm \sqrt{(47.4)^2 - 4(0.07)(-677)}}{2(0.07)}$$

$x \approx 14, \quad x \approx -691$ (rejected)

The system's income will be \$1177 billion 14 years after 2004, or 2018.

26. The formulas model the data quite well.

Chapter 7
Algebra: Graphs, Functions, and Linear Systems

Check Points 7.1

1.

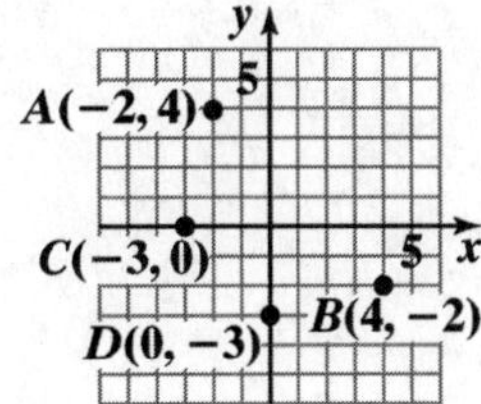

2.

x	$y = 4 - x$	(x, y)
−3	$y = 4 - (-3) = 4 + 3 = 7$	$(-3, 7)$
−2	$y = 4 - (-2) = 4 + 2 = 6$	$(-2, 6)$
−1	$y = 4 - (-1) = 4 + 1 = 5$	$(-1, 5)$
0	$y = 4 - (0) = 4 - 0 = 4$	$(0, 4)$
1	$y = 4 - (1) = 4 - 1 = 3$	$(1, 3)$
2	$y = 4 - (2) = 4 - 2 = 2$	$(2, 2)$
3	$y = 4 - (3) = 4 - 3 = 1$	$(3, 1)$

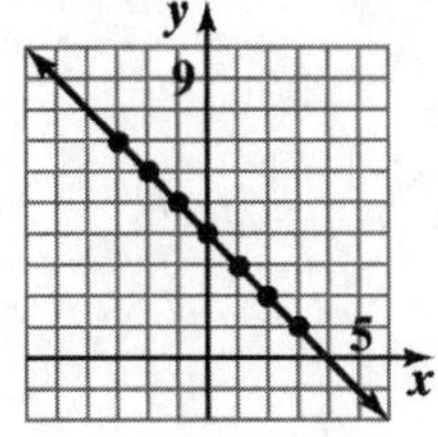

3. a. Without the discount pass

x	$y = 2x$	(x, y)
0	$y = 2(0) = 0$	$(0, 0)$
2	$y = 2(2) = 4$	$(2, 4)$
4	$y = 2(4) = 8$	$(4, 8)$
6	$y = 2(6) = 12$	$(6, 12)$
8	$y = 2(8) = 16$	$(8, 16)$
10	$y = 2(10) = 20$	$(10, 20)$
12	$y = 2(12) = 24$	$(12, 24)$

With the discount pass

x	$y = 10 + x$	(x, y)
0	$y = 10 + 0 = 10$	$(0, 10)$
2	$y = 10 + 2 = 12$	$(2, 12)$
4	$y = 10 + 4 = 14$	$(4, 14)$
6	$y = 10 + 6 = 16$	$(6, 16)$
8	$y = 10 + 8 = 18$	$(8, 18)$
10	$y = 10 + 10 = 20$	$(10, 20)$
12	$y = 10 + 12 = 22$	$(12, 22)$

b.

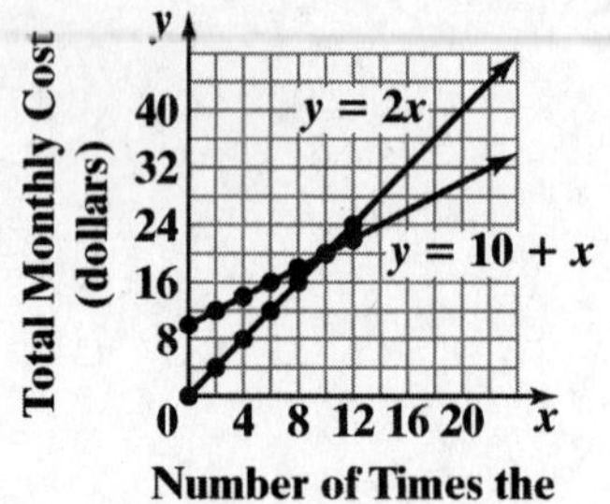

c. The graphs intersect at $(10, 20)$. This means that if the bridge is used ten times in a month, the total monthly cost is \$20 with or without the discount pass.

4. a.

$$f(x) = 4x + 5$$
$$f(6) = 4(6) + 5$$
$$= 29$$

b.

$$g(x) = 3x^2 - 10$$
$$g(-5) = 3(-5)^2 - 10$$
$$= 65$$

c.

$$h(r) = r^2 - 7r + 2$$
$$h(-4) = (-4)^2 - 7(-4) + 2$$
$$= 46$$

5. a. A car's required stopping distance at 40 miles an hour on dry pavement is about 190 feet.

b.

$$f(x) = 0.0875x^2 - 0.4x + 66.6$$
$$f(40) = 0.0875(40)^2 - 0.4(40) + 66.6 \approx 191$$

6.

x	$f(x) = 2x$	(x, y) or $(x, f(x))$
-2	$f(-2) = 2(-2) = -4$	$(-2, -4)$
-1	$f(-1) = 2(-1) = -2$	$(-1, -2)$
0	$f(0) = 2(0) = 0$	$(0, 0)$
1	$f(1) = 2(1) = 2$	$(1, 2)$
2	$f(2) = 2(2) = 4$	$(2, 4)$

x	$g(x) = 2x - 3$	(x, y) or $(x, f(x))$
-2	$g(-2) = 2(-2) - 3 = -7$	$(-2, -7)$
-1	$g(-1) = 2(-1) - 3 = -5$	$(-1, -5)$
0	$g(0) = 2(0) - 3 = -3$	$(0, -3)$
1	$g(1) = 2(1) - 3 = -1$	$(1, -1)$
2	$g(2) = 2(2) - 3 = 1$	$(2, 1)$

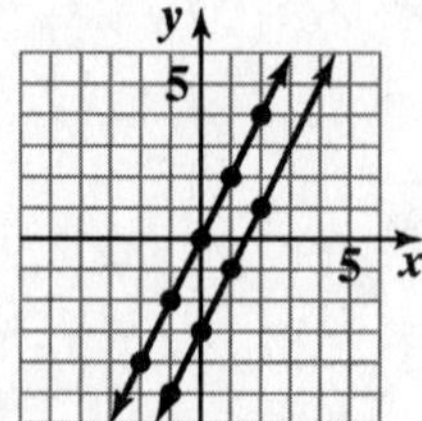

The graph of g is the graph of f shifted vertically down 3 units.

7. a. y is a function of x.

b. y is a function of x.

c. y is not a function of x. Two values of y correspond to an x-value.

8. a. The concentration is increasing from 0 to 3 hours.

b. The concentration is decreasing from 3 to 13 hours.

c. The maximum concentration of 0.05 mg per 100 ml occurs after 3 hours.

d. None of the drug is left in the body.

e. The graph defines y as a function of x because no vertical line intersects the graph in more than one point.

Concept and Vocabulary Check 7.1

1. x-axis
2. y-axis
3. origin
4. quadrants; four
5. x-coordinate; y-coordinate
6. solution; satisfies
7. y; x; function
8. x; 6
9. more than once; function

Exercise Set 7.1

1.

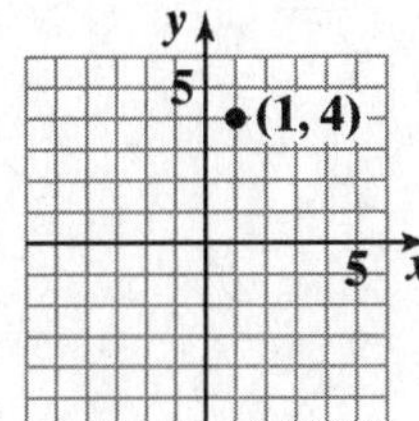

3.

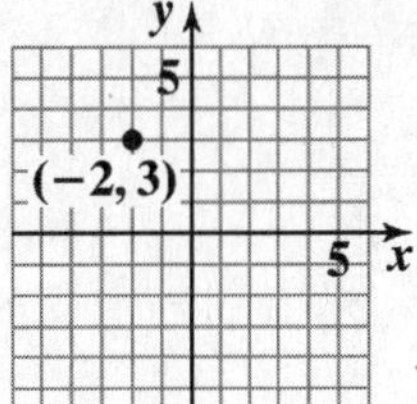

5.

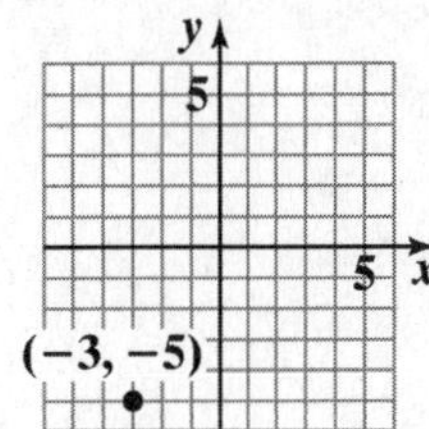

7.

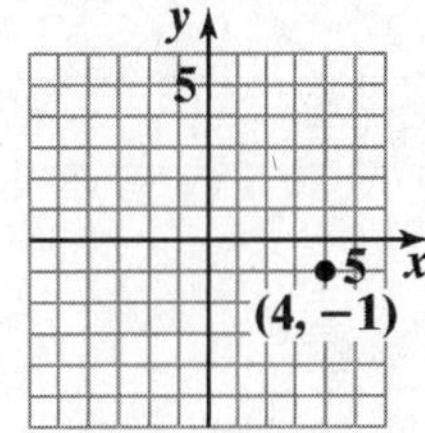

9.

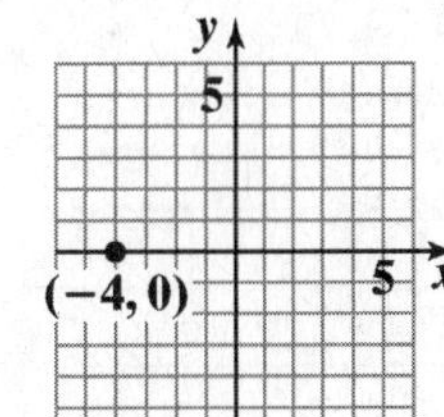

11.

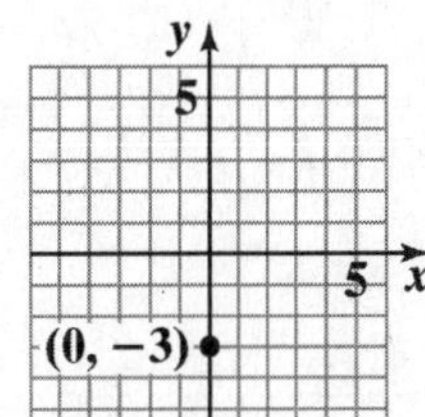

13.

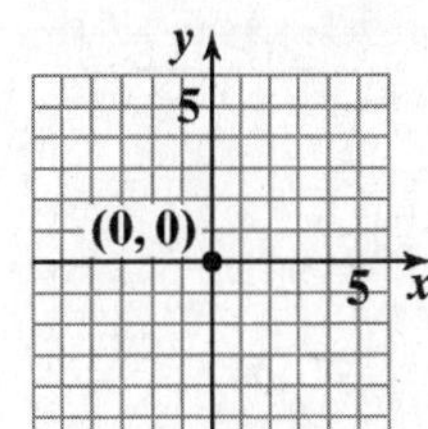

15.

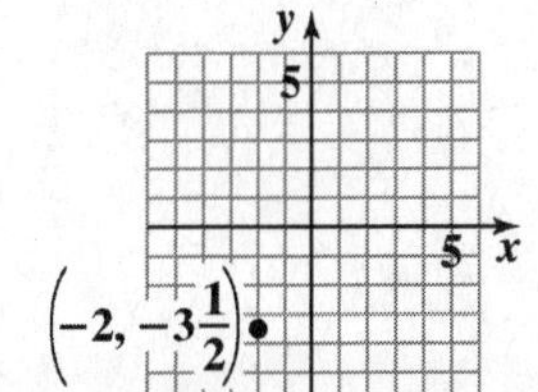

17.

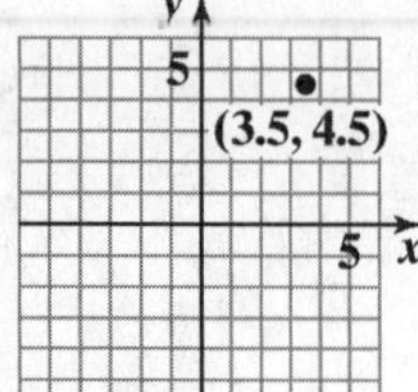

19.

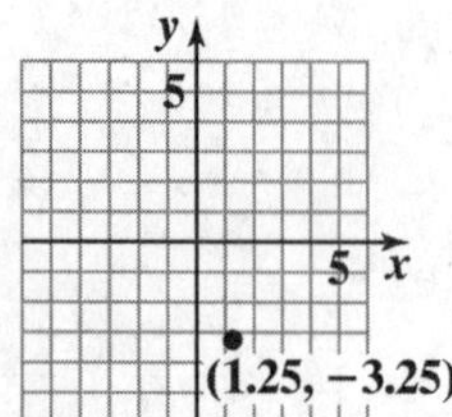

21.

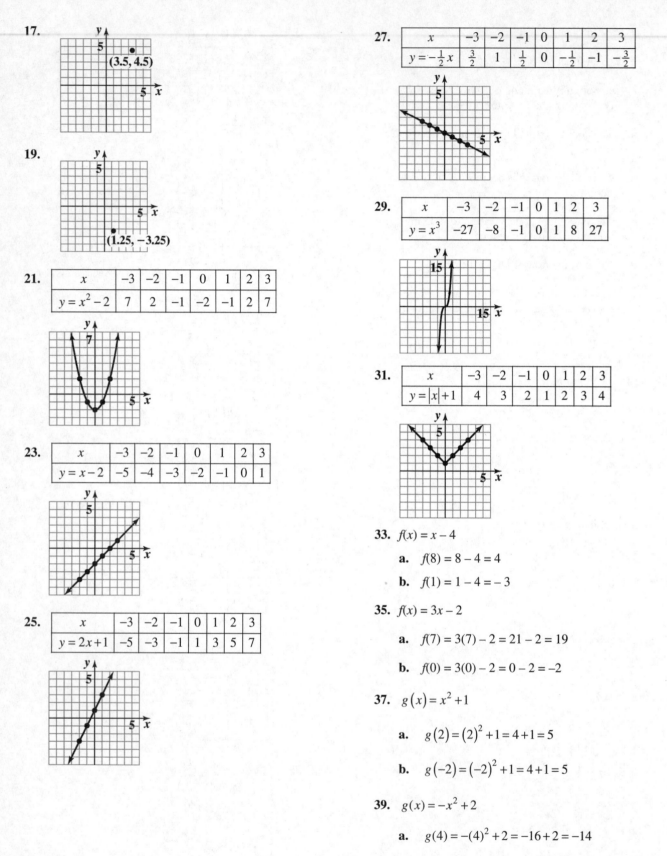

x	−3	−2	−1	0	1	2	3
$y = x^2 - 2$	7	2	−1	−2	−1	2	7

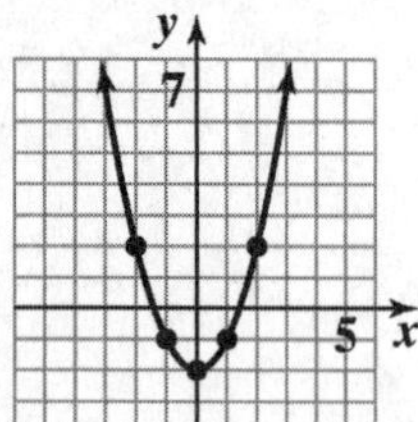

23.

x	−3	−2	−1	0	1	2	3
$y = x - 2$	−5	−4	−3	−2	−1	0	1

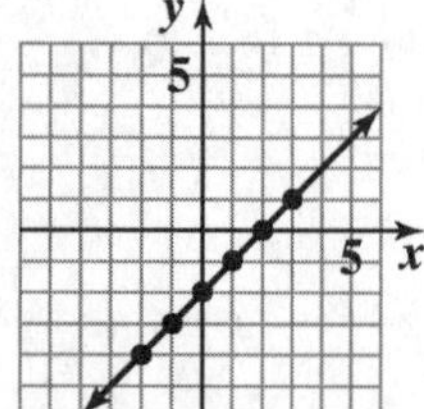

25.

x	−3	−2	−1	0	1	2	3
$y = 2x + 1$	−5	−3	−1	1	3	5	7

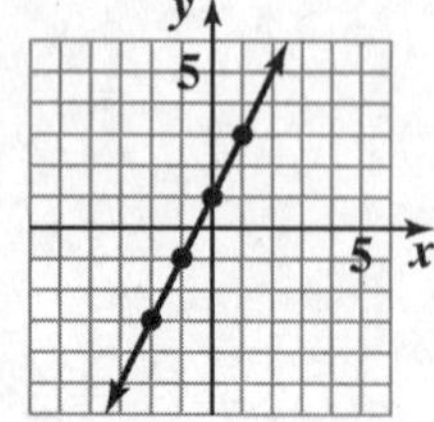

27.

x	−3	−2	−1	0	1	2	3
$y = -\frac{1}{2}x$	$\frac{3}{2}$	1	$\frac{1}{2}$	0	$-\frac{1}{2}$	−1	$-\frac{3}{2}$

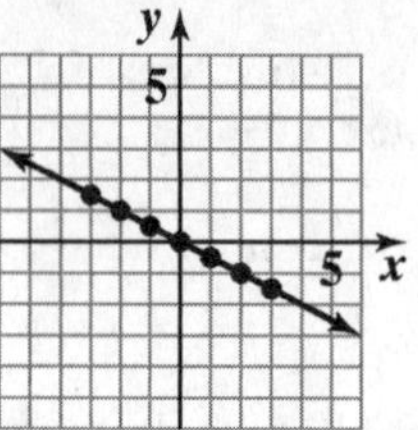

29.

x	−3	−2	−1	0	1	2	3
$y = x^3$	−27	−8	−1	0	1	8	27

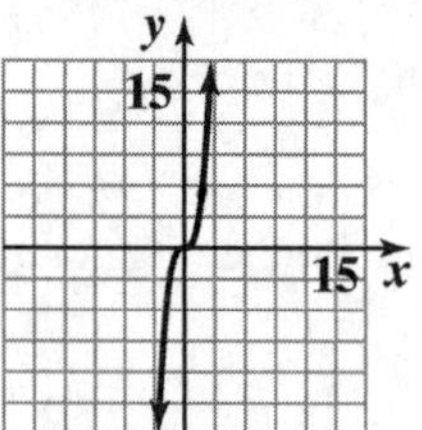

31.

x	−3	−2	−1	0	1	2	3
$y = \|x\| + 1$	4	3	2	1	2	3	4

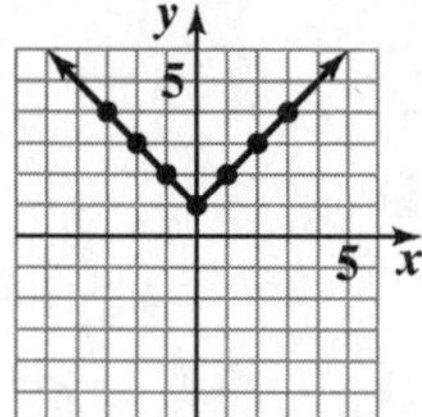

33. $f(x) = x - 4$

a. $f(8) = 8 - 4 = 4$

b. $f(1) = 1 - 4 = -3$

35. $f(x) = 3x - 2$

a. $f(7) = 3(7) - 2 = 21 - 2 = 19$

b. $f(0) = 3(0) - 2 = 0 - 2 = -2$

37. $g(x) = x^2 + 1$

a. $g(2) = (2)^2 + 1 = 4 + 1 = 5$

b. $g(-2) = (-2)^2 + 1 = 4 + 1 = 5$

39. $g(x) = -x^2 + 2$

a. $g(4) = -(4)^2 + 2 = -16 + 2 = -14$

b. $g(-3) = -(-3)^2 + 2 = -9 + 2 = -7$

41. $h(r) = 3r^2 + 5$

a. $h(4) = 3(4)^2 + 5$
$= 3(16) + 5$
$= 48 + 5$
$= 53$

b. $h(-1) = 3(-1)^2 + 5 = 3 + 5 = 8$

43. $f(x) = 2x^2 + 3x - 1$

a. $f(3) = 2(3)^2 + 3(3) - 1$
$= 2(9) + 9 - 1$
$= 18 + 9 - 1$
$= 26$

b. $f(-4) = 2(-4)^2 + 3(-4) - 1$
$= 2(16) - 12 - 1$
$= 32 - 12 - 1$
$= 19$

45. $f(x) = \dfrac{x}{|x|}$

a. $f(6) = \dfrac{6}{|6|} = 1$

b. $f(-6) = \dfrac{-6}{|-6|} = \dfrac{-6}{6} = -1$

47.

x	$f(x) = x^2 - 1$
−2	3
−1	0
0	−1
1	0
2	3

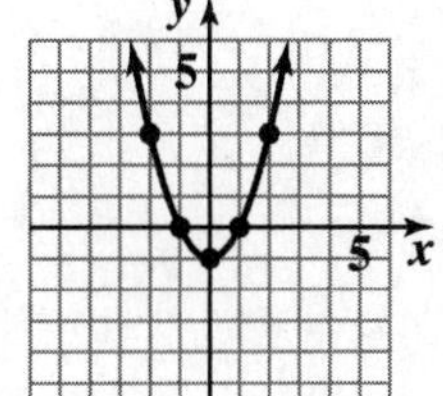

49.

x	$f(x) = x - 1$
−2	−3
−1	−2
0	−1
1	0
2	1

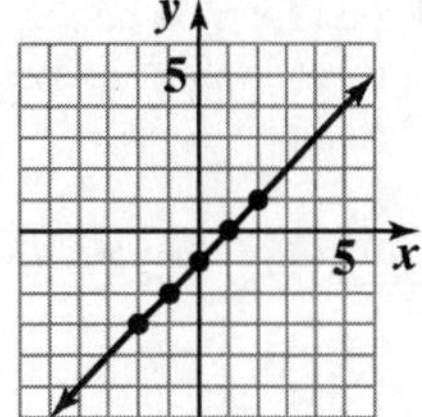

51.

x	$f(x) = (x - 2)^2$
0	4
1	1
2	0
3	1
4	4

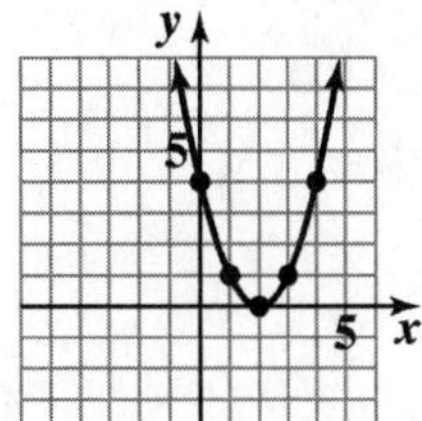

53.

x	$f(x) = x^3 + 1$
−3	−26
−2	−7
−1	0
0	1
1	2

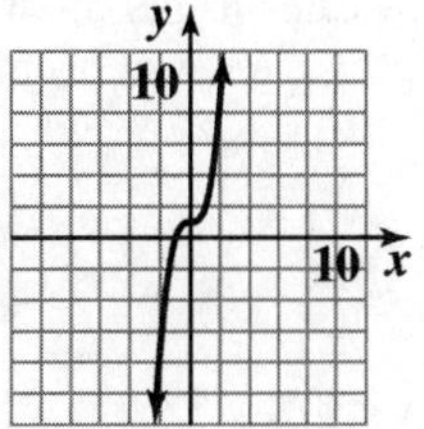

55. y is a function of x.

57. y is a function of x.

69.

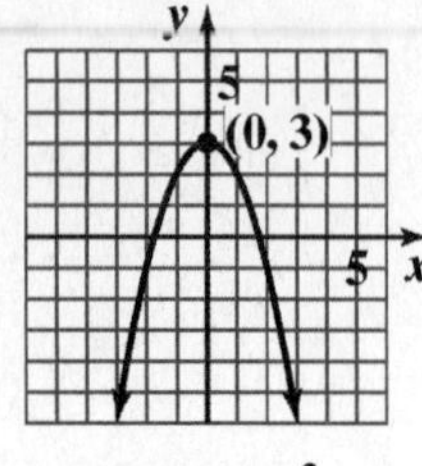

$y = 3 - x^2$

71. The coordinates of point A are (2,7). When the football is 2 yards from the quarterback, its height is 7 feet.

73. The coordinates of point C are approximately (6, 9.25).

75. The football's maximum height is 12 feet. It reaches this height when it is 15 yards from the quarterback.

77. **a.** $G(30) = -0.01(30)^2 + (30) + 60 = 81$
In 2010, the wage gap was 81%. This is represented as $(30, 81)$ on the graph.

b. $G(30)$ underestimates the actual data shown by the bar graph by 2%.

79. $f(20) = 0.4(20)^2 - 36(20) + 1000$
$= 0.4(400) - 720 + 1000$
$= 160 - 720 + 1000$
$= -560 + 1000 = 440$
Twenty-year-old drivers have 440 accidents per 50 million miles driven.
This is represented on the graph by point (20,440).

81. The graph reaches its lowest point at $x = 45$.
$f(45) = 0.4(45)^2 - 36(45) + 1000$
$= 0.4(2025) - 1620 + 1000$
$= 810 - 1620 + 1000$
$= -810 + 1000$
$= 190$
Drivers at age 45 have 190 accidents per 50 million miles driven. This is the least number of accidents for any driver between ages 16 and 74.

89. makes sense

91. makes sense

93. $f(-1) + g(-1) = 1 + (-3) = -2$

95. $f(g(-1)) = f(-3) = 1$

Check Points 7.2

1. Find the x-intercept by setting $y = 0$
$2x + 3(0) = 6$
$2x = 6$
$x = 3$; resulting point (3, 0)
Find the y-intercept by setting $x = 0$
$2(0) + 3y = 6$
$3y = 6$
$y = 2$; resulting point (0, 2)
Find a checkpoint by substituting any value.
$2(1) + 3y = 6$
$2 + 3y = 6$
$3y = 4$
$y = \frac{4}{3}$; resulting point $\left(1, \frac{4}{3}\right)$

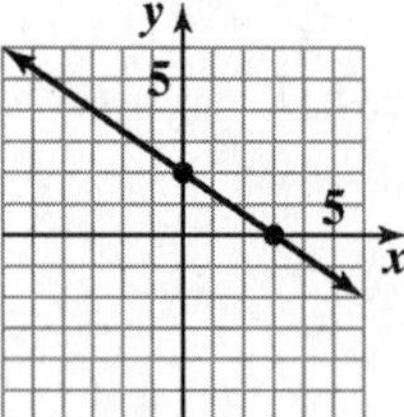

2. **a.** $m = \frac{-2-4}{-4-(-3)} = \frac{-6}{-1} = 6$

b. $m = \frac{5-(-2)}{-1-4} = \frac{7}{-5} = -\frac{7}{5}$

3. Step 1. Plot the y-intercept of (0, 1)

Step 2. Obtain a second point using the slope m.
$m = \frac{3}{5} = \frac{\text{Rise}}{\text{Run}}$
Starting from the y-intercept move up 3 units and move 5 units to the right. This puts the second point at (3, 6).

Step 3. Draw the line through the two points.

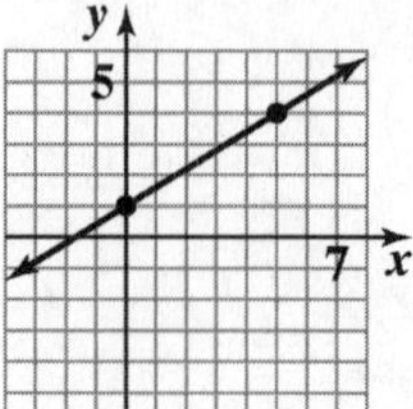

4. Solve for y.
$$3x+4y=0$$
$$4y=-3x+0$$
$$\frac{4y}{4}=\frac{-3x}{4}+\frac{0}{4}$$
$$y=\frac{-3}{4}x+0$$
$m=\frac{-3}{4}$ and the y-intercept is (0, 0)

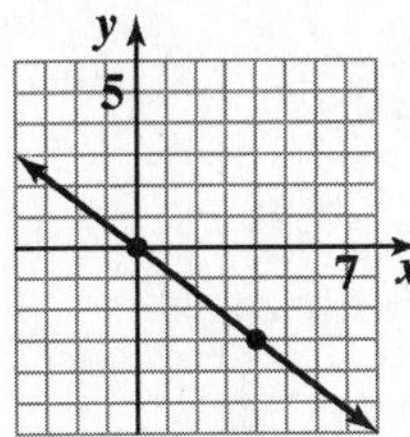

5. Draw horizontal line that intersects the y-axis at 3.

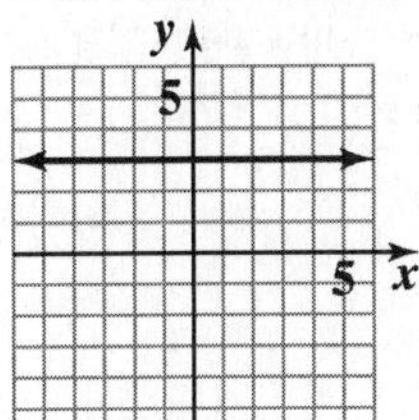

6. Draw vertical line that intersects the x-axis at -2.

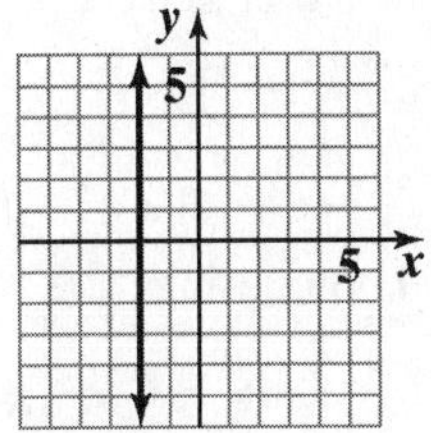

7. The two points shown on the line segment for Medicare are (2007, 446) and (2016, 909).
$$m=\frac{11-45}{2010-1970}=\frac{-34}{40}=-0.85$$
For the period from 1970 through 2010, the percentage of married men ages 20 to 24 decreased by 0.85 per year. The rate of change -0.85% is per year.

8. a. The y-intercept is 8 and the slope is
$$m=\frac{\text{Change in } y}{\text{Change in } x}=\frac{24-8}{50-0}=\frac{16}{50}=0.32$$
The equation is $C(x)=0.32x+8$.

b.
$$C(x)=0.32x+8$$
$$C(60)=0.32(60)+8$$
$$=27.2$$
The model projects that 27.2% of the U.S. population will be college graduates in 2020.

Concept and Vocabulary Check 7.2

1. x-intercept
2. y-intercept
3. $\frac{y_2-y_1}{x_2-x_1}$
4. $y=mx+b$; slope; y-intercept
5. -4; 3
6. $(0,3)$; 2; 5
7. horizontal
8. vertical

Exercise Set 7.2

1. Find the x-intercept by setting $y=0$
$$x-y=3$$
$$x-0=3$$
$x=3$; resulting point (3, 0)
Find the y-intercept by setting $x=0$
$$0-y=3$$
$$-y=3$$
$y=-3$; resulting point (0, – 3)

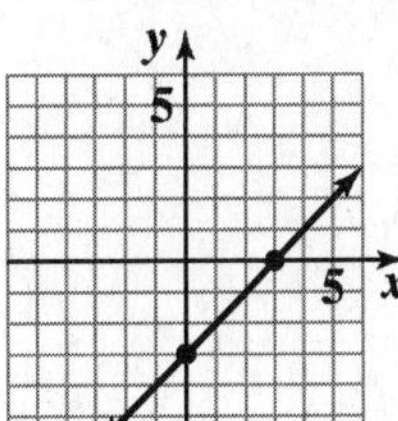

3. Find the x-intercept by setting $y = 0$

$3x - 4(0) = 12$

$3x = 12$

$x = 4$; resulting point (4, 0)

Find the y-intercept by setting $x = 0$

$3(0) - 4y = 12$

$-4y = 12$

$y = -3$; resulting point (0, – 3)

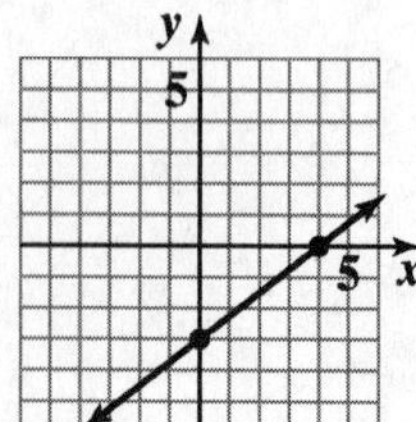

5. Find the x-intercept by setting $y = 0$

$2x + 0 = 6$

$2x = 6$

$x = 3$; resulting point (3, 0)

Find the y-intercept by setting $x = 0$

$2(0) + y = 6$

$y = 6$; resulting point (0, 6)

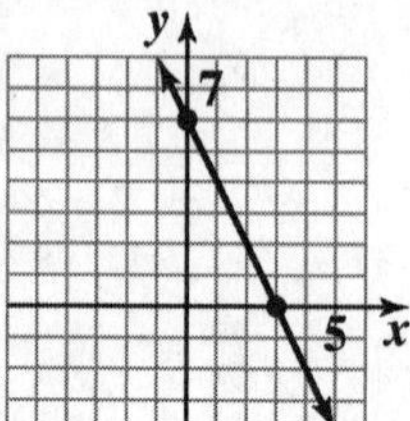

7. Find the x-intercept by setting $y = 0$

$5x = 3(0) - 15$

$5x = -15$

$x = -3$; resulting point (–3, 0)

Find the y-intercept by setting $x = 0$

$5(0) = 3y - 15$

$0 = 3y - 15$

$-3y = -15$

$y = 5$; resulting point (0, 5)

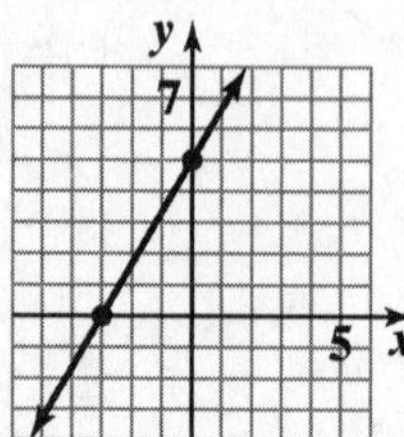

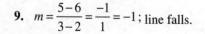

9. $m = \dfrac{5-6}{3-2} = \dfrac{-1}{1} = -1$; line falls.

11. $m = \dfrac{2-1}{2-(-2)} = \dfrac{1}{4}$; line rises.

13. $m = \dfrac{-1-4}{-1-(-2)} = \dfrac{-5}{1} = -5$; line falls.

15. $m = \dfrac{-2-3}{5-5} = \dfrac{-5}{0}$;

Slope undefined. Line is vertical.

17. $m = \dfrac{8-0}{0-2} = \dfrac{8}{-2} = -4$; line falls.

19. $m = \dfrac{1-1}{-2-5} = \dfrac{0}{-7} = 0$; line is horizontal.

21. $y = 2x + 3$

Slope: 2, y-intercept: 3

Plot point (0, 3) and second point using

$m = \dfrac{2}{1} = \dfrac{\text{rise}}{\text{run}}$

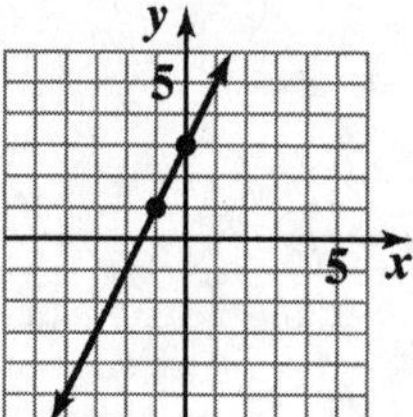

23. $y = -2x + 4$

Slope: – 2, y-intercept: 4

Plot point (0, 4) and second point using

$m = \dfrac{-2}{1} = \dfrac{\text{rise}}{\text{run}}$

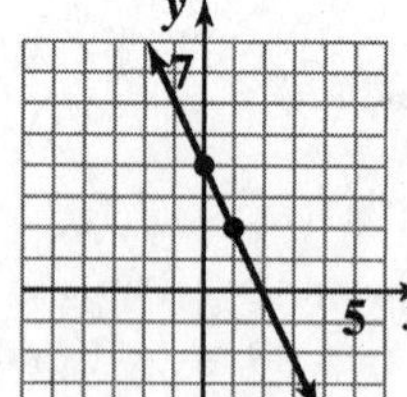

25. $y = \frac{1}{2}x + 3$

Slope: $\frac{1}{2}$, y-intercept: 3

Plot point (0, 3) and second point using

$m = \frac{1}{2} = \frac{\text{rise}}{\text{run}}$.

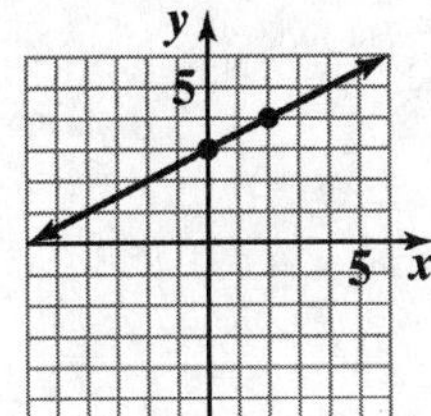

27. $f(x) = \frac{2}{3}x - 4$

Slope: $\frac{2}{3}$, y-intercept: – 4

Plot point (0, – 4) and second point using

$m = \frac{2}{3} = \frac{\text{rise}}{\text{run}}$.

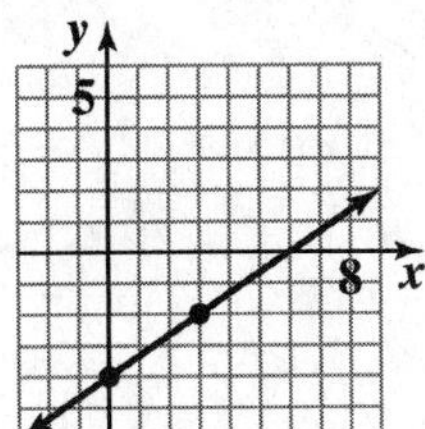

29. $y = -\frac{3}{4}x + 4$

Slope: $-\frac{3}{4}$, y-intercept: 4

Plot point (0, 4) and second point using

$m = \frac{-3}{4} = \frac{\text{rise}}{\text{run}}$.

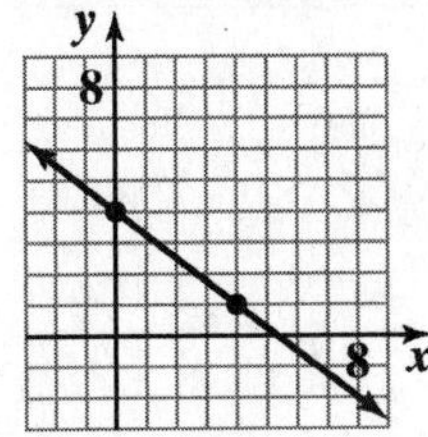

31. $f(x) = -\frac{5}{3}x$ or $f(x) = -\frac{5}{3}x + 0$

Slope: $-\frac{5}{3}$, y-intercept: 0

Plot point (0, 0) and second point using

$m = \frac{-5}{3} = \frac{\text{rise}}{\text{run}}$.

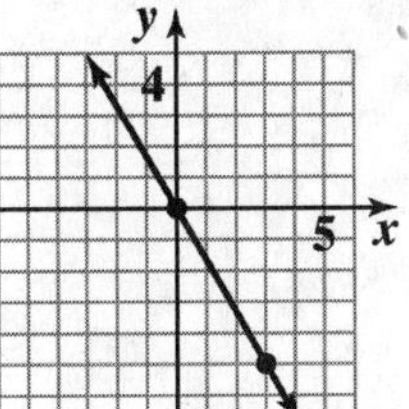

33. a. $3x + y = 0$

$y = -3x$ or $y = -3x + 0$

b. Slope = – 3

y-intercept = 0

c.

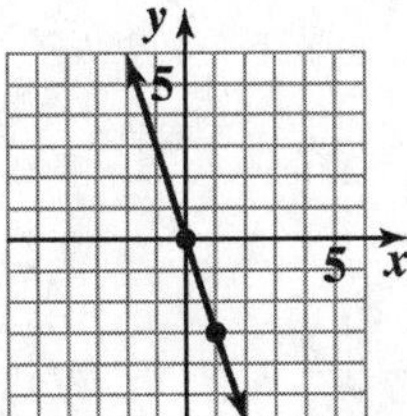

35. a. $3y = 4x$

$y = \frac{4}{3}x$ or $y = \frac{4}{3}x + 0$

b. Slope = $\frac{4}{3}$

y-intercept = 0

c.

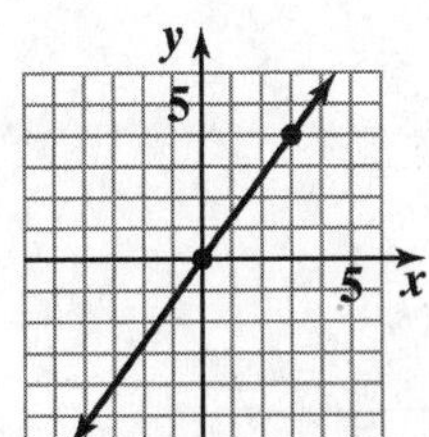

37. a. $2x + y = 3$

$y = -2x + 3$

b. Slope = – 2
y-intercept = 3

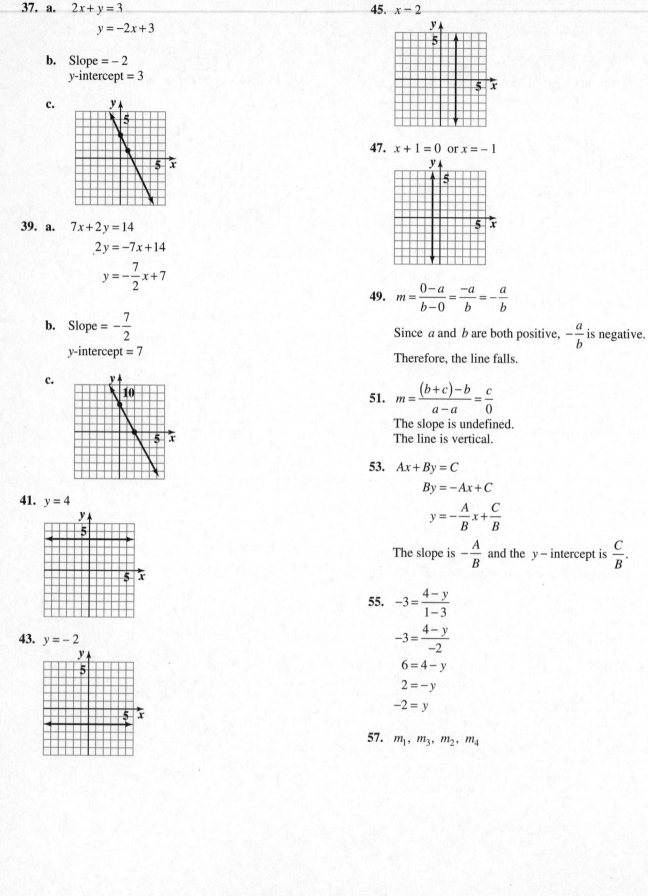

c.

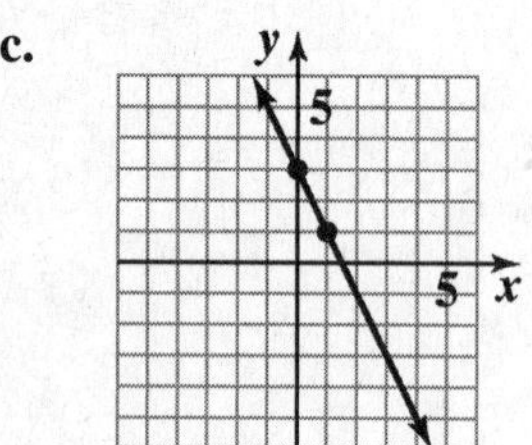

39. a. $7x + 2y = 14$

$2y = -7x + 14$

$y = -\frac{7}{2}x + 7$

b. Slope = $-\frac{7}{2}$
y-intercept = 7

c.

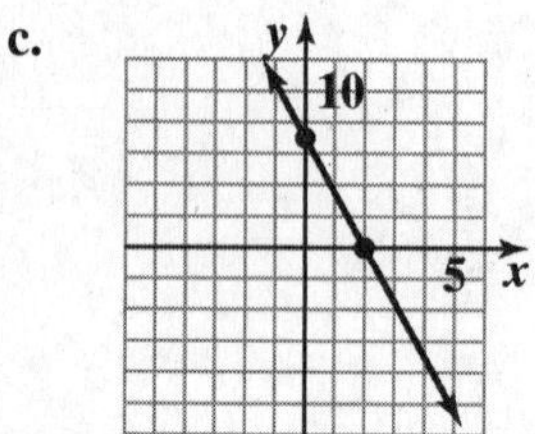

41. $y = 4$

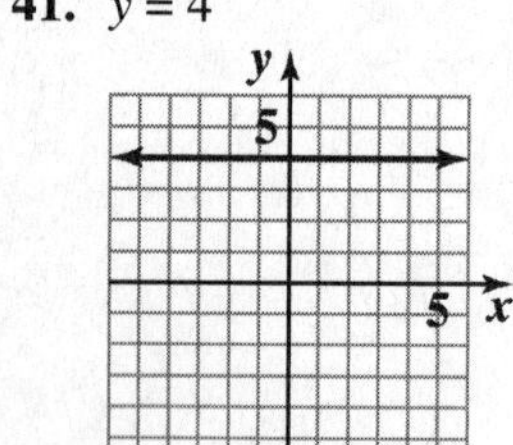

43. $y = -2$

45. $x = 2$

47. $x + 1 = 0$ or $x = -1$

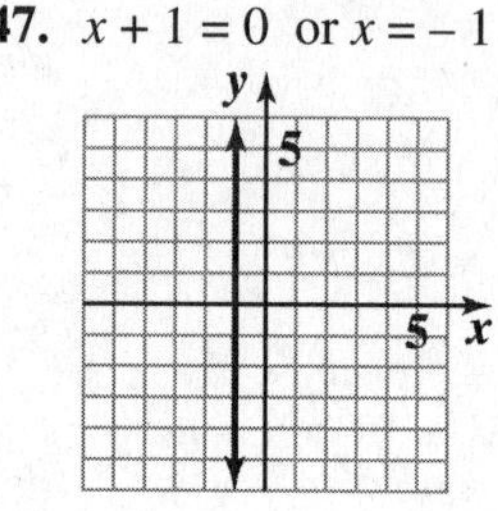

49. $m = \frac{0-a}{b-0} = \frac{-a}{b} = -\frac{a}{b}$

Since a and b are both positive, $-\frac{a}{b}$ is negative. Therefore, the line falls.

51. $m = \frac{(b+c)-b}{a-a} = \frac{c}{0}$
The slope is undefined.
The line is vertical.

53. $Ax + By = C$

$By = -Ax + C$

$y = -\frac{A}{B}x + \frac{C}{B}$

The slope is $-\frac{A}{B}$ and the y – intercept is $\frac{C}{B}$.

55. $-3 = \frac{4-y}{1-3}$

$-3 = \frac{4-y}{-2}$

$6 = 4 - y$

$2 = -y$

$-2 = y$

57. $m_1,\ m_3,\ m_2,\ m_4$

59. a. $m = \dfrac{\text{Change in } y}{\text{Change in } x} = \dfrac{29-49}{62-22} = \dfrac{-20}{40} = -0.5$

b. For each year of aging, the percentage of Americans reporting "a lot" of stress decreases by 0.5%. The rate of change is –0.5% per year of aging.

61. $P(x) = 0.725x + 18$

63. a. Find slope by using the endpoints of the line segment.

$m = \dfrac{940-460}{2010-1980} = \dfrac{480}{30} = 16$

The value of b is the y-intercept, or 460.

$W(x) = mx + b$

$W(x) = 16x + 460$

b. $W(x) = 16x + 460$

$W(x) = 16(40) + 460$

$= 1100$

In the year 2020, the number of bachelor's degrees that will be awarded to women will be about 1,100,000.

75. does not make sense; Explanations will vary. Sample explanation: Since college cost are going up, this function has a positive slope.

77. makes sense

79. false; Changes to make the statement true will vary. A sample change is: Vertical lines can not be expressed in slope-intercept forn.

81. **false; Changes to make the statement true will vary. A sample change is: The line $2y = 3x + 7$ is equivalent to $y = \frac{3}{2}x + \frac{7}{2}$ which has a y-intercept of $\frac{7}{2}$.**

Check Points 7.3

1. Replace x with -4 and y with 3.

$x + 2y = 2$ $x - 2y = 6$

$-4 + 2(3) = 2$ $-4 - 2(3) = 6$

$-4 + 6 = 2$ $-4 - 6 = 6$

$2 = 2$ true $-10 = 6$ false

The pair $(-4, 3)$ does not satisfy both equations. Therefore it is not a solution of the system.

2.

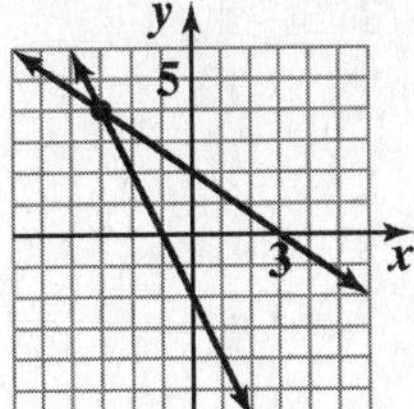

Check coordinates of intersection:

$2x + 3y = 6$ $2x + y = -2$

$2(-3) + 3(4) = 6$ $2(-3) + (4) = -2$

$-6 + 12 = 6$ $-6 + 2 = -2$

$6 = 6$, true $-2 = -2$, true

The solution set is $\{(-3, 4)\}$.

3. Step 1. Solve one of the equations for one variable: $y = 3x - 7$

Step 2. Substitute into the other equation:

$5x - 2y = 8$

$5x - 2\overbrace{(3x-7)}^{y} = 8$

Step 3. Solve: $5x - 2(3x - 7) = 8$

$5x - 6x + 14 = 8$

$-x + 14 = 8$

$-x = -6$

$x = 6$

Step 4. Back-substitute the obtained value into the equation from step 1:

$y = 3x - 7$

$y = 3(6) - 7$

$y = 11$

Step 5. Check (6, 11) in both equations:

$y = 3x - 7$ $5x - 2y = 8$

$11 = 3(6) - 7$ $5(6) - 2(11) = 8$

$11 = 11$, true $8 = 8$, true

The solution set is $\{(6, 11)\}$.

4. Step 1. Solve one of the equations for one variable:

$x - y = 3$

$x = y + 3$

Step 2. Substitute into the other equation:

$3x + 2y = -1$

$3\overbrace{(y+3)}^{x} + 2y = -1$

Step 3. Solve: $3(y+3)+2y=-1$

$$\begin{aligned}3y+9+2y&=-1\\5y+9&=-1\\5y&=-10\\y&=-2\end{aligned}$$

Step 4. Back-substitute the obtained value into the equation from step 1:

$$\begin{aligned}x&=y+3\\x&=-2+3\\x&=1\end{aligned}$$

Step 5. Check $(1,-2)$ in both equations:

$$\begin{aligned}x-y&=3 & 3x+2y&=-1\\1-(-2)&=3 & 3(1)+2(-2)&=-1\\3&=3,\text{ true} & -1&=-1,\text{ true}\end{aligned}$$

The solution set is $\{(1,-2)\}$.

5. Rewrite one or both equations:

$$\begin{aligned}4x+5y=3 &\xrightarrow{\text{No change}} & 4x+5y&=3\\2x-3y=7 &\xrightarrow{\text{Mult. by }-2} & -4x+6y&=-14\\ && 11y&=-11\\ && y&=-1\end{aligned}$$

Back-substitute into either equation:

$$\begin{aligned}4x+5y&=3\\4x+5(-1)&=3\\4x-5&=3\\4x&=8\\x&=2\end{aligned}$$

Checking confirms the solution set is {(2, –1)}.

6. Rewrite both equations in the form $Ax+By=C$:

$$\begin{aligned}3x=2-4y &\rightarrow 3x+4y=2\\5y=-1-2x &\rightarrow 2x+5y=-1\end{aligned}$$

Rewrite with opposite coefficients, then add and solve:

$$\begin{aligned}3x+4y=2 &\xrightarrow{\text{Mult. by }2} & 6x+8y&=4\\2x+5y=-1 &\xrightarrow{\text{Mult. by }-3} & -6x-15y&=3\\ && -7y&=7\\ && y&=-1\end{aligned}$$

Back-substitute into either equation:

$$\begin{aligned}3x&=2-4y\\3x&=2-4(-1)\\3x&=6\\x&=2\end{aligned}$$

Checking confirms the solution set is {(2, –1)}.

7. Rewrite with a pair of opposite coefficients, then add:

$$\begin{aligned}x+2y=4 &\xrightarrow{\text{Mult. by }-3} & -3x-6y&=-12\\3x+6y=13 &\xrightarrow{\text{No change}} & 3x+6y&=13\\ && 0&=1\end{aligned}$$

The statement 0 = 1 is false which indicates that the system has no solution. The solution set is the empty set, ∅.

8. Substitute $4x-4$ for y in the other equation:

$$\begin{aligned}8x-2\overbrace{(4x-4)}^{y}&=8\\8x-8x+8&=8\\8&=8\end{aligned}$$

The statement 8 = 8 is true which indicates that the system has infinitely many solutions. The solution set is $\{(x,y)|\,y=4x-4\}$ **or** $\{(x,y)|\,8x-2y=8\}$.

9. a. $C(x)=300{,}000+30x$

b. $R(x)=80x$

c. $R(x)=C(x)$

$$\begin{aligned}80x&=300{,}000+30x\\50x&=300{,}000\\x&=6000\end{aligned}$$

$C(6000)=300{,}000+30(6000)=480{,}000$

Break even point (6000, 480000)

The company will need to make 6000 pairs of shoes and earn $480,000 to break even.

Concept and Vocabulary Check 7.3

1. satisfies both equation in the system
2. the intersection point
3. $\left\{\left(\frac{1}{3},-2\right)\right\}$
4. –2
5. –3
6. ∅; parallel
7. $\{(x,y)|\,x=3y+2\}$ or $\{(x,y)|\,5x-15y=10\}$; are identical or coincide
8. revenue; profit
9. break-even point

Exercise Set 7.3

1. Replace x with 2 and y with 3.

$x+3y=11 \qquad x-5y=-13$

$2+3(3)=11 \qquad 2-5(3)=13$

$2+9=11 \qquad 2-15=13$

$11=11$, true $\qquad 13=13$, true

The pair (2, 3) is a solution of the system.

3. Replace x with 2 and y with 5.

$2x+3y=17$

$2(2)+3(5)=17$

$4+15=17$

$19=17$, false.

The pair (2, 5) is not a solution of the system.

5.

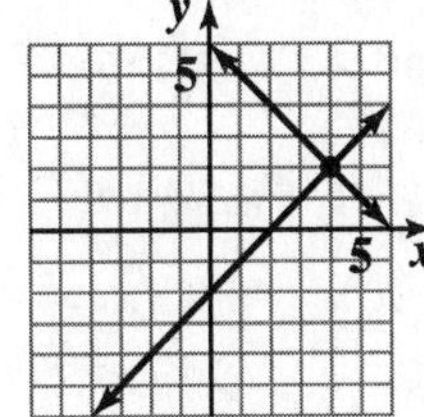

Check coordinates of intersection:

$x+y=6 \qquad x-y=2$

$4+2=6 \qquad 4-2=2$

$6=6$, true $\qquad 2=2$, true

The solution set is $\{(4, 2)\}$.

7.

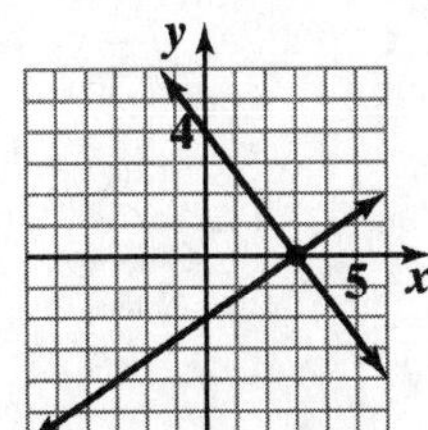

Check coordinates of intersection:

$2x-3y=6 \qquad 4x+3y=12$

$2(3)-3(0)=6 \qquad 4(3)+(0)=12$

$6=6$, true $\qquad 12=12$, true

The solution set is $\{(3, 0)\}$.

9.

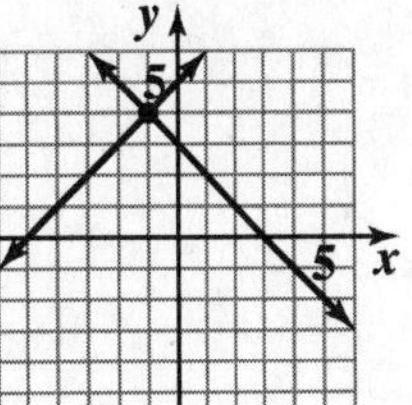

Check coordinates of intersection:

$y=x+5 \qquad y=-x+3$

$4=-1+5 \qquad 4=-(-1)+3$

$4=4$, true $\qquad 4=4$, true

The solution set is $\{(-1, 4)\}$.

11.

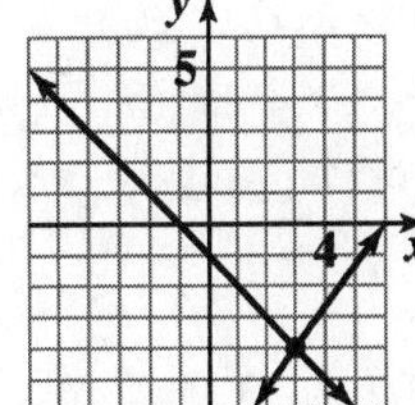

Check coordinates of intersection:

$y=-x-1 \qquad 4x-3y=24$

$-4=-(3)-1 \qquad 4(3)-3(-4)=24$

$-4=-4$, true $\qquad 24=24$, true

The solution set is $\{(3, -4)\}$.

13. $y=3x \qquad x+y=4$

$x+3x=4$

$4x=4$

$x=1$

$y=3(1)=3$

The proposed solution is (1, 3)

Check: $3=3(1) \qquad 1+3=4$

$3=3$, true $\qquad 4=4$, true

The pair (1, 3) satisfies both equations.
The system's solution set is $\{(1, 3)\}$.

15. $y=2x-9 \qquad x+3y=8$

$x+3(2x-9)=8$

$x+6x-27=8$

$7x=35$

$x=5$

$y=2(5)-9=1$

The proposed solution is (5, 1).

Check:

$1=2(5)-9 \qquad 5+3(1)=8$

$1=10-9 \qquad 5+3=8$

$1=1$, true $\qquad 8=8$, true

The pair (5, 1) satisfies both equations.
The system's solution set is $\{(5, 1)\}$.

17. $x + 3y = 5$

$x = 5 - 3y \quad 4x + 5y = 13$

$4(5-3y)+5y=13$

$20-12y+5y=13$

$20-7y=13$

$-7y=-7$

$y=1$

$x=5-3(1)=2$

The proposed solution is (2, 1).

Check:

$2+3(1)=5 \qquad 4(2)+5(1)=13$

$5=5$, true $\qquad 8+5=13$

$13=13$, true

The pair (2, 1) satisfies both equations. The system's solution set is $\{(2, 1)\}$.

19. $2x - y = -5$

$y = 2x + 5 \quad x + 5y = 14$

$x + 5(2x + 5) = 14$

$x + 10x + 25 = 14$

$11x = -11$

$x = -1$

$y = 2(-1) + 5 = -2 + 5 = 3$

The proposed solution is (–1, 3).

Check:

$2(-1)-3=-5 \qquad -1+5(3)=14$

$-2-3=-5 \qquad -1+15=14$

$-5=-5$, true $\qquad 14=14$, true

The pair (– 1, 3) satisfies both equations. The system's solution set is $\{(-1, 3)\}$.

21. $2x - y = 3$

$y = 2x - 3 \quad 5x - 2y = 10$

$5x-2(2x-3)=10$

$5x-4x+6=10$

$x=4$

$y = 2(4) - 3 = 8 - 3 = 5$

The proposed solution is (4, 5).

Check:

$2(4)-5=3 \qquad 5(4)-2(5)=10$

$8-5=3 \qquad 20-10=10$

$3=3$, true $\qquad 10=10$, true

The pair (4, 5) satisfies both equations. The system's solution set is $\{(4, 5)\}$.

23. $x + 8y = 6$

$x = 6 - 8y \quad 2x + 4y = -3$

$2(6-8y)+4y=-3$

$12-16y+4y=-3$

$-12y=-15$

$\frac{-12y}{-12}=\frac{-15}{-12}$

$y=\frac{15}{12}=\frac{5}{4}$

$x=6-8\left(\frac{5}{4}\right)=6-10=-4$

The proposed solution is $\left(-4, \frac{5}{4}\right)$

Check:

$-4+8\left(\frac{5}{4}\right)=6 \quad 2(-4)+4\left(\frac{5}{4}\right)=-3$

$-4+10=6 \qquad -8+5=-3$

$6=6$, true $\qquad -3=-3$, true

The pair $\left(-4, \frac{5}{4}\right)$ satisfies both equations.

The system's solution set is $\left\{\left(-4, \frac{5}{4}\right)\right\}$.

25. $x+y=1$

$x-y=3$

$2x=4$

$x=2$

$x+y=1$

$2+y=1$

$y=-1$

Check: $2+(-1)=1 \quad 2-(-1)=3$

$1=1$, true $\quad 3=3$, true

The solution set is $\{(2, -1)\}$.

27. $2x+3y=6$
$\underline{2x-3y=6}$
$4x=12$
$x=3$
$2x+3y=6$
$2\cdot 3+3y=6$
$6+3y=6$
$3y=0$
$y=0$
Check:
$2(3)+3(0)=6$ $\quad$ $2(3)-3(0)=6$
$6+0=6$ $\quad$ $6-0=6$
$6=6$, true $\quad$ $6=6$, true
The solution set is $\{(3, 0)\}$.

29. $x+2y=2$ Mult. by 3. $3x+6y=6$
$-4x+3y=25$ Mult. by -2. $\underline{8x-6y=-50}$
$11x=-44$
$x=-4$

$x+2y=2$
$-4+2y=2$
$2y=6$
$y=3$
Check:
$-4+2(3)=2$ $\quad$ $-4(-4)+3(3)=25$
$-4+6=2$ $\quad$ $16+9=25$
$2=2$, true $\quad$ $25=25$, true
The solution set is $\{(-4, 3)\}$.

31. $4x+3y=15$ Mult. by 5. $20x+15y=75$
$2x-5y=1$ Mult. by 3. $\underline{6x-15y=3}$
$26x=78$
$x=3$

$4x+3y=15$
$4\cdot 3+3y=15$
$12+3y=15$
$3y=3$
$y=1$
Check:
$4(3)+3(1)=15$ $\quad$ $2(3)-5(1)=1$
$12+3=15$ $\quad$ $6-5=1$
$15=15$, true $\quad$ $1=1$, true
The solution set is $\{(3, 1)\}$.

33. $3x-4y=11$ Mult. by 3. $9x-12y=33$
$2x+3y=-4$ Mult. by 4. $\underline{8x+12y=-16}$
$17x=17$
$x=1$

$2x+3y=-4$
$2\cdot 1+3y=-4$
$2+3y=-4$
$3y=-6$
$y=-2$
Check:
$3(1)-4(-2)=11$
$3+8=11$
$11=11$, true
$2(1)+3(-2)=-4$
$2-6=-4$
$-4=-4$, true
The solution set is $\{(1, -2)\}$.

35. $2x=3y-4$ Rearrange and Mult. by 3. $6x-9y=-12$
$-6x+12y=6$ No change. $\underline{-6x+12y=6}$
$3y=-6$
$y=-2$

$2x=3y-4$
$2x=3(-2)-4$
$2x=-6-4$
$2x=-10$
$x=-5$
Check:
$2(-5)=3(-2)-4$ $\quad$ $-6(-5)+12(-2)=6$
$-10=-6-4$ $\quad$ $30-24=6$
$-10=-10$, true $\quad$ $6=6$, true
The solution set is $\{(-5, -2)\}$.

37. $x=9-2y$ $\quad$ $x+2y=13$
$(9-2y)+2y=13$
$9=13$ false
The system has no solution.
The solution set is the empty set, $\varnothing$.

39. $y = 3x - 5 \quad 21x - 35 = 7y$

$$21x - 35 = 7(3x - 5)$$
$$21x - 35 = 21x - 35$$
$$21x - 21x = 35 - 35$$
$$0 = 0, \text{ true}$$

The system has infinitely many solutions.
The solution set is $\{(x, y) | y = 3x - 5\}$.

41. $3x - 2y = -5$ No change. $3x - 2y = -5$
$4x + y = 8$ Mult. by 2. $8x + 2y = 16$

$$11x = 11$$
$$x = 1$$

$$4x + y = 8$$
$$4(1) + y = 8$$
$$y = 4$$

Check:

$3(1) - 2(4) = -5 \qquad 4(1) + (4) = 8$
$3 - 8 = -5 \qquad 4 + 4 = 8$
$-5 = -5, \text{ true} \qquad 8 = 8, \text{ true}$

The solution set is $\{(1, 4)\}$.

43. $x + 3y = 2$
$x = 2 - 3y \quad 3x + 9y = 6$

$$3(2 - 3y) + 9y = 6$$
$$6 - 9y + 9y = 6$$
$$6 = 6 \text{ true}$$

The system has infinitely many solutions.
The solution set is $\{(x, y) | x + 3y = 2\}$.

45. The solution to a system of linear equations is the point of intersection of the graphs of the equations in the system. If $(6, 2)$ is a solution, then we need to find the lines that intersect at that point.
Looking at the graph, we see that the graphs of $x + 3y = 12$ and $x - y = 4$ intersect at the point $(6, 2)$. Therefore, the desired system of equations is

$x + 3y = 12$ or $y = -\frac{1}{3}x + 4$
$x - y = 4 \qquad y = x - 4$

47. $5ax + 4y = 17$
$ax + 7y = 22$

Multiply the second equation by -5 and add the equations.

$$5ax + 4y = 17$$
$$-5ax - 35y = -110$$
$$-31y = -93$$
$$y = 3$$

Back-substitute into one of the original equations to solve for x.

$$ax + 7y = 22$$
$$ax + 7(3) = 22$$
$$ax + 21 = 22$$
$$ax = 1$$
$$x = \frac{1}{a}$$

The solution is $\left(\frac{1}{a}, 3\right)$.

49. $f(-2) = 11 \rightarrow -2m + b = 11$
$f(3) = -9 \rightarrow 3m + b = -9$

We need to solve the resulting system of equations:

$$-2m + b = 11$$
$$3m + b = -9$$

Subtract the two equations:

$$-2m + b = 11$$
$$3m + b = -9$$
$$-5m = 20$$
$$m = -4$$

Back-substitute into one of the original equations to solve for b.

$$-2m + b = 11$$
$$-2(-4) + b = 11$$
$$8 + b = 11$$
$$b = 3$$

Therefore, $m = -4$ and $b = 3$.

51. At the break-even point, $R(x) = C(x)$.

$$10000 + 30x = 50x$$
$$10000 = 20x$$
$$10000 = 20x$$
$$500 = x$$

Five hundred radios must be produced and sold to break-even.

53. $R(x) = 50x$
$R(200) = 50(200) = 10000$

$C(x) = 10000 + 30x$
$C(200) = 10000 + 30(200)$
$= 10000 + 6000 = 16000$

$R(200) - C(200) = 10000 - 16000$
$= -6000$
This means that if 200 radios are produced and sold the company will lose $6,000.

55. a. $P(x) = R(x) - C(x)$
$= 50x - (10000 + 30x)$
$= 50x - 10000 - 30x$
$= 20x - 10000$
$P(x) = 20x - 10000$

b. $P(10000) = 20(10000) - 10000$
$= 200000 - 10000 = 190000$
If 10,000 radios are produced and sold the profit will be $190,000.

57. a. The cost function is:
$C(x) = 18{,}000 + 20x$

b. The revenue function is:
$R(x) = 80x$

c. At the break-even point, $R(x) = C(x)$.
$80x = 18000 + 20x$
$60x = 18000$
$x = 300$

$R(x) = 80x$
$R(300) = 80(300)$
$= 24{,}000$
When approximately 300 canoes are produced the company will break-even with cost and revenue at $24,000.

59. a. The cost function is:
$C(x) = 30000 + 2500x$

b. The revenue function is:
$R(x) = 3125x$

c. At the break-even point, $R(x) = C(x)$.
$3125x = 30000 + 2500x$
$625x = 30000$
$x = 48$
After 48 sold out performances, the investor will break-even. ($150,000)

61. a. Substitute $0.375x + 3$ for *p* in the first equation.
$p = -0.325x + 5.8$

$\overbrace{0.375x + 3}^{p} = -0.325x + 5.8$
$0.375x + 3 = -0.325x + 5.8$
$0.375x + 0.325x + 3 = -0.325x + 0.325x + 5.8$
$0.7x + 3 = 5.8$
$0.7x + 3 - 3 = 5.8 - 3$
$0.7x = 2.8$
$\frac{0.7x}{0.7} = \frac{2.8}{0.7}$
$x = 4$
Back-substitute to find *p*.
$p = -0.325x + 5.8$
$p = -0.325(4) + 5.8 = 4.5$

The ordered pair is (4,4.5).
Equilibrium number of workers: 4 million
Equilibrium hourly wage: $4.50

b. If workers are paid <u>$4.50</u> per hour, there will be <u>4</u> million available workers and <u>4</u> million workers will be hired. In this state of market equilibrium, there is no unemployment.

c. $p = -0.325x + 5.8$
$5.15 = -0.325x + 5.8$
$0.65 = -0.325x$
$\frac{-0.65}{-0.325} = \frac{-0.325x}{-0.325}$
$2 = x$
At $5.15 per hour, 2 million workers will be hired.

d. $p = 0.375x + 3$
$5.15 = 0.375x + 3$
$2.15 = 0.375x$
$\frac{2.15}{0.375} = \frac{0.375x}{0.375}$
$x \approx 5.7$
At $5.15 per hour, there will be about 5.7 million available workers.

e. $5.7-2=3.7$
At \$5.15 per hour, there will be about 3.7 million more people looking for work than employers are willing to hire.

63. a. $y=0.45x+0.8$

b. $y=0.15x+2.6$

c. To find the week in the semester when both groups report the same number of symptoms, we set the two equations equal to each other and solve for x.

$$0.45x+0.8=0.15x+2.6$$
$$0.3x=1.8$$
$$x=6$$

The number of symptoms will be the same in week 6.

$$y=0.15x+2.6$$
$$y=0.15(6)+2.6$$
$$y=3.5$$

The number of symptoms in week 6 will be 3.5 for both groups. This is shown in the graph by the intersection point (6, 3.5).

75. makes sense

77. does not make sense; Explanations will vary. Sample explanation: Some linear systems have one ordered pair solution and some linear systems have no solutions.

79. Answers will vary.

81. x = first lucky number
y = second lucky number
$3x + 6y = 12$
$x + 2y = 5$
Eliminate x by multiplying the second equation by –3 and adding the resulting equations.

$$\begin{array}{r} 3x+6y=12 \\ -3x-6y=-15 \\ \hline 0=-3 \end{array}$$

The false statement $0 = -3$ indicates that the system has no solution. Therefore, the twin who always lies is talking.

Check Points 7.4

1. $2x-4y\geq 8$
Graph the equation $2x-4y=8$ as a solid line.
Choose a test point that is not on the line.
Test (0,0)

$$2x-4y\geq 8$$
$$2(0)-4(0)\geq 8$$
$$0\geq 8,\ \text{false}$$

Since the statement is false, shade the other half-plane.

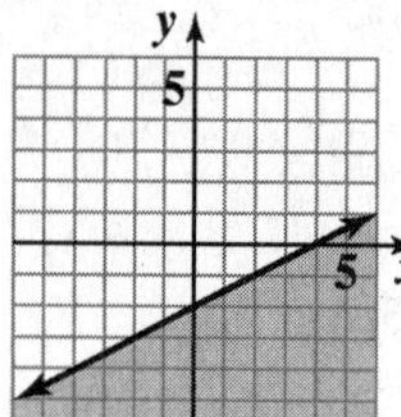

2. $y>-\frac{3}{4}x$

Graph the equation $y=-\frac{3}{4}x$ as a dashed line.
Choose a test point that is not on the line.
Test (1,1)

$$y>-\frac{3}{4}x$$
$$1>-\frac{3}{4}(1)$$
$$1>-\frac{3}{4},\ \text{true}$$

Since the statement is true, shade the half-plane containing the point.

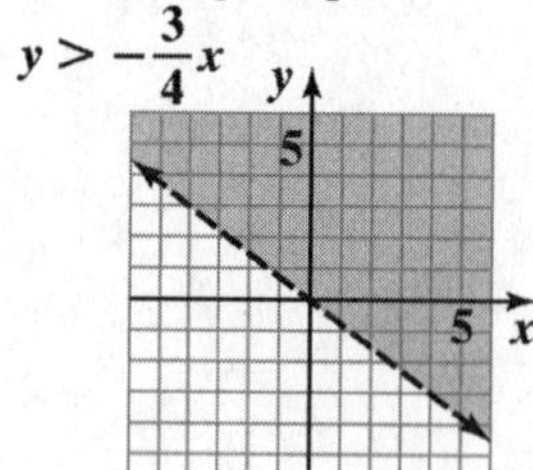

3. a. $y > 1$

Graph the equation $y = 1$ as a dashed line.

Choose a test point that is not on the line.

Test (0,0)

$y > 1$

$0 > 1$, false

Since the statement is false, shade the other half-plane.

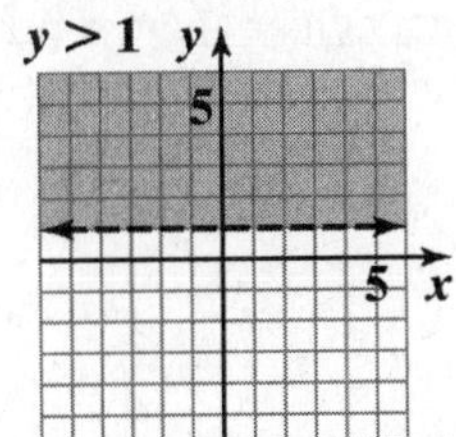

b. Graph the equation $x = -2$ as a solid line.

Choose a test point that is not on the line.

Test (0,0)

$x \le -2$

$0 \le -2$, false

Since the statement is false, shade the other half-plane.

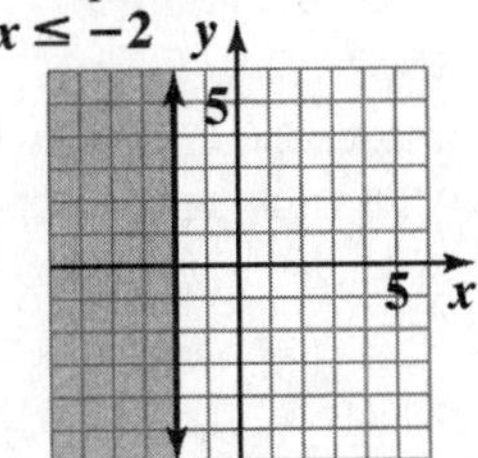

4. Point $B = (66, 130)$

$$4.9x - y \ge 165$$
$$4.9(66) - 130 \ge 165$$
$$193.4 \ge 165, \text{ true}$$

$$3.7x - y \le 125$$
$$3.7(66) - 130 \le 125$$
$$114.2 \le 125, \text{ true}$$

Point B is a solution of the system.

5. $x + 2y > 4$

$2x - 3y \le -6$

Graph the equation $x + 2y = 4$ as a dashed line.

Choose a test point that is not on the line.

Test (0,0)

$x + 2y > 4$

$0 + 2(0) > 4$

$0 > 4$, false

Since the statement is false, shade the other half-plane.

Next, graph the equation $2x - 3y = -6$ as a solid line.

Choose a test point that is not on the line.

Test (0,0)

$2x - 3y \le -6$

$2(0) - 3(0) \le -6$

$0 \le -6$, false

Since the statement is false, shade the other half-plane.

The graph is the intersection (overlapping) of the two half-planes.

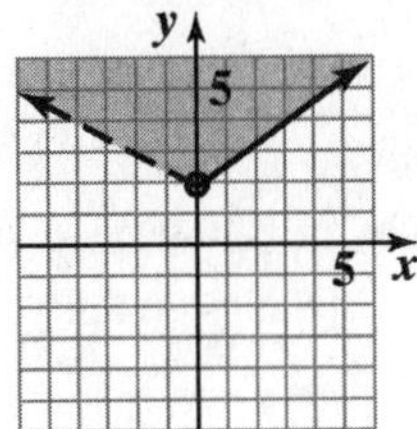

6. $x < 3$

$y \ge -1$

Graph the equation $x = 3$ as a dashed line.

Choose a test point that is not on the line.

Test (0,0)

$x < 3$

$0 < 3$, true

Since the statement is true, shade the half-plane that contains the test point.

Next, graph the equation $y = -1$ as a solid line.

Choose a test point that is not on the line.

Test (0,0)

$y \ge -1$

$0 \ge -1$, true

Since the statement is true, shade the half-plane that contains the test point.

The graph is the intersection (overlapping) of the two half-planes.

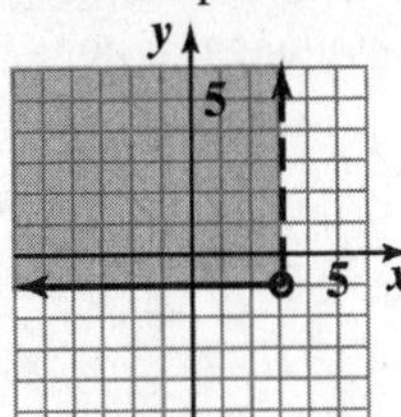

Concept and Vocabulary Check 7.4

1. solution; x; y; $5>1$
2. graph
3. half-plane
4. false
5. true
6. false
7. $x-y<1$; $2x+3y\geq 12$
8. false

Exercise Set 7.4

1. To graph $x+y\geq 2$, begin by graphing $x+y=2$ with a solid line because $\geq$ includes equality.

   test point (0, 0):

   $x+y\geq 2$

   $0+0\geq 2$

   $0\geq 2$, false

   Since the test point makes the inequality false, shade the half-plane not containing test point (0, 0).

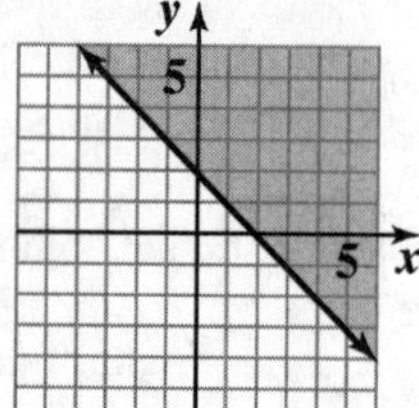

3. To graph $3x-y\geq 6$, begin by graphing $3x-y=6$ with a solid line because $\geq$ includes equality.

   test point (0, 0):

   $3x-y\geq 6$

   $3(0)-0\geq 6$

   $0\geq 6$, false

   Since the test point makes the inequality false, shade the half-plane not containing test point (0, 0).

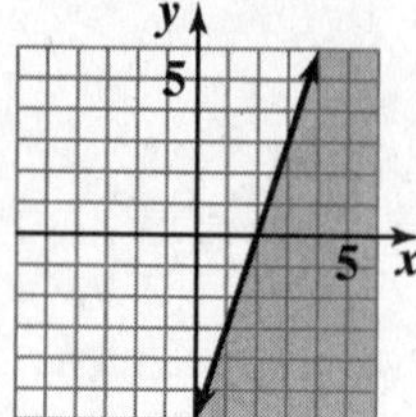

5. To graph $2x+3y>12$, begin by graphing $2x+3y=12$ with a dashed line because $>$ does not include equality.

   test point (0, 0):

   $2x+3y>12$

   $2(0)+3(0)>12$

   $0>12$, false

   Since the test point makes the inequality false, shade the half-plane not containing test point (0, 0).

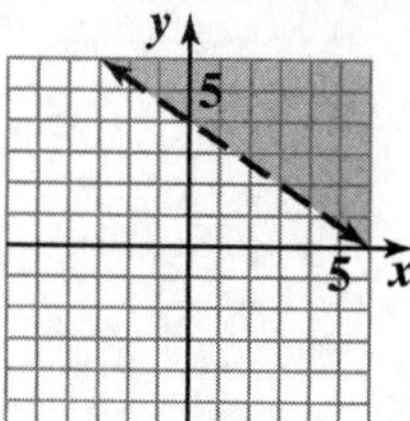

7. To graph $5x+3y\leq -15$, begin by graphing $5x+3y=-15$ with a solid line because $\leq$ includes equality.

   test point (0, 0):

   $5x+3y\leq -15$

   $5(0)+3(0)\leq -15$

   $0\leq -15$, false

   Since the test point makes the inequality false, shade the half-plane not containing test point (0, 0).

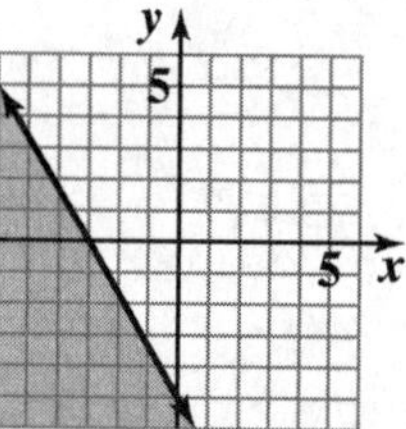

9. To graph $2y-3x>6$, begin by graphing $2y-3x=6$ with a dashed line because $>$ does not include equality.

   test point (0, 0):

   $2y-3x>6$

   $2(0)-3(0)>6$

   $0>6$, false

   Since the test point makes the inequality false, shade the half-plane not containing test point (0, 0).

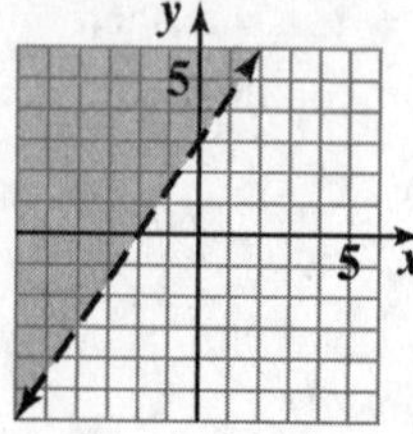

11. $y > \frac{1}{3}x$

Graph the equation $y = \frac{1}{3}$ with a dashed line.

Next, select a test point. We cannot use the origin because it lies on the line. Use $(1,1)$.

$1 > \frac{1}{3}(1)$

$1 > \frac{1}{3}$

This is a true statement, so we know the point $(1,1)$ lies in the shaded half-plane.

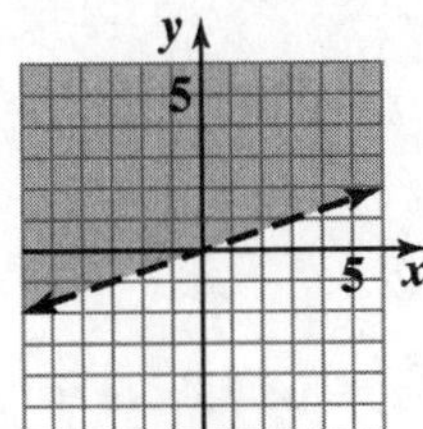

13. $y \le 3x + 2$

Graph the equation $y = 3x + 2$ with a solid line.

Next, use the origin as a test point.

$0 \le 3(0) + 2$

$0 \le 2$

This is a true statement. This means that the point $(0,0)$ will fall in the shaded half-plane.

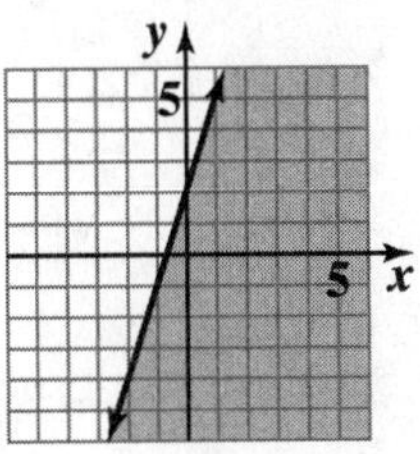

15. $y < -\frac{1}{4}x$

Graph the equation $y = -\frac{1}{4}x$ with a dashed line.

Next, select a test point. We cannot use the origin because it lies on the line. Use $(1,1)$.

$1 < -\frac{1}{4}(1)$

$1 < -\frac{1}{4}$

This is a false statement, so we know the point $(1,1)$ does not lie in the shaded half-plane.

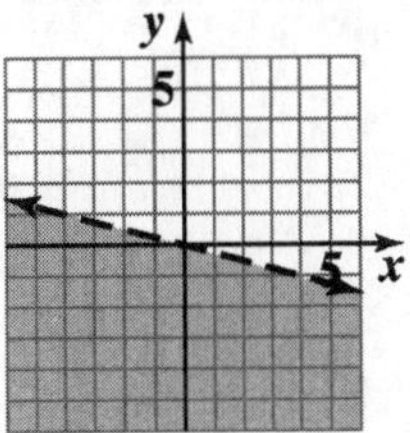

17. $x \le 2$

Graph the equation $x = 2$ with a solid line.

Next, use the origin as a test point.

$x \le 2$

$0 \le 2$

This is a true statement, so we know the point $(0,0)$ lies in the shaded half-plane.

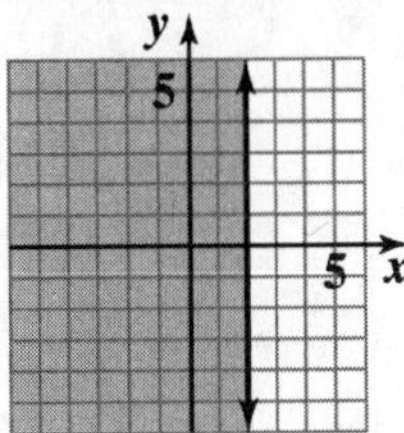

19. $y > -4$

Graph the equation $y = -4$ with a dashed line.

Next, use the origin as a test point.

$y > -4$

$0 > -4$

This is a true statement, so we know the point $(0,0)$ lies in the shaded half-plane.

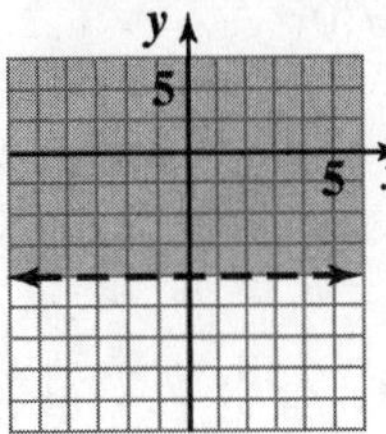

21. $y \geq 0$
Graph the equation $y = 0$ with a solid line.
Next, select a test point. We cannot use the origin because it lies on the line. Use $(1,1)$.
$y \geq 0$
$1 \geq 0$
This is a true statement, so we know the point $(1,1)$ lies in the shaded half-plane.

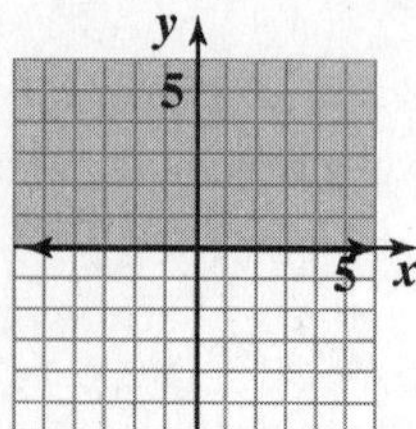

23. $3x + 6y \leq 6$
$2x + y \leq 8$
Graph the equations using the intercepts.

$3x + 6y = 6$	$2x + y = 8$
x – intercept = 2	x – intercept = 4
y – intercept = 1	y – intercept = 8

Use the origin as a test point to determine shading.

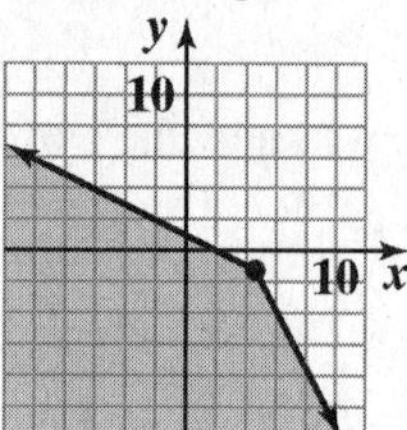

The solution set is the intersection of the shaded half-planes.

25. $2x + y < 3$
$x - y > 2$
Graph $2x + y = 3$ as a dashed line.
If $x = 0$, then $y = 3$ and if $y = 0$, then $x = \frac{3}{2}$.
Because (0, 0) makes the inequality true, shade the half-plane containing (0, 0).
Graph $x - y = 2$ as a dashed line.
If $x = 0$, then $y = -2$ and if $y = 0$, then $x = 2$.
Because (0, 0) makes the inequality false, shade the half-plane not containing (0, 0).

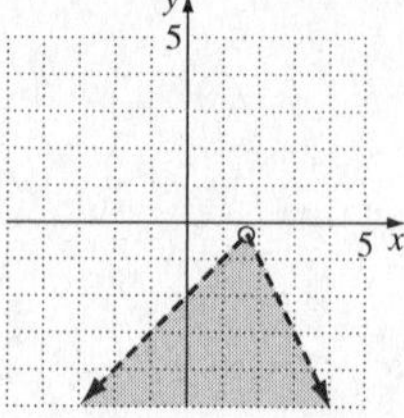

27. $2x + y < 4$
$x - y > 4$
Graph $2x + y = 4$ as a dashed line.
If $x = 0$, then $y = 4$ and if $y = 0$, then $x = 2$.
Because (0, 0) makes the inequality true, shade the half-plane containing (0, 0)
Graph $x - y = 4$ as a dashed line.
If $x = 0$, then $y = -4$. and if $y = 0$, then $x = 4$.
Because (0, 0) makes the inequality false, shade the half-plane not containing (0, 0).

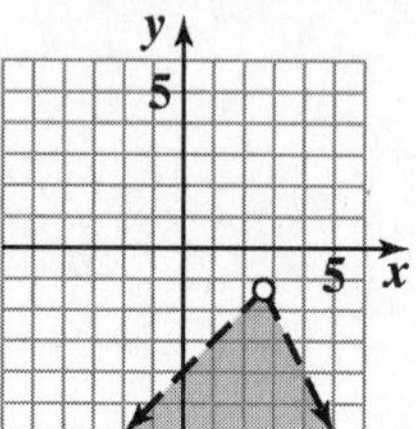

29. $x \geq 2$
$y \leq 3$
Graph $x = 2$ as a solid line.
The points in the half-plane to the right of the line satisfy $x > 2$.
Graph $y = 3$ as a solid line.
The points in the half-plane below the line satisfy $y < 3$.

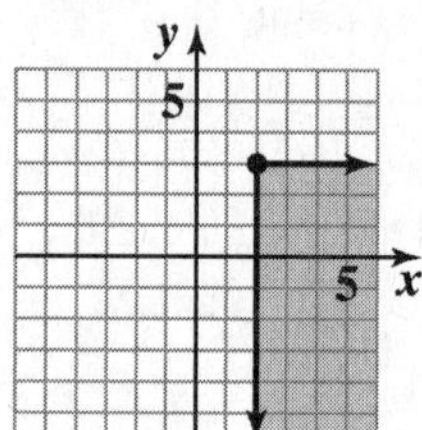

31. $x \leq 5$
$y > -3$
Graph $x = 5$ as a solid line.
The points in the half-plane to the left of the line satisfy $x < 5$.
Graph $y = -3$ as a dashed line.
The points in the half-plane above the line satisfy $y > -3$.

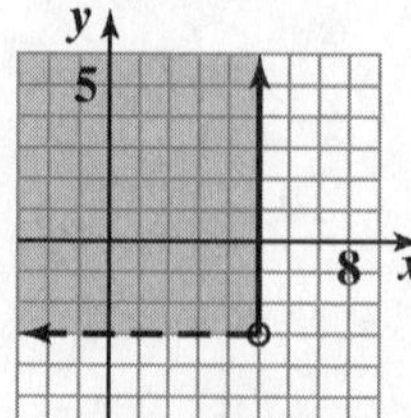

33. $x - y \le 1$
$x \ge 2$
Graph $x - y = 1$ as a solid line.
If $x = 0$, then $y = -1$ and if $y = 0$, then $x = 1$.
Because (0, 0) satisfies the inequality, shade the half-plane containing (0, 0).
Graph $x = 2$ as a solid line.
The points in the half-plane to the right of $x = 2$ satisfy the inequality $x \ge 2$.

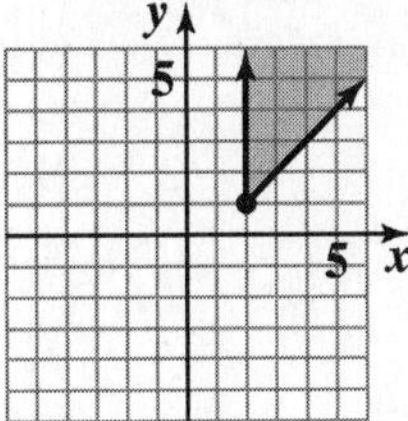

35. $y > 2x - 3$
$y < -x + 6$
Graph the equations using the intercepts.

$y = 2x - 3$	$y = -x + 6$
$x - \text{intercept} = \frac{3}{2}$	$x - \text{intercept} = 6$
$y - \text{intercept} = -3$	$y - \text{intercept} = 6$

Use the origin as a test point to determine shading.

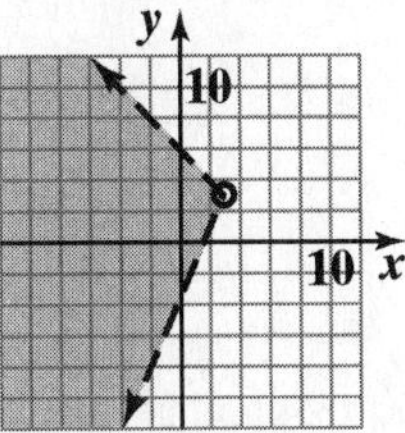

The solution set is the intersection of the shaded half-planes.

37. $x + 2y \le 4$
$y \ge x - 3$
Graph the equations using the intercepts.

$x + 2y = 4$	$y = x - 3$
$x - \text{intercept} = 4$	$x - \text{intercept} = 3$
$y - \text{intercept} = 2$	$y - \text{intercept} = -3$

Use the origin as a test point to determine shading.

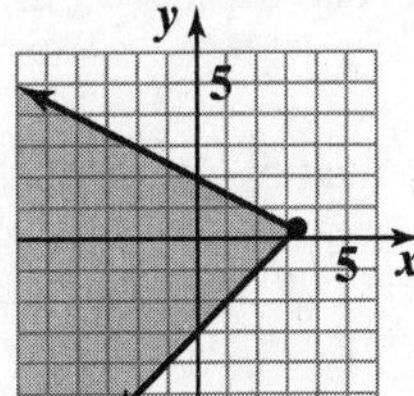

The solution set is the intersection of the shaded half-planes.

39. Graph:
$y \ge -2x + 4$

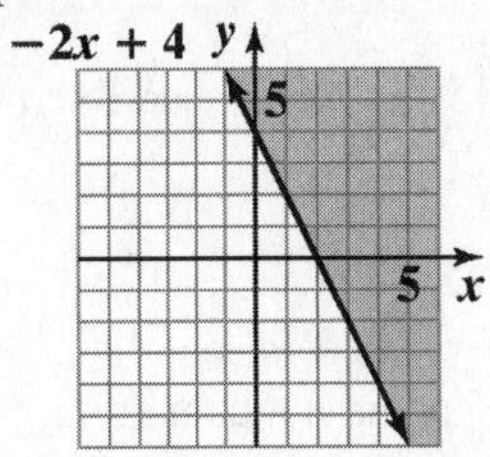

41. Find the union of the solutions.
$x + y \le 4$
$3x + y \le 6$

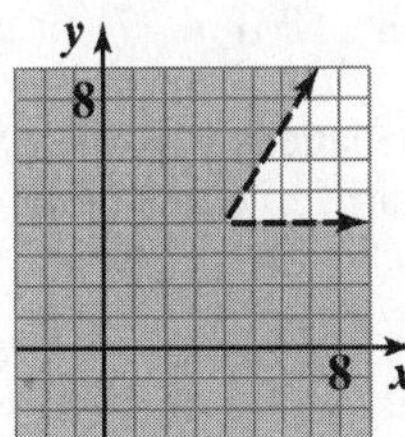

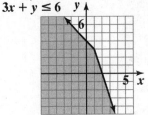

43. Find the union of solutions of $y > \frac{3}{2}x - 2$ and $y < 4$.

y
8
8
x

45. Point A = (66,160)
$$5.3x - y \ge 180$$
$$5.3(66) - 160 \ge 180$$
$$189.8 \ge 180, \text{ true}$$

$$4.1x - y \le 14$$
$$4.1(66) - 160 \le 140$$
$$110.6 \le 140, \text{ true}$$
Point A is a solution of the system.

47. Point = (72,205)
$$5.3x - y \ge 180$$
$$5.3(72) - 205 \ge 180$$
$$176.6 \ge 180, \text{ false}$$

$$4.1x - y \le 14$$
$$4.1(72) - 205 \le 140$$
$$90.2 \le 140, \text{ true}$$
The data does not satisfy both inequalities. The person is not within the healthy weight region.

49. a. $50x + 150y > 2000$

b. Graph $50x + 150y$ as a dashed line using its x-intercept, (40, 0), and its y-intercept, $\left(0, \frac{40}{3}\right)$.

Test (0, 0):
$50(0) + 150(0) > 2000?$
$0 > 2000$ false
Shade the half-plane not containing (0, 0).

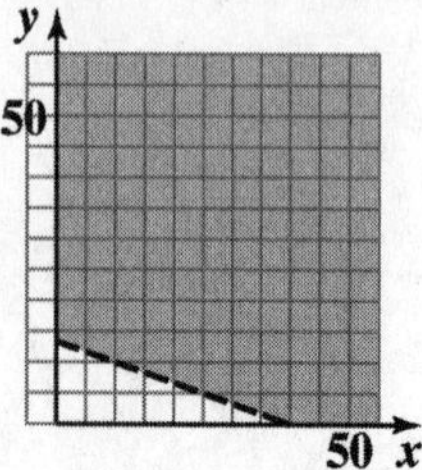

50x + 150y > 2000

c. Ordered pairs may vary.

51. a. $\text{BMI} = \frac{703W}{H^2} = \frac{703(200)}{72^2} \approx 27.1$

b. A 20 year old man with a BMI of 27.1 is classified as overweight.

59. does not make sense; Explanations will vary. Sample explanation: It is necessary to graph the linear equation with a dashed line to represent its role as a borderline.

61. makes sense

63. $y > x - 3$
$y \leq x$

65. The system $\begin{matrix} 6x - y \leq 24 \\ 6x - y > 24 \end{matrix}$ has no solution. The number $6x - y$ cannot both be less than or equal to 24 and greater than 24 at the same time.

67. The system $\begin{matrix} 6x - y \leq 24 \\ 6x - y \geq 24 \end{matrix}$ has infinitely many solutions. The solutions are all points on the line $6x - y = 24$.

Section 7.5

Check Point Exercises

1. The total profit is 25 times the number of bookshelves, x, plus 55 times the number of desks, y. The objective function is $z = 25x + 55y$

2. Not more than a total of 80 bookshelves and desks can be manufactured per day. This is represented by the inequality $x + y \leq 80$.

3. Objective function: $z = 25x + 55y$
Constraints: $x + y \leq 80$
$30 \leq x \leq 80$
$10 \leq y \leq 30$

4. Graph the constraints and find the corners, or vertices, of the region of intersection.

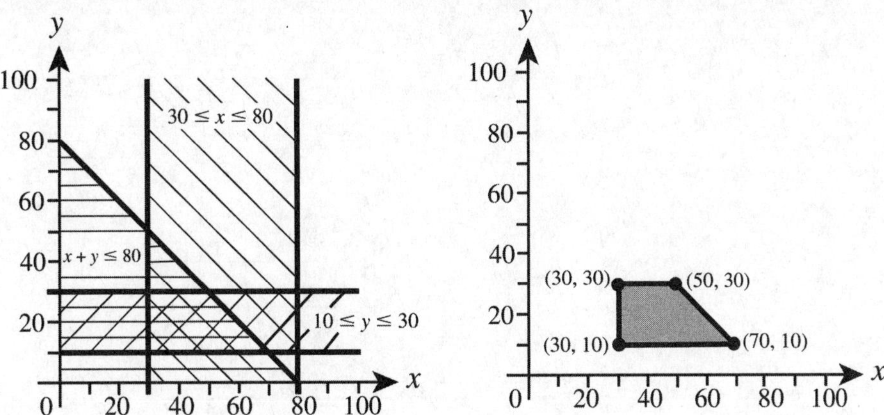

Find the value of the objective function at each corner of the graphed region.

Corner (x, y)	Objective Function $z = 25x + 55y$
(30, 10)	$z = 25(30) + 55(10)$ $= 750 + 550 = 1300$
(30, 30)	$z = 25(30) + 55(30)$ $= 750 + 1650 = 2400$
(50, 30)	$z = 25(50) + 55(30)$ $= 1250 + 1650 = 2900 \leftarrow$ Maximum
(70, 10)	$z = 25(70) + 55(10)$ $= 1750 + 550 = 2300$

The maximum value of z is 2900 and it occurs at the point (50, 30).
In order to maximize profit, 50 bookshelves and 30 desks must be produced each day for a profit of $2900.

Concept and Vocabulary Check 7.5

1. linear programming
2. objective
3. constraints; corner

Exercise Set 7.5

1. $z = 5x + 6y$
(1, 2): 5(1) + 6(2) = 5 + 12 = 17
(2, 10): 5(2) + 6(10) = 10 + 60 = 70
(7, 5): 5(7) + 6(5) = 35 + 30 = 65
(8, 3): 5(8) + 6(3) = 40 + 18 = 58
The maximum value is $z = 70$; the minimum value is $z = 17$.

3. $z = 40x + 50y$
(0, 0): 40(0) + 50(0) = 0 + 0 = 0
(0, 8): 40(0) + 50(8) = 0 + 400 = 400
(4, 9): 40(4) + 50(9) = 160 + 450 = 610
(8, 0): 40(8) + 50(0) = 320 + 0 = 320
The maximum value is $z = 610$; the minimum value is $z = 0$.

5. a.

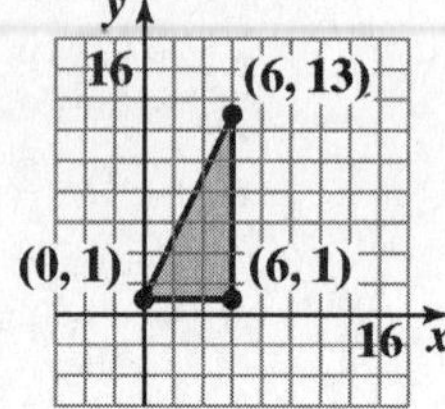

b. at (0, 1) $z = 0 + 1 = 1$
at (6, 13) $z = 6 + 13 = 19$
at (6, 1) $z = 6 + 1 = 7$

c. Maximum = 19
occurs at $x = 6$ and $y = 13$

7. a.

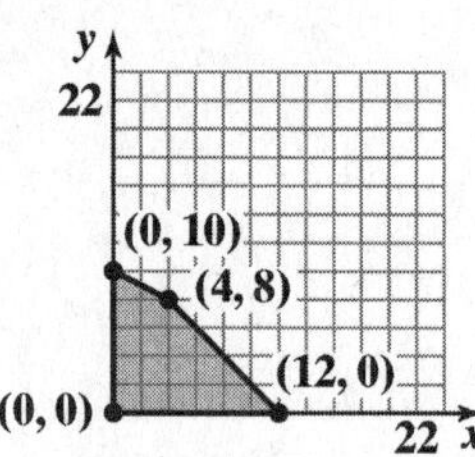

b. at (0, 10) $z = 6(0) + 10(10) = 100$
at (4, 8) $z = 6(4) + 10(8) = 104$
at (12, 0) $z = 6(12) + 10(0) = 72$
at (0, 0) $z = 6(0) + 10(0) = 0$

c. Maximum = 104
occurs at $x = 4$ and $y = 8$

9. $z = 5x - 2y$
$0 \le x \le 5$
$0 \le y \le 3$
$x + y \ge 2$

a.

(0, 3) (5, 3) (5, 0) (0, 2) (2, 0)

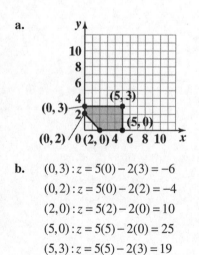

b. $(0,3): z = 5(0) - 2(3) = -6$
$(0,2): z = 5(0) - 2(2) = -4$
$(2,0): z = 5(2) - 2(0) = 10$
$(5,0): z = 5(5) - 2(0) = 25$
$(5,3): z = 5(5) - 2(3) = 19$

c. The maximum value is 25 at $x = 5$ and $y = 0$.

11. $z = 10x + 12y$
$x \ge 0, y \ge 0$
$x + y \le 7$
$2x + y \le 10$
$2x + 3y \le 18$

a.

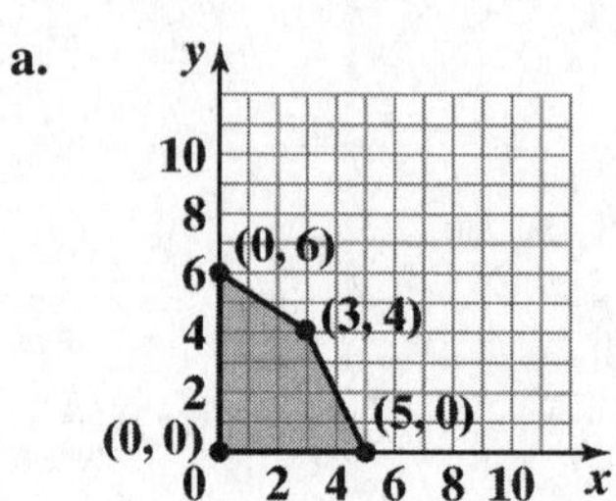

b. (0, 6): $z = 10(0) + 12(6) = 72$
(0, 0): $z = 10(0) + 12(0) = 0$
(5, 0): $z = 10(5) + 12(0) = 50$
(3, 4): $z = 10(3) + 12(4)$
$= 30 + 48 = 78$

c. The maximum value is 78 at $x = 3$ and $y = 4$.

13. a. Let x = number of hours spent tutoring and y = number of hours spent as a teacher's aid. The objective is to maximize $z = 10x + 7y$.

b. The constraints are:
$x + y \le 20$
$x \ge 3$
$x \le 8$

c.

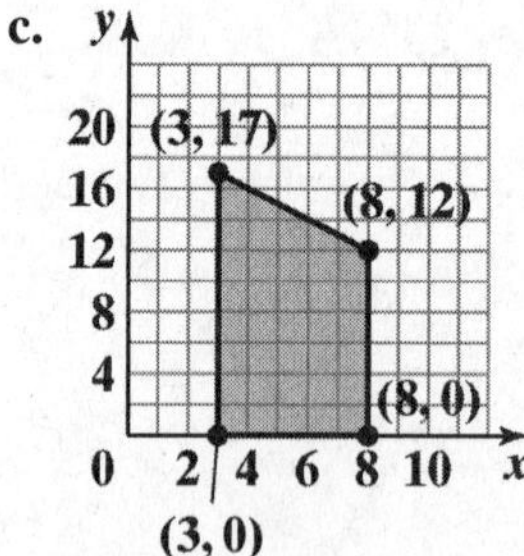

d. (3, 0): $10(3) + 7(0) = 30 + 0 = 30$
(3, 17): $10(3) + 7(17) = 30 + 119 = 149$
(8, 12): $10(8) + 7(12) = 80 + 84 = 164$
(8, 0): $10(8) + 7(0) = 80 + 0 = 80$

e. The student can earn the maximum amount per week by tutoring for 8 hours a week and working as a teacher's aid for 12 hours a week. The maximum that the student can earn each week is $164.

15. Let x = the number of cartons of food and
y = the number of cartons of clothing.
The constraints are:
$20x + 10y \le 8{,}000$ or $2x + y \le 8000$
$50x + 20y \le 19{,}000$ or $5x + 2y \le 1900$
Graph these inequalities in the first quadrant, since x and y cannot be negative.

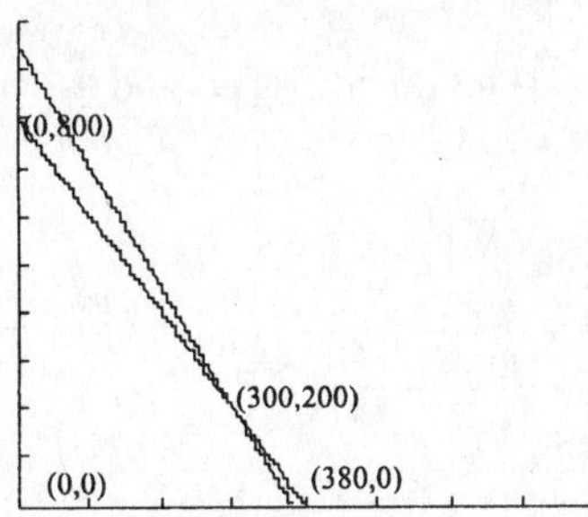

The quantity to be maximized is the number of people helped, which is $12x + 5y$.
(0, 0): $12(0) + 5(0) = 0 + 0 = 0$
(0, 800): $12(0) + 5(800) = 0 + 4000 = 4000$
(300, 200): $12(300) + 5(200) = 4600$
(380, 0): $12(380) + 5(0) = 4500$
300 cartons of food and 200 cartons of clothing should be shipped. This will help 4600 people.

17. Let x = number of students attending and
y = number of parents attending.
The constraints are
$x + y \le 150$
$2x \ge y$
or
$x + y \le 150$
$2x - y \ge 0$
Graph these inequalities in the first quadrant, since x and y cannot be negative.

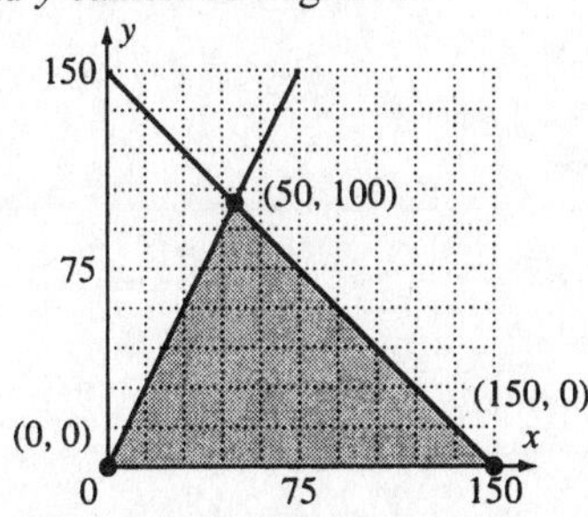

The quantity to be maximized is the amount of money raised, which is $x + 2y$.
(0, 0): $0 + 2(0) = 0 + 0 = 0$
(50, 100): $50 + 2(100) = 50 + 200 = 250$
(150, 0): $150 + 2(0) = 150 + 0 = 150$
50 students and 100 parents should attend.

25. makes sense

27. makes sense

Section 7.6

Check Point Exercises

1.

x	$f(x) = 3^x$
–2	$\frac{1}{9}$
–1	$\frac{1}{3}$
0	1
1	3
2	9

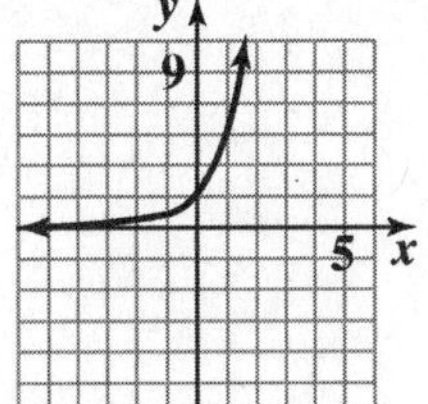

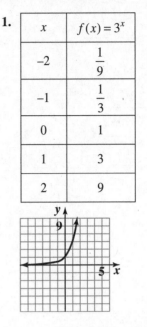

2. a. $f(x) = 0.074x + 2.294$
$f(21) = 0.074(21) + 2.294$
$f(21) \approx 3.8$

$g(x) = 2.577(1.017)^x$
$g(21) = 2.577(1.017)^{21}$
$g(21) \approx 3.7$
When rounded to one decimal place, the result from the exponential function serves as the better model for the year 1970.

b. $f(x) = 0.074x + 2.294$
$f(101) = 0.074(101) + 2.294$
$f(101) \approx 9.8$

$g(x) = 2.577(1.017)^x$
$g(101) = 2.577(1.017)^{101}$
$g(101) \approx 14.1$
The linear function, $f(x)$, serves as the better model for 2050.

3. $R = 6e^{12.77x}$
$= 6e^{12.77(0.01)}$
$= 6.8\%$
The risk of a car accident with a blood alcohol concentration of 0.01 is 6.8%.

4. $y = \log_3 x$ is equivalent to $x = 3^y$.

$x = 3^y$	y	(x, y)
$\frac{1}{9}$	−2	$\left(\frac{1}{9}, -2\right)$
$\frac{1}{3}$	−1	$\left(\frac{1}{3}, -1\right)$
1	0	$(1, 0)$
3	1	$(3, 1)$
9	2	$(9, 2)$

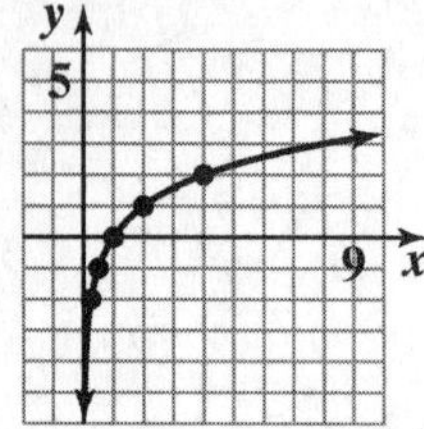

5. $f(x) = -11.6 + 13.4 \ln x$

$f(30) = -11.6 + 13.4 \ln 30$

$f(30) \approx 34°$

The function models the actual data extremely well.

6. Step 1. Since $a > 0$, the parabola opens upward ($a = 1$).

Step 2. Find the vertex given $a = 1$ and $b = 6$.

x-coordinate of vertex

$= \frac{-b}{2a} = \frac{-6}{2(1)} = \frac{-6}{2} = -3$

y-coordinate of vertex

$= (-3)^2 + 6(-3) + 5 = 9 - 18 + 5 = -4$

Thus, the vertex is the point $(-3, -4)$.

Step 3. Replace y with 0 and solve the equation for x by factoring.

$x^2 + 6x + 5 = 0$

$(x + 5)(x + 1) = 0$

$x + 5 = 0$ or $x + 1 = 0$

$x = -5$ $\quad$ $x = -1$

Thus the x-intercepts are -5 and -1, , which are located at the points $(-5, 0)$ and $(-1, 0)$.

Step 4. Replace x with 0 and solve the equation for y.

$y = x^2 + 6x + 5$

$y = (0)^2 + 6(0) + 5$

$y = 5$

Thus the y-intercept is 5, which is located at the point (0, 5).

Steps 5 and 6. Plot the intercepts and the vertex. Connect these points with a smooth curve.

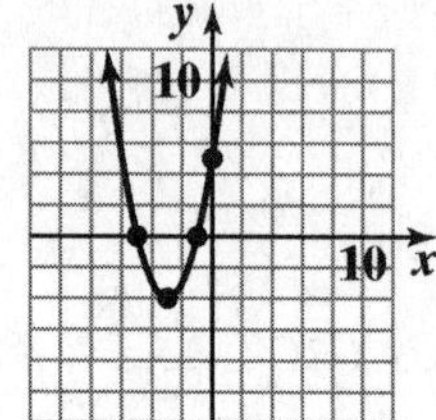

7. $f(x) = -0.01x^2 + 1.18x + 2$

$f(8) = -0.01(8)^2 + 1.18(8) + 2$

$= 10.8$

The defensive player would have needed to reach 10.8 feet. It would be unlikely any player could reach that far. This would be represented on the graph by the point $(8, 10.8)$.

Concept and Vocabulary Check 7.6

1. scatter plot; regression
2. logarithmic
3. exponential
4. quadratic
5. linear
6. b^x
7. 2.72; natural
8. $b^y = x$
9. $\log x$; common
10. $\ln x$; natural
11. quadratic; parabola; $\frac{-b}{2a}$

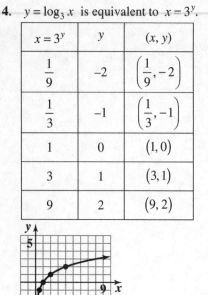

Exercise Set 7.6

1.

x	$y = 4^x$
−2	$\frac{1}{16}$
−1	$\frac{1}{4}$
0	1
1	4
2	16

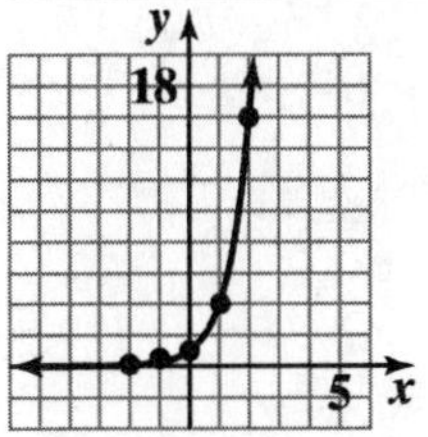

3.

x	$y = 2^{x+1}$
−2	$\frac{1}{2}$
−1	1
0	2
1	4
2	8

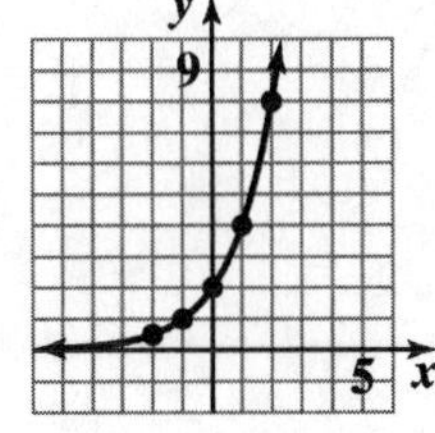

5.

x	$y = 3^{x-1}$
−2	$\frac{1}{27}$
−1	$\frac{1}{9}$
0	$\frac{1}{3}$
1	1
2	3

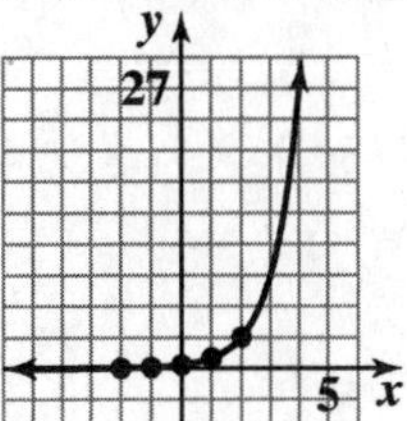

7. a. $y = \log_4 x$ is equivalent to $x = 4^y$.

b.

$x = 4^y$	y
$\frac{1}{16}$	−2
$\frac{1}{4}$	−1
1	0
4	1
16	2

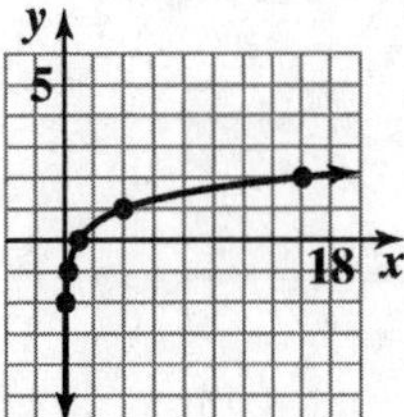

9. a. $a > 0$, thus the parabola opens upward.

b. x-coordinate: $x = \frac{-b}{2a} = \frac{-8}{2(1)} = -4$

y-coordinate: $y = x^2 + 8x + 7$

$$= (-4)^2 + 8(-4) + 7$$

$$= -9$$

vertex: $(-4, -9)$

c. x-intercepts: $y = x^2 + 8x + 7$

$$0 = x^2 + 8x + 7$$
$$0 = (x+7)(x+1)$$

$x + 7 = 0$ or $x + 1 = 0$

$x = -7$ $\quad$ $x = -1$

d. y-intercept: $y = x^2 + 8x + 7$

$$y = 0^2 + 8(0) + 7$$
$$y = 7$$

e.

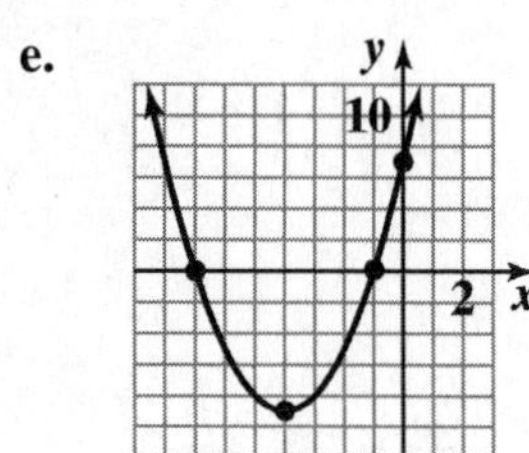

11. a. $a > 0$, thus the parabola opens upward.

b. x-coordinate: $x = \dfrac{-b}{2a} = \dfrac{-(-2)}{2(1)} = 1$

y-coordinate: $f(x) = x^2 - 2x - 8$

$$f(1) = (1)^2 - 2(1) - 8$$
$$= -9$$

vertex: $(1, -9)$

c. x-intercepts: $f(x) = x^2 - 2x - 8$

$$0 = x^2 - 2x - 8$$
$$0 = (x+2)(x-4)$$

$x + 2 = 0$ or $x - 4 = 0$

$x = -2$ $\quad$ $x = 4$

d. y-intercept: $f(x) = x^2 - 2x - 8$

$$f(0) = 0^2 - 2(0) - 8$$
$$y = -8$$

e.

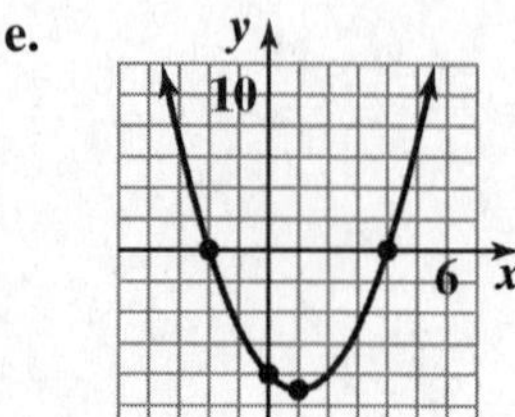

13. a. $a < 0$, thus the parabola opens downward.

b. x-coordinate: $x = \dfrac{-b}{2a} = \dfrac{-4}{2(-1)} = 2$

y-coordinate: $y = -x^2 + 4x - 3$

$$= -(2)^2 + 4(2) - 3$$
$$= 1$$

vertex: $(2, 1)$

c. x-intercepts: $y = -x^2 + 4x - 3$

$$0 = -x^2 + 4x - 3$$
$$0 = x^2 - 4x + 3$$
$$0 = (x-3)(x-1)$$

$x - 3 = 0$ or $x - 1 = 0$

$x = 3$ $\quad$ $x = 1$

d. y-intercept: $y = -x^2 + 4x - 3$

$$y = -0^2 + 4(0) - 3$$
$$y = -3$$

e.

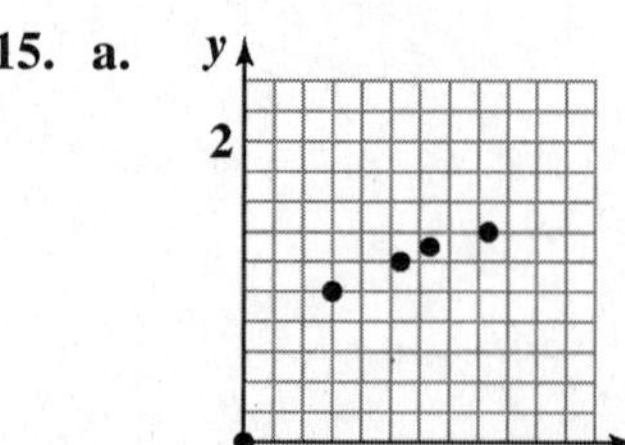

15. a.

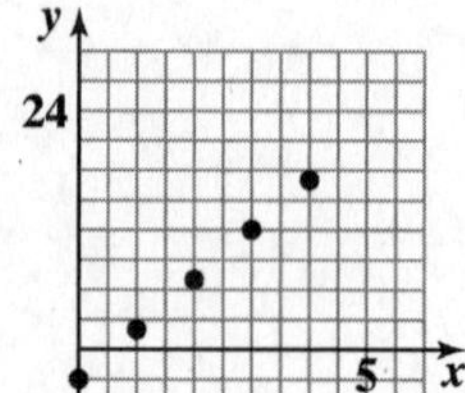

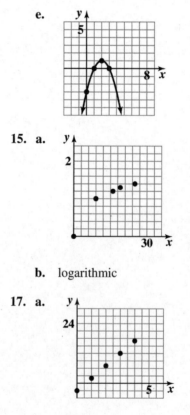

b. logarithmic

17. a.

y

24

5 x

b. linear

19. a.

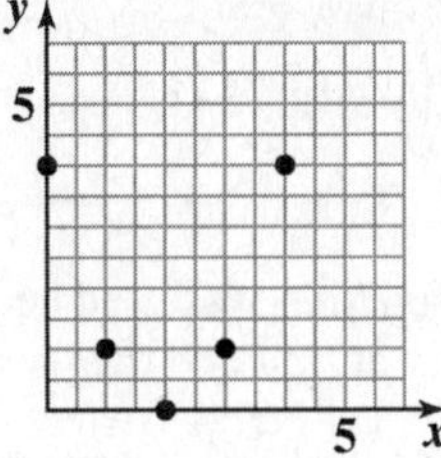

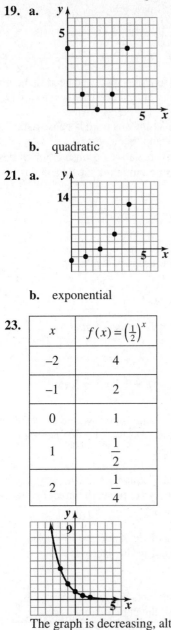

b. quadratic

21. a.

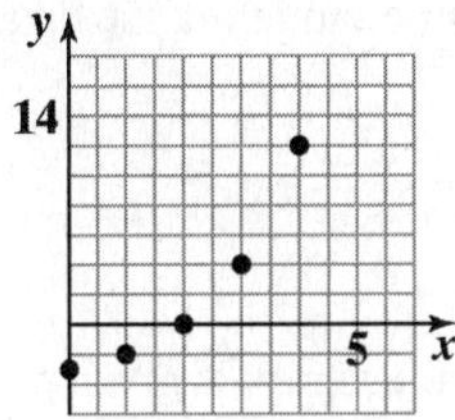

b. exponential

23.

x	$f(x)=\left(\frac{1}{2}\right)^x$
–2	4
–1	2
0	1
1	$\frac{1}{2}$
2	$\frac{1}{4}$

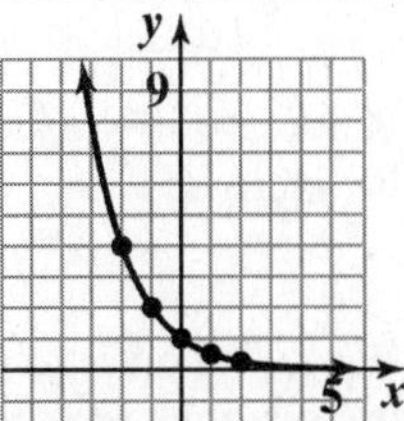

The graph is decreasing, although the rate of decrease is slowing down.

25.

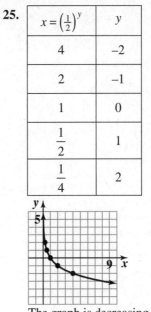

$x=\left(\frac{1}{2}\right)^y$	y
4	–2
2	–1
1	0
$\frac{1}{2}$	1
$\frac{1}{4}$	2

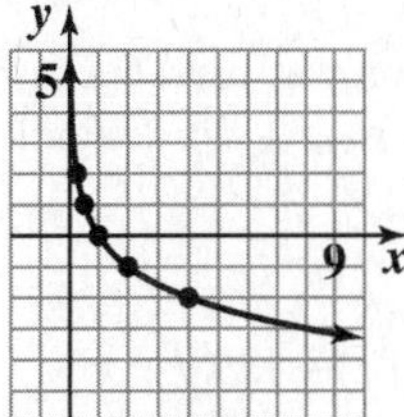

The graph is decreasing, although the rate of decrease is slowing down.

27. a. $a < 0$, thus the parabola opens downward.

b. x-coordinate: $x = \dfrac{-b}{2a} = \dfrac{-4}{2(-2)} = 1$

y-coordinate: $f(x) = -2x^2 + 4x + 5$

$$f(1) = -2(1)^2 + 4(1) + 5$$
$$= 7$$

vertex: $(1, 7)$

c. x-intercepts: $f(x) = -2x^2 + 4x + 5$

$$0 = -2x^2 + 4x + 5$$
$$0 = 2x^2 - 4x - 5$$
$$x = \frac{-b \pm \sqrt{b^2 - 4ac}}{2a}$$
$$x = \frac{-(-4) \pm \sqrt{(-4)^2 - 4(2)(-5)}}{2(2)}$$

$x \approx -0.9$ or $x \approx 2.9$

d. y-intercept: $f(x) = -2x^2 + 4x + 5$

$$f(0) = -2(0)^2 + 4(0) + 5$$
$$f(0) = 5$$

e.

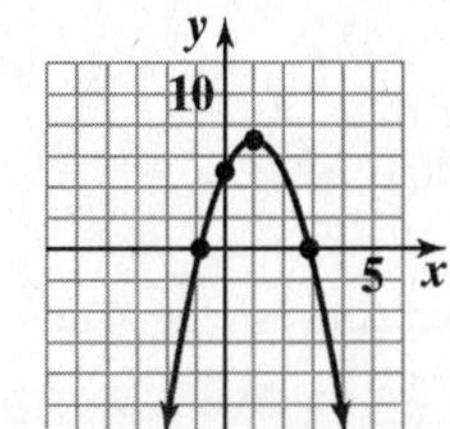

29. $y=(x-3)^2+2$

$y=x^2-6x+9+2$

$y=x^2-6x+11$

x-coordinate: $x=\frac{-b}{2a}=\frac{-(-6)}{2(1)}=3$

y-coordinate: $y=x^2-6x+11$

$y=3^2-6(3)+11$

$y=2$

vertex: (3, 2)

31. a. An exponential function was used because the graph is increasing more and more rapidly.

b. $f(x)=3.476(1.023)^x$

c. $f(111)=3.476(1.023)^{111}\approx 43.4$

43.4 million

The function underestimates the actual value by 1.2 million.

d. $f(121)=3.476(1.023)^{121}\approx 54.5$

54.5 million

The function overestimates the actual value by 0.8 million.

33. a. $f(x)=782x+6564$

$f(11)=782(11)+6564\approx 15{,}166$

According to the linear model, the average cost of a family health insurance plan was $15,166 in 2011.

b. $g(x)=6875e^{0.077x}$

$g(11)=6875e^{0.077(11)}\approx 16{,}037$

According to the exponential model, the average cost of a family health insurance plan was $16,037 in 2011.

c. The linear model is the better model for the data in 2011.

35. a. An logarithmic function was used because the data increase rapidly and then begin to level off.

b. $f(x)=32+29\ln x$

c. $f(x)=32+29\ln x$

$f(10)=32+29\ln 10\approx 99$

About 99%

The function overestimates the actual value by 4%.

37. a. $f(x)=62+35\log(x-4)$

$f(13)=62+35\log(13-4)$

$f(13)\approx 95.4\%$

b. A logarithmic function was used because height increases rapidly at first and then more slowly.

39. a. A quadratic function was used because data values increase and then decrease.

The value of *a* is negative because graph of the quadratic function modeling the data opens down.

b. $f(x)=-0.8x^2+2.4x+6$

c. The *x* value of the vertex is given by $x=-\frac{b}{2a}$

$x=-\frac{2.4}{2(-0.8)}=1.5$

The *y* value of the vertex is found by substitution.

$f(x)=-0.8x^2+2.4x+6$

$f(1.5)=-0.8(1.5)^2+2.4(1.5)+6$

$=7.8$

The maximum height of the ball occurs 1.5 feet from where it was thrown, and the maximum height is 7.8 feet.

47. does not make sense; Explanations will vary. Sample explanation: An exponential model is better than a linear model.

49. does not make sense; Explanations will vary. Sample explanation: The risk increases exponentially.

51. There are two *x*-intercepts because the vertex is above the *x*-axis and the parabola opens downward ($a<0$).

53. There are no *x*-intercepts because the vertex is above the *x*-axis and the parabola opens upward ($a>0$).

Chapter 7 Review Exercises

1\.

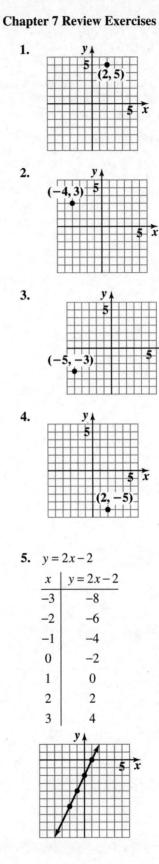

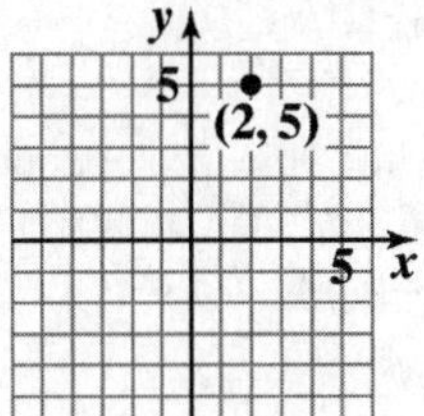

2\.

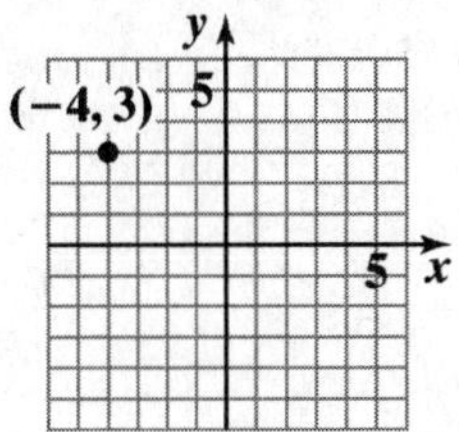

3\.

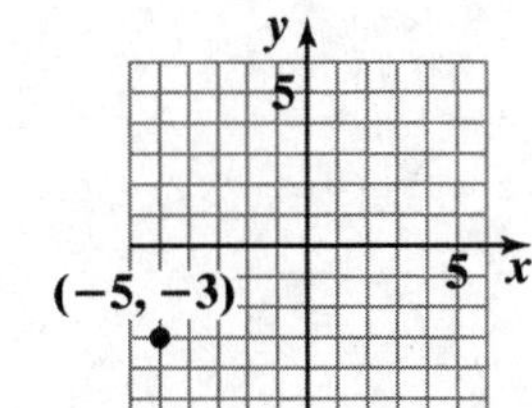

4\.

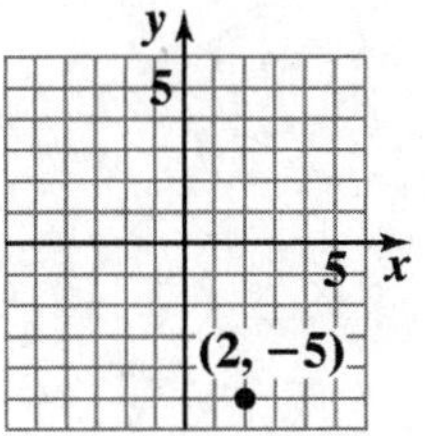

5\. $y = 2x - 2$

x	$y = 2x - 2$
−3	−8
−2	−6
−1	−4
0	−2
1	0
2	2
3	4

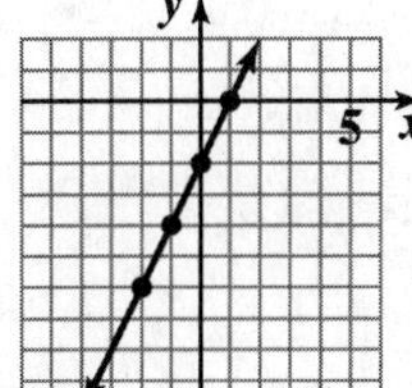

6\. $y = |x| + 2$

x	$y = \lvert x \rvert + 2$
−3	5
−2	4
−1	3
0	2
1	3
2	4
3	5

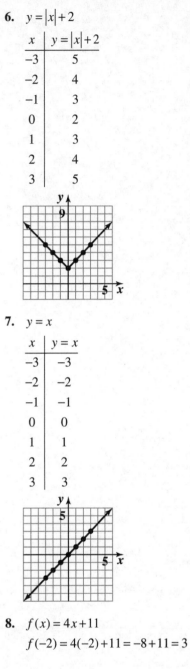

7\. $y = x$

x	$y = x$
−3	−3
−2	−2
−1	−1
0	0
1	1
2	2
3	3

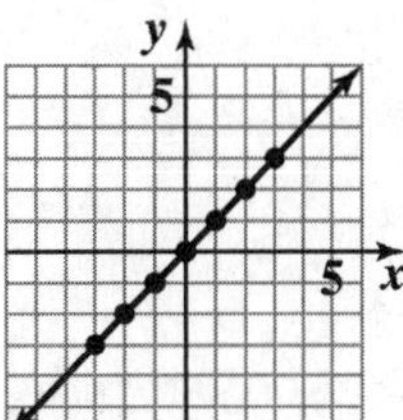

8\. $f(x) = 4x + 11$

$f(-2) = 4(-2) + 11 = -8 + 11 = 3$

9\. $f(x) = -7x + 5$

$f(-3) = -7(-3) + 5 = 21 + 5 = 26$

10\. $f(x) = 3x^2 - 5x + 2$

$f(4) = 3(4)^2 - 5(4) + 2 = 48 - 20 + 2 = 30$

11\. $f(x) = -3x^2 + 6x + 8$

$f(-4) = -3(-4)^2 + 6(-4) + 8$

$= -48 - 24 + 8 = -64$

12. $f(x)=\frac{1}{2}|x|$

x	$f(x)=\frac{1}{2}\lvert x\rvert$
–6	3
–4	2
–2	1
0	0
2	1
4	2
6	3

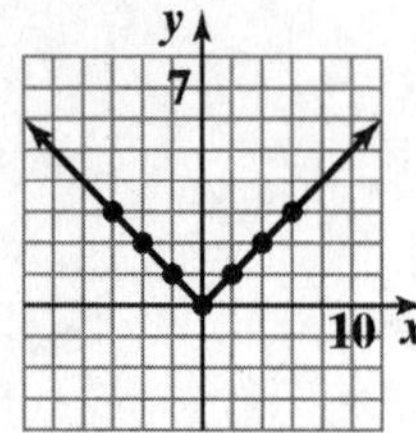

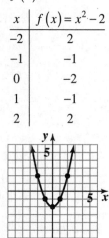

13. $f(x)=x^2-2$

x	$f(x)=x^2-2$
–2	2
–1	–1
0	–2
1	–1
2	2

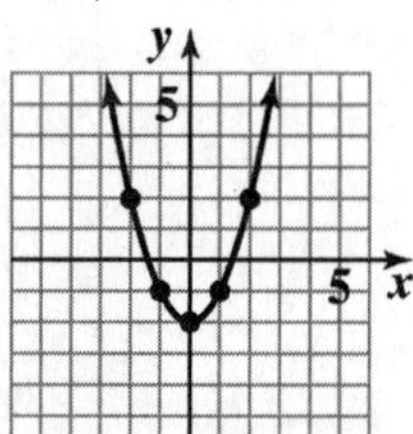

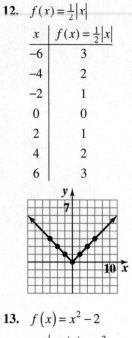

14. The graph passes the vertical line test. Thus y is a function of x.

15. The graph does not pass the vertical line test. Thus y is not a function of x.

16. a. $D(x)=0.8x^2-17x+109$

$D(1)=0.8(1)^2-17(1)+109$

$=92.8$

Skin damage begins for burn-prone people after 92.8 minutes when the sun's UV index is 1: This is shown on the graph as the point (1,92.8).

b. $D(x)=0.8x^2-17x+109$

$D(10)=0.8(10)^2-17(10)+109$

$=19$

Skin damage begins for burn-prone people after 19 minutes when the sun's UV index is 10: This is shown on the graph as the point (10,19).

17. $2x+y=4$

x-intercept is 2; y-intercept is 4.

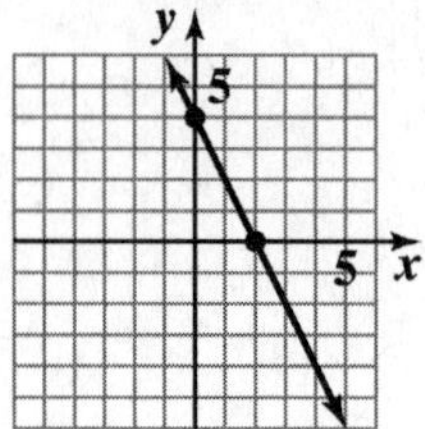

18. $2x-3y=6$

x-intercept is 3; y-intercept is –2.

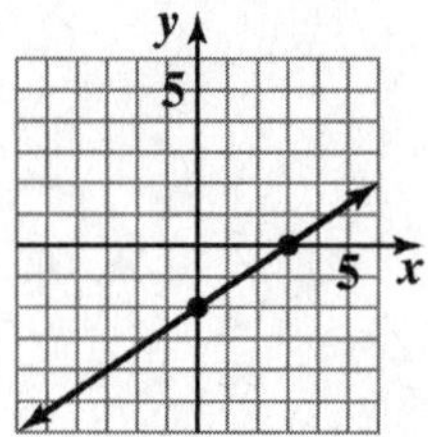

19. $5x-3y=15$

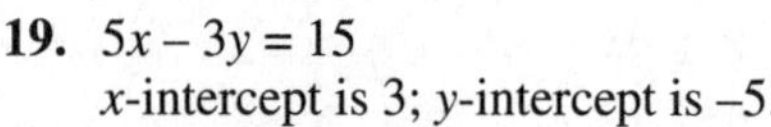

x-intercept is 3; y-intercept is –5.

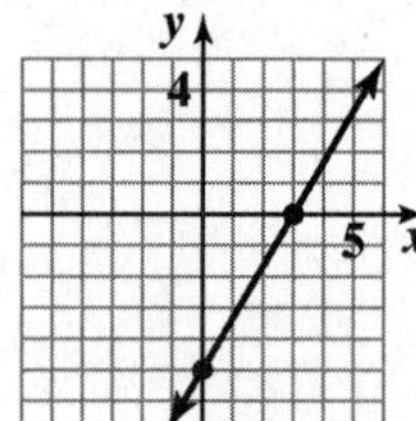

20. Slope $=\dfrac{1-2}{5-3}=-\dfrac{1}{2}$; line falls

21. Slope $=\dfrac{-4-2}{-3-(-1)}=\dfrac{-6}{-2}=3$; line rises

22. Slope $=\dfrac{4-4}{6-(-3)}=0$; line horizontal

23. Slope $=\dfrac{-3-3}{5-5}=\dfrac{-6}{0}$ is undefined, vertical line

24. $y = 2x - 4$; Slope: 2, y-intercept: –4
Plot point (0, –4) and second point using
$m = \frac{2}{1} = \frac{\text{rise}}{\text{run}}$.

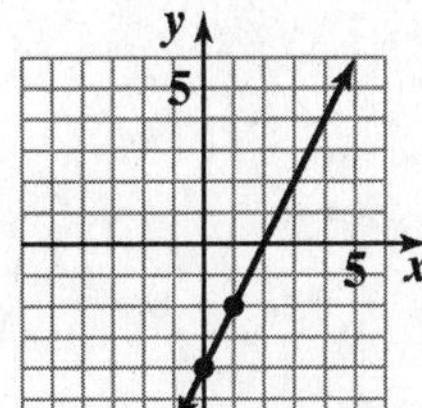

25. $y = -\frac{2}{3}x + 5$; Slope: $-\frac{2}{3}$, y-intercept: 5
Plot point (0, 5) and second point using
$m = \frac{-2}{3} = \frac{\text{rise}}{\text{run}}$.

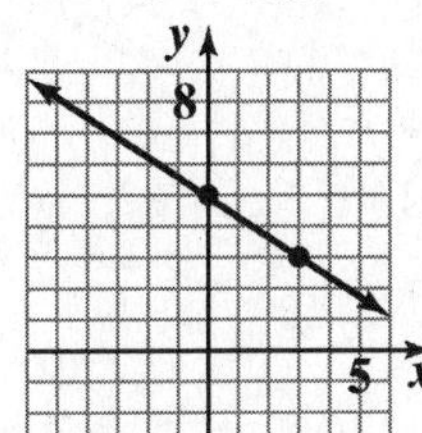

26. $y = \frac{3}{4}x - 2$; Slope: $\frac{3}{4}$, y-intercept: –2
Plot point (0, –2) and second point using
$m = \frac{3}{4} = \frac{\text{rise}}{\text{run}}$.

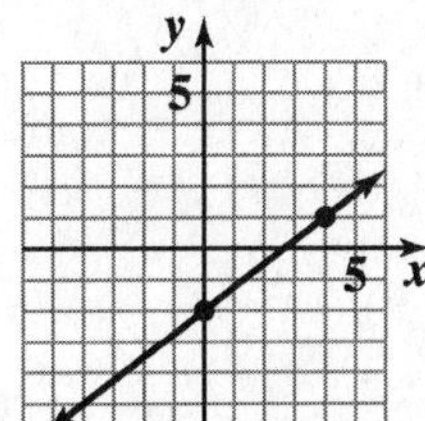

27. $y = \frac{1}{2}x + 0$; Slope: $\frac{1}{2}$, y-intercept: 0
Plot point (0, 0) and second point using
$m = \frac{1}{2} = \frac{\text{rise}}{\text{run}}$.

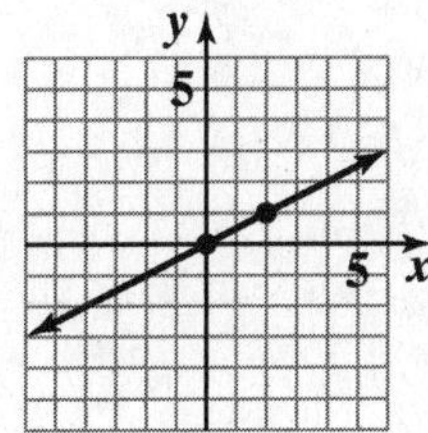

28. a. $2x + y = 0$
$y = -2x$

b. Slope = –2
y-intercept = 0

c.

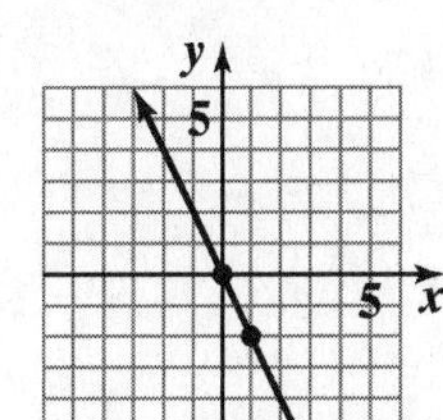

29. a. $3y = 5x$
$y = \frac{5}{3}x$

b. Slope = $\frac{5}{3}$
y-intercept = 0

c.

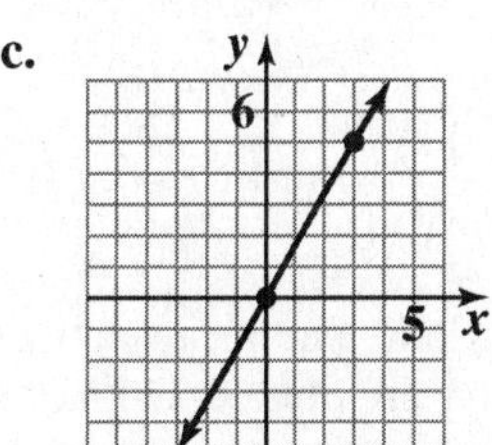

30. a. $3x + 2y = 4$
$2y = -3x + 4$
$y = -\frac{3}{2}x + 2$

b. Slope $= -\frac{3}{2}$
y-intercept = 2

c.

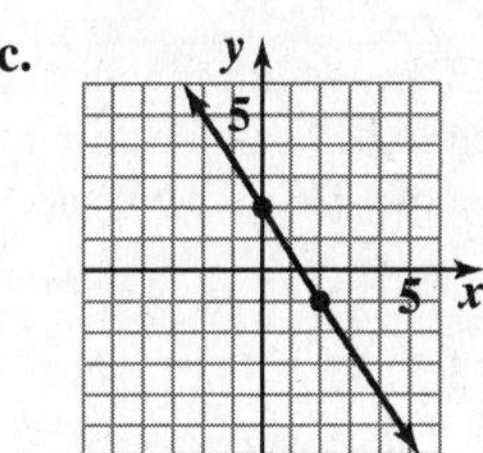

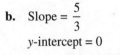

31. $x = 3$

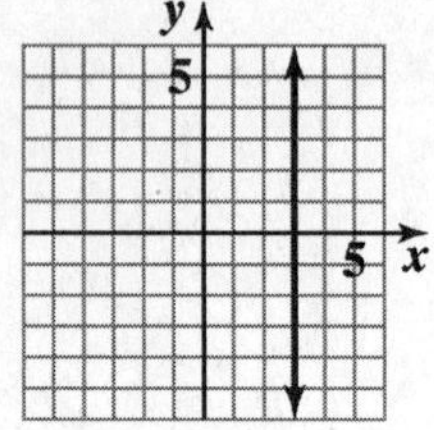

32. $y = -4$

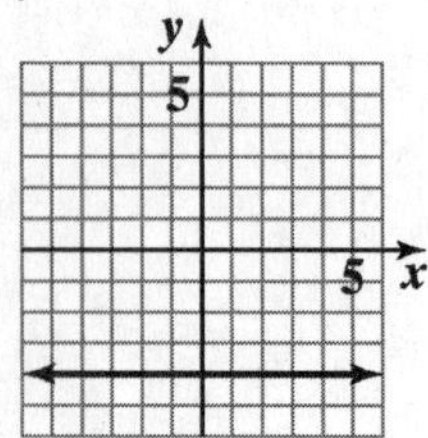

33. $x + 2 = 0$ or $x = -2$

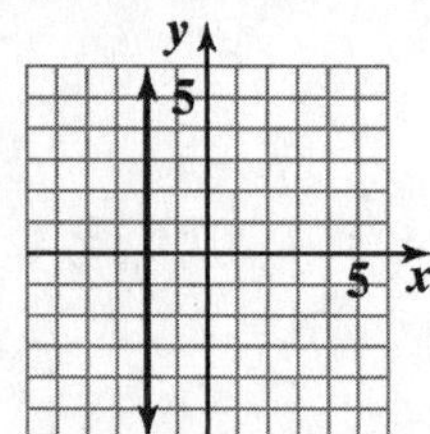

34. a. The y-intercept is 254. This represents if no women in a country are literate, the mortality rate of children under five is 254 per thousand.

b. $m = \dfrac{y_2 - y_1}{x_2 - x_1} = \dfrac{110 - 254}{60 - 0} = \dfrac{-144}{60} = -2.4$

For each 1% of adult females who are literate, the mortality rate of children under five decreases by 2.4 per thousand.

c. $f(x) = -2.4x + 254$

d. $f(50) = -2.4(50) + 254 = 134$

A country where 50% of adult females are literate is predicted to have a mortality rate of children under five of 134 per thousand.

35. The intersection is (2, 3).

Check: $2 + 3 = 5$ $\quad 3(2) - 3 = 3$

$5 = 5$ true $\quad 6 - 3 = 3$

$3 = 3$ true

The solution set is $\{(2, 3)\}$.

36. The intersection is (–2, –3).

Check: $2(-2) - (-3) = -1$ $\quad -2 - 3 = -5$

$-4 + 3 = -1$ $\quad -5 = -5$ true

$-1 = -1$ true

The solution set is $\{(-2, -3)\}$.

37. The intersection is (3, 2).

Check: $2 = -3 + 5$ $\quad 2(3) - 2 = 4$

$2 = 2$ true $\quad 6 - 2 = 4$

$4 = 4$ true

The solution set is $\{(3, 2)\}$.

38. $x = 3y + 10 \quad 2x + 3y = 2$

$2(3y + 10) + 3y = 2$

$6y + 20 + 3y = 2$

$9y = -18$

$y = -2$

$x = 3(-2) + 10 = -6 + 10 = 4$

The solution set is $\{(4, -2)\}$.

39. $y = 4x + 1 \quad 3x + 2y = 13$

$3x + 2(4x + 1) = 13$

$3x + 8x + 2 = 13$

$11x = 11$

$x = 1$

$y = 4(1) + 1 = 5$

The solution set is $\{(1, 5)\}$.

40. $x + 4y = 14$

$x = 14 - 4y \quad 2x - y = 1$

$2(14 - 4y) - y = 1$

$28 - 8y - y = 1$

$-9y = -27$

$y = 3$

$x = 14 - 4(3) = 2$

The solution set is $\{(2, 3)\}$.

41. $x + 2y = -3$ No change. $\quad x + 2y = -3$

$x - y = -12$ Multiply by –1. $\quad \underline{-x + y = 12}$

$3y = 9$

$y = 3$

$x - y = -12$

$x - 3 = -12$

$x = -9$

The solution set is $\{(-9, 3)\}$.

42. $2x - y = 2$ Mult. by 2. $4x - 2y = 4$
$x + 2y = 11$ No change $x + 2y = 11$

$$5x = 15$$
$$x = 3$$

$$x + 2y = 11$$
$$3 + 2y = 11$$
$$2y = 8$$
$$y = 4$$

The solution set is $\{(3, 4)\}$.

43. $5x + 3y = 1$ Mult. by 3. $15x + 9y = 3$
$3x + 4y = -6$ Mult. by -5. $-15x - 20y = 30$

$$-11y = 33$$
$$y = -3$$

$$5x + 3y = 1$$
$$5x + 3(-3) = 1$$
$$5x = 10$$
$$x = 2$$

The solution set is $\{(2, -3)\}$.

44. $y = -x + 4$ $3x + 3y = -6$
$3x + 3(-x + 4) = -6$
$3x - 3x + 12 = -6$
$12 = -6$, false
There is no solution or $\{\ \}$.

45. $3x + y = 8$
$y = 8 - 3x$ $2x - 5y = 11$
$2x - 5(8 - 3x) = 11$
$2x - 40 + 15x = 11$
$17x = 51$
$x = 3$
$y = 8 - 3(3) = -1$
The solution set is $\{(3, -1)\}$.

46. $3x - 2y = 6$ Mult. by -2. $-6x + 4y = -12$
$6x - 4y = 12$ No change. $6x - 4y = 12$

$$0 = 0$$

The system has infinitely many solutions.
The solution set is $\{(x, y) | 3x - 2y = 6\}$.

47. **a.** $C(x) = 60{,}000 + 200x$

b. $R(x) = 450x$

c. $450x = 60000 + 200x$
$250x = 60000$
$x = 240$
$450(240) = 108{,}000$
The company must make 240 desks at a cost of \$108,000 to break even.

48. **a.** Answers will vary. Approximate point is (2016, 325). This means that in 2016 the the population and the number of firearms will both be 325 million.

b. $y = 6x + 200$

c. Using substitution,

$$y - 3x = 200$$
$$\overbrace{6x + 200}^{y} - 3x = 263$$
$$3x + 200 = 263$$
$$3x = 63$$
$$x = 21$$

According to the models, the population and the number of firearms will be the same 21 years after 1995, or 2016.

$$y = 6x + 200$$
$$y = 6(21) + 200$$
$$= 326$$

According to the models, in 2016 the the population and the number of firearms will both be 326 million.

d. The models describe the point of intersection quite well.

49. To graph $x - 3y \le 6$, begin by graphing $x - 3y = 6$ with a solid line because $\le$ includes equality.
test point (0, 0):

$$x - 3y \le 6$$
$$0 - 3(0) \le 6$$
$$0 \le 6, \text{ true}$$

Since the test point makes the inequality true, shade the half-plane containing test point (0, 0).

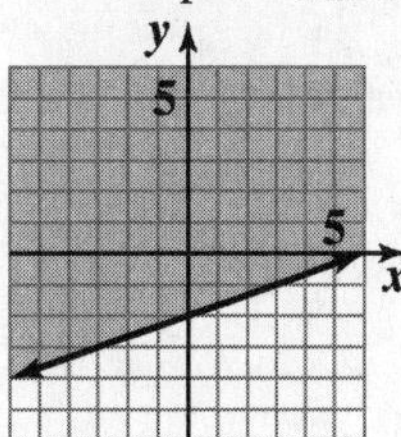

50. To graph $2x+3y \geq 12$, begin by graphing $2x+3y=12$ with a solid line because $\geq$ includes equality.

test point (0, 0):

$2x+3y \geq 12$

$2(0)+3(0) \geq 12$

$0 \geq 12$, false

Since the test point makes the inequality false, shade the half-plane not containing test point (0, 0).

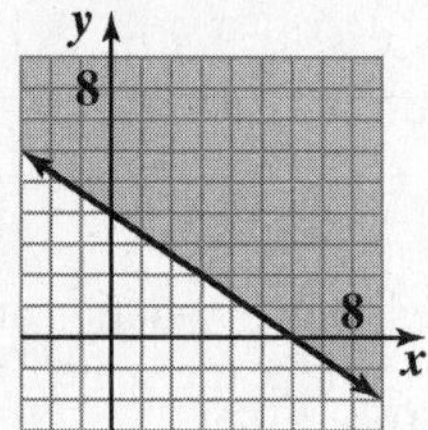

51. To graph $2x-7y>14$, begin by graphing $2x-7y=14$ with a dashed line because $>$ does not include equality.

test point (0, 0):

$2x-7y>14$

$2(0)-7(0)>14$

$0>14$, false

Since the test point makes the inequality false, shade the half-plane not containing test point (0, 0).

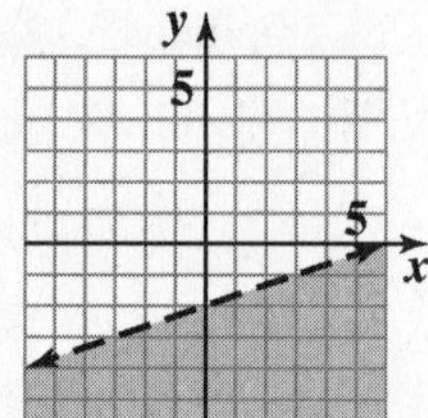

52. To graph $y>\frac{3}{5}x$, begin by graphing $y=\frac{3}{5}x$ as a dashed line passing through the origin with a slope of $\frac{3}{5}$, then shade above the line.

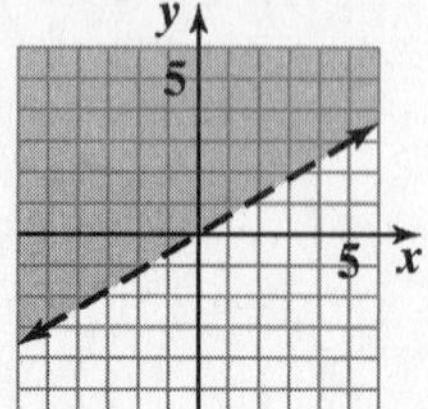

53. To graph $y \leq -\frac{1}{2}x+2$, begin by graphing $y=-\frac{1}{2}x+2$ as a solid line passing through (0, 2) with a slope of $\frac{-1}{2}$, then shade below the line.

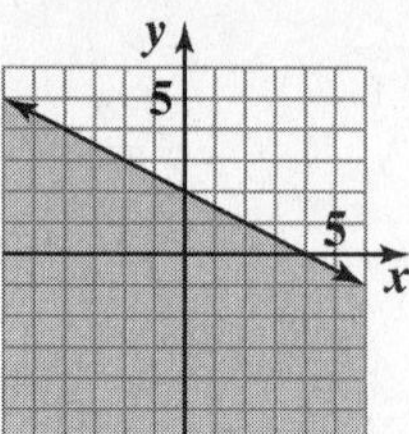

54. To graph $x \leq 2$, begin by graphing $x=2$ as a solid vertical line passing through $x=2$, then shade to the left of the line.

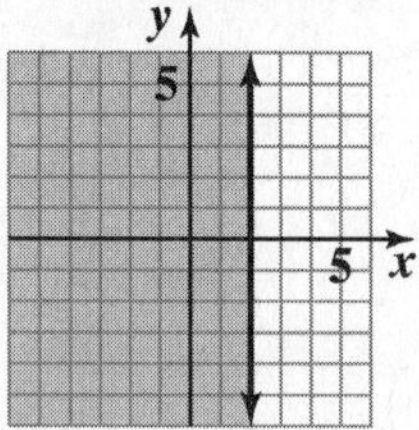

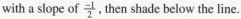

55. To graph $y>-3$, begin by graphing $y=-3$ as a dashed horizontal line passing through $y=-3$, then shade above the line.

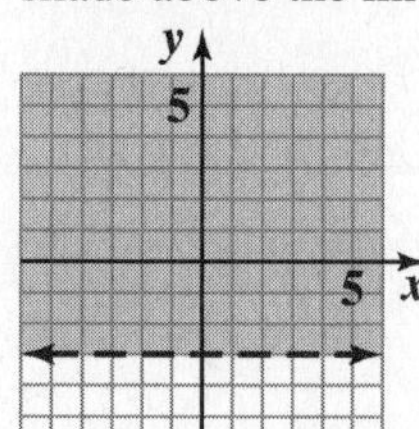

56. $3x-y \leq 6$

$x+y \geq 2$

Graph $3x-y=6$ as a solid line.
Because (0, 0) makes the inequality true, shade the half-plane containing (0,0).
Graph $x+y=2$ as a solid line.
Because (0, 0) makes the inequality false, shade the half-plane not containing (0, 0).

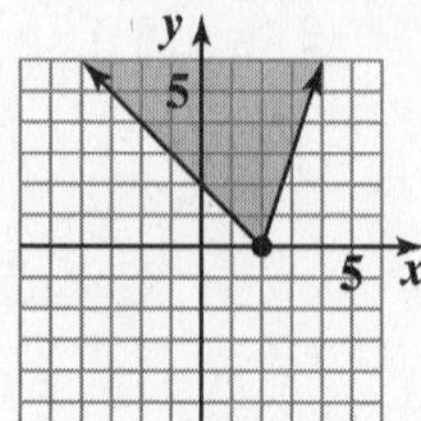

57. $x + y < 4$
$x - y < 4$
Graph $x + y = 4$ as a dashed line.
Because (0, 0) makes the inequality true, shade the half-plane containing (0, 0).
Graph $x - y = 4$ as a dashed line.
Because (0, 0) makes the inequality true, shade the half-plane containing (0, 0).

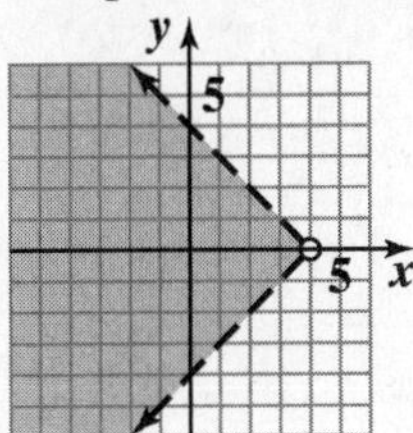

58. $x \le 3$
$y > -2$
Graph $x = 3$ as a solid line.
The points in the half-plane to the left of the line satisfy $x < 3$.
Graph $y = -2$ as a dashed line.
The points in the half-plane above the line satisfy $y > -2$.

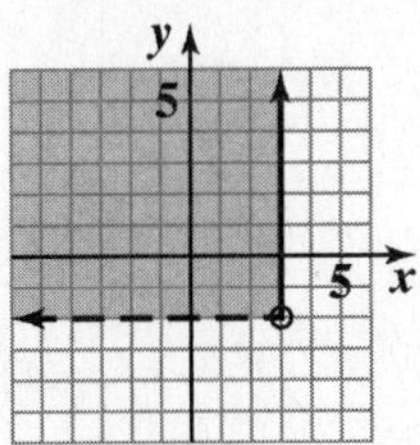

59. $4x + 6y = 24$
$y > 2$
Graph $4x + 6y = 24$ as a solid line.
Because (0, 0) makes the inequality true, shade the half-plane containing (0, 0).
Graph $y = 2$ as a dashed line.
The points in the half-plane above the line satisfy $y > 2$.

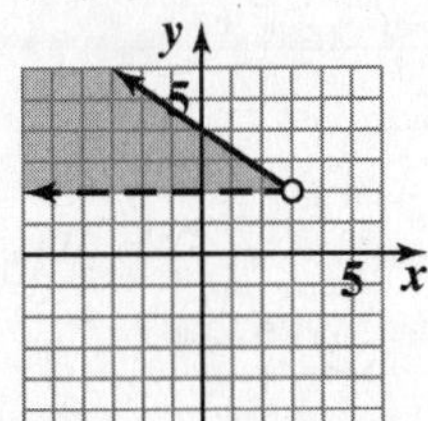

60. $x + y \le 6$
$y \ge 2x - 3$
Graph $x + y = 6$ as a solid line.
Because (0, 0) makes the inequality true, shade the half-plane containing (0, 0).
Graph $y = 2x - 3$ as a solid line.
Because (0, 0) makes the inequality true, shade the half-plane containing (0, 0).

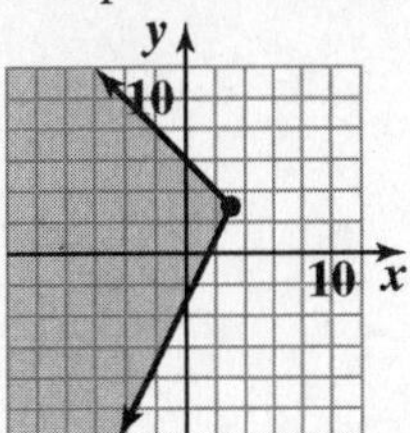

61. $y < -x + 4$
$y > x - 4$
Graph $y < -x + 4$ as a dashed line.
Because (0, 0) makes the inequality true, shade the half-plane containing (0, 0).
Graph $y = x - 4$ as a dashed line.
Because (0, 0) makes the inequality true, shade the half-plane containing (0, 0).

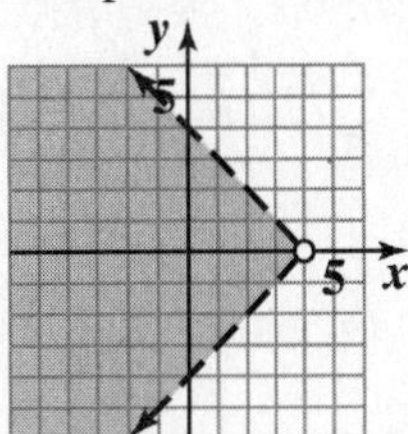

62. $z = 2x + 3y$
at (1, 0) $z = 2(1) + 3(0) = 2$
at $\left(\frac{1}{2}, \frac{1}{2}\right)$ $z = 2\left(\frac{1}{2}\right) + 3\left(\frac{1}{2}\right) = \frac{5}{2}$
at (2, 2) $z = 2(2) + 3(2) = 10$
at (4, 0) $z = 2(4) + 3(0) = 8$
Maximum value of the objective function is 10.
Minimum value of the objective function is 2.

63. $z = 2x + 3y$

Constraints: $x \le 6$

$y \le 5$

$x + y \ge 2$

$x \ge 0$

$y \ge 0$

a.

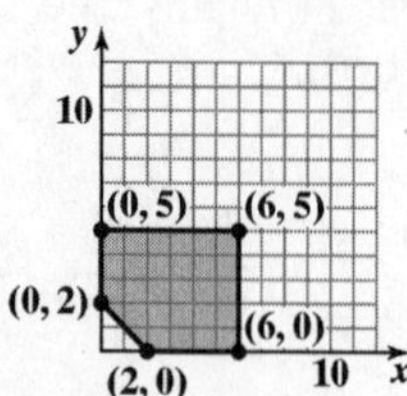

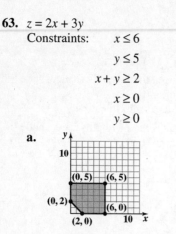

b. at (0, 2) $z = 2(0) + 3(2) = 6$
at (0, 5) $z = 2(0) + 3(5) = 15$
at (6, 5) $z = 2(6) + 3(5) = 27$
at (6, 0) $z = 2(6) + 3(0) = 12$
at (2, 0) $z = 2(2) + 3(0) = 4$

c. The maximum value of the objective function is 27. It occurs at $x = 6$ and $y = 5$.
The minimum value of the objective function is 4. It occurs at $x = 2$ and $y = 0$.

64. a. $z = 500x + 350y$

b. $x + y \le 200$

$x \ge 10$

$y \ge 80$

c.

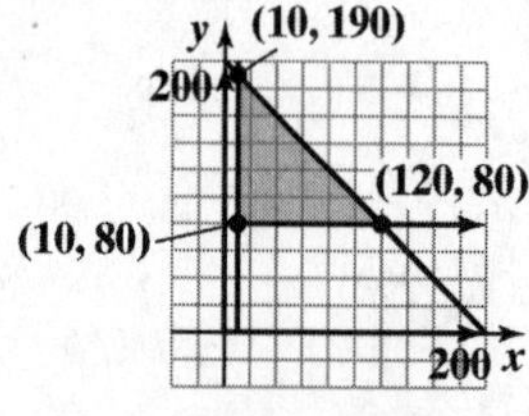

d.

Vertex	Objective Function $z = 500x + 350y$
(10, 80)	$z = 500(10) + 350(80)$ $= 33{,}000$
(10, 190)	$z = 500(10) + 350(190)$ $= 71{,}500$
(120, 80)	$z = 500(120) + 350(80)$ $= 88{,}000$

e. The company will make the greatest profit by producing 120 units of writing paper and 80 units of newsprint each day. The maximum daily profit is $88,000.

65.

x	$y = 2^x$
−2	$\frac{1}{4}$
−1	$\frac{1}{2}$
0	1
1	2
2	4

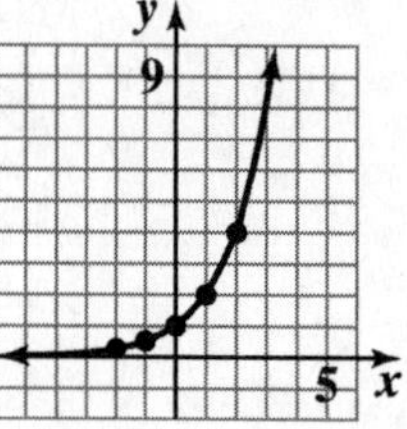

66.

x	$y = 2^{x+1}$
−2	$\frac{1}{2}$
−1	1
0	2
1	4
2	8

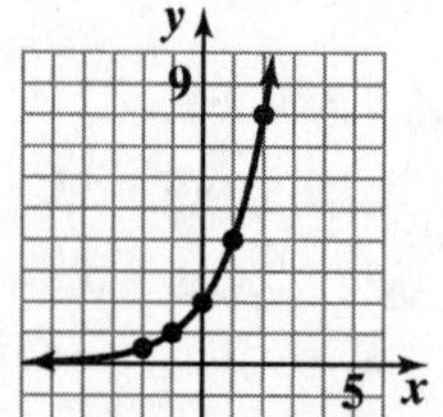

67. $y = \log_2 x$ is equivalent to $x = 2^y$.

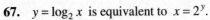

$x = 2^y$	y
$\frac{1}{4}$	-2
$\frac{1}{2}$	-1
1	0
2	1
4	2

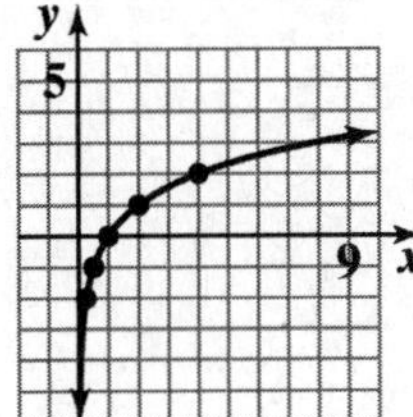

68. a. $a > 0$, thus the parabola opens upward.

b. x-coordinate: $x = \frac{-b}{2a} = \frac{-(-6)}{2(1)} = 3$

y-coordinate: $f(x) = x^2 - 6x - 7$

$f(3) = (3)^2 - 6(3) - 7$

$= -16$

vertex: $(3, -16)$

c. x-intercepts: $f(x) = x^2 - 6x - 7$

$0 = x^2 - 6x - 7$

$0 = (x+1)(x-7)$

$x + 1 = 0$ or $x - 7 = 0$

$x = -1$ $\quad$ $x = 7$

d. y-intercept: $f(x) = x^2 - 6x - 7$

$f(0) = 0^2 - 6(0) - 7$

$y = -7$

e.

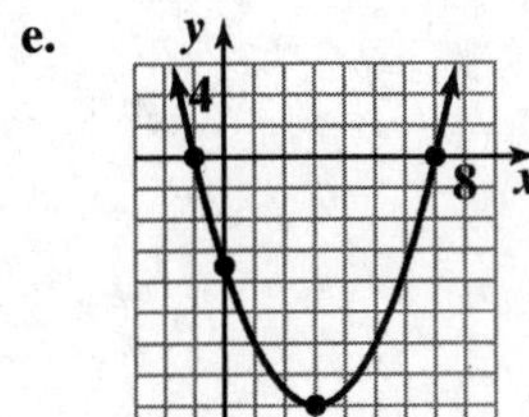

69. a. $a < 0$, thus the parabola opens downward.

b. x-coordinate: $x = \frac{-b}{2a} = \frac{-(-2)}{2(-1)} = -1$

y-coordinate: $f(x) = -x^2 - 2x + 3$

$f(-1) = -(-1)^2 - 2(-1) + 3$

$= 4$

vertex: $(-1, 4)$

c. x-intercepts: $f(x) = -x^2 - 2x + 3$

$0 = -x^2 - 2x + 3$

$0 = x^2 + 2x - 3$

$0 = (x+3)(x-1)$

$x + 3 = 0$ or $x - 1 = 0$

$x = -3$ $\quad$ $x = 1$

d. y-intercept: $f(x) = -x^2 - 2x + 3$

$f(0) = -0^2 - 2(0) + 3$

$y = 3$

e. graph:

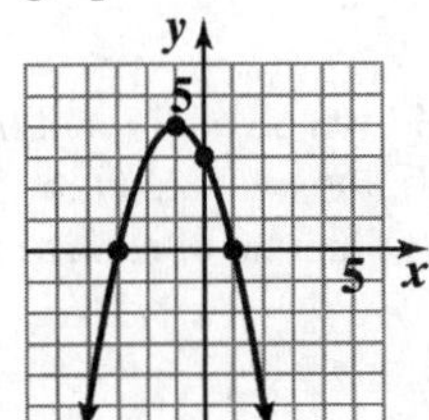

70. a. graph:

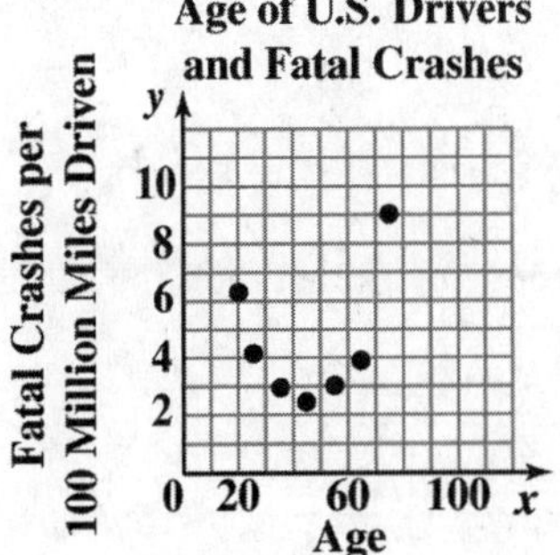

b. quadratic

71. a. graph:

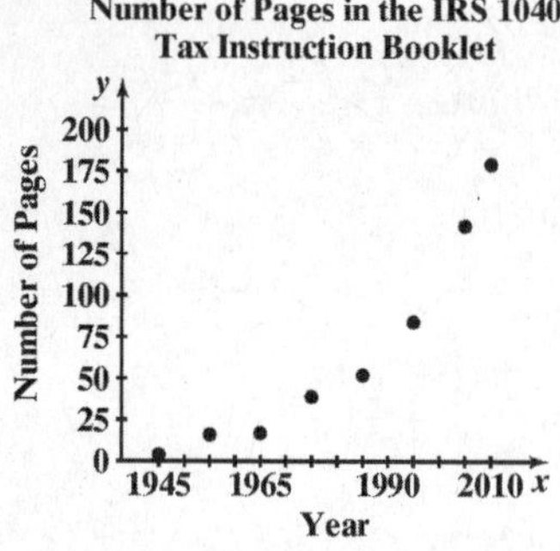

b. exponential

72. a. graph:

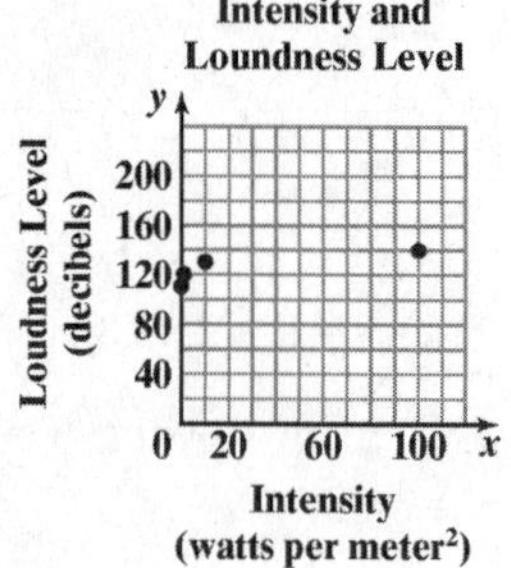

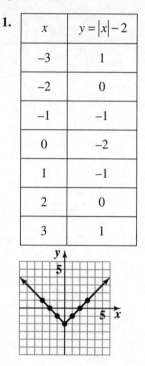

b. logarithmic

73. a. The slope is 47. For each additional hour spent at a shopping mall, the average amount spent increases by \$47. The rate of change is \$47 per hour.

b. $f(x) = 47x + 22$
$f(3.5) = 47(3.5) + 22 = 186.5$

$g(x) = 42.2(1.56)^x$
$g(3.5) = 42.2(1.56)^{3.5} = 200.1$

The exponential function is the better model.

74. $f(x) = -0.4x + 25.4$
$f(60) = -0.4(60) + 25.4 = 1.4$

$g(x) = 54.8 - 12.3\ln x$
$g(60) = 54.8 - 12.3\ln(60) \approx 4.4$

The logarithmic function is the better model.

Chapter 7 Test

1.

x	$y = \lvert x \rvert - 2$
–3	1
–2	0
–1	–1
0	–2
1	–1
2	0
3	1

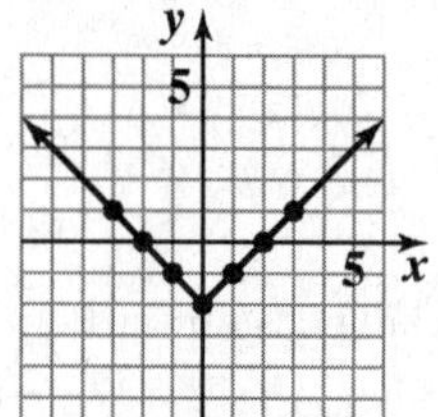

2. $f(-2) = 3(-2)^2 - 7(-2) - 5 = 12 + 14 - 5 = 21$

3. The graph does not pass the vertical line test. Thus y is not a function of x.

4. The graph passes the vertical line test. Thus y is a function of x.

5. a. Yes, it is a function. The graph passes the vertical line test.

b. $f(15) = 0$ means that the eagle was on the ground after 15 seconds.

c. The maximum height was 45 meters.

d. The eagle was descending between second 3 and second 12.

6. Set $y = 0$

$$4x - 2\cdot 0 = -8$$
$$4x = -8$$
$$x = -2$$

x-intercept is –2.

Set $x = 0$

$$4\cdot 0 - 2y = -8$$
$$-2y = -8$$
$$y = 4$$

y-intercept is 4.

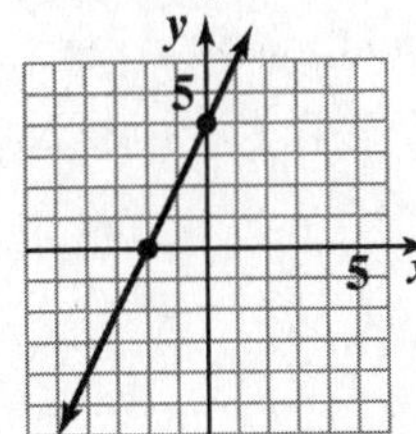

7. $\text{Slope} = \dfrac{-2-4}{-5-(-3)} = \dfrac{-6}{-2} = 3$

8. $y = \dfrac{2}{3}x - 1$

Slope: $\dfrac{2}{3}$, y-intercept: –1

Plot the point (0, –1) and a second point using $m = \dfrac{2}{3} = \dfrac{\text{rise}}{\text{run}}$.

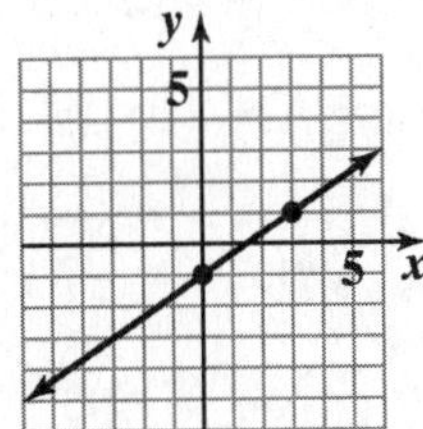

9. $f(x) = -2x + 3$

Slope: –2, y-intercept: 3

Plot the point (0, 3) and a second point using $m = \dfrac{-2}{1} = \dfrac{\text{rise}}{\text{run}}$.

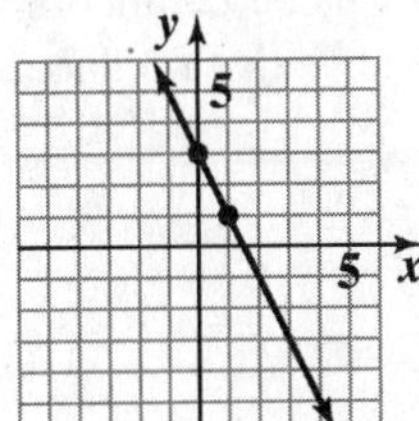

10. a. $m = \dfrac{52-64}{2010-1985} = \dfrac{-12}{25} = -0.48$

b. For each year from 1985 through 2010, the percentage of U.S. college freshmen rating their emotional health high or above average decreased by 0.48. The rate of change was –0.48% per year.

11. a. The y-intercept is 4571. There were 4571 deaths involving distracted driving 0 years after 2005, or in 2005.

b. $m = \dfrac{5870-4571}{3-0} = \dfrac{1299}{3} = 433$

The rate of change in the number of deaths involving distracted driving is 433 deaths per year.

c.

$$y = mx + b$$
$$f(x) = 433x + 4571$$

d.

$$f(x) = 433x + 4571$$
$$f(10) = 433(10) + 4571$$
$$= 8901$$

The linear function projects 8901 fatalities in the United States in 2015 involving distracted driving.

12. The intersection is (2, 4)

Check: $2 + 4 = 6$, $6 = 6$ true; $4(2) - 4 = 4$, $8 - 4 = 4$, $4 = 4$ true

The solution set is {(2, 4)}.

13. $x = y + 4$ $\quad 3x + 7y = -18$

$$3(y+4) + 7y = -18$$
$$3y + 12 + 7y = -18$$
$$10y = -30$$
$$y = -3$$

$x = -3 + 4 = 1$

The solution set is {(1, –3)}.

14.

$$5x + 4y = 10 \xrightarrow{\text{Mult. by } 3} 15x + 12y = 30$$
$$3x + 5y = -7 \xrightarrow{\text{Mult. by } -5} -15x - 25y = 35$$
$$-13y = 65$$
$$y = -5$$

$$5x + 4y = 10$$
$$5x + 4(-5) = 10$$
$$5x = 30$$
$$x = 6$$

The solution set is {(6, –5)}.

15. a. $C(x) = 360{,}000 + 850x$

b. $R(x) = 1150x$

c. $1150x = 360{,}000 + 850x$
$300x = 360{,}000$
$x = 1200$
Substitute 1200 into either equation to find the amount of cost and revenue at $x = 1200$.
$R(1200) = 1150(1200) = \$1{,}380{,}000$
The company will break even if it produces and sells 1200 computers.

16. $3x - 2y < 6$
Graph $3x - 2y = 6$ as a dashed line.
x-intercept:
$3x - 2 \cdot 0 = 6$
$3x = 6$
$x = 2$
y-intercept:
$3 \cdot 0 - 2y = 6$
$-2y = 6$
$y = -3$
Test point: (0, 0).
Is $3 \cdot 0 - 2 \cdot 0 < 6$?
$0 < 6$, true
Shade the half-plane containing (0, 0).

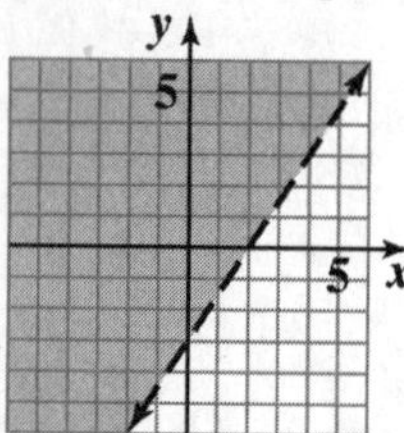

17. Graph $y = \frac{1}{2}x - 1$ as a solid line.
Use y-intercept of –1 and slope of $\frac{1}{2}$
Shade below this line.

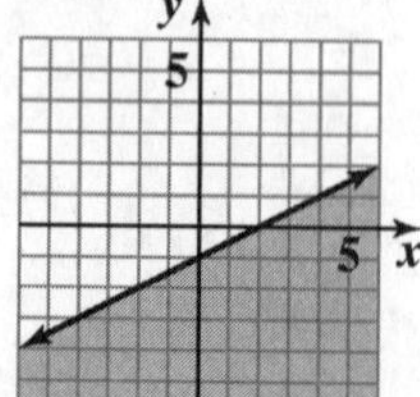

18. $y > -1$
Graph $y = -1$ as a dashed line.
Test point: (0, 0).
Is $0 > -1$?
$0 > -1$, true
Shade the half-plane containing (0, 0).

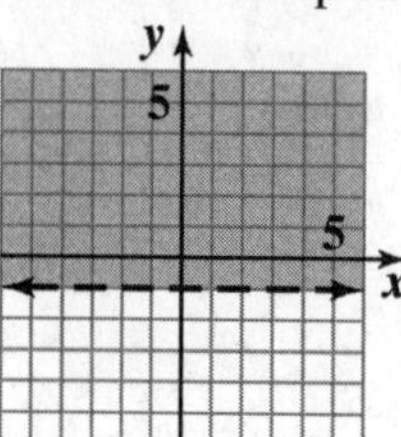

19. $2x - y \le 4$
$2x - y > -1$
Graph $2x - y = 4$ as a solid line.
Because (0, 0) makes the inequality true, shade the half-plane containing (0, 0).
Graph $2x - y = -1$ as a dashed line.
Because (0, 0) makes the inequality true, shade the half-plane containing (0, 0).

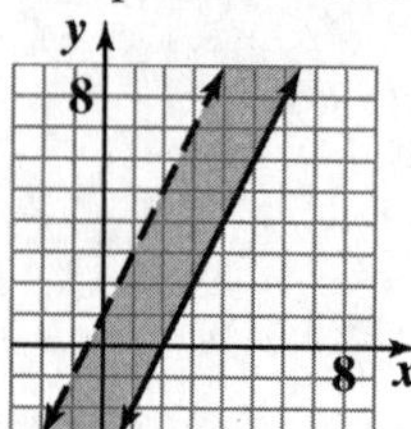

20. $z = 3x + 2y$
at (2, 0) $z = 3(2) + 2(0) = 6$
at (2, 6) $z = 3(2) + 2(6) = 18$
at (6, 3) $z = 3(6) + 2(3) = 24$
at (8, 0) $z = 3(8) + 2(0) = 24$
The maximum value of the objective function is 24.
The minimum value of the objective function is 6.

21.

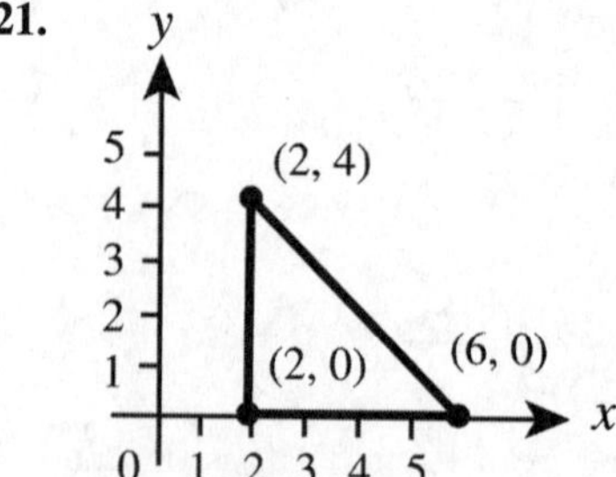

Objective function: $z = 3x + 5y$
at (2, 0) $z = 3(2) + 5(0) = 6$
at (6, 0) $z = 3(6) + 5(0) = 18$
at (2, 4) $z = 3(2) + 5(4) = 26$
The maximum value of the objective function is 26.

22.

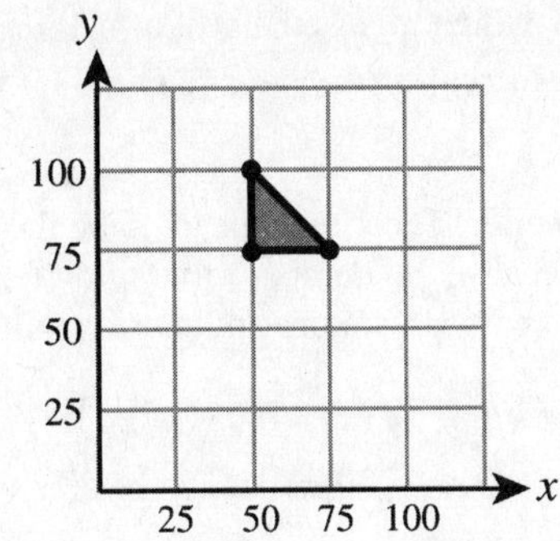

Objective function: $z = 200x + 250y$

Constraints: $x \geq 50$; $y \geq 75$; $x + y \leq 150$

Substitute vertices into objective function:

at $(50, 100)$ $z = 200(50) + 250(100) = 35{,}000$

at $(75, 75)$ $z = 200(75) + 250(75) = 33{,}750$

at $(50, 75)$ $z = 200(50) + 250(75) = 28{,}750$

The company will make the greatest profit by producing 50 regular jet skis and 100 deluxe jet skis each week. The maximum weekly profit is \$35,000.

23.

x	$f(x) = 3^x$
−2	$\frac{1}{9}$
−1	$\frac{1}{3}$
0	1
1	3
2	9

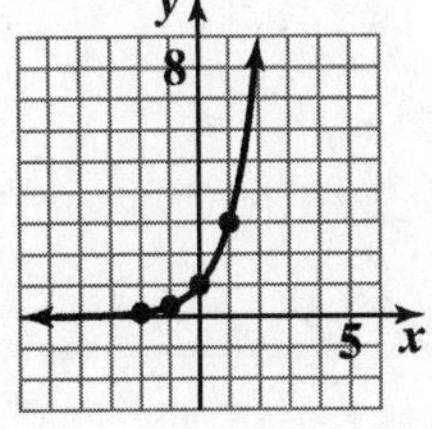

24. $y = \log_2 x$ is equivalent to $x = 3^y$.

$x = 3^y$	y
$\frac{1}{9}$	−2
$\frac{1}{3}$	−1
1	0
3	1
9	2

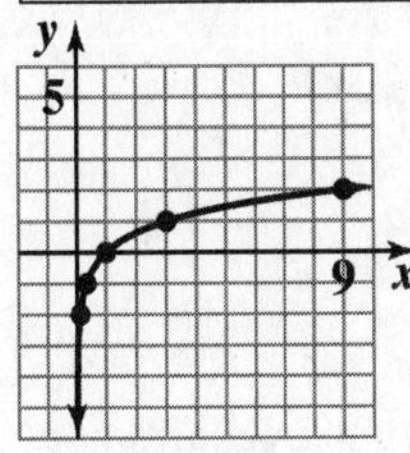

25. x-coordinate: $x = \dfrac{-b}{2a} = \dfrac{-(-2)}{2(1)} = 1$

y-coordinate: $f(x) = x^2 - 2x - 8$

$f(1) = 1^2 - 2(1) - 8$

$y = -9$

vertex: $(1, -9)$

x-intercepts: $f(x) = x^2 - 2x - 8$

$0 = x^2 - 2x - 8$

$0 = (x+2)(x-4)$

$x + 2 = 0$ or $x - 4 = 0$

$x = -2$ $\quad x = 4$

y-intercept: $f(x) = x^2 - 2x - 8$

$f(0) = 0^2 - 2(0) - 8$

$y = -8$

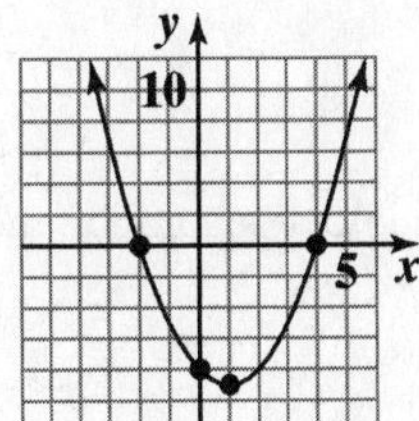

26. Plot the ordered pairs.

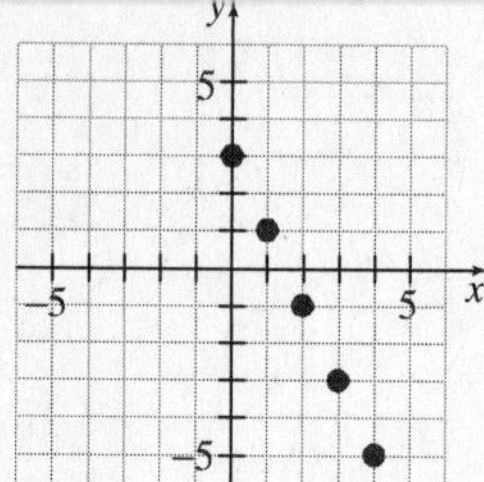

The values appear to belong to a linear function.

27. Plot the ordered pairs.

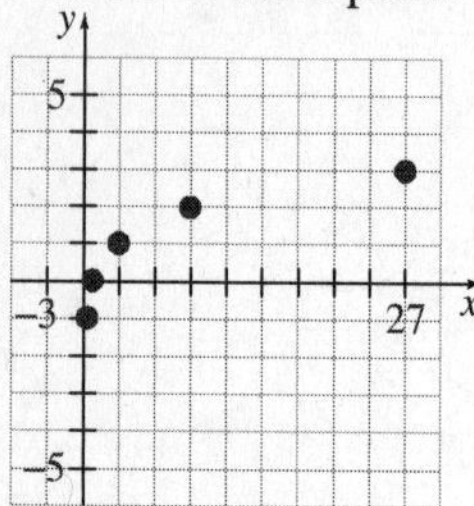

The values appear to belong to a logarithmic function.

28. Plot the ordered pairs.

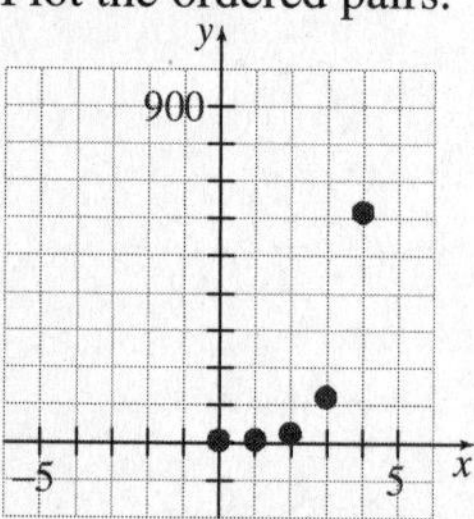

The values appear to belong to an exponential function.

29. Plot the ordered pairs.

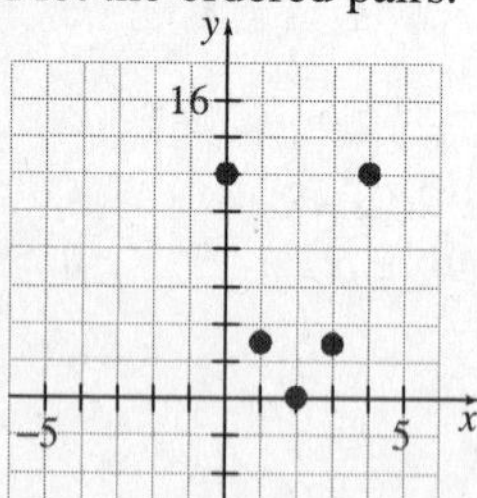

The values appear to belong to a quadratic function.

30. a. $m = 0.03$, which means the cost of making a penny is increasing an average of 0.03 cents per year.

b. An exponential function appears to be the better model because the number of monthly text messages increases more and more rapidly.

c. linear function: $f(x) = 0.03x + 0.63$

$$f(30) = 0.03(30) + 0.63$$
$$= 1.53¢$$

exponential function: $g(x) = 0.72(1.03)^x$

$$g(30) = 0.72(1.03)^{30}$$
$$\approx 1.75¢$$

The exponential function serves better for 2012. Yes, this is consistent with the answer for part b.

Chapter 8
Personal Finance

Checkpoints 8.1

1. Step 1: $\frac{1}{8} = 1 \div 8 = 0.125$
   Step 2: $0.125 \cdot 100 = 12.5$
   Step 3: 12.5%

2. $0.023 = 2.3\%$

3. **a.** $67\% = 0.67$

   b. $250\% = 2.50 = 2.5$

4. **a.** 6% of $\$1260 = 0.06 \times \$1260 = \$75.60$
   The tax paid is \$75.60

   b. $\$1260.00 + \$75.60 = \$1335.60$
   The total cost is \$1335.60

5. **a.** 35% of $\$380 = 0.35 \times \$380 = \$133$
   The discount is \$133

   b. $\$380 - \$133 = \$247$
   The sale price is \$247

6. **a.** $\text{Percent of increase} = \dfrac{\text{amount of increase}}{\text{original amount}}$

   $= \dfrac{4}{6} = 0.66\tfrac{2}{3} = 66\tfrac{2}{3}\%$

   b. $\text{Percent of decrease} = \dfrac{\text{amount of decrease}}{\text{original amount}}$

   $= \dfrac{4}{10} = 0.4 = 40\%$

7. Amount of decrease: $\$940 - \$611 = \$329$
   $\dfrac{\text{amount of decrease}}{\text{original amount}} = \dfrac{\$329}{\$940} = 0.35 = 35\%$
   There was a 35% decrease in price.

8. Amount of increase: $12\% - 10\% = 2\%$
   $\dfrac{\text{amount of increase}}{\text{original amount}} = \dfrac{2\%}{10\%} = 0.2 = 20\%$
   There was a 20% increase for this episode.

9. **a.** 20% of $\$1200 = 0.20 \times \$1200 = \$240$
   Taxes for year 1 are $\$1200 - \$240 = \$960$
   20% of $\$960 = 0.20 \times \$960 = \$192$
   Taxes for year 2 are $\$960 + \$192 = \$1152$

   b. $\dfrac{\$1200 - \$1152}{\$1200} = \dfrac{\$48}{\$1200} = 0.04 = 4\%$
   Taxes for year 2 are 4% less than the original amount.

Concept and Vocabulary Check 8.1

1. 100
2. 7; 8; 100; a percent sign
3. two; right; a percent sign
4. two; left; a percent sign
5. tax rate; item's cost
6. discount rate; original price
7. the amount of increase; the original amount
8. the amount of decrease; the original amount
9. false; Changes to make the statement true will vary. A sample change is: Only 6 reindeer remain.
10. false; Changes to make the statement true will vary. A sample change is: You spent \$500 on gifts.

Exercise Set 8.1

1. $\frac{2}{5} = 2 \div 5 = 0.4 = 40\%$

3. $\frac{1}{4} = 1 \div 4 = 0.25 = 25\%$

5. $\frac{3}{8} = 3 \div 8 = 0.375 = 37.5\%$

7. $\frac{1}{40} = 1 \div 40 = 0.025 = 2.5\%$

9. $\frac{9}{80} = 9 \div 80 = 0.1125 = 11.25\%$

11. $0.59 = 59\%$

13. $0.3844 = 38.44\%$

15. $2.87 = 287\%$

17. $14.87 = 1487\%$

19. $100 = 10{,}000\%$

21. $72\% = 0.72$

23. $43.6\% = 0.436$

25. $130\% = 1.3$

27. $2\% = 0.02$

29. $\frac{1}{2}\% = 0.5\% = 0.005$

31. $\frac{5}{8}\% = 0.625\% = 0.00625$

33. $62\frac{1}{2}\% = 62.5\% = 0.625$

35.
$$\begin{aligned} A &= PB \\ A &= 0.03 \cdot 200 \\ A &= 6 \end{aligned}$$

37.
$$\begin{aligned} A &= PB \\ A &= 0.18 \cdot 40 \\ A &= 7.2 \end{aligned}$$

39.
$$\begin{aligned} A &= PB \\ 3 &= 0.60 \cdot B \\ \frac{3}{0.60} &= \frac{0.60B}{0.60} \\ 5 &= B \end{aligned}$$

41.
$$\begin{aligned} A &= PB \\ 40.8 &= 0.24 \cdot B \\ \frac{40.8}{0.24} &= \frac{0.24B}{0.24} \\ 170 &= B \end{aligned}$$

43.
$$\begin{aligned} A &= PB \\ 3 &= P \cdot 15 \\ \frac{3}{15} &= \frac{P \cdot 15}{15} \\ 0.2 &= P \\ P &= 20\% \end{aligned}$$

45.
$$\begin{aligned} A &= PB \\ 0.3 &= P \cdot 2.5 \\ \frac{0.3}{2.5} &= \frac{P \cdot 2.5}{2.5} \\ 0.12 &= P \\ P &= 12\% \end{aligned}$$

47. **a.** $(0.06)(32{,}800) = \$1968$

b. $32{,}800 + 1968 = \$34{,}768$

49. **a.** $(0.12)(860) = \$103.20$

b. $860 - 103.20 = \$756.80$

51. $\frac{70}{365} \approx 0.192 = 19.2\%$

53. $\frac{76-38}{38} = \frac{38}{38} = 1 = 100\%$

55. $\frac{840-714}{840} = 0.15 = 15\%$

57. Amount after first year
$= 10{,}000 - (0.3)(10{,}000)$
$= \$7000$
Amount after second year
$= 7000 + (0.4)(7000)$
$= \$9800$
Your adviser is not using percentages properly.
Actual change:
$\frac{10{,}000 - 9800}{10{,}000} = 0.02 = 2\%$ loss.

65. does not make sense; Explanations will vary. Sample explanation: 20% of \$80 is \$16. This will make the total \$96.

67. does not make sense; Explanations will vary. Sample explanation: Since $1.01 \times 1.01 = 1.0201$ the percent of increase is 2.01%.

69. First, find the discount amount.
$15\% \times \$720 = 0.15 \times \$720 = \$108$
Next, find the sales price.
$\$720 - \$108 = \$612$
Then, find the tax.
$6\% \times \$612 = 0.06 \times \$612 = \$36.72$
Finally, find the total cost.
$\$612 + \$36.72 = \$648.72$
Percent reduction $= 30\% + 14\% = 44\%$

71. January sales = $60 \cdot \$500 = \$30,000$
Number of customers in February
$= 60 - (0.10)(60) = 60 - 6 = 54$
Price of washing machine in February
$= 500 + (0.20)(500) = 500 + 100 = \$600$
February sales = $54 \cdot \$600 = \$32,400$
$32,400 – $30,000 = $2400 increase.

Checkpoints 8.2

1. a. Gross income $= \$87,200 + \$2680 = \$89,880$

b. $$\text{Adjusted gross income} = \overbrace{\$89,880}^{\text{Gross income}} - \overbrace{\$3200}^{\text{Contribution}} = \$86,680$$

c. $$\text{Itemized deductions} = \overbrace{\$11,700}^{\text{Interest}} + \overbrace{\$4300}^{\text{Property tax}} + \overbrace{\$5220}^{\text{State tax}} + \overbrace{\$15,000}^{\text{Charity}} = \$36,220$$

This person is entitled to a standard deduction of $5950. However, the itemized deduction is greater than the standard deduction.

$$\text{Taxable income} = \overbrace{\$86,680}^{\text{Adj. gross income}} - \overbrace{(\$3800 + \$36,220)}^{\text{Exemptions and deductions}}$$
$$= \$86,680 - \$40,020$$
$$= \$46,660$$

2. Step 1. Determine the adjusted gross income.

$$\text{Adjusted gross income} = \overbrace{\$40,000}^{\text{Gross income}} - \overbrace{\$1000}^{\text{Adjustments}} = \$39,000$$

Step 2. Determine the taxable income.
Since the total deduction of $4800 is less than the standard deduction of $5950, use $5950.

$$\text{Taxable income} = \overbrace{\$39,000}^{\text{Adj. gross income}} - \overbrace{(\$3800 + \$5950)}^{\text{Exemptions and deductions}}$$
$$= \$39,000 - \$9750$$
$$= \$29,250$$

Step 3. Determine the income tax.
$$\text{Tax Computation} = 0.10(8700) + 0.15(29,250 - 8700) = \$3952.50$$

$$\text{Income tax} = \overbrace{\$3952.50}^{\text{Tax Computation}} - \overbrace{0}^{\text{Tax credits}} = \$3952.50$$

3. FICA Tax (not self-employed):

$$\begin{aligned}\text{FICA Tax} &= \overbrace{0.0565\times\$110,000}^{\substack{5.65\%\text{ on first}\\ \$110,000}}+\overbrace{0.0145\times(\$200,000-\$110,000)}^{\substack{1.45\%\text{ on income in}\\ \text{excess of }\$110,000}}\\ &=0.0565\times\$110,000+0.0145\times\$90,000\\ &=\$6215+\$1305\\ &=\$7520\end{aligned}$$

4. a. Gross pay $= 15 \text{ hours} \times \dfrac{\$12}{\text{hour}} = \$180$

b. Federal taxes $= 10\% \times \$180 = 0.10 \times \$180 = \$18$

c. FICA taxes $= 5.65\% \times \$180 = 0.0565 \times \$180 = \$10.17$

d. State taxes $= 4\% \times \$180 = 0.04 \times \$180 = \$7.20$

e. $$\begin{aligned}\text{Net pay} &= \overbrace{\$180}^{\text{Gross pay}} - \overbrace{(\$18+\$10.17+\$7.20)}^{\text{Federal, FICA, and state taxes}}\\ &=\$180-\$35.37\\ &=\$144.63\end{aligned}$$

f. Percent of gross pay withheld for taxes

$$=\frac{\text{Taxes}}{\text{Gross pay}}=\frac{\$35.37}{\$180}=0.1965\approx 19.7\%$$

Concept and Vocabulary Check 8.2

1. gross
2. adjusted gross; adjustments
3. exemption
4. adjusted gross; exemptions; deductions
5. credits
6. FICA
7. gross
8. net
9. false; Federal income tax is a percentage of your taxable income.
10. true
11. true
12. true

Exercise Set 8.2

1. Gross income = $\$52,600 + \$720 = \$53,320$

$$\text{Adjusted gross income} = \overbrace{\$53,320}^{\text{Gross income}} - \overbrace{\$3200}^{\text{Contribution}} = \$50,120$$

This person is entitled to a standard deduction of $5950. However, the itemized deduction is greater than the standard deduction.

$$\text{Taxable income} = \overbrace{\$50,120}^{\text{Adj. gross income}} - \overbrace{(\$3800 + \$7250)}^{\text{Exemptions and deductions}} = \$39,070$$

3. Gross income = $\$86,250 + \$1240 = \$87,490$

$$\text{Adjusted gross income} = \overbrace{\$87,490}^{\text{Gross income}} - \overbrace{\$2200}^{\text{Contribution}} = \$85,290$$

This person is entitled to a standard deduction of $5950. However, the itemized deduction is greater than the standard deduction.

$$\text{Itemized deductions} = \overbrace{\$8900}^{\text{Interest}} + \overbrace{\$1725}^{\text{State tax}} + \overbrace{\$2400}^{\text{Charity}} = \$13,025$$

$$\text{Taxable income} = \overbrace{\$85,290}^{\text{Adj. gross income}} - \overbrace{(\$3800 + \$13,025)}^{\text{Exemptions and deductions}} = \$85,290 - \$16,825 = \$68,465$$

5.
$$\begin{aligned}\text{Tax Computation} &= 0.10(\$8700) + 0.15(\$35,350 - \$8700) + 0.25(\$40,000 - \$35,350)\\ &= 0.10(\$8700) + 0.15(\$26,650) + 0.25(\$4650)\\ &= \$870 + \$3997.50 + \$1162.50\\ &= \$6030\end{aligned}$$

$$\text{Income tax} = \overbrace{\$6030}^{\text{Tax Computation}} - \overbrace{0}^{\text{Tax credits}} = \$6030$$

7. Tax Computation

$$\begin{aligned}&= 0.10(\$8700) + 0.15(\$35,350 - \$8700) + 0.25(\$71,350 - \$35,350)\\ &\qquad + 0.28(\$108,725 - \$71,350) + 0.33(\$120,000 - \$108,725)\\ &= 0.10(\$8700) + 0.15(\$26,650) + 0.25(\$36,000) + 0.28(\$37,375) + 0.33(\$11,275)\\ &= \$870 + \$3997.50 + \$9000 + \$10,465 + \$3720.75\\ &= \$28,053.25\end{aligned}$$

$$\text{Income tax} = \overbrace{\$28,053.25}^{\text{Tax Computation}} - \overbrace{0}^{\text{Tax credits}} = \$28,053.25$$

9.
$$\begin{aligned}\text{Tax Computation} &= 0.10(\$8700) + 0.15(\$15,000 - \$8700)\\ &= 0.10(\$8700) + 0.15(\$6,300)\\ &= \$870 + \$945\\ &= \$1815\end{aligned}$$

$$\text{Income tax} = \overbrace{\$1815}^{\text{Tax Computation}} - \overbrace{\$2500}^{\text{Tax credits}} = -\$685$$

11. Tax Computation

$= 0.10(\$17{,}400) + 0.15(\$70{,}700 - \$17{,}400) + 0.25(\$142{,}700 - \$70{,}700)$

$+ 0.28(\$217{,}450 - \$142{,}700) + 0.33(\$250{,}000 - \$217{,}450)$

$= 0.10(\$17{,}400) + 0.15(\$53{,}300) + 0.25(\$72{,}000) + 0.28(\$74{,}750) + 0.33(\$32{,}550)$

$= \$1740 + \$7995 + \$18{,}000 + \$20{,}930 + \$10{,}741.50$

$= \$59{,}406.50$

$\text{Income tax} = \overbrace{\$59{,}406.50}^{\text{Tax Computation}} - \overbrace{4500}^{\text{Tax credits}} = \$51{,}906.50$

13. Tax Computation

$= 0.10(\$12{,}400) + 0.15(\$47{,}350 - \$12{,}400) + 0.25(\$58{,}000 - \$47{,}350)$

$= 0.10(\$12{,}400) + 0.15(\$34{,}950) + 0.25(\$10{,}650)$

$= \$1240 + \$5242.50 + \$2662.50$

$= \$9145$

$\text{Income tax} = \overbrace{\$9145}^{\text{Tax Computation}} - \overbrace{\$6500}^{\text{Tax credits}} = \$2645$

15. Step 1. Determine the adjusted gross income.
Adj. gross income = Gross income – Adjustments
Adj. gross income $= \$75{,}000 - \$4000$
$= \$71{,}000$

Step 2. Determine the taxable income.
Since the total deduction of \$35,200 is greater than the standard deduction of \$5950, use \$35,200.
Taxable inc. = Adj. gross inc– (Exempt.+Deduct.)
Taxable inc. $= \$71{,}000 - (\$3800 + \$35{,}200)$
$= \$32{,}000$

Step 3. Determine the income tax.
Tax Computation $= 0.10(8700) + 0.15(32{,}000 - 8700)$
$= \$4365$
Income tax = Tax Computation – Tax credits
Income tax $= \$4365 - \$0$
$= \$4365$

17. Step 1. Determine the adjusted gross income.
Adj. gross income = Gross income – Adjustments
Adj. gross income $= \$50{,}000 - \$0$
$= \$50{,}000$

Step 2. Determine the taxable income.
Since the total deduction of \$6500 is less than the standard deduction of \$8700, use \$8700.
Taxable inc. = Adj. gross inc– (Exempt.+Deduct.)
Taxable inc. $= \$50{,}000 - (\$3800 \cdot 3 + \$8700)$
$= \$29{,}900$

Step 3. Determine the income tax.
Tax Computation $= 0.10(12{,}400) + 0.15(29{,}900 - 12{,}400)$
$= \$3865$
Income tax = Tax Computation – Tax credits
Income tax $= \$3865 - \$2000$
$= \$1865$

19. FICA tax $= 0.0565(110,000) + 0.0145(120,000 - 110,000)$
$= \$6360$

21. FICA tax $= 0.133(110,000) + 0.029(150,000 - 110,000)$
$= \$15,790$

23. a. FICA tax $= 0.0565(20,000) = \$1130$

b. Step 1. Determine the adjusted gross income.
Adj. gross income = Gross income – Adjustments
Adj. gross income $= \$20,000 - \$0 = \$20,000$

Step 2. Determine the taxable income.
The standard deduction is $5450.
Taxable inc. = Adj. gross inc– (Exempt.+Deduct.)
Taxable inc. $= \$20,000 - (\$3800 + \$5950)$
$= \$10,250$

Step 3. Determine the income tax.
Tax Computation $= 0.10(8700) + 0.15(10,250 - 8700)$
$= \$1102.50$
Income tax = Tax Computation – Tax credits
Income tax $= \$1102.50 - \$0$
$= \$1102.50$

c. $\dfrac{1130 + 1102.50}{20,000} \approx 0.112 = 11.2\%$

25. a. Gross pay $= 20 \text{ hours} \times \dfrac{\$8.50}{\text{hour}} = \$170$

b. Federal taxes $= 10\% \times \$170 = 0.10 \times \$170 = \$17$

c. FICA taxes $= 5.65\% \times \$170 = 0.0565 \times \$170 \approx \$9.61$

d. State taxes $= 3\% \times \$170 = 0.03 \times \$170 = \$5.10$

e. Net pay $= \overbrace{\$170}^{\text{Gross pay}} - \overbrace{(\$17 + \$9.61 + \$5.10)}^{\text{Federal, FICA, and state taxes}}$
$= \$170 - \$31.71$
$= \$138.29$

f. Percent of gross pay withheld for taxes
$= \dfrac{\text{Taxes}}{\text{Gross pay}} = \dfrac{\$31.71}{\$170} \approx 0.187 = 18.7\%$

39. does not make sense; Explanations will vary.

41. makes sense

43. First compute amount of tax deduction: $10\% \times \$4000 = 0.10 \times \$4000 = \$400$
The tax credit of $2500 is the greater option.
The difference is $\$2500 - \$400 = \$2100$.

45. yes; Explanations will vary.

Check Points 8.3

1. $I = Prt = (\$3000)(0.05)(1) = \$150$

2. $I = Prt = (\$2400)(0.07)(2) = \$336$

3. $A = P(1+rt) = 2040\left[1+(0.075)\left(\frac{4}{12}\right)\right] = \$2091$

4. a. $\frac{\$5}{\text{day}} \times \frac{7 \text{ days}}{\text{week}} \times \frac{52 \text{ weeks}}{\text{year}} = \frac{\$1820}{\text{year}}$

   ...or...

   $\frac{\$5}{\text{day}} \times \frac{365 \text{ days}}{\text{year}} = \frac{\$1825}{\text{year}}$

   b. $A = P(1+rt) = 1820[1+(0.04)(1)] = \$1892.80$

   ...or...

   $A = P(1+rt) = 1825[1+(0.04)(1)] = \$1898$

5. $$\begin{aligned} A &= P(1+rt) \\ 6800 &= 5000[1+r(2)] \\ 6800 &= 5000+10,000r \\ 1800 &= 10,000r \\ \frac{1800}{10,000} &= \frac{10,000r}{10,000} \\ 0.18 &= r \\ r &= 18\% \end{aligned}$$

6. $$\begin{aligned} A &= P(1+rt) \\ 4000 &= P\left[1+(0.08)\left(\tfrac{6}{12}\right)\right] \\ 4000 &= P(1.04) \\ \frac{4000}{1.04} &= \frac{P(1.04)}{1.04} \\ 3846.153 &\approx P \\ P &\approx \$3846.16 \end{aligned}$$

Concept and Vocabulary Check 8.3

1. $I = Prt$; principal; rate; time

2. $A = P(1+rt)$

3. 360

4. false

5. true

6. false

Exercise Set 8.3

1. $I = (\$4000)(0.06)(1) = \$240$

3. $I = (\$180)(0.03)(2) = \$10.80$

5. $I = (\$5000)(0.085)\left(\frac{9}{12}\right) = \$318.75$

7. $I = (\$15,500)(0.11)\left(\frac{90}{360}\right) = \$426.25$

9. $A = P(1+rt) = 3000[1+(0.07)(2)] = \$3420$

11. $A = P(1+rt) = 26,000[1+(0.095)(5)] = \$38,350$

13. $A = P(1+rt) = 9000\left[1+(0.065)\left(\tfrac{8}{12}\right)\right] = \$9390$

15. $$\begin{aligned} A &= P(1+rt) \\ 2150 &= 2000[1+r(1)] \\ 2150 &= 2000+2000r \\ 150 &= 2000r \\ \frac{150}{2000} &= \frac{2000r}{2000} \\ 0.075 &= r \\ r &= 7.5\% \end{aligned}$$

17. $$\begin{aligned} A &= P(1+rt) \\ 5900 &= 5000[1+r(2)] \\ 900 &= 5000+10,000r \\ 900 &= 10,000r \\ \frac{900}{10,000} &= \frac{10,000r}{10,000} \\ 0.09 &= r \\ r &= 9\% \end{aligned}$$

19. $$\begin{aligned} A &= P(1+rt) \\ 2840 &= 2300\left[1+r\left(\tfrac{9}{12}\right)\right] \\ 2840 &= 2300+1725r \\ 540 &= 1725r \\ \frac{540}{1725} &= \frac{1725r}{1725} \\ 0.313 &= r \\ r &= 31.3\% \end{aligned}$$

21.
$$A = P(1+rt)$$
$$6000 = P\left[1+(0.08)(2)\right]$$
$$6000 = P(1.16)$$
$$\frac{6000}{1.16} = \frac{P(1.16)}{1.16}$$
$$5172.414 \approx P$$
$$P \approx \$5172.42$$

23.
$$A = P(1+rt)$$
$$14{,}000 = P\left[1+(0.095)(6)\right]$$
$$14{,}000 = P(1.57)$$
$$\frac{14{,}000}{1.57} = \frac{P(1.57)}{1.57}$$
$$8917.197 \approx P$$
$$P \approx \$8917.20$$

25.
$$A = P(1+rt)$$
$$5000 = P\left[1+(0.145)\left(\tfrac{9}{12}\right)\right]$$
$$5000 = P(1.10875)$$
$$\frac{5000}{1.10875} = \frac{P(1.10875)}{1.10875}$$
$$4509.583 \approx P$$
$$P \approx \$4509.59$$

27.
$$A = P(1+rt)$$
$$A = P + Prt$$
$$A - P = Prt$$
$$\frac{A-P}{Pt} = \frac{Prt}{Pt}$$
$$\frac{A-P}{Pt} = r$$
$$r = \frac{A-P}{Pt}$$

29.
$$A = P(1+rt)$$
$$\frac{A}{1+rt} = \frac{P(1+rt)}{1+rt}$$
$$\frac{A}{1+rt} = P$$
$$P = \frac{A}{1+rt}$$

31. a.
$$I = Prt$$
$$= (\$4000)(0.0825)\left(\frac{9}{12}\right)$$
$$= \$247.50$$

b. $4000 + $247.50 = $4247.50

33.
$$A = P(1+rt)$$
$$2000 = 1400\left[1+r(2)\right]$$
$$2000 = 1400 + 2800r$$
$$600 = 2800r$$
$$\frac{600}{2800} = \frac{2800r}{2800}$$
$$0.214 = r$$
$$r = 21.4\%$$

35.
$$A = P(1+rt)$$
$$1472 = 960\left[1+r\left(\frac{1}{12}\right)\right]$$
$$1472 = 960 + 80r$$
$$512 = 80r$$
$$\frac{512}{80} = \frac{80r}{80}$$
$$6.4 = r$$
$$r = 640\%$$

37.
$$A = P(1+rt)$$
$$3000 = P\left[1+(0.065)(2)\right]$$
$$3000 = P(1.13)$$
$$\frac{3000}{1.13} = \frac{P(1.13)}{1.13}$$
$$2654.867 \approx P$$
$$P \approx \$2654.87$$

41. does not make sense; Explanations will vary. Sample explanation: This would be the amount of interest after one year.

43. does not make sense; Explanations will vary. Sample explanation: The principal should be rounded up to $3846.16 to make sure there is enough money.

45. a.
$$A = P(1+rt)$$
$$A = 5000\left[1+(0.055)t\right]$$
$$A = 5000 + 275t$$

b. The slope is 275. This means the *rate of change* for the account is $275 per year.

Check Points 8.4

1. a. $A = \$1000(1+0.04)^5 \approx \$1216.65$

b. $\$1216.65 - \$1000 = \$216.65$

2. a. $A = \$4200\left(1+\frac{0.04}{4}\right)^{4\cdot 10} \approx \$6253.23$

b. $\$6253.23 - \$4200 = \$2053.23$

3. a. $A = P\left(1+\frac{r}{n}\right)^{nt}$

$$A = 10{,}000\left(1+\frac{0.08}{4}\right)^{4(5)}$$
$$= \$14{,}859.47$$

b. $A = Pe^{rt}$

$$A = 10{,}000e^{0.08(5)}$$
$$= \$14{,}918.25$$

4. $P = \dfrac{A}{\left(1+\frac{r}{n}\right)^{nt}}$

$A = \$10{,}000,\ r = 0.07,\ n = 52,\ t = 8$

$$P = \frac{10{,}000}{\left(1+\frac{0.07}{52}\right)^{52\cdot 8}} \approx \frac{10{,}000}{1.750013343} \approx \$5714.25$$

5. a. $A = \$6000\left(1+\frac{0.10}{12}\right)^{12\cdot 1} \approx \$6628.28$

b.
$$A = P(1+rt)$$
$$6628.28 = 6000[1+(r)(1)]$$
$$6628.28 = 6000 + 6000r$$
$$628.28 = 6000r$$
$$\frac{628.28}{6000} = \frac{6000r}{6000}$$
$$0.105 \approx r$$
$$r \approx 10.5\%$$

6. $Y = \left(1+\frac{r}{n}\right)^n - 1$

$$Y = \left(1+\frac{0.08}{4}\right)^4 - 1 \approx 0.0824 = 8.24\%$$

Concept and Vocabulary Check 8.4

1. principal; interest
2. *t*; *r*; *n*
3. $A = P(1+r)^t$
4. six; semiannually
5. three; quarterly
6. continuous
7. *P*; *A*; *t*; *r*; *n*
8. effective annual yield; simple
9. true
10. true
11. true
12. true

Exercise Set 8.4

1. a. $A = \$10{,}000(1+0.04)^2 = \$10{,}816$

b. $\$10{,}816 - \$10{,}000 = \$816$

3. a. $A = \$3000\left(1+\frac{0.05}{2}\right)^{2\cdot 4}$

$$= \$3000(1.025)^8$$
$$= \$3655.21$$

b. $\$3655.21 - \$3000 = \$655.21$

5. a. $A = \$9500\left(1+\frac{0.06}{4}\right)^{4\cdot 5}$

$$= \$9500(1.015)^{20}$$
$$= \$12{,}795.12$$

b. $\$12{,}795.12 - \$9500 = \$3295.12$

7. a. $A = \$4500\left(1+\frac{0.045}{12}\right)^{12\cdot 3}$

$$= \$4500(1.0038)^{36}$$
$$= \$5149.12$$

b. $\$5149.12 - \$4500 = \$649.12$

9. a. $A = \$1500\left(1+\frac{0.085}{360}\right)^{360\cdot 2.5}$

$= \$1500(1.000236)^{900}$

$= \$1855.10$

b. $1855.10 – $1500 = $355.10

11. a. $A = \$20{,}000\left(1+\frac{0.045}{360}\right)^{360\cdot 20}$

$= \$20{,}000(1.000125)^{7200}$

$= \$49{,}189.30$

b. $49,189.30 – $20,000 = $29,189.30

13. a. $A = 10{,}000\left(1+\frac{0.055}{2}\right)^{2(5)}$

$\approx \$13{,}116.51$

b. $A = 10{,}000\left(1+\frac{0.055}{4}\right)^{4(5)}$

• $13,140.67

c. $A = 10{,}000\left(1+\frac{0.055}{12}\right)^{12(5)}$

$\approx \$13{,}157.04$

d. $A = 10{,}000e^{0.055(5)}$

$\approx \$13{,}165.31$

15. $A = 12{,}000\left(1+\frac{0.07}{12}\right)^{12(3)}$

$\approx 14{,}795.11$ (7% yield)

$A = 12{,}000e^{0.0685(3)}$

$\approx 14{,}737.67$ (6.85% yield)

Investing $12,000 for 3 years at 7% compounded monthly yields the greater return.

17. $A =$ $10,000, $r = 0.06$, $n = 2$, $t = 3$

$$P = \frac{10{,}000}{\left(1+\frac{0.06}{2}\right)^{2\cdot 3}} = \frac{10{,}000}{(1.03)^6} = \$8374.85$$

19. $A = \$10{,}000$, $r = 0.095$, $n = 12$, $t = 3$

$$P = \frac{10{,}000}{\left(1+\frac{0.095}{12}\right)^{12\cdot 3}} = \frac{10{,}000}{(1.00791667)^{36}} = \$7528.59$$

21. a. $A = \$10{,}000\left(1+\frac{0.045}{4}\right)^{4\cdot 1}$

$= \$10{,}000(1.01125)^4$

$= \$10{,}457.65$

b. $A = P(1+rt)$

$10{,}457.65 = 10{,}000[1+r(1)]$

$10{,}457.65 = 10{,}000 + 10{,}000r$

$457.65 = 10{,}000r$

$\frac{457.65}{10{,}000} = \frac{10{,}000r}{10{,}000}$

$0.046 \approx r$

$r \approx 4.6\%$

23. $Y = \left(1+\frac{0.06}{2}\right)^2 - 1 = 0.061 = 6.1\%$

25. $Y = \left(1+\frac{0.06}{12}\right)^{12} - 1 \approx 0.062 = 6.2\%$

27. $Y = \left(1+\frac{0.06}{1000}\right)^{1000} - 1 \approx 0.062 = 6.2\%$

29. $Y = \left(1+\frac{0.08}{12}\right)^{12} - 1 \approx 0.0830 = 8.3\%$

$Y = \left(1+\frac{0.0825}{1}\right)^{1} - 1 \approx 0.0825 = 8.25\%$

8% compounded monthly is better..

31. $Y = \left(1+\frac{0.055}{2}\right)^2 - 1 \approx 0.0558 = 5.6\%$

$Y = \left(1+\frac{0.054}{360}\right)^{360} - 1 \approx 0.05548 = 5.5\%$

5.5% compounded semiannually is better.

33. First investment: $A = P(1+r)^t$

$A = \$25{,}000(1+0.12)^{40}$

$= \$2{,}326{,}274.26$

Second investment: $A = P(1+r)^t$

$A = \$25{,}000(1+0.06)^{40}$

$= \$257{,}142.95$

Additional earnings:

$\$2{,}326{,}274.26 - \$257{,}142.95 \approx \$2{,}069{,}131$

35. First investment: $A = P(1+r)^t$

$$A = \$50{,}000(1+0.10)^{30}$$
$$= \$872{,}470.11$$

Second investment: $A = P\left(1+\frac{r}{n}\right)^{nt}$

$$A == \$50{,}000\left(1+\frac{0.05}{12}\right)^{12\cdot 30}$$
$$= \$223{,}387.22$$

Additional earnings: $\$872{,}470.11 - \$223{,}387.22 = \$649{,}083$

37. $A = P\left(1+\frac{r}{n}\right)^{nt} = 12{,}000\left(1+\frac{0.06}{2}\right)^{2\cdot 21} \approx \$41{,}528$

39. **a.** $A = P\left(1+\frac{r}{n}\right)^{nt} = 2600\left(1+\frac{0.04}{1}\right)^{1\cdot 1} \approx \$2704$

$A = P\left(1+\frac{r}{n}\right)^{nt} = 2200\left(1+\frac{0.05}{12}\right)^{12\cdot 1} \approx \$2312.56$

You will have $\$2704 - \$2312.56 = \$391.44$ or approximately \$391 more.

b. $A = P\left(1+\frac{r}{n}\right)^{nt} = 2600\left(1+\frac{0.04}{1}\right)^{1\cdot 5} \approx \$3163.30$

$A = P\left(1+\frac{r}{n}\right)^{nt} = 2200\left(1+\frac{0.05}{12}\right)^{12\cdot 5} \approx \$2823.39$

You will have $\$3163.30 - \$2823.39 = \$339.91$ or approximately \$340 more.

c. $A = P\left(1+\frac{r}{n}\right)^{nt} = 2600\left(1+\frac{0.04}{1}\right)^{1\cdot 20} \approx \$5696.92$

$A = P\left(1+\frac{r}{n}\right)^{nt} = 2200\left(1+\frac{0.05}{12}\right)^{12\cdot 20} \approx \$5967.81$

Your friend will have $\$5967.81 - \$5696.92 = \$270.89$ or approximately \$271 more.

41. $A = P\left(1+\frac{r}{n}\right)^{nt} = 3000\left(1+\frac{0.07}{2}\right)^{2\cdot 10} \approx \$5969.37$

$A = P\left(1+\frac{r}{n}\right)^{nt} = 5969.37\left(1+\frac{0.0725}{4}\right)^{4\cdot 6} \approx \$9186.60$

The value of the account will be approximately \$9187.

43. **a.** $A = 24\left(1+\frac{0.05}{12}\right)^{12\cdot 384} \approx \$5{,}027{,}400{,}000$

b. $A = 24\left(1+\frac{0.05}{360}\right)^{360\cdot 384} \approx \$5{,}225{,}000{,}000$

45. $I = Prt = 2000(0.06)(1) = \$120$

$$A = P\left(1+\frac{r}{n}\right)^{nt} = 2000\left(1+\frac{0.059}{360}\right)^{360\cdot 1} \approx \$2122$$

$I = \$2122 - 2000 = \$122$

The account that pays 5.9% compounded daily earns $\$122 - \$120 = \$2$ more interest.

47. For compound interest once per year, use the formula $A = 5000(1+0.055)^t$.

For compound interest continuously, use the formula $A = 5000e^{0.055t}$.

Years	Once a Year Amount	Once a Year Interest	Continous Amount	Continous Interest
1	\$5275	\$275	\$5283	\$283
5	\$6535	\$1535	\$6583	\$1583
10	\$8541	\$3541	\$8666	\$3666
20	\$14,589	\$9589	\$15,021	\$10,021

49. $$P = \frac{A}{\left(1+\frac{r}{n}\right)^{nt}}$$

$A = \$80,000, r = 0.06, n = 2, t = 13$

$$P = \frac{80,000}{\left(1+\frac{0.06}{2}\right)^{2\cdot 13}} = \frac{80,000}{(1.03)^{26}} = \$37,096$$

51. $$P = \frac{A}{\left(1+\frac{r}{n}\right)^{nt}} = \frac{75,000}{\left(1+\frac{0.045}{1}\right)^{1\cdot 15}} \approx \$38,755$$

$$P = \frac{A}{\left(1+\frac{r}{n}\right)^{nt}} = \frac{75,000}{\left(1+\frac{0.04}{360}\right)^{360\cdot 15}} \approx \$41,163$$

53. $$Y = \left(1+\frac{r}{n}\right)^{n} - 1 = \left(1+\frac{0.054}{360}\right)^{360} - 1 \approx 0.0555 = 5.55\%$$

55. $$Y = \left(1+\frac{r}{n}\right)^{n} - 1 = \left(1+\frac{0.042}{4}\right)^{4} - 1 \approx 0.043 = 4.3\%$$

$$Y = \left(1+\frac{r}{n}\right)^{n} - 1 = \left(1+\frac{0.042}{12}\right)^{12} - 1 \approx 0.043 = 4.3\%$$

$$Y = \left(1+\frac{r}{n}\right)^{n} - 1 = \left(1+\frac{0.042}{360}\right)^{360} - 1 \approx 0.043 = 4.3\%$$

As the number of compounding periods increases, the effective annual yield increases slightly. However, with the rates rounded to the nearest tenth of a percent, this increase is not evident.

57. $Y=\left(1+\frac{r}{n}\right)^n-1=\left(1+\frac{0.045}{2}\right)^2-1\approx 0.0455=4.55\%$

$Y=\left(1+\frac{r}{n}\right)^n-1=\left(1+\frac{0.044}{360}\right)^{360}-1\approx 0.0450=4.50\%$

The account paying 4.5% compounded semiannually is the better investment.

63. does not make sense; Explanations will vary. Sample explanation: At the same rate, any compounding period will be a better deal than simple interest.

65. does not make sense; Explanations will vary. Sample explanation: Compounding continuously does not result in an infinite amount of money.

67. $A=P\left(1+\frac{r}{n}\right)^{nt}$

Have \$6000 in the account for 6 years:

$A=\$6000\left(1+\frac{0.05}{2}\right)^{2\cdot 6}=\$8069.33$

Have \$4000 in the account for 4 years:

$A=\$4000\left(1+\frac{0.05}{2}\right)^{2\cdot 4}=\$4873.61$

$$\begin{aligned}\text{Balance after 6 years} &= \$8069.33+\$4873.61\\ &= \$12{,}942.94\end{aligned}$$

69. Substitute Y for r in $A=P(1+rt)$

Thus, $A=P(1+Yt)$

Substitute $P(1+Yt)$ for A in $A=P\left(1+\frac{r}{n}\right)^{nt}$ and substitute 1 for t.

$$P(1+Yt)=P\left(1+\frac{r}{n}\right)^{nt}$$

$$\frac{P[1+Y(1)]}{P}=\frac{P\left(1+\frac{r}{n}\right)^{n(1)}}{P}$$

$$1+Y=\left(1+\frac{r}{n}\right)^{n}$$

$$Y=\left(1+\frac{r}{n}\right)^{n}-1$$

Checkpoints 8.5

1. a. Value at end of year 1
$2000
Value at end of year 2
$\$2000(1+0.10)+\$2000=\$4200$
Value at end of year 3
$\$4200(1+0.10)+\$2000=\$6620$

b. $\$6620-\$2000\cdot 3=\$620$

2. a. $A=\dfrac{P\left[(1+r)^t-1\right]}{r}$

$A=\dfrac{3000\left[(1+0.08)^{40}-1\right]}{0.08}$

$\approx \$777{,}170$

b. $\$777{,}170-40\times\$3000=\$657{,}170$

3. a. $A=\dfrac{P\left[\left(1+\frac{r}{n}\right)^{nt}-1\right]}{\frac{r}{n}}$

$A=\dfrac{100\left[\left(1+\frac{0.095}{12}\right)^{12\times 35}-1\right]}{\frac{0.095}{12}}$

$\approx \$333{,}946$

b. $\$333{,}946-\$100\cdot 12\cdot 35=\$291{,}946$

4. a. $P=\dfrac{A\left(\frac{r}{n}\right)}{\left[\left(1+\frac{r}{n}\right)^{nt}-1\right]}$

$P=\dfrac{100{,}000\left(\frac{0.09}{12}\right)}{\left[\left(1+\frac{0.09}{12}\right)^{12\times 18}-1\right]}$

$\approx \$187$

b. Deposits: $\$187\times 18\times 12=\$40{,}392$
Interest: $\$100{,}000-\$40{,}392=\$59{,}608$

5. a. High price = $63.38,
Low price = $42.37

b. Dividend $=\$0.72\cdot 3000=\$2160$

c. Annual return for dividends alone = 1.5%
1.5% is much lower than the 3.5% bank rate.

d. Shares traded $=72{,}032\cdot 100=7{,}203{,}200$ shares

e. High price = $49.94,
Low price = $48.33

f. Price at close = $49.50

g. The price went up $0.03 per share.

h. Annual earnings per share $=\dfrac{\$49.50}{37}\approx\$1.34$

6. a. $A=\dfrac{P\left[(1+r)^t-1\right]}{r}$

$A=\dfrac{3000\left[(1+0.08)^{15}-1\right]}{0.08}$

$\approx \$81{,}456$

b. $A=P(1+r)^t$

$A=\$81{,}456(1+0.08)^{25}$

$\approx \$557{,}849$

c. $\$557{,}849-\$2000(15)=\$527{,}849$

Concept and Vocabulary Check 8.5

1. annuity
2. P; r; n; value of the annuity; t
3. stock; capital; dividends
4. bonds
5. portfolio; diversified
6. mutual fund
7. Roth; $59\frac{1}{2}$
8. true
9. false
10. true
11. true

Exercise Set 8.5

1. a. $A=\frac{P\left[(1+r)^t-1\right]}{r}$

$A=\frac{2000\left[(1+0.05)^{20}-1\right]}{0.05}$

$\approx \$66,132$

b. $\$66,132-20\times\$2000=\$26,132$

3. a. $A=\frac{P\left[(1+r)^t-1\right]}{r}$

$A=\frac{4000\left[(1+0.065)^{40}-1\right]}{0.065}$

$\approx \$702,528$

b. $\$702,528-40\times\$4000=\$542,528$

5. a. $A=\frac{P\left[\left(1+\frac{r}{n}\right)^{nt}-1\right]}{\frac{r}{n}}$

$A=\frac{50\left[\left(1+\frac{0.06}{12}\right)^{12\times 30}-1\right]}{\frac{0.06}{12}}$

$\approx \$50,226$

b. $\$50,226-\$50\cdot 12\cdot 30=\$32,226$

7. a. $A=\frac{P\left[\left(1+\frac{r}{n}\right)^{nt}-1\right]}{\frac{r}{n}}$

$A=\frac{100\left[\left(1+\frac{0.045}{2}\right)^{2\times 25}-1\right]}{\frac{0.045}{2}}$

$\approx \$9076$

b. $\$9076-\$100\cdot 2\cdot 25=\$4076$

9. a. $A=\frac{P\left[\left(1+\frac{r}{n}\right)^{nt}-1\right]}{\frac{r}{n}}$

$A=\frac{1000\left[\left(1+\frac{0.0625}{4}\right)^{4\times 6}-1\right]}{\frac{0.0625}{4}}$

$\approx \$28,850$

b. $\$28,850-\$1000\cdot 4\cdot 6=\$4850$

11. a. $P=\frac{A\left(\frac{r}{n}\right)}{\left[\left(1+\frac{r}{n}\right)^{nt}-1\right]}$

$P=\frac{140,000\left(\frac{0.06}{1}\right)}{\left[\left(1+\frac{0.06}{1}\right)^{1\times 18}-1\right]}$

$\approx \$4530$

b. Deposits: $\$4530\times 1\times 18=\$81,540$
Interest: $\$140,000-\$81,540=\$58,460$

13. a. $P=\frac{A\left(\frac{r}{n}\right)}{\left[\left(1+\frac{r}{n}\right)^{nt}-1\right]}$

$P=\frac{200,000\left(\frac{0.045}{12}\right)}{\left[\left(1+\frac{0.045}{12}\right)^{12\times 10}-1\right]}$

$\approx \$1323$

b. Deposits: $\$1323\times 12\times 10=\$158,760$
Interest: $\$200,000-\$158,760=\$41,240$

15. a. $P=\frac{A\left(\frac{r}{n}\right)}{\left[\left(1+\frac{r}{n}\right)^{nt}-1\right]}$

$P=\frac{1,000,000\left(\frac{0.0725}{12}\right)}{\left[\left(1+\frac{0.0725}{12}\right)^{12\times 40}-1\right]}$

$\approx \$356$

b. Deposits: $\$356\times 12\times 40=\$170,880$
Interest: $\$1,000,000-\$170,880=\$829,120$

17. a. $P=\frac{A\left(\frac{r}{n}\right)}{\left[\left(1+\frac{r}{n}\right)^{nt}-1\right]}$

$P=\frac{20,000\left(\frac{0.035}{4}\right)}{\left[\left(1+\frac{0.035}{4}\right)^{4\times 5}-1\right]}$

$\approx \$920$

b. Deposits: $\$920\times 4\times 5=\$18,400$
Interest: $\$20,000-\$18,400=\$1600$

19. a. High price = \$73.25,
Low price = \$45.44

b. Dividend = $\$1.20 \cdot 700 = \$840$

c. Annual return for dividends alone = 2.2%
2.2% is lower than a 3% bank rate.

d. Shares traded = $5915 \cdot 100 = 591{,}500$ shares

e. High price = \$56.38,
Low price = \$54.38

f. Price at close = \$55.50

g. The price went up \$1.25 per share.

h. Annual earnings per share

$$= \frac{\text{close}}{\text{PE}} = \frac{\$55.50}{17} \approx \$3.26$$

21. a. Lump-Sum Deposit:

$$A = P(1+r)^t$$
$$A = 30{,}000(1+0.05)^{20}$$
$$\approx \$79{,}599$$

Periodic Deposit:

$$A = \frac{P\left[(1+r)^t - 1\right]}{r}$$
$$A = \frac{1500\left[(1+0.05)^{20} - 1\right]}{0.05}$$
$$\approx \$49{,}599$$

The lump-sum investment will have
$\$79{,}599 - \$49{,}599 = \$30{,}000$ more.

b. Lump-Sum Interest:
$\$79{,}599 - \$30{,}000 = \$49{,}599$
Periodic Deposit Interest:
$\$49{,}599 - \$30{,}000 = \$19{,}599$
The lump-sum investment will have
$\$49{,}599 - \$19{,}599 = \$30{,}000$ more.

23.

$$A = \frac{P\left[(1+r)^t - 1\right]}{r}$$
$$Ar = P\left[(1+r)^t - 1\right]$$
$$\frac{Ar}{\left[(1+r)^t - 1\right]} = \frac{P\left[(1+r)^t - 1\right]}{\left[(1+r)^t - 1\right]}$$
$$\frac{Ar}{(1+r)^t - 1} = P$$
$$P = \frac{Ar}{(1+r)^t - 1}$$

This formula describes the deposit necessary at the end of each year that yields *A* dollars after *t* years with interest rate *r* compounded annually.

25. a.

$$A = \frac{P\left[(1+r)^t - 1\right]}{r}$$
$$A = \frac{2000\left[(1+0.075)^5 - 1\right]}{0.075}$$
$$\approx \$11{,}617$$

b. $\$11{,}617 - 5 \times \$2000 = \$1617$

27. a.

$$A = \frac{P\left[\left(1+\frac{r}{n}\right)^{nt} - 1\right]}{\frac{r}{n}}$$
$$A = \frac{50\left[\left(1+\frac{0.055}{12}\right)^{12\times 40} - 1\right]}{\frac{0.055}{12}}$$
$$\approx \$87{,}052$$

b. $\$87{,}052 - \$50 \cdot 12 \cdot 40 = \$63{,}052$

29. a.

$$A = \frac{P\left[\left(1+\frac{r}{n}\right)^{nt} - 1\right]}{\frac{r}{n}}$$
$$A = \frac{10{,}000\left[\left(1+\frac{0.105}{4}\right)^{4\times 10} - 1\right]}{\frac{0.105}{4}}$$
$$\approx \$693{,}031$$

b. $\$693{,}031 - \$10{,}000 \cdot 4 \cdot 10 = \$293{,}031$

31. a. $P = \dfrac{A\left(\frac{r}{n}\right)}{\left[\left(1+\frac{r}{n}\right)^{nt}-1\right]}$

$P = \dfrac{3500\left(\frac{0.05}{2}\right)}{\left[\left(1+\frac{0.05}{2}\right)^{2\times 4}-1\right]}$

$\approx \$401$

b. Deposits: $\$401 \times 2 \times 4 = \$3208$
Interest: $\$3500 - \$3208 = \$292$

33. $P = \dfrac{A\left(\frac{r}{n}\right)}{\left[\left(1+\frac{r}{n}\right)^{nt}-1\right]}$

$P = \dfrac{2{,}000{,}000\left(\frac{0.065}{12}\right)}{\left[\left(1+\frac{0.065}{12}\right)^{12\times 45}-1\right]}$

$\approx \$620$

You must invest \$620 per month.

Amount from interest:
$\$2{,}000{,}000 - \$620 \cdot 12 \cdot 45 = \$1{,}665{,}200$

35. a. $A = \dfrac{P\left[(1+r)^t - 1\right]}{r}$

$A = \dfrac{4500\left[(1+0.083)^{18}-1\right]}{0.083}$

$\approx \$173{,}527$

b. $A = P(1+r)^t$

$A = \$173{,}527(1+0.083)^{25}$

$\approx \$1{,}273{,}733$

c. $\$1{,}273{,}733 - \$3000(18) = \$1{,}219{,}733$

47. does not make sense; Explanations will vary.

49. makes sense

51. does not make sense; Explanations will vary.

53. does not make sense; Explanations will vary.

55. a. $P = \dfrac{A\left(\frac{r}{n}\right)}{\left[\left(1+\frac{r}{n}\right)^{nt}-1\right]}$

$P = \dfrac{650{,}000\left(\frac{0.07}{12}\right)}{\left[\left(1+\frac{0.07}{12}\right)^{12\times 40}-1\right]}$

$\approx \$248$

b. Adjusted gross income *with* IRA:
Adj. gross income $= \$50{,}000 - \$248 \cdot 12$
$= \$47{,}024$
Taxable income *with* IRA:
Taxable inc $= \$47{,}024 - (\$3800 + \$5950)$
$= \$37{,}274$
Income tax *with* IRA:
$= 0.10(8700) + 0.15(35{,}350 - 8700)$
$+ 0.25(37{,}274 - 35{,}350)$
$= \$5348.50$

Adjusted gross income *without* IRA:
Adj. gross income $= \$50{,}000 - \$0$
$= \$50{,}000$
Taxable income *without* IRA:
Taxable inc $= \$50{,}000 - (\$3800 + \$5950)$
$= \$41{,}800$
Income tax *without* IRA:
$= 0.10(8700) + 0.15(35{,}350 - 8700)$
$+ 0.25(40{,}250 - 35{,}350)$
$= \$6092.50$

c. Percent of gross income *with* IRA:
$\dfrac{5348.50}{50{,}000} \approx 10.7\%$
Percent of gross income *without* IRA:
$\dfrac{6092.50}{50{,}000} \approx 12.2\%$

Checkpoints 8.6

1. a. $PMT = \dfrac{P\left(\frac{r}{n}\right)}{1-\left(1+\frac{r}{n}\right)^{-nt}} = \dfrac{15{,}000\left(\frac{0.08}{12}\right)}{1-\left(1+\frac{0.08}{12}\right)^{-12(4)}} \approx \$366$

Total interest for loan A: $\$366 \cdot 12 \cdot 4 - \$15{,}000 = \$2568$

b. $PMT = \dfrac{P\left(\frac{r}{n}\right)}{1-\left(1+\frac{r}{n}\right)^{-nt}} = \dfrac{15{,}000\left(\frac{0.10}{12}\right)}{1-\left(1+\frac{0.10}{12}\right)^{-12(6)}} \approx \$278$

Total interest for loan B: $\$278 \cdot 12 \cdot 6 - \$15{,}000 = \$5016$

c. Monthly payments are lower with the longer-term loan, but there is more interest with the longer-term loan.

2. New car: $PMT = \dfrac{P\left(\frac{r}{n}\right)}{1-\left(1+\frac{r}{n}\right)^{-nt}} = \dfrac{19{,}000\left(\frac{0.0618}{12}\right)}{1-\left(1+\frac{0.0618}{12}\right)^{-12(3)}} \approx \$580$

Used car: $PMT = \dfrac{P\left(\frac{r}{n}\right)}{1-\left(1+\frac{r}{n}\right)^{-nt}} = \dfrac{11{,}500\left(\frac{0.075}{12}\right)}{1-\left(1+\frac{0.075}{12}\right)^{-12(3)}} \approx \$358$

The difference is $\$580 - \$358 = \$222$

3. a. Annual fuel expense for the hybrid

$= \dfrac{\text{annual miles driven}}{\text{miles per gallon}} \times \text{price per gallon}$

$= \dfrac{36{,}000}{40} \times \$3.50$

$= \$3150$

Annual fuel expense for the SUV

$= \dfrac{\text{annual miles driven}}{\text{miles per gallon}} \times \text{price per gallon}$

$= \dfrac{36{,}000}{15} \times \$3.50$

$= \$8400$

The difference is $\$8400 - \$3150 = \$5250$

b. Monthly savings $= \dfrac{\$5250}{12} \approx \$438$

Thus, $A = \dfrac{P\left[\left(1+\frac{r}{n}\right)^{nt} - 1\right]}{\frac{r}{n}}$

$A = \dfrac{438\left[\left(1+\frac{0.0725}{12}\right)^{12\times 7} - 1\right]}{\frac{0.0725}{12}}$

$\approx \$47{,}746$

Concept and Vocabulary Check 8.6

1. *PMT*; *P*; *n*; *t*; *r*
2. closed-end; open-end
3. residual value
4. bodily injury; property damage
5. collision
6. comprehensive
7. true
8. false
9. false
10. true
11. false
12. true

Exercise Set 8.6

1. $PMT = \dfrac{P\left(\frac{r}{n}\right)}{1-\left(1+\frac{r}{n}\right)^{-nt}} = \dfrac{10,000\left(\frac{0.08}{12}\right)}{1-\left(1+\frac{0.08}{12}\right)^{-12(4)}} \approx \$244$

   Total interest: $\$244 \cdot 12 \cdot 4 - \$10,000 = \$1712$

3. **a.** $PMT = \dfrac{P\left(\frac{r}{n}\right)}{1-\left(1+\frac{r}{n}\right)^{-nt}} = \dfrac{15,000\left(\frac{0.051}{12}\right)}{1-\left(1+\frac{0.051}{12}\right)^{-12(3)}} \approx \$450$

   Total interest for loan A: $\$450 \cdot 12 \cdot 3 - \$15,000 = \$1200$

   b. $PMT = \dfrac{P\left(\frac{r}{n}\right)}{1-\left(1+\frac{r}{n}\right)^{-nt}} = \dfrac{15,000\left(\frac{0.064}{12}\right)}{1-\left(1+\frac{0.064}{12}\right)^{-12(5)}} \approx \$293$

   Total interest for loan B: $\$293 \cdot 12 \cdot 5 - \$15,000 = \$2580$

   c. Monthly payments are lower with the longer-term loan, but there is more interest with the longer-term loan.

5. New car: $PMT = \dfrac{P\left(\frac{r}{n}\right)}{1-\left(1+\frac{r}{n}\right)^{-nt}} = \dfrac{28,000\left(\frac{0.0612}{12}\right)}{1-\left(1+\frac{0.0612}{12}\right)^{-12(4)}} \approx \$659$

   Used car: $PMT = \dfrac{P\left(\frac{r}{n}\right)}{1-\left(1+\frac{r}{n}\right)^{-nt}} = \dfrac{16,000\left(\frac{0.0686}{12}\right)}{1-\left(1+\frac{0.0686}{12}\right)^{-12(4)}} \approx \$382$

   The difference is $\$659 - \$382 = \$277$

7. Amount financed $\$29,635-\$9000=\$20,635$

$$PMT=\frac{P\left(\frac{r}{n}\right)}{1-\left(1+\frac{r}{n}\right)^{-nt}}=\frac{20,635\left(\frac{0.0662}{12}\right)}{1-\left(1+\frac{0.0662}{12}\right)^{-12(5)}}\approx \$405$$

Total interest for loan: $\$405\cdot 12\cdot 5-\$20,635=\$3665$

9. Amount financed for incentive A: $\$60,000-\$10,000-\$5000=\$45,000$

$$PMT=\frac{P\left(\frac{r}{n}\right)}{1-\left(1+\frac{r}{n}\right)^{-nt}}=\frac{45,000\left(\frac{0.0734}{12}\right)}{1-\left(1+\frac{0.0734}{12}\right)^{-12(5)}}\approx \$898$$

Amount financed for incentive B: $\$60,000-\$10,000=\$50,000$

$$PMT=\frac{\$50,000}{60}\approx \$833$$

The difference in monthly payments is $\$898-\$863=\$65$.
Incentive B is the better deal.

11. a. Annual fuel expense for the hybrid

$$=\frac{\text{annual miles driven}}{\text{miles per gallon}}\times \text{price per gallon}$$

$$=\frac{40,000}{40}\times \$4$$

$$=\$4000$$

Annual fuel expense for the SUV

$$=\frac{\text{annual miles driven}}{\text{miles per gallon}}\times \text{price per gallon}$$

$$=\frac{40,000}{16}\times \$4$$

$$=\$10,000$$

The difference is $\$10,000-\$4000=\$6000$

b. Monthly savings $=\frac{\$6000}{12}=\$500$

Thus, $A=\dfrac{P\left[\left(1+\frac{r}{n}\right)^{nt}-1\right]}{\frac{r}{n}}$

$$A=\frac{500\left[\left(1+\frac{0.052}{12}\right)^{12\times 6}-1\right]}{\frac{0.052}{12}}$$

$$\approx \$42,142$$

13. a. Annual expense $= \$0.98 \times 20{,}000 = \$19{,}600$

b.
$$A = \frac{P\left[\left(1+\frac{r}{n}\right)^{nt} - 1\right]}{\frac{r}{n}}$$

$$A = \frac{19{,}600\left[\left(1+\frac{0.085}{1}\right)^{6} - 1\right]}{\frac{0.085}{1}}$$

$$\approx \$145{,}609$$

15. 6-year expense for Cadillac STS
$= \$0.98 \times 30{,}000 \times 6 = \$176{,}400$

6-year expense for Corolla CE
$= \$0.40 \times 30{,}000 \times 6 = \$72{,}000$

The expense of a Cadillac STS exceeds that of a Corolla CE by $\$176{,}400 - \$72{,}000 = \$104{,}400$.

25. makes sense

27. makes sense

29. makes sense

31.
$$P\left(1+\frac{r}{n}\right)^{nt} = \frac{PMT\left[\left(1+\frac{r}{n}\right)^{nt} - 1\right]}{\frac{r}{n}}$$

$$P\left(\frac{r}{n}\right)\left(1+\frac{r}{n}\right)^{nt} = PMT\left[\left(1+\frac{r}{n}\right)^{nt} - 1\right]$$

$$\frac{P\left(\frac{r}{n}\right)\left(1+\frac{r}{n}\right)^{nt}}{\left(1+\frac{r}{n}\right)^{nt} - 1} = \frac{PMT\left[\left(1+\frac{r}{n}\right)^{nt} - 1\right]}{\left(1+\frac{r}{n}\right)^{nt} - 1}$$

$$\frac{P\left(\frac{r}{n}\right)\left(1+\frac{r}{n}\right)^{nt}}{\left(1+\frac{r}{n}\right)^{nt} - 1} = PMT$$

$$\frac{\frac{P\left(\frac{r}{n}\right)\left(1+\frac{r}{n}\right)^{nt}}{\left(1+\frac{r}{n}\right)^{nt}}}{\frac{\left(1+\frac{r}{n}\right)^{nt} - 1}{\left(1+\frac{r}{n}\right)^{nt}}} = PMT$$

$$\frac{P\left(\frac{r}{n}\right)}{\frac{\left(1+\frac{r}{n}\right)^{nt}}{\left(1+\frac{r}{n}\right)^{nt}} - \frac{1}{\left(1+\frac{r}{n}\right)^{nt}}} = PMT$$

$$\frac{P\left(\frac{r}{n}\right)}{1-\left(1+\frac{r}{n}\right)^{-nt}} = PMT$$

Checkpoints 8.7

1. a. $PMT = \dfrac{P\left(\frac{r}{n}\right)}{1-\left(1+\frac{r}{n}\right)^{-nt}} = \dfrac{175{,}500\left(\frac{0.075}{12}\right)}{1-\left(1+\frac{0.075}{12}\right)^{-12\cdot 15}} \approx \$1627$

b. $\$1627\cdot 12\cdot 15-\$175{,}500=\$117{,}360$

c. $\$266{,}220-\$117{,}360=\$148{,}860$

2. Interest for first month = $Prt=\$200{,}000\times 0.07\times\dfrac{1}{12}\approx\$1166.67$
Principle payment = $\$1550.00-\$1166.67=\$383.33$
Balance of loan = $\$200{,}000-\$383.33=\$199{,}616.67$

Interest for second month = $Prt=\$199{,}616.67\times 0.07\times\dfrac{1}{12}\approx\$1164.43$
Principle payment = $\$1550.00-\$1164.43=\$385.57$
Balance of loan = $\$199{,}616.67-\$385.57=\$199{,}231.10$

Payment Number	Interest Payment	Principal Payment	Balance of Loan
1	$1166.67	$383.33	$199,616.67
2	$1164.43	$385.57	$199,231.10

3. Monthly gross income $=\dfrac{\$240{,}000}{12}=\$20{,}000$

a. You should spend no more than 28% on a mortgage payment:
$28\%\times\$20{,}000=0.28\times\$20{,}000=\$5600$

b. You should spend no more than 36% on total monthly debt:
$36\%\times\$20{,}000=0.36\times\$20{,}000=\$7200$

c. $\$7200-\$5600(0.90)=\$2160$

Concept and Vocabulary Check 8.7

1. mortgage; down payment
2. loan amortization schedule
3. false
4. false
5. true
6. false

Exercise Set 8.7

1. a. $\$220,000(0.20)=\$44,000$

b. $\$220,000-\$44,000=\$176,000$

c. $\$176,000(0.03)=\$5280$

d. $PMT=\dfrac{P\left(\frac{r}{n}\right)}{1-\left(1+\frac{r}{n}\right)^{-nt}}=\dfrac{176,000\left(\frac{0.07}{12}\right)}{1-\left(1+\frac{0.07}{12}\right)^{-12(30)}}\approx\$1171$

e. $\$1171(12)(30)-\$176,000=\$245,560$

3. Mortgage amount: $\$100,000-\$100,000(0.05)=\$95,000$

Payment for 20-year loan: $PMT=\dfrac{P\left(\frac{r}{n}\right)}{1-\left(1+\frac{r}{n}\right)^{-nt}}=\dfrac{95,000\left(\frac{0.08}{12}\right)}{1-\left(1+\frac{0.08}{12}\right)^{-12(20)}}\approx\$795$

Interest for 20-year loan: $\$795(12)(20)-\$100,000=\$90,800$

Payment for 30-year loan: $PMT=\dfrac{P\left(\frac{r}{n}\right)}{1-\left(1+\frac{r}{n}\right)^{-nt}}=\dfrac{95,000\left(\frac{0.08}{12}\right)}{1-\left(1+\frac{0.08}{12}\right)^{-12(30)}}\approx\$697$

Interest for 30-year loan: $\$697(12)(30)-\$100,000=\$150,920$

The buyer saves $\$150,920-\$90,800=\$60,120$

5. Payment for 30-year 8% loan: $PMT=\dfrac{P\left(\frac{r}{n}\right)}{1-\left(1+\frac{r}{n}\right)^{-nt}}=\dfrac{150,000\left(\frac{0.08}{12}\right)}{1-\left(1+\frac{0.08}{12}\right)^{-12(30)}}\approx\$1101$

Interest for 30-year loan: $\$1101(12)(30)-\$150,000=\$246,360$

Payment for 20-year 7.5% loan: $PMT=\dfrac{P\left(\frac{r}{n}\right)}{1-\left(1+\frac{r}{n}\right)^{-nt}}=\dfrac{150,000\left(\frac{0.075}{12}\right)}{1-\left(1+\frac{0.075}{12}\right)^{-12(20)}}\approx\$1208$

Interest for 20-year loan: $\$1208(12)(20)-\$150,000=\$139,920$

The 20-year 7.5% loan is more economical. The buyer saves $\$246,360-139,920=\$106,440$

7. Payment for Mortgage A: $PMT=\dfrac{P\left(\frac{r}{n}\right)}{1-\left(1+\frac{r}{n}\right)^{-nt}}=\dfrac{120,000\left(\frac{0.07}{12}\right)}{1-\left(1+\frac{0.07}{12}\right)^{-12(30)}}\approx\$798$

Interest for Mortgage A: $\$798(12)(30)-\$120,000=\$167,280$

Points for Mortgage A: $\$120,000(0.01)=\$1200$

Cost for Mortgage A: $\$2000+\$1200+\$167,280=\$170,480$

Payment for Mortgage B: $PMT=\dfrac{P\left(\frac{r}{n}\right)}{1-\left(1+\frac{r}{n}\right)^{-nt}}=\dfrac{120,000\left(\frac{0.065}{12}\right)}{1-\left(1+\frac{0.065}{12}\right)^{-12(30)}}\approx\$758$

Interest for Mortgage B: $\$758(12)(30)-\$120,000=\$152,880$

Points for Mortgage B: $\$120,000(0.04)=\$4800$

Cost for Mortgage B: $\$1500+\$4800+\$152,880=\$159,180$

Mortgage A has the greater cost by $\$170,480-\$159,180=\$11,300$

9. a. $PMT = \dfrac{P\left(\frac{r}{n}\right)}{1-\left(1+\frac{r}{n}\right)^{-nt}} = \dfrac{120{,}000\left(\frac{0.045}{12}\right)}{1-\left(1+\frac{0.045}{12}\right)^{-12(30)}} \approx \$608$

Total interest $= \$608 \times 12 \times 30 - \$120{,}000 = \$98{,}880$

b. Interest for first month $= Prt = \$120{,}000 \times 0.045 \times \dfrac{1}{12} \approx \$450.00$

Principle payment $= \$608.00 - \$450.00 = \$158.00$

Balance of loan $= \$120{,}000 - \$158.00 = \$119{,}842.00$

Interest for second month $= Prt = \$119{,}842 \times 0.045 \times \dfrac{1}{12} \approx \$449.41$

Principle payment $= \$608.00 - \$449.41 = \$158.59$

Balance of loan $= \$119{,}842.00 - \$158.59 = \$119{,}683.41$

Interest for third month $= Prt = \$119{,}683.41 \times 0.045 \times \dfrac{1}{12} \approx \$448.81$

Principle payment $= \$608.00 - \$448.81 = \$159.19$

Balance of loan $= \$119{,}683.41 - \$159.19 = \$119{,}524.22$

Payment Number	Interest	Principal	Loan Balance
1	$450.00	$158.00	$119,842.00
2	$449.41	$158.59	$119,683.41
3	$448.81	$159.19	$119,524.22

11. Monthly gross income $= \dfrac{\$36{,}000}{12} = \$3000$

a. You should spend no more than 28% on a mortgage payment:
$28\% \times \$3000 = 0.28 \times \$3000 = \$840$

b. You should spend no more than 36% on total monthly debt:
$36\% \times \$3000 = 0.36 \times \$3000 = \$1080$

c. $\$1080 - \$840(0.70) = \$492$

23. makes sense

25. does not make sense; Explanations will vary.

27. Monthly gross income $= \dfrac{\$75{,}000}{12} \approx \$6250$

You should spend no more than 28% on a mortgage payment:
$28\% \times \$6250 = 0.28 \times \$6250 = \$1750$

$PMT = \dfrac{P\left(\frac{r}{n}\right)}{1-\left(1+\frac{r}{n}\right)^{-nt}} = \dfrac{200{,}000\left(\frac{0.055}{12}\right)}{1-\left(1+\frac{0.055}{12}\right)^{-12(30)}} \approx \$1136$

The payment of $1136 is less than the maximum of $1750. Thus, you can afford the mortgage.

Checkpoints 8.8

1. a. Make a table that shows the unpaid balance for each transaction date, the number of days at each unpaid balance, and then multiply each unpaid balance by the number of days that the balance was outstanding.

Date	Unpaid Balance	Number of Days at Each Unpaid Balance	$\begin{pmatrix}\text{Unpaid}\\ \text{Balance}\end{pmatrix}\cdot\begin{pmatrix}\text{Number}\\ \text{of Days}\end{pmatrix}$
May 1	\$8240.00	6	\$49,440.00
May 7	\$8240.00 − \$350.00 = \$7890.00	8	\$63,120.00
May 15	\$7890.00 + \$1405.00 = \$9295.00	2	\$18,590.00
May 17	\$9295.00 + \$45.20 = \$9340.20	13	\$121,422.60
May 30	\$9340.20 + \$180.72 = \$9520.92	2	\$19,041.84
		Total days: 31	Total: \$271,614.44

$$\begin{aligned}\text{Average daily balance} &= \frac{\text{Sum of unpaid balances}}{\text{Number of days in the billing period}}\\ &= \frac{\$271{,}614.44}{31}\\ &\approx \$8{,}761.76\end{aligned}$$

b.

$$\begin{aligned} I &= Prt\\ &= (\$8761.76)(0.016)(1)\\ &\approx \$140.19\end{aligned}$$

c. Balance due = \$9520.92 + \$140.19 = \$9661.11

d. Because the balance exceeds \$360, the minimum payment is $\frac{1}{36}$ of the balance due.

$$\text{Minimum Payment} = \frac{\$9661.11}{36} \approx \$269$$

Concept and Vocabulary Check 8.8

1. open-end
2. the sum of the unpaid balances for each day in the billing period; the number of days in the billing period
3. debit
4. credit report
5. 300; 850; better credit (worthiness)
6. false
7. false
8. true
9. true

Exercise Set 8.8

1. a. Make a table that shows the unpaid balance for each transaction date, the number of days at each unpaid balance, and then multiply each unpaid balance by the number of days that the balance was outstanding.

Date	Unpaid Balance	Number of Days at Each Unpaid Balance	$\begin{pmatrix}\text{Unpaid}\\\text{Balance}\end{pmatrix}\cdot\begin{pmatrix}\text{Number}\\\text{of Days}\end{pmatrix}$
March 1	\$6240.00	4	\$24,960.00
March 5	\$6240.00 − \$300.00 = \$5940.00	2	\$11,880.00
March 7	\$5940.00 + \$40.00 = \$5980.00	5	\$29,900.00
March 12	\$5980.00 + \$90.00 = \$6070.00	9	\$54,630.00
March 21	\$6070.00 + \$230.00 = \$6300.00	11	\$69,300.00
		Total days: 31	Total: \$190,670.00

$$\begin{aligned}\text{Average daily balance} &= \frac{\text{Sum of unpaid balances}}{\text{Number of days in the billing period}}\\ &= \frac{\$190{,}670.00}{31}\\ &\approx \$6150.65\end{aligned}$$

b. $$\begin{aligned} I &= Prt\\ &= (\$6150.65)(0.015)(1)\\ &\approx \$92.26\end{aligned}$$

c. Balance due $= \$6300.00 + \$92.26 = \$6392.26$

d. Because the balance exceeds \$360, the minimum payment is $\frac{1}{36}$ of the balance due.

$$\text{Minimum Payment} = \frac{\$6392.26}{36} \approx \$178$$

3. a. Make a table that shows the unpaid balance for each transaction date, the number of days at each unpaid balance, and then multiply each unpaid balance by the number of days that the balance was outstanding.

Date	Unpaid Balance	Number of Days at Each Unpaid Balance	$\begin{pmatrix}\text{Unpaid}\\\text{Balance}\end{pmatrix}\cdot\begin{pmatrix}\text{Number}\\\text{of Days}\end{pmatrix}$
June 1	\$2653.48	5	\$13,267.40
June 6	\$2653.48 − \$1000.00 = \$1653.48	2	\$3306.96
June 8	\$1653.48 + \$36.25 = \$1689.73	1	\$1689.73
June 9	\$1689.73 + \$138.43 = \$1828.16	8	\$14,625.28
June 17	\$1828.16 + \$42.36 + \$127.19 = \$1997.71	10	\$19,977.10
June 27	\$1997.71 + \$214.83 = \$2212.54	4	\$8850.16
		Total days: 30	Total: \$61,716.63

$$\begin{aligned}\text{Average daily balance} &= \frac{\text{Sum of unpaid balances}}{\text{Number of days in the billing period}}\\ &= \frac{\$61{,}716.63}{30}\\ &\approx \$2057.22\end{aligned}$$

b. $I = Prt$
$= (\$2057.22)(0.012)(1)$
$\approx \$24.69$

c. Balance due $= \$2212.54 + \$24.69 = \$2237.23$

d. Because the balance exceeds \$400, the minimum payment is $\frac{1}{25}$ of the balance due.

Minimum Payment $= \frac{\$2237.24}{25} \approx \$90$

5. a. $PMT = \frac{P\left(\frac{r}{n}\right)}{1-\left(1+\frac{r}{n}\right)^{-nt}} = \frac{4200\left(\frac{0.18}{12}\right)}{1-\left(1+\frac{0.18}{12}\right)^{-12(2)}} \approx \$210$

b. $\$210(12)(2) - \$4200 = \$840$

7. a. $PMT = \frac{P\left(\frac{r}{n}\right)}{1-\left(1+\frac{r}{n}\right)^{-nt}} = \frac{4200\left(\frac{0.105}{12}\right)}{1-\left(1+\frac{0.105}{12}\right)^{-12(3)}} \approx \$137$; This payment is lower.

b. $\$137(12)(3) - \$4200 = \$732$; This loan has less interest.

9. $PMT = \frac{P\left(\frac{r}{n}\right)}{1-\left(1+\frac{r}{n}\right)^{-nt}} = \frac{4200\left(\frac{0.18}{12}\right)}{1-\left(1+\frac{0.18}{12}\right)^{-12(1)}} \approx \$385$

Total interest: $\$385(12)(1) - \$4200 = \$420$
Additional each month: $\$385 - \$210 = \$175$
Less total interest: $\$840 - \$420 = \$420$

19. does not make sense; Explanations will vary. Sample explanation: Paying the minimum payment will cost more money in interest over the long run.

21. makes sense

23. does not make sense; Explanations will vary. Sample explanation: Very low rates on car loans typically require higher credit scores.

25. does not make sense; Explanations will vary.

Chapter 8 Review Exercises

1. $\frac{4}{5} = 4 \div 5 = 0.80 = 80\%$

2. $\frac{1}{8} = 1 \div 8 = 0.125 = 12.5\%$

3. $\frac{3}{4} = 3 \div 4 = 0.75 = 75\%$

4. $0.72 = 72\%$

5. $0.0035 = 0.35\%$

6. $4.756 = 475.6\%$

7. $65\% = 0.65$

8. $99.7\% = 0.997$

9. $150\% = 1.50$

10. $3\% = 0.03$

11. $0.65\% = 0.0065$

12. $\frac{1}{4}\% = 0.25\% = 0.0025$

13. $A = PB$
$A = 0.08 \cdot 120$
$A = 9.6$

14. a. Tax = 0.06($24) = $1.44

b. Total cost = $24 + $1.44 = $25.44

15. a. Amount of discount = 0.35($850)
= $297.50

b. Sale price = $850 – $297.50 = $552.50

16. $\frac{45-40}{40} = 0.125 = 12.5\%$ increase.

17. $\frac{\$56.00-\$36.40}{\$56.00} = 0.35 = 35\%$ decrease.

18. The statement is not true.
The 10% loss is $1000.
$[0.10 \times 10{,}000 = 1000]$
This leaves $9000.
The 10% rise is $900.
$[0.10 \times 9{,}000 = 900]$
Thus there is $9900 in the portfolio.
Find the percent of decrease:
$\frac{\text{amount of decrease}}{\text{original amount}} = \frac{100}{10{,}000} = 0.01 = 1\%$
The net loss of $100 is a 1% decrease from the original.

19. Gross income $= \$30,200 + \$130 = \$30,330$

Adjusted gross income $= \overbrace{\$30,330}^{\text{Gross income}} - \overbrace{\$1100}^{\text{Contribution}} = \$29,230$

Taxable income $= \overbrace{\$29,230}^{\text{Adj. gross income}} - \overbrace{(\$3800 + \$5950)}^{\text{Exemptions and deductions}} = \$19,480$

20. Gross income $= \$86,400 + \$350,000 = \$436,400$

Adjusted gross income $= \overbrace{\$436,400}^{\text{Gross income}} - \overbrace{\$50,000}^{\text{Contribution}} = \$386,400$

This person is entitled to a standard deduction of \$5950. However, the itemized deduction is greater than the standard deduction.

Itemized deductions $= \overbrace{\$9200}^{\text{Interest}} + \overbrace{\$95,000}^{\text{Charity}} = \$104,200$

Taxable income $= \overbrace{\$386,400}^{\text{Adj. gross income}} - \overbrace{(\$3800 + \$104,200)}^{\text{Exemptions and deductions}} = \$386,400 - \$108,000 = \$278,400$

21. Tax Computation

$$= 0.10(\$8700) + 0.15(\$35,350 - \$8700) + 0.25(\$85,650 - \$35,350) + 0.28(\$178,650 - \$85,650)$$
$$+ 0.33(\$388,350 - \$178,650) + 0.35(\$600,000 - \$388,350)$$
$$= 0.10(\$8700) + 0.15(\$26,650) + 0.25(\$50,300) + 0.28(\$93,000) + 0.33(\$209,700) + 0.35(\$211,650)$$
$$= \$870 + \$3997.50 + \$12,575 + \$26,040 + \$69,201 + \$74,077.50$$
$$= \$186,761$$

22. Tax Computation

$$= 0.10(\$17,400) + 0.15(\$70,700 - \$17,400) + 0.25(\$82,000 - \$70,700)$$
$$= 0.10(\$17,400) + 0.15(\$53,300) + 0.25(\$11,300)$$
$$= \$1740 + \$7995 + \$2825$$
$$= \$12,560$$

Income tax $= \overbrace{\$12,560}^{\text{Tax Computation}} - \overbrace{7500}^{\text{Tax credits}} = \$5060$

23. Step 1. Determine the adjusted gross income.
Adj. gross income = Gross income – Adjustments
Adj. gross income $= \$40,000 - \$2500$
$= \$37,500$

Step 2. Determine the taxable income.
Since the total deduction of \$8300 is greater than the standard deduction of \$5950, use \$8300.
Taxable inc. = Adj. gross inc– (Exempt.+Deduct.)
Taxable inc. $= \$37,500 - (\$3800 + \$8300)$
$= \$25,400$

Step 3. Determine the income tax.
Tax Computation $= 0.10(8700) + 0.15(25,400 - 8700)$
$= \$3375$

Income tax = Tax Computation – Tax credits
Income tax $= \$3375 - \$0$
$= \$3375$

24. $\text{FICA tax} = 0.0565(86,000)$
$= \$4859$

25. $\text{FICA tax} = 0.133(110,000) + 0.029(260,000 - 110,000)$
$= \$18,980$

26. **a.** $\text{Gross pay} = 16 \text{ hours} \times \dfrac{\$8.50}{\text{hour}} = \$136$

b. $\text{Federal taxes} = 10\% \times \$136 = 0.10 \times \$136 = \$13.60$

c. $\text{FICA taxes} = 5.65\% \times \$136 = 0.0565 \times \$136 \approx \$7.68$

d. $\text{State taxes} = 4\% \times \$136 = 0.04 \times \$136 = \$5.44$

e. $$\text{Net pay} = \overbrace{\$136}^{\text{Gross pay}} - \overbrace{(\$13.60 + \$7.68 + \$5.44)}^{\text{Federal, FICA, and state taxes}}$$
$= \$136 - \$26.72$
$= \$109.28$

f. Percent of gross pay withheld for taxes
$= \dfrac{\text{Taxes}}{\text{Gross pay}} = \dfrac{\$26.72}{\$136} \approx 0.196 = 19.6\%$

27. $I = Prt = (\$6000)(0.03)(1) = \$180$

28. $I = Prt = (\$8400)(0.05)(6) = \$2520$

29. $I = Prt = (\$20,000)(0.08)\left(\dfrac{9}{12}\right) = \$1200$

30. $I = Prt = (\$36,000)(0.15)\left(\dfrac{60}{360}\right) = \$900$

31. **a.** $I = Prt = (\$3500)(0.105)\left(\dfrac{4}{12}\right)$
$= \$122.50$

b. $\text{Maturity value} = \$3500 + \$122.50$
$= \$3622.50$

32. $A = P(1 + rt)$
$A = 12,000(1 + 0.082 \times \frac{9}{12})$
$A = \$12,738$

33.
$$\begin{aligned} A &= P(1+rt) \\ 5750 &= 5000(1+r(2)) \\ 5750 &= 5000+10{,}000r \\ 750 &= 10{,}000r \\ 0.075 &= r \\ r &= 7.5\% \end{aligned}$$

34.
$$\begin{aligned} A &= P(1+rt) \\ 16{,}000 &= P(1+(0.065)(3)) \\ 16{,}000 &= 1.195P \\ 13{,}389.12 &= P \\ P &= \$13{,}389.12 \end{aligned}$$

35.
$$\begin{aligned} A &= P(1+rt) \\ 12{,}000 &= P(1+(0.073)(4)) \\ 12{,}000 &= 1.292P \\ 9287.93 &= P \\ P &= \$9287.93 \end{aligned}$$

36.
$$\begin{aligned} A &= P(1+rt) \\ 1800 &= 1500\left(1+r\left(\tfrac{1}{2}\right)\right) \\ 1800 &= 1500+750r \\ 300 &= 750r \\ 0.4 &= r \\ r &= 40\% \end{aligned}$$

37. a.
$$\begin{aligned} A &= \$7000(1+0.03)^5 \\ &= \$7000(1.03)^5 \\ &\approx \$8114.92 \end{aligned}$$

b. Interest = \$8114.92 – \$7000 = \$1114.92

38. a.
$$\begin{aligned} A &= \$30{,}000\left(1+\frac{0.025}{4}\right)^{4\cdot 10} \\ &= \$30{,}000(1.00625)^{40} \\ &\approx \$38{,}490.80 \end{aligned}$$

b. Interest = \$38,490.80 – \$30,000 = \$8490.80

39. a.
$$\begin{aligned} A &= \$2500\left(1+\frac{0.04}{12}\right)^{12\cdot 20} \\ &= \$2500(1.003333)^{240} \\ &\approx \$5556.46 \end{aligned}$$

b. Interest = \$5556.46 – \$2500 = \$3056.46

40.
$$\begin{aligned} A &= P\left(1+\tfrac{r}{n}\right)^{nt} \\ A &= 14{,}000\left(1+\tfrac{0.07}{12}\right)^{12(10)} \\ &\approx \$28{,}135 \end{aligned}$$

$$\begin{aligned} A &= Pe^{rt} \\ A &= 14{,}000e^{0.0685(10)} \\ &\approx \$27{,}773 \end{aligned}$$

The 7% compounded monthly is the better investment by $\$28{,}135-\$27{,}773=\$362$.

41. $P=\dfrac{100{,}000}{\left(1+\dfrac{0.07}{12}\right)^{12\cdot 18}}\approx \$28{,}469.44$

42. $P=\dfrac{75{,}000}{\left(1+\dfrac{0.05}{4}\right)^{4\cdot 35}}\approx \$13{,}175.19$

43. a.
$$\begin{aligned} A &= \$2000\left(1+\frac{0.06}{4}\right)^{4\cdot 1} \\ &= \$2000(1.015)^4 \\ &= \$2122.73 \end{aligned}$$

b.
$$\begin{aligned} A &= P(1+rt) \\ 2122.73 &= 2000[1+r(1)] \\ 2122.73 &= 2000+2000r \\ 122.73 &= 2000r \\ 0.061365 &\approx r \\ r &\approx 6.1\% \end{aligned}$$

44. $Y=\left(1+\dfrac{0.055}{4}\right)^4-1\approx 0.0561=5.6\%$

5.5% compounded quarterly is equivalent to 5.6% compounded annually.

45. 6.25% compounded monthly:

$$Y=\left(1+\frac{0.0625}{12}\right)^{12}-1\approx 0.0643=6.4\%$$

6.3% compounded annually:

$$Y=\left(1+\frac{0.063}{1}\right)^{1}-1\approx 0.063=6.3\%$$

6.25% compounded monthly is better than 6.3% compounded annually.

46. **a.** $A=\dfrac{P\left[(1+r)^t-1\right]}{r}$

$$A=\frac{520\left[(1+0.06)^{20}-1\right]}{0.06}$$
$$\approx \$19{,}129$$

b. $\$19{,}129-20\times\$520=\$8729$

47. **a.** $A=\dfrac{P\left[\left(1+\frac{r}{n}\right)^{nt}-1\right]}{\frac{r}{n}}$

$$A=\frac{100\left[\left(1+\frac{0.055}{12}\right)^{12(30)}-1\right]}{\frac{0.055}{12}}$$
$$\approx \$91{,}361$$

b. $\$91{,}361-30\times 12\times\$100=\$55{,}361$

48. **a.** $P=\dfrac{A\left(\frac{r}{n}\right)}{\left[\left(1+\frac{r}{n}\right)^{nt}-1\right]}$

$$P=\frac{25{,}000\left(\frac{0.0725}{4}\right)}{\left[\left(1+\frac{0.0725}{4}\right)^{4(5)}-1\right]}$$
$$\approx \$1049$$

b. Deposits: $5\times 4\times\$1049=\$20{,}980$
Interest: $\$25{,}000-\$20{,}980=\$4020$

49. High = \$64.06, Low = \$26.13

50. Dividend = \$0.16(900) = \$144

51. Annual return for dividends alone = 0.3%

52. Shares traded yesterday = 5458 · 100
= 545,800 shares

53. High = \$61.25, Low = \$59.25

54. Price at close = \$61

55. Change in price = \$1.75 increase

56. Annual earnings per share $\dfrac{\$61}{41}\approx\$1.49$

59. **a.** Payment for Loan A:

$$PMT=\frac{P\left(\frac{r}{n}\right)}{1-\left(1+\frac{r}{n}\right)^{-nt}}=\frac{100{,}000\left(\frac{0.072}{12}\right)}{1-\left(1+\frac{0.072}{12}\right)^{-12(3)}}\approx\$465$$

Interest for Loan A:
$\$465(12)(3)-\$15{,}000=\$1740$

b. Payment for Loan B:

$$PMT=\frac{P\left(\frac{r}{n}\right)}{1-\left(1+\frac{r}{n}\right)^{-nt}}=\frac{100{,}000\left(\frac{0.081}{12}\right)}{1-\left(1+\frac{0.081}{12}\right)^{-12(5)}}\approx\$305$$

Interest for Loan B:
$\$305(12)(5)-\$15{,}000=\$3300$

c. The longer term has a lower monthly payment but greater total interest.

63. **a.** Annual fuel expense for the hybrid

$$=\frac{\text{annual miles driven}}{\text{miles per gallon}}\times\text{price per gallon}$$
$$=\frac{36{,}000}{40}\times\$3.60$$
$$=\$3240$$

Annual fuel expense for the SUV

$$=\frac{\text{annual miles driven}}{\text{miles per gallon}}\times\text{price per gallon}$$
$$=\frac{36{,}000}{12}\times\$3.60$$
$$=\$10{,}800$$

The difference is $\$10{,}800-\$3240=\$7560$

b. Monthly savings $=\dfrac{\$7560}{12}=\$630$

Thus, $A=\dfrac{P\left[\left(1+\frac{r}{n}\right)^{nt}-1\right]}{\frac{r}{n}}$

$$A=\frac{630\left[\left(1+\frac{0.052}{12}\right)^{12\times 6}-1\right]}{\frac{0.052}{12}}$$
$$\approx\$53{,}099$$

64. a. $\$240{,}000(0.20) = \$48{,}000$

b. $\$240{,}000 - \$48{,}000 = \$192{,}000$

c. $\$192{,}000(0.02) = \$3840$

d.
$$PMT = \frac{P\left(\frac{r}{n}\right)}{1-\left(1+\frac{r}{n}\right)^{-nt}} = \frac{192{,}000\left(\frac{0.07}{12}\right)}{1-\left(1+\frac{0.07}{12}\right)^{-12(30)}} \approx \$1277$$

e. $\$1277(12)(30) - \$192{,}000 = \$267{,}720$

65. Payment for 30-year mortgage:

$$PMT = \frac{P\left(\frac{r}{n}\right)}{1-\left(1+\frac{r}{n}\right)^{-nt}} = \frac{70{,}000\left(\frac{0.085}{12}\right)}{1-\left(1+\frac{0.085}{12}\right)^{-12(30)}} \approx \$538$$

Interest for 30-year mortgage:
$\$538(12)(30) - \$70{,}000 = \$123{,}680$

Payment for 20-year mortgage:

$$PMT = \frac{P\left(\frac{r}{n}\right)}{1-\left(1+\frac{r}{n}\right)^{-nt}} = \frac{70{,}000\left(\frac{0.08}{12}\right)}{1-\left(1+\frac{0.08}{12}\right)^{-12(20)}} \approx \$586$$

Interest for 20-year mortgage:
$\$586(12)(20) - \$70{,}000 = \$70{,}640$

The 20-year mortgage saves
$\$123{,}680 - \$70{,}640 = \$53{,}040$.

An advantage of the 30-year loan is the lower monthly payment. A disadvantage of the 30-year loan is the greater total interest.

An advantage of the 20-year loan is the lower total interest. A disadvantage of the 20-year loan is the higher monthly payment.

66. a. Payment for Mortgage A:

$$PMT = \frac{P\left(\frac{r}{n}\right)}{1-\left(1+\frac{r}{n}\right)^{-nt}} = \frac{100{,}000\left(\frac{0.085}{12}\right)}{1-\left(1+\frac{0.085}{12}\right)^{-12(30)}} \approx \$769$$

Payment for Mortgage B:

$$PMT = \frac{P\left(\frac{r}{n}\right)}{1-\left(1+\frac{r}{n}\right)^{-nt}} = \frac{100{,}000\left(\frac{0.075}{12}\right)}{1-\left(1+\frac{0.075}{12}\right)^{-12(30)}} \approx \$699$$

b. Interest for Mortgage A:
$\$769(12)(30) - \$100{,}000 = \$176{,}840$
Cost for Mortgage A:
$\$0 + \$0 + \$176{,}840 = \$176{,}840$
Interest for Mortgage B:
$\$699(12)(30) - \$100{,}000 = \$151{,}640$
Points for Mortgage B:
$\$100{,}000(0.03) = \$3000$
Cost for Mortgage B:
$\$1300 + \$3000 + \$151{,}640 = \$155{,}940$
Mortgage A has the greater cost by
$\$176{,}840 - \$155{,}940 = \$20{,}900$.

67. a.
$$PMT = \frac{P\left(\frac{r}{n}\right)}{1-\left(1+\frac{r}{n}\right)^{-nt}} = \frac{300{,}000\left(\frac{0.065}{12}\right)}{1-\left(1+\frac{0.065}{12}\right)^{-12(30)}} \approx \$1896$$

b. Interest for first month =

$$Prt = \$300{,}000 \times 0.065 \times \frac{1}{12} \approx \$1625.00$$

Principle payment =
$\$1896.00 - \$1625.00 = \$271.00$
Balance of loan =
$\$300{,}000 - \$271.00 = \$299{,}729.00$

Interest for second month =

$$Prt = \$299{,}729.00 \times 0.065 \times \frac{1}{12} \approx \$1623.53$$

Principle payment =
$\$1896.00 - \$1623.53 = \$272.47$
Balance of loan =
$\$299{,}729.00 - \$272.47 = \$299{,}456.53$

Interest for third month =

$$Prt = \$299{,}456.53 \times 0.065 \times \frac{1}{12} \approx \$1622.06$$

Principle payment =
$\$1896.00 - \$1622.06 = \$273.94$
Balance of loan =
$\$299{,}456.53 - \$273.94 = \$299{,}182.59$

Payment Number	Interest	Principal	Loan Balance
1	\$1625.00	\$271.00	\$299,729.00
2	\$1623.53	\$272.47	\$299,456.53
3	\$1622.06	\$273.94	\$299,182.59

68. Monthly gross income $= \dfrac{\$54,000}{12} = \$4500$

a. You should spend no more than 28% on a mortgage payment:
$28\% \times \$4500 = 0.28 \times \$4500 = \$1260$

b. You should spend no more than 36% on total monthly debt:
$36\% \times \$4500 = 0.36 \times \$4500 = \$1620$

c. $\$1620 - \$1260(0.80) = \$612$

71. a. Make a table that shows the unpaid balance for each transaction date, the number of days at each unpaid balance, and then multiply each unpaid balance by the number of days that the balance was outstanding.

Date	Unpaid Balance	Number of Days at Each Unpaid Balance	$\begin{pmatrix}\text{Unpaid}\\\text{Balance}\end{pmatrix}\cdot\begin{pmatrix}\text{Number}\\\text{of Days}\end{pmatrix}$
November 1	$4620.80	6	$27,724.80
November 7	$\$4620.80 - \$650.00 = \$3970.80$	4	$15,883.20
November 11	$\$3970.80 + \$350.25 = \$4,321.05$	14	$60,494.70
November 25	$\$4321.05 + \$125.70 = \$4446.75$	3	$13,340.25
November 28	$\$4446.75 + \$38.25 = \$4485.00$	3	$13,455.00
		Total days: 30	Total: $130,897.95

$$\begin{aligned}\text{Average daily balance} &= \frac{\text{Sum of unpaid balances}}{\text{Number of days in the billing period}}\\ &= \frac{\$130,897.95}{30}\\ &\approx \$4363.27\end{aligned}$$

b.
$$\begin{aligned}I &= \Pr t\\ &= (\$4363.27)(0.011)(1)\\ &\approx \$48.00\end{aligned}$$

c. Balance due $= \$4485.00 + \$48.00 = \$4533.00$

d. Because the balance exceeds \$360, the minimum payment is $\frac{1}{36}$ of the balance due.

Minimum Payment $= \dfrac{\$4533.00}{36} \approx \$126$

72. a. $PMT = \dfrac{P\left(\frac{r}{n}\right)}{1-\left(1+\frac{r}{n}\right)^{-nt}} = \dfrac{15,374\left(\frac{0.18}{12}\right)}{1-\left(1+\frac{0.18}{12}\right)^{-12(2)}} \approx \$768$

b. $\$768(12)(2) - \$15,374 = \$3058$

Chapter 8 Test

1. a. Discount = 0.15($120) = $18

b. Sale price = $120 – $18 = $102

2. $\frac{3500-2000}{2000} = 0.75 = 75\%$ increase

3. a. Gross income $= \$46,500 + \$790 = \$47,290$

b. Adjusted gross income $= \overbrace{\$47,290}^{\text{Gross income}} - \overbrace{\$1100}^{\text{Contribution}} = \$46,190$

c. Itemized deductions $= \overbrace{\$7300}^{\text{Interest}} + \overbrace{\$350}^{\text{Charity}} + \overbrace{\$1395}^{\text{State tax}} = \$9045$
This person is entitled to a standard deduction of $5950. However, the itemized deduction is greater than the standard deduction.

Taxable income $= \overbrace{\$46,190}^{\text{Adj. gross income}} - \overbrace{(\$3800 + \$9045)}^{\text{Exemptions and deductions}} = \$46,190 - \$12,845 = \$33,345$

4. Step 1. Determine the adjusted gross income.
Adj. gross income = Gross income – Adjustments
Adj. gross income $= \$36,500 - \$2000 = \$34,500$

Step 2. Determine the taxable income.
Since the total deduction of $6000 is greater than the standard deduction of $5950, use $6000.
Taxable inc. = Adj. gross inc– (Exempt.+Deduct.) $= \$34,500 - (\$3800 + \$6000) = \$24,700$

Step 3. Determine the income tax.
Tax Computation $= 0.10(8700) + 0.15(24,700 - 8700) = \$3270$
Income tax = Tax Computation – Tax credits
Income tax $= \$3270 - \$0 = \$3270$

5. FICA Tax (not self-employed):

$$\begin{aligned}\text{FICA Tax} &= \overbrace{0.0565 \times \$110,000}^{5.65\% \text{ on first } \$110,000} + \overbrace{0.0145 \times (\$150,000 - \$110,000)}^{1.45\% \text{ on income in excess of } \$110,000} \\ &= 0.0565 \times \$110,000 + 0.0145 \times \$40,000 \\ &= \$6215 + \$580 \\ &= \$6795\end{aligned}$$

6. a. Gross pay $= 15 \text{ hours} \times \frac{\$10}{\text{hour}} = \$150$

b. Federal taxes $= 10\% \times \$150 = 0.10 \times \$150 = \$15$

c. FICA taxes $= 5.65\% \times \$150 = 0.0565 \times \$150 \approx \$8.48$

d. State taxes $= 3\% \times \$150 = 0.03 \times \$150 = \$4.50$

e. $$\text{Net pay} = \underbrace{\$150}_{\text{Gross pay}} - \underbrace{(\$15+\$8.48+\$4.50)}_{\text{Federal, FICA, and state taxes}}$$
$$= \$150 - \$27.98$$
$$= \$122.02$$

f. Percent of gross pay withheld for taxes
$$= \frac{\text{Taxes}}{\text{Gross pay}} = \frac{\$27.98}{\$150} \approx 0.187 = 18.7\%$$

7. $$A = P(1+rt)$$
$$A = 2400\left(1+(0.12)\left(\tfrac{3}{12}\right)\right)$$
$$A = \$2472$$
The future value is \$2472.
The interest earned is \$72.

8. $$A = P(1+rt)$$
$$3000 = 2000(1+r(2))$$
$$3000 = 2000 + 4000r$$
$$1000 = 4000r$$
$$0.25 = r$$
$$r = 25\%$$

9. $$A = P(1+rt)$$
$$7000 = P\left(1+(0.09)\left(\tfrac{6}{12}\right)\right)$$
$$7000 = 1.045P$$
$$6698.57 = P$$
$$P = \$6698.57$$

10. $$Y = \left(1+\frac{0.045}{4}\right)^4 - 1 \approx 0.0458 = 4.58\%$$
4.5% compounded quarterly is equivalent to 4.58% compounded annually.

11. a. $$A = P\left(1+\tfrac{r}{n}\right)^{nt}$$
$$A = \$20{,}000\left(1+\tfrac{0.065}{12}\right)^{12\cdot 40}$$
$$\approx \$267{,}392$$

b. $\$267{,}392 - \$20{,}000 = \$247{,}392$

12. $$P = \frac{A}{\left(1+\frac{r}{n}\right)^{nt}}$$
$$P = \frac{\$3000}{\left(1+\frac{0.095}{2}\right)^{2(4)}}$$
$$\approx \$2070$$

13. a. $$A = P\left(1+\tfrac{r}{n}\right)^{nt}$$
$$A = 6000\left(1+\tfrac{0.065}{12}\right)^{12(5)}$$
$$\approx \$8297$$

b. $\$8297 - \$6000 = \$2297$

14. a. $$A = \frac{P\left[\left(1+\frac{r}{n}\right)^{nt} - 1\right]}{\frac{r}{n}}$$
$$A = \frac{100\left[\left(1+\frac{0.065}{12}\right)^{12(5)} - 1\right]}{\frac{0.065}{12}}$$
$$\approx \$7067$$

b. $\$7067 - \$6000 = \$1067$

c. Only part of the \$6000 is invested for the entire five years. Reasons for selecting the annuity will vary

15. $$P = \frac{A\left(\frac{r}{n}\right)}{\left[\left(1+\frac{r}{n}\right)^{nt} - 1\right]}$$
$$P = \frac{1{,}500{,}000\left(\frac{0.0625}{12}\right)}{\left[\left(1+\frac{0.0625}{12}\right)^{12(40)} - 1\right]} \approx \$704$$
$$\text{Interest} = \$1{,}500{,}000 - \$704(12)(40)$$
$$= \$1{,}162{,}080$$

16. High = \$25.75, Low = \$25.50

17. Dividend $= \$2.03 \times 1000 = \$2030$

18. Total price paid $= 600(\$25.75) = \$15{,}450$
Broker's commission $= 0.025(\$15{,}450) = \$386.25$

19. Annual fuel expense for the hybrid
$$= \frac{\text{annual miles driven}}{\text{miles per gallon}} \times \text{price per gallon}$$
$$= \frac{30{,}000}{50} \times \$3.80$$
$$= \$2280$$

Annual fuel expense for the SUV
$$= \frac{\text{annual miles driven}}{\text{miles per gallon}} \times \text{price per gallon}$$
$$= \frac{30{,}000}{15} \times \$3.80$$
$$= \$7600$$

The difference is $\$7600 - \$2280 = \$5320$

20. Down payment $= 0.10(\$120{,}000) = \$12{,}000$

21. Amount of mortgage $= \$120{,}000 - \$12{,}000$
$= \$108{,}000$

22. Two points $= 0.02(\$108{,}000) = \$2160$

23. $$PMT = \frac{P\left(\frac{r}{n}\right)}{1-\left(1+\frac{r}{n}\right)^{-nt}} = \frac{108{,}000\left(\frac{0.085}{12}\right)}{1-\left(1+\frac{0.085}{12}\right)^{-12(30)}} \approx \$830$$

24. Total cost of interest $= 360(\$830) - \$108{,}000$
$= \$190{,}800$

25. Interest for first month = $Prt = \$108{,}000 \times 0.085 \times \frac{1}{12} \approx \$765.00$
Principle payment = $\$830.00 - \$765.00 = \$65.00$
Balance of loan = $\$108{,}000 - \$65.00 = \$107{,}935.00$

Interest for second month = $Prt = \$107{,}935.00 \times 0.085 \times \frac{1}{12} \approx \$764.54$
Principle payment = $\$830.00 - \$764.54 = \$65.46$
Balance of loan = $\$107{,}935.00 - \$65.46 = \$107{,}869.54$

Payment Number	Interest	Principal	Loan Balance
1	$765.00	$65.00	$107,935.00
2	$764.54	$65.46	$107,869.54

26. Monthly gross income $= \frac{\$66{,}000}{12} = \$5500$

a. You should spend no more than 28% on a mortgage payment:
$28\% \times \$5500 = 0.28 \times \$5500 = \$1540$

b. You should spend no more than 36% on total monthly debt:
$36\% \times \$5500 = 0.36 \times \$5500 = \$1980$

c. $\$1980 - \$1540(0.90) = \$594$

27. a. Make a table that shows the unpaid balance for each transaction date, the number of days at each unpaid balance, and then multiply each unpaid balance by the number of days that the balance was outstanding.

Date	Unpaid Balance	Number of Days at Each Unpaid Balance	$\begin{pmatrix}\text{Unpaid}\\\text{Balance}\end{pmatrix}\cdot\begin{pmatrix}\text{Number}\\\text{of Days}\end{pmatrix}$
September 1	$3800.00	4	$15,200.00
September 5	$3800.00 − $800.00 = $3000.00	4	$12,000.00
September 9	$3000.00 + $40.00 = $3040.00	10	$30,400.00
September 19	$3040.00 + $160.00 = $3200.00	8	$25,600.00
September 27	$3200.00 + $200.00 = $3400.00	4	$13,600.00
		Total days: 30	Total: $96,800.00

$$\begin{aligned}\text{Average daily balance} &= \frac{\text{Sum of unpaid balances}}{\text{Number of days in the billing period}}\\ &= \frac{\$96{,}800.00}{30}\\ &\approx \$3226.67\end{aligned}$$

b. $$\begin{aligned}I &= Prt\\ &= (\$3226.67)(0.02)(1)\\ &\approx \$64.53\end{aligned}$$

c. Balance due $= \$3400.00 + \$64.53 = \$3464.53$

d. Because the balance exceeds $360, the minimum payment is $\frac{1}{36}$ of the balance due.

$$\text{Minimum Payment} = \frac{\$3464.53}{36} \approx \$97$$

28. false; Changes to make the statement true will vary.

29. true

30. false; Changes to make the statement true will vary.

31. false; Changes to make the statement true will vary

32. true

33. false; Changes to make the statement true will vary.

34. false; Changes to make the statement true will vary.

Chapter 9
Measurement

Check Points 9.1

1. a. $78 \text{ in.} = \frac{78 \cancel{\text{in.}}}{1} \cdot \frac{1 \text{ ft}}{12 \cancel{\text{in.}}} = 6.5 \text{ ft}$

b. $17{,}160 \text{ ft} = \frac{17{,}160 \cancel{\text{ft}}}{1} \cdot \frac{1 \text{ mi}}{5280 \cancel{\text{ft}}} = 3.25 \text{ mi}$

c. $3 \text{ in.} = \frac{3 \cancel{\text{in.}}}{1} \cdot \frac{1 \text{ yd}}{36 \cancel{\text{in.}}} = \frac{1}{12} \text{ yd}$

2. a. 8000 m = 8 km

b. 53 m = 53,000 mm

c. 604 cm = 0.0604 hm

d. 6.72 dam = 6720 cm

3. a. $8 \text{ ft} = \frac{8 \cancel{\text{ft}}}{1} \cdot \frac{30.48 \text{ cm}}{1 \cancel{\text{ft}}} = 243.84 \text{ cm}$

b. $20 \text{ m} = \frac{20 \cancel{\text{m}}}{1} \cdot \frac{1 \text{ yd}}{0.9 \cancel{\text{m}}} \approx 22.22 \text{ yd}$

c. 30 m = 3000 cm

$= \frac{3000 \cancel{\text{cm}}}{1} \cdot \frac{1 \text{ in.}}{2.54 \cancel{\text{cm}}}$

$\approx 1181.1 \text{ in.}$

4. $\frac{60 \text{ km}}{\text{hr}} = \frac{60 \cancel{\text{km}}}{\text{hr}} \cdot \frac{1 \text{ mi}}{1.6 \cancel{\text{km}}} = 37.5 \text{ mi/hr}$

Concept and Vocabulary Check 9.1

1. linear; linear
2. 12; 3; 36; 5280
3. unit; 1
4. 1000; 100; 10; 0.1; 0.01; 0.001
5. false
6. false
7. false
8. false

Exercise Set 9.1

1. $30 \text{ in.} = \frac{30 \cancel{\text{in.}}}{1} \cdot \frac{1 \text{ ft}}{12 \cancel{\text{in.}}} = 2.5 \text{ ft}$

3. $30 \text{ ft} = \frac{30 \cancel{\text{ft}}}{1} \cdot \frac{12 \text{ in.}}{1 \cancel{\text{ft}}} = 360 \text{ in.}$

5. $6 \text{ in.} = \frac{6 \cancel{\text{in.}}}{1} \cdot \frac{1 \text{ yd}}{36 \cancel{\text{in.}}} \approx 0.17 \text{ yd}$

7. $6 \text{ yd} = \frac{6 \cancel{\text{yd}}}{1} \cdot \frac{36 \text{ in.}}{1 \cancel{\text{yd}}} = 216 \text{ in.}$

9. $6 \text{ yd} = \frac{6 \cancel{\text{yd}}}{1} \cdot \frac{3 \text{ ft}}{1 \cancel{\text{yd}}} = 18 \text{ ft}$

11. $6 \text{ ft} = \frac{6 \cancel{\text{ft}}}{1} \cdot \frac{1 \text{ yd}}{3 \cancel{\text{ft}}} = 2 \text{ yd}$

13. $23{,}760 \text{ ft} = \frac{23{,}760 \cancel{\text{ft}}}{1} \cdot \frac{1 \text{ mi}}{5280 \cancel{\text{ft}}} = 4.5 \text{ mi}$

15. $0.75 \text{ mi} = \frac{0.75 \cancel{\text{mi}}}{1} \cdot \frac{5280 \text{ ft}}{1 \cancel{\text{mi}}} = 3960 \text{ ft}$

17. 5 m = 500 cm

19. 16.3 hm = 1630 m

21. 317.8 cm = 0.03178 hm

23. 0.023 mm = 0.000023 m

25. 2196 mm = 21.96 dm

27. $14 \text{ in.} = \frac{14 \cancel{\text{in.}}}{1} \cdot \frac{2.54 \text{ cm}}{1 \cancel{\text{in.}}} \approx 35.56 \text{ cm}$

29. $14 \text{ cm} = \frac{14 \cancel{\text{cm}}}{1} \cdot \frac{1 \text{ in.}}{2.54 \cancel{\text{cm}}} \approx 5.51 \text{ in.}$

31. $265 \text{ mi} = \frac{265 \cancel{\text{mi}}}{1} \cdot \frac{1.6 \text{ km}}{1 \cancel{\text{mi}}} \approx 424 \text{ km}$

33. $265 \text{ km} = \frac{265 \cancel{\text{km}}}{1} \cdot \frac{1 \text{ mi}}{1.6 \cancel{\text{km}}} \approx 165.625 \text{ mi}$

35. $12\text{ m} = \frac{12\cancel{\text{m}}}{1}\cdot\frac{1\text{ yd}}{0.9\cancel{\text{m}}} \approx 13.33\text{ yd}$

37. $14\text{ dm} = 140\text{ cm} = \frac{140\cancel{\text{cm}}}{1}\cdot\frac{1\text{ in.}}{2.54\cancel{\text{cm}}} \approx 55.12\text{ in.}$

39. $160\text{ in.} = \frac{160\cancel{\text{in.}}}{1}\cdot\frac{2.54\text{ cm}}{1\cancel{\text{in.}}}$
$\approx 406.4\text{ cm}$
$= 0.4064\text{ dam}$

41. $5\text{ ft} = \frac{5\cancel{\text{ft}}}{1}\cdot\frac{30.48\text{ cm}}{1\cancel{\text{ft}}} \approx 152.4\text{ cm} \approx 1.524\text{ m}$

43. $5\text{ m} = 500\text{ cm} = \frac{500\cancel{\text{cm}}}{1}\cdot\frac{1\text{ ft}}{30.48\cancel{\text{cm}}} \approx 16.40\text{ ft}$

45. $\frac{96\text{ km}}{\text{hr}} = \frac{96\cancel{\text{km}}}{\text{hr}}\cdot\frac{1\text{ mi}}{1.6\cancel{\text{km}}} \approx 60\text{ mi/hr}$

47. $\frac{45\text{ mi}}{\text{hr}} = \frac{45\cancel{\text{mi}}}{\text{hr}}\cdot\frac{1.6\text{ km}}{1\cancel{\text{mi}}} \approx 72\text{ km/hr}$

49. $5\text{ yd} = \frac{5\cancel{\text{yd}}}{1}\cdot\frac{36\cancel{\text{in.}}}{1\cancel{\text{yd}}}\cdot\frac{2.54\text{ cm}}{1\cancel{\text{in.}}} \approx 457.2\text{ cm}$

51. $762\text{ cm} = \frac{762\cancel{\text{cm}}}{1}\cdot\frac{1\cancel{\text{in.}}}{2.54\cancel{\text{cm}}}\cdot\frac{1\text{ yd}}{36\cancel{\text{in.}}} \approx 8\frac{1}{3}\text{ yd}$

53. $30\text{ mi} = \frac{30\cancel{\text{mi}}}{1}\cdot\frac{5280\cancel{\text{ft}}}{1\cancel{\text{mi}}}\cdot\frac{12\cancel{\text{in.}}}{1\cancel{\text{ft}}}\cdot\frac{2.54\cancel{\text{cm}}}{1\cancel{\text{in.}}}\cdot\frac{1\cancel{\text{m}}}{100\cancel{\text{cm}}}\cdot\frac{1\text{ km}}{1000\cancel{\text{m}}} \approx 48.28032\text{ km}$

55. $\frac{120\text{ mi}}{\text{hr}} = \frac{120\cancel{\text{mi}}}{\cancel{\text{hr}}}\cdot\frac{5280\text{ ft}}{1\cancel{\text{mi}}}\cdot\frac{1\cancel{\text{hr}}}{60\cancel{\text{min.}}}\cdot\frac{1\cancel{\text{min.}}}{60\text{ sec}} = \frac{176\text{ ft}}{1\text{ sec}} = 176\text{ ft/sec}$

57. meter

59. millimeter

61. meter

63. millimeter

65. millimeter

67. b.

69. a.

71. c.

73. a.

75. $2 \cdot 4 \cdot 27 \text{ m} = 216 \text{ m} = 0.216 \text{ km}$

77. $93 \text{ million miles} = \frac{93{,}000{,}000 \cancel{\text{mi}}}{1} \cdot \frac{1.6 \text{ km}}{1 \cancel{\text{mi}}}$
$= 148.8 \text{ million kilometers}$

79. Amazon: 6400 km

Nile: $4130 \text{ miles} = \frac{4130 \cancel{\text{mi}}}{1} \cdot \frac{1.6 \text{ km}}{1 \cancel{\text{mi}}} = 6608 \text{ km}$

Difference: $6608 - 6400 = 208$
The Nile is 208 km longer.

81. K2: 8611 meters

Everest: $29{,}035 \text{ feet} = \frac{29{,}035 \cancel{\text{ft}}}{1} \cdot \frac{30.48 \text{ cm}}{1 \cancel{\text{ft}}} \approx 884986.8 \text{ cm} = 8849.868 \text{ m} \approx 8850 \text{ m}$

Difference: $8850 - 8611 = 239$
Everest is 239 meters higher.

83. Waialeale: 451 inches

Debundscha: $10{,}280 \text{ mm} = 1028 \text{ cm} = \frac{1028 \cancel{\text{cm}}}{1} \cdot \frac{1 \text{ in.}}{2.54 \cancel{\text{cm}}} \approx 405 \text{ in.}$

Difference: $451 - 405 = 46$
Waialeale has 46 inches greater average rainfall.

93. makes sense

95. does not make sense; Explanations will vary. Sample explanation: To introduce a unit of measure when using dimensional analysis, that unit of measure should be placed in the numerator.

97. $900 \text{ m} = 9 \text{ hm}$

99. $11{,}000 \text{ mm} = 11 \text{ m}$

Check Points 9.2

1. The area is 8 square units.

2. $\frac{37{,}691{,}912 \text{ people}}{158{,}633 \text{ square miles}} \approx 237.6 \text{ people per sq. mile}$

3. $84{,}000{,}000 \text{ acres} = \frac{84{,}000{,}000 \cancel{\text{acres}}}{1} \cdot \frac{1 \text{ mi}^2}{640 \cancel{\text{acres}}} = \frac{84{,}000{,}000}{640} \text{mi}^2 = 131{,}250 \text{ mi}^2$

4. a. $1.8 \text{ acres} = \frac{1.8 \cancel{\text{acres}}}{1} \cdot \frac{0.4 \text{ ha}}{1 \cancel{\text{acre}}} = 0.72 \text{ ha}$

b. $\frac{\$415{,}000}{0.72 \text{ ha}} = \$576{,}389 \text{ per hectare}$

5. The volume is 9 cubic units.

6. $10{,}000\text{ ft}^3 = \frac{10{,}000\cancel{\text{ft}^3}}{1}\cdot\frac{7.48\text{ gal}}{1\cancel{\text{ft}^3}} = 74{,}800\text{ gal}$

7. $220{,}000\text{ cm}^3 = \frac{220{,}000\cancel{\text{cm}^3}}{1}\cdot\frac{1\text{ L}}{1000\cancel{\text{cm}^3}} = 220\text{ L}$

8. a. $1\text{ cc} = 1\text{ mL}$
So $20\text{ cc} = 20\text{ mL}$.

b. $20\text{ mL} = \frac{20\cancel{\text{mL}}}{1}\cdot\frac{1\text{ fl oz}}{30\cancel{\text{mL}}} = \frac{20}{30}\text{ fl oz} \approx 0.67\text{ fl oz}$

Concept and Vocabulary Check 9.2

1. square; cubic

2. 144; 9

3. $\frac{1\text{ mi}^2}{640\text{ acres}};\ \frac{640\text{ acres}}{1\text{ mi}^2}$

4. 2; 4

5. capacity; liter

6. area; 1

7. false

8. false

9. false

10. false

Exercise Set 9.2

1. $4\cdot 4 = 16$ square units

3. 8 square units

5. $14\text{ cm}^2 = \frac{14\cancel{\text{cm}^2}}{1}\cdot\frac{1\text{ in.}^2}{6.5\cancel{\text{cm}^2}} \approx 2.15\text{ in.}^2$

7. $30\text{ m}^2 = \frac{30\cancel{\text{m}^2}}{1}\cdot\frac{1\text{ yd}^2}{0.8\cancel{\text{m}^2}} = 37.5\text{ yd}^2$

9. $10.2\text{ ha} = \frac{10.2\cancel{\text{ha}}}{1}\cdot\frac{1\text{ acre}}{0.4\cancel{\text{ha}}} = 25.5\text{ acres}$

11. $14\text{ in.}^2 = \frac{14\cancel{\text{in.}^2}}{1}\cdot\frac{6.5\text{ cm}^2}{1\cancel{\text{in.}^2}} = 91\text{ cm}^2$

13. $2\cdot 4\cdot 3 = 24$ cubic units

15. $10{,}000\text{ ft}^3 = \frac{10{,}000\cancel{\text{ft}^3}}{1}\cdot\frac{7.48\text{ gal}}{1\cancel{\text{ft}^3}}$
$= 74{,}800\text{ gal}$

17. $8\text{ yd}^3 = \frac{8\cancel{\text{yd}^3}}{1}\cdot\frac{200\text{ gal}}{1\cancel{\text{yd}^3}} = 1600\text{ gal}$

19. $2079\text{ in.}^3 = \frac{2079\cancel{\text{in.}^3}}{1}\cdot\frac{1\text{ gal}}{231\cancel{\text{in.}^3}} = 9\text{ gal}$

21. $2700\text{ gal} = \frac{2700\cancel{\text{gal}}}{1}\cdot\frac{1\text{ yd}^3}{200\cancel{\text{gal}}} = 13.5\text{ yd}^3$

23. $45{,}000\text{ cm}^3 = \frac{45{,}000\cancel{\text{cm}^3}}{1}\cdot\frac{1\text{ L}}{1000\cancel{\text{cm}^3}} = 45\text{ L}$

25. $17\text{ cm}^3 = \frac{17\cancel{\text{cm}^3}}{1}\cdot\frac{1\cancel{\text{L}}}{1000\cancel{\text{cm}^3}}\cdot\frac{1\text{ mL}}{0.001\cancel{\text{L}}} = 17\text{ mL}$

27. $1.5\text{ L} = \frac{1.5\cancel{\text{L}}}{1}\cdot\frac{1000\text{ cm}^3}{1\cancel{\text{L}}} = 1500\text{ cm}^3$

29. $150\text{ mL} = \frac{150\cancel{\text{mL}}}{1}\cdot\frac{0.001\cancel{\text{L}}}{\cancel{\text{mL}}}\cdot\frac{1000\text{ cm}^3}{1\cancel{\text{L}}}$
$= 150\text{ cm}^3$

31. $12\text{ kL} = \frac{12\cancel{\text{kL}}}{1}\cdot\frac{1000\cancel{\text{L}}}{1\cancel{\text{kL}}}\cdot\frac{1\text{ dm}^3}{1\cancel{\text{L}}}$
$= 12{,}000\text{ dm}^3$

33. $12\text{ mL} = \frac{12\cancel{\text{mL}}}{1}\cdot\frac{1\text{ tsp}}{5\cancel{\text{mL}}} = \frac{12}{5}\text{ tsp} = 2.4\text{ tsp}$

35. $3\text{ tbsp} = \frac{3\cancel{\text{tbsp}}}{1}\cdot\frac{15\text{ mL}}{1\cancel{\text{tbsp}}} = 45\text{ mL}$

37. $70\text{ mL} \approx \frac{70\cancel{\text{mL}}}{1}\cdot\frac{1\text{ fl oz}}{30\cancel{\text{mL}}} \approx 2.33\text{ fl oz}$

39. $1.4\text{ L} \approx \frac{1.4\cancel{\text{L}}}{1}\cdot\frac{1\text{ c}}{0.24\cancel{\text{L}}} \approx 5.83\text{ c}$

41. $6\text{ pt} \approx \frac{6\cancel{\text{pt}}}{1} \cdot \frac{0.47\text{ L}}{1\cancel{\text{pt}}} \approx 2.82\text{ L}$

43. $4\text{ L} \approx \frac{4\cancel{\text{L}}}{1} \cdot \frac{1\text{ qt}}{0.95\cancel{\text{L}}} \approx 4.21\text{ qt}$

45. $3\text{ gal} \approx \frac{3\cancel{\text{gal}}}{1} \cdot \frac{3.8\text{ L}}{1\cancel{\text{gal}}} \approx 11.4\text{ L}$

47. $2000\text{ mL} \approx \frac{2000\cancel{\text{mL}}}{1} \cdot \frac{1\cancel{\text{L}}}{1000\cancel{\text{mL}}} \cdot \frac{1\text{ qt}}{0.95\cancel{\text{L}}} \approx 2.11\text{ qt}$

49. a. Population density in 1900:

$\frac{75{,}994{,}575\text{ people}}{2{,}969{,}834\text{ square miles}}$

≈ 25.6 people per square mile

Population density in 2010:

$\frac{308{,}745{,}538\text{ people}}{3{,}531{,}905\text{ square miles}}$

≈ 87.4 people per square mile

b. $\frac{87.4-25.6}{25.6} \approx 2.414 = 241.4\%$ increase

51. $\frac{131{,}669{,}275\text{ people}}{2{,}977{,}128\text{ square miles}}$

$= \frac{131{,}669{,}275\text{ people}}{2{,}977{,}128\cancel{\text{mi}^2}} \cdot \frac{1\cancel{\text{mi}^2}}{2.6\text{ km}^2}$

≈ 17.0 people per square kilometer

53. Population density in Illinois:

$\frac{12{,}869{,}257\text{ people}}{57{,}914\text{ square miles}}$

≈ 222.2 people per square mile

Population density in Ohio:

$\frac{11{,}544{,}951\text{ people}}{44{,}826\text{ square miles}}$

≈ 257.6 people per square mile

Ohio has the greater population density by 35.4 people per square mile.

55. $1{,}509{,}154\text{ acres} = \frac{1{,}509{,}154\ \cancel{\text{acres}}}{1} \cdot \frac{1\text{ m}^2}{640\ \cancel{\text{acres}}} \approx 2358\text{ m}^2$

57. **a.** $8 \text{ ha} = \frac{8 \cancel{\text{ha}}}{1} \cdot \frac{1 \text{ acre}}{0.4 \cancel{\text{ha}}} = 20 \text{ acres}$

b. $\frac{\$250,000}{20 \text{ acres}} = \$12,500 \text{ per acre}$

59. square centimeters or square meters

61. square kilometers

63. b

65. b

67. $45,000 \text{ ft}^3 = \frac{45,000 \cancel{\text{ft}^3}}{1} \cdot \frac{7.48 \text{ gal}}{1 \cancel{\text{ft}^3}}$

$= 336,600 \text{ gal}$

69. $4000 \text{ cm}^3 = \frac{4000 \cancel{\text{cm}^3}}{1} \cdot \frac{1 \text{ L}}{1000 \cancel{\text{cm}^3}} = 4 \text{ L}$

71. Philippines: $300,000 \text{ km}^2$

Japan: $145,900 \text{ mi}^2 = \frac{145,900 \cancel{\text{mi}^2}}{1} \cdot \frac{2.6 \text{ km}^2}{1 \cancel{\text{mi}^2}} \approx 379,000 \text{ km}^2$ Difference: $379,000 - 300,000 = 79,000$

Japan's area is approximately $79,000 \text{ km}^2$ greater.

73. Baffin Island: $194,574 \text{ mi}^2$

Sumatra: $443,070 \text{ km}^2 = \frac{443,070 \cancel{\text{km}^2}}{1} \cdot \frac{1 \text{ mi}^2}{2.6 \cancel{\text{km}^2}} \approx 170,412 \text{ mi}^2$

Difference: $194,574 - 170,412 = 24,162$

Sumatra's area is approximately $24,162 \text{ mi}^2$ greater.

75. **a.** $3 \text{ tsp} = \frac{3 \cancel{\text{tsp}}}{1} \cdot \frac{5 \text{ mL}}{1 \cancel{\text{tsp}}} = 15 \text{ mL}$

b. $1 \text{ mL} = 1 \text{ cc}$
So $15 \text{ mL} = 15 \text{ cc}$.

c. $15 \text{ mL} = \frac{15 \cancel{\text{mL}}}{1} \cdot \frac{1 \text{ fl oz}}{30 \cancel{\text{mL}}} = \frac{15}{30} \text{ fl oz} \approx 0.5 \text{ fl oz}$

d. $0.5 \text{ fl oz} \div 3 = \frac{0.5 \text{ fl oz}}{3} \approx 0.17 \text{ fl oz}$

83. does not make sense; Explanations will vary. Sample explanation: The capacity unit must be a measure of volume. Meters measure length.

85. makes sense

87. $\dfrac{46{,}690 \text{ people}}{1000 \text{ ha}}$

$\approx \dfrac{46{,}690 \text{ people}}{1000 \text{ ha}} \cdot \dfrac{0.4 \text{ ha}}{1 \text{ acre}} \cdot \dfrac{640 \text{ acre}}{1 \text{ square mile}}$

$\approx 11{,}952.64$ people per square mile

89. Answers will vary.

91. Approximately 6.5 liters. 6.5 mL is only a little more than a teaspoon and 6.5 kL is thousands of gallons.

Check Points 9.3

1. a. 4.2 dg = 420 mg

b. 620 cg = 6.2 g

2. $0.145 \text{ m}^3 = \dfrac{0.145 \text{ m}^3}{1} \cdot \dfrac{1000 \text{ kg}}{1 \text{ m}^3} = 145 \text{ kg}$

The water weighs 145 kg.

3. a. $120 \text{ lb} \approx \dfrac{120 \text{ lb}}{1} \cdot \dfrac{0.45 \text{ kg}}{1 \text{ lb}} \approx 54 \text{ kg}$

b. $500 \text{ g} \approx \dfrac{500 \text{ g}}{1} \cdot \dfrac{1 \text{ oz}}{28 \text{ g}} \approx 17.9 \text{ oz}$

4. First, Convert 150 pounds to kilograms.

$150 \text{ lb} \approx \dfrac{150 \text{ lb}}{1} \cdot \dfrac{0.45 \text{ kg}}{1 \text{ lb}} \approx 68 \text{ kg}$

Next, determine the dosage based on the given 6 mg/kg.

$\text{Dosage} = \dfrac{68 \text{ kg}}{1} \cdot \dfrac{6 \text{ mg}}{1 \text{ kg}} = 408 \text{ mg}$

Finally, determine the number of tablets that should be given each day.

$\text{Number of tablets} = \dfrac{408 \text{ mg}}{200 \text{ mg}} = 2.04$

The patient should receive 2 tablets daily

5. $F = \dfrac{9}{5} \cdot 50 + 32 = 122$

$50°C = 122°F$

6. $C = \dfrac{5}{9}(59 - 32) = 15$

$59°F = 15°C$

Concept and Vocabulary Check 9.3

1. 16; 2000

2. gram

3. 2.2

4. 1

5. 32; 212

6. 0; 100

7. false

8. false

9. false

10. false

Exercise Set 9.3

1. 7.4 dg = 740 mg

3. 870 mg = 0.87 g

5. 8 g = 800 cg

7. 18.6 kg = 18,600 g

9. 0.018 mg = 0.000018 g

11. $0.05 \text{ m}^3 = \dfrac{0.05 \text{ m}^3}{1} \cdot \dfrac{1000 \text{ kg}}{1 \text{ m}^3} = 50 \text{ kg}$

13. $4.2 \text{ kg} = \dfrac{4.2 \text{ kg}}{1} \cdot \dfrac{1000 \text{ cm}^3}{1 \text{ kg}} = 4200 \text{ cm}^3$

15. $1100 \text{ m}^3 = 1100 \text{ t}$

17. $0.04 \text{ kL} = \dfrac{0.04 \text{ kL}}{1} \cdot \dfrac{1000 \text{ kg}}{1 \text{ kL}} \cdot \dfrac{1000 \text{ g}}{1 \text{ kg}} = 40{,}000 \text{ g}$

19. $36 \text{ oz} = \dfrac{36 \text{ oz}}{1} \cdot \dfrac{1 \text{ lb}}{16 \text{ oz}} = 2.25 \text{ lb}$

21. $36 \text{ oz} = \dfrac{36 \text{ oz}}{1} \cdot \dfrac{28 \text{ g}}{1 \text{ oz}} = 1008 \text{ g}$

23. $540 \text{ lb} = \frac{540 \cancel{\text{lb}}}{1} \cdot \frac{0.45 \text{ kg}}{1 \cancel{\text{lb}}} = 243 \text{ kg}$

25. $80 \text{ lb} = \frac{80 \cancel{\text{lb}}}{1} \cdot \frac{0.45 \cancel{\text{kg}}}{1 \cancel{\text{lb}}} \cdot \frac{1000 \text{ g}}{1 \cancel{\text{kg}}} = 36{,}000 \text{ g}$

or $80 \text{ lb} = \frac{80 \cancel{\text{lb}}}{1} \cdot \frac{16 \cancel{\text{oz}}}{1 \cancel{\text{lb}}} \cdot \frac{28 \text{ g}}{1 \cancel{\text{oz}}} = 35{,}840 \text{ g}$

27. $540 \text{ kg} = \frac{540 \cancel{\text{kg}}}{1} \cdot \frac{1 \text{ lb}}{0.45 \cancel{\text{kg}}} = 1200 \text{ lb}$

29. $200 \text{ t} = \frac{200 \cancel{t}}{1} \cdot \frac{1 \text{ T}}{0.9 \cancel{t}} \approx 222.22 \text{ T}$

31. 10° C

$F = \frac{9}{5} \cdot 10 + 32$

10° C = 50° F

33. 35° C

$F = \frac{9}{5} \cdot 35 + 32$

35°C = 95°F

35. 57° C

$F = \frac{9}{5} \cdot 57 + 32$

57° C = 134.6°F

37. –5° C

$F = \frac{9}{5}(-5) + 32$

–5°C = 23°F

39. 68° F

$C = \frac{5}{9}(68 - 32)$

68°F = 20°C

41. 41° F

$C = \frac{5}{9}(41 - 32)$

41°F = 5°C

43. 72° F

$C = \frac{5}{9}(72 - 32)$

72°F ≈ 22.2°C

45. 23° F

$C = \frac{5}{9}(23 - 32)$

23°F = –5°C

47. 350° F

$C = \frac{5}{9}(350 - 32)$

350°F ≈ 176.7°C

49. –22° F

$C = \frac{5}{9}(-22 - 32)$

–22°F = –30°C

51. a. $m = \frac{68 - 32}{20 - 0} = \frac{36}{20} = \frac{9}{5}$

This means that the Fahrenheit temperature increases by $\frac{9}{5}^{\circ}$ for each 1° change in Celsius temperature.

b. $y = mx + b$

$F = mC + b$

$F = \frac{9}{5}C + 32$

53. milligram

55. gram

57. kilogram

59. kilogram

61. b

63. a

65. c

67. 720 g = 0.720 kg

14 – 0.720 = 13.28 kg

69. $86\text{ g}=\frac{86\not{g}}{1}\cdot\frac{1\text{ oz}}{28\not{g}}\approx 3.07\text{ oz}$

The cost will be for 4 ounces.
Cost: $44¢+3(24¢)=116¢=\$1.16$

71. $\frac{\$3.15}{3\text{ kg}}=\$1.05$ per kg for economy size
$720\text{ g}=0.72\text{ kg}$
$\frac{\$.60}{0.72\text{ kg}}=\$.83$ per kg for regular size
It is more economical to purchase the regular size.

73. First, Convert 120 pounds to kilograms.
$120\text{ lb}\approx\frac{120\not{lb}}{1}\cdot\frac{0.45\text{ kg}}{1\not{lb}}\approx 54\text{ kg}$
Next, determine the dosage based on the given 15 mg/kg.
$\text{Dosage}=\frac{54\not{kg}}{1}\cdot\frac{15\text{ mg}}{1\not{kg}}=810\text{ mg}$
Finally, determine the number of tablets that should be given each day.
$\text{Number of tablets}=\frac{810\text{ mg}}{200\text{ mg}}=4.05$
The patient should receive 4 tablets daily

75. a. $\frac{21.5\text{ mg}}{\text{tsp}}=\frac{21.5\text{ mg}}{\not{tsp}}\cdot\frac{2\not{tsp}}{1\text{ dose}}=43\text{ mg/dose}$

b. $\frac{21.5\text{ mg}}{\text{tsp}}$
$=\frac{21.5\text{ mg}}{\not{tsp}}\cdot\frac{\not{tsp}}{5\not{ml}}\cdot\frac{30\not{ml}}{1\not{oz}}\cdot\frac{4\not{oz}}{1\text{ bottle}}$
$=516\text{ mg/bottle}$

77. a

79. c

81. Berbera: 86.8°F
Néma: $F=\frac{9}{5}C+32$
$=\frac{9}{5}(30.3)+32$
$\approx 86.5°\text{F}$
Difference: $86.8-86.5=0.3$
Néma's average temperature is 0.3°F hotter.

83. Eismitte: −29.2°C
Resolute: $C=\frac{5}{9}(F-32)$
$=\frac{5}{9}(-11.6-32)$
$\approx -24.2°\text{F}$
Difference: $-24.2-(-29.2)=5$
Eismitte's average temperature is 5°C colder.

91. does not make sense; Explanations will vary. Sample explanation: 500 mg is 0.5 g.

93. makes sense

95. false; $100\text{ mg}=0.1\text{ g}=\frac{0.1\not{g}}{1}\cdot\frac{1\text{ oz}}{28\not{g}}\approx 0.0036\text{ oz}$

97. true, $4\text{ kg}=\frac{4\not{kg}}{1}\cdot\frac{1\text{ lb}}{0.45\not{kg}}\approx 8.9\text{ lb}$

99. true

101. false; $350\text{ kg}=\frac{350\not{kg}}{1}\cdot\frac{1\text{ lb}}{0.45\not{kg}}\approx 778\text{ lb}$

Chapter 9 Review Exercises

1. $69\text{ in.}=\frac{69\not{in.}}{1}\cdot\frac{1\text{ ft}}{12\not{in.}}=5.75\text{ ft}$

2. $9\text{ in.}=\frac{9\not{in.}}{1}\cdot\frac{1\text{ yd}}{36\not{in.}}=0.25\text{ yd}$

3. $21\text{ ft}=\frac{21\not{ft}}{1}\cdot\frac{1\text{ yd}}{3\not{ft}}=7\text{ yd}$

4. $13{,}200\text{ ft}=\frac{13{,}200\not{ft}}{1}\cdot\frac{1\text{ mi}}{5280\not{ft}}=2.5\text{ mi}$

5. 22.8 m = 2280 cm

6. 7 dam = 70 m

7. 19.2 hm = 1920 m

8. 144 cm = 0.0144 hm

9. 0.5 mm = 0.0005 m

10. 18 cm = 180 mm

11. $23 \text{ in.} = \frac{23 \cancel{\text{in.}}}{1} \cdot \frac{2.54 \text{ cm}}{1 \cancel{\text{in.}}} = 58.42 \text{ cm}$

12. $19 \text{ cm} = \frac{19 \cancel{\text{cm}}}{1} \cdot \frac{1 \text{ in.}}{2.54 \cancel{\text{cm}}} \approx 7.48 \text{ in.}$

13. $330 \text{ mi} = \frac{330 \cancel{\text{mi}}}{1} \cdot \frac{1.6 \text{ km}}{1 \cancel{\text{mi}}} = 528 \text{ km}$

14. $600 \text{ km} = \frac{600 \cancel{\text{km}}}{1} \cdot \frac{1 \text{ mi}}{1.6 \cancel{\text{km}}} = 375 \text{ mi}$

15. $14 \text{ m} = \frac{14 \cancel{\text{m}}}{1} \cdot \frac{1 \text{ yd}}{0.9 \cancel{\text{m}}} \approx 15.56 \text{ yd}$

16. $12 \text{ m} = \frac{12 \cancel{\text{m}}}{1} \cdot \frac{100 \cancel{\text{cm}}}{1 \cancel{\text{m}}} \cdot \frac{1 \text{ in.}}{2.54 \cancel{\text{cm}}} \cdot \frac{1 \text{ ft}}{12 \cancel{\text{in.}}} = 39.37 \text{ ft}$

17. $45 \text{ km per hour} = \frac{45 \cancel{\text{km}}}{1 \text{ hr}} \cdot \frac{1 \text{ mi}}{1.6 \cancel{\text{km}}}$
$\approx 28.13 \text{ miles/hour}$

18. $60 \text{ mi per hour} = \frac{60 \cancel{\text{mi}}}{1 \text{ hr}} \cdot \frac{1.6 \text{ km}}{1 \cancel{\text{mi}}}$
$= 96 \text{ km/hr}$

19. 0.024 km; 24,000 cm; 2400 m

20. $6 \cdot 800 \text{ m} = 4800 \text{ m} = 4.8 \text{ km}$

21. $3 \cdot 8 = 24$ square units

22. $\frac{4,425,700 \text{ people}}{268 \text{ square miles}}$
$\approx 16,513.8$ people per square mile
In Singapore there are an average of 16,513.8 people for each square mile.

23. $47,453 \text{ acres} = \frac{47,453 \cancel{\text{acres}}}{1} \cdot \frac{1 \text{ mi}^2}{640 \cancel{\text{acres}}} \approx 74 \text{ mi}^2$

24. $7.2 \text{ ha} = \frac{7.2 \cancel{\text{ha}}}{1} \cdot \frac{1 \text{ acre}}{0.4 \cancel{\text{ha}}} = 18 \text{ acres}$

25. $30 \text{ m}^2 = \frac{30 \cancel{\text{m}^2}}{1} \cdot \frac{1 \text{ ft}^2}{0.09 \cancel{\text{m}^2}} \approx 333.33 \text{ ft}^2$

26. $12 \text{ mi}^2 = \frac{12 \cancel{\text{mi}^2}}{1} \cdot \frac{2.6 \text{ km}^2}{1 \cancel{\text{mi}^2}} = 31.2 \text{ km}^2$

27. a

28. $2 \cdot 4 \cdot 3 = 24$ cubic units

29. $33,600 \text{ cubic feet} = \frac{33,600 \cancel{\text{ft}^3}}{1} \cdot \frac{7.48 \text{ gal}}{1 \cancel{\text{ft}^3}}$
$= 251,328 \text{ gal}$

30. $76,000 \text{ cm}^3 = \frac{76,000 \cancel{\text{cm}^3}}{1} \cdot \frac{1 \text{ L}}{1000 \cancel{\text{cm}^3}} = 76 \text{ L}$

31. $22 \text{ mL} \approx \frac{22 \cancel{\text{mL}}}{1} \cdot \frac{1 \text{ tsp}}{5 \cancel{\text{mL}}} \approx 4.4 \text{ tsp}$

32. $5.4 \text{ L} \approx \frac{5.4 \cancel{\text{L}}}{1} \cdot \frac{1 \text{ c}}{0.24 \cancel{\text{L}}} \approx 22.5 \text{ c}$

33. $8 \text{ L} \approx \frac{8 \cancel{\text{L}}}{1} \cdot \frac{1 \text{ qt}}{0.95 \cancel{\text{L}}} \approx 8.42 \text{ qt}$

34. $6 \text{ gal} \approx \frac{6 \cancel{\text{gal}}}{1} \cdot \frac{3.8 \text{ L}}{1 \cancel{\text{gal}}} \approx 22.8 \text{ L}$

35. **a.** $1 \text{ cc} = 1 \text{ mL}$
So $15 \text{ cc} = 15 \text{ mL}$

b. $15 \text{ mL} = \frac{15 \cancel{\text{mL}}}{1} \cdot \frac{1 \text{ fl oz}}{30 \cancel{\text{mL}}} = \frac{15}{30} \text{ fl oz} \approx 0.5 \text{ fl oz}$

36. c

37. There are $3 \times 3 = 9$ square feet in a square yard.

38. "Cubic miles" is a unit of volume, not area.

39. 12.4 dg = 1240 mg

40. 12 g = 1200 cg

41. 0.012 mg = 0.000012 g

42. 450 mg = 0.00045 kg

43. $50 \text{ kg} = \frac{50 \cancel{\text{kg}}}{1} \cdot \frac{1000 \text{ cm}^3}{1 \cancel{\text{kg}}} = 50,000 \text{ cm}^3$

44. $4 \text{ kL} = \frac{4 \cancel{\text{kL}}}{1} \cdot \frac{1000 \cancel{\text{kg}}}{1 \cancel{\text{kL}}} \cdot \frac{1 \text{ dm}^3}{1 \cancel{\text{kg}}} = 4000 \text{ dm}^3$

$4000 \text{ dm}^3 = \frac{4000 \cancel{\text{dm}^3}}{1} \cdot \frac{1000 \text{ g}}{1 \cancel{\text{dm}^3}} = 4,000,000 \text{ g}$

45. $210 \text{ lb} \approx \frac{210 \cancel{\text{lb}}}{1} \cdot \frac{0.45 \text{ kg}}{1 \cancel{\text{lb}}} \approx 94.5 \text{ kg}$

46. $392 \text{ g} \approx \frac{392 \cancel{\text{g}}}{1} \cdot \frac{1 \text{ oz}}{28 \cancel{\text{g}}} \approx 14 \text{ oz}$

47. First, Convert 220 pounds to kilograms.

$220 \text{ lb} \approx \frac{175 \cancel{\text{lb}}}{1} \cdot \frac{0.45 \text{ kg}}{1 \cancel{\text{lb}}} \approx 99 \text{ kg}$

Next, determine the dosage based on the given 12 mg/kg.

$\text{Dosage} = \frac{99 \cancel{\text{kg}}}{1} \cdot \frac{12 \text{ mg}}{1 \cancel{\text{kg}}} = 1188 \text{ mg}$

Finally, determine the number of tablets that should be given each day.

$\text{Number of tablets} = \frac{1188 \text{ mg}}{400 \text{ mg}} = 2.97$

The patient should receive 3 tablets daily

48. Kilograms; Answers will vary.

49. $36 \text{ oz} = \frac{36 \cancel{\text{oz}}}{1} \cdot \frac{1 \text{ lb}}{16 \cancel{\text{oz}}} = 2.25 \text{ lb}$

50. a

51. c

52. $\text{F}=\frac{9}{5} \cdot 15+32=59° \text{ F}$

53. $F=\frac{9}{5} \cdot 100+32=212° \text{ F}$

54. $F=\frac{9}{5} \cdot 5+32=41° \text{F}$

55. $F=\frac{9}{5} \cdot 0+32=32° \text{ F}$

56. $-F=\frac{9}{5}(-25)+32=-13° \text{ F}$

57. $C=\frac{5}{9}(59-32)=15° \text{ C}$

58. $C=\frac{5}{9}(41-32)=5° \text{C}$

59. $C=\frac{5}{9}(212-32)=100° \text{ C}$

60. $C=\frac{5}{9}(98.6-32)=37° \text{ C}$

61. $C=\frac{5}{9}(0-32) \approx -17.8° \text{C}$

62. $C=\frac{5}{9}(14-32)=-10° \text{ C}$

63. A decrease of $15°C$ is more than a decrease of $15°F$; Explanations will vary.

Chapter 9 Test

1. 807 mm = 0.00807 hm

2. $635 \text{ cm} = \frac{635 \cancel{\text{cm}}}{1} \cdot \frac{1 \text{ in.}}{2.54 \cancel{\text{cm}}} = 250 \text{ in.}$

3. $8 \cdot 600 \text{ m} = 4800 \text{ m} = 4.8 \text{ km}$

4. mm

5. cm

6. km

7. $80 \text{ miles per hour} = \frac{80 \cancel{\text{mi}}}{1 \text{ hr}} \cdot \frac{1.6 \text{ km}}{1 \cancel{\text{mi}}}$

$= 128 \text{ km/hr}$

8. $1 \text{ yd}^2 = (3 \text{ ft})(3 \text{ ft}) = 9 \text{ ft}^2$

A square yard is 9 times greater than a square foot.

9. $\frac{20{,}090{,}400 \text{ people}}{2{,}967{,}908 \text{ square miles}}$

≈ 6.8 people per square mile

In Australia, there is an average of 6.8 people for each square mile.

10. $18 \text{ ha} = \frac{18 \cancel{\text{ha}}}{1} \cdot \frac{1 \text{ acre}}{0.4 \cancel{\text{ha}}} = 45 \text{ acres}$

11. b

12. Answers will vary.

$1 \text{ m}^3 = (10 \text{ dm})(10 \text{ dm})(10 \text{ dm}) = 1000 \text{ dm}^3$

A cubic meter is 1000 times greater than a cubic decimeter.

13. $16 \text{ tbsp} = \frac{16 \text{ tbsp}}{1} \cdot \frac{15 \text{ mL}}{1 \text{ tbsp}} \cdot \frac{1 \text{ fl oz}}{30 \text{ mL}} = 8 \text{ fl oz}$

14. $10{,}000 \text{ ft}^3 = \frac{10{,}000 \text{ ft}^3}{1} \cdot \frac{7.48 \text{ gal}}{1 \text{ ft}^3}$

$= 74{,}800 \text{ gal}$

15. b

16. $137 \text{ g} = 0.137 \text{ kg}$

17. First, Convert 130 pounds to kilograms.

$130 \text{ lb} \approx \frac{120 \text{ lb}}{1} \cdot \frac{0.45 \text{ kg}}{1 \text{ lb}} \approx 59 \text{ kg}$

Next, determine the dosage based on the given 10 mg/kg.

$\text{Dosage} = \frac{59 \text{ kg}}{1} \cdot \frac{10 \text{ mg}}{1 \text{ kg}} = 590 \text{ mg}$

Finally, determine the number of tablets that should be given each day.

$\text{Number of tablets} = \frac{590 \text{ mg}}{200 \text{ mg}} = 2.95$

The patient should receive 3 tablets daily

18. kg

19. mg

20. $F = \frac{9}{5} \cdot 30 + 32 = 86° \text{ F}$

21. $C = \frac{5}{9}(176 - 32) = 80°\text{C}$

22. d

Chapter 10
Geometry

Check Points 10.1

1. Hand moves $\frac{1}{12}$ of a rotation

$\frac{1}{12} \cdot 360° = 30°$

2. $90° - 19° = 71°$

3. $m\measuredangle DBC + m\measuredangle ABD = 180°$

$$x + (x + 88°) = 180°$$
$$2x + 88° = 180°$$
$$2x = 92°$$
$$x = 46°$$

Thus, $m\measuredangle DBC = 46°$ and $m\measuredangle ABD = 134°$

4. $m\measuredangle 1 = 57°$
$m\measuredangle 2 = 180° - 57° = 123°$
$m\measuredangle 3 = m\measuredangle 2 = 123°$

5. $m\measuredangle 1 = m\measuredangle 8 = 29°$
$m\measuredangle 5 = m\measuredangle 8 = 29°$
$m\measuredangle 2 = m\measuredangle 8 = 29°$
$m\measuredangle 6 = 180° - m\measuredangle 8 = 180° - 29° = 151°$
$m\measuredangle 7 = m\measuredangle 6 = 151°$
$m\measuredangle 3 = m\measuredangle 7 = 151°$
$m\measuredangle 4 = m\measuredangle 3 = 151°$

Concept and Vocabulary Check 10.1

1. line; half-line; ray; line segment

2. acute; right; obtuse; straight

3. complementary; supplementary

4. vertical

5. parallel; transversal;

6. perpendicular

7. false

8. false

9. false

10. false

11. true

12. true

Exercise Set 10.1

1. Hand moves $\frac{5}{12}$ of a rotation

$\frac{5}{12} \cdot 360° = 150°$

3. Hand moves $\frac{4-1}{12} = \frac{3}{12} = \frac{1}{4}$ of a rotation

$\frac{1}{4} \cdot 360° = 90°$

5. $20°$ is acute.

7. $160°$ is obtuse.

9. $180°$ is straight.

11. $90° - 25° = 65°$

13. $180° - 34° = 146°$

15. Complement:
$90° - 48° = 42°$
Supplement:
$180° - 48° = 132°$

17. Complement:
$90° - 89° = 1°$
Supplement:
$180° - 89° = 91°$

19. Complement:
$90° - 37.4° = 52.6°$
Supplement:
$180° - 37.4° = 142.6°$

21. Let x = the measure of the angle's complement.
Then $x+12°$ represents the angle.
$$x+(x+12°)=90°$$
$$2x+12°=90°$$
$$2x=78°$$
$$x=39°$$
$$x+12°=51°$$
The complements are $39°$ and $51°$.

23. Let x = the measure of the angle's supplement.
Then $3x$ represents the angle.
$$x+3x=180°$$
$$4x=180°$$
$$x=45°$$
$$3x=135°$$
The supplements are $45°$ and $135°$.

25. $m\measuredangle 1=180°-72°=108°$
$m\measuredangle 2=72°$
$m\measuredangle 3=m\measuredangle 1=108°$

27. $m\measuredangle 1=90°-40°=50°$
$m\measuredangle 2=90°$
$m\measuredangle 3=m\measuredangle 1=50°$

29. $m\measuredangle 1=180°-112°=68°$
$m\measuredangle 2=m\measuredangle 1=68°$
$m\measuredangle 3=112°$
$m\measuredangle 4=112°$
$m\measuredangle 5=m\measuredangle 1=68°$
$m\measuredangle 6=m\measuredangle 2=68°$
$m\measuredangle 7=m\measuredangle 3=112°$

31. $m\measuredangle 1=38°$
$m\measuredangle 2=90°-38°=52°$
$m\measuredangle 3=180°-38°=142°$

33. $m\measuredangle 1=65°$
$$m\measuredangle 2=180°-m\measuredangle 1-59°$$
$$=180°-65°-59°$$
$$=56°$$
$$m\measuredangle 3=m\measuredangle 1+59°$$
$$=65°+59°$$
$$=124°$$

35. false; Changes to make the statement true will vary.
A sample change is: $m\measuredangle 2=53°$

37. true

39. false; Changes to make the statement true will vary.
A sample change is: $m\measuredangle 1=108°$

41. false; Changes to make the statement true will vary.
A sample change is: $m\measuredangle 2=108°$

43. The two angles are complementary.
$$(2x+50°)+(4x+10°)=90°$$
$$6x+60°=90°$$
$$6x=30°$$
$$x=5°$$
Angle 1: $2x+50°=2(5°)+50°=60°$
Angle 2: $4x+10°=4(5°)+10°=30°$

45. The two angles are equal.
$$11x-20°=7x+28°$$
$$4x=48°$$
$$x=12°$$
Angle 1: $11x-20°=11(12°)-20°=112°$
Angle 2: $7x+28°=7(12°)+28°=112°$

47. $\overline{AC}\cap\overline{BD}=\overline{BC}$

49. $\overline{AC}\cup\overline{BD}=\overline{AD}$

51. $\overrightarrow{BA}\cup\overrightarrow{BC}=\overleftrightarrow{AD}$

53. $\overline{AD}\cap\overrightarrow{BD}=\overline{AD}$

55. $\dfrac{360°}{8}=45°$

57. When two parallel lines are intersected by a transversal, corresponding angles have the same measure.

59. E, F, H, and T contain perpendicular line segments.

61. long-distance riding and mountain biking

63. $116°-89°=27°$

73. does not make sense; Explanations will vary. Sample explanation: Two distinct lines cannot intersect twice.

75. does not make sense; Explanations will vary. Sample explanation: Two angles can be neither complementary nor supplementary.

77. d, since $m\measuredangle 1=m\measuredangle 4$ and $m\measuredangle 4+m\measuredangle 5=90°$, then $m\measuredangle 1+m\measuredangle 5=90°$

Check Points 10.2

1. $m\angle A + 116° + 15° = 180°$
$m\angle A + 131° = 180°$
$m\angle A = 180° - 131°$
$m\angle A = 49°$

2. $m\angle 1 = 180° - 90° = 90°$
$m\angle 2 = 180° - 36° - m\angle 1$
$= 180° - 36° - 90°$
$= 54°$
$m\angle 3 = m\angle 2 = 54°$
$m\angle 4 = 180° - 58° - m\angle 3$
$= 180° - 58° - 54°$
$= 68°$
$m\angle 5 = 180° - m\angle 4$
$= 180° - 68°$
$= 112°$

3. Two angles of the small triangle are equal in measure to two angles of the large triangle. One angle pair is given to have the same measure (right angles). Another angle pair consists of vertical angles with the same measure.
Corresponding sides are proportional.
$\frac{8}{12} = \frac{10}{x}$
$8 \cdot x = 10 \cdot 12$
$8x = 120$
$\frac{8x}{8} = \frac{120}{8}$
$x = 15 \text{ cm}$

4. $\frac{h}{2} = \frac{56}{3.5}$
$3.5 \cdot h = 2 \cdot 56$
$3.5h = 112$
$\frac{3.5h}{3.5} = \frac{112}{3.5}$
$h = 32 \text{ yd}$

5. $c^2 = a^2 + b^2$
$c^2 = 7^2 + 24^2$
$c^2 = 49 + 576$
$c^2 = 625$
$c = \sqrt{625}$
$c = 25 \text{ ft}$

6. $a^2 + b^2 = c^2$
$a^2 + (50)^2 = (130)^2$
$a^2 + 2500 = 16,900$
$a^2 = 14,400$
$a = \pm 120$
–120 must be rejected.
The tower is 120 yards tall.

Concept and Vocabulary Check 10.2

1. 180°

2. acute

3. obtuse

4. isosceles

5. equilateral

6. scalene

7. similar; the same measure; proportional

8. right; legs; the square of the length of the hypotenuse

9. true

10. true

11. false

12. false

13. false

Exercise Set 10.2

1. $m\angle A = 180° - 46° - 67° = 67°$

3. $m\angle A = 180° - 58° - 90° = 32°$

5. $= 50 \text{ yd} \cdot 30 \text{ yd} \cdot 14 \text{ yd} = 21,000 \text{ yd}^3$
$m\angle 2 = 180° - m\angle 1 = 180° - 50° = 130°$
$m\angle 3 = m\angle 1 = 50°$
$m\angle 4 = m\angle 2 = 130°$
$m\angle 5 = 180° - 80° - m\angle 3$
$= 180° - 80° - 50°$
$= 50°$

7. $m\measuredangle 1 = 180° - 130° = 50°$
$m\measuredangle 2 = m\measuredangle 1 = 50°$
$m\measuredangle 3 = 180° - m\measuredangle 1 - m\measuredangle 2$
$= 180° - 50° - 50°$
$= 80°$
$m\measuredangle 4 = 180° - m\measuredangle 2 = 180° - 50° = 130°$
$m\measuredangle 5 = m\measuredangle 4 = 130°$

9. $m\measuredangle 1 = 55°$
$m\measuredangle 1 + m\measuredangle 2 = 120°$
$55° + m\measuredangle 2 = 120°$
$m\measuredangle 2 = 65°$
$m\measuredangle 1 + m\measuredangle 2 + m\measuredangle 3 = 180°$
$55° + 65° + m\measuredangle 3 = 180°$
$m\measuredangle 3 = 60°$
$m\measuredangle 4 = m\measuredangle 2 = 65°$
$m\measuredangle 5 = m\measuredangle 3 = 60°$
$m\measuredangle 6 = 120°$
$m\measuredangle 7 = m\measuredangle 3 = 60°$
$m\measuredangle 8 = m\measuredangle 7 = 60°$
$m\measuredangle 9 = m\measuredangle 1 = 55°$
$m\measuredangle 10 = m\measuredangle 9 = 55°$

11. The three angles of the large triangle are given to have the same measures as the three angles of the small triangle.
$\frac{18}{9} = \frac{10}{x}$
$18 \cdot x = 9 \cdot 10$
$18x = 90$
$\frac{18x}{18} = \frac{90}{18}$
$x = 5$ in.

13. Two angles of the large triangle are given to have the same measures as two angles of the small triangle.
$\frac{30}{10} = \frac{18}{x}$
$30 \cdot x = 10 \cdot 18$
$30x = 180$
$\frac{30x}{30} = \frac{180}{30}$
$x = 6$ m

15. One angle pair is given to have the same measure (right angles). Another angle pair consists of vertical angles with the same measure.
$\frac{20}{15} = \frac{x}{12}$
$15x = 20 \cdot 12$
$15x = 240$
$\frac{15x}{15} = \frac{240}{15}$
$x = 16$ in.

17. Let $x = \overline{CA}$
$\frac{CA}{EA} = \frac{BC}{DE}$
$\frac{x}{15} = \frac{3}{9}$
$9x = 3 \cdot 15$
$9x = 45$
$x = 5$
$\overline{CA} = 5$

19. Let $x = \overline{DA}$
$\frac{DA}{BA} = \frac{DE}{BC}$
$\frac{x}{3} = \frac{9}{3}$
$x = 9$
$\overline{DA} = 9$

21. $c^2 = 8^2 + 15^2$
$c^2 = 64 + 225$
$c^2 = 289$
$c = 17$ m

23. $c^2 = 15^2 + 36^2$
$c^2 = 225 + 1296$
$c^2 = 1521$
$c = 39$ m

25. $a^2 + 16^2 = 20^2$
$a^2 + 256 = 400$
$a^2 = 144$
$a = 12$ cm

27. congruent; SAS

29. congruent; SSS

31. congruent; SAS

33. not necessarily congruent

35. congruent; ASA

37. Let x = height of tree.

$$\frac{x}{5}=\frac{86}{6}$$
$$6\cdot x=5\cdot 86$$
$$6x=430$$
$$x\approx 71.7 \text{ ft}$$

39. Let x = distance from home to second base.

$$x^2=90^2+90^2$$
$$x^2=8100+8100$$
$$x^2=16,200$$
$$x\approx 127.3 \text{ ft}$$

41. Let x = the length of each cable.
Let $3x$ = the total length of the 3 cables.

$$x^2=9^2+(16-4)^2$$
$$x^2=81+144$$
$$x^2=225$$
$$x=15 \text{ yd}$$
$$3x=45 \text{ yd}$$

43. Let x = the length of the diagonal.

$$x^2=5^2+12^2$$
$$x^2=25+144$$
$$x^2=169$$
$$x=13 \text{ ft}$$

45. Let c = the length of the new road.

$$c^2=3000^2+4000^2$$
$$c^2=9,000,000+16,000,000$$
$$c^2=25,000,000$$
$$c=5000 \text{ m}$$
$$c=5 \text{ km}$$

Thus, the cost is $5\times\$150,000=\$750,000$

57. makes sense

59. does not make sense; Explanations will vary. Sample explanation: The Pythagorean Theorem can only apply to right triangles.

61. Let x = the left portion of $\overline{AB}$
Let y = the right portion of $\overline{AB}$

$$x^2+12^2=13^2$$
$$x^2+144=169$$
$$x^2=25$$
$$x=5 \text{ ft}$$

$$y^2+12^2=20^2$$
$$y^2+144=400$$
$$y^2=256$$
$$y=16 \text{ ft}$$
$$\overline{AB}=x+y=5+16=21 \text{ ft}$$

Check Points 10.3

1. Note: 50 yds equals 150 ft and 30 yds equals 90 ft

$$P=2l+2w$$
$$P=2\cdot 150 \text{ ft}+2\cdot 90 \text{ ft}=480 \text{ ft}$$
$$\text{Cost}=\frac{480\,\text{feet}}{1}\cdot\frac{\$6.50}{\text{foot}}=\$3120$$

2. a.
$$\text{Sum}=(n-2)180^\circ$$
$$=(12-2)\,180^\circ$$
$$=10\cdot 180^\circ$$
$$=1800^\circ$$

b. $m\measuredangle A=\dfrac{1800^\circ}{12}=150^\circ$

3. Each angle is $\dfrac{(n-2)\,180^\circ}{n}=\dfrac{(8-2)\,180^\circ}{8}=135^\circ$
Regular octagons cannot be used to create a tessellation because 360° is not a multiple of 135°.

Concept and Vocabulary Check 10.3

1. perimeter

2. quadrilateral; pentagon; hexagon; heptagon; octagon

3. regular

4. equal in measure; parallel

5. rhombus

6. rectangle

7. square

8. trapezoid

9. $P = 2l + 2w$

10. $(n-2)180°$

11. tessellation

12. false

13. true

14. true

15. true

16. false

17. false

18. true

Exercise Set 10.3

1. Quadrilateral (4 sides)

3. Pentagon (5 sides)

5. a (square), b (rhombus), d (rectangle), and e (parallelogram) all have two pairs of parallel sides.

7. a (square), d (rectangle)

9. c (trapezoid)

11. $P = 2 \cdot 3 \text{ cm} + 2 \cdot 12 \text{ cm}$
$= 6 \text{ cm} + 24 \text{ cm}$
$= 30 \text{ cm}$

13. $P = 2 \cdot 6 \text{ yd} + 2 \cdot 8 \text{ yd}$
$= 12 \text{ yd} + 16 \text{ yd}$
$= 28 \text{ yd}$

15. $P = 4 \cdot 250 \text{ in.} = 1000 \text{ in.}$

17. $P = 9 \text{ ft} + 7 \text{ ft} + 11 \text{ ft} = 27 \text{ ft}$

19. $P = 3 \cdot 6 \text{ yd} = 18 \text{ yd}$

21. $P = 12 \text{ yd} + 12 \text{ yd} + 9 \text{ yd} + 9 \text{ yd} + 21 \text{ yd} + 21 \text{ yd}$
$= 84 \text{ yd}$

23. First determine lengths of unknown sides.

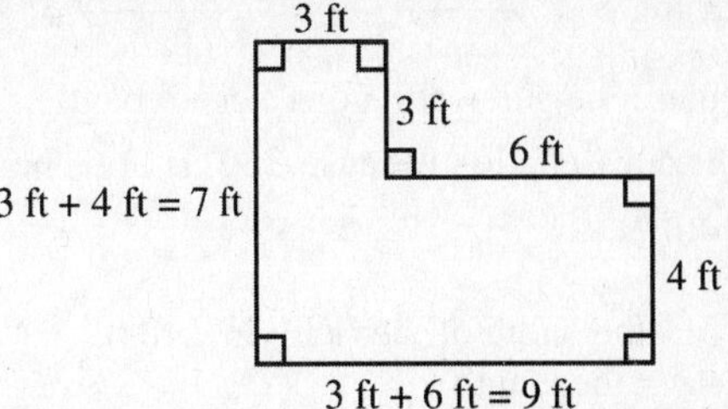

$P = 3 \text{ ft} + 3 \text{ ft} + 6 \text{ ft} + 4 \text{ ft} + 9 \text{ ft} + 7 \text{ ft} = 32 \text{ ft}$

25. Sum $= (n-2)180°$
$= (5-2)\,180°$
$= 3 \cdot 180°$
$= 540°$

27. Sum$=(n-2)180°$
$= (4-2)180°$
$= 2 \cdot 180°$
$= 360°$

29. From Exercise 25, we know the sum of the measures of the angles of a pentagon is 540°. Since all 5 angles have the same degree measure, $m\measuredangle A = \frac{540°}{5} = 108°$.
$m\measuredangle B = 180° - 108° = 72°$

31. **a.** From Exercise 25, we know the sum of the measures of the angles of a pentagon is 540°.

b. $m\measuredangle A = 540° - 70° - 150° - 90° - 90° = 140°$ and $m\measuredangle B = 180° - 140° = 40°$

33. **a.** squares, hexagons, dodecagons

b. The 3 angles that come together are $90°$, $120°$, and $150°$.

c. The tessellation is possible because $90° + 120° + 150° = 360°$.

35. **a.** triangles, hexagons

b. The 4 angles that come together are $60°$, $60°$, $120°$, and $120°$.

c. The tessellation is possible because $60° + 60° + 120° + 120° = 360°$.

37. Each angle is $\frac{(n-2)\,180°}{n} = \frac{(9-2)\,180°}{9} = 140°$

Regular nine-sided polygons can not be used to create a tessellation because 360° is not a multiple of 140°.

39. Let w = the width of the field (in yards).
Let $4w$ = the length.
The perimeter of a rectangle is twice the width plus twice the length, so $2w+2(4w)=500$

$$2w+8w=500$$
$$10w=500$$
$$w=50$$

The width is 50 yards and the length is 4(50) = 200 yards. This checks because 2(50) + 2(200) = 500.

41. Let w = the width of a football field (in feet).
Let w + 200 = the length.

$$2w+2(w+200)=1040$$
$$2w+2w+400=1040$$
$$4w+400=1040$$
$$4w=640$$
$$w=160$$

The width 160 feet and the length is 160 + 200 = 360 feet. This checks because 2(160) + 2(200) = 720.

43. $x+x+(x+5°)+(x+5°)+120°+130°=(6-2)180°$

$$4x+260°=720°$$
$$4x=460°$$
$$x=115°$$
$$x+5°=120°$$

The angles are 115°, 115°, 120°, and 120°.

45. $\frac{(8-2)180°}{8}+\frac{(6-2)180°}{6}+\frac{(5-2)180°}{5}=363°$

If the polygons were all regular polygons, the sum would be 363°. The tessellation is fake because the sum is not 360°.

47. $P = 2 \cdot 400 \text{ ft} + 2 \cdot 200 \text{ ft}$
$= 800 \text{ ft} + 400 \text{ ft}$
$= 1200 \text{ ft}$

$$\text{Cost} = \frac{1200\,\text{ft}}{1}\cdot\frac{1\,\text{yd}}{3\,\text{ft}}\cdot\frac{\$14}{1\,\text{yd}} = \$5600$$

49. Since the side of the square is 8 ft, its perimeter is 32 ft.
32 ft. is equivalent to 384 inches.
Thus, the total number of
flowers $=\frac{384}{8}=48$ flowers.

59. makes sense

61. does not make sense; Explanations will vary. Sample explanation: A tessellation cannot be created using only regular pentagons.

63. All sides have length a, therefore $P = 6a$.

Check Points 10.4

1. Area of large rectangle:

$$A_{\text{large}} = lw$$
$$= (13 \text{ ft}+3 \text{ ft})\times(3 \text{ ft}+6 \text{ ft})$$
$$= 16 \text{ ft}\cdot 9 \text{ ft}$$
$$= 144 \text{ ft}^2$$

Area of small rectangle:

$$A_{\text{small}} = lw$$
$$= 13 \text{ ft}\cdot 6 \text{ ft}$$
$$= 78 \text{ ft}^2$$

Area of path = $144 \text{ ft}^2 - 78 \text{ ft}^2 = 66 \text{ ft}^2$

2. First convert the linear measures in feet to linear yards.

$$18 \text{ ft} = \frac{18\,\text{ft}}{1}\cdot\frac{1\text{ yd}}{3\,\text{ft}} = 6 \text{ yd}$$

$$21 \text{ ft} = \frac{21\,\text{ft}}{1}\cdot\frac{1\text{ yd}}{3\,\text{ft}} = 7 \text{ yd}$$

Area of floor $= 6 \text{ yd}\cdot 7 \text{ yd} = 42 \text{ yd}^2$

$$\text{Cost of carpet} = \frac{42\,\text{yd}^2}{1}\cdot\frac{\$16}{1\,\text{yd}^2} = \$672$$

3. $A = bh$

$A = 10 \text{ in.}\cdot 6 \text{ in.} = 60 \text{ in.}^2$

4. $A = \frac{1}{2}bh$

$A = \frac{1}{2}\cdot 12 \text{ ft}\cdot 5 \text{ ft} = 30 \text{ ft}^2$

5. $A = \frac{1}{2}h(a+b)$
$= \frac{1}{2} \cdot 7 \text{ ft} \cdot (20 \text{ ft} + 10 \text{ ft})$
$= \frac{1}{2} \cdot 7 \text{ ft} \cdot 30 \text{ ft}$
$= 105 \text{ ft}^2$

6. $C = \pi d$
$= \pi(10 \text{ in.})$
$= 10\pi \text{ in.}$
$\approx 31.4 \text{ in.}$

7. Find the circumference of the semicircle:
$C_{\text{semicircle}} = \frac{1}{2}\pi d$
$\approx \frac{1}{2}\pi(10 \text{ ft})$
$\approx 15.7 \text{ ft}$
Length of trim $= 10 \text{ ft} + 12 \text{ ft} + 12 \text{ ft} + 15.7 \text{ ft}$
$= 49.7 \text{ ft}$

8. First, find the area of pizzas.

Large:	Medium:
$A = \pi r^2$	$A = \pi r^2$
$= \pi(9 \text{ in.})^2$	$= \pi(7 \text{ in.})^2$
$= 81\pi \text{ in.}^2$	$= 49\pi \text{ in.}^2$
$\approx 254 \text{ in.}^2$	$\approx 154 \text{ in.}^2$

Next, find the price per square inch.

Large:	Medium:
$\frac{\$20.00}{81\pi \text{ in.}^2}$	$\frac{\$14.00}{49\pi \text{ in.}^2}$
$\approx \frac{\$20.00}{254 \text{ in.}^2}$	$\approx \frac{\$14.00}{154 \text{ in.}^2}$
$\approx \frac{\$0.08}{\text{in.}^2}$	$\approx \frac{\$0.09}{\text{in.}^2}$

The large pizza is a better buy.

Concept and Vocabulary Check 10.4

1. $A = lw$

2. $A = s^2$

3. $A = bh$

4. $A = \frac{1}{2}bh$

5. $A = \frac{1}{2}h(a+b)$

6. $C = \pi d$

7. $C = 2\pi r$

8. $A = \pi r^2$

9. false

10. true

11. true

12. false

13. true

Exercise Set 10.4

1. $A = 6 \text{ m} \cdot 3 \text{ m} = 18 \text{ m}^2$

3. $A = (4 \text{ in.})^2 = 16 \text{ in.}^2$

5. $A = 50 \text{ cm} \cdot 42 \text{ cm} = 2100 \text{ cm}^2$

7. $A = \frac{1}{2} \cdot 14 \text{ in.} \cdot 8 \text{ in.} = 56 \text{ in.}^2$

9. $A = \frac{1}{2} \cdot 9.8 \text{ yd} \cdot 4.2 \text{ yd} = 20.58 \text{ yd}^2$

11. $a^2 + b^2 = c^2$
$h^2 + 12^2 = 13^2$
$h^2 + 144 = 169$
$h^2 = 25$
$h = 5$
$A = \frac{1}{2} \cdot 12 \text{ in.} \cdot 5 \text{ in.} = 30 \text{ in.}^2$

13. $A = \frac{1}{2} \cdot 18 \text{ m} \cdot (37 \text{ m} + 26 \text{ m})$
$= 9 \text{ m}(63 \text{ m})$
$= 567 \text{ m}^2$

15. $C = 2\pi \cdot 4 \text{ cm} = 8\pi \text{ cm} \approx 25.1 \text{ cm}$
$A = \pi(4 \text{ cm})^2 = 16\pi \text{ cm}^2 \approx 50.3 \text{ cm}^2$

17. $C = \pi \cdot 12 \text{ yd} = 12\pi \text{ yd} \approx 37.7 \text{ yd}$

$r = \frac{d}{2} = \frac{12 \text{ yd}}{2} = 6 \text{ yd}$

$A = \pi(6 \text{ yd})^2 = 36\pi \text{ yd}^2 \approx 113.1 \text{ yd}^2$

19. The figure breaks into a lower rectangle and an upper rectangle.

Area of lower rectangle:
$A = lw$
$A = (12 \text{ m})(3 \text{ m})$
$A = 36 \text{ m}^2$

Area of upper rectangle:
$A = lw$
$A = (9 \text{ m})(4 \text{ m})$
$A = 36 \text{ m}^2$

Total area $= 36 \text{ m}^2 + 36 \text{ m}^2 = 72 \text{ m}^2$

21. The figure breaks into a lower rectangle and an upper triangle.

Area of rectangle:
$A = lw$
$A = (24 \text{ m})(10 \text{ m})$
$A = 240 \text{ m}^2$

Area of triangle:
$A = \frac{1}{2}bh$
$A = \frac{1}{2}(24 \text{ m})(5 \text{ m})$
$A = 60 \text{ m}^2$

Total area $= 240 \text{ m}^2 + 60 \text{ m}^2 = 300 \text{ m}^2$

23. The figure's area can be obtained by adding the area of a square of side 10 cm, to twice the area of a circle of radius 5 cm.

Area of square:
$A = s^2$
$A = (10 \text{ cm})^2$
$A = 100 \text{ cm}^2$

Area of circles:
$A = \pi r^2$
$A = \pi(5 \text{ cm})^2$
$A = 25\pi \text{ cm}^2$

Total area $= 100 \text{ cm}^2 + 25\pi \text{ cm}^2 + 25\pi \text{ cm}^2$
$= (100 + 50\pi) \text{ cm}^2$
$\approx 257.1 \text{ cm}^2$

25. $A = ab + \frac{1}{2}(c-a)b$
$= b\left(a + \frac{1}{2}(c-a)\right)$
$= b\left(a + \frac{1}{2}c - \frac{1}{2}a\right)$
$= b\left(\frac{1}{2}a + \frac{1}{2}c\right)$
$= \frac{1}{2}b(a+c)$

27. $A = a^2 + \frac{1}{2}b(a+a) + a^2$
$= 2a^2 + \frac{1}{2}b(2a)$
$= 2a^2 + ab$

29. Area of larger triangle:
$A = \frac{1}{2}bh$
$A = \frac{1}{2} \cdot (8 \text{ cm} + 8 \text{ cm} + 8 \text{ cm}) \cdot (12 \text{ cm} + 6 \text{ cm})$
$A = \frac{1}{2} \cdot 24 \text{ cm} \cdot 18 \text{ cm}$
$A = 216 \text{ cm}^2$
Area of smaller triangle:
$A = \frac{1}{2}bh$
$A = \frac{1}{2} \cdot 8 \text{ cm} \cdot 6 \text{ cm}$
$A = 24 \text{ cm}^2$
Shaded area $= 216 \text{ cm}^2 - 24 \text{ cm}^2 = 192 \text{ cm}^2$

31. $A =$ (area of large circle) $-$ 2(area of small circle)
$A = \pi(4 \text{ cm})^2 - 2\left[\pi(2 \text{ cm})^2\right]$
$A = 16\pi \text{ cm}^2 - 8\pi \text{ cm}^2$
$A = 8\pi \text{ cm}^2$

33. Use the Pythagorean theorem to find the radius, r.
$c^2 = a^2 + b^2$
$(2r)^2 = (6)^2 + (8)^2$
$4r^2 = 36 + 64$
$4r^2 = 100$
$r^2 = 25$
$r = 5$
$A =$ (area of semicircle) $-$ (area of triangle)
$A = \frac{1}{2}\pi(5 \text{ in.})^2 - \frac{1}{2}(6 \text{ in.})(8 \text{ in.})$
$A = 12.5\pi \text{ in.}^2 - 24 \text{ in.}^2$
$A = (12.5\pi - 24) \text{ in.}^2$

35. Perimeter:

$$2\sqrt{8^2+15^2}+2\sqrt{6^2+8^2} = 2\sqrt{289}+2\sqrt{100}$$
$$= 2\cdot 17+2\cdot 10$$
$$= 54 \text{ ft}$$

Area:

$$\tfrac{1}{2}(15)(8)+\tfrac{1}{2}(15)(8)+\tfrac{1}{2}(6)(8)+\tfrac{1}{2}(6)(8) = 168 \text{ ft}^2$$

37. First convert the linear measures in feet to linear yards.

$$9 \text{ ft} = \frac{9\cancel{\text{ft}}}{1}\cdot\frac{1 \text{ yd}}{3\cancel{\text{ft}}} = 3 \text{ yd}$$

$$21 \text{ ft} = \frac{21\cancel{\text{ft}}}{1}\cdot\frac{1 \text{ yd}}{3\cancel{\text{ft}}} = 7 \text{ yd}$$

$$\text{Area of floor } = 3\text{ yd}\cdot 7\text{ yd} = 21\text{ yd}^2$$

$$\text{Cost of carpet } = \frac{21\cancel{\text{yd}^2}}{1}\cdot\frac{\$26.50}{1\cancel{\text{yd}^2}} = \$556.50$$

39. Area of tile = (Area of floor) – (Area of store) – (Area of refrigerator)

$$= (12 \text{ ft}\cdot 15 \text{ ft})-(3 \text{ ft}\cdot 4 \text{ ft})-(4 \text{ ft}\cdot 5 \text{ ft})$$
$$= 180 \text{ ft}^2 - 12 \text{ ft}^2 - 20 \text{ ft}^2 = 148 \text{ ft}^2$$

41. a. Area of lawn = (Area of lot) – (Area of house) – (Area of shed) – (Area of driveway)

$$= 200\text{ft}\cdot 500 \text{ ft} - 60 \text{ ft}\cdot 100 \text{ ft} - (20 \text{ ft})^2 - 100 \text{ ft}\cdot 20 \text{ ft}$$
$$= 100{,}000 \text{ ft}^2 - 6000 \text{ ft}^2 - 400 \text{ ft}^2 - 2000 \text{ ft}^2$$
$$= 91{,}600 \text{ ft}^2$$

$$\text{Maximum number of bags of fertilizer } = \frac{1 \text{ bag}}{4000\cancel{\text{ft}^2}}\cdot\frac{91{,}600\cancel{\text{ft}^2}}{1} = 22.9 \text{ bags} \to 23 \text{ bags}$$

b. $\text{Total cost of fertilizer } = \frac{\$25.00}{1\cancel{\text{bag}}}\cdot\frac{23\cancel{\text{bags}}}{2} = \$575$

43. a. Area of a front wall $= [20 \text{ ft}\cdot 40 \text{ ft}]+\left[\tfrac{1}{2}\cdot 40 \text{ ft}\cdot 10 \text{ ft}\right] = 1000 \text{ ft}^2$

Area of a side wall $= 50 \text{ ft}\cdot 20 \text{ ft} = 1000 \text{ ft}^2$

Area of windows $= 4[8 \text{ ft}\cdot 5 \text{ ft}]+2[30 \text{ ft}\cdot 2 \text{ ft}] = 280 \text{ ft}^2$

Area of doors $= 2[80 \text{ in.}\cdot 36 \text{ in.}] = 2\left[6\tfrac{2}{3} \text{ ft}\cdot 3 \text{ ft}\right] = 40 \text{ ft}^2$

Area of paint = 2(Area of front wall) + 2(Area of side wall) – (Area of windows and doors)

$$= 2\left(1000 \text{ ft}^2\right)+2\left(1000 \text{ ft}^2\right)-\left(280 \text{ ft}^2+40 \text{ ft}^2\right)$$
$$= 2000 \text{ ft}^2 + 2000 \text{ ft}^2 - 320 \text{ ft}^2$$
$$= 3680 \text{ ft}^2$$

b. Two coats will require enough paint for $2\cdot 3680 \text{ ft}^2 = 7360 \text{ ft}^2$.

$$7360 \text{ ft}^2 = \frac{7360 \text{ ft}^2}{1}\cdot\frac{1 \text{ gallon}}{500 \text{ ft}^2} = 14.72 \text{ gallons} \approx 15 \text{ gallons}.$$

c. $\$26.95\times 15 = \$404.25$ is the cost to buy the paint.

45. Area of Master Bedroom $= 14 \text{ ft} \cdot 14 \text{ ft} = 196 \text{ ft}^2$

Area of Bedroom #2 $= 11 \text{ ft} \cdot 12 \text{ ft} = 132 \text{ ft}^2$

Area of Bedroom #3 $= 12 \text{ ft} \cdot 11 \text{ ft} = 132 \text{ ft}^2$

Total area $= 196 \text{ ft}^2 + 132 \text{ ft}^2 + 132 \text{ ft}^2 = 460 \text{ ft}^2$

Since there are 9 square feet in a square yard, $460 \text{ ft}^2 \approx 51.1 \text{ yd}^2$.

52 yd^2 at \$17.95 per square yard costs \$933.40.

47. Amount of fencing $= C = 2\pi \cdot 20 \text{ m} = 40\pi \text{ m} \approx 125.7 \text{ m}$

49. $C = 2\pi \cdot 30 \text{ ft} \approx 188.5 \text{ ft}$

$$188.5 \text{ ft} = \frac{188.5 \cancel{\text{ft}}}{1} \cdot \frac{12 \text{ in.}}{1 \cancel{\text{ft}}} = 2262 \text{ in.}$$

$$\text{Number of plants} = \frac{1 \text{ plant}}{6 \cancel{\text{in.}}} \cdot \frac{2262 \cancel{\text{in.}}}{1} = 377 \text{ plants}$$

51. First, find the area of the pizzas.

Large:	Medium:
$A = \pi r^2$	$A = \pi r^2$
$= \pi(7 \text{ in.})^2$	$= \pi(3.5 \text{ in.})^2$
$= 49\pi \text{ in.}^2$	$= 12.25\pi \text{ in.}^2$
$\approx 153.9 \text{ in.}^2$	$\approx 38.5 \text{ in.}^2$

Next, find the price per square inch.

Large:	Medium:
$\dfrac{\$12.00}{49\pi \text{ in.}^2}$	$\dfrac{\$5.00}{12.25\pi \text{ in.}^2}$
$\approx \dfrac{\$12.00}{153.9 \text{ in.}^2}$	$\approx \dfrac{\$5.00}{38.5 \text{ in.}^2}$
$\approx \dfrac{\$0.08}{\text{in.}^2}$	$\approx \dfrac{\$0.13}{\text{in.}^2}$

The large pizza is a better buy.

59. makes sense

61. does not make sense; Explanations will vary. Sample explanation: A pizza with twice the radius would be four times as large as the smaller pizza.

63. Original Area $= 8 \text{ ft} \cdot 10 \text{ ft} = 80 \text{ ft}^2$

New area $= 12 \text{ ft} \cdot 15 \text{ ft} = 180 \text{ ft}^2$

$$\text{Ratio} = \frac{180 \text{ ft}^2}{80 \text{ ft}^2} = \frac{9}{4}$$

The cost will increase by a factor of $\frac{9}{4}$, or 2.25.

65. Length of pipeline $= \frac{16.8\text{ mi}}{1} \cdot \frac{5280\text{ ft}}{1\text{ mi}} = 88{,}704\text{ ft}$

Area of land=88,704 ft · 200 ft =17,740,800 ft^2

Area of land in acres $= \frac{17{,}740{,}800\text{ ft}^2}{1} \cdot \frac{1\text{ acre}}{43{,}560\text{ ft}^2} \approx 407.2727\text{ acres}$

Total cost $= \frac{\$32}{1\text{ acre}} \cdot \frac{407.2727\text{ acres}}{1} = \$13{,}032.73$

Check Points 10.5

1. $V = 5\text{ ft} \cdot 3\text{ ft} \cdot 7\text{ ft} = 105\text{ ft}^3$

2. $= \frac{6\text{ ft}}{1} \cdot \frac{1\text{ yd}}{3\text{ ft}} = 2\text{ yd}$

$V = (2\text{ yd})^3 = 8\text{ yd}^3$

3. $B = (6\text{ ft})^2 = 36\text{ ft}^2$

$V = \frac{1}{3} \cdot 36\text{ ft}^2 \cdot 4\text{ ft}$

$= 48\text{ ft}^3$

4. $r = \frac{1}{2}(8\text{ cm}) = 4\text{ cm}$

$V = \pi(4\text{ in.})^2 \cdot 6\text{ in.} \approx 302\text{ in.}^3$

5. $V = \frac{1}{3}\pi(4\text{ in.})^2 \cdot 6\text{ in.} \approx 101\text{ in.}^3$

6. No, it is not enough air.

$V = \frac{4}{3}\pi(4.5\text{ in.})^3 \approx 382\text{ in.}^3$

7. New dimensions: $l = 16$ yd, $w = 10$ yd, $h = 6$ yd

$SA = 2lw + 2lh + 2wh$

$= 2 \cdot 16\text{ yd} \cdot 10\text{ yd} + 2 \cdot 16\text{ yd} \cdot 6\text{ yd} + 2 \cdot 10\text{ yd} \cdot 6\text{ yd}$

$= 320\text{ yd}^2 + 192\text{ yd}^2 + 120\text{ yd}^2$

$= 632\text{ yd}^2$

Concept and Vocabulary Check 10.5

1. $V = lwh$

2. $V = s^2$

3. polyhedron

4. $V = \frac{1}{3}Bh$

5. $V = \pi r^2 h$

6. $V = \frac{1}{3}\pi r^2 h$

7. $V = \frac{4}{3}\pi r^3$

8. true

9. true

10. false

11. true

12. true

13. true

14. false

Exercise Set 10.5

1. $V = 3 \text{ in.} \cdot 3 \text{ in.} \cdot 4 \text{ in.} = 36 \text{ in.}^3$

3. $V = (4 \text{ cm})^3 = 64 \text{ cm}^3$

5. $B = 7 \text{ yd} \cdot 5 \text{ yd} = 35 \text{ yd}^2$
   $V = \frac{1}{3} \cdot 35 \text{ yd}^2 \cdot 15 \text{ yd}$
   $= 175 \text{ yd}^3$

7. $B = 4 \text{ in.} \cdot 7 \text{ in.} = 28 \text{ in.}^2$
   $V = \frac{1}{3} \cdot 28 \text{ in.}^2 \cdot 6 \text{ in.}$
   $= 56 \text{ in.}^3$

9. $V = \pi(5 \text{ cm})^2 \cdot 6 \text{ cm} = 150\pi \text{ cm}^3 \approx 471 \text{ cm}^3$

11. $r = \frac{1}{2}(24 \text{ in.}) = 12 \text{ in.}$
    $V = \pi(12 \text{ in.})^2 \cdot 21 \text{ in.} = 3024\pi \text{ in.}^3 \approx 9500 \text{ in.}^3$

13. $V = \frac{1}{3}\pi(4 \text{ m})^2 \cdot 9 \text{ m} = 48\pi \text{ m}^3 \approx 151 \text{ m}^3$

15. $r = \frac{1}{2} \cdot 6 \text{ yd} = 3 \text{ yd}$

$V = \frac{1}{3}\pi(3 \text{ yd})^2 \cdot 5 \text{ yd} = 15\pi \text{ yd}^3 \approx 47 \text{ yd}^3$

17. $V = \frac{4}{3}\pi(6\text{m})^3 = 288\pi \text{m}^3 \approx 905\text{m}^3$

19. $r = \frac{1}{2} \cdot 18 \text{ cm} = 9 \text{ cm}$

$V = \frac{4}{3}\pi(9 \text{ cm})^3 = 972\pi \text{ cm}^3 \approx 3054 \text{ cm}^3$

21. $\text{Surface Area} = 2(5 \text{ m} \cdot 3 \text{ m}) + 2(2 \text{ m} \cdot 3 \text{ m}) + 2(5 \text{ m} \cdot 2 \text{ m})$

$= 2 \cdot 15 \text{ m}^2 + 2 \cdot 6 \text{ m}^2 + 2 \cdot 10 \text{ m}^2$

$= 30 \text{ m}^2 + 12 \text{ m}^2 + 20 \text{ m}^2$

$= 62 \text{ m}^2$

23. $\text{Surface Area} = 6(4\text{ft})^2 = 96\text{ft}^2$

25. Volume = (volume of cone) + (volume of hemisphere)

$V = \frac{1}{3}\pi(6 \text{ cm})^2 \cdot 15 \text{ cm} + \frac{1}{2}\left[\frac{4}{3}\pi(6 \text{ cm})^3\right] = 324\pi \text{ cm}^3 \approx 1018 \text{ cm}^3$

27. Volume = (volume of right circular cylinder) + (volume of cone)

$V = \pi(6 \text{ in.})^2 \cdot 11 \text{ in.} + \frac{1}{3}\pi(6 \text{ in.})^2(14 \text{ in.} - 11 \text{ in.}) = 432\pi \text{ in.}^3 \approx 1357 \text{ in.}^3$

29. Volume = (volume of right circular cylinder) + (volume hemisphere)

$V = \pi(7 \text{ m})^2 \cdot 18 \text{ m} + \frac{1}{2}\left[\frac{4}{3}\pi(7 \text{ m})^3\right] = \frac{3332}{3}\pi \text{ m}^3 \approx 3489 \text{ m}^3$

31. Surface area:

$\underbrace{2[(5)(5)+(4)(3)]}_{\text{front and back}} + \underbrace{[(5)(4)+(3)(4)+(2)(4)]}_{\text{left and right sides}} + \underbrace{[(5)(4)+(4)(4)+(9)(4)]}_{\text{top(s) and bottom}} = 186 \text{ yd}^2$

Volume:

$\underbrace{(5)(5)(4)}_{\text{left part of block}} + \underbrace{(4)(4)(3)}_{\text{right part of block}} = 100 + 48 = 148 \text{ yd}^3$

33. Surface area:

$\underbrace{2[(10)(5)+\frac{1}{2}(4)(10+4)]}_{\text{front and back}} + \underbrace{4(15)(5)}_{\text{left, right, and 2 upper slants}} + \underbrace{(15)(4)}_{\text{top}} + \underbrace{(15)(10)}_{\text{bottom}} = \underbrace{2[50+28]}_{\text{front and back}} + \underbrace{300}_{\text{left, right, and 2 upper slants}} + \underbrace{60}_{\text{top}} + \underbrace{150}_{\text{bottom}} = 666 \text{ yd}^2$

35. $\frac{\frac{4}{3}\pi 3^3}{\frac{4}{3}\pi 6^3} = \frac{\cancel{\frac{4}{3}}\cancel{\pi}3^3}{\cancel{\frac{4}{3}}\cancel{\pi}6^3} = \left(\frac{3}{6}\right)^3 = \left(\frac{1}{2}\right)^3 = \frac{1}{8}$

37. Smaller cylinder: $r = 3$ in, $h = 4$ in.

$V = \pi r^2 h = \pi(3)^2 \cdot 4 = 36\pi$

The volume of the smaller cylinder is $36\pi\, in^3$.

Larger cylinder: r = 3(3 in) = 9 in, h = 4 in.

$V = \pi r^2 h = \pi(9)^2 \cdot 4 = 324\pi$

The volume of the larger cylinder is 324π. The ratio of the volumes of the two cylinders is $\frac{V_{\text{larger}}}{V_{\text{smaller}}} = \frac{324\pi}{36\pi} = \frac{9}{1}$.

So, the volume of the larger cylinder is 9 times the volume of the smaller cylinder.

39. First convert all linear measures in feet to linear yards.

$$12 \text{ ft} = \frac{12 \cancel{\text{ft}}}{1} \cdot \frac{1 \text{ yd}}{3 \cancel{\text{ft}}} = 4 \text{ yd}$$

$$9 \text{ ft} = \frac{9 \cancel{\text{ft}}}{1} \cdot \frac{1 \text{ yd}}{3 \cancel{\text{ft}}} = 3 \text{ yd}$$

$$6 \text{ ft} = \frac{6 \cancel{\text{ft}}}{1} \cdot \frac{1 \text{ yd}}{3 \cancel{\text{ft}}} = 2 \text{ yd}$$

Total dirt $= 4 \text{ yd} \cdot 3 \text{ yd} \cdot 2 \text{ yd} = 24 \text{ yd}^3$

$$\text{Total cost} = \frac{24 \cancel{\text{yd}^3}}{1} \cdot \frac{1 \cancel{\text{truck}}}{6 \cancel{\text{yd}^3}} \cdot \frac{\$85}{1 \cancel{\text{truck}}} = \$340$$

41. Volume of house $= 1400 \text{ ft}^2 \cdot 9 \text{ ft} = 12{,}600 \text{ ft}^3$

No. This furnace will not be adequate.

43. a. First convert linear measures in feet to linear yards.

$$756 \text{ ft} = \frac{756 \cancel{\text{ft}}}{1} \cdot \frac{1 \text{ yd}}{3 \cancel{\text{ft}}} = 252 \text{ yd}$$

$$480 \text{ ft} = \frac{480 \cancel{\text{ft}}}{1} \cdot \frac{1 \text{ yd}}{3 \cancel{\text{ft}}} = 160 \text{ yd}$$

$$B = (252 \text{ yd})^2 = 63{,}504 \text{ yd}^2$$

$$V = \frac{1}{3} \cdot 63{,}504 \text{ yd}^2 \cdot 160 \text{ yd}$$

$$= 3{,}386{,}880 \text{ yd}^3$$

b. $$\frac{1 \text{ block}}{1.5 \cancel{\text{yd}^3}} \cdot \frac{3{,}386{,}880 \cancel{\text{yd}^3}}{1} = 2{,}257{,}920 \text{ blocks}$$

45. Volume of tank $= \pi(3\text{ft})^2 \cdot \frac{7}{3} \text{ ft} \approx 66 \text{ ft}^3$

Yes. The volume of the tank is less than 67 cubic feet.

47. Volume of pool (in cubic feet) $= \pi(12 \text{ ft})^2 \cdot 4 \text{ ft} = 576\pi \text{ ft}^3 \approx 1809.6 \text{ ft}^3$

Volume of pool (in gallons) $= 1809.6 \text{ ft}^3 = \frac{1809.6 \cancel{\text{ft}^3}}{1} \cdot \frac{7.48 \text{ gallons}}{1 \cancel{\text{ft}^3}} \approx 13{,}536 \text{ gallons}$

Cost to fill the pool $= \$2 \cdot 13.535 \approx \$27$

51. does not make sense; Explanations will vary. Sample explanation: Basketballs are spheres.

53. does not make sense; Explanations will vary. Sample explanation: You must divide by 12^3, or 1728.

55. New volume $= \frac{4}{3}\pi(2r)^3 = \frac{4}{3}\pi \cdot 8r^3 = 8\left(\frac{4}{3}\pi r^3\right)$

The volume is multiplied by 8.

57. Volume of darkly shaded region = (Volume of rectangular solid) – (Volume of pyramid)

$$= 6 \text{ cm} \cdot 6 \text{ cm} \cdot 7 \text{ cm} - \frac{1}{3}(6 \text{ cm})^2 \cdot 7 \text{ cm}$$

$$= 168 \text{ cm}^3$$

59. Surface area = (Areas of 3 rectangles) + (Area of 2 triangles)

$$= (5 \text{ cm} \cdot 6 \text{ cm} + 4 \text{ cm} \cdot 6 \text{ cm} + 3 \text{ cm} \cdot 6 \text{ cm}) + 2\left(\frac{1}{2} \cdot 3 \text{ cm} \cdot 4 \text{ cm}\right)$$

$$= 72 \text{ cm}^2 + 12 \text{ cm}^2$$

$$= 84 \text{ cm}^2$$

Check Points 10.6

1. Begin by finding the measure of the hypotenuse c using the Pythagorean Theorem.

$$c^2 = a^2 + b^2 = 3^2 + 4^2 = 25$$

$$c = \sqrt{25} = 5$$

$$\sin A = \frac{3}{5}$$

$$\cos A = \frac{4}{5}$$

$$\tan A = \frac{3}{4}$$

2. $\tan A = \frac{a}{b}$

$$\tan 62° = \frac{a}{140}$$

$$a = 140 \tan 62° \approx 263 \text{ cm}$$

3. $\cos A = \frac{b}{c}$

$$\cos 62° = \frac{140}{c}$$

$$c \cos 62° = 140$$

$$c = \frac{140}{\cos 62°}$$

$$c \approx 298 \text{ cm}$$

4. Let a = the height of the tower.

$$\tan 85.4° = \frac{a}{80}$$

$$a = 80 \tan 85.4° \approx 994 \text{ ft}$$

5. $\tan A = \frac{14}{10}$

   $A = \tan^{-1}\left(\frac{14}{10}\right) \approx 54°$

Concept and Vocabulary Check 10.6

1. sine; opposite; hypotenuse; $\frac{a}{c}$
2. cosine; adjacent to; hypotenuse; $\frac{b}{c}$
3. tangent; opposite; adjacent to; $\frac{a}{b}$
4. elevation
5. depression
6. false
7. false
8. true
9. false

Exercise Set 10.6

1. $\sin A = \frac{3}{5}$

   $\cos A = \frac{4}{5}$

   $\tan A = \frac{3}{4}$

3. First find the length of missing side.

   $a^2 = 29^2 - 21^2 = 400$

   $a = 20$

   $\sin A = \frac{20}{29}$

   $\cos A = \frac{21}{29}$

   $\tan A = \frac{20}{21}$

5. First find the length of missing side.

   $b^2 = 26^2 - 10^2 = 576$

   $b = 24$

   $\sin A = \frac{10}{26} = \frac{5}{13}$

   $\cos A = \frac{24}{26} = \frac{12}{13}$

   $\tan A = \frac{10}{24} = \frac{5}{12}$

7. First find the length of missing side.

   $a^2 = 35^2 - 21^2 = 784$

   $a = 28$

   $\sin A = \frac{28}{35} = \frac{4}{5}$

   $\cos A = \frac{21}{35} = \frac{3}{5}$

   $\tan A = \frac{28}{21} = \frac{4}{3}$

9. $\tan A = \frac{a}{b}$

   $\tan 37° = \frac{a}{250}$

   $a = 250 \tan 37° \approx 188$ cm

11. $\cos 34° = \frac{b}{220}$

    $b = 220 \cos 34° \approx 182$ in.

13. $\sin 34° = \frac{a}{13}$

    $a = 13 \sin 34° \approx 7$ m

15. $\tan 33° = \frac{14}{b}$

    $b = \frac{14}{\tan 33°} \approx 22$ yd

17. $\sin 30° = \frac{20}{c}$

    $c = \frac{20}{\sin 30°} = 40$ m

19. $m\measuredangle B = 90° - 40° = 50°$

Side a: $\tan 40° = \dfrac{a}{22}$

$a = 22\tan 40° \approx 18$ yd

Side c: $\cos 40° = \dfrac{22}{c}$

$c = \dfrac{22}{\cos 40°} \approx 29$ yd

$m\measuredangle B = 50°,\ a \approx 18$ yd, $c \approx 29$ yd

21. $m\measuredangle B = 90° - 52° = 38°$

Side a: $\sin 52° = \dfrac{a}{54}$

$a = 54\sin 52° \approx 43$ cm

Side b: $\cos 52° = \dfrac{b}{54}$

$b = 54\cos 52° \approx 33$ cm

$m\measuredangle B = 38°,\ a \approx 43$ cm, $b \approx 33$ cm

23. $\sin A = \dfrac{30}{50}$

$A = \sin^{-1}\left(\dfrac{30}{50}\right) \approx 37°$

25. $\cos A = \dfrac{15}{17}$

$A = \cos^{-1}\left(\dfrac{15}{17}\right) \approx 28°$

27. $x = 500\tan 40° + 500\tan 25°$

$x \approx 653$

29. $x = 600\tan 28° - 600\tan 25°$

$x \approx 39$

31. $x = \dfrac{300}{\tan 34°} - \dfrac{300}{\tan 64°}$

$x \approx 298$

33. $x = \dfrac{400\tan 40° \tan 20°}{\tan 40° - \tan 20°}$

$x \approx 257$

35. $\tan 40° = \dfrac{a}{630}$

$a = 630\tan 40° \approx 529$ yd

37. $\sin 10° = \dfrac{500}{c}$

$c = \dfrac{500}{\sin 10°} \approx 2879$ ft

39. Let h = the height of the tower.

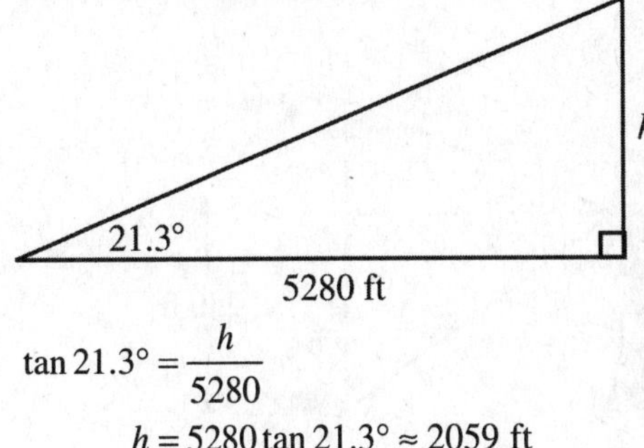

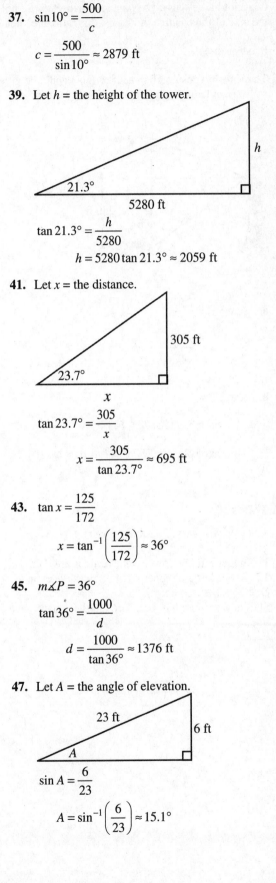

$\tan 21.3° = \dfrac{h}{5280}$

$h = 5280\tan 21.3° \approx 2059$ ft

41. Let x = the distance.

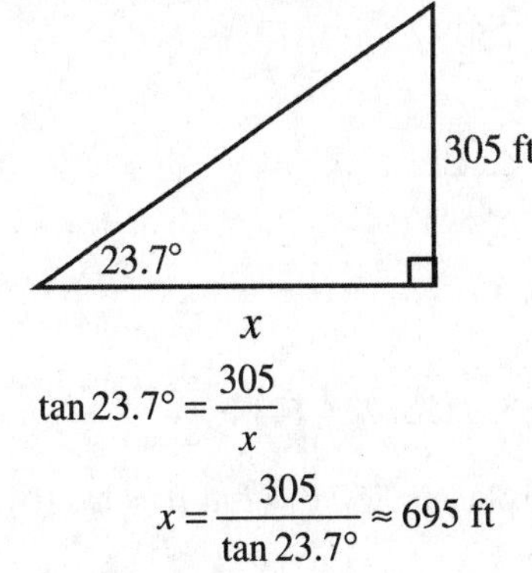

$\tan 23.7° = \dfrac{305}{x}$

$x = \dfrac{305}{\tan 23.7°} \approx 695$ ft

43. $\tan x = \dfrac{125}{172}$

$x = \tan^{-1}\left(\dfrac{125}{172}\right) \approx 36°$

45. $m\measuredangle P = 36°$

$\tan 36° = \dfrac{1000}{d}$

$d = \dfrac{1000}{\tan 36°} \approx 1376$ ft

47. Let A = the angle of elevation.

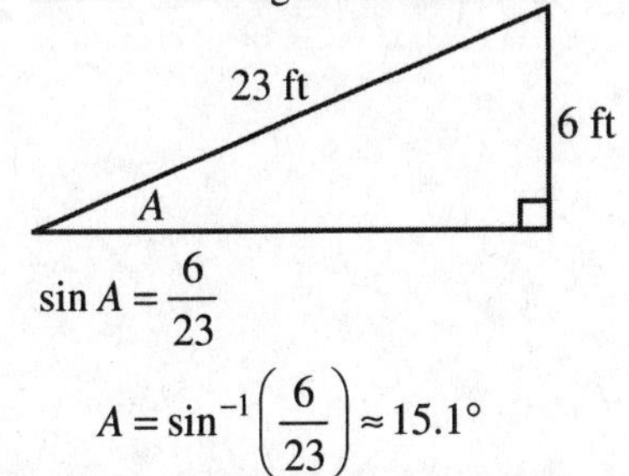

$\sin A = \dfrac{6}{23}$

$A = \sin^{-1}\left(\dfrac{6}{23}\right) \approx 15.1°$

57. does not make sense; Explanations will vary. Sample explanation: The sine is the ratio of two sides of the triangle. As the size of the triangle increases, this ratio does not change.

59. makes sense

61. The sine and cosine of an acute angle cannot be greater than or equal to 1 because they are each the ratio of a leg of a right triangle to the hypotenuse. The hypotenuse of a right triangle is always the longest side; this results in a value less than 1.

63.

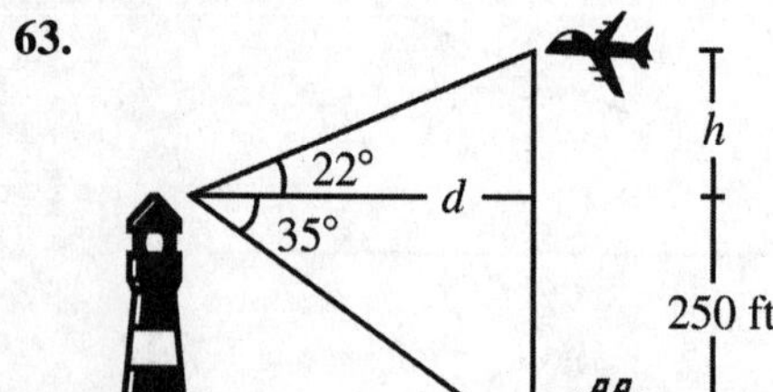

a. $\tan 35° = \dfrac{250}{d}$

$d = \dfrac{250}{\tan 35°} \approx 357 \text{ ft}$

b. $\tan 22° = \dfrac{h}{d} = \dfrac{h}{357}$

$h = 357 \tan 22° \approx 144 \text{ ft}$

Height of plane = 250 ft + 144 ft = 394 ft.

Check Points 10.7

1. Answers will vary. Possible answer:

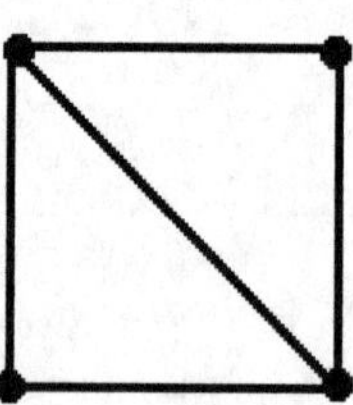

The upper left and lower right vertices are odd.
The lower left and upper right vertices are even.
One possible tracing:
Start at the upper left, trace around the square, then trace down the diagonal.

Concept and Vocabulary Check 10.7

1. vertex; edge; graph
2. traversable
3. genus
4. parallel
5. non-Euclidean; parallel
6. self-similarity; iteration
7. true
8. false
9. true
10. true

Exercise Set 10.7

1. **a.** *A* and *C* are even vertices.
   B and *D* are odd vertices.
   Because this graph has two odd vertices, by Euler's second rule, it is traversable.

   b. Sample path: *D, A, B, D, C, B*

3. **a.** *C, D, E* are even vertices.
   A and *B* are odd vertices.
   Because this graph has two odd vertices, by Euler's second rule, it is traversable.

   b. Sample path: *A, D, C, B, D, E, A, B*

5. *A, B, D, E* are odd vertices.
   Because this graph has more than two odd vertices, by Euler's third rule, it is not traversable.

7. 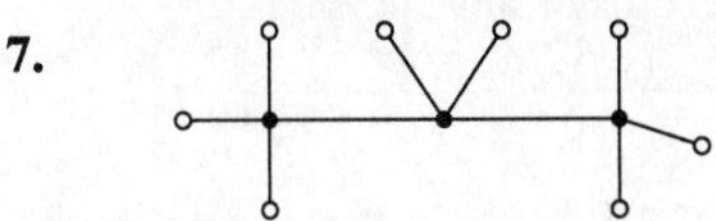

9. No, the graph is not traversable because there are more than 2 odd vertices.

11. 2 doors connect room *C* to the outside. This is shown in the graph by connecting 2 edges from *C* to *E*.

13. Sample path: *B, E, A, B, D, C, A, E, C, E, D*

15. 2

17. 4

19. Answers will vary.

21. The sum of the angles of such a quadrilateral is greater than 360°.

23. Yes

43. makes sense

45. does not make sense; Explanations will vary. Sample explanation: Euclidean geometry is limited in this regard.

Chapter 10 Review Exercises

1. $\measuredangle 3$
2. $\measuredangle 5$
3. $\measuredangle 4$ and $\measuredangle 6$
4. $\measuredangle 1$ and $\measuredangle 6$
5. $\measuredangle 1$ and $\measuredangle 4$
6. $\measuredangle 2$
7. $\measuredangle 5$
8. $180° - 115° = 65°$
9. $90° - 41° = 49°$
10. Measure of complement $= 90° - 73° = 17°$
11. Measure of supplement $= 180° - 46° = 134°$
12. $m\measuredangle 1 = 180° - 70° = 110°$
    $m\measuredangle 2 = 70°$
    $m\measuredangle 3 = m\measuredangle 1 = 110°$

13. $m\measuredangle 1 = 180° - 42° = 138°$
$m\measuredangle 2 = 42°$
$m\measuredangle 3 = m\measuredangle 1 = 138°$
$m\measuredangle 4 = m\measuredangle 1 = 138°$
$m\measuredangle 5 = m\measuredangle 2 = 42°$
$m\measuredangle 6 = 42°$
$m\measuredangle 7 = m\measuredangle 3 = 138°$

14. $m\measuredangle A = 180° - 60° - 48° = 72°$

15. $m\measuredangle A = 90° - 39° = 51°$

16. $m\measuredangle 1 = 180° - 50° - 40° = 90°$
$m\measuredangle 2 = 180° - 90° = 90°$
$m\measuredangle 3 = 180° - 40° = 140°$
$m\measuredangle 4 = 40°$
$m\measuredangle 5 = m\measuredangle 3 = 140°$

17. $m\measuredangle 2 = 180° - 115° = 65°$
$\measuredangle 1$ is in a triangle with angles of $65°$ and $35°$.
Thus, $m\measuredangle 1 = 180° - 65° - 35° = 80°$
$m\measuredangle 3 = 115°$
$m\measuredangle 4 = m\measuredangle 1 = 80°$
$m\measuredangle 5 = 180° - 80° = 100°$
$m\measuredangle 6 = m\measuredangle 1 = 80°$

18. $\frac{8}{4} = \frac{10}{x}$
$8x = 40$
$x = 5$ ft

19. $\frac{9}{x} = \frac{7+5}{5}$
$\frac{9}{x} = \frac{12}{5}$
$12x = 45$
$x = \frac{45}{12} = 3.75$ ft

20. $c^2 = 8^2 + 6^2$
$c^2 = 64 + 36$
$c^2 = 100$
$c = 10$ ft

21. $c^2 = 6^2 + 4^2$
$c^2 = 36 + 16$
$c^2 = 52$
$c \approx 7.2$ in.

22. $b^2 = 15^2 - 11^2$
$b^2 = 225 - 121$
$b^2 = 104$
$b \approx 10.2$ cm

23. $\frac{x}{5} = \frac{9+6}{6}$
$\frac{x}{5} = \frac{15}{6}$
$6x = 75$
$x = 12.5$ ft

24. $a^2 = 25^2 - 20^2$
$a^2 = 625 - 400$
$a^2 = 225$
$a = 15$ ft

25. $b^2 = 13^2 + 5^2$
$b^2 = 169 - 25$
$b^2 = 144$
$b = 12$ yd

26. Rectangle, square

27. Rhombus, square

28. Parallelogram, rhombus, trapezoid

29. $P = 2\ (6\text{ cm}) + 2(9\text{ cm})$
$= 12\text{ cm} + 18\text{ cm}$
$= 30\text{ cm}$

30. $P = 2 \cdot 1000\text{ yd} + 2 \cdot 1240\text{ yd}$
$= 2000\text{ yd} + 2480\text{ yd}$
$= 4480\text{ yd}$

31. First find the lengths of missing sides.

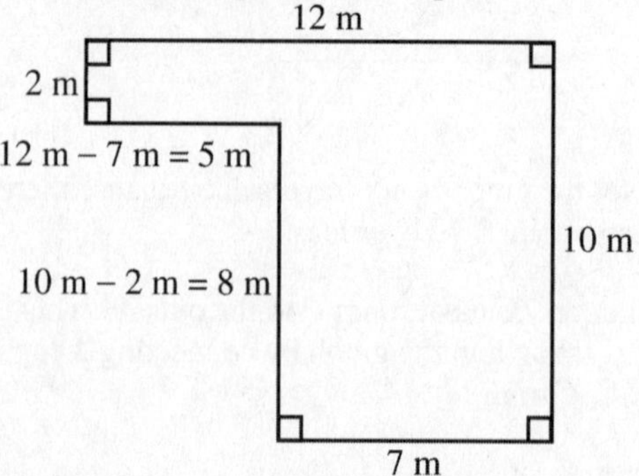

$P = 12\text{ m} + 10\text{ m} + 7\text{ m} + 8\text{ m} + 5\text{ m} + 2\text{ m}$
$= 44\text{ m}$

32. $\text{Sum} = (n-2)\ 180°$
$= (12-2)\ 180°$
$= 10 \cdot 180°$
$= 1800°$

33. $\text{Sum} = (n-2)\ 180°$
$= (8-2)\ 180°$
$= 6 \cdot 180°$
$= 1080°$

34. $\text{Sum of measures of angles} = (n-2)180°$
$= (8-2)180°$
$= 6 \cdot 180°$
$= 1080°$

$m\measuredangle 1 = \frac{1080°}{8} = 135°$
$m\measuredangle 2 = 180° - 135° = 45°$

35. Amount of baseboard
= Perimeter of room – Lengths of doorways
$= 2 \cdot 35 \text{ ft} + 2 \cdot 15 \text{ ft} - 4 \cdot 3 \text{ ft}$
$= 70 \text{ ft} + 30 \text{ ft} - 12 \text{ ft}$
$= 88 \text{ ft}$

$\text{Cost} = \frac{\$1.50}{1 \cancel{\text{ft}}} \cdot \frac{88 \cancel{\text{ft}}}{1} = \$132$

36. a. triangles, hexagons

b. The 5 angles that come together are $60°$, $60°$, $60°$, $60°$, and $120°$.

c. The tessellation is possible because $60° + 60° + 60° + 60° + 120° = 360°$.

37. Each angle is $\frac{(n-2)\ 180°}{n} = \frac{(6-2)\ 180°}{6} = 120°$
Regular hexagons can be used to create a tessellation because $360°$ is a multiple of $120°$.

38. $A = 5 \text{ ft} \cdot 6.5 \text{ ft} = 32.5 \text{ft}^2$

39. $A = 5 \text{ m} \cdot 4 \text{ m} = 20 \text{ m}^2$

40. $A = \frac{1}{2} \cdot 20 \text{ cm} \cdot 5 \text{ cm} = 50 \text{cm}^2$

41. $A = \frac{1}{2} \cdot 10 \text{ yd} \cdot (22 \text{ yd} + 5 \text{ yd})$
$= \frac{1}{2} \cdot 10 \text{ yd} \cdot (27 \text{ yd})$
$= 135 \text{ yd}^2$

42. $C = \pi \cdot 20 \text{ m} = 20\pi \text{ m} \approx 62.8 \text{ m}$
$r = \frac{1}{2} d = \frac{1}{2} \cdot 20 \text{ m} = 10 \text{ m}$
$A = \pi r^2 = \pi (10 \text{m})^2 = 100\pi \text{m}^2 \approx 314.2 \text{ m}^2$

43. Area = (Area of square) + (Area of triangle)
$= (12 \text{ in.})^2 + \frac{1}{2} \cdot 12 \text{ in.} \cdot 8 \text{ in.}$
$= 144 \text{ in.}^2 + 48 \text{ in.}^2$
$= 192 \text{ in.}^2$

44. Area = (Area of top rectangle)
+ (Area of bottom rectangle)
$= 8 \text{ m} \cdot 2 \text{ m} + 6 \text{ m} \cdot 2 \text{ m}$
$= 16 \text{ m}^2 + 12 \text{ m}^2$
$= 28 \text{ m}^2$

45. $A = (\text{area of rectange}) - (\text{area of triangle})$
$A = (13 \text{ ft})(24 \text{ ft}) - \frac{1}{2}(5 \text{ ft})(13 \text{ ft})$
$A = 312 \text{ ft}^2 - 32.5 \text{ ft}^2$
$A = 279.5 \text{ ft}^2$

46. $A = (\text{area of rectange}) - 2(\text{area of small circle})$
$A = (8 \text{ in.})(16 \text{ in.}) - 2\left[\pi (4 \text{ in.})^2\right]$
$A = 128 \text{ in.}^2 - 32\pi \text{ in.}^2$
$A = (128 - 32\pi) \text{ in.}^2$
$A \approx 27.5 \text{ in.}^2$

47. First convert linear measurements in feet to linear yards.

$15 \text{ ft} = \frac{15 \cancel{\text{ft}}}{1} \cdot \frac{1 \text{ yd}}{3 \cancel{\text{ft}}} = 5 \text{ yd}$

$21 \text{ ft} = \frac{21 \cancel{\text{ft}}}{1} \cdot \frac{1 \text{ yd}}{3 \cancel{\text{ft}}} = 7 \text{ yd}$

$\text{Area} = 5 \text{ yd} \cdot 7 \text{ yd} = 35 \text{ yd}^2$

$\text{Cost} = \frac{\$22.50}{1 \cancel{\text{yd}^2}} \cdot \frac{35 \cancel{\text{yd}^2}}{1} = \$787.50$

48. $\text{Area of floor} = 40 \text{ ft} \cdot 50 \text{ ft} = 2000 \text{ ft}^2$
$\text{Area of each tile} = (2 \text{ft})^2 = 4 \text{ft}^2$

$\text{Number of tiles} = \frac{2000 \text{ ft}^2}{4 \text{ ft}^2} = 500 \text{ tiles}$

$\text{Cost} = \frac{\$13}{10 \cancel{\text{tiles}}} \cdot \frac{500 \cancel{\text{tiles}}}{1} = \$650$

49. $C = \pi d = \pi \cdot 10 \text{ yd} = 10\pi \text{ yd} \approx 31 \text{ yd}$

50. $V = 5 \text{ cm} \cdot 3 \text{ cm} \cdot 4 \text{ cm} = 60 \text{ cm}^3$

51. $V =$ (Volume of rectangular solid) + (Volume of Pyramid)

$= 8 \text{ m} \cdot 9 \text{ m} \cdot 10 \text{ m} + \frac{1}{3}(8 \text{ m} \cdot 9 \text{ m})\ 10 \text{ m}$

$\approx 720 \text{ m}^3 + 240 \text{ m}^3 = 960 \text{ m}^3$

52. $V = \pi(4 \text{ yd})^2 \cdot 8 \text{ yd} = 128\pi \text{ yd}^3 \approx 402 \text{ yd}^3$

53. $V = \frac{1}{3}\pi(40 \text{ in.})^2 \cdot 28 \text{ in.}$

$= \frac{44{,}800}{3}\pi \text{ in.}^3 \approx 46{,}914 \text{ in.}^3$

54. $V = \frac{4}{3}\pi(6 \text{ m})^3 = 288\pi \text{ m}^3 \approx 905 \text{ m}^3$

55. Surface area

$= 2(5 \text{ m})(3 \text{ m}) + 2(3 \text{ m})(6 \text{ m}) + 2(5 \text{ m})(6 \text{ m})$

$= 30 \text{ m}^2 + 36 \text{ m}^2 + 60 \text{ m}^2$

$= 126 \text{ m}^2$

56. Volume of one box $= 8 \text{ m} \cdot 4 \text{ m} \cdot 3 \text{ m} = 96 \text{ m}^3$

Volume of 50 boxes $= 50 \cdot 96 \text{ m}^3 = 4800 \text{ m}^3$

57. $V = \frac{1}{3}(145 \text{ m})^2 \cdot 93 \text{ m} = 651{,}775 \text{ m}^3$

58. First convert linear measures in feet to linear yards.

$27 \text{ ft} = \frac{27 \cancel{\text{ft}}}{1} \cdot \frac{1 \text{ yd}}{3 \cancel{\text{ft}}} = 9 \text{ yd}$

$4 \text{ ft} = \frac{4 \cancel{\text{ft}}}{1} \cdot \frac{1 \text{ yd}}{3 \cancel{\text{ft}}} = \frac{4}{3} \text{ yd}$

$6 \text{ in.} = \frac{6 \cancel{\text{in.}}}{1} \cdot \frac{1 \text{ yd}}{36 \cancel{\text{in.}}} = \frac{1}{6} \text{ yd}$

Volume $= 9 \text{ yd} \cdot \frac{4}{3} \text{ yd} \cdot \frac{1}{6} \text{ yd} = 2 \text{ yd}^3$

Cost $= \frac{\$40}{1 \cancel{\text{yd}^3}} \cdot \frac{2 \cancel{\text{yd}^3}}{1} = \$80$

59. First compute length of hypotenuse

$c^2 = 12^2 + 9^2 = 144 + 81 = 225$

$c = 15$

$\sin A = \frac{9}{15} = \frac{3}{5}$

$\cos A = \frac{12}{15} = \frac{4}{5}$

$\tan A = \frac{9}{12} = \frac{3}{4}$

60. $\tan 23° = \frac{a}{100}$

$a = 100 \tan 23° \approx 42 \text{ mm}$

61. $\sin 61° = \frac{20}{c}$

$c = \frac{20}{\sin 61°} \approx 23 \text{ cm}$

62. $\sin 48° = \frac{a}{50}$

$a = 50 \sin 48° \approx 37 \text{ in.}$

63. $\sin A = \frac{17}{20}$

$A = \sin^{-1}\left(\frac{17}{20}\right) \approx 58°$

64. $\frac{1}{2} \text{ mi} = \frac{0.5 \cancel{\text{mi}}}{1} \cdot \frac{5280 \text{ ft}}{1 \cancel{\text{mi}}} = 2640 \text{ ft}$

$\sin 17° = \frac{h}{2640}$

$h = 2640 \sin 17° \approx 772 \text{ ft}$

65. $\tan 32° = \frac{d}{50}$

$d = 50 \tan 32° \approx 31 \text{ m}$

66.

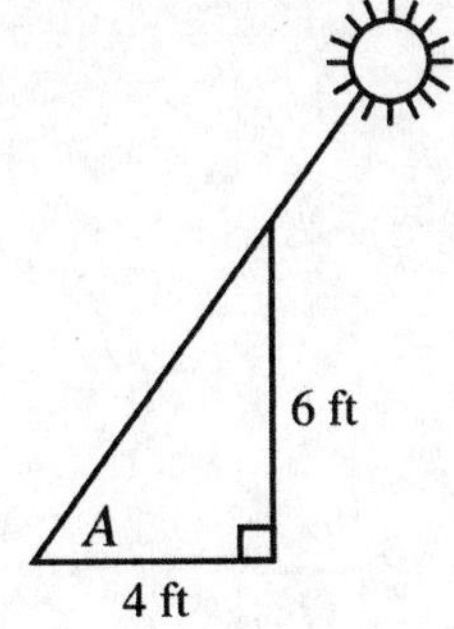

$\tan A = \frac{6}{4}$

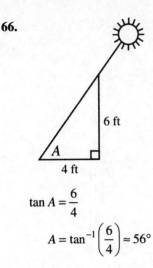

$A = \tan^{-1}\left(\frac{6}{4}\right) \approx 56°$

67. The graph is not traversable because there are more than two odd vertices.

68. All vertices have even degrees, so the graph is traversable. Possible path: *A, B, C, D, A, B, C, D, A*

69. 0

70. 2

71. 1

72. 2

Chapter 10 Test

1. Measure of complement = 90° – 54° = 36°
Measure of supplement = 180° – 54° = 126°

2. $m\measuredangle 1 = 133°$ because alternate exterior angles are equal.

3. $m\measuredangle 1 = 180° - 40° - 70° = 70°$

4. First find measures of other angles of triangle.

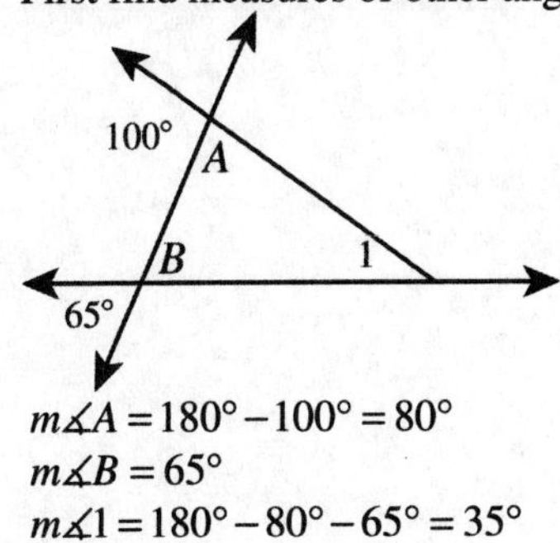

$m\measuredangle A = 180° - 100° = 80°$
$m\measuredangle B = 65°$
$m\measuredangle 1 = 180° - 80° - 65° = 35°$

5. $\frac{x}{8} = \frac{4}{10}$

$10x = 4 \cdot 8$

$10x = 32$

$x = \frac{32}{10} = 3.2 \text{ in.}$

6. $b^2 = 26^2 - 24^2$

$b^2 = 676 - 576$

$b^2 = 100$

$b = 10 \text{ ft}$

7. Sum = (*n* – 2) 180°
= (10 – 2) 180°
= 8 · 180°
= 1440°

8. First find lengths of missing sides.

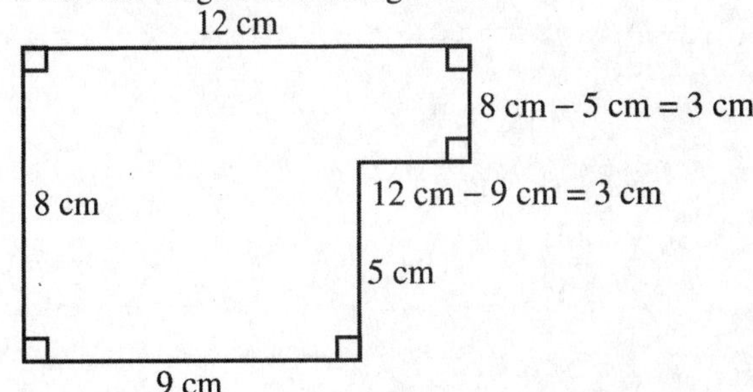

P = 12 cm + 3 cm + 3 cm + 5 cm + 9 cm + 8 cm
= 40 cm

9. d

10. **a.** triangles, squares

b. The 5 angles that come together are 60°, 60°, 60°, 90°, and 90°.

c. The tessellation is possible because $60° + 60° + 60° + 90° + 90° = 360°$.

11. $A = \frac{1}{2}bh$

$A = \frac{1}{2} \cdot 47\text{ m} \cdot 22\text{ m} = 517\text{ m}^2$

12. $A = \frac{1}{2} \cdot 15\text{ in.}(40\text{ in.} + 30\text{ in.})$

$= \frac{1}{2} \cdot 15\text{ in.}(70\text{ in.})$

$= 525\text{ in.}^2$

13. **a.**
$$a^2 + b^2 = c^2$$
$$a^2 + 5^2 = 13^2$$
$$a^2 + 25 = 169$$
$$a^2 = 144$$
$$a = 12 \text{ cm}$$

b. $P = 5 \text{ cm} + 12 \text{ cm} + 13 \text{ cm} = 30 \text{ cm}$

c. $A = \frac{1}{2}bh = \frac{1}{2} \cdot 12 \text{ cm} \cdot 5 \text{ cm} = 30 \text{ cm}^2$

14. $C = \pi d = \pi \cdot 40 \text{ m} = 40\pi \text{ m} \approx 125.7 \text{ m}$
$A = \pi r^2 = \pi(20 \text{ m})^2 = 400\pi \text{ m}^2 \approx 1256.6 \text{ m}^2$

15. Area of floor $8 \text{ ft} \cdot 6 \text{ ft} = 48 \text{ ft}^2$
Convert inches to feet:
$$8 \text{ in.} = \frac{8 \cancel{\text{in.}}}{1} \cdot \frac{1 \text{ ft}}{12 \cancel{\text{in.}}} = \frac{2}{3} \text{ ft}$$
Area of one tile
$$= \left(\frac{2}{3} \text{ft}\right)^2 = \frac{4}{9} \text{ft}^2$$
Number of tiles
$$= \frac{48 \text{ ft}^2}{\frac{4}{9} \text{ft}^2} = 108 \text{ tiles}$$

16. $V = 3 \text{ ft} \cdot 2 \text{ ft} \cdot 3 \text{ ft} = 18 \text{ ft}^3$

17. $V = \frac{1}{3}(4 \text{ m} \cdot 3 \text{ m}) 4 \text{ m} = 16 \text{ m}^3$

18. $V = \pi(5 \text{cm})^2 \cdot 7 \text{ cm} = 175\pi \text{ cm}^3 \approx 550 \text{ cm}^3$

19. $\sin 28° = \frac{40}{c}$
$$c = \frac{40}{\sin 28°} \approx 85 \text{ cm}$$

20.

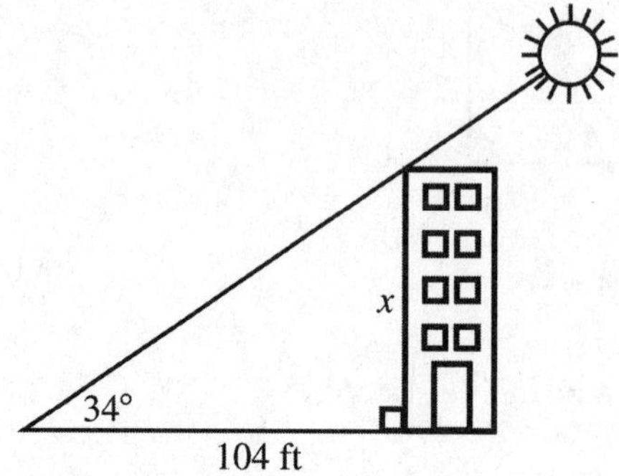

$$\tan 34° = \frac{h}{104}$$
$$h = 104 \tan 34° \approx 70 \text{ ft}$$

21. The graph is traversable because there are two odd vertices (*B* and *E*). Sample path: *B*,*C*,*A*,*E*,*C*,*D*,*E*

Chapter 11
Counting Methods and Probability Theory

Check Points 11.1

1. Multiply the number of choices for each of the two courses of the meal:

   $\underline{\text{Appetizers}}: \ \underline{\text{Main Courses:}}$

   $10 \times 15 = 150$

2. Multiply the number of choices for each of the two courses:

   $\underline{\text{Psychology}}: \ \underline{\text{Social Science:}}$

   $10 \times 4 = 40$

3. Multiply the number of choices for each of the three decisions:

   $\underline{\text{Size}}: \ \underline{\text{Crust}}: \ \underline{\text{Topping:}}$

   $2 \times 3 \times 5 = 30$

4. Multiply the number of choices for each of the five options:

   $\underline{\text{Color:}} \ \underline{\text{A/C:}} \ \underline{\text{Electric/Gas:}} \ \underline{\text{Onboard Computer:}} \ \underline{\text{Global Positioning System:}}$

   $10 \times 2 \times 2 \times 2 \times 2 = 160$

5. Multiply the number of choices for each of the six questions:

   $\underline{\text{Question \#1:}} \ \underline{\text{Question \#2:}} \ \underline{\text{Question \#3:}} \ \underline{\text{Question \#4:}} \ \underline{\text{Question \#5:}} \ \underline{\text{Question \#6:}}$

   $3 \times 3 \times 3 \times 3 \times 3 \times 3 = 3^6 = 729$

6. Multiply the number of choices for each of the five digits:

   $\overbrace{\underline{\text{Digit 1:}}}^{1-9} \ \overbrace{\underline{\text{Digit 2:}}}^{0-9} \ \overbrace{\underline{\text{Digit 3:}}}^{0-9} \ \overbrace{\underline{\text{Digit 4:}}}^{0-9} \ \overbrace{\underline{\text{Digit 5:}}}^{0-9}$

   $9 \times 10 \times 10 \times 10 \times 10 = 90{,}000$

Concept and Vocabulary Check 11.1

1. $M \cdot N$
2. multiplying; Fundamental Counting
3. false
4. true

Exercise Set 11.1

1. $8 \cdot 10 = 80$

3. $3 \cdot 4 = 12$

5. $3 \cdot 2 = 6$

7. Multiply the number of choices for each of the three decisions:

Drink:		Size:		Flavor:		
2	×	4	×	5	=	40

9. Multiply the number of choices for each of the four menu categories:

Main Course:		Vegetables:		Beverages:		Desserts:		
4	×	3	×	4	×	3	=	144

This includes, for example, an order of ham and peas with tea and cake.
This also includes an order of beef and peas with milk and pie.

11. Multiply the number of choices for each of the three categories:

Gender:		Age:		Payment method:		
2	×	2	×	2	=	8

13. Multiply the number of choices for each of the five options:

Color:		A/C:		Transmission:		Windows:		CD Player:		
6	×	2	×	2	×	2	×	2	=	96

15. Multiply the number of choices for each of the five questions:

Question 1:		Question 2:		Question 3:		Question 4:		Question 5:		
3	×	3	×	3	×	3	×	3	=	243

17. Multiply the number of choices for each of the three digits:

Digit 1:		Digit 2:		Digit 3:		
8	×	2	×	9	=	144

19. Multiply the number of choices for each of the letters and digits:

Letter 1:		Letter 2:		Digit 1:		Digit 2:		Digit 3:		
26	×	26	×	10	×	10	×	10	=	676,000

21. This situation involves making choices with seven groups of items. Each stock is a group, and each group has three choices. Multiply choices: $3\times3\times3\times3\times3\times3\times3 = 3^7 = 2187$

27. makes sense

29. makes sense

31. Multiply the number of choices for each of the four groups of items:

Bun:		Sauce:		Lettuce:		Tomatoes:		
12	×	30	×	4	×	3	=	4320

Total time $= 10\times4320 = 43,200$ minutes, which is $43,200 \div 60 = 720$ hours.

Check Points 11.2

1. There are 5 men to choose from for the first joke. This leaves 5 choices for the second joke. The number of choices then decreases by 1 each time a joke is selected.

1st joke:		2nd joke:		3rd joke:		4th joke:		5th joke:		6th joke:	
5	×	5	×	4	×	3	×	2	×	1	= 600

2. The number of choices decreases by 1 each time a book is selected.

1st Book:		2nd Book:		3rd Book:		4th Book:		5th Book:	
5	×	4	×	3	×	2	×	1	= 120

3. a. $\frac{9!}{6!}=\frac{9\cdot 8\cdot 7\cdot 6!}{6!}=\frac{9\cdot 8\cdot 7\cdot \cancel{6!}}{\cancel{6!}}=9\cdot 8\cdot 7=504$

b. $\frac{16!}{11!}=\frac{16\cdot 15\cdot 14\cdot 13\cdot 12\cdot 11!}{11!}=\frac{16\cdot 15\cdot 14\cdot 13\cdot 12\cdot \cancel{11!}}{\cancel{11!}}=16\cdot 15\cdot 14\cdot 13\cdot 12=524{,}160$

c. $\frac{100!}{99!}=\frac{100\cdot 99!}{99!}=\frac{100\cdot \cancel{99!}}{\cancel{99!}}=100$

4. ${}_7P_4=\frac{7!}{(7-4)!}=\frac{7!}{3!}=\frac{7\cdot 6\cdot 5\cdot 4\cdot 3!}{3!}=\frac{7\cdot 6\cdot 5\cdot 4\cdot \cancel{3!}}{\cancel{3!}}=7\cdot 6\cdot 5\cdot 4=840$

5. ${}_9P_5=\frac{9!}{(9-5)!}=\frac{9!}{4!}=\frac{9\cdot 8\cdot 7\cdot 6\cdot 5\cdot 4!}{4!}=\frac{9\cdot 8\cdot 7\cdot 6\cdot 5\cdot \cancel{4!}}{\cancel{4!}}=9\cdot 8\cdot 7\cdot 6\cdot 5=15{,}120$

6. There a 7 letters with 2 O's and 3 S's. Thus, $\frac{n!}{p!q!}=\frac{7!}{2!3!}=\frac{7\cdot 6\cdot 5\cdot 4\cdot \cancel{3!}}{2\cdot 1\cdot \cancel{3!}}=420$

Concept and Vocabulary Check 11.2

1. factorial; 5; 1; 1

2. $\frac{n!}{(n-r)!}$

3. $\frac{n!}{p!q!}$

4. false

5. false

6. true

7. false

Exercise Set 11.2

1. The number of choices decreases by 1 each time a performer is selected.

1st Performer:		2nd Performer:		3rd Performer:		4th Performer:		5th Performer:		6th Performer:	
6	×	5	×	4	×	3	×	2	×	1	= 720

3. The number of choices decreases by 1 each time a sentence is selected.

1st Sentence:		2nd Sentence:		3rd Sentence:		4th Sentence:		5th Sentence:	
5	×	4	×	3	×	2	×	1	= 120

5. There is only one choice for the 6th performer. The number of choices decreases by 1 each time a performer is selected.

1st Performer:	2nd Performer:	3rd Performer:	4th Performer:	5th Performer:	6th Performer:	
5 ×	4 ×	3 ×	2 ×	1 ×	1	= 120

7. The number of choices decreases by 1 each time a book is selected.

1st Book:	2nd:	3rd Book:	4th:	5th Book:	6th:	7th Book:	8th:	9th Book:	
9 ×	8 ×	7 ×	6 ×	5 ×	4 ×	3 ×	2 ×	1	= 362,880

9. There is only one choice each for the first and last sentences. For the other values, the number of choices decreases by 1 each time a sentence is selected.

1st Sentence:	2nd Sentence:	3rd Sentence:	4th Sentence:	5th Sentence:	
1 ×	3 ×	2 ×	1 ×	1	= 6

11. There are two choices for the first movie and one for the second. There is only one choice for the last movie. This leaves two choices for the third movie and one for the fourth.

G rated		Other two movies		NC-17 Rated	
1st Movie:	2nd Movie:	3rd Movie:	4th Movie:	5th Movie:	
2 ×	1 ×	2 ×	1 ×	1	= 4

13. $\frac{9!}{6!} = \frac{9 \cdot 8 \cdot 7 \cdot 6!}{6!} = 9 \cdot 8 \cdot 7 = 504$

15. $\frac{29!}{25!} = \frac{29 \cdot 28 \cdot 27 \cdot 26 \cdot 25!}{25!}$
$= 29 \cdot 28 \cdot 27 \cdot 26$
$= 570,024$

17. $\frac{19!}{11!} = \frac{19 \cdot 18 \cdot 17 \cdot 16 \cdot 15 \cdot 14 \cdot 13 \cdot 12 \cdot 11!}{11!}$
$= 19 \cdot 18 \cdot 17 \cdot 16 \cdot 15 \cdot 14 \cdot 13 \cdot 12$
$= 3,047,466,240$

19. $\frac{600!}{599!} = \frac{600 \cdot 599!}{599!} = 600$

21. $\frac{104!}{102!} = \frac{104 \cdot 103 \cdot 102!}{102!} = 104 \cdot 103 = 10,712$

23. $7! - 3! = 5040 - 6 = 5034$

25. $(7-3)! = 4! = 4 \cdot 3 \cdot 2 \cdot 1 = 24$

27. $\left(\frac{12}{4}\right)! = 3! = 3 \cdot 2 \cdot 1 = 6$

29. $\frac{7!}{(7-2)!} = \frac{7!}{5!} = \frac{7 \cdot 6 \cdot 5!}{5!} = 7 \cdot 6 = 42$

31. $\dfrac{13!}{(13-3)!}=\dfrac{13!}{10!}$
$=\dfrac{13\cdot 12\cdot 11\cdot 10!}{10!}$
$=13\cdot 12\cdot 11$
$=1716$

33. ${}_9P_4=\dfrac{9!}{(9-4)!}$
$=\dfrac{9!}{5!}$
$=\dfrac{9\cdot 8\cdot 7\cdot 6\cdot 5!}{5!}$
$=9\cdot 8\cdot 7\cdot 6$
$=3024$

35. ${}_8P_5=\dfrac{8!}{(8-5)!}$
$=\dfrac{8!}{3!}$
$=\dfrac{8\cdot 7\cdot 6\cdot 5\cdot 4\cdot 3!}{3!}$
$=8\cdot 7\cdot 6\cdot 5\cdot 4$
$=6720$

37. ${}_6P_6=\dfrac{6!}{(6-6)!}=\dfrac{6!}{0!}=\dfrac{6\cdot 5\cdot 4\cdot 3\cdot 2\cdot 1}{1}=720$

39. ${}_8P_0=\dfrac{8!}{(8-0)!}=\dfrac{8!}{8!}=1$

41. ${}_{10}P_3=\dfrac{10!}{(10-3)!}$
$=\dfrac{10!}{7!}$
$=\dfrac{10\cdot 9\cdot 8\cdot 7!}{7!}$
$=10\cdot 9\cdot 8$
$=720$

43. ${}_{13}P_7=\dfrac{13!}{(13-7)!}$
$=\dfrac{13!}{6!}$
$=\dfrac{13\cdot 12\cdot 11\cdot 10\cdot 9\cdot 8\cdot 7\cdot 6!}{6!}$
$=13\cdot 12\cdot 11\cdot 10\cdot 9\cdot 8\cdot 7$
$=8,648,640$

45. ${}_6P_3=\dfrac{6!}{(6-3)!}$
$=\dfrac{6!}{3!}$
$=\dfrac{6\cdot 5\cdot 4\cdot 3!}{3!}$
$=6\cdot 5\cdot 4$
$=120$

47. ${}_9P_5=\dfrac{9!}{(9-5)!}$
$=\dfrac{9!}{4!}$
$=\dfrac{9\cdot 8\cdot 7\cdot 6\cdot 5\cdot 4!}{4!}$
$=9\cdot 8\cdot 7\cdot 6\cdot 5$
$=15,120$

49. $\dfrac{n!}{p!q!}=\dfrac{6!}{2!2!}=\dfrac{6\cdot 5\cdot 4\cdot 3\cdot 2\cdot 1}{2\cdot 1\cdot 2\cdot 1}=180$

51. $\dfrac{n!}{p!q!r!s!}=\dfrac{11!}{3!2!2!2!}$
$=\dfrac{11\cdot 10\cdot 9\cdot 8\cdot 7\cdot 6\cdot 5\cdot 4\cdot \cancel{3!}}{\cancel{3!}\cdot 2\cdot 1\cdot 2\cdot 1\cdot 2\cdot 1}$
$=831,600$

53. $\dfrac{n!}{p!q!}=\dfrac{7!}{4!2!}=\dfrac{7\cdot 6\cdot 5\cdot \cancel{4!}}{\cancel{4!}\cdot 2\cdot 1}=105$

55. $\dfrac{n!}{p!q!}=\dfrac{8!}{4!3!}=\dfrac{8\cdot 7\cdot 6\cdot 5\cdot \cancel{4!}}{\cancel{4!}\cdot 3\cdot 2\cdot 1}=280$

63. Because the letter B is repeated in the word BABE, the number of permutations is given by
$\dfrac{n!}{p!}=\dfrac{4!}{2!}=\dfrac{4\cdot 3\cdot 2\cdot 1}{2\cdot 1}=12$

65. makes sense

67. does not make sense; Explanations will vary. Sample explanation: This situation calls for the formula for permutations of duplicate items.

69. Multiply the number of ways to select the two first place horses by the number of orders in which the remaining four horses can finish.
${}_6C_2\times {}_4P_4=15\times 24=360$

71. There are 5! ways to arrange the women, and 5! ways to arrange the men. The total number of arrangements is found by multiplying these values: (5!)(5!) = 120 · 120 = 14,400

73. $_nP_{n-2} = \dfrac{n!}{(n-(n-2))!} = \dfrac{n!}{(n-n+2)!} = \dfrac{n!}{2!} = \dfrac{n(n-1)(n-2)\times\cdots\times 3\times 2\times 1}{2} = n(n-1)(n-2)\times\cdots\times 3$

Check Points 11.3

1. a. The order in which you select the DVDs does not matter. This problem involves combinations.

b. Order matters. This problem involves permutations.

2. $_7C_3 = \dfrac{7!}{(7-3)!3!} = \dfrac{7!}{4!3!} = \dfrac{7\cdot6\cdot5\cdot4!}{4!\cdot3\cdot2\cdot1} = \dfrac{7\cdot6\cdot5\cdot\cancel{4!}}{\cancel{4!}\cdot3\cdot2\cdot1} = \dfrac{7\cdot6\cdot5}{3\cdot2\cdot1} = 35$

35 such combinations are possible.

3. $_{16}C_4 = \dfrac{16!}{(16-4)!4!} = \dfrac{16!}{12!4!} = \dfrac{16\cdot15\cdot14\cdot13\cdot12!}{12!\cdot4\cdot3\cdot2\cdot1} = \dfrac{16\cdot15\cdot14\cdot13\cdot\cancel{12!}}{\cancel{12!}\cdot4\cdot3\cdot2\cdot1} = \dfrac{16\cdot15\cdot14\cdot13}{4\cdot3\cdot2\cdot1} = 1820$

1820 such hands can be dealt.

4. Choose the male bears: $_6C_2 = \dfrac{6!}{(6-2)!2!} = \dfrac{6!}{4!2!} = \dfrac{6\cdot5\cdot4!}{4!\cdot2\cdot1} = \dfrac{6\cdot5\cdot\cancel{4!}}{\cancel{4!}\cdot2\cdot1} = \dfrac{30}{2} = 15$

Choose the female bears: $_7C_3 = \dfrac{7!}{(7-3)!3!} = \dfrac{7!}{4!3!} = \dfrac{7\cdot6\cdot5\cdot4!}{4!\cdot3\cdot2\cdot1} = \dfrac{7\cdot6\cdot5\cdot\cancel{4!}}{\cancel{4!}\cdot3\cdot2\cdot1} = \dfrac{210}{6} = 35$

Multiply the choices: $15\times35 = 525$
There are 525 five-bear collections possible.

Concept and Vocabulary Check 11.3

1. $\dfrac{n!}{(n-r)!r!}$

2. $r!$

3. false

4. false

Exercise Set 11.3

1. Order does not matter. This problem involves combinations.

3. Order matters. This problem involves permutations.

5. $_6C_5 = \dfrac{6!}{(6-5)!5!} = \dfrac{6!}{1!5!} = \dfrac{6\cdot5!}{1\cdot5!} = 6$

7. $_9C_5=\frac{9!}{(9-5)!5!}=\frac{9!}{4!5!}=\frac{9\cdot 8\cdot 7\cdot 6\cdot 5!}{4\cdot 3\cdot 2\cdot 1\cdot 5!}=126$

9. $_{11}C_4=\frac{11!}{(11-4)!4!}=\frac{11!}{7!4!}=\frac{11\cdot 10\cdot 9\cdot 8\cdot 7!}{7!\cdot 4\cdot 3\cdot 2\cdot 1}=330$

11. $_8C_1=\frac{8!}{(8-1)!1!}=\frac{8!}{7!1!}=\frac{8\cdot 7!}{7!1}=8$

13. $_7C_7=\frac{7!}{(7-7)!7!}=\frac{7!}{0!7!}=1$

15. $_{30}C_3=\frac{30!}{(30-3)!3!}=\frac{30!}{27!3!}=\frac{30\cdot 29\cdot 28\cdot 27!}{27!\cdot 3\cdot 2\cdot 1}=4060$

17. $_5C_0=\frac{5!}{(5-0)!0!}=\frac{5!}{5!0!}=1$

19. $\frac{_7C_3}{_5C_4}=\frac{\frac{7!}{(7-3)!3!}}{\frac{5!}{(5-4)!4!}}=\frac{\frac{7!}{4!3!}}{\frac{5!}{1!4!}}=\frac{\frac{7\cdot 6\cdot 5\cdot 4!}{4!\cdot 3\cdot 2\cdot 1}}{\frac{5\cdot 4!}{1\cdot 4!}}=\frac{35}{5}=7$

21. $\frac{_7P_3}{3!}-{_7C_3}=\frac{\frac{7!}{(7-3)!}}{3!}-\frac{7!}{(7-3)!3!}=\frac{\frac{7!}{4!}}{3!}-\frac{7!}{4!3!}=\frac{7!}{4!3!}-\frac{7!}{4!3!}=0$

23. $1-\frac{_3P_2}{_4P_3}=1-\frac{\frac{3!}{(3-2)!}}{\frac{4!}{(4-3)!}}=\frac{\frac{3!}{1!}}{\frac{4!}{1!}}=1-\frac{3!}{4!}=1-\frac{3!}{4\cdot 3!}=1-\frac{1}{4}=\frac{3}{4}$

25. $\frac{_7C_3}{_5C_4}-\frac{98!}{96!}=\frac{\frac{7!}{(7-3)!3!}}{\frac{5!}{(5-4)!4!}}-\frac{98\cdot 97\cdot \cancel{96!}}{\cancel{96!}}=\frac{\frac{7!}{4!3!}}{\frac{5!}{1!4!}}-95067=\frac{\frac{7\cdot 6\cdot 5\cdot \cancel{4!}}{\cancel{4!}3\cdot 2\cdot 1}}{\frac{5\cdot \cancel{4!}}{1!\cancel{4!}}}-9506=\frac{35}{5}-9506=7-9506=-9499$

27. $\frac{_4C_2\cdot{_6C_1}}{_{18}C_3}=\frac{\frac{4!}{(4-2)!2!}\cdot\frac{6!}{(6-1)!1!}}{\frac{18!}{(18-3)!3!}}=\frac{\frac{4!}{2!2!}\cdot\frac{6!}{5!1!}}{\frac{18!}{15!3!}}=\frac{\frac{4\cdot 3\cdot \cancel{2!}}{\cancel{2!}2\cdot 1}\cdot\frac{6\cdot \cancel{5!}}{\cancel{5!}1!}}{\frac{18\cdot 17\cdot 16\cdot \cancel{15!}}{\cancel{15!}3\cdot 2\cdot 1}}=\frac{36}{816}=\frac{3}{68}$

29. $_6C_3=\frac{6!}{(6-3)!3!}=\frac{6!}{3!3!}=\frac{6\cdot 5\cdot 4\cdot 3!}{3!3\cdot 2\cdot 1}=20$

31. $_{12}C_4=\frac{12!}{(12-4)!4!}=\frac{12!}{8!4!}=\frac{12\cdot 11\cdot 10\cdot 9\cdot 8!}{8!4\cdot 3\cdot 2\cdot 1}=495$

33. $_{17}C_8=\frac{17!}{(17-8)!8!}=\frac{17!}{9!8!}=\frac{17\cdot 16\cdot 15\cdot 14\cdot 13\cdot 12\cdot 11\cdot 10\cdot 9!}{9!8\cdot 7\cdot 6\cdot 5\cdot 4\cdot 3\cdot 2\cdot 1}=24,310$

35. $_{53}C_6 = \frac{53!}{(53-6)!6!} = \frac{53!}{47!6!} = \frac{53\cdot 52\cdot 51\cdot 50\cdot 49\cdot 48\cdot 47!}{47!6\cdot 5\cdot 4\cdot 3\cdot 2\cdot 1} = 22,957,480$

37. Choose the men: $_7C_4 = \frac{7!}{(7-4)!4!} = \frac{7!}{3!4!} = \frac{7\cdot 6\cdot 5\cdot 4!}{3\cdot 2\cdot 1\cdot 4!} = 35$

Choose the women: $_7C_5 = \frac{7!}{(7-5)!5!} = \frac{7!}{2!5!} = \frac{7\cdot 6\cdot 5!}{2\cdot 1\cdot 5!} = 21$

Multiply the choices: $35 \cdot 21 = 735$

39. Choose the Republicans: $_{55}C_4 = \frac{55!}{(55-4)!4!} = \frac{55!}{51!4!} = \frac{55\cdot 54\cdot 53\cdot 52\cdot 51!}{51!\cdot 4\cdot 3\cdot 2\cdot 1} = 341,055$

Choose the Democrats: $_{44}C_3 = \frac{44!}{(44-3)!3!} = \frac{44!}{41!3!} = \frac{44\cdot 43\cdot 42\cdot 41!}{3\cdot 2\cdot 1\cdot 41!} = 13,244$

Multiply the choices: $341,055 \times 13,244 = 4,516,932,420$

41. $_6P_4 = \frac{6!}{2!} = 6\cdot 5\cdot 4\cdot 3 = 360$ ways

43. $_{13}C_6 = \frac{13!}{7!6!} = \frac{13\cdot 12\cdot 11\cdot 10\cdot 9\cdot 8}{6\cdot 5\cdot 4\cdot 3\cdot 2\cdot 1}$
$= 1716$ ways

45. $_{20}C_3 = \frac{20!}{17!3!} = \frac{20\cdot 19\cdot 18}{3\cdot 2\cdot 1} = 1140$ ways

47. $_7P_4 = \frac{7!}{3!} = 840$ passwords

49. $_{15}P_3 = \frac{15!}{12!} = 15\cdot 14\cdot 13 = 2730$ cones

51. $_5C_2 = \frac{5!}{3!2!} = \frac{5\cdot 4}{2\cdot 1} = 10$ outcomes

53. $3\times 2\times 2 = 12$ outcomes

55. $_5C_3 = \frac{5!}{2!3!} = \frac{5\cdot 4}{2\cdot 1} = 10$ outcomes

57. Choose the Democrats: $_4C_2 = \frac{4!}{2!2!} = \frac{4\cdot 3}{2\cdot 1} = 6$

Choose the Republicans: $_5C_2 = \frac{5!}{3!2!} = \frac{5\cdot 4}{2\cdot 1} = 10$

Multiply the choices: $6\cdot 10 = 60$

59. $_{12}P_5 = \frac{12!}{(12-5)!} = 12\cdot 11\cdot 10\cdot 9\cdot 8 = 95,040$ ways

61. $_6P_6 = \frac{6!}{(6-6)!} = 6\cdot 5\cdot 4\cdot 3\cdot 2\cdot 1 = 720$ ways

63. ${}_6C_3 = \dfrac{6!}{(6-3)!3!} = \dfrac{6!}{3!3!} = \dfrac{6\cdot5\cdot4\cdot3!}{3\cdot2\cdot1\cdot3!} = 20$ ways

65. ${}_4P_4 = \dfrac{4!}{(4-4)!} = 4\cdot3\cdot2\cdot1 = 24$ ways

67. $2\cdot{}_4C_2 = 2\cdot\dfrac{4!}{(4-2)!2!} = 2\cdot\dfrac{4!}{2!2!} = 2\cdot\dfrac{4\cdot3\cdot2!}{2\cdot1\cdot2!} = 12$ ways

73. does not make sense; Explanations will vary. Sample explanation: Since order matters, the permutation formula is necessary.

75. makes sense

77. Selections for 6/53 lottery: ${}_{53}C_6 = \dfrac{53!}{(53-6)!6!} = \dfrac{53!}{47!6!} = \dfrac{53\cdot52\cdot51\cdot50\cdot49\cdot48\cdot47!}{47!6\cdot5\cdot4\cdot3\cdot2\cdot1} = 22{,}957{,}480$

Selections for 5/36 lottery: ${}_{36}C_5 = \dfrac{36!}{(36-5)!5!} = \dfrac{36!}{31!5!} = \dfrac{36\cdot35\cdot34\cdot33\cdot32\cdot31!}{31!5\cdot4\cdot3\cdot2\cdot1} = 376{,}992$

The 5/36 lottery is easier to win because there are fewer possible selections.

79. For a group of 20 people:

${}_{20}C_2 = \dfrac{20!}{(20-2)!2!} = \dfrac{20!}{18!2!} = \dfrac{20\cdot19\cdot18!}{18!2\cdot1} = 190$ handshakes

Time $= 3\times190 = 570$ seconds, which gives $570\div60 = 9.5$ minutes.

For a group of 40 people:

${}_{40}C_2 = \dfrac{40!}{(40-2)!2!} = \dfrac{40!}{38!2!} = \dfrac{40\cdot39\cdot38!}{38!2\cdot1} = 780$ handshakes

Time $= 3\times780 = 2340$ seconds, which gives $2340\div60 = 39$ minutes.

Check Points 11.4

1. a. The event of getting a 2 can occur in one way.

$P(2) = \dfrac{\text{number of ways a 2 can occur}}{\text{total number of possible outcomes}} = \dfrac{1}{6}$

b. The event of getting a number less than 4 can occur in three ways: 1, 2, 3.

$P(\text{less than } 4) = \dfrac{\text{number of ways a number less than 4 can occur}}{\text{total number of possible outcomes}} = \dfrac{3}{6} = \dfrac{1}{2}$

c. The event of getting a number greater than 7 cannot occur.

$P(\text{greater than } 7) = \dfrac{\text{number of ways a number greater than 7 can occur}}{\text{total number of possible outcomes}} = \dfrac{0}{6} = 0$

The probability of an event that cannot occur is 0.

d. The event of getting a number less than 7 can occur in six ways: 1, 2, 3, 4, 5, 6.

$P(\text{less than } 7) = \dfrac{\text{number of ways a number less than 7 can occur}}{\text{total number of possible outcomes}} = \dfrac{6}{6} = 1$

The probability of any certain event is 1.

2. a. $P(\text{ace}) = \dfrac{\text{number of ways a ace can occur}}{\text{total number of possibilities}} = \dfrac{4}{52} = \dfrac{1}{13}$

b. $P(\text{red card}) = \dfrac{\text{number of ways a red card can occur}}{\text{total number of possible outcomes}} = \dfrac{26}{52} = \dfrac{1}{2}$

c. $P(\text{red king}) = \dfrac{\text{number of ways a red king can occur}}{\text{total number of possible outcomes}} = \dfrac{2}{52} = \dfrac{1}{26}$

3. The table shows the four equally likely outcomes. The *Cc* and *cC* children will be carriers who are not actually sick.

$P(\text{carrier, not sick}) = P(Cc) = \dfrac{\text{number of ways } Cc \text{ or } cC \text{ can occur}}{\text{total number of possible outcomes}} = \dfrac{2}{4} = \dfrac{1}{2}$

4. a. $P(\text{never married}) = \dfrac{\text{number of persons never married}}{\text{total number of U.S. adults}} = \dfrac{74}{242} \approx 0.31$

b. $P(\text{male}) = \dfrac{\text{number of males}}{\text{total number of U.S. adults}} = \dfrac{118}{242} \approx 0.49$

Concept and Vocabulary Check 11.4

1. sample space

2. $P(E)$; number of outcomes in *E*; total number of possible outcomes

3. 52; hearts; diamonds; clubs; spades

4. empirical

5. true

6. false

7. true

8. false

Exercise Set 11.4

1. $P(4) = \dfrac{\text{number of ways a 4 can occur}}{\text{total number of possible outcomes}} = \dfrac{1}{6}$

3. $P(\text{odd number}) = \dfrac{\text{number of ways an odd number can occur}}{\text{total number of possible outcomes}} = \dfrac{3}{6} = \dfrac{1}{2}$

5. $P(\text{less than 3}) = \dfrac{\text{number of ways a number less than 3 can occur}}{\text{total number of possible outcomes}} = \dfrac{2}{6} = \dfrac{1}{3}$

7. $P(\text{less than } 20) = \dfrac{\text{number of ways a number less than 20 can occur}}{\text{total number of possible outcomes}} = \dfrac{6}{6} = 1$

9. $P(\text{greater than } 20) = \dfrac{\text{number of ways a number greater than 20 can occur}}{\text{total number of possible outcomes}} = \dfrac{0}{6} = 0$

11. $P(\text{queen}) = \dfrac{\text{number of ways a queen can occur}}{\text{total number of possibilities}} = \dfrac{4}{52} = \dfrac{1}{13}$

13. $P(\text{club}) = \dfrac{\text{number of ways a club can occur}}{\text{total number of possibilities}} = \dfrac{13}{52} = \dfrac{1}{4}$

15. $P(\text{picture card}) = \dfrac{\text{number of ways a picture card can occur}}{\text{total number of possibilities}} = \dfrac{12}{52} = \dfrac{3}{13}$

17. $P(\text{queen of spades}) = \dfrac{\text{number of ways a queen of spades can occur}}{\text{total number of possibilities}} = \dfrac{1}{52}$

19. $P(\text{diamond and spade}) = \dfrac{\text{number of ways a diamond and a spade can occur}}{\text{total number of possibilities}} = \dfrac{0}{52} = 0$

21. $P(\text{two heads}) = \dfrac{\text{number of ways two heads can occur}}{\text{total number of possibilities}} = \dfrac{1}{4}$

23. $P(\text{same on each toss}) = \dfrac{\text{number of ways the same outcome on each toss can occur}}{\text{total number of possibilities}} = \dfrac{2}{4} = \dfrac{1}{2}$

25. $P(\text{head on second toss}) = \dfrac{\text{number of ways a head on the second toss can occur}}{\text{total number of possibilities}} = \dfrac{2}{4} = \dfrac{1}{2}$

27. $P(\text{exactly one female child}) = \dfrac{\text{number of ways exactly one female child can occur}}{\text{total number of possibilities}} = \dfrac{3}{8}$

29. $P(\text{exactly two male children}) = \dfrac{\text{number of ways exactly two male children can occur}}{\text{total number of possibilities}} = \dfrac{3}{8}$

31. $P(\text{at least one male child}) = \dfrac{\text{number of ways at least one male child can occur}}{\text{total number of possiblities}} = \dfrac{7}{8}$

33. $P(\text{four male children}) = \dfrac{\text{number of ways four male children can occur}}{\text{total number of possibilities}} = \dfrac{0}{8} = 0$

35. $P(\text{two even numbers}) = \dfrac{\text{number of ways two even numbers can occur}}{\text{total number of possibilities}} = \dfrac{9}{36} = \dfrac{1}{4}$

37. $P(\text{two numbers whose sum is 5}) = \dfrac{\text{number of ways two numbers whose sum is 5 can occur}}{\text{total number of possibilities}} = \dfrac{4}{36} = \dfrac{1}{9}$

39. $P(\text{two numbers whose sum exceeds 12})$

$$= \frac{\text{number of ways two numbers whose sum exceeds 12 can occur}}{\text{total number of possibilities}} = \frac{0}{36} = 0$$

41. $P(\text{red region}) = \frac{\text{number of ways a red region can occur}}{\text{total number of possibilities}} = \frac{3}{10}$

43. $P(\text{blue region}) = \frac{\text{number of ways a blue region can occur}}{\text{total number of possibilities}} = \frac{2}{10} = \frac{1}{5}$

45. $P(\text{region that is red or blue}) = \frac{\text{number of ways a region that is red or blue can occur}}{\text{total number of possibilities}} = \frac{5}{10} = \frac{1}{2}$

47. $P(\text{region that is red and blue}) = \frac{\text{number of ways a region that is red and blue can occur}}{\text{total number of possibilities}} = \frac{0}{10} = 0$

49. $P(\text{sickle cell anemia}) = \frac{\text{number of ways sickle cell anemia can occur}}{\text{total number of possibilities}} = \frac{1}{4}$

51. $P(\text{healthy}) = \frac{\text{number of ways a healthy child can occur}}{\text{total number of possibilities}} = \frac{1}{4}$

53. $P(\text{sickle cell trait}) = \frac{\text{number of ways sickle cell trait can occur}}{\text{total number of possibilities}} = \frac{2}{4} = \frac{1}{2}$

55. $P(\text{male}) = \frac{\text{number of males}}{\text{total number of Americans living alone}} = \frac{12.5}{29.3} \approx 0.43$

57. $P(25-34 \text{ age range}) = \frac{\text{number in } 25-34 \text{ age range}}{\text{total number of Americans living alone}} = \frac{3.8}{29.3} \approx 0.13$

59. $P(\text{woman in } 15-24 \text{ age range}) = \frac{\text{number of women in } 15-24 \text{ age range}}{\text{total number of Americans living alone}} = \frac{0.8}{29.3} \approx 0.03$

61. $P(\text{owner}) = \frac{\text{number of owners}}{\text{total number of Americans who moved in 2004}} = \frac{14.8}{39.0} \approx 0.38$

63. $P(\text{moved within state}) = \frac{\text{number that moved within state}}{\text{total number of Americans who moved in 2004}} = \frac{30.4}{39.0} \approx 0.78$

65. $P(\text{renter who moved to different state}) = \frac{\text{number of renters who moved to a different state}}{\text{total number of Americans who moved in 2004}} = \frac{4.5}{39.0} \approx 0.12$

67. $P(\text{had less than 4 years of high school}) = \frac{\text{number with less than 4 years of high school}}{\text{total number of Americans aged 25 and older}} = \frac{29}{174} = \frac{1}{6}$

69. $P(\text{a woman with 4 years of college or more}) = \frac{\text{number of women with 4 years of college or more}}{\text{total number of Americans aged 25 and older}} = \frac{22}{174} = \frac{11}{87}$

79. does not make sense; Explanations will vary. Sample explanation: Even if there are only two choices, it does not necessarily follow that they are equally likely to be selected.

81. makes sense

83. The area of the target is $(12 \text{ in.})^2 = 144 \text{ in.}^2$

The area of the yellow region is $(9 \text{ in.})^2 - (6 \text{ in.})^2 + (3 \text{ in.})^2 = 54 \text{ in.}^2$

The probability that the dart hits a yellow region is $\dfrac{54 \text{ in.}^2}{144 \text{ in.}^2} = 0.375$

Check Points 11.5

1. total number of permutations = 6! = 6 · 5 · 4 · 3 · 2 · 1 = 720
For the given outcome there is 1 choice (first name beginning with G) for the first joke, which would leave 4 choices for the last joke (the 4 remaining men). The remaining jokes have 4, 3, 2, and 1 choice respectively.

$$\underbrace{\underline{\text{1st:}}}_{\text{First name begins with G}} \quad \overbrace{\underline{\text{2nd:}} \quad \underline{\text{3rd:}} \quad \underline{\text{4th:}} \quad \underline{\text{5th:}}}^{\text{4 jokes other than first and last}} \quad \overbrace{\underline{\text{6th:}}}^{\text{man (other than first joke)}}$$

$$1 \times 4 \times 3 \times 2 \times 1 \times 4 = 96$$

$P(\text{first joke is by a man whose name begins with G and the last is by a man}) = \dfrac{96}{720} = \dfrac{2}{15}$

2. Total number of Powerball selections:
$$\begin{aligned} {}_{59}C_5 \cdot 35 &= \frac{59!}{(59-5)!5!} \cdot 35 \\ &= \frac{59!}{54!5!} \cdot 35 \\ &= \frac{59 \cdot 58 \cdot 57 \cdot 56 \cdot 55 \cdot 54!}{54!5 \cdot 4 \cdot 3 \cdot 2 \cdot 1} \cdot 35 \\ &= 5,006,386 \cdot 35 \\ &= 175,223,510 \end{aligned}$$

Number of selections that match 4 out of 5 white balls and the Powerball:

$$\overbrace{{}_5C_4}^{\text{match 4 of the 5 selected white balls}} \times \overbrace{{}_{54}C_1}^{\text{any 1 of the 54 non-selected white balls}} \times \overbrace{1}^{\text{the Powerball}} = 270$$

$$\begin{aligned} P(\text{matching 4 of the 5 white balls and the powerball}) &= \frac{270}{175,223,510} \\ &= \frac{27}{17,522,351} \\ &\approx 0.000001541 \\ &\approx 1.541 \times 10^{-6} \end{aligned}$$

3. total number of combinations: $_{10}C_3 = \frac{10!}{(10-3)!3!} = \frac{10!}{7!3!} = \frac{10\cdot 9\cdot 8\cdot 7!}{7!3\cdot 2\cdot 1} = 120$

a. total number of combinations of 3 men: $_6C_3 = \frac{6!}{(6-3)!3!} = \frac{6!}{3!3!} = \frac{6\cdot 5\cdot 4\cdot 3!}{3\cdot 2\cdot 1\cdot 3!} = 20$

$P(3\text{ men}) = \frac{\text{number of combinations with 3 men}}{\text{total number of combinations}} = \frac{20}{120} = \frac{1}{6}$

b. Select 2 out of 6 men: $_6C_2 = \frac{6!}{(6-2)!2!} = \frac{6!}{4!2!} = \frac{6\cdot 5\cdot 4!}{4!2\cdot 1} = 15$

Select 1 out of 4 women: $_4C_1 = \frac{4!}{(4-1)!1!} = \frac{4!}{3!1!} = \frac{4\cdot 3!}{3!} = \frac{4\cdot \cancel{3!}}{\cancel{3!}} = 4$

total number of combinations of 2 men and 1 woman: $15\times 4 = 60$

$P(2\text{ men, 1 woman}) = \frac{\text{number of combinations with 2 men, 1 woman}}{\text{total number of combinations}} = \frac{60}{120} = \frac{1}{2}$

Concept and Vocabulary Check 11.5

1. permutations; the total number of possible permutations
2. 1; combinations
3. true
4. false

Exercise Set 11.5

1. a. $5! = 5\cdot 4\cdot 3\cdot 2\cdot 1 = 120$

b.

Martha	Lee, Nancy, Paul			Armando	
1st:	2nd:	3rd:	4th:	5th:	
1 ×	3 ×	2 ×	1 ×	1	= 6

c. $P(\text{Martha first and Armando last}) = \frac{6}{120} = \frac{1}{20}$

3. a. total number of permutations $= 6! = 6\cdot 5\cdot 4\cdot 3\cdot 2\cdot 1 = 720$
number of permutations with E first $= 1\cdot 5\cdot 4\cdot 3\cdot 2\cdot 1 = 120$

$P(\text{E first}) = \frac{\text{number of permutations with E first}}{\text{total number of permutations}} = \frac{120}{720} = \frac{1}{6}$

b. number of permutations with C fifth and B last $= 4\cdot 3\cdot 2\cdot 1\cdot 1\cdot 1 = 24$

$P(\text{C fifth and B last}) = \frac{\text{number of permutations with C fifth and B last}}{\text{total number of permutations}} = \frac{24}{720} = \frac{1}{30}$

c. $P(\text{D, E, C, A, B, F}) = \frac{\text{number of permutations with order D, E, C, A, B, F}}{\text{total number of permutations}} = \frac{1}{720}$

d. number of permutations with A or B first $= 2\cdot 5\cdot 4\cdot 3\cdot 2\cdot 1 = 240$

$P(\text{A or B first}) = \frac{\text{number of permutations with A or B first}}{\text{total number of permutations}} = \frac{240}{720} = \frac{1}{3}$

5. a. $_9C_3 = \frac{9!}{(9-3)!3!} = \frac{9!}{6!3!} = \frac{9 \cdot 8 \cdot 7 \cdot 6!}{6!3 \cdot 2 \cdot 1} = 84$

b. $_5C_3 = \frac{5!}{(5-3)!3!} = \frac{5!}{2!3!} = \frac{5 \cdot 4 \cdot 3!}{2 \cdot 1 \cdot 3!} = 10$

c. $P(\text{all women}) = \frac{\text{number of ways to select 3 women}}{\text{total number of possible combinations}} = \frac{10}{84} = \frac{5}{42}$

7. $_{56}C_5 \times 46 = \frac{56!}{(56-5)!5!} \times 46 = \frac{56!}{51!5!} \times 46 = \frac{56 \cdot 55 \cdot 54 \cdot 53 \cdot 52 \cdot 51!}{51!5 \cdot 4 \cdot 3 \cdot 2 \cdot 1} \times 46 = 3{,}819{,}816 \times 46 = 175{,}711{,}536$

$P(\text{winning}) = \frac{\text{number of ways of winning}}{\text{total number of possible combinations}} = \frac{1}{175{,}711{,}536}$

9. Total number of combinations:

$_{56}C_5 \times 46 = \frac{56!}{(56-5)!5!} \times 46 = \frac{56!}{51!5!} \times 46 = \frac{56 \cdot 55 \cdot 54 \cdot 53 \cdot 52 \cdot 51!}{51!5 \cdot 4 \cdot 3 \cdot 2 \cdot 1} \times 46 = 3{,}819{,}816 \times 46 = 175{,}711{,}536$

Number of selections that match 3 out of 5 white balls and the gold Mega Ball:

$$\underbrace{_5C_3}_{\text{match 3 of the 5 selected white balls}} \times \underbrace{_{51}C_2}_{\text{any 2 of the 51 non-selected white balls}} \times \underbrace{1}_{\text{gold Mega Ball}} = 10 \times 1275 \times 1 = 12{,}750$$

$P(\text{matching 3 of the 5 white balls and the gold Mega Ball}) = \frac{12{,}750}{175{,}711{,}536} = \frac{2125}{29{,}285{,}256}$

11. a. $_{25}C_6 = \frac{25!}{(25-6)!6!} = \frac{25!}{19!6!} = \frac{25 \cdot 24 \cdot 23 \cdot 22 \cdot 21 \cdot 20 \cdot 19!}{19!6 \cdot 5 \cdot 4 \cdot 3 \cdot 2 \cdot 1} = 177{,}100$

$P(\text{all are defective}) = \frac{\text{number of ways to choose 6 defective transistors}}{\text{total number of possible combinations}} = \frac{1}{177{,}100} \approx 0.00000565$

b. $_{19}C_6 = \frac{19!}{(19-6)!6!} = \frac{19!}{13!6!} = \frac{19 \cdot 18 \cdot 17 \cdot 16 \cdot 15 \cdot 14 \cdot 13!}{13!6 \cdot 5 \cdot 4 \cdot 3 \cdot 2 \cdot 1} = 27{,}132$

$P(\text{none are defective}) = \frac{\text{number of ways to choose 6 good transistors}}{\text{total number of possible permutations}} = \frac{27{,}132}{177{,}100} = \frac{969}{6325} \approx 0.153$

13. total number of possible combinations: $_{10}C_3 = \frac{10!}{(10-3)!3!} = \frac{10!}{7!3!} = \frac{10 \cdot 9 \cdot 8 \cdot 7!}{7!3 \cdot 2 \cdot 1} = 120$

number of ways to select one Democrat: $_6C_1 = \frac{6!}{(6-1)!1!} = \frac{6!}{5!1!} = \frac{6 \cdot 5!}{5!1} = 6$

number of ways to select two Republicans: $_4C_2 = \frac{4!}{(4-2)!2!} = \frac{4!}{2!2!} = \frac{4 \cdot 3 \cdot 2!}{2!2 \cdot 1} = 6$

number of ways to select one Democrat and two Republicans: $_6C_1 \cdot {_4C_2} = 6 \cdot 6 = 36$

$P(\text{one Democrat and two Republicans}) = \frac{36}{120} = \frac{3}{10} = 0.3$

15. **a.** $_{52}C_5 = \frac{52!}{(52-5)!5!} = \frac{52!}{47!5!} = \frac{52 \cdot 51 \cdot 50 \cdot 49 \cdot 48 \cdot 47!}{47!5 \cdot 4 \cdot 3 \cdot 2 \cdot 1} = 2{,}598{,}960$

b. $_{13}C_5 = \frac{13!}{(13-5)!5!} = \frac{13!}{8!5!} = \frac{13 \cdot 12 \cdot 11 \cdot 10 \cdot 9 \cdot 8!}{8!5 \cdot 4 \cdot 3 \cdot 2 \cdot 1} = 1287$

c. $P(\text{diamond flush}) = \frac{\text{number of possible 5-card diamond flushes}}{\text{total number of possible combinations}} = \frac{1287}{2{,}598{,}960} \approx 0.000495$

17. total number of possible combinations: $_{52}C_3 = \frac{52!}{(52-3)!3!} = \frac{52!}{49!3!} = \frac{52 \cdot 51 \cdot 50 \cdot 49!}{49!3 \cdot 2 \cdot 1} = 22{,}100$

number of ways to select 3 picture cards: $_{12}C_3 = \frac{12!}{(12-3)!3!} = \frac{12!}{9!3!} = \frac{12 \cdot 11 \cdot 10 \cdot 9!}{9!3 \cdot 2 \cdot 1} = 220$

$P(\text{3 picture cards}) = \frac{220}{22{,}100} = \frac{11}{1105} \approx 0.00995$

19. total number of possible combinations: $_{52}C_4 = \frac{52!}{(52-4)!4!} = \frac{52!}{48!4!} = \frac{52 \cdot 51 \cdot 50 \cdot 49 \cdot 48!}{48!4 \cdot 3 \cdot 2 \cdot 1} = 270{,}725$

number of ways to select 2 queens: $_4C_2 = \frac{4!}{(4-2)!2!} = \frac{4!}{2!2!} = \frac{4 \cdot 3 \cdot 2!}{2!2 \cdot 1} = 6$

number of ways to select 2 kings: $_4C_2 = 6$

number of ways to select 2 queens and 2 kings: $_4C_2 \cdot {_4C_2} = 6 \cdot 6 = 36$

$P(\text{2 queens and 2 kings}) = \frac{36}{270{,}725} \approx 0.000133$

25. does not make sense; Explanations will vary. Sample explanation: Each possible combination is equally likely.

27. makes sense

29. Other players could also purchase the winning combination and share the prize money, possibly making this person's share of the prize less than what this person paid for the tickets.

31. total number of possible combinations: $_{52}C_5 = \frac{52!}{(52-5)!5!} = \frac{52!}{47!5!} = \frac{52 \cdot 51 \cdot 50 \cdot 49 \cdot 48 \cdot 47!}{47!5 \cdot 4 \cdot 3 \cdot 2 \cdot 1} = 2{,}598{,}960$

number of ways to select one ace: $_4C_1 = \frac{4!}{(4-1)!1!} = \frac{4!}{3!1!} = \frac{4 \cdot 3!}{3!1} = 4$

Note: one card is an ace, so the other four must not be aces.
number of ways to select 4 cards with no face cards and no aces:

$_{36}C_4 = \frac{36!}{(36-4)!4!} = \frac{36!}{32!4!} = \frac{36 \cdot 35 \cdot 34 \cdot 33 \cdot 32!}{32!4 \cdot 3 \cdot 2 \cdot 1} = 58{,}905$

number of hands with one ace and no face cards: $_4C_1 \cdot {_{36}C_4} = 4 \cdot 58{,}905 = 235{,}620$

$P(\text{one ace and no face cards}) = \frac{\text{number of hands with one ace and no face cards}}{\text{total number of possible combinations}} = \frac{235{,}620}{2{,}598{,}960} \approx 0.0907$

Check Points 11.6

1. $P(\text{not a diamond}) = 1 - P(\text{diamond}) = 1 - \frac{13}{52} = \frac{39}{52} = \frac{3}{4}$

2. a. $P(\text{not } 50-59) = 1 - P(50-59) = 1 - \frac{31}{191} = \frac{160}{191}$

b. $P(\text{at least 20 years old}) = 1 - P(\text{less than 20 years}) = 1 - \frac{9}{191} = \frac{182}{191}$

3. $P(4 \text{ or } 5) = P(4) + P(5) = \frac{1}{6} + \frac{1}{6} = \frac{2}{6} = \frac{1}{3}$

4. $P(\text{math or psychology}) = P(\text{math}) + P(\text{psychology}) - P(\text{math and psychology}) = \frac{23}{50} + \frac{11}{50} - \frac{7}{50} = \frac{27}{50}$

5. $P(\text{odd or less than 5}) = P(\text{odd}) + P(\text{less than 5}) - P(\text{odd and less than 5}) = \frac{4}{8} + \frac{4}{8} - \frac{2}{8} = \frac{6}{8} = \frac{3}{4}$

6. a. These events are not mutually exclusive.

$P(\text{married or female}) = P(\text{married}) + P(\text{female}) - P(\text{married and female})$

$$= \frac{130}{242} + \frac{124}{242} - \frac{65}{242}$$

$$= \frac{189}{242} \approx 0.78$$

b. These events are mutually exclusive.

$P(\text{divorced or widowed}) = P(\text{divorced}) + P(\text{widowed})$

$$= \frac{24}{242} + \frac{14}{242}$$

$$= \frac{38}{242}$$

$$= \frac{19}{121} \approx 0.16$$

7. There are 2 red queens. Number of favorable outcomes = 2, Number of unfavorable outcomes = 50

a. Odds in favor of getting a red queen are 2 to 50 or 2:50 which reduces to 1:25.

b. Odds against getting a red queen are 50 to 2 or 50:2 which reduces to 25:1.

8. number of unfavorable outcomes = 995, number of favorable outcomes = 5
Odds against winning the scholarship are 995 to 5 or 995:5 which reduces to 199:1.

9. number of unfavorable outcomes = 15, number of favorable outcomes = 1
Odds in favor of the horse winning the race are 1 to 15

$P(\text{the horse wins race}) = \frac{1}{1+15} = \frac{1}{16} = 0.0625$ or 6.3%.

Concept and Vocabulary Check 11.6

1. $1-P(E)$; $1-P(\text{not } E)$

2. mutually exclusive; $P(A)+P(B)$

3. $P(A)+P(B)-P(A \text{ and } B)$

4. E will occur; E will not occur

5. $P(E)=\dfrac{a}{a+b}$

6. false

7. false

8. true

9. false

Exercise Set 11.6

1. $P(\text{not an ace}) = 1 - P(\text{ace}) = 1 - \frac{4}{52} = \frac{48}{52} = \frac{12}{13}$

3. $P(\text{not a heart}) = 1 - P(\text{heart}) = 1 - \frac{13}{52} = \frac{39}{52} = \frac{3}{4}$

5. $P(\text{not a picture card}) = 1 - P(\text{picture card}) = 1 - \frac{12}{52} = \frac{40}{52} = \frac{10}{13}$

7. $P(\text{not a straight flush}) = 1 - P(\text{straight flush}) = 1 - \frac{36}{2{,}598{,}960} = \frac{2{,}598{,}924}{2{,}598{,}960} \approx 0.999986$

9. $P(\text{not a full house}) = 1 - P(\text{full house}) = 1 - \frac{3744}{2{,}598{,}960} = \frac{2{,}595{,}216}{2{,}598{,}960} \approx 0.998559$

11. **a.** 0.10 (read from graph)

    b. $1.00 - 0.10 = 0.90$

13. $P(\text{not age } 25-44) = 1 - P(\text{age } 25-44) = 1 - \frac{1080}{3000} = \frac{1920}{3000} = \frac{16}{25}$

15. $P(\text{age less than } 65) = 1 - P(\text{age } 65-74) = 1 - \frac{180}{3000} = \frac{2820}{3000} = \frac{47}{50}$

17. $P(2 \text{ or } 3) = P(2) + P(3) = \frac{4}{52} + \frac{4}{52} = \frac{8}{52} = \frac{2}{13}$

19. $P(\text{red 2 or black 3}) = P(\text{red 2}) + P(\text{black 3}) = \frac{2}{52} + \frac{2}{52} = \frac{4}{52} = \frac{1}{13}$

21. $P(\text{2 of hearts or 3 of spades}) = P(\text{2 of hearts}) + P(\text{3 of spades}) = \frac{1}{52} + \frac{1}{52} = \frac{2}{52} = \frac{1}{26}$

23. $P(\text{professor or instructor}) = P(\text{professor}) + P(\text{instructor}) = \frac{8}{44} + \frac{10}{44} = \frac{18}{44} = \frac{9}{22}$

25. $P(\text{even or less than 5}) = P(\text{even}) + P(\text{less than 5}) - P(\text{even and less than 5}) = \frac{3}{6} + \frac{4}{6} - \frac{2}{6} = \frac{5}{6}$

27. $P(\text{7 or red}) = P(7) + P(\text{red}) - P(\text{red 7}) = \frac{4}{52} + \frac{26}{52} - \frac{2}{52} = \frac{28}{52} = \frac{7}{13}$

29. $P(\text{heart or picture card}) = P(\text{heart}) + P(\text{picture card}) - P(\text{heart and picture card}) = \frac{13}{52} + \frac{12}{52} - \frac{3}{52} = \frac{22}{52} = \frac{11}{26}$

31. $P(\text{odd or less than 6}) = P(\text{odd}) + P(\text{less than 6}) - P(\text{odd and less than 6}) = \frac{4}{8} + \frac{5}{8} - \frac{3}{8} = \frac{6}{8} = \frac{3}{4}$

33. $P(\text{even or greater than 5}) = P(\text{even}) + P(\text{greater than 5}) - P(\text{even and greater than 5}) = \frac{4}{8} + \frac{3}{8} - \frac{2}{8} = \frac{5}{8}$

35. $P(\text{professor or male}) = P(\text{professor}) + P(\text{male}) - P(\text{male professor}) = \frac{19}{40} + \frac{22}{40} - \frac{8}{40} = \frac{33}{40}$

37. $P(\text{teach. assist. or female}) = P(\text{teach. assist.}) + P(\text{female}) - P(\text{female teach. assist.}) = \frac{21}{40} + \frac{18}{40} - \frac{7}{40} = \frac{32}{40} = \frac{4}{5}$

39. $P(\text{Democrat or business major}) = P(\text{Democrat}) + P(\text{business major}) - P(\text{Democrat and business major})$

$$= \frac{29}{50} + \frac{11}{50} - \frac{5}{50} = \frac{35}{50} = \frac{7}{10}$$

41. $P(\text{not completed 4 years or more}) = 1 - P(\text{completed 4 years or more}) = 1 - \frac{45}{174} = \frac{129}{174} = \frac{43}{58}$

43. $P(\text{completed 4 years of high school only or less than four years of college})$

$= P(\text{completed 4 years of high school only}) + P(\text{less than four years of college})$

$= \frac{56}{174} + \frac{44}{174} = \frac{100}{174} = \frac{50}{87}$

45. $P(\text{completed 4 years of high school only or is a man})$

$= P(\text{completed 4 years of high school only}) + P(\text{male}) - P(\text{completed 4 years of high school only and is a man})$

$= \frac{56}{174} + \frac{82}{174} - \frac{25}{174} = \frac{113}{174}$

47. The number that meets the characteristic is 45. The number that does not meet the characteristic is $174 - 45 = 129$.
Odds in favor: 45 to 129 which reduces to 15 to 43
Odds against: 129 to 45 which reduces to 43 to 5

49. $P(\text{not in the Army}) = 1 - P(\text{in the Army}) = 1 - \frac{490+80}{1420} = 1 - \frac{570}{1420} = \frac{85}{142}$

51. $P(\text{in the Navy or a man}) = P(\text{in the Navy}) + P(\text{a man}) - P(\text{in the Navy and a man})$

$$= \frac{270+50}{1420} + \frac{270+490+190+270}{1420} - \frac{270}{1420}$$
$$= \frac{320}{1420} + \frac{1220}{1420} - \frac{270}{1420}$$
$$= \frac{1270}{1420}$$
$$= \frac{127}{142}$$

53. $P(\text{in the Air Force or the Marines}) = P(\text{in the Air Force}) + P(\text{in the Marines}) = \frac{270+60}{1420} + \frac{190+10}{1420} = \frac{530}{1420} = \frac{53}{142}$

55. The number that meets the characteristic is 270 + 50 = 320.
The number that does not meet the characteristic is 1420 – 320 = 1100.
Odds in favor: 320 to 1100 which reduce 16 to 55
Odds against: 1100 to 320 which reduce 55 to 16

57. The number that meets the characteristic is 10. The number that does not meet the characteristic is 1420 – 10 = 1410.
Odds in favor: 10 to 1410 which reduce 1 to 141
Odds against: 1410 to 10 which reduce 141 to 1

59. The number that meets the characteristic is 270 + 490 + 190 + 270 = 1220.
The number that does not meet the characteristic is 1420 –1220 = 200.
Odds in favor: 1220 to 200 which reduce 61 to 10
Odds against: 200 to 1220 which reduce 10 to 61

61. number of favorable outcomes = 4, number of unfavorable outcomes = 2
Odds in favor of getting a number greater than 2 are 4:2, or 2:1.

63. number of unfavorable outcomes = 2, number of favorable outcomes = 4
Odds against getting a number greater than 2 or 2:4, or 1:2.

65. number of favorable outcomes = 9, number of unfavorable outcomes $= 100 - 9 = 91$

a. Odds in favor of a child in a one-parent household having a parent who is a college graduate are 9:91.

b. Odds against a child in a one-parent household having a parent who is a college graduate are 91:9.

67. number of favorable outcomes = 13, number of unfavorable outcomes = 39
Odds in favor of a heart are 13:39, or 1:3.

69. number of favorable outcomes = 26, number of unfavorable outcomes = 26
Odds in favor of a red card are 26:26, or 1:1.

71. number of unfavorable outcomes = 48, number of favorable outcomes = 4
Odds against a 9 are 48:4, or 12:1.

73. number of unfavorable outcomes = 50, number of favorable outcomes = 2
Odds against a black king are 50:2, or 25:1.

75. number of unfavorable outcomes = 47, number of favorable outcomes = 5
Odds against a spade greater than 3 and less than 9 are 47:5.

77. number of unfavorable outcomes = 980, number of favorable outcomes = 20
Odds against winning are 980:20, or 49:1.

79. The number that meets the characteristic is 18. The number that does not meet the characteristic is 38 – 18 = 20.
Odds in favor: 18 to 20 which reduce 9 to 10

81. The number that meets the characteristic is 10. The number that does not meet the characteristic is 38 – 10 = 28.
Odds against: 28 to 10 which reduce 14 to 5

83. The number that meets the characteristic is 18 + 10 = 28.
The number that does not meet the characteristic is 38 – 28 = 10.
Odds in favor: 28 to 10 which reduce 14 to 5

85. The number that meets the characteristic is 10 + 10 = 20.
The number that does not meet the characteristic is 38 – 20 = 18.
Odds against: 18 to 20 which reduce 9 to 10

87. $P(\text{winning}) = \frac{3}{3+4} = \frac{3}{7}$

89. $P(\text{miss free throw}) = \frac{4}{21+4} = \frac{4}{25} = 0.16 = 16\%$
In 100 free throws, on average he missed 16, so he made 100 – 16 = 84.

91. $P(\text{contracting an airborn illness}) = \frac{1}{1+999} = \frac{1}{1000}$

101. does not make sense; Explanations will vary. Sample explanation: Since 1 card is a heart *and* a king, the probability is
$\frac{4}{52} + \frac{13}{52} - \frac{1}{52} = \frac{16}{52} = \frac{4}{13}$.

103. does not make sense; Explanations will vary. Sample explanation: The odds are more likely 1:9.

105. $P(\text{driving intoxicated or driving accident})$
$= P(\text{driving intoxicated}) + P(\text{driving accident}) - P(\text{driving accident while intoxicated})$

Substitute the three given probabilities and solve for the unknown probability:

$$0.35 = 0.32 + 0.09 - P(\text{driving accident while intoxicated})$$

$P(\text{driving accident while intoxicated}) = 0.32 + 0.09 - 0.35$
$P(\text{driving accident while intoxicated}) = 0.06$

Check Points 11.7

1. $P(\text{green and green}) = P(\text{green}) \cdot P(\text{green}) = \frac{2}{38} \cdot \frac{2}{38} = \frac{1}{19} \cdot \frac{1}{19} = \frac{1}{361} \approx 0.00277$

2. $P(\text{4 boys in a row}) = P(\text{boy and boy and boy and boy}) = P(\text{boy}) \cdot P(\text{boy}) \cdot P(\text{boy}) \cdot P(\text{boy}) = \frac{1}{2} \cdot \frac{1}{2} \cdot \frac{1}{2} \cdot \frac{1}{2} = \frac{1}{16}$

3. **a.** $P(\text{hit four years in a row}) = P(\text{hit}) \cdot P(\text{hit}) \cdot P(\text{hit}) \cdot P(\text{hit}) = \frac{5}{19} \cdot \frac{5}{19} \cdot \frac{5}{19} \cdot \frac{5}{19} = \frac{625}{130{,}321} \approx 0.005$

b. Note: $P(\text{not hit in any single year}) = 1 - P(\text{hit in any single year}) = 1 - \frac{5}{19} = \frac{14}{19}$,. Therefore,

$P(\text{not hit in next four years})$

$= P(\text{not hit}) \cdot P(\text{not hit}) \cdot P(\text{not hit}) \cdot P(\text{not hit}) = \frac{14}{19} \cdot \frac{14}{19} \cdot \frac{14}{19} \cdot \frac{14}{19} = \frac{38,416}{130,321} \approx 0.295$

c. $P(\text{hit at least once in next four years}) = 1 - P(\text{not hit in next four years}) = 1 - \frac{38,416}{130,321} = \frac{91,905}{130,321} \approx 0.705$

4. $P(2 \text{ kings}) = P(\text{king}) \cdot P(\text{king given the first card was a king}) = \frac{4}{52} \cdot \frac{3}{51} = \frac{1}{13} \cdot \frac{1}{17} = \frac{1}{221} \approx 0.00452$

5. $P(3 \text{ hearts}) = P(\text{heart}) \cdot P(\text{heart given the first card was a heart}) \cdot P(\text{heart given the first two cards were hearts})$

$= \frac{13}{52} \cdot \frac{12}{51} \cdot \frac{11}{50} = \frac{1}{4} \cdot \frac{4}{17} \cdot \frac{11}{50} = \frac{1}{1} \cdot \frac{1}{17} \cdot \frac{11}{50} = \frac{11}{850} \approx 0.0129$

6. The sample space is given by $S = \{a, e, i, o, u\}$.
Of these 5 elements, only a and e precede h.
Thus the probability is $P(\text{letter precedes h} | \text{vowel}) = \frac{2}{5}$.

7. a. The sample space is the set of 13 spades.
Of these 13 elements, all 13 cards are black.
Thus the probability is $P(\text{black card} | \text{spade}) = \frac{13}{13} = 1$.

b. The sample space is the set of 26 black cards.
Of these 26 elements, 13 cards are spades.
Thus the probability is $P(\text{spade} | \text{black card}) = \frac{13}{26} = \frac{1}{2}$.

8. a. $P(\text{positive mammogram} | \text{breast cancer}) = \frac{720}{800} = \frac{9}{10} = 0.9$.

b. $P(\text{breast cancer} | \text{positive mammogram}) = \frac{720}{7664} = \frac{45}{479} = 0.094$.

Concept and Vocabulary Check 11.7

1. independent; $P(A) \cdot P(B)$
2. the event does not occur
3. dependent; $P(A) \cdot P(B \text{ given that } A \text{ occurred})$
4. conditional; $P(B|A)$
5. false
6. false
7. true
8. true

Exercise Set 11.7

1. $P(\text{green and then red}) = P(\text{green}) \cdot P(\text{red}) = \frac{2}{6} \cdot \frac{3}{6} = \frac{1}{3} \cdot \frac{1}{2} = \frac{1}{6}$

3. $P(\text{yellow and then yellow}) = P(\text{yellow}) \cdot P(\text{yellow}) = \frac{1}{6} \cdot \frac{1}{6} = \frac{1}{36}$

5. $P(\text{color other than red each time}) = P(\text{not red}) \cdot P(\text{not red}) = \frac{3}{6} \cdot \frac{3}{6} = \frac{1}{2} \cdot \frac{1}{2} = \frac{1}{4}$

7. $P(\text{green and then red and then yellow}) = P(\text{green}) \cdot P(\text{red}) \cdot P(\text{yellow}) = \frac{2}{6} \cdot \frac{3}{6} \cdot \frac{1}{6} = \frac{1}{3} \cdot \frac{1}{2} \cdot \frac{1}{6} = \frac{1}{36}$

9. $P(\text{red every time}) = P(\text{red}) \cdot P(\text{red}) \cdot P(\text{red}) = \frac{3}{6} \cdot \frac{3}{6} \cdot \frac{3}{6} = \frac{1}{2} \cdot \frac{1}{2} \cdot \frac{1}{2} = \frac{1}{8}$

11. $P(2 \text{ and then } 3) = P(2) \cdot P(3) = \frac{1}{6} \cdot \frac{1}{6} = \frac{1}{36}$

13. $P(\text{even and then greater than 2}) = P(\text{even}) \cdot P(\text{greater than 2}) = \frac{3}{6} \cdot \frac{4}{6} = \frac{1}{2} \cdot \frac{2}{3} = \frac{1}{3}$

15. $P(\text{picture card and then heart}) = P(\text{picture card}) \cdot P(\text{heart}) = \frac{12}{52} \cdot \frac{13}{52} = \frac{3}{13} \cdot \frac{1}{4} = \frac{3}{52}$

17. $P(2 \text{ kings}) = P(\text{king}) \cdot P(\text{king}) = \frac{4}{52} \cdot \frac{4}{52} = \frac{1}{13} \cdot \frac{1}{13} = \frac{1}{169}$

19. $P(\text{red each time}) = P(\text{red}) \cdot P(\text{red}) = \frac{26}{52} \cdot \frac{26}{52} = \frac{1}{2} \cdot \frac{1}{2} = \frac{1}{4}$

21. $P(\text{all heads}) = P(\text{heads}) \cdot P(\text{heads}) \cdot P(\text{heads}) \cdot P(\text{heads}) \cdot P(\text{heads}) \cdot P(\text{heads}) = \frac{1}{2} \cdot \frac{1}{2} \cdot \frac{1}{2} \cdot \frac{1}{2} \cdot \frac{1}{2} \cdot \frac{1}{2} = \frac{1}{64}$

23. $P(\text{head and number greater than 4}) = P(\text{head}) \cdot P(\text{number greater than 4}) = \frac{1}{2} \cdot \frac{2}{6} = \frac{1}{6}$

25. a. $P(\text{hit two years in a row}) = P(\text{hit}) \cdot P(\text{hit}) = \frac{1}{16} \cdot \frac{1}{16} = \frac{1}{256} \approx 0.00391$

b. $P(\text{Hit three consecutive years}) = P(\text{hit}) \cdot P(\text{hit}) \cdot P(\text{hit}) = \frac{1}{16} \cdot \frac{1}{16} \cdot \frac{1}{16} = \frac{1}{4096} \approx 0.000244$

c. $P(\text{not hit in next ten years}) = [P(\text{not hit})]^{10} = \left(1 - \frac{1}{16}\right)^{10} = \left(\frac{15}{16}\right)^{10} \approx 0.524$

d. $P(\text{hit at least once in next ten years}) = 1 - P(\text{not hit in next ten years}) \approx 1 - 0.524 \approx 0.476$

27. $P(\text{both suffer from depression - from general population}) = P(\text{depression}) \cdot P(\text{depression}) = 0.12 \cdot 0.12 = 0.0144$

29. $P(\text{all three suffer from frequent hangovers - from population of smokers})$
$= P(\text{frequent hangovers}) \cdot P(\text{frequent hangovers}) \cdot P(\text{frequent hangovers}) = 0.20 \cdot 0.20 \cdot 0.20 = 0.008$

31. $P(\text{at least one of three suffers from anxiety/panic disorder - from population of smokers})$

$$\begin{aligned}
&= 1 - [1 - P(\text{anxiety/panic disorder})] \cdot [1 - P(\text{anxiety/panic disorder})] \cdot [1 - P(\text{anxiety/panic disorder})] \\
&= 1 - [1 - 0.19] \cdot [1 - 0.19] \cdot [1 - 0.19] \\
&= 1 - [0.81] \cdot [0.81] \cdot [0.81] \\
&\approx 1 - 0.5314 \\
&= 0.4686
\end{aligned}$$

33. $P(\text{solid and solid}) = P(\text{solid}) \cdot P(\text{solid given first was solid}) = \frac{15}{30} \cdot \frac{14}{29} = \frac{1}{2} \cdot \frac{14}{29} = \frac{7}{29}$

35. $P(\text{coconut then caramel}) = P(\text{coconut}) \cdot P(\text{caramel given first was coconut}) = \frac{5}{30} \cdot \frac{10}{29} = \frac{1}{6} \cdot \frac{10}{29} = \frac{5}{87}$

37. $P(\text{two Democrats}) = P(\text{Democrat}) \cdot P(\text{Democrat given first was Democrat}) = \frac{5}{15} \cdot \frac{4}{14} = \frac{1}{3} \cdot \frac{2}{7} = \frac{2}{21}$

39. $P(\text{Independent then Republican}) = P(\text{Independent}) \cdot P(\text{Republican given first was Independent})$

$$= \frac{4}{15} \cdot \frac{6}{14} = \frac{4}{15} \cdot \frac{3}{7} = \frac{4}{35}$$

41. $P(\text{no Independents}) = P(\text{not Independent}) \cdot P(\text{not Independent given first was not Independent})$

$$= \frac{11}{15} \cdot \frac{10}{14} = \frac{11}{15} \cdot \frac{5}{7} = \frac{11}{21}$$

43. $P(\text{three cans of apple juice})$

$$= P(\text{apple juice}) \cdot P\begin{pmatrix}\text{apple juice given} \\ \text{first was apple juice}\end{pmatrix} \cdot P\begin{pmatrix}\text{apple juice given first} \\ \text{two were apple juice}\end{pmatrix} = \frac{6}{20} \cdot \frac{5}{19} \cdot \frac{4}{18} = \frac{1}{57}$$

45. $P(\text{grape juice then orange juice then mango juice})$

$$= P(\text{grape juice}) \cdot P\begin{pmatrix}\text{orange juice given} \\ \text{first was grape juice}\end{pmatrix} \cdot P\begin{pmatrix}\text{mango juice given first was grape juice} \\ \text{and second was orange juice}\end{pmatrix} = \frac{8}{20} \cdot \frac{4}{19} \cdot \frac{2}{18} = \frac{8}{855}$$

47. $P(\text{no grape juice})$

$$= P(\text{not grape juice}) \cdot P\begin{pmatrix}\text{not grape juice given} \\ \text{first was not grape juice}\end{pmatrix} \cdot P\begin{pmatrix}\text{not grape juice given first} \\ \text{two were not grape juice}\end{pmatrix} = \frac{12}{20} \cdot \frac{11}{19} \cdot \frac{10}{18} = \frac{11}{57}$$

49. $P(3 | \text{red}) = \frac{1}{5}$

51. $P(\text{even} | \text{yellow}) = \frac{2}{3}$

53. $P(\text{red} | \text{odd}) = \frac{3}{4}$

55. $P(\text{red}|\text{at least 5}) = \frac{3}{4}$

57. $P(\text{surviving}|\text{wore seat belt}) = \frac{412{,}368}{412{,}878} = \frac{68{,}728}{68{,}813} \approx 0.999$

59. $P(\text{wore seat belt}|\text{driver survived}) = \frac{412{,}368}{574{,}895} \approx 0.717$

61. $P(\text{not divorced}) = 1 - P(\text{divorced}) = 1 - \frac{24}{242} = \frac{218}{242} = \frac{109}{121} \approx 0.90$

63. $P(\text{widowed or divorced}) = P(\text{widowed}) + P(\text{divorced}) = \frac{14}{242} + \frac{24}{242} = \frac{38}{242} = \frac{19}{121} \approx 0.16$

65. $P(\text{male or is divorced}) = P(\text{male}) + P(\text{divorced}) - P(\text{male and is divorced}) = \frac{118}{242} + \frac{24}{242} - \frac{10}{242} = \frac{132}{242} = \frac{6}{11} \approx 0.55$

67. $P(\text{male}|\text{divorced}) = \frac{10}{24} = \frac{5}{12} \approx 0.42$

69. $P(\text{widowed}|\text{woman}) = \frac{11}{124} \approx 0.09$

71. $P(\text{never married or married}|\text{man}) = \frac{40}{118} + \frac{65}{118} = \frac{105}{118} \approx 0.89$

73. **a.** The first person can have any of 365 birthdays. To not match, the second person can then have any of the remaining 364 birthdays.

b. $P(\text{three different birthdays}) = \frac{365}{365} \cdot \frac{364}{365} \cdot \frac{363}{365} \approx 0.992$

c. $P(\text{at least two have same birthday}) = 1 - P(\text{three different birthdays}) = 1 - 0.992 = 0.008$

d. $P(\text{20 different birthdays})$

$$= \frac{365 \cdot 364 \cdot 363 \cdot 362 \cdot 361 \cdot 360 \cdot 359 \cdot 358 \cdot 357 \cdot 356 \cdot 355 \cdot 354 \cdot 353 \cdot 352 \cdot 351 \cdot 350 \cdot 349 \cdot 348 \cdot 347 \cdot 346}{365 \cdot 365 \cdot 365 \cdot 365 \cdot 365 \cdot 365 \cdot 365 \cdot 365 \cdot 365 \cdot 365 \cdot 365 \cdot 365 \cdot 365 \cdot 365 \cdot 365 \cdot 365 \cdot 365 \cdot 365 \cdot 365 \cdot 365} \approx 0.589$$

$P(\text{at least two have same birthday}) = 1 - P(\text{20 different birthdays}) = 1 - 0.589 = 0.411$

e. 23 people (determine by trial-and-error using method shown in part d)

$P(\text{23 different birthdays})$

$$= \frac{365 \cdot 364 \cdot 363 \cdot 362 \cdot 361 \cdot 360 \cdot 359 \cdot 358 \cdot 357 \cdot 356 \cdot 355 \cdot 354 \cdot 353 \cdot 352 \cdot 351 \cdot 350 \cdot 349 \cdot 348 \cdot 347 \cdot 346 \cdot 345 \cdot 344 \cdot 343}{365 \cdot 365}$$

≈ 0.493

$P(\text{at least two have same birthday}) = 1 - P(\text{23 different birthdays}) = 1 - 0.493 = 0.507$

83. does not make sense; Explanations will vary. Sample explanation: The probability of the second selection being a man, given that the first was a man is $\frac{4}{9}$.

85. does not make sense; Explanations will vary. Sample explanation: $P(A|B)$ does not necessarily equal $P(B|A)$.

87. $P(\text{2 on 1st, 3rd, and 4th rolls only}) = P(2)\cdot P(\text{not }2)\cdot P(2)\cdot P(2)\cdot P(\text{not }2) = \frac{1}{6}\cdot\frac{5}{6}\cdot\frac{1}{6}\cdot\frac{1}{6}\cdot\frac{5}{6} = \frac{25}{7776} \approx 0.00322$

89. The sample space has 36 elements. Of these elements, the following 11 fit the given condition: 1&5, 1&6, 3&5, 3&6, 5&1, 5&3, 5&5, 5&6, 6&1, 6&3, 6&5. Thus the probability is $\frac{11}{36}$.

Check Points 11.8

1. $E = 1\cdot\frac{1}{4} + 2\cdot\frac{1}{4} + 3\cdot\frac{1}{4} + 4\cdot\frac{1}{4} = \frac{1+2+3+4}{4} = \frac{10}{4} = 2.5$

2. $E = 0\cdot\frac{1}{16} + 1\cdot\frac{4}{16} + 2\cdot\frac{6}{16} + 3\cdot\frac{4}{16} + 4\cdot\frac{1}{16} = \frac{0+4+12+12+4}{16} = \frac{32}{16} = 2$

3. a. $E = \$0(0.01)+\$2000(0.15) + \$4000(0.08) + \$6000(0.05) + \$8000(0.01) + \$10{,}000(0.70) = \$8000$
This means that in the long run, the average cost of a claim is expected to be $8000.

b. An average premium charge of $8000 would cause the company to neither lose nor gain money.

4. $E = (1)\left(\frac{1}{5}\right) + \left(-\frac{1}{4}\right)\left(\frac{4}{5}\right) = \frac{1}{5} + \left(-\frac{1}{5}\right) = 0$
Since the expected value is 0, there is nothing to gain or lose on average by guessing.

5. Values of gain or loss:
Grand Prize: $\$1000 - \$2 = \$998$, Consolation Prize: $\$50 - \$2 = \$48$, Nothing: $\$0 - \$2 = -\$2$

$$E = (-\$2)\left(\frac{997}{1000}\right) + (\$48)\left(\frac{2}{1000}\right) + (\$998)\left(\frac{1}{1000}\right) = \frac{-\$1994 + \$96 + \$998}{1000} = -\frac{\$900}{1000} = -\$0.90$$

The expected value for one ticket is $-\$0.90$. This means that in the long run a player can expect to lose $0.90 for each ticket bought. Buying five tickets will make your likelihood of winning five times greater, however there is no advantage to this strategy because the *cost* of five tickets is also five times greater than one ticket.

6. $E = (\$2.20)\left(\frac{20}{80}\right) + (-\$1.00)\left(\frac{60}{80}\right) = \frac{\$44 - \$60}{80} = \frac{-\$16}{80} = -\$0.20$
This means that in the long run a player can expect to lose an average of $0.20 for each $1 bet.

Concept and Vocabulary Check 11.8

1. expected; probability; add

2. loss; probability; add

3. false

4. true

Exercise Set 11.8

1. $E=1\cdot\frac{1}{2}+2\cdot\frac{1}{4}+3\cdot\frac{1}{4}=1.75$

3. a. E = \$0(0.65)+\$50,000(0.20) + \$100,000(0.10) + \$150,000(0.03) + \$200,000(0.01) + \$250,000(0.01) = \$29,000
This means that in the long run the average cost of a claim is \$29,000.

b. \$29,000

c. \$29,050

5. E = –\$10,000(0.9) + \$90,000(0.1) = \$0. This means on the average there will be no gain or loss.

7. $E=-\$99{,}999\left(\frac{27}{10{,}000{,}000}\right)+\$1\left(\frac{9{,}999{,}973}{10{,}000{,}000}\right)=\$0.73$

9. Probabilities after eliminating one possible answer: Guess Correctly: $\frac{1}{4}$, Guess Incorrectly: $\frac{3}{4}$

$E=(1)\left(\frac{1}{4}\right)+\left(-\frac{1}{4}\right)\left(\frac{3}{4}\right)=\frac{1}{4}+\left(-\frac{3}{16}\right)=\frac{1}{16}$ expected points on a guess if one answer is eliminated.
Yes, it is advantageous to guess after eliminating one possible answer.

11. First mall: $E=\$300{,}000\left(\frac{1}{2}\right)-\$100{,}000\left(\frac{1}{2}\right)=\$100{,}000$

Second mall: $E=\$200{,}000\left(\frac{3}{4}\right)-\$60{,}000\left(\frac{1}{4}\right)=\$135{,}000$

Choose the second mall.

13. a. E = \$700,000(0.2) + \$0(0.8) = \$140,000

b. No

15. $E=\$4\left(\frac{1}{6}\right)-\$1\left(\frac{5}{6}\right)=-\$\frac{1}{6}\approx-\$0.17$. This means an expected loss of approximately \$0.17 per game.

17. $E=\$1\left(\frac{18}{38}\right)-\$1\left(\frac{20}{38}\right)\approx-\$0.053$. This means an expected loss of approximately \$0.053 per \$1.00 bet.

19. $E=\$499\left(\frac{1}{1000}\right)-\$1\left(\frac{999}{1000}\right)=-\$0.50$. This means an expected loss of \$0.50 per \$1.00 bet.

27. makes sense

29. does not make sense; Explanations will vary. Sample explanation: The expected value of a lottery game is less than the cost of the ticket.

31. Let x = the charge for the policy. Note, the expected value, E = \$60.

$\$60=(x-\$200{,}000)(0.0005)+(x)(0.9995)$

$\$60=0.0005x-\$100+0.9995x$

$\$160=x$

The insurance company should charge \$160 for the policy.

Chapter 11 Review Exercises

1. Use the Fundamental Counting Principle with two groups of items. $20 \cdot 40 = 800$

2. Use the Fundamental Counting Principle with two groups of items. $4 \cdot 5 = 20$

3. Use the Fundamental Counting Principle with two groups of items. $100 \cdot 99 = 9900$

4. Use the Fundamental Counting Principle with three groups of items. $5 \cdot 5 \cdot 5 = 125$

5. Use the Fundamental Counting Principle with five groups of items. $3 \cdot 3 \cdot 3 \cdot 3 \cdot 3 = 243$

6. Use the Fundamental Counting Principle with four groups of items. $5 \cdot 2 \cdot 2 \cdot 3 = 60$

7. $\frac{16!}{14!} = \frac{16 \cdot 15 \cdot 14!}{14!} = 240$

8. $\frac{800!}{799!} = \frac{800 \cdot 799!}{799!} = 800$

9. $5! - 3! = 5 \cdot 4 \cdot 3 \cdot 2 \cdot 1 - 3 \cdot 2 \cdot 1 = 120 - 6 = 114$

10. $\frac{11!}{(11-3)!} = \frac{11!}{8!} = \frac{11 \cdot 10 \cdot 9 \cdot 8!}{8!} = 990$

11. ${}_{10}P_6 = \frac{10!}{(10-6)!} = \frac{10!}{4!} = \frac{10 \cdot 9 \cdot 8 \cdot 7 \cdot 6 \cdot 5 \cdot 4!}{4!} = 151,200$

12. ${}_{100}P_2 = \frac{100!}{(100-2)!} = \frac{100!}{98!} = \frac{100 \cdot 99 \cdot 98!}{98!} = 9900$

13. ${}_{11}C_7 = \frac{11!}{(11-7)!7!} = \frac{11!}{4!7!} = \frac{11 \cdot 10 \cdot 9 \cdot 8 \cdot 7!}{4 \cdot 3 \cdot 2 \cdot 1 \cdot 7!} = 330$

14. ${}_{14}C_5 = \frac{14!}{(14-5)!5!} = \frac{14!}{9!5!} = \frac{14 \cdot 13 \cdot 12 \cdot 11 \cdot 10 \cdot 9!}{9! \cdot 5 \cdot 4 \cdot 3 \cdot 2 \cdot 1} = 2002$

15. Order does not matter. This problem involves combinations.

16. Order matters. This problem involves permutations.

17. Order does not matter. This problem involves combinations.

18. Use the Fundamental Counting Principle with six groups of items. $6 \cdot 5 \cdot 4 \cdot 3 \cdot 2 \cdot 1 = 720$

19. ${}_{15}P_4 = \frac{15!}{(15-4)!} = \frac{15!}{11!} = \frac{15 \cdot 14 \cdot 13 \cdot 12 \cdot 11!}{11!} = 32,760$

20. ${}_{10}C_4 = \frac{10!}{(10-4)!4!} = \frac{10!}{6!4!} = \frac{10 \cdot 9 \cdot 8 \cdot 7 \cdot 6!}{6!4 \cdot 3 \cdot 2 \cdot 1} = 210$

21. $\frac{n!}{p!q!} = \frac{7!}{3!2!} = \frac{7 \cdot 6 \cdot 5 \cdot 4 \cdot \cancel{3!}}{\cancel{3!} \cdot 2 \cdot 1} = 420$

22. $_{20}C_3 = \frac{20!}{(20-3)!3!} = \frac{20!}{17!3!} = \frac{20 \cdot 19 \cdot 18 \cdot 17!}{17!3 \cdot 2 \cdot 1} = 1140$

23. Use the Fundamental Counting Principle with seven groups of items. $1 \cdot 5 \cdot 4 \cdot 3 \cdot 2 \cdot 1 \cdot 1 = 120$

24. $_{20}P_5 = \frac{20!}{(20-5)!} = \frac{20!}{15!} = \frac{20 \cdot 19 \cdot 18 \cdot 17 \cdot 16 \cdot 15!}{15!} = 1{,}860{,}480$

25. Use the Fundamental Counting Principle with five groups of items. $5 \cdot 4 \cdot 3 \cdot 2 \cdot 1 = 120$

26. $_{13}C_5 = \frac{13!}{(13-5)!5!} = \frac{13!}{8!5!} = \frac{13 \cdot 12 \cdot 11 \cdot 10 \cdot 9 \cdot 8!}{8!5 \cdot 4 \cdot 3 \cdot 2 \cdot 1} = 1287$

27. Choose the Republicans: $_{12}C_5 = \frac{12!}{(12-5)!5!} = \frac{12!}{7!5!} = \frac{12 \cdot 11 \cdot 10 \cdot 9 \cdot 8 \cdot 7!}{7!5 \cdot 4 \cdot 3 \cdot 2 \cdot 1} = 792$

Choose the Democrats: $_8C_4 = \frac{8!}{(8-4)!4!} = \frac{8!}{4!4!} = \frac{8 \cdot 7 \cdot 6 \cdot 5 \cdot 4!}{4!4 \cdot 3 \cdot 2 \cdot 1} = 70$

Multiply the choices: $792 \cdot 70 = 55{,}440$

28. $\frac{n!}{p!q!} = \frac{6!}{3!2!} = \frac{6 \cdot 5 \cdot 4 \cdot \cancel{3!}}{\cancel{3!} \cdot 2 \cdot 1} = 60$

29. $P(6) = \frac{\text{number of ways a 6 can occur}}{\text{total number of possible outcomes}} = \frac{1}{6}$

30. $P(\text{less than 5}) = \frac{\text{number of ways a number less than 5 can occur}}{\text{total number of possible outcomes}} = \frac{4}{6} = \frac{2}{3}$

31. $P(\text{less than 7}) = \frac{\text{number of ways a number less than 7 can occur}}{\text{total number of possible outcomes}} = \frac{6}{6} = 1$

32. $P(\text{greater than 6}) = \frac{\text{number of ways a number greater than 6 can occur}}{\text{total number of possible outcomes}} = \frac{0}{6} = 0$

33. $P(5) = \frac{\text{number of ways a 5 can occur}}{\text{total number of possible outcomes}} = \frac{4}{52} = \frac{1}{13}$

34. $P(\text{picture card}) = \frac{\text{number of ways a picture card can occur}}{\text{total number of possible outcomes}} = \frac{12}{52} = \frac{3}{13}$

35. $P(\text{greater than 4 and less than 8}) = \frac{\text{number of ways a card greater than 4 and less than 8 can occur}}{\text{total number of possible outcomes}} = \frac{12}{52} = \frac{3}{13}$

36. $P(\text{4 of diamonds}) = \frac{\text{number of ways a 4 of diamonds can occur}}{\text{total number of possible outcomes}} = \frac{1}{52}$

37. $P(\text{red ace}) = \frac{\text{number of ways a red ace can occur}}{\text{total number of possible outcomes}} = \frac{2}{52} = \frac{1}{26}$

38. $P(\text{chocolate}) = \dfrac{\text{number of ways a chocolate can occur}}{\text{total number of possible outcomes}} = \dfrac{15}{30} = \dfrac{1}{2}$

39. $P(\text{caramel}) = \dfrac{\text{number of ways a caramel can occur}}{\text{total number of possible outcomes}} = \dfrac{10}{30} = \dfrac{1}{3}$

40. $P(\text{peppermint}) = \dfrac{\text{number of ways a peppermint can occur}}{\text{total number of possible outcomes}} = \dfrac{5}{30} = \dfrac{1}{6}$

41. **a.** $P(\text{carrier without the disease}) = \dfrac{\text{number of ways to be a carrier without the disease}}{\text{total number of possible outcomes}} = \dfrac{2}{4} = \dfrac{1}{2}$

b. $P(\text{disease}) = \dfrac{\text{number of ways to have the disease}}{\text{total number of possible outcomes}} = \dfrac{0}{4} = 0$

42. $P(\text{employed}) = \dfrac{140}{240} = \dfrac{7}{12}$

43. $P(\text{female}) = \dfrac{124}{240} = \dfrac{31}{60}$

44. $P(\text{unemployed male}) = \dfrac{8}{240} = \dfrac{1}{30}$

45. number of ways to visit in order D, B, A, C = 1
total number of possible permutations $= 4 \cdot 3 \cdot 2 \cdot 1 = 24$

$P(\text{D, B, A, C}) = \dfrac{1}{24}$

46. number of permutations with C last $= 5 \cdot 4 \cdot 3 \cdot 2 \cdot 1 \cdot 1 = 120$
total number of possible permutations $= 6 \cdot 5 \cdot 4 \cdot 3 \cdot 2 \cdot 1 = 720$

$P(\text{C last}) = \dfrac{120}{720} = \dfrac{1}{6}$

47. number of permutations with B first and A last $= 1 \cdot 4 \cdot 3 \cdot 2 \cdot 1 \cdot 1 = 24$
total number of possible permutations $= 6 \cdot 5 \cdot 4 \cdot 3 \cdot 2 \cdot 1 = 720$

$P(\text{B first and A last}) = \dfrac{24}{720} = \dfrac{1}{30}$

48. number of permutations in order F, E, A, D, C, B = 1
total number of possible permutations $= 6 \cdot 5 \cdot 4 \cdot 3 \cdot 2 \cdot 1 = 720$

$P(\text{F, E, A, D, C, B}) = \dfrac{1}{720}$

49. number of permutations with A or C first $= 2 \cdot 5 \cdot 4 \cdot 3 \cdot 2 \cdot 1 = 240$
total number of possible permutations $= 6 \cdot 5 \cdot 4 \cdot 3 \cdot 2 \cdot 1 = 720$

$P(\text{A or C first}) = \dfrac{240}{720} = \dfrac{1}{3}$

50. a. number of ways to win = 1
total number of possible combinations:
$${}_{20}C_5 = \frac{20!}{(20-5)!5!} = \frac{20!}{15!5!} = \frac{20 \cdot 19 \cdot 18 \cdot 17 \cdot 16 \cdot 15!}{15!5 \cdot 4 \cdot 3 \cdot 2 \cdot 1} = 15{,}504$$
$$P(\text{winning with one ticket}) = \frac{1}{15{,}504} \approx 0.0000645$$

b. number of ways to win = 100
$$P(\text{winning with 100 different tickets}) = \frac{100}{15{,}504} \approx 0.00645$$

51. a. number of ways to select 4 Democrats: ${}_6C_4 = \frac{6!}{(6-4)!4!} = \frac{6!}{2!4!} = \frac{6 \cdot 5 \cdot 4!}{2 \cdot 1 \cdot 4!} = 15$

total number of possible combinations: ${}_{10}C_4 = \frac{10!}{(10-4)!4!} = \frac{10!}{6!4!} = \frac{10 \cdot 9 \cdot 8 \cdot 7 \cdot 6!}{6!4 \cdot 3 \cdot 2 \cdot 1} = 210$

$$P(\text{all Democrats}) = \frac{15}{210} = \frac{1}{14}$$

b. number of ways to select 2 Democrats: ${}_6C_2 = \frac{6!}{(6-2)!2!} = \frac{6!}{4!2!} = \frac{6 \cdot 5 \cdot 4!}{4!2 \cdot 1} = 15$

number of ways to select 2 Republicans: ${}_4C_2 = \frac{4!}{(4-2)!2!} = \frac{4!}{2!2!} = \frac{4 \cdot 3 \cdot 2!}{2!2 \cdot 1} = 6$

number of ways to select 2 Democrats and 2 Republicans = 15 · 6 = 90

$$P(\text{2 Democrats and 2 Republicans}) = \frac{90}{210} = \frac{3}{7}$$

52. number of ways to get 2 picture cards: ${}_6C_2 = \frac{6!}{(6-2)!2!} = \frac{6!}{4!2!} = \frac{6 \cdot 5 \cdot 4!}{4!2 \cdot 1} = 15$
number of ways to get one non-picture card = 20
number of ways to get 2 picture cards and one non-picture card = 15 · 20 = 300
total number of possible combinations: ${}_{26}C_3 = \frac{26!}{(26-3)!3!} = \frac{26!}{23!3!} = \frac{26 \cdot 25 \cdot 24 \cdot 23!}{23!3 \cdot 2 \cdot 1} = 2600$

$$P(\text{2 picture cards}) = \frac{300}{2600} = \frac{3}{26}$$

53. $P(\text{not a }5) = 1 - P(5) = 1 - \frac{1}{6} = \frac{5}{6}$

54. $P(\text{not less than }4) = 1 - P(\text{less than }4) = 1 - \frac{3}{6} = 1 - \frac{1}{2} = \frac{1}{2}$

55. $P(3\text{ or }5) = P(3) + P(5) = \frac{1}{6} + \frac{1}{6} = \frac{2}{6} = \frac{1}{3}$

56. $P(\text{less than 3 or greater than 4}) = P(\text{less than 3}) + P(\text{greater than 4}) = \frac{2}{6} + \frac{2}{6} = \frac{1}{3} + \frac{1}{3} = \frac{2}{3}$

57. $P(\text{less than 5 or greater than 2}) = P(\text{less than 5}) + P(\text{greater than 2}) - P(\text{less than 5 and greater than 2})$

$$= \frac{4}{6} + \frac{4}{6} - \frac{2}{6} = 1$$

58. $P(\text{not a picture card}) = 1 - P(\text{picture card}) = 1 - \frac{12}{52} = 1 - \frac{3}{13} = \frac{10}{13}$

59. $P(\text{not a diamond}) = 1 - P(\text{diamond}) = 1 - \frac{13}{52} = 1 - \frac{1}{4} = \frac{3}{4}$

60. $P(\text{ace or king}) = P(\text{ace}) + P(\text{king}) = \frac{4}{52} + \frac{4}{52} = \frac{1}{13} + \frac{1}{13} = \frac{2}{13}$

61. $P(\text{black 6 or red 7}) = P(\text{black 6}) + P(\text{red 7}) = \frac{2}{52} + \frac{2}{52} = \frac{1}{26} + \frac{1}{26} = \frac{2}{26} = \frac{1}{13}$

62. $P(\text{queen or red card}) = P(\text{queen}) + P(\text{red card}) - P(\text{red queen}) = \frac{4}{52} + \frac{26}{52} - \frac{2}{52} = \frac{28}{52} = \frac{7}{13}$

63. $P(\text{club or picture card}) = P(\text{club}) + P(\text{picture card}) - P(\text{club and picture card}) = \frac{13}{52} + \frac{12}{52} - \frac{3}{52} = \frac{22}{52} = \frac{11}{26}$

64. $P(\text{not 4}) = 1 - P(4) = 1 - \frac{1}{6} = \frac{5}{6}$

65. $P(\text{not yellow}) = 1 - P(\text{yellow}) = 1 - \frac{1}{6} = \frac{5}{6}$

66. $P(\text{not red}) = 1 - P(\text{red}) = 1 - \frac{3}{6} = 1 - \frac{1}{2} = \frac{1}{2}$

67. $P(\text{red or yellow}) = P(\text{red}) + P(\text{yellow}) = \frac{3}{6} + \frac{1}{6} = \frac{4}{6} = \frac{2}{3}$

68. $P(\text{red or even}) = P(\text{red}) + P(\text{even}) - P(\text{red and even}) = \frac{3}{6} + \frac{3}{6} - \frac{0}{6} = 1$

69. $P(\text{red or greater than 3}) = P(\text{red}) + P(\text{greater than 3}) - P(\text{red and greater than 3}) = \frac{3}{6} + \frac{3}{6} - \frac{1}{6} = \frac{5}{6}$

70. $P(\text{African American or male}) = P(\text{African American}) + P(\text{male}) - P(\text{African American male})$

$$= \frac{50+20}{200} + \frac{50+90}{200} - \frac{50}{200} = \frac{160}{200} = \frac{4}{5}$$

71. $P(\text{female or white}) = P(\text{female}) + P(\text{white}) - P(\text{white female}) = \frac{20+40}{200} + \frac{90+40}{200} - \frac{40}{200} = \frac{150}{200} = \frac{3}{4}$

72. $P(\text{public college}) = \frac{252}{350} = \frac{18}{25}$

73. $P(\text{not from high-income family}) = 1 - P(\text{from high-income family}) = 1 - \frac{50}{350} = \frac{350}{350} - \frac{50}{350} = \frac{300}{350} = \frac{6}{7}$

74. $P(\text{from middle-income family or high-income family}) = \frac{160+50}{350} = \frac{210}{350} = \frac{3}{5}$

75. $P(\text{attended private college or is from a high income family})$
$= P(\text{private college}) + P(\text{high income family}) - P(\text{attended private college and is from a high income family})$
$= \frac{98}{350} + \frac{50}{350} - \frac{28}{350} = \frac{120}{350} = \frac{12}{35}$

76. number of favorable outcomes = 4, number of unfavorable outcomes = 48
Odds in favor of getting a queen are 4:48, or 1:12. Odds against getting a queen are 12:1.

77. number of favorable outcomes = 20, number of unfavorable outcomes = 1980
Odds against winning are 1980: 20, or 99:1.

78. $P(\text{win}) = \frac{3}{3+1} = \frac{3}{4}$

79. $P(\text{yellow then red}) = P(\text{yellow}) \cdot P(\text{red}) = \frac{2}{6} \cdot \frac{4}{6} = \frac{1}{3} \cdot \frac{2}{3} = \frac{2}{9}$

80. $P(1 \text{ then } 3) = P(1) \cdot P(3) = \frac{1}{6} \cdot \frac{1}{6} = \frac{1}{36}$

81. $P(\text{yellow both times}) = P(\text{yellow}) \cdot P(\text{yellow}) = \frac{2}{6} \cdot \frac{2}{6} = \frac{1}{3} \cdot \frac{1}{3} = \frac{1}{9}$

82. $P(\text{yellow then 4 then odd}) = P(\text{yellow}) \cdot P(4) \cdot P(\text{odd}) = \frac{2}{6} \cdot \frac{1}{6} \cdot \frac{3}{6} = \frac{1}{3} \cdot \frac{1}{6} \cdot \frac{1}{2} = \frac{1}{36}$

83. $P(\text{red every time}) = P(\text{red}) \cdot P(\text{red}) \cdot P(\text{red}) = \frac{4}{6} \cdot \frac{4}{6} \cdot \frac{4}{6} = \frac{2}{3} \cdot \frac{2}{3} \cdot \frac{2}{3} = \frac{8}{27}$

84. $P(\text{five boys in a row}) = P(\text{boy}) \cdot P(\text{boy}) \cdot P(\text{boy}) \cdot P(\text{boy}) \cdot P(\text{boy}) = \frac{1}{2} \cdot \frac{1}{2} \cdot \frac{1}{2} \cdot \frac{1}{2} \cdot \frac{1}{2} = \frac{1}{2^5} = \frac{1}{32}$

85. a. $P(\text{flood two years in a row}) = P(\text{flood}) \cdot P(\text{flood}) = (0.2)(0.2) = 0.04$

b. $P(\text{flood for three consecutive years}) = P(\text{flood}) \cdot P(\text{flood}) \cdot P(\text{flood}) = (0.2)(0.2)(0.2) = 0.008$

c. $P(\text{no flooding for four consecutive years}) = [1 - P(\text{flood})]^4 = (1-0.2)^4 = (0.8)^4 = 0.4096$

d. $P(\text{flood at least once in next four years}) = 1 - P(\text{no flooding for four consecutive years})$
$= 1 - 0.4096 = 0.5904$

86. $P(\text{music major then psychology major}) = P(\text{music major}) \cdot P\begin{pmatrix}\text{psychology major given} \\ \text{first was music major}\end{pmatrix} = \frac{2}{9} \cdot \frac{4}{8} = \frac{2}{9} \cdot \frac{1}{2} = \frac{1}{9}$

87. $P(\text{two business majors}) = P(\text{bus. major}) \cdot P(\text{bus. major given first was bus. major}) = \frac{3}{9} \cdot \frac{2}{8} = \frac{1}{3} \cdot \frac{1}{4} = \frac{1}{12}$

88. $P(\text{solid then two cherry})$
$= P(\text{solid}) \cdot P\begin{pmatrix}\text{cherry given} \\ \text{first was solid}\end{pmatrix} \cdot P\begin{pmatrix}\text{cherry given first was solid} \\ \text{and second was cherry}\end{pmatrix} = \frac{30}{50} \cdot \frac{5}{49} \cdot \frac{4}{48} = \frac{3}{5} \cdot \frac{5}{49} \cdot \frac{1}{12} = \frac{1}{196}$

89. $P(5|\text{odd}) = \frac{1}{3}$

90. $P(\text{vowel}|\text{precedes the letter k}) = \frac{3}{10}$

91. a. $P(\text{odd}|\text{red}) = \frac{2}{4} = \frac{1}{2}$

b. $P(\text{yellow}|\text{at least 3}) = \frac{2}{7}$

92. $P(\text{does not have TB}) = \frac{11+124}{9+1+11+124} = \frac{135}{145} = \frac{27}{29}$

93. $P(\text{tests positive}) = \frac{9+11}{9+1+11+124} = \frac{20}{145} = \frac{4}{29}$

94. $P(\text{does not have TB or tests positive})$
$= P(\text{does not have TB}) + P(\text{tests positive}) - P(\text{does not have TB and tests positive})$
$= \frac{11+124}{145} + \frac{9+11}{145} - \frac{11}{145}$
$= \frac{144}{145}$

95. $P(\text{does not have TB}|\text{positive test}) = \frac{11}{9+11} = \frac{11}{20}$

96. $P(\text{tests positive}|\text{does not have TB}) = \frac{11}{11+124} = \frac{11}{135}$

97. $P(\text{has TB}|\text{negative Test}) = \frac{1}{1+124} = \frac{1}{125}$

98. $P(\text{two people with TB}) = P(\text{TB}) \cdot P(\text{TB}|\text{first person selected has TB}) = \frac{10}{145} \cdot \frac{9}{144} = \frac{1}{232}$

99. $P(\text{two people with positive tests}) = P(\text{positive test}) \cdot P(\text{positive test}|\text{first person has positive test}) = \frac{20}{145} \cdot \frac{19}{144} = \frac{19}{1044}$

100. $P(\text{male}) = \frac{27,336}{31,593} \approx 0.865$

101. $P(\text{age } 25-44) = \frac{11,161}{31,593} \approx 0.353$

102. $P(\text{less than }75) = 1 - P(\text{greater than or equal to }75) = 1 - \frac{2379}{31{,}593} = \frac{29{,}214}{31{,}593} \approx 0.925$

103. $P(\text{age }20-24\text{ or }25-44) = P(\text{age }20-24) + P(\text{age }25-44) = \frac{4095}{31{,}593} + \frac{11{,}161}{31{,}593} = \frac{15{,}256}{31{,}593} \approx 0.483$

104. $P(\text{female or younger than }5) = P(\text{female}) + P(\text{younger than }5) - P(\text{female and younger than }5)$

$$= \frac{4257}{31{,}593} + \frac{88}{31{,}593} - \frac{33}{31{,}593} = \frac{4312}{31{,}593} \approx 0.136$$

105. $P(\text{age }20-24 | \text{male}) = \frac{3684}{27{,}336} \approx 0.135$

106. $P(\text{male} | \text{at least }75) = \frac{2169}{2379} \approx 0.912$

107. $E = 1 \cdot \frac{1}{4} + 2 \cdot \frac{1}{8} + 3 \cdot \frac{1}{8} + 4 \cdot \frac{1}{4} + 5 \cdot \frac{1}{4} = 3.125$

108. a. E = \$0(0.9999995) + (–\$1,000,000)(0.0000005) = –\$.50
The insurance company spends an average of \$0.50 per person insured.

b. charge \$9.50 – (–\$0.50) = \$10.00

109. $E = \$27{,}000\left(\frac{1}{4}\right) + (-\$3000)\left(\frac{3}{4}\right) = \$4500.$ The expected gain is \$4500 per bid.

110. $E = \$1\left(\frac{2}{4}\right) + \$1\left(\frac{1}{4}\right) + (-\$4)\left(\frac{1}{4}\right) = -\$0.25.$ The expected loss is \$0.25 per game.

Chapter 11 Test

1. Use the Fundamental Counting Principle with five groups of items. $10 \cdot 2 \cdot 2 \cdot 2 \cdot 3 = 240$

2. Use the Fundamental Counting Principle with four groups of items. $4 \cdot 3 \cdot 2 \cdot 1 = 24$

3. Use the Fundamental Counting Principle with seven groups of items. $1 \cdot 6 \cdot 5 \cdot 4 \cdot 3 \cdot 2 \cdot 1 = 720$

4. ${}_{11}P_3 = \frac{11!}{(11-3)!} = \frac{11!}{8!} = \frac{11 \cdot 10 \cdot 9 \cdot 8!}{8!} = 990$

5. ${}_{10}C_4 = \frac{10!}{(10-4)!4!} = \frac{10!}{6!4!} = \frac{10 \cdot 9 \cdot 8 \cdot 7 \cdot 6!}{6!4 \cdot 3 \cdot 2 \cdot 1} = 210$

6. $\frac{n!}{p!q!} = \frac{7!}{3!2!} = \frac{7 \cdot 6 \cdot 5 \cdot 4 \cdot \cancel{3!}}{\cancel{3!} \cdot 2 \cdot 1} = 420$

7. $P(\text{freshman}) = \frac{12}{50} = \frac{6}{25}$

8. $P(\text{not a sophomore}) = 1 - P(\text{sophomore}) = 1 - \frac{16}{50} = 1 - \frac{8}{25} = \frac{17}{25}$

9. $P(\text{junior or senior}) = P(\text{junior}) + P(\text{senior}) = \frac{20}{50} + \frac{2}{50} = \frac{22}{50} = \frac{11}{25}$

10. $P(\text{greater than 4 and less than 10}) = \frac{20}{52} = \frac{5}{13}$

11. $P(C \text{ first, } A \text{ next-to-last, } E \text{ last})$

$= P(C) \cdot P(A \text{ given } C \text{ was first}) \cdot P(E \text{ given } C \text{ was first and } A \text{ was next-to-last}) = \frac{1}{7} \cdot \frac{1}{6} \cdot \frac{1}{5} = \frac{1}{210}$

12. total number of possible combinations: ${}_{15}C_6 = \frac{15!}{(15-6)!6!} = \frac{15!}{9!6!} = \frac{15 \cdot 14 \cdot 13 \cdot 12 \cdot 11 \cdot 10 \cdot 9!}{9!6 \cdot 5 \cdot 4 \cdot 3 \cdot 2 \cdot 1} = 5005$

$P(\text{winning with 50 tickets}) = \frac{50}{5005} = \frac{10}{1001} \approx 0.00999$

13. $P(\text{red or blue}) = P(\text{red}) + P(\text{blue}) = \frac{2}{8} + \frac{2}{8} = \frac{4}{8} = \frac{1}{2}$

14. $P(\text{red then blue}) = P(\text{red}) \cdot P(\text{blue}) = \frac{2}{8} \cdot \frac{2}{8} = \frac{1}{4} \cdot \frac{1}{4} = \frac{1}{16}$

15. $P(\text{flooding for three consecutive years}) = P(\text{flood}) \cdot P(\text{flood}) \cdot P(\text{flood}) = \frac{1}{20} \cdot \frac{1}{20} \cdot \frac{1}{20} = \frac{1}{8000}$

16. $P(\text{black or picture card}) = P(\text{black}) + P(\text{picture card}) - P(\text{black picture card}) = \frac{26}{52} + \frac{12}{52} - \frac{6}{52} = \frac{32}{52} = \frac{8}{13}$

17. $P(\text{freshman or female}) = P(\text{freshman}) + P(\text{female}) - P(\text{female freshman}) = \frac{10+15}{50} + \frac{15+5}{50} - \frac{15}{50} = \frac{30}{50} = \frac{3}{5}$

18. $P(\text{both red}) = P(\text{red}) \cdot P(\text{red given first ball was red}) = \frac{5}{20} \cdot \frac{4}{19} = \frac{1}{4} \cdot \frac{4}{19} = \frac{1}{19}$

19. $P(\text{all correct}) = P(\text{correct}) \cdot P(\text{correct}) \cdot P(\text{correct}) \cdot P(\text{correct}) = \frac{1}{4} \cdot \frac{1}{4} \cdot \frac{1}{4} \cdot \frac{1}{4} = \left(\frac{1}{4}\right)^4 = \frac{1}{256}$

20. number of favorable outcomes = 20, number of unfavorable outcomes = 15
Odds against being a man are 15:20, or 3:4.

21. **a.** Odds in favor are 4:1. **b.** $P(\text{win}) = \frac{4}{1+4} = \frac{4}{5}$

22. $P(\text{not brown eyes}) = \frac{18+10+20+12}{22+18+10+18+20+12} = \frac{60}{100} = \frac{3}{5}$

23. $P(\text{brown eyes or blue eyes}) = \frac{22+18+18+20}{22+18+10+18+20+12} = \frac{78}{100} = \frac{39}{50}$

24. $P(\text{female or green eyes}) = P(\text{female}) + P(\text{green eyes}) - P(\text{female and green eyes})$

$$= \frac{18+20+12}{100} + \frac{10+12}{100} - \frac{12}{100}$$

$$= \frac{50}{100} + \frac{22}{100} - \frac{12}{100}$$

$$= \frac{60}{100}$$

$$= \frac{3}{5}$$

25. $P(\text{male} | \text{blue eyes}) = \frac{18}{18+20} = \frac{18}{38} = \frac{9}{19}$

26. $P(\text{two people with green eyes}) = P(\text{green eyes}) \cdot P(\text{green eyes} | \text{first person has green eyes}) = \frac{22}{100} \cdot \frac{21}{99} = \frac{7}{150}$

27. $E = \$65{,}000(0.2) + (-\$15{,}000)(0.8) = \$1000$. This means the expected gain is \$1000 for this bid.

28. $E = (-\$19) \cdot \frac{10}{20} + (-\$18) \cdot \frac{5}{20} + (-\$15) \cdot \frac{3}{20} + (-\$10) \cdot \frac{1}{20} + (\$80) \cdot \frac{1}{20}$

$$= \frac{-\$190 - \$90 - \$45 - \$10 + \$80}{20} = \frac{-\$255}{20} = -\$12.75$$

This expected value of $-\$12.75$ means that a player will lose an average of \$12.75 per play in the long run.

Chapter 12
Statistics

Check Points 12.1

1. **a.** The population is the set containing all the of the city's homeless people.

   b. This is not a good idea. This sample of people currently in a shelter is more likely to hold opinions that favor required residence in city shelters than the population of all the city's homeless.

2. The sampling technique described in Check Point 1b does not produce a random sample because homeless people who do not go to shelters have no chance of being selected for the survey. In this instance, an appropriate method would be to randomly select neighborhoods of the city and then randomly survey homeless people within the selected neighborhood.

3.

Grade	Number of students
A	3
B	5
C	9
D	2
F	1
	20

4.

Exam Scores (class)	Tally	Number of students (frequency)
40 – 49	|	1
50 – 59	~~||||~~	5
60 – 69	||||	4
70 – 79	~~||||~~ ~~||||~~ ~~||||~~	15
80 – 89	~~||||~~	5
90 – 99	~~||||~~ ||	7
		37

5.

Stems	Leaves
4	1
5	8 2 8 0 7
6	8 2 9 9
7	3 5 9 9 7 5 5 3 3 6 7 1 7 1 5
8	7 3 9 9 1
9	4 6 9 7 5 8 0

Concept and Vocabulary Check 12.1

1. random
2. frequency distribution
3. grouped frequency distribution; 80; 89
4. histogram; frequencies
5. frequency polygon; horizontal axis
6. stem-and-leaf plot
7. false
8. true
9. false
10. true

Exercise Set 12.1

1. c

3. A stress rating of 7 was reported by 31 students.

5. Totaling the frequency column shows that 151 students were involved in the study.

7.

Time Spent on Homework (in hours)	Number of students
15	4
16	5
17	6
18	5
19	4
20	2
21	2
22	0
23	0
24	2
	30

9. The lower class limits are 0, 5, 10, 15, 20, 25, 30, 35, 40, and 45.

11. The class width is 5, the difference between successive lower limits.

13. $4 + 3 + 3 + 3 = 13$. Thus, 13 students had at least 30 social interactions.

15. The 5 – 9 class.

17.

Age	Frequency
41–45	2
46–50	9
51–55	15
56–60	9
61–65	7
66–70	2
	44

19. Histogram for Stress Rating:

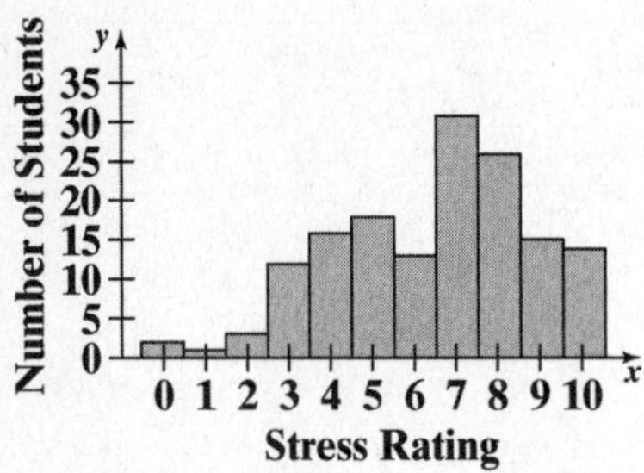

Frequency Polygon for Stress Rating:

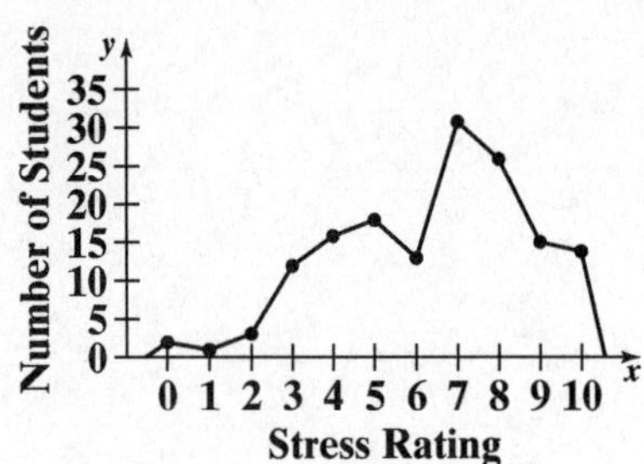

21. Histogram for Height:

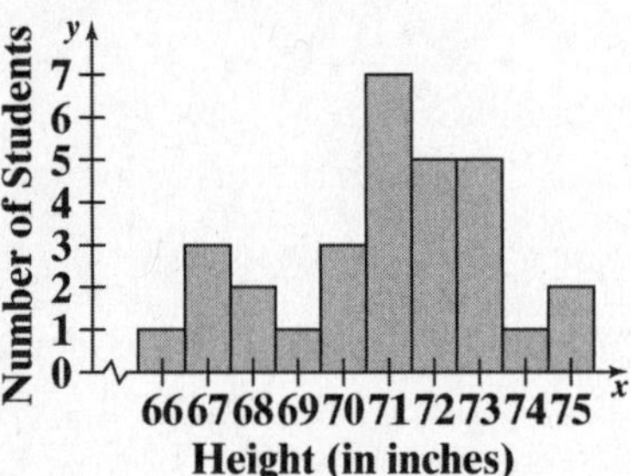

Frequency Polygon for Height:

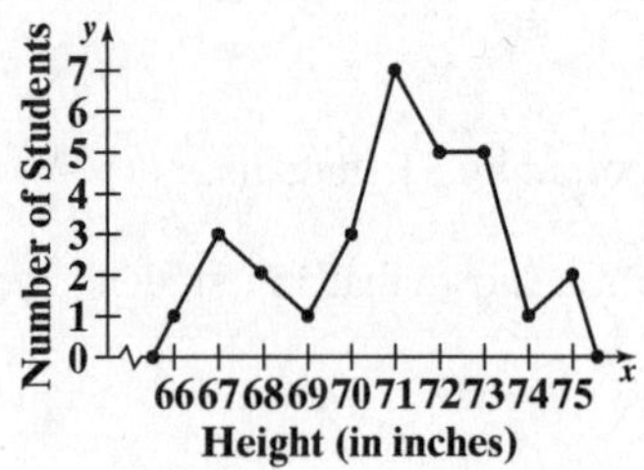

23. false

25. false

27. true

29. false

31.

Stems	Leaves
2	8 8 9 5
3	8 7 0 1 2 7 6 4 0 5
4	8 2 2 1 4 5 4 6 2 0 8 2 7 9
5	9 4 1 9 1 0
6	3 2 3 6 6 3

The greatest number of college professors are in their 40s.

33. The bars on the horizontal axis are evenly spaced, yet the time intervals that they represent vary greatly. This may give the misleading impression of linear growth.

35. The sectors representing these six countries use up 100% of the pie graph, yet the percentages for these six countries total only 57%. This may give the misleading impression that the U.S. has about 50% of the world's computer use.

37. Each film's star extends above the bar giving a misimpression of the data represented.

49. does not make sense; Explanations will vary. Sample explanation: The decline has not been rapid.

51. makes sense

Check Points 12.2

1. $\text{Mean} = \frac{\sum x}{n} = \frac{13+13+10+10+10+9+9+7+7+7}{10} = \frac{95}{10} = 9.5$
$9.5 million

2.

x	f	xf
30	3	$30 \cdot 3 = 90$
33	4	$33 \cdot 4 = 132$
40	4	$40 \cdot 4 = 160$
50	1	$50 \cdot 1 = 50$
	12	$\sum xf = 432$

$\text{Mean} = \frac{\sum xf}{n} = \frac{432}{12} = 36$

3. a. First arrange the data items from smallest to largest: 25, 28, <u>35</u>, 40, 42
The number of data items is odd, so the median is the middle number. The median is 35.

b. First arrange the data items from smallest to largest: 61, 72, <u>79</u>, <u>85</u>, 87, 93
The number of data items is even, so the median is the mean of the two middle data items.
The median is $\frac{79+85}{2} = \frac{164}{2} = 82$.

4. The data items are arranged from smallest to largest with $n = 19$, which gives $\frac{n+1}{2} = \frac{19+1}{2} = \frac{20}{2} = 10$
The median is in the 10th position, which means the median is 5.

5. The eating times from smallest to largest are 1:06, 1:09, 1:14, 1:21, 1:22, 1:25, 1:29, 1:29, 1:34, 1:34, 1:36, 1:45, 1:46, 1:49, 1:54, 1:57, 2:10, 2:15.
There are 18 data items so $n = 18$, which gives $\frac{n+1}{2} = \frac{18+1}{2} = \frac{19}{2} = 9.5$ position
The median is the mean of the data items in positions 9 and 10.
Both the 9th and 10th positions are 1:34.
Thus, the median is 1 hour, 34 minutes.

6. The total frequency is $1+1+1+3+1+2+2+2+1+2+1+1=18$, therefore $n = 18$
The median's position is $\frac{n+1}{2} = \frac{18+1}{2} = \frac{19}{2} = 9.5$.
Therefore, the median is the mean of the data items in positions 9 and 10.
Counting through the frequency row identifies that the 9th data item is 54 and the 10th data item is 55.
Thus, the median is $\frac{54+55}{2} = \frac{109}{2} = 54.5$.

7. a. Mean $= \dfrac{\$1000+\$98+\$15+\$7+\$7+\$13+\$23+\$38+\$20+\$5}{10} = \$122.6$ million

b. Position of median: $\dfrac{n+1}{2} = \dfrac{10+1}{2} = 5.5$ position

The median is the mean of the data items in positions 5 and 6.
First, order the data: 5, 7, 7, 13, 15, 20, 23, 38, 98, 1000

Thus, the median is $\dfrac{\$15+\$20}{2} = \$17.5$ million .

c. The mean is so much greater than the median because one data item, Kennedy's net worth, was much greater than the other presidents..

8. a. The mode is 8 (because 8 occurs most often).

b. The modes are 3 and 8 (because both 3 and 8 occur most often).

c. There is no mode (because each data item occurs the same number of times).

9. Midrange $= \dfrac{0.0+29.0}{2} = 14.5$

10. a. Mean $= \dfrac{173+191+182+190+172+147+146+138+175+136+179+153+107+195+135+140+138}{17}$

$= \dfrac{2697}{17} = 158.6$ calories

b. Order the data items: 107, 135, 136, 138, 138, 140, 146, 147, <u>153</u>, 172, 173, 175, 179, 182, 190, 191, 195
The number of data items is odd, so the median is the middle number. The median is 153 calories.

c. The number 138 occurs more often than any other. The mode is 138 calories.

d. Midrange $= \dfrac{107+195}{2} = \dfrac{302}{2} = 151$ calories

Concept and Vocabulary Check 12.2

1. mean

2. median

3. $\dfrac{n+1}{2}$

4. mode

5. midrange

6. true

7. false

8. false

9. false

Exercise Set 12.2

1. $\frac{7+4+3+2+8+5+1+3}{8}=\frac{33}{8}=4.125$

3. $\frac{91+95+99+97+93+95}{6}=\frac{570}{6}=95$

5. $\frac{100+40+70+40+60}{5}=\frac{310}{5}=62$

7. $\frac{1.6+3.8+5.0+2.7+4.2+4.2+3.2+4.7+3.6+2.5+2.5}{11}=\frac{38}{11}\approx 3.45$

9.

x	f	xf
1	1	$1\cdot 1=1$
2	3	$2\cdot 3=6$
3	4	$3\cdot 4=12$
4	4	$4\cdot 4=16$
5	6	$5\cdot 6=30$
6	5	$6\cdot 5=30$
7	3	$7\cdot 3=21$
8	2	$8\cdot 2=16$
	28	$\sum xf=132$

$\text{Mean}=\frac{\sum xf}{n}=\frac{132}{28}\approx 4.71$

11.

x	f	xf
1	1	$1\cdot 1=1$
2	1	$2\cdot 1=2$
3	2	$3\cdot 2=6$
4	5	$4\cdot 5=20$
5	7	$5\cdot 7=35$
6	9	$6\cdot 9=54$
7	8	$7\cdot 8=56$
8	6	$8\cdot 6=48$
9	4	$9\cdot 4=36$
10	3	$10\cdot 3=30$
	46	$\sum xf=288$

$\text{Mean}=\frac{\sum xf}{n}=\frac{288}{46}\approx 6.26$

13. First arrange the data items from smallest to largest: 1, 2, 3, 3, 4, 5, 7, 8
The number of data items is even, so the median is the mean of the two middle data items. The median is 3.5.

15. First arrange the data items from smallest to largest: 91, 93, 95, 95, 97, 99
The number of data items is even, so the median is the mean of the two middle data items.

$\text{Median}=\frac{95+95}{2}=95$

17. First arrange the data items from smallest to largest: 40, 40, 60, 70, 100
The number of data items is odd, so the median is the middle number. The median is 60.

19. First arrange the data items from smallest to largest: 1.6, 2.5, 2.5, 2.7, 3.2, 3.6, 3.8, 4.2, 4.2, 4.7, 5.0
The number of data items is odd, so the median is the middle number. The median is 3.6.

21. $n = 28$

$$\frac{n+1}{2} = \frac{28+1}{2} = \frac{29}{2} = 14.5$$

The median is in the 14.5 position, which means the median is the mean of the data items in positions 14 and 15. Counting down the frequency column, the 14th and 15th data items are both 5.

$$\text{Median} = \frac{5+5}{2} = 5$$

23. $n = 46$

$$\frac{n+1}{2} = \frac{46+1}{2} = 23.5$$

The median is in the 23.5 position, which means the median is the mean of the data items in positions 23 and 24. Counting down the frequency column, the 23rd and 24th data items are both 6.

$$\text{Median} = \frac{6+6}{2} = 6$$

25. The mode is 3.

27. The mode is 95.

29. The mode is 40.

31. The modes are 2.5 and 4.2 (bimodal).

33. The mode is 5.

35. The mode is 6.

37. lowest data value = 1, highest data value = 8

$$\text{Midrange} = \frac{1+8}{2} = 4.5$$

39. lowest data value = 91, highest data value = 99

$$\text{Midrange} = \frac{91+99}{2} = 95$$

41. lowest data value = 40, highest data value = 100

$$\text{Midrange} = \frac{40+100}{2} = 70$$

43. lowest data value = 1.6, highest data value = 5.0

$$\text{Midrange} = \frac{1.6+5.0}{2} = 3.3$$

45. $\text{Midrange} = \frac{1+8}{2} = 4.5$

47. $\text{Midrange} = \frac{1+10}{2} = 5.5$

49.

x	f	xf
10	1	10
20	2	40
30	4	120
40	2	80
50	1	50
	10	$\sum xf = 300$

$$\text{Mean} = \frac{\sum xf}{n} = \frac{300}{10} = 30$$

The median is the mean of the 5th and 6th data items. Since these items are both 30, the median is 30.
The mode is 30 (it has the highest frequency).

$$\text{Midrange} = \frac{10+50}{2} = 30$$

51.

x	f	xf
10	2	20
11	2	22
12	3	36
13	4	52
14	1	14
15	2	30
	14	$\sum xf = 174$

$$\text{Mean} = \frac{\sum xf}{n} = \frac{174}{14} \approx 12.4$$

The median is the mean of the 7th and 8th data items. Median $= \dfrac{12+13}{2} = 12.5$

The mode is 13 (it has the highest frequency).

$$\text{Midrange} = \frac{10+15}{2} = 12.5$$

53. The data items are 21, 24, 25, 30, 31, 31, 33, 42, 45

$$\text{Mean} = \frac{21+24+25+30+31+31+33+42+45}{9} = \frac{282}{9} \approx 31.3$$

The median is the 5th data item, or 31.
The mode is 31.

$$\text{Midrange} = \frac{21+45}{2} = 33$$

55. a. Mean $= \dfrac{\sum x}{n} = \dfrac{876}{13} \approx 67.4$ thousand

b. The median is 51 thousand, which is the 7th data item.

c. The modes are 51 and 92 thousand.

d. Midrange $= \dfrac{27+200}{2} = 113.5$ thousand

57.

x	f	xf
2	12	$2 \cdot 12 = 24$
7	16	$7 \cdot 16 = 112$
12	16	$12 \cdot 16 = 192$
17	16	$17 \cdot 16 = 272$
22	10	$22 \cdot 10 = 220$
27	11	$27 \cdot 11 = 297$
32	4	$32 \cdot 4 = 128$
37	3	$37 \cdot 3 = 111$
42	3	$42 \cdot 3 = 126$
47	3	$47 \cdot 3 = 141$
	94	$\sum xf = 1623$

a. $\text{Mean} = \dfrac{\sum xf}{n} = \dfrac{1623}{94} \approx 17.27$

b. The median is 17 because the 47th and 48th data items both are 17.

c. The modes are 7, 12, and 17.

d. $\text{Midrange} = \dfrac{47+2}{2} = \dfrac{49}{2} = 24.5$

59. $n = 40,\ \dfrac{n+1}{2} = \dfrac{40+1}{2} = \dfrac{41}{2} = 20.5$

The median is in the 20.5 position, which means the median is the mean of the data items in positions 20 and 21.

$\text{Median} = \dfrac{175+175}{2} = 175 \text{ lb}$

61. $\text{Midrange} = \dfrac{150+205}{2} = 177.5 \text{ lb}$

63. Find the weighted mean by treating the number of credits as the "frequency."

Course	Grade	Value (x)	Credits (f)	xf
Sociology	A	4	3	$4 \cdot 3 = 12$
Biology	C	2	3.5	$2 \cdot 3.5 = 7$
Music	B	3	1	$3 \cdot 1 = 3$
Math	B	3	4	$3 \cdot 4 = 12$
English	C	2	3	$2 \cdot 3 = 6$
			14.5	$\sum xf = 40$

$\text{Mean} = \dfrac{\sum xf}{n} = \dfrac{40}{14.5} \approx 2.76$

73. makes sense

75. makes sense

77. Answers will vary. Sample answers:

a. 75, 80, 80, 90, 91, 94

b. 50, 80, 80, 85, 90, 95

c. 70, 75, 80, 85, 90, 100

d. 75, 80, 85, 90, 95, 95

e. 75, 80, 85, 85, 90, 95

f. 68, 70, 72, 72, 74, 76

Check Points 12.3

1. Range $= 11 - 2 = 9$

2. Mean $= \dfrac{2+4+7+11}{4} = \dfrac{24}{4} = 6$

Data item	Deviation: Data item – mean
2	$2 - 6 = -4$
4	$4 - 6 = -2$
7	$7 - 6 = 1$
11	$11 - 6 = 5$

3. Mean $= \dfrac{2+4+7+11}{4} = \dfrac{24}{4} = 6$

Data item	Deviation: Data item – mean	(Deviation)^2: (Data item–mean)^2
2	$2 - 6 = -4$	$(-4)^2 = 16$
4	$4 - 6 = -2$	$(-2)^2 = 4$
7	$7 - 6 = 1$	$1^2 = 1$
11	$11 - 6 = 5$	$5^2 = 25$
		$\sum(\text{data item–mean})^2 = 46$

Standard deviation $= \sqrt{\dfrac{46}{4-1}} = \sqrt{\dfrac{46}{3}} \approx 3.92$

4. *Sample A*

$$\text{Mean} = \frac{73+75+77+79+81+83}{6} = \frac{468}{6} = 78$$

Data item	Deviation: Data item – mean	$(\text{Deviation})^2$: $(\text{Data item–mean})^2$
73	$73-78=-5$	$(-5)^2 = 25$
75	$75-78=-3$	$(-3)^2 = 9$
77	$77-78=-1$	$(-1)^2 = 1$
79	$79-78=1$	$1^2 = 1$
81	$81-78=3$	$3^2 = 9$
83	$83-78=5$	$5^2 = 25$
		$\sum(\text{data item–mean})^2 = 70$

$$\text{Standard deviation} = \sqrt{\frac{70}{6-1}} = \sqrt{\frac{70}{5}} \approx 3.74$$

Sample B

$$\text{Mean} = \frac{40+44+92+94+98+100}{6} = \frac{468}{6} = 78$$

Data item	Deviation: Data item – mean	$(\text{Deviation})^2$: $(\text{Data item–mean})^2$
40	$40-78=-38$	$(-38)^2 = 1444$
44	$44-78=-34$	$(-34)^2 = 1156$
92	$92-78=14$	$14^2 = 196$
94	$94-78=16$	$16^2 = 256$
98	$98-78=20$	$20^2 = 400$
100	$100-78=22$	$22^2 = 484$
		$\sum(\text{data item–mean})^2 = 3936$

$$\text{Standard deviation} = \sqrt{\frac{3936}{6-1}} = \sqrt{\frac{3936}{5}} \approx 28.06$$

5. a. Small-company stocks had a greater return on investment.

b. Small-company stocks had the greater risk. The higher standard deviation indicates that small-company stocks are more likely to lose money.

Concept and Vocabulary Check 12.3

1. range
2. standard deviation
3. true
4. true
5. false

Exercise Set 12.3

1. Range $= 5 - 1 = 4$

3. Range $= 15 - 7 = 8$

5. Range $= 5 - 3 = 2$

7. a.

Data item	Deviation: Data item – mean
3	$3 - 12 = -9$
5	$5 - 12 = -7$
7	$7 - 12 = -5$
12	$12 - 12 = 0$
18	$18 - 12 = 6$
27	$27 - 12 = 15$

b. $-9 - 7 - 5 + 0 + 6 + 15 = 0$

9. a.

Data item	Deviation: Data item – mean
29	$29 - 49 = -20$
38	$38 - 49 = -11$
48	$48 - 49 = -1$
49	$49 - 49 = 0$
53	$53 - 49 = 4$
77	$77 - 49 = 28$

b. $-20 - 11 - 1 + 0 + 4 + 28 = 0$

11. a. $\text{Mean} = \dfrac{85+95+90+85+100}{5} = 91$

b.

Data item	Deviation: Data item – mean
85	$85 - 91 = -6$
95	$95 - 91 = 4$
90	$90 - 91 = -1$
85	$85 - 91 = -6$
100	$100 - 91 = 9$

c. $-6 + 4 - 1 - 6 + 9 = 0$

13. a. $\text{Mean} = \dfrac{146+153+155+160+161}{5} = 155$

b.

Data item	Deviation: Data item – mean
146	$146 - 155 = -9$
153	$153 - 155 = -2$
155	$155 - 155 = 0$
160	$160 - 155 = 5$
161	$161 - 155 = 6$

c. $-9 - 2 + 0 + 5 + 6 = 0$

15. a. $\text{Mean} = \dfrac{2.25+3.50+2.75+3.10+1.90}{5} = 2.70$

b.

Data item	Deviation: Data item – mean
2.25	2.25 – 2.70 = – 0.45
3.50	3.50 – 2.70 = 0.80
2.75	2.75 – 2.70 = 0.05
3.10	3.10 – 2.70 = 0.40
1.90	1.90 – 2.70 = – 0.80

c. $-0.45 + 0.80 + 0.05 + 0.40 - 0.80 = 0$

17. $\text{Mean} = \dfrac{1+2+3+4+5}{5} = 3$

Data item	Deviation: Data item – mean	(Deviation)^2 : (Data item–mean)^2
1	$1 - 3 = -2$	$(-2)^2 = 4$
2	$2 - 3 = -1$	$(-1)^2 = 1$
3	$3 - 3 = 0$	$0^2 = 0$
4	$4 - 3 = 1$	$1^2 = 1$
5	$5 - 3 = 2$	$2^2 = 4$
		$\sum(\text{data item–mean})^2 = 10$

$$\text{Standard deviation} = \sqrt{\frac{10}{5-1}} = \sqrt{\frac{10}{4}} \approx 1.58$$

19. $\text{Mean} = \dfrac{7+9+9+15}{4} = 10$

Data item	Deviation: Data item – mean	(Deviation)^2 : (Data item–mean)^2
7	$7 - 10 = -3$	$(-3)^2 = 9$
9	$9 - 10 = -1$	$(-1)^2 = 1$
9	$9 - 10 = -1$	$(-1)^2 = 1$
15	$15 - 10 = 5$	$5^2 = 25$
		$\sum(\text{data item–mean})^2 = 36$

$$\text{Standard deviation} = \sqrt{\frac{36}{4-1}} = \sqrt{\frac{36}{3}} \approx 3.46$$

21. Mean $= \frac{3+3+4+4+5+5}{6} = 4$

Data item	Deviation: Data item – mean	$(\text{Deviation})^2$: $(\text{Data item–mean})^2$
3	$3-4=-1$	$(-1)^2=1$
3	$3-4=-1$	$(-1)^2=1$
4	$4-4=0$	$0^2=0$
4	$4-4=0$	$0^2=0$
5	$5-4=1$	$1^2=1$
5	$5-4=1$	$1^2=1$
		$\sum(\text{data item–mean})^2=4$

Standard deviation $= \sqrt{\frac{4}{6-1}} = \sqrt{\frac{4}{5}} \approx 0.89$

23. Mean $= \frac{1+1+1+4+7+7+7}{7} = 4$

Data item	Deviation: Data item – mean	$(\text{Deviation})^2$: $(\text{Data item–mean})^2$
1	$1-4=-3$	$(-3)^2=9$
1	$1-4=-3$	$(-3)^2=9$
1	$1-4=-3$	$(-3)^2=9$
4	$4-4=0$	$0^2=0$
7	$7-4=3$	$3^2=9$
7	$7-4=3$	$3^2=9$
7	$7-4=3$	$3^2=9$
		$\sum(\text{data item–mean})^2=54$

Standard deviation $= \sqrt{\frac{54}{7-1}} = \sqrt{\frac{54}{6}} = 3$

25. Mean $= \dfrac{9+5+9+5+9+5+9+5}{8} = 7$

Data item	Deviation: Data item – mean	(Deviation)^2: (Data item–mean)^2
9	$9-7=2$	$2^2=4$
5	$5-7=-2$	$(-2)^2=4$
9	$9-7=2$	$2^2=4$
5	$5-7=-2$	$(-2)^2=4$
9	$9-7=2$	$2^2=4$
5	$5-7=-2$	$(-2)^2=4$
9	$9-7=2$	$2^2=4$
5	$5-7=-2$	$(-2)^2=4$
		$\sum(\text{data item–mean})^2 = 32$

Standard deviation $= \sqrt{\dfrac{32}{8-1}} = \sqrt{\dfrac{32}{7}} \approx 2.14$

27. *Sample A*

Mean $= \dfrac{6+8+10+12+14+16+18}{7} = 12$

Range $= 18-6=12$

Data item	Deviation: Data item – mean	(Deviation)^2: (Data item–mean)^2
6	$6-12=-6$	$(-6)^2=36$
8	$8-12=-4$	$(-4)^2=16$
10	$10-12=-2$	$(-2)^2=4$
12	$12-12=0$	$0^2=0$
14	$14-12=2$	$2^2=4$
16	$16-12=4$	$4^2=16$
18	$18-12=6$	$6^2=36$
		$\sum(\text{data item–mean})^2 = 112$

Standard deviation $= \sqrt{\dfrac{112}{7-1}} = \sqrt{\dfrac{112}{6}} \approx 4.32$

Sample B

$$\text{Mean} = \frac{6+7+8+12+16+17+18}{7} = 12$$

Range = 18 – 6 = 12

Data item	Deviation: Data item – mean	(Deviation)^2 : (Data item–mean)^2
6	$6 - 12 = -6$	$(-6)^2 = 36$
7	$7 - 12 = -5$	$(-5)^2 = 25$
8	$8 - 12 = -4$	$(-4)^2 = 16$
12	$12 - 12 = 0$	$0^2 = 0$
16	$16 - 12 = 4$	$4^2 = 16$
17	$17 - 12 = 5$	$5^2 = 25$
18	$18 - 12 = 6$	$6^2 = 36$
		$\sum(\text{data item–mean})^2 = 154$

$$\text{Standard deviation} = \sqrt{\frac{154}{7-1}} = \sqrt{\frac{154}{6}} \approx 5.07$$

Sample C

$$\text{Mean} = \frac{6+6+6+12+18+18+18}{7} = 12$$

Range = 18 – 6 = 12

Data item	Deviation: Data item – mean	(Deviation)^2 : (Data item–mean)^2
6	$6 - 12 = -6$	$(-6)^2 = 36$
6	$6 - 12 = -6$	$(-6)^2 = 36$
6	$6 - 12 = -6$	$(-6)^2 = 36$
12	$12 - 12 = 0$	$0^2 = 0$
18	$18 - 12 = 6$	$6^2 = 36$
18	$18 - 12 = 6$	$6^2 = 36$
18	$18 - 12 = 6$	$6^2 = 36$
		$\sum(\text{data item–mean})^2 = 216$

$$\text{Standard deviation} = \sqrt{\frac{216}{7-1}} = \sqrt{\frac{216}{6}} = 6$$

The samples have the same mean and range, but different standard deviations.

29. Mean $= \dfrac{9+9+9+9+9+9+9}{7} = \dfrac{63}{7} = 9$

Data item	Deviation: Data item – mean	$(\text{Deviation})^2$: $(\text{Data item–mean})^2$
9	$9-9=0$	$(0)^2=0$
9	$9-9=0$	$(0)^2=0$
9	$9-9=0$	$(0)^2=0$
9	$9-9=0$	$(0)^2=0$
9	$9-9=0$	$(0)^2=0$
9	$9-9=0$	$(0)^2=0$
9	$9-9=0$	$(0)^2=0$
		$\sum(\text{data item}-\text{mean})^2=0$

Standard deviation $= \sqrt{\dfrac{0}{7-1}} = \sqrt{\dfrac{0}{6}} = 0$

31. Mean $= \dfrac{8+8+8+9+10+10+10}{7} = \dfrac{63}{7} = 9$

Data item	Deviation: Data item – mean	$(\text{Deviation})^2$: $(\text{Data item–mean})^2$
8	$8-9=-1$	$(-1)^2=1$
8	$8-9=-1$	$(-1)^2=1$
8	$8-9=-1$	$(-1)^2=1$
9	$9-9=0$	$(0)^2=0$
10	$10-9=1$	$(-1)^2=1$
10	$10-9=1$	$(-1)^2=1$
10	$10-9=1$	$(-1)^2=1$
		$\sum(\text{data item}-\text{mean})^2=6$

Standard deviation $= \sqrt{\dfrac{6}{7-1}} = \sqrt{\dfrac{6}{6}} = 1$

33. Mean $= \frac{5+10+15+20+25}{5} = \frac{75}{5} = 15$

Data item	Deviation: Data item – mean	(Deviation)^2: (Data item–mean)^2
5	$5-15=-10$	$(-10)^2=100$
10	$10-15=-5$	$(-5)^2=25$
15	$15-15=0$	$(0)^2=0$
20	$20-15=5$	$(5)^2=25$
25	$25-15=10$	$(10)^2=100$
		$\sum(\text{data item}-\text{mean})^2=250$

Standard deviation $= \sqrt{\frac{250}{5-1}} = \sqrt{\frac{250}{4}} \approx 7.91$

35. Mean $= \frac{17+18+18+18+19+19+20+20+21+22}{10} = \frac{192}{10} = 19.2$

Data item	Deviation: Data item – mean	(Deviation)^2: (Data item–mean)^2
17	$17-19.2=-2.2$	$(-2.2)^2=4.84$
18	$18-19.2=-2.2$	$(-1.2)^2=1.44$
18	$18-19.2=-2.2$	$(-1.2)^2=1.44$
18	$18-19.2=-2.2$	$(-1.2)^2=1.44$
19	$19-19.2=-0.2$	$(-0.2)^2=0.04$
19	$19-19.2=-0.2$	$(-0.2)^2=0.04$
20	$20-19.2=0.8$	$(0.8)^2=0.64$
20	$20-19.2=0.8$	$(0.8)^2=0.64$
21	$21-19.2=1.8$	$(1.8)^2=3.24$
22	$22-19.2=2.8$	$(2.8)^2=7.84$
		$\sum(\text{data item}-\text{mean})^2=21.6$

Standard deviation $= \sqrt{\frac{21.6}{10-1}} = \sqrt{\frac{21.6}{9}} \approx 1.55$

37. a. The male artists' data set has the greater mean. This can be seen without calculating by observing that at each rank, the male artist had more platinum albums than the corresponding female artist.

b. Mean (male artists) $= \frac{465}{5} = 93$; Mean (female artists) $= \frac{290}{5} = 58$

c. The male artists' data set has the greater standard deviation. This can be seen without calculating by observing that the male artists' data set data has a greater spread.

d. Standard deviation (male artists) $= \sqrt{\dfrac{4262}{5-1}} \approx 32.64$

Standard deviation (female artists) $= \sqrt{\dfrac{186}{5-1}} \approx 6.82$

47. makes sense

49. makes sense

53. a is the best approximation

Check Points 12.4

1. a. $\text{Height} = \text{mean} + 3 \cdot \text{standard deviation}$
$= 65 + 3 \cdot 3.5 = 75.5 \text{ in.}$

b. $\text{Height} = \text{mean} - 2 \cdot \text{standard deviation}$
$= 65 - 2 \cdot 3.5 = 58 \text{ in.}$

2. a. The 68-95-99.7 Rule states that approximately 95% of the data items fall within 2 standard deviations of the mean. The figure shows that 95% of male adults have heights between 62 inches and 78 inches.

b. The 68-95-99.7 Rule states that approximately 95% of the data items fall within 2 standard deviations of the mean. Since the mean is 70 inches, the figure shows that half of the 95%, or 47.5% of male adults have heights between 70 inches and 78 inches.

c. The 68-95-99.7 Rule states that approximately 68% of the data items fall within 1 standard deviation of the mean, thus 32% of the data falls outside this range. Half of the 32%, or 16% of male adults will have heights above 74 inches.

3. a. $z_{342} = \dfrac{\text{data item} - \text{mean}}{\text{standard deviation}} = \dfrac{342-336}{3} = \dfrac{6}{3} = 2$

b. $z_{336} = \dfrac{\text{data item} - \text{mean}}{\text{standard deviation}} = \dfrac{336-336}{3} = \dfrac{0}{3} = 0$

c. $z_{333} = \dfrac{\text{data item} - \text{mean}}{\text{standard deviation}} = \dfrac{333-336}{3} = \dfrac{-3}{3} = -1$

4. Find the z-score for each test taken.

SAT: $z_{550} = \dfrac{\text{data item} - \text{mean}}{\text{standard deviation}} = \dfrac{550-500}{100} = \dfrac{50}{100} = 0.5$

ACT: $z_{24} = \dfrac{\text{data item} - \text{mean}}{\text{standard deviation}} = \dfrac{24-18}{6} = \dfrac{6}{6} = 1$

You scored better on the ACT test because the score is 1 standard deviation above the mean. The SAT score is only half a standard deviation above the mean.

5. a. $\text{Score} = \text{mean} - 2.25 \cdot \text{standard deviation} = 100 - 2.25(16) = 64$

b. $\text{Score} = \text{mean} + 1.75 \cdot \text{standard deviation} = 100 + 1.75(16) = 128$

6. This means that 75% of the scores on the SAT are less than this student's score.

7. a. The sample size is $n = 2513$. The margin of

error is $\pm\frac{1}{\sqrt{n}}\times 100\% = \pm\frac{1}{\sqrt{2513}}\times 100\% \approx \pm 0.020\times 100\% = \pm 2.0\%$.

b. There is a 95% probability that the true population percentage lies between
the sample percent $-\frac{1}{\sqrt{n}}\times 100\% = 36\% - 2.0\% = 34\%$ and the sample percent $+\frac{1}{\sqrt{n}}\times 100\% = 36\% + 2.0\% = 38\%$.
We can be 95% confident that between 34% and 38% of Americans read more than ten books per year.

c. Sample answer: Some people may be embarrassed to admit that they read few or no books in a year.

Concept and Vocabulary Check 12.4

1. 68; 95; 99.7
2. mean
3. percentile
4. margin of error
5. true
6. true
7. false
8. true

Exercise Set 12.4

1. Score = 100 + 1 · 20 = 100 + 20 = 120

3. Score = 100 + 3 · 20 = 100 + 60 = 160

5. Score = 100 + 2.5(20) = 100 + 50 = 150

7. Score = 100 – 2 · 20 = 100 – 40 = 60

9. Score = 100 – 0.5(20) = 100 – 10 = 90

11. \$16,500 is 1 standard deviation below the mean and \$17,500 is 1 standard deviation above the mean. The Rule and the figure indicate that 68% of the buyers paid between \$16,500 and \$17,500.

13. \$17,500 is 1 standard deviation above the mean. 68% of the buyers paid between \$16,500 and \$17,500. Because of symmetry, the percent that paid between \$17,000 and \$17,500 is $\frac{1}{2}(68\%) = 34\%$.

15. \$16,000 is 2 standard deviations below the mean. 95% of the buyers paid between \$16,000 and \$18,000. Because of symmetry, the percent that paid between \$16,000 and \$17,000 is $\frac{1}{2}(95\%) = 47.5\%$.

17. \$15,500 is 3 standard deviations below the mean. 99.7% of the buyers paid between \$15,500 and \$18,500. Because of symmetry, the percent that paid between \$15,500 and \$17,000 is
$\frac{1}{2}(99.7\%) = 49.85\%$.

19. \$17,500 is 1 standard deviation above the mean. Since 68% of the data items fall within 1 standard deviation of the mean, 100% – 68% = 32% fall farther than 1 standard deviation from the mean. Because of symmetry, the percent that paid more than \$17,500 is $\frac{1}{2}(32\%) = 16\%$.

21. \$16,000 is 2 standard deviations below the mean. Since 95% of the data items fall within 2 standard deviations of the mean, 100% – 95% = 5% fall farther than 2 standard deviations from the mean. Because of symmetry, the percent that paid less than \$16,000 is $\frac{1}{2}(5\%) = 2.5\%$.

23. The 68-95-99.7 Rule states that approximately 95% of the data items fall within 2 standard deviations of the mean.
95% of people will have IQs between 68 and 132.

25. The 68-95-99.7 Rule states that approximately 95% of the data items fall within 2 standard deviations of the mean.
Half of the 95%, or 47.5% of people will have IQs between 68 and 100.

27. The 68-95-99.7 Rule states that approximately 68% of the data items fall within 1 standard deviation of the mean.
Thus, 100% – 68% = 32% will fall outside this range. Half of the 32%, or 16% of people will have IQs above 116.

29. The 68-95-99.7 Rule states that approximately 95% of the data items fall within 2 standard deviations of the mean.
Thus, 100% – 95% = 5% will fall outside this range. Half of the 5%, or 2.5% of people will have IQs below 68.

31. The 68-95-99.7 Rule states that approximately 99.7% of the data items fall within 3 standard deviations of the mean.
Thus, 100% – 99.7% = 0.3% will fall outside this range. Half of the 0.3%, or 0.15% of people will have IQs above 148.

33. $z_{68} = \frac{68-60}{8} = \frac{8}{8} = 1$

35. $z_{84} = \frac{84-60}{8} = \frac{24}{8} = 3$

37. $z_{64} = \frac{64-60}{8} = \frac{4}{8} = 0.5$

39. $z_{74} = \frac{74-60}{8} = \frac{14}{8} = 1.75$

41. $z_{60} = \frac{60-60}{8} = \frac{0}{8} = 0$

43. $z_{52} = \frac{52-60}{8} = \frac{-8}{8} = -1$

45. $z_{48} = \frac{48-60}{8} = \frac{-12}{8} = -1.5$

47. $z_{34} = \frac{34-60}{8} = \frac{-26}{8} = -3.25$

49. $z = \frac{\text{data item} - \text{mean}}{\text{standard deviation}} = \frac{17-11}{4} = 1.5$

51. $z = \frac{\text{data item} - \text{mean}}{\text{standard deviation}} = \frac{20-11}{4} = 2.25$

53. $z = \frac{\text{data item} - \text{mean}}{\text{standard deviation}} = \frac{6-11}{4} = -1.25$

55. $z = \frac{\text{data item} - \text{mean}}{\text{standard deviation}} = \frac{5-11}{4} = -1.5$

57. z-score of 128 on the Stanford-Binet:
$z = \frac{\text{data item} - \text{mean}}{\text{standard deviation}} = \frac{128-100}{16} = 1.75$
z-score of 127 on the Wechsler:
$z = \frac{\text{data item} - \text{mean}}{\text{standard deviation}} = \frac{127-100}{15} = 1.8$
The person who scores 127 on the Wechsler has the higher IQ.

59. $2 \cdot 50 = 100$
The data item is 100 units above the mean.
$400 + 100 = 500$

61. $1.5(50) = 75$
The data item is 75 units above the mean.
$400 + 75 = 475$

63. $-3 \cdot 50 = -150$
The data item is 150 units below the mean.
$400 - 150 = 250$

65. $-2.5(50) = -125$
The data item is 125 units below the mean.
$400 - 125 = 275$

67. a.
$$\begin{aligned}\text{margin of error} &= \pm\frac{1}{\sqrt{814}}\times 100\% \\ &\approx \pm 0.035\times 100\% \\ &= \pm 3.5\%\end{aligned}$$

b. $69\% - 3.5\% = 21.9\%$
$69\% + 3.5\% = 28.1\%$
We can be 95% confident that between 65.5% and 72.5% of the population favor required gun registration as a means to reduce gun violence.

69. a.
$$\begin{aligned}\text{margin of error} &= \pm\frac{1}{\sqrt{4000}}\times 100\% \\ &\approx \pm 0.016\times 100\% \\ &= \pm 1.6\%\end{aligned}$$

b. $60.2\% - 1.6\% = 58.6\%$
$60.2\% + 1.6\% = 61.8\%$
We can be 95% confident that between 58.6% and 61.8% of all TV households watched the final episode of *M*A*S*H*.

71.
$$\begin{aligned}\text{new margin of error} &= \pm\frac{1}{\sqrt{5000}}\times 100\% \\ &\approx \pm 0.014\times 100\% \\ &= \pm 1.4\%\end{aligned}$$
improvement $= 1.6\% - 1.4\% = 0.2\%$

73. a. The graph is skewed to the right.

b.

x	f	xf
1	3	$1 \cdot 3 = 3$
2	9	$2 \cdot 9 = 18$
3	8	$3 \cdot 8 = 24$
4	2	$4 \cdot 2 = 8$
5	7	$5 \cdot 7 = 35$
6	9	$6 \cdot 9 = 54$
7	5	$7 \cdot 5 = 35$
8	4	$8 \cdot 4 = 32$
9	1	$9 \cdot 1 = 9$
10	1	$10 \cdot 1 = 10$
12	1	$123 \cdot 1 = 12$
29	1	$29 \cdot 1 = 29$
	51	$\sum xf = 269$

$$\text{Mean} = \frac{\sum xf}{n} = \frac{269}{51} \approx 5.3$$
The mean rate is 5.3 murders per 100,000 residents.

c. The median is in the 26th position. The median rate is 5 murders per 100,000 residents.

d. Yes, these rates are consistent with the graph. The mean is greater than the median, which is expected with a distribution that is skewed to the right.

e. $z_{29} = \dfrac{29-5.3}{4.2} \approx 5.6$
Yes, this is unusually high. For a normal distribution, almost 100% of the z-scores are between –3 and 3.

87. does not make sense; Explanations will vary. Sample explanation: The standard deviation is too big for this case.

89. does not make sense; Explanations will vary. Sample explanation: The margin of error is approximately ±2.9%. So we are 95% confident that between 48.1% and 53.9% of voters will vote for candidate A which does not mean they will definitely win.

Check Points 12.5

1. $z_{83.60} = \dfrac{\text{data item} - \text{mean}}{\text{standard deviation}} = \dfrac{83.60 - 62}{18} = 1.2$

A z-score of 1.2 corresponds to a percentile of 88.49. Thus, 88.49% of plans have charges less than $83.60.

2. $z_{69.9} = \dfrac{\text{data item} - \text{mean}}{\text{standard deviation}} = \dfrac{69.9 - 65}{3.5} = 1.4$

A z-score of 1.4 corresponds to a percentile of 91.93. Thus, 100% – 91.92% = 8.08% of women have heights greater than 69.9 inches.

3. $z_{11} = \dfrac{\text{data item} - \text{mean}}{\text{standard deviation}} = \dfrac{11 - 14}{2.5} = -1.2$ which corresponds to a percentile of 11.51.

$z_{18} = \dfrac{\text{data item} - \text{mean}}{\text{standard deviation}} = \dfrac{18 - 14}{2.5} = 1.6$ which corresponds to a percentile of 94.52.

Thus, 94.52% – 11.51% = 83.01% of refrigerators have lives between 11 and 18 years.

Concept and Vocabulary Check 12.5

1. 98.93%

2. 1.07%

3. 88.49%

4. 87.42%

5. true

Exercise Set 12.5

1. a. 72.57%

b. 100% – 72.57% = 27.43%

3. a. 88.49%

b. 100% – 88.49% = 11.51%

5. a. 24.20%

b. 100% – 24.20% = 75.8%

7. a. 11.51%

b. 100% – 11.51% = 88.49%

9. $z = 0.2 \rightarrow 57.93\%$
$z = 1.4 \rightarrow 91.92\%$
91.92% – 57.93% = 33.99%

11. $z = 1 \rightarrow 84.13\%$
$z = 3 \rightarrow 99.87\%$
$99.87\% - 84.13\% = 15.74\%$

13. $z = -1.5 \rightarrow 6.68\%$
$z = 1.5 \rightarrow 93.32\%$
$93.32\% - 6.68\% = 86.64\%$

15. $z = -2 \rightarrow 2.28\%$
$z = -0.5 \rightarrow 30.85\%$
$30.85\% - 2.28\% = 28.57\%$

17. $z_{142} = \frac{\text{data item} - \text{mean}}{\text{standard deviation}} = \frac{142-121}{15} = 1.4$
A z-score of 1.4 corresponds to a percentile of 91.92. Thus, 91.92% of people have blood pressure below 142

19. $z_{130} = \frac{\text{data item} - \text{mean}}{\text{standard deviation}} = \frac{130-121}{15} = 0.6$
A z-score of 0.6 corresponds to a percentile of 72.57. Thus, 100% – 72.97% = 27.43% of people have blood pressure above 130.

21. $z_{103} = \frac{\text{data item} - \text{mean}}{\text{standard deviation}} = \frac{103-121}{15} = -1.2$
A z-score of –1.2 corresponds to a percentile of 11.51. Thus, 100% – 11.51% = 88.49% of people have blood pressure above 103.

23. $z_{142} = \frac{\text{data item} - \text{mean}}{\text{standard deviation}} = \frac{142-121}{15} = 1.4$
A z-score of 1.4 corresponds to a percentile of 91.92.
$z_{154} = \frac{\text{data item} - \text{mean}}{\text{standard deviation}} = \frac{154-121}{15} = 2.2$
A z-score of 2.2 corresponds to a percentile of 98.61. Thus, 98.61% – 91.92% = 6.69% of people have blood pressure between 142 and 154.

25. $z_{112} = \frac{\text{data item} - \text{mean}}{\text{standard deviation}} = \frac{112-121}{15} = -0.6$
A z-score of –0.6 corresponds to a percentile of 27.43.
$z_{130} = \frac{\text{data item} - \text{mean}}{\text{standard deviation}} = \frac{130-121}{15} = 0.6$
A z-score of 0.6 corresponds to a percentile of 72.57. Thus, 72.57% – 27.43% = 45.14% of people have blood pressure between 112 and 130.

27. $z_{25.8} = \frac{25.8 - 22.5}{2.2} = 1.5$
$z = 1.5 \rightarrow 93.32\%$
$100\% - 93.32\% = 6.68\%$ weigh more than 25.8 pounds.

29. $z_{19.2} = \dfrac{19.2-22.5}{2.2} = -1.5$
$z = -1.5 \rightarrow 6.68\%$
$z_{21.4} = \dfrac{21.4-22.5}{2.2} = -0.5$
$z = -0.5 \rightarrow 30.85\%$
$30.85\% - 6.68\% = 24.17\%$ weigh between 19.2 and 21.4 pounds.

31. The 77th percentile means that 77% of U.S. drivers are younger than 55.

33. The 14th percentile means that 14% of U.S. drivers are younger than 25. So $100\% - 14\% = 86\%$ which are at least 25.

35. 88% are younger than 65 and 98% are younger than 75. So $98\% - 88\% = 10\%$ which are at least 65 and younger than 75.

39. does not make sense; Explanations will vary. Sample explanation: Percentiles are always positive.

41. makes sense

45. A z-score of 1.3 has 90.32% of the data items below it, and 9.68% above it. So find the score corresponding to $z = 1.3$.
500 + 1.3(100) = 630
The cutoff score is 630.

Check Points 12.6

1. 0.51 would indicate a moderate correlation between the two.

2.

x	y	xy	x^2	y^2
8	2.2	17.6	64	4.84
15	2.3	34.5	225	5.29
18	3.8	68.4	324	14.44
31	2.8	86.8	961	7.84
31	3.5	108.5	961	12.25
32	2.7	86.4	1024	7.29
32	5.0	160	1024	25
44	6.5	286	1936	42.25
58	4.5	261	3364	20.25
90	11.0	990	8100	121

$\sum x = 359 \quad \sum y = 44.3 \quad \sum xy = 2099.2 \quad \sum x^2 = 17{,}983 \quad \sum y^2 = 260.45$

$\left(\sum x\right)^2 = (359)^2 = 128{,}881$ and $\left(\sum y\right)^2 = (44.3)^2 = 1962.49$

$$r = \frac{10(2099.2)-(359)(44.3)}{\sqrt{10(17{,}983)-128{,}881}\sqrt{10(260.45)-1962.49}} = \frac{5088.3}{\sqrt{50949}\sqrt{642.01}} \approx 0.89$$

This value for r is fairly close to 1 and indicates a moderately strong positive correlation. This means the higher the rate of firearm ownership, the higher the rate of deaths.

3. $m = \dfrac{10(2099.2)-(359)(44.3)}{10(17,983)-128,881} = \dfrac{5088.3}{50949} \approx 0.1$

$b = \dfrac{44.3-(0.1)(359)}{10} = \dfrac{8.4}{10} \approx 0.8$

The equation of the regression line is $y = 0.1x + 0.8$.

The predicted rate in a country with 80 firearms per 100 persons can be found by substituting 80 for x.

$y = 0.1x + 0.8$
$= 0.1(80) + 0.8$
$= 8.8$

The death rate would be 8.8 per 100,000 people.

4. Yes, $|r| = 0.89$. Since $0.89 > 0.632$ and 0.765 (using table 12.16), we may conclude that a correlation does exist.

Concept and Vocabulary Check 12.6

1. scatter plot
2. regression line
3. correlation coefficient; -1; 1
4. true
5. false
6. false
7. true

Exercise Set 12.6

1. There appears to be a positive correlation.

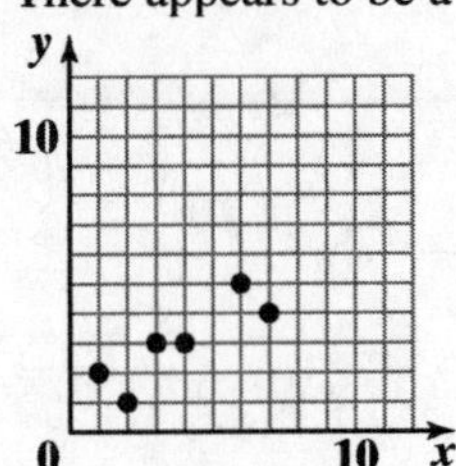

3. There appears to be a negative correlation.

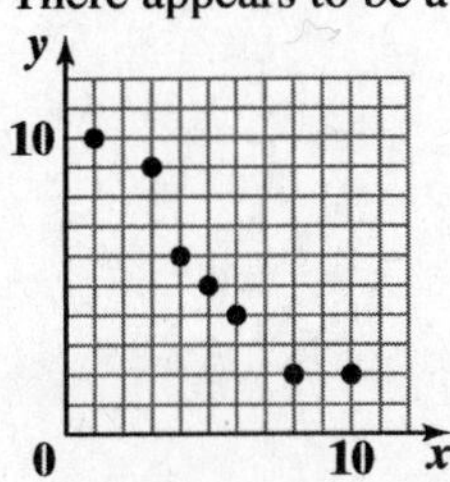

5. There appears to be a positive correlation.

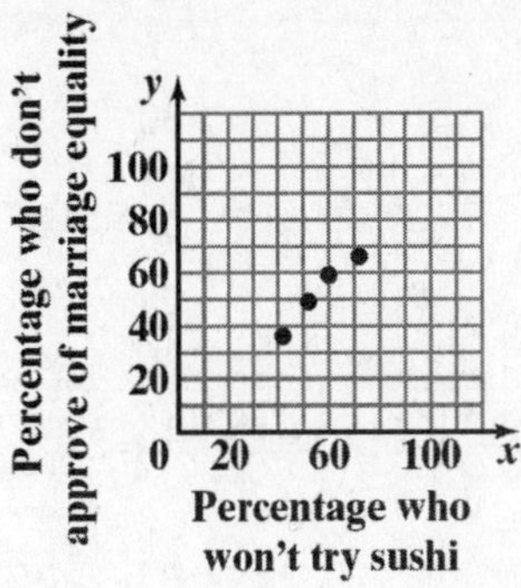

7. There appears to be a positive correlation.

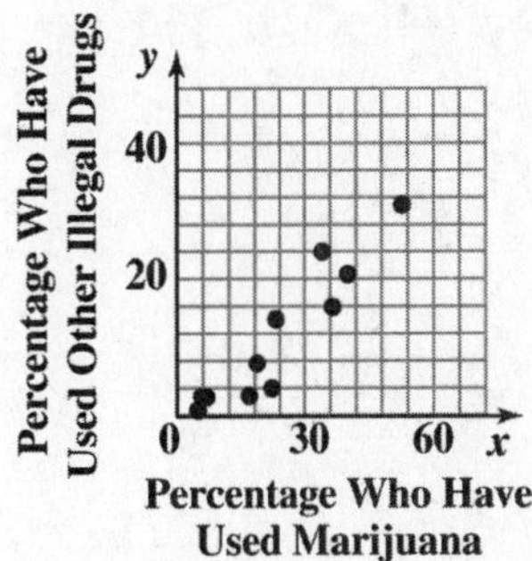

9. false; The correlation is negative.
11. true
13. true
15. false; See for example, Syria and Vietnam.
17. true
19. false; Generally speaking, as per capita income rises, the percentage of people who call themselves "happy" rises.
21. true
23. false; The lowest the lowest level was reported by the Ukraine, yet several countries have lower per capita income (points to the left).
25. false; The correlation is positive, but not that strong..
27. a
29. d

31.

x	y	xy	x^2	y^2
1	2	2	1	4
6	5	30	36	25
4	3	12	16	9
3	3	9	9	9
7	4	28	49	16
2	1	2	4	1
$\sum x = 23$	$\sum y = 18$	$\sum xy = 83$	$\sum x^2 = 115$	$\sum y^2 = 64$

$\left(\sum x\right)^2 = (23)^2 = 529$ and $\left(\sum y\right)^2 = (18)^2 = 324$

$$r = \frac{6(83)-(23)(18)}{\sqrt{6(115)-529}\sqrt{6(64)-(324)}}$$
$$= \frac{84}{\sqrt{161}\sqrt{60}}$$
$$\approx 0.85$$

33.

x	y	xy	x^2	y^2
8	2	16	64	4
6	4	24	36	16
1	10	10	1	100
5	5	25	25	25
4	6	24	16	36
10	2	20	100	4
3	9	27	9	81
$\sum x = 37$	$\sum y = 38$	$\sum xy = 146$	$\sum x^2 = 251$	$\sum y^2 = 266$

$\left(\sum x\right)^2 = (37)^2 = 1369$ and $\left(\sum y\right)^2 = (38)^2 = 1444$

$$r = \frac{7(146)-(37)(38)}{\sqrt{7(251)-1369}\sqrt{7(266)-1444}}$$
$$= \frac{-384}{\sqrt{388}\sqrt{418}}$$
$$\approx -0.95$$

35. a.

x	y	xy	x^2	y^2
42	36	1512	1764	1296
52	49	2548	2704	2401
60	59	3540	3600	3481
72	66	4752	5184	4356
$\sum x = 226$	$\sum y = 210$	$\sum xy = 12{,}352$	$\sum x^2 = 13{,}252$	$\sum y^2 = 11{,}534$

$\left(\sum x\right)^2 = (226)^2 = 51{,}076$ and $\left(\sum y\right)^2 = (210)^2 = 44{,}100$

$$r = \frac{5(12{,}352)-(226)(210)}{\sqrt{4(13{,}252)-51{,}076}\sqrt{4(11{,}534)-44{,}100}}$$
$$\approx 0.98$$

b. Answers will vary.

c. $m = \frac{4(12{,}352) - (226)(210)}{4(13{,}252) - 51{,}076} = \frac{1948}{1932} \approx 1.008282 \approx 1.01$

$b = \frac{210 - (1.008282)(226)}{4} \approx \frac{-17.87}{4} \approx -4.47$

$y = mx + b$

$y = 1.01x - 4.47$

c. $y = 1.01x - 4.47$

$y = 1.01(30) - 4.47$

$= 25.83$

≈ 26

We can anticipate that 26% of such people will not approve of marriage equality.

37. a.

x	y	xy	x^2	y^2
22	4	88	484	16
17	3	51	289	9
40	21	840	1600	441
5	1	5	25	1
37	16	592	1369	256
19	8	152	361	64
23	14	322	529	196
6	3	18	36	9
7	3	21	49	9
53	31	1643	2809	961
34	24	816	1156	576
$\sum x = 263$	$\sum y = 128$	$\sum xy = 4548$	$\sum x^2 = 8707$	$\sum y^2 = 2538$

$\left(\sum x\right)^2 = (263)^2 = 69{,}169$ and $\left(\sum y\right)^2 = (128)^2 = 16{,}384$

$r = \frac{11(4548) - (263)(128)}{\sqrt{11(8707) - 69{,}169}\sqrt{11(2538) - 16{,}384}}$

$= \frac{16{,}364}{\sqrt{26{,}608}\sqrt{11{,}534}}$

≈ 0.93

b. $m = \frac{11(4548) - (263)(128)}{11(8707) - 69{,}169} = \frac{16{,}364}{26{,}608} \approx 0.62$

$b = \frac{128 - 0.6150(263)}{11} = \frac{-33.745}{11} \approx -3.07$

$y = mx + b$

$y = 0.62x - 3.07$

c. $y = 0.62x - 3.07$

$y = 0.62(10) - 3.07$

$= 3.13$

≈ 3

We can anticipate that a country where 10% of teenagers have used marijuana will have 3% of teenagers using other illegal drugs.

39. $|r| = 0.5$

Since 0.5 > 0.444, conclude that a correlation does exist.

41. $|r| = 0.5$

Since 0.5 < 0.576, conclude that a correlation does not exist.

43. $|r| = 0.351$

Since 0.351 > 0.232, conclude that a correlation does exist.

45. $|r| = 0.37$

Since 0.37 < 0.444, conclude that a correlation does not exist.

59. does not make sense; Explanations will vary. Sample explanation: Increasing literacy does not necessarily decrease undernourishment.

61. does not make sense; Explanations will vary. Sample explanation: The correlation would be higher for identical twins reared together.

Chapter 12 Review Exercises

1. a

2.

Time Spent on Homework (in hours)	Number of students
6	1
7	3
8	3
9	2
10	1
	10

3.

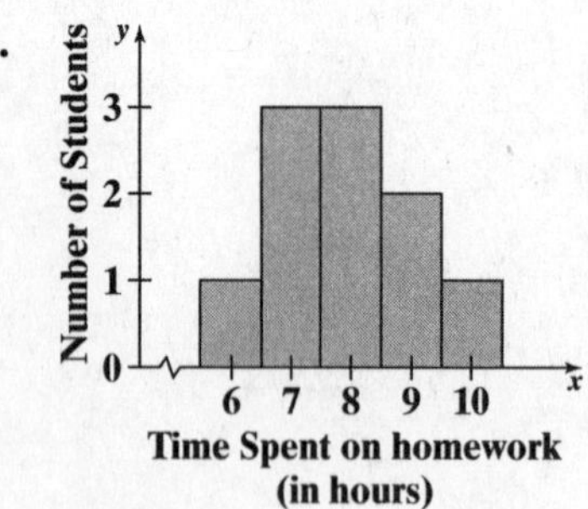

4.

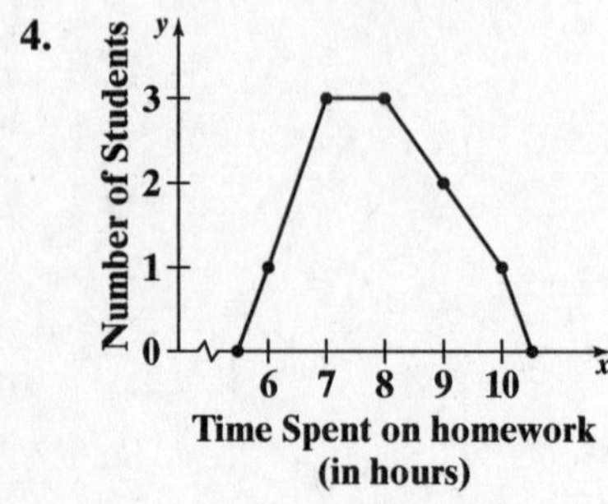

5.

Grades	Number of students
0–39	19
40–49	8
50–59	6
60–69	6
70–79	5
80–89	3
90–100	3
	50

6.

Stems	Leaves
1	3 4 1 3 7 8
2	4 9 6 9 2 7
3	4 9 6 5 1 1 1
4	4 0 2 7 9 1 2 5
5	7 9 6 4 0 1
6	3 3 7 0 8 9
7	2 3 4 0 5
8	7 1 6
9	5 1 0

7. The sizes of the barrels are not scaled proportionally in terms of the data they represent.

8. $\text{Mean} = \dfrac{84+90+95+89+98}{5} = \dfrac{456}{5} = 91.2$

9. $\text{Mean} = \dfrac{33+27+9+10+6+7+11+23+27}{9} = \dfrac{153}{9} = 17$

10. $\text{Mean} = \dfrac{1\cdot 2+2\cdot 4+3\cdot 3+4\cdot 1}{10} = \dfrac{2+8+9+4}{10} = \dfrac{23}{10} = 2.3$

11. First arrange the data items from smallest to largest.
6, 7, 9, 10, <u>11</u>, 23, 27, 27, 33
There is an odd number of data items, so the median is the middle number. The median is 11.

12. First arrange the data items from smallest to largest.
16, 22, <u>28</u>, 28, 34
There is an odd number of data items, so the median is the middle number. The median is 28.

13. The median is the value in the $\dfrac{n+1}{2} = \dfrac{10+1}{2} = \dfrac{11}{2} = 5.5$ position, which means the median is the mean of the 5th and 6th values. The 5th and 6th values are both 2, therefore the median is 2.

14. The number 27 occurs most frequently, so the mode is 27.

15. Bimodal; 585 and 587 each occur twice.

16. The number 2 occurs most frequently, so the mode is 2.

17. lowest data value = 84, highest data value = 98

$\text{Midrange} = \dfrac{84+98}{2} = \dfrac{182}{2} = 91$

18. lowest data value = 6, highest data value = 33

$\text{Midrange} = \dfrac{6+33}{2} = \dfrac{39}{2} = 19.5$

19. lowest data value = 1, highest data value = 4

$\text{Midrange} = \frac{1+4}{2} = \frac{5}{2} = 2.5$

21. a.

Age at first inauguration	Number of Presidents
42	1
43	1
44	0
45	0
46	2
47	2
48	1
49	2
50	1
51	5
52	2
53	0
54	5
55	4
56	3
57	4
58	1
59	0
60	1
61	3
62	1
63	0
64	2
65	1
66	0
67	0
68	1
69	1
	44

b. $$\text{Mean} = \frac{\begin{pmatrix} 42\cdot 1+43\cdot 1+46\cdot 2+47\cdot 2+48\cdot 1+49\cdot 2+50\cdot 1+51\cdot 5+52\cdot 2+54\cdot 5+55\cdot 4 \\ +56\cdot 3+57\cdot 4+58\cdot 1+60\cdot 1+61\cdot 3+62\cdot 1+64\cdot 2+65\cdot 1+68\cdot 1+69\cdot 1 \end{pmatrix}}{44} = \frac{2405}{44} \approx 54.66 \text{ years}$$

The median is the value in the $\frac{n+1}{2} = \frac{44+1}{2} = \frac{45}{2} = 22.5$ position, which means the median is the mean of the data in positions 22 and 23.

$\text{Median} = \frac{54+55}{2} = 54.5 \text{ years}$

The model ages are 51 and 54 years (bimodal).

$\text{Midrange} = \frac{42+69}{2} = 55.5 \text{ years}$

22. Range = 34 – 16 = 18

23. Range = 783 – 219 = 564

24. a.

Data item	Deviation: Data item – mean
29	29 – 35 = –6
9	9 – 35 = –26
8	8 – 35 = –27
22	22 – 35 = –13
46	46 – 35 = 11
51	51 – 35 = 16
48	48 – 35 = 13
42	42 – 35 = 7
53	53 – 35 = 18
42	42 – 35 = 7

b. –6 – 26 – 27 – 13 + 11 + 16 + 13 + 7 + 18 + 7 = 0

25. a. $\text{Mean} = \dfrac{36+26+24+90+74}{5} = \dfrac{250}{5} = 50$

b.

Data item	Deviation: Data item – mean
36	36 – 50 = –14
26	26 – 50 = –24
24	24 – 50 = –26
90	90 – 50 = 40
74	74 – 50 = 24

c. –14 – 24 – 26 + 40 + 24 = 0

26. $\text{Mean} = \dfrac{3+3+5+8+10+13}{6} = \dfrac{42}{6} = 7$

Data item	Deviation: Data item – mean	$(\text{Deviation})^2$: $(\text{Data item–mean})^2$
3	3 – 7 = –4	$(-4)^2 = 16$
3	3 – 7 = –4	$(-4)^2 = 16$
5	5 – 7 = –2	$(-2)^2 = 4$
8	8 – 7 = 1	$1^2 = 1$
10	10 – 7 = 3	$3^2 = 9$
13	13 – 7 = 6	$6^2 = 36$
		$\sum(\text{data item–mean})^2 = 82$

$$\text{Standard deviation} = \sqrt{\frac{82}{6-1}} = \sqrt{\frac{82}{5}} \approx 4.05$$

27. Mean $= \dfrac{20+27+23+26+28+32+33+35}{8} = \dfrac{224}{8} = 28$

Data item	Deviation: Data item – mean	(Deviation)^2: (Data item–mean)^2
20	$20-28=-8$	$(-8)^2=64$
27	$27-28=-1$	$(-1)^2=1$
23	$23-28=-5$	$(-5)^2=25$
26	$26-28=-2$	$(-2)^2=4$
28	$28-28=0$	$0^2=0$
32	$32-28=4$	$4^2=16$
33	$33-28=5$	$5^2=25$
35	$35-28=7$	$7^2=49$
		$\sum(\text{data item–mean})^2=184$

Standard deviation $= \sqrt{\dfrac{184}{8-1}} = \sqrt{\dfrac{184}{7}} \approx 5.13$

28. Mean $= \dfrac{10+30+37+40+43+44+45+69+86+86}{10} = \dfrac{490}{10} = 49$

Range $= 86 - 10 = 76$

Data item	Deviation: Data item – mean	(Deviation)^2: (Data item–mean)^2
10	$10-49=-39$	$(-39)^2=1521$
30	$30-49=-19$	$(-19)^2=361$
37	$37-49=-12$	$(-12)^2=144$
40	$40-49=-9$	$(-9)^2=81$
43	$43-49=-6$	$(-6)^2=36$
44	$44-49=-5$	$(-5)^2=25$
45	$45-49=-4$	$(-4)^2=16$
69	$69-49=20$	$20^2=400$
86	$86-49=37$	$37^2=1369$
86	$86-49=37$	$37^2=1369$
		$\sum(\text{data item–mean})^2=5322$

Standard deviation $= \sqrt{\dfrac{5322}{10-1}} = \sqrt{\dfrac{5322}{9}} \approx 24.32$

29. Set A:

$$\text{Mean} = \frac{80+80+80+80}{4} = \frac{320}{4} = 80$$

Data item	Deviation: Data item – mean	$(\text{Deviation})^2$: $(\text{Data item–mean})^2$
80	$80 - 80 = 0$	$0^2 = 0$
80	$80 - 80 = 0$	$0^2 = 0$
80	$80 - 80 = 0$	$0^2 = 0$
80	$80 - 80 = 0$	$0^2 = 0$
		$\sum(\text{data item–mean})^2 = 0$

$$\text{Standard deviation} = \sqrt{\frac{0}{4-1}} = \sqrt{\frac{0}{3}} = 0$$

Set B:

$$\text{Mean} = \frac{70+70+90+90}{4} = \frac{320}{4} = 80$$

Data item	Deviation: Data item – mean	$(\text{Deviation})^2$: $(\text{Data item–mean})^2$
70	$70 - 80 = -10$	$(-10)^2 = 100$
70	$70 - 80 = -10$	$(-10)^2 = 100$
90	$90 - 80 = 10$	$10^2 = 100$
90	$90 - 80 = 10$	$10^2 = 100$
		$\sum(\text{data item–mean})^2 = 400$

$$\text{Standard deviation} = \sqrt{\frac{400}{4-1}} = \sqrt{\frac{400}{3}} \approx 11.55$$

Written descriptions of the similarities and differences between the two sets of data will vary.

30. Answers will vary.

31. $70 + 2 \cdot 8 = 70 + 16 = 86$

32. $70 + 3.5(8) = 70 + 28 = 98$

33. $70 - 1.25(8) = 70 - 10 = 60$

34. 64 is one standard deviation below the mean and 72 is one standard deviation above the mean, so 68% of the people in the retirement community are between 64 and 72 years old.

35. 60 is two standard deviations below the mean and 76 is two standard deviations above the mean, so 95% of the people in the retirement community are between 60 and 76 years old.

36. 68 is the mean and 72 is one standard deviation above the mean, so half of 68%, or 34% of the people in the retirement community are between 68 and 72 years old.

37. 56 is three standard deviations below the mean and 80 is three standard deviations above the mean, so 99.7% of the people in the retirement community are between 56 and 80 years old.

38. 72 is one standard deviation above the mean, so 16% of the people in the retirement community are over 72 years old. (Note: 100% – 68% = 32%, half of 32% is 16%).

39. 72 is one standard deviation above the mean, so 84% of the people in the retirement community are under 72 years old. (Note: Question #41 showed that 16% is above 72, 100% – 16% = 84%)

40. 76 is two standard deviations above the mean, so 2.5% of the people in the retirement community are over 76 years old. (Note: 100% – 95% = 5%, half of 5% is 2.5%).

41. $z_{50} = \dfrac{50-50}{5} = \dfrac{0}{5} = 0$

42. $z_{60} = \dfrac{60-50}{5} = \dfrac{10}{5} = 2$

43. $z_{58} = \dfrac{58-50}{5} = \dfrac{8}{5} = 1.6$

44. $z_{35} = \dfrac{35-50}{5} = \dfrac{-15}{5} = -3$

45. $z_{44} = \dfrac{44-50}{5} = \dfrac{-6}{5} = -1.2$

46. vocabulary test: $z_{60} = \dfrac{60-50}{5} = \dfrac{10}{5} = 2$

grammar test: $z_{80} = \dfrac{80-72}{6} = \dfrac{8}{6} \approx 1.3$

The student scored better on the vocabulary test because it has a higher z-score.

47. 1.5(4000) = 6000
32,000 + 6000 = 38,000 miles

48. 2.25(4000) = 9000
32,000 + 9000 = 41,000 miles

49. –2.5(4000) = –10,000
32,000 – 10,000 = 22,000 miles

50. **a.** $\text{margin of error} = \pm\dfrac{1}{\sqrt{2281}}$
$\approx \pm 0.021$
$\approx \pm 2.1\%$

b. 31% – 2.1% = 28.9%
31% + 2.1% = 33.1%
We can be 95% confident that between 28.9% and 33.1% of American adults would be willing to sacrifice a percentage of their salary to work for an environmentally friendly company.

51. a. The graph is skewed to the right.

b.

x	f	xf
1	36	$1 \cdot 36 = 36$
2	34	$2 \cdot 34 = 68$
3	18	$3 \cdot 18 = 54$
4	9	$4 \cdot 9 = 36$
5	2	$5 \cdot 2 = 10$
6	1	$6 \cdot 1 = 6$
	100	$\sum xf = 210$

$$\text{Mean} = \frac{\sum xf}{n} = \frac{210}{100} = 2.1 \text{ syllables}$$

The median is the mean of the 50th and 51st positions. Since these data items are both 2, the median is 2 syllables. The mode is 1 syllable.

c. Yes, these measures of central tendency are consistent with the graph. The mean is greater than the median, which is expected with a distribution that is skewed to the right.

52. $z_{221} = \dfrac{221-200}{15} = \dfrac{21}{15} = 1.4$

$z = 1.4 \rightarrow 91.92\%$

91.92% have cholesterol less than 221.

53. $z_{173} = \dfrac{173-200}{15} = \dfrac{-27}{15} = -1.8$

$z = -1.8 \rightarrow 3.59\%$

100% – 3.59% = 96.41% have cholesterol greater than 173.

54. $z_{173} = \dfrac{173-200}{15} = \dfrac{-27}{15} = -1.8$

and $z = -1.8 \rightarrow 3.59\%$

$z_{221} = \dfrac{221-200}{15} = \dfrac{21}{15} = 1.4$

and $z = 1.4 \rightarrow 91.92\%$

91.92% – 3.59% = 88.33% have cholesterol between 173 and 221.

55. $z_{164} = \dfrac{164-200}{15} = \dfrac{-36}{15} = -2.4$

and $z = -2.4 \rightarrow 0.82\%$

$z_{182} = \dfrac{182-200}{15} = \dfrac{-18}{15} = -1.2$

and $z = -1.2 \rightarrow 11.51\%$

11.51% – 0.82% = 10.69% have cholesterol between 164 and 182.

56. 75%

57. 100% – 86% = 14%

58. 86% – 75% = 11%

59. There appears to be a positive correlation.

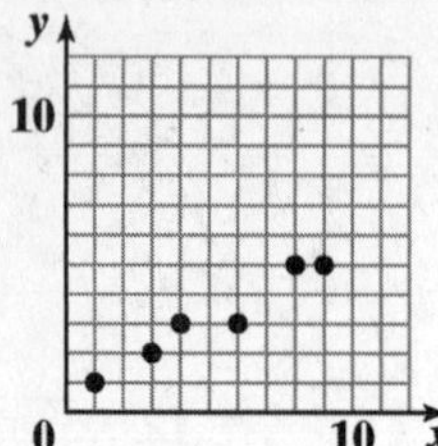

60. There appears to be a negative correlation.

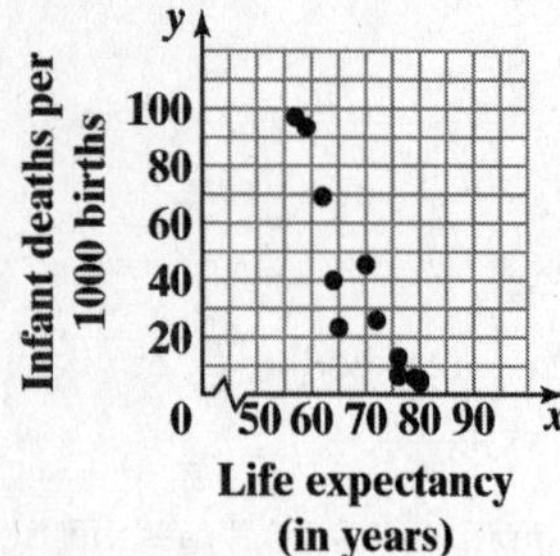

61. false; The correlation is only moderate.

62. true

63. false

64. false; Data points that are vertically aligned dispute this statement.

65. true

66. false; There is a moderate negative correlation.

67. true

68. c

69. a.

x	y	xy	x^2	y^2
1	1	1	1	1
3	2	6	9	4
4	3	12	16	9
6	3	18	36	9
8	5	40	64	25
9	5	45	81	25
$\sum x = 31$	$\sum y = 19$	$\sum xy = 122$	$\sum x^2 = 207$	$\sum y^2 = 73$

$\left(\sum x\right)^2 = (31)^2 = 961$ and $\left(\sum y\right)^2 = (19)^2 = 361$

$$r = \frac{6(122)-(31)(19)}{\sqrt{6(207)-961}\sqrt{6(73)-361}} = \frac{143}{\sqrt{281}\sqrt{77}} \approx 0.972$$

b. $m = \dfrac{6(122)-(31)(19)}{6(207)-961} = \dfrac{143}{281} \approx 0.509$

$b = \dfrac{19-(0.509)(31)}{6} = \dfrac{3.221}{6} \approx 0.537$

$y = 0.509x + 0.537$

70. a.

x	y	xy	x^2	y^2
22	26	1	1	1
32	32	6	9	4
42	34	12	16	9
52	39	18	36	9
62	44	45	81	25
$\sum x = 210$	$\sum y = 175$	$\sum xy = 7780$	$\sum x^2 = 9820$	$\sum y^2 = 6313$

$\left(\sum x\right)^2 = (210)^2 = 44{,}100$ and $\left(\sum y\right)^2 = (175)^2 = 30{,}625$

$$r = \frac{5(7780) - (210)(175)}{\sqrt{5(9820) - 44{,}100}\sqrt{5(6313) - 30{,}625}} = \frac{2150}{\sqrt{5000}\sqrt{940}} \approx 0.99$$

b. There is a correlation.

Chapter 12 Test

1. d

2.

Score	Frequency
3	1
4	2
5	3
6	2
7	2
8	3
9	2
10	1
	16

3.

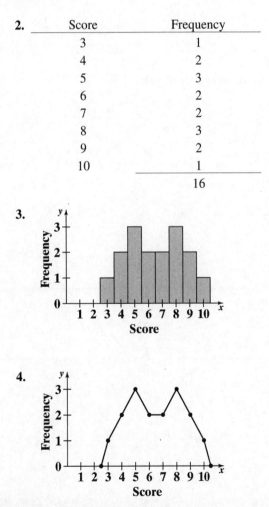

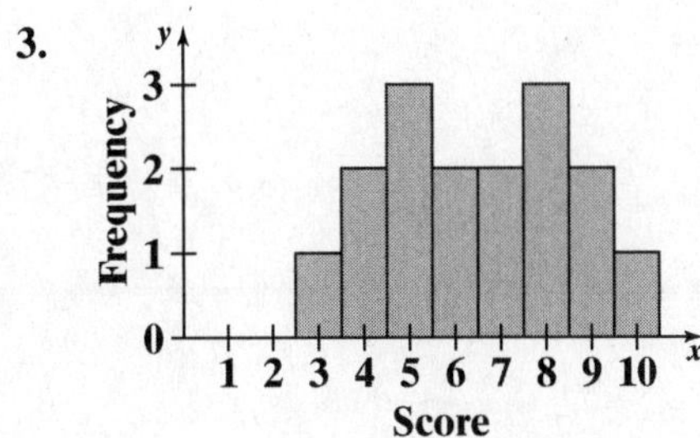

4.

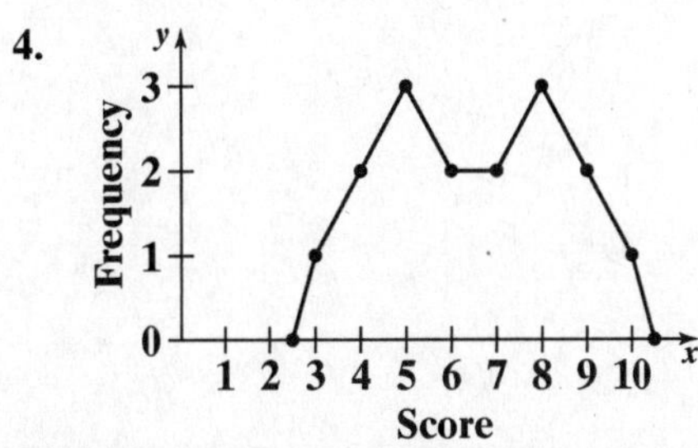

5.

Class	Frequency
40–49	3
50–59	6
60–69	6
70–79	7
80–89	6
90–99	2
	30

6.

Stems	Leaves
4	1 8 6
5	9 1 0 5 0 0
6	2 3 7 0 1 1
7	9 3 1 5 8 9 1
8	8 9 9 1 3 0
9	0 3

7. The roofline gives the impression that the percentage of home schooled students grew at the same rate each year between the years shown. This may be misleading if the growth rate was not constant from year to year.

8. $\text{Mean} = \frac{3+6+2+1+7+3}{6} = \frac{22}{6} \approx 3.67$

9. First arrange the numbers from smallest to largest.
1, 2, 3, 3, 6, 7
There is an even number of data items, so the median is the mean of the middle two data values.

$\text{Median} = \frac{3+3}{2} = \frac{6}{2} = 3$

10. lowest data value = 1
highest data value = 7

$\text{Midrange} = \frac{1+7}{2} = \frac{8}{2} = 4$

11.

Data item	Deviation: Data item – mean	(Deviation)^2 : (Data item–mean)^2
3	$3 - 3.7 = -0.7$	$(-0.7)^2 = 0.49$
6	$6 - 3.7 = 2.3$	$(2.3)^2 = 5.29$
2	$2 - 3.7 = -1.7$	$(-1.7)^2 = 2.89$
1	$1 - 3.7 = -2.7$	$(-2.7)^2 = 7.29$
7	$7 - 3.7 = 3.3$	$(3.3)^2 = 10.89$
3	$3 - 3.7 = -0.7$	$(-0.7)^2 = 0.49$
		$\sum(\text{data item–mean})^2 = 27.34$

$\text{Standard deviation} = \sqrt{\frac{27.34}{6-1}} = \sqrt{\frac{27.34}{5}} \approx 2.34$

12. $\text{Mean} = \frac{1\cdot 3+2\cdot 5+3\cdot 2+4\cdot 2}{12}$

$= \frac{3+10+6+8}{12}$

$= \frac{27}{12}$

$= 2.25$

13. The median is in the $\frac{n+1}{2} = \frac{12+1}{2} = \frac{13}{2} = 6.5$ position, which means the median is the mean of the values in the 6th and 7th positions.

$\text{Median} = \frac{2+2}{2} = \frac{4}{2} = 2$

14. Mode = 2

15. Answers will vary.

16. 7 + 1(5.3) = 12.3

68% of the data values are within 1 standard deviation of the mean. Because of symmetry, $\frac{1}{2}(68\%) = 34\%$ of college freshmen study between 7 and 12.3 hours per week.

17. 7 + 2(5.3) = 17.6

95% of the data values are within 2 standard deviations of the mean. 100% – 95% = 5% of the values are farther than 2 standard deviations from the mean. Because of symmetry, $\frac{1}{2}(5\%) = 2.5\%$ of college freshmen study more than 17.6 hours per week.

18. student: $z_{120} = \frac{120-100}{10} = \frac{20}{10} = 2$

professor: $z_{128} = \frac{128-100}{15} = \frac{28}{15} \approx 1.9$

The student scored better, because the student's *z*-score is higher.

19. $z_{88} = \frac{88-74}{10} = \frac{14}{10} = 1.4$

$z = 1.4 \to 91.92\%$

100% – 91.92% = 8.08% of the scores are above 88.

20. 49% – 8% = 41%

21. a. $\text{margin of error} = \pm\frac{1}{\sqrt{n}}$

$= \pm\frac{1}{\sqrt{100}}$

$= \pm 0.1$

$= \pm 10\%$

b. We can be 95% confident that between 50% and 70% of all students are very satisfied with their professors.

22. There appears to be a strong negative correlation.

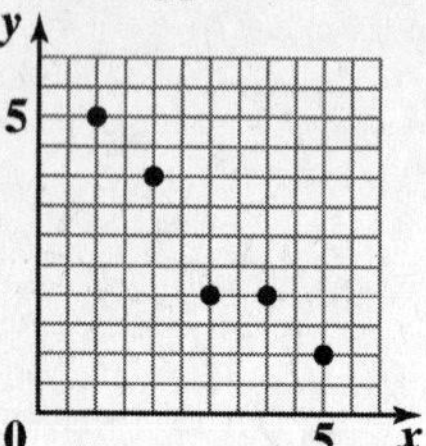

23. false; Though the data shows that there is a <u>correlation</u>, it does not prove <u>causation</u>.

24. false

25. true

26. Answers will vary.

Chapter 13
Voting and Apportionment

Check Points 13.1

1. **a.** We find the number of people who voted in the election by adding the numbers in the row labeled Number of Votes: 2100 + 1305 + 765 + 40 = 4210. Thus, 4210 people voted in the election.

   b. We find how many people selected the candidates in the order B, S, A, C by referring to the fourth column of letters in the preference table. Above this column is the number 40. Thus, 40 people voted in the order B, S, A, C.

   c. We find the number of people who selected S as their first choice by reading across the row that says First Choice: 2100 + 765 = 2865. Thus, 2865 students selected S (Samir) as their first choice for student body president.

2. The candidate with the most first-place votes is the winner. When using Table 13.2, it is only necessary to look at the row which indicates the number of first-place votes. This indicates that A (Antonio) gets 130 first-place votes, C (Carmen) gets 150 first-place votes, and D (Donna) gets 120 + 100 = 220 first-place votes. Thus Donna is declared the winner using the plurality method.

3. Because there are four candidates, a first-place vote is worth 4 points, a second-place vote is worth 3 points, a third-place vote is worth 2 points, and a fourth-place vote is worth 1 point. We show the points produced by the votes in the preference table.

Number of Votes	**130**	**120**	**100**	**150**
First Choice: 4 points	A: $130 \times 4 = 520$ pts	D: $120 \times 4 = 480$ pts	D: $100 \times 4 = 400$ pts	C: $150 \times 4 = 600$ pts
Second Choice: 3 points	B: $130 \times 3 = 390$ pts	B: $120 \times 3 = 360$ pts	B: $100 \times 3 = 300$ pts	B: $150 \times 3 = 450$ pts
Third Choice: 2 points	C: $130 \times 2 = 260$ pts	C: $120 \times 2 = 240$ pts	A: $100 \times 2 = 200$ pts	A: $150 \times 2 = 300$ pts
Fourth Choice: 1 point	D: $130 \times 1 = 130$ pts	A: $120 \times 1 = 120$ pts	C: $100 \times 1 = 100$ pts	D: $150 \times 1 = 150$ pts

Now we read down each column and total the points for each candidate separately.

A gets 520 + 120 + 200 + 300 = 1140 points
B gets 390 + 360 + 300 + 450 = 1500 points
C gets 260 + 240 + 100 + 600 = 1200 points
D gets 130 + 480 + 400 + 150 = 1160 points

Because B (Bob) has received the most points, he is the winner and the new mayor of Smallville.

4. There are 130 + 120 + 100 + 150, or 500, people voting. In order to receive a majority, a candidate must receive more than 50% of the votes, meaning more than 250 votes. The number of first-place votes for each candidate is
A (Antonio) = 130 B (Bob) = 0 C (Carmen) = 150 D (Donna) = 220

   We see that no candidate receives a majority of first-place votes. Because Bob received the fewest first-place votes, he is eliminated in the next round. We construct a new preference table in which B is removed. Each candidate below B moves up one place, while the positions of candidates above B remain unchanged.

Number of Votes	**130**	**120**	**100**	**150**
First Choice	A	D	D	C
Second Choice	C	C	A	A
Third Choice	D	A	C	D

The number of first-place votes for each candidate is now A (Antonio) = 130; C (Carmen) = 150; D (Donna) = 220

No candidate receives a majority of first-place votes. Because Antonio received the fewest first-place votes, he is eliminated in the next round.

Number of Votes	**130**	**120**	**100**	**150**
First Choice	C	D	D	C
Second Choice	D	C	C	D

The number of first-place votes for each candidate is now C (Carmen) = 280; D (Donna) = 220

Because Carmen has received the majority of first-place votes, she is the winner and the new mayor of Smallville.

5. **A vs. B**

130	120	100	150
A	D	D	C
B	**B**	**B**	**B**
C	C	*A*	*A*
D	*A*	C	D

130 voters prefer A to B.
120 + 100 + 150 = 370 voters prefer B to A.

Conclusion: B wins this comparison and gets one point.

A vs. C

130	120	100	150
A	D	D	**C**
B	B	B	B
C	**C**	**A**	*A*
D	*A*	*C*	D

130 + 100 = 230 voters prefer A to C.
120 + 150 = 270 voters prefer C to A.

Conclusion: C wins this comparison and gets one point.

A vs. D

130	120	100	150
A	**D**	**D**	C
B	B	B	B
C	C	*A*	**A**
D	*A*	C	*D*

130 + 150 = 280 voters prefer A to D.
120 + 100 = 220 voters prefer D to A.

Conclusion: A wins this comparison and gets one point.

B vs. C

130	120	100	150
A	D	D	**C**
B	**B**	**B**	*B*
C	*C*	A	A
D	A	*C*	D

130 + 120 + 100 = 350 voters prefer B to C.
150 voters prefer C to B.

Conclusion: B wins this comparison and gets one point.

B vs. D

130	120	100	150
A	**D**	**D**	C
B	*B*	*B*	**B**
C	C	A	A
D	A	C	*D*

130 + 150 = 280 voters prefer B to D.
120 + 100 = 220 voters prefer D to B.

Conclusion: B wins this comparison and gets one point.

C vs. D

130	120	100	150
A	**D**	**D**	**C**
B	B	B	B
C	*C*	A	A
D	A	*C*	*D*

130 + 150 = 280 voters prefer C to D.
120 + 100 = 220 voters prefer D to C.

Conclusion: C wins this comparison and gets one point.

We now use each of the six conclusions and add points for the six comparisons.
A gets 1 point.
B gets 1 + 1 + 1 = 3 points.
C gets 1 + 1 = 2 points.

After all comparisons have been made, the candidate receiving the most points is B (Bob). He is the winner and the new mayor of Smallville.

Concept and Vocabulary Check 13.1

1. preference; preference
2. majority
3. pairwise comparison; 1; $\frac{1}{2}$; most points
4. $\frac{n(n-1)}{2}$
5. plurality
6. plurality
7. Borda count; most points
8. true

Exercise Set 13.1

1.

Number of Votes	7	5	4
First Choice	A	B	C
Second Choice	B	C	B
Third Choice	C	A	A

3.

Number of Votes	5	1	4	2
First Choice	A	B	C	C
Second Choice	B	D	B	B
Third Choice	C	C	D	A
Fourth Choice	D	A	A	D

5. **a.** $14 + 8 + 3 + 1 = 26$

   b. 8

   c. $14 + 8 = 22$

   d. 3

7. "Musical" received 12 first-place votes, "comedy" received 10 first-place votes, and "drama" received 8 first-place votes, so the type of play selected is a musical.

9. Darwin received 30 first-place votes, Einstein received 22 first-place votes, Freud received 20 first-place votes, and Hawking received 14 first-place votes, so the professor declared chair is Darwin.

11.

Number of Votes	**10**	**6**	**6**	**4**	**2**	**2**
First Choice: 3 points	M: $10\times3=30$	C: $6\times3=18$	D: $6\times3=18$	C: $4\times3=12$	D: $2\times3=6$	M: $2\times3=6$
Second Choice: 2 points	C: $10\times2=20$	M: $6\times2=12$	C: $6\times2=12$	D: $4\times2=8$	M: $2\times2=4$	D: $2\times2=4$
Third Choice: 1 point	D: $10\times1=10$	D: $6\times1=6$	M: $6\times1=6$	M: $4\times1=4$	C: $2\times1=2$	C: $2\times1=2$

C gets $20+18+12+12+2+2=66$ points.
D gets $10+6+18+8+6+4=52$ points.
M gets $30+12+6+4+4+6=62$ points.

C (Comedy) receives the most points, and is selected.

13.

Number of Votes	**30**	**22**	**20**	**12**	**2**
First Choice: 4 points	D: $30\times4=120$	E: $22\times4=88$	F: $20\times4=80$	H: $12\times4=48$	H: $2\times4=8$
Second Choice: 3 points	H: $30\times3=90$	F: $22\times3=66$	E: $20\times3=60$	E: $12\times3=36$	F: $2\times3=6$
Third Choice: 2 points	F: $30\times2=60$	H: $22\times2=44$	H: $20\times2=40$	F: $12\times2=24$	D: $2\times2=4$
Fourth Choice: 1 point	E: $30\times1=30$	D: $22\times1=22$	D: $20\times1=20$	D: $12\times1=12$	E: $2\times1=2$

D gets $120+22+20+12+4=178$ points.
E gets $30+88+60+36+2=216$ points.
F gets $60+66+80+24+6=236$ points.
H gets $90+44+40+48+8=230$ points.

F (Freud) receives the most points and is declared the new division chair.

15. There are 30 people voting, so the winner needs more than 15 votes for a majority.
The number of first-place votes for each candidate is

C (Comedy) = 10   D (Drama) = 8   M (Musical) = 12

No candidate has a majority. Drama received the fewest first-place votes, so we eliminate it in the next round.

Number of Votes	**10**	**6**	**6**	**4**	**2**	**2**
First Choice	M	C	C	C	M	M
Second Choice	C	M	M	M	C	C

The number of first-place votes for each candidate is now

C (Comedy) = 16   M (Musical) = 14

C (Comedy) has 16 votes, which is a majority, so "Comedy" is selected.

17. There are 86 people voting, so the winner needs more than 43 votes for a majority. The number of first-place votes for each candidate is

D (Darwin) = 30 E (Einstein) = 22
F (Freud) = 20 H (Hawking) = 14

No candidate has a majority. Hawking received the fewest first-place votes, so we eliminate him in the next round.

Number of Votes	**30**	**22**	**20**	**12**	**2**
First Choice	D	E	F	E	F
Second Choice	F	F	E	F	D
Third Choice	E	D	D	D	E

The number of first-place votes for each candidate is now
D (Darwin) = 30 E (Einstein) = 34 F (Freud) = 22

No candidate has a majority. Freud received the fewest first-place votes, so we eliminate him in the next round:

Number of Votes	**30**	**22**	**20**	**12**	**2**
First Choice	D	E	E	E	D
Second Choice	E	D	D	D	E

The number of first-place votes for each candidate is now
D (Darwin) = 32 E (Einstein) = 54

E (Einstein) has 54 votes, which is a majority, so Einstein is declared the new division chair.

19. With $n = 5$, there are $\frac{5(5-1)}{2} = 10$ comparisons.

21. With $n = 8$, there are $\frac{8(8-1)}{2} = 28$ comparisons.

23.

10	**6**	**6**	**4**	**2**	**2**
M	C	D	C	D	M
C	M	C	D	M	D
D	D	M	M	C	C

C vs. D
10 + 6 + 4 = 20 voters prefer C to D.
6 + 2 + 2 = 10 voters prefer D to C.
C wins this comparison and gets one point.

D vs. M
6 + 4 + 2 = 12 voters prefer D to M.
10 + 6 + 2 = 18 voters prefer M to D.
M wins this comparison and gets one point.

C vs. M
6 + 6 + 4 = 16 voters prefer C to M.
10 + 2 + 2 = 14 voters prefer M to C.
C wins this comparison and gets one point

Adding points for the three comparisons:
C gets 1 + 1 = 2 points.
D gets 0 points.
M gets 1 point.

C (Comedy) receives the most points, so a comedy is selected.

25.

30	22	20	12	2
D	E	F	H	H
H	F	E	E	F
F	H	H	F	D
E	D	D	D	E

D vs. E
30 + 2 = 32 voters prefer D to E.
22 + 20 + 12 = 54 voters prefer E to D.
E wins the comparison and gets one point

D vs. H
30 voters prefer D to H.
22 + 20 + 12 + 2 = 56 voters prefer H to D.
H wins this comparison and gets one point.

E vs. H
22 + 20 = 42 voters prefer E to H.
30 + 12 + 2 = 44 voters prefer H to E.
H wins this comparison and gets one point.

D vs. F
30 voters prefer D to F.
22 + 20 + 12 + 2 = 56 voters prefer F to D.
F wins this comparison and gets one point.

E vs. F
22 + 12 = 34 voters prefer E to F.
30 + 20 + 2 = 52 voters prefer F to E.
F wins this comparison and gets one point

F vs. H
22 + 20 = 42 voters prefer F to H.
30 + 12 + 2 = 44 voters prefer H to F.
H wins this comparison and gets one point.

Adding points for the six comparisons:
D gets 0 points.
E gets 1 point.
F gets 1 + 1 = 2 points.
H gets 1 + 1 + 1 = 3 points.

H (Hawking) receives the most points, so Hawking is declared the new division chair.

27. A received 34 first-place votes, B received 30 first-place votes, C received 6 first-place votes, and D received 2 first-place votes, so A is the winner.

29. There are 72 people voting, so the winner needs more than 36 votes for a majority. The number of first-place votes for each candidate is: A = 34; B = 30; C = 6; D = 2

No candidate has a majority. D received the fewest first-place votes, so we eliminate it in the next round.

Number of Voters	34	30	6	2
First Choice	A	B	C	B
Second Choice	B	C	B	C
Third Choice	C	A	A	A

The number of first-place votes for each candidate is now A = 34; B = 32; C = 6

No candidate has a majority. C received the fewest first-place votes, so we eliminate it in the next round.

Number of Voters	34	30	6	2
First Choice	A	B	B	B
Second Choice	B	A	A	A

The number of first-place votes for each candidate is now A = 34; B = 38

B has 38 votes, which is a majority, so B is selected.

31.

Number of Votes	5	5	4	3	3	2
First choice: 5 points	C: $5 \times 5 = 25$	S: $5 \times 5 = 25$	C: $4 \times 5 = 20$	W: $3 \times 5 = 15$	W: $3 \times 5 = 15$	P: $2 \times 5 = 10$
Second choice: 4 points	R: $5 \times 4 = 20$	R: $5 \times 4 = 20$	P: $4 \times 4 = 16$	P: $3 \times 4 = 12$	R: $3 \times 4 = 12$	S: $2 \times 4 = 8$
Third choice: 3 points	P: $5 \times 3 = 15$	W: $5 \times 3 = 15$	R: $4 \times 3 = 12$	R: $3 \times 3 = 9$	S: $3 \times 3 = 9$	C: $2 \times 3 = 6$
Fourth choice: 2 points	W: $5 \times 2 = 10$	P: $5 \times 2 = 10$	S: $4 \times 2 = 8$	S: $3 \times 2 = 6$	C: $3 \times 2 = 6$	R: $2 \times 2 = 4$
Fifth choice: 1 point	S: $5 \times 1 = 5$	C: $5 \times 1 = 5$	W: $4 \times 1 = 4$	C: $3 \times 1 = 3$	P: $3 \times 1 = 3$	W: $2 \times 1 = 2$

C gets $25 + 5 + 20 + 3 + 6 + 6 = 65$ points.
P gets $15 + 10 + 16 + 12 + 3 + 10 = 66$ points.
R gets $20 + 20 + 12 + 9 + 12 + 4 = 77$ points.
S gets $5 + 25 + 8 + 6 + 9 + 8 = 61$ points.
W gets $10 + 15 + 4 + 15 + 15 + 2 = 61$ points.

R (Rent) receives the most points and is selected.

33.

5	5	4	3	3	2
C	S	C	W	W	P
R	R	P	P	R	S
P	W	R	R	S	C
W	P	S	S	C	R
S	C	W	C	P	W

C vs. P
$5 + 4 + 3 = 12$ voters prefer C to P.
$5 + 3 + 2 = 10$ voters prefer P to C.
C wins this comparison and gets one point.

C vs. S
$5 + 4 = 9$ voters prefer C to S.
$5 + 3 + 3 + 2 = 13$ voters prefer S to C.
S wins this comparison and gets one point.

P vs. R
$4 + 3 + 2 = 9$ voters prefer P to R.
$5 + 5 + 3 = 13$ voters prefer R to P.
R wins this comparison and gets one point.

P vs. W
$5 + 4 + 2 = 11$ voters prefer P to W.
$5 + 3 + 3 = 11$ voters prefer W to P.
P and W are tied. Each gets $\frac{1}{2}$ point.

R vs. W
$5 + 5 + 4 + 2 = 16$ voters prefer R to W.
$3 + 3 = 6$ voters prefer W to R.
R wins this comparison and gets one point.

C vs. R
$5 + 4 + 2 = 11$ voters prefer C to R.
$5 + 3 + 3 = 11$ voters prefer R to C.
C and R are tied. Each gets $\frac{1}{2}$ point.

C vs. W
$5 + 4 + 2 = 11$ voters prefer C to W.
$5 + 3 + 3 = 11$ voters prefer W to C.
C and W are tied. Each gets $\frac{1}{2}$ point.

P vs. S
$5 + 4 + 3 + 2 = 14$ voters prefer P to S.
$5 + 3 = 8$ voters prefer S to P.
P wins this comparison and gets one point.

R vs. S
$5 + 4 + 3 + 3 = 15$ voters prefer R to S.
$5 + 2 = 7$ voters prefer S to R.
R wins this comparison and gets one point.

S vs. W
$5 + 4 + 2 = 11$ voters prefer S to W.
$5 + 3 + 3 = 11$ voters prefer W to S.
S and W are tied. Each gets $\frac{1}{2}$ point.

Adding points for 10 comparisons:
C gets $1 + \frac{1}{2} + \frac{1}{2} = 2$ points.
P gets $1 + \frac{1}{2} = 1\frac{1}{2}$ points.
R gets $\frac{1}{2} + 1 + 1 + 1 = 3\frac{1}{2}$ points.
S gets $1 + \frac{1}{2} = 1\frac{1}{2}$ points.
W gets $\frac{1}{2} + \frac{1}{2} + \frac{1}{2} = 1\frac{1}{2}$ points.

R (Rent) receives the most points, so Rent is the winner.

35. a.

Number of Votes	**5**	**5**	**3**	**3**	**3**	**2**
First Choice: 5 points	A: 5 × 5 = 25	C: 5 × 5 = 25	D: 3 × 5 = 15	A: 3 × 5 = 15	B: 3 × 5 = 15	D: 2 × 5 = 10
Second Choice: 4 points	B: 5 × 4 = 20	E: 5 × 4 = 20	C: 3 × 4 = 12	D: 3 × 4 = 12	E: 3 × 4 = 12	C: 2 × 4 = 8
Third Choice: 3 points	C: 5 × 3 = 15	D: 5 × 3 = 15	B: 3 × 3 = 9	B: 3 × 3 = 9	A: 3 × 3 = 9	B: 2 × 3 = 6
Fourth Choice: 2 points	D: 5 × 2 = 10	A: 5 × 2 = 10	E: 3 × 2 = 6	C: 3 × 2 = 6	C: 3 × 2 = 6	A: 2 × 2 = 4
Fifth Choice: 1 point	E: 5 × 1 = 5	B: 5 × 1 = 5	A: 3 × 1 = 3	E: 3 × 1 = 3	D: 3 × 1 = 3	E: 2 × 1 = 2

A gets 25 + 10 + 3 + 15 + 9 + 4 = 66 points.
B gets 20 + 5 + 9 + 9 + 15 + 6 = 64 points.
C gets 15 + 25 + 12 + 6 + 6 + 8 = 72 points.
D gets 10 + 15 + 15 + 12 + 3 + 10 = 65 points.
E gets 5 + 20 + 6 + 3 + 12 + 2 = 48 points.

C receives the most points and is the winner.

b.

Number of Votes	**5**	**5**	**3**	**3**	**3**	**2**
First Choice: 4 points	A: 5 × 4 = 20	C: 5 × 4 = 20	D: 3 × 4 = 12	A: 3 × 4 = 12	B: 3 × 4 = 12	D: 2 × 4 = 8
Second Choice: 3 points	B: 5 × 3 = 15	D: 5 × 3 = 15	C: 3 × 3 = 9	D: 3 × 3 = 9	A: 3 × 3 = 9	C: 2 × 3 = 6
Third Choice: 2 points	C: 5 × 2 = 10	A: 5 × 2 = 10	B: 3 × 2 = 6	B: 3 × 2 = 6	C: 3 × 2 = 6	B: 2 × 2 = 4
Fourth Choice: 1 points	D: 5 × 1 = 5	B: 5 × 1 = 5	A: 3 × 1 = 3	C: 3 × 1 = 3	D: 3 × 1 = 3	A: 2 × 1 = 2

A gets 20 + 10 + 3 + 12 + 9 + 2 = 56 points.
B gets 15 + 5 + 6 + 6 + 12 + 4 = 48 points.
C gets 10 + 20 + 9 + 3 + 6 + 6 = 54 points.
D gets 5 + 15 + 12 + 9 + 3 + 8 = 52 points.

A receives the most points and is the winner.

37. First use the plurality method: C receives 12,000 first-place votes, and A receives 12,000 first-place votes. This results in a tie, so we use the Borda count method.

Number of Votes	12,000	7500	4500
First Choice: 3 points	C: $12{,}000 \times 3 = 36{,}000$	A: $7500 \times 3 = 22{,}500$	A: $4500 \times 3 = 13{,}500$
Second Choice: 2 points	B: $12{,}000 \times 2 = 24{,}000$	B: $7500 \times 2 = 15{,}000$	C: $4500 \times 3 = 9000$
Third Choice: 1 points	A: $12{,}000 \times 1 = 12{,}000$	C: $7500 \times 1 = 7500$	B: $4500 \times 1 = 4500$

A gets $12{,}000 + 22{,}500 + 13{,}500 = 48{,}000$ points.
B gets $24{,}000 + 15{,}000 + 4500 = 43{,}500$ points.
C gets $36{,}000 + 7500 + 9000 = 52{,}500$ points.
C receives the most points and is the winner.

We have a tie. We next try the Borda count method.

Number of Votes	60,000	40,000	40,000	20,000	20,000
First Choice: 3 points	A: $60{,}000 \times 3 =$ 180,000	C: $40{,}000 \times 3 =$ 120,000	B: $40{,}000 \times 3 =$ 120,000	A: $20{,}000 \times 3 =$ 60,000	C: $20{,}000 \times 3 =$ 60,000
Second Choice: 2 points	B: $60{,}000 \times 2 =$ 120,000	A: $40{,}000 \times 2 =$ 80,000	C: $40{,}000 \times 2 =$ 80,000	C: $20{,}000 \times 2 =$ 40,000	B: $20{,}000 \times 2 =$ 40,000
Third Choice: 1 point	C: $60{,}000 \times 1 =$ 60,000	B: $40{,}000 \times 1 =$ 40,000	A: $40{,}000 \times 1 =$ 40,000	B: $20{,}000 \times 1 =$ 20,000	A: $20{,}000 \times 1 =$ 20,000

A gets $180{,}000 + 80{,}000 + 40{,}000 + 60{,}000 + 20{,}000 = 380{,}000$ points.
B gets $120{,}000 + 40{,}000 + 120{,}000 + 20{,}000 + 40{,}000 = 340{,}000$ points.
C gets $60{,}000 + 120{,}000 + 80{,}000 + 40{,}000 + 60{,}000 = 360{,}000$ points.

A receives the most points, so A becomes the new mayor.

49. does not make sense; Explanations will vary. Sample explanation: A candidate with a majority must win using the plurality method.

51. makes sense

Check Points 13.2

1. a. There are 14 first-place votes. A candidate with more than half of these receives a majority. The first-choice row shows that candidate A received 8 first-place votes. Thus, candidate A has a majority of first-place votes.

b. Using the Borda count method with four candidates, a first-place vote is worth 4 points, a second-place vote is worth 3 points, a third-place vote is worth 2 points, and a fourth-place vote is worth 1 point.

Number of Votes	**6**	**4**	**2**	**2**
First Choice: 4 points	A: $6 \times 4 = 24$ pts	B: $4 \times 4 = 16$ pts	B: $2 \times 4 = 8$ pts	A: $2 \times 4 = 8$ pts
Second Choice: 3 points	B: $6 \times 3 = 18$ pts	C: $4 \times 3 = 12$ pts	D: $2 \times 3 = 6$ pts	B: $2 \times 3 = 6$ pts
Third Choice: 2 points	C: $6 \times 2 = 12$ pts	D: $4 \times 2 = 8$ pts	C: $2 \times 2 = 4$ pts	D: $2 \times 2 = 4$ pts
Fourth Choice: 1 point	D: $6 \times 1 = 6$ pts	A: $4 \times 1 = 4$ pts	A: $2 \times 1 = 2$ pts	C: $2 \times 1 = 2$ pts

Now we read down the columns and total the points for each candidate.
A gets $24 + 4 + 2 + 8 = 38$ points.
B gets $18 + 16 + 8 + 6 = 48$ points.
C gets $12 + 12 + 4 + 2 = 30$ points.
D gets $6 + 8 + 6 + 4 = 24$ points.

Because candidate B has received the most points, candidate B is declared the new principal using the Borda count method.

2. a. We begin by comparing A and B. A is favored over B in column 1, giving A 3 votes. B is favored over A in columns 2 and 3, giving B 2 + 2, or 4, votes. Thus, B is favored when compared to A.

Now we compare B to C. B is favored over C in columns 1 and 2, giving B 3 + 2, or 5, votes. C is favored over B in column 3, giving C 2 votes. Thus, B is favored when compared to C.

We see that B is favored over both A and C using a head-to-head comparison.

b. Using the plurality method, the brand with the most first-place votes is the winner. In the row indicating first choice, A received 3 votes, B received 2 votes, and C received 2 votes. A wins using the plurality method.

3. a. There are 120 people voting. No candidate initially receives more than 60 votes. Because C receives the fewest first-place votes, C is eliminated in the next round. The new preference table is

Number of Votes	**42**	**34**	**28**	**16**
First Choice	A	A	B	B
Second Choice	B	B	A	A

Because A has received a majority of first-place votes, A is the winner of the straw poll.

b. No candidate initially receives more than 60 votes. Because B receives the fewest first-place votes, B is eliminated in the next round. The new preference table is

Number of Votes	**54**	**34**	**28**	**4**
First Choice	A	C	C	A
Second Choice	C	A	A	C

Because C has received a majority of first-place votes, C is the winner of the second election.

c. A won the first election. A then gained additional support with the 12 voters who changed their ballots to make A their first choice. A lost the second election. This violates the monotonicity criterion.

4. **a.** Because there are 4 candidates, $n = 4$ and the number of comparisons we must make is $\frac{n(n-1)}{2} = \frac{4(4-1)}{2} = \frac{4 \cdot 3}{2} = \frac{12}{2} = 6$.

The following table shows the results of these 6 comparisons.

Comparison	**Vote Results**	**Conclusion**
A vs. B	270 voters prefer A to B. 90 voters prefer B to A.	A wins and gets 1 point.
A vs. C	270 voters prefer A to C. 90 voters prefer C to A.	A wins and gets 1 point.
A vs. D	150 voters prefer A to D. 210 voters prefer D to A.	D wins and gets 1 point.
B vs. C	180 voters prefer B to C. 180 voters prefer C to B.	B and C tie. Each gets $\frac{1}{2}$ point.
B vs. D	240 voters prefer B to D. 120 voters prefer D to B.	B wins and gets 1 point.
C vs. D	240 voters prefer C to D. 120 voters prefer D to C.	C wins and gets 1 point.

Thus A gets 2 points, B gets $1\frac{1}{2}$ points, C gets $1\frac{1}{2}$ points, and D gets 1 point. Therefore A is the winner.

b. After B and C withdraw, there is a new preference table:

Number of Votes	**150**	**90**	**90**	**30**
First Choice	A	D	D	D
Second Choice	D	A	A	A

Using the pairwise comparison test with 2 candidates, there is only one comparison to make namely A vs. D. 150 voters prefer A to D, and 210 voters prefer D to A. D gets 1 point, A gets 0 points, and D wins the election.

c. The first election count produced A as the winner. The removal of B and C from the ballots produced D as the winner. This violates the irrelevant alternatives criterion.

Concept and Vocabulary Check 13.2

1. majority
2. head-to-head
3. monotonicity
4. irrelevant alternatives
5. Borda count
6. true

Exercise Set 13.2

1. a. D has 300 first-place votes, which is more than half of the 570 total votes, so D has a majority of first-place votes.

b.

Number of Votes	**300**	**120**	**90**	**60**
First Choice: 4 points	D: $300 \times 4 = 1200$	C: $120 \times 4 = 480$	C: $90 \times 4 = 360$	A: $60 \times 4 = 240$
Second Choice: 3 points	A: $300 \times 3 = 900$	A: $120 \times 3 = 360$	A: $90 \times 3 = 270$	D: $60 \times 3 = 180$
Third Choice: 2 points	B: $300 \times 2 = 600$	B: $120 \times 2 = 240$	D: $90 \times 2 = 180$	B: $60 \times 2 = 120$
Fourth Choice: 1 point	C: $300 \times 1 = 300$	D: $120 \times 1 = 120$	B: $90 \times 1 = 90$	C: $60 \times 1 = 60$

A gets $900 + 360 + 270 + 240 = 1770$ points.
B gets $600 + 240 + 90 + 120 = 1050$ points.
C gets $300 + 480 + 360 + 60 = 1200$ points.
D gets $1200 + 120 + 180 + 180 = 1680$ points.

A receives the most points, so A is the chosen design.

c. No. D receives a majority of first-place votes, but A is chosen by the Borda count method.

3. a. A is favored over R in columns 1 and 3, giving A $12 + 4$, or 16, votes. R is favored over A in columns 2 and 4, giving R $9 + 4$, or 13, votes. Thus, A is favored when compared to R.

A is favored over V in columns 1 and 4, giving A $12 + 4$, or 16, votes. V is favored over A in columns 2 and 3, giving V $9 + 4$, or 13, votes. Thus, A is favored when compared to V.

We see that A is favored over the other two cities using a head-to-head comparison.

b. A gets 12 first-place votes, V gets 13 first-place votes, and R gets 4 first-place votes, so V wins using the plurality method.

c. No. A wins the head-to-head comparison, but V wins the election.

5. a. A is favored over B in columns 1 and 4, giving A $120 + 30$, or 150, votes. B is favored over A in columns 2, 3, and 5, giving B $60 + 30 + 30$, or 120 votes. Thus, A is favored when compared to B.

A is favored over C in columns 1 and 3, giving A $120 + 30$, or 150 votes. C is favored over A in columns 2, 4, and 5, giving C $60 + 30 + 30$, or 120, votes. Thus, A is favored when compared to C.

We see that A is favored over the other two options using a head-to-head comparison.

b.

Number of Votes	**120**	**60**	**30**	**30**	**30**
First Choice: 3 points	A: $120 \times 3 = 360$	C: $60 \times 3 = 180$	B: $30 \times 3 = 90$	C: $30 \times 3 = 90$	B: $30 \times 3 = 90$
Second Choice: 2 points	C: $120 \times 2 = 240$	B: $60 \times 2 = 120$	A: $30 \times 2 = 60$	A: $30 \times 2 = 60$	C: $30 \times 2 = 60$
Third Choice: 1 point	B: $120 \times 1 = 120$	A: $60 \times 1 = 60$	C: $30 \times 1 = 30$	B: $30 \times 1 = 30$	A: $30 \times 1 = 30$

A gets $360 + 60 + 60 + 60 + 30 = 570$ points.
B gets $120 + 120 + 90 + 30 + 90 = 450$ points.
C gets $240 + 180 + 30 + 90 + 60 = 600$ points.

C receives the most points, so C is the winner.

c. No. A wins the head-to-head comparison, but C wins the election.

7. a. There are 29 people voting. No one receives the 15 first-place votes needed for a majority. B receives the fewest first-place votes and is eliminated in the next round.

Number of Votes	18	11
First Choice	C	A
Second Choice	A	C

C receives the majority of first-place votes, so C is the winner.

b. With the voting change, a new preference table results.

Number of Votes	14	8	7
First Choice	C	B	A
Second Choice	A	C	B
Third Choice	B	A	C

No one receives a majority of first-place votes. A receives the fewest first-place votes, and is eliminated in the next round.

Number of Votes	14	15
First Choice	C	B
Second Choice	B	C

B receives the majority of first-place votes, so B is the winner.

c. No. C wins the straw vote, and the only change increases the number of first-place votes for C, but B wins the election.

9. a. There are 3 candidates, so $n = 3$ and the number of comparisons we must make is $\frac{n(n-1)}{2} = \frac{3(2)}{2} = 3$.

Comparison	Vote Results	Conclusion
H vs. L	10 voters prefer H to L. 13 voters prefer L to H.	L wins and gets one point.
H vs. S	10 voters prefer H to S. 13 voters prefer S to H.	S wins and gets one point.
L vs. S	8 voters prefer L to S. 15 voters prefer S to L.	S wins and gets one point.

Thus, L gets 1 point and S gets 2 points. Therefore, S is the winner when candidates H and L are included.

b. New preference table:

Number of Votes	15	8
First Choice	S	L
Second Choice	L	S

With only two candidates, we can only make one comparison. We see that S wins, defeating L by 15 votes to 8 votes. Thus S gets 1 point, L gets 0 points, and S is the winner.

c. Yes. S wins whether or not H withdraws.

11. a.

Number of Votes	20	16	10	4
First Choice: 4 points	D: $20 \times 4 = 80$	C: $16 \times 4 = 64$	C: $10 \times 4 = 40$	A: $4 \times 4 = 16$
Second Choice: 3 points	A: $20 \times 3 = 60$	A: $16 \times 3 = 48$	B: $10 \times 3 = 30$	B: $4 \times 3 = 12$
Third Choice: 2 points	B: $20 \times 2 = 40$	B: $16 \times 2 = 32$	D: $10 \times 2 = 20$	D: $4 \times 2 = 8$
Fourth Choice: 1 point	C: $20 \times 1 = 20$	D: $16 \times 1 = 16$	A: $10 \times 1 = 10$	C: $4 \times 1 = 4$

A gets $60 + 48 + 10 + 16 = 134$ points.
B gets $40 + 32 + 30 + 12 = 114$ points.
C gets $20 + 64 + 40 + 4 = 128$ points.
D gets $80 + 16 + 20 + 8 = 124$ points.

A receives the most points, so A is the winner.

b. No. A has only 4 first-place votes, out of 50 total votes. C has 26 first-place votes, which is a majority, but A wins the election.

13. a. There are 70 people voting. No one receives the 36 first-place votes needed for a majority. B receives the fewest first-place votes and is eliminated in the next round.

Number of Votes	24	20	10	8	8
First Choice	D	C	A	A	C
Second Choice	A	A	D	C	D
Third Choice	C	D	C	D	A

No one receives a majority of first-place votes. A receives the fewest first-place votes and is eliminated in the next round.

Number of Votes	34	36
First Choice	D	C
Second Choice	C	D

C receives 36 first-place votes, which is a majority, so C is the winner.

b. No. When compared individually to B, A wins with 60 votes to 10. Compared with C, A wins with 42 votes to 28. Compared with D, A wins with 38 votes to 32. So A is favored in all head-to-head contests but C wins the election.

15. a.

Number of Votes	14	8	4
First Choice: 4 points	A: $14 \times 4 = 56$	B: $8 \times 4 = 32$	D: $4 \times 4 = 16$
Second Choice: 3 points	B: $14 \times 3 = 42$	D: $8 \times 3 = 24$	A: $4 \times 3 = 12$
Third Choice: 2 points	C: $14 \times 2 = 28$	C: $8 \times 2 = 16$	C: $4 \times 2 = 8$
Fourth Choice: 1 point	D: $14 \times 1 = 14$	A: $8 \times 1 = 8$	B: $4 \times 1 = 4$

A gets $56 + 8 + 12 = 76$ points.
B gets $42 + 32 + 4 = 78$ points.
C gets $28 + 16 + 8 = 52$ points.
D gets $14 + 24 + 16 = 54$ points.

B receives the most points, so B is the winner.

b. No. A receives the majority of first-place votes, but B wins the election.

c. No. A wins all head-to-head comparisons, but B wins the election.

d. Using the Borda count method with C removed:

Number of Votes	14	8	4
First Choice: 3 points	A: $14 \times 3 = 42$	B: $8 \times 3 = 24$	D: $4 \times 3 = 12$
Second Choice: 2 points	B: $14 \times 2 = 28$	D: $8 \times 2 = 16$	A: $4 \times 2 = 8$
Third Choice: 1 point	D: $14 \times 1 = 14$	A: $8 \times 1 = 8$	B: $4 \times 1 = 4$

A gets $42 + 8 + 8 = 58$ points.
B gets $28 + 24 + 4 = 56$ points.
D gets $14 + 16 + 12 = 42$ points.

A receives the most points, and wins the election.

The irrelevant alternatives criterion is not satisfied. Candidate C's dropping out changed the outcome of the election.

17. a.

Number of Votes	16	14	12	4	2
First Choice: 5 points	A: $16 \times 5 = 80$	D: $14 \times 5 = 70$	D: $12 \times 5 = 60$	C: $4 \times 5 = 20$	E: $2 \times 5 = 10$
Second Choice: 4 points	B: $16 \times 4 = 64$	B: $14 \times 4 = 56$	B: $12 \times 4 = 48$	A: $4 \times 4 = 16$	A: $2 \times 4 = 8$
Third Choice: 3 points	C: $16 \times 3 = 48$	A: $14 \times 3 = 42$	E: $12 \times 3 = 36$	B: $4 \times 3 = 12$	D: $2 \times 3 = 6$
Fourth Choice: 2 points	D: $16 \times 2 = 32$	C: $14 \times 2 = 28$	C: $12 \times 2 = 24$	D: $4 \times 2 = 8$	B: $2 \times 2 = 4$
Fifth Choice: 1 point	E: $16 \times 1 = 16$	E: $14 \times 1 = 14$	A: $12 \times 1 = 12$	E: $4 \times 1 = 4$	C: $2 \times 1 = 2$

A gets $80 + 42 + 12 + 16 + 8 = 158$ points.
B gets $64 + 56 + 48 + 12 + 4 = 184$ points.
C gets $48 + 28 + 24 + 20 + 2 = 122$ points.
D gets $32 + 70 + 60 + 8 + 6 = 176$ points.
E gets $16 + 14 + 36 + 4 + 10 = 80$ points.

B receives the most points, so B is the winner.

b. No. D gets a majority of first-place votes, but B wins the election.

c. No. D wins all head-to-head comparisons, but B wins the election.

19. a. A receives the most first-place votes, and is the winner.

b. Yes. A has a majority of the first-place votes, and wins.

c. Yes. A wins in comparisons to B and C.

d. New preference table:

Number of Votes	7	3	2
First Choice	A	B	A
Second Choice	B	C	C
Third Choice	C	A	B

A has the majority of first-place votes, and wins using the plurality method.

e. Yes. A still receives the most first-place votes, and wins.

f. No. The fact that all four criteria are satisfied in a particular case does not mean that the method used always satisfies all four criteria.

29. makes sense

31. does not make sense; Explanations will vary. Sample explanation: The majority criterion could be violated. For instance, suppose candidate A is the first choice of 51% of voters and is approved by 60% of voters, yet candidate B is the first choice of 49% of voters and is approved by 70% of voters.

Check Points 13.3

1. a. $\text{Standard divisor} = \dfrac{\text{total population}}{\text{number of allocated items}} = \dfrac{10{,}000}{200} = 50$

b. $\text{Standard quota for state A} = \dfrac{\text{population of state A}}{\text{standard divisor}} = \dfrac{1112}{50} = 22.24$

$\text{Standard quota for state B} = \dfrac{\text{population of state B}}{\text{standard divisor}} = \dfrac{1118}{50} = 22.36$

$\text{Standard quota for state C} = \dfrac{\text{population of state C}}{\text{standard divisor}} = \dfrac{1320}{50} = 26.4$

$\text{Standard quota for state D} = \dfrac{\text{population of state D}}{\text{standard divisor}} = \dfrac{1515}{50} = 30.3$

$\text{Standard quota for state E} = \dfrac{\text{population of state E}}{\text{standard divisor}} = \dfrac{4935}{50} = 98.7$

Table 13.27 **Population of Amador by State**

State	A	B	C	D	E	Total
Population (in thousands)	1112	1118	1320	1515	4935	10,000
Standard quota	22.24	22.36	26.4	30.3	98.7	200

2.

State	Population (in thousands)	Standard Quota	Lower Quota	Fractional Part	Surplus	Final Apportionment
A	1112	22.24	22	0.24		22
B	1118	22.36	22	0.36		22
C	1320	26.4	26	0.4 (next largest)	1	27
D	1515	30.3	30	0.3		30
E	4935	98.7	98	0.7 (largest)	1	99
Total	10,000	200	198			200

3.

State	Population (in thousands)	Modified Quota (using $d = 49.3$)	Modified Lower Quota	Final Apportionment
A	1112	22.56	22	22
B	1118	22.68	22	22
C	1320	26.77	26	26
D	1515	30.73	30	30
E	4935	100.10	100	100
Total	10,000		200	200

4.

State	Population (in thousands)	Modified Quota (using $d = 50.5$)	Modified Upper Quota
A	1112	22.02	23
B	1118	22.14	23
C	1320	26.14	27
D	1515	30	30
E	4935	97.72	98
Total	10,000		201

This sum should be 200, not 201.

State	Population (in thousands)	Modified Quota (using $d = 50.6$)	Modified Upper Quota	Final Apportionment
A	1112	21.98	22	22
B	1118	22.09	23	23
C	1320	26.09	27	27
D	1515	29.94	30	30
E	4935	97.53	98	98
Total	10,000		200	200

5.

State	Population (in thousands)	Modified Quota (using $d = 49.8$)	Modified Rounded Quota
A	1112	22.33	22
B	1118	22.45	22
C	1320	26.51	27
D	1515	30.42	30
E	4935	99.10	99
Total	10,000		200

Concept and Vocabulary Check 13.3

1. divisor; quota
2. quotas
3. lower; upper; lower quota; upper quota
4. Hamilton's; decimal
5. modified; Jefferson's; Adams's; Webster's
6. quota; Jefferson's; Adams's; Webster's
7. true

Exercise Set 13.3

1. a. Standard divisor = $\frac{1600}{80} = 20$. There are 20,000 people for each seat in congress.

b–c.

State	A	B	C	D
Standard quota	$\frac{138}{20} = 6.9$	$\frac{266}{20} = 13.3$	$\frac{534}{20} = 26.7$	$\frac{662}{20} = 33.1$
Lower quota	6	13	26	33
Upper Quota	7	14	27	34

3.

State	Population (in thousands)	Standard Quota	Lower Quota	Fractional Part	Surplus	Final Apportionment
A	138	6.9	6	0.9	1	7
B	266	13.3	13	0.3		13
C	534	26.7	26	0.7	1	27
D	662	33.1	33	0.1		33
Total	1600	80	78			80

5.

School	Enrollment	Standard Quota	Lower Quota	Fractional Part	Surplus	Final Apportionment
Humanities	1050	30.26	30	0.26		30
Social Science	1410	40.63	40	0.63	1	41
Engineering	1830	52.74	52	0.74	1	53
Business	2540	73.20	73	0.20		73
Education	3580	103.17	103	0.17		103
Total	10,410	300	298			300

We use $\frac{10,410}{300} = 34.7$ as the standard divisor.

7.

State	Population	Modified Quota (d = 32,920)	Modified Lower Quota	Final Apportionment
A	126,316	3.84	3	3
B	196,492	5.97	5	5
C	425,264	12.92	12	12
D	526,664	15.998	15	15
E	725,264	22.03	22	22
Total	2,000,000		57	57

9. There are 15,000 patients. The standard divisor is $\frac{15,000}{150}$, or 100. Try a modified divisor of 98.

Clinic	Average Weekly Patient Load	Modified Quota	Modified Lower Quota	Final Apportionment
A	1714	17.49	17	17
B	5460	55.71	55	55
C	2440	24.90	24	24
D	5386	54.96	54	54
Total	15,000		150	150

11.

Precinct	Crimes	Modified Quota ($d = 16$)	Modified Upper Quota	Final Apportionment
A	446	27.88	28	28
B	526	32.88	33	33
C	835	52.19	53	53
D	227	14.19	15	15
E	338	21.13	22	22
F	456	28.5	29	29
Total	2828		180	180

13. There is a total of \$2025 to be invested. The standard divisor is $\frac{2025}{30}$, or 67.5. Try a modified divisor of 72.

Person	Amount	Modified Quota	Modified Upper Quota	Final Apportionment
A	795	11.04	12	12
B	705	9.79	10	10
C	525	7.29	8	8
Total	2025		30	30

15.

Course	Enrollment	Modified Quota ($d = 29.6$)	Modified Rounded Quota	Final Apportionment
Introductory Algebra	130	4.39	4	4
Intermediate Algebra	282	9.53	10	10
Liberal Arts Math	188	6.35	6	6
Total	600		20	20

17. The total number of passengers is 11,060. The standard divisor is $\frac{11,060}{200}$ or 55.3. Try a modified divisor of 55.5.

Route	Average Number of Passengers	Modified Quota	Modified Rounded Quota	Final Apportionment
A	1087	19.59	20	20
B	1323	23.84	24	24
C	1592	28.68	29	29
D	1596	28.76	29	29
E	5462	98.41	98	98
Total	11,060		200	200

19. The total number of patients is 2000. The standard divisor is $\frac{2000}{250}$, or 8. Use Hamilton's method.

Shift	Average Number of Patients	Standard Quota	Lower Quota	Fractional Part	Surplus	Final Apportionment
A	453	56.625	56	0 .625	1	57
B	650	81.25	81	0.25		81
C	547	68.375	68	0.375		68
D	350	43.75	43	0.75	1	44
Total	2000	250	248			250

21. Try a modified divisor of 8.06. Use Adams' method.

Shift	Average Number of Patients	Modified Quota	Modified Upper Quota	Final Apportionment
A	453	56.20	57	57
B	650	80.65	81	81
C	547	67.87	68	68
D	350	43.42	44	44
Total	2000		250	250

23. The total population is 3,615,920. The standard divisor is $\frac{3,615,920}{105}$, or 34,437.333. Use Hamilton's method.

State	Population	Standard Quota	Lower Quota	Fractional Part	Surplus	Final Apportionment
Connecticut	236,841	6.88	6	0.88	1	7
Delaware	55,540	1.61	1	0.61	1	2
Georgia	70,835	2.06	2	0.06		2
Kentucky	68,705	1.995	1	0.995	1	2
Maryland	278,514	8.09	8	0.09		8
Massachusetts	475,327	13.80	13	0.80	1	14
New Hampshire	141,822	4.12	4	0.12		4
New Jersey	179,570	5.21	5	0.21		5
New York	331,589	9.63	9	0.63	1	10
North Carolina	353,523	10.27	10	0.27		10
Pennsylvania	432,879	12.57	12	0.57	1	13
Rhode Island	68,446	1.99	1	0.99	1	2
South Carolina	206,236	5.99	5	0.99	1	6
Vermont	85,533	2.48	2	0.48		2
Virginia	630,560	18.31	18	0.31		18
Total	3,615,920	105.005	97			105

25. Use Adams' method with $d = 36,100$.

State	Population	Modified Quota	Modified Upper Quota	Final Apportionment
Connecticut	236,841	6.56	7	7
Delaware	55,540	1.54	2	2
Georgia	70,835	1.96	2	2
Kentucky	68,705	1.90	2	2
Maryland	278,514	7.72	8	8
Massachusetts	475,327	13.17	14	14
New Hampshire	141,822	3.93	4	4
New Jersey	179,570	4.97	5	5
New York	331,589	9.19	10	10
North Carolina	353,523	9.79	10	10
Pennsylvania	432,879	11.99	12	12
Rhode Island	68,446	1.90	2	2
South Carolina	206,236	5.71	6	6
Vermont	85,533	2.37	3	3
Virginia	630,560	17.47	18	18
Total	3,615,920		105	105

43. does not make sense; Explanations will vary. Sample explanation: For the U.S. Senate, each state is allocated two representatives.

45. does not make sense; Explanations will vary. Sample explanation: These data indicate an apportionment that match the upper quota and thus do not violate the quota rule.

Check Points 13.4

1. We begin with 99 seats in the Congress.

First we compute the standard divisor: Standard divisor = $\dfrac{\text{total population}}{\text{number of allocated items}} = \dfrac{20{,}000}{99} = 202.02$

Using this value, make a table showing apportionment using Hamilton's method.

State	Population	Standard Quota	Lower Quota	Fractional Part	Surplus Seats	Final Apportionment
A	2060	10.20	10	0.20		10
B	2080	10.30	10	0.30	1	11
C	7730	38.26	38	0.26		38
D	8130	40.24	40	0.24		40
Total	20,000	99	98			99

Now let's see what happens with 100 seats in Congress.

First we compute the standard divisor: Standard divisor $\dfrac{\text{total population}}{\text{number of allocated items}} = \dfrac{20{,}000}{100} = 200$.

Using this value, make a table showing apportionment using Hamilton's method.

State	Population	Standard Quota	Lower Quota	Fractional Part	Surplus Seats	Final Apportionment
A	2060	10.3	10	0.3		10
B	2080	10.4	10	0.4		10
C	7730	38.65	38	0.65	1	39
D	8130	40.65	40	0.65	1	41
Total	20,000	100	98			100

The final apportionments are summarized in the following table.

State	Apportionment with 99 seats	Apportionment with 100 seats
A	10	10
B	11	10
C	38	39
D	40	41

When the number of seats increased from 99 to 100, B's apportionment decreased from 11 to 10.

2. a. **We use Hamilton's method to find the apportionment for each state with its original population. First we compute the standard divisor.**

$$\text{Standard divisor} = \frac{\text{total population}}{\text{number of allocated items}} = \frac{200,000}{100} = 2000$$

Using this value, we show the apportionment in the following table.

State	Original Population	Standard Quota	Lower Quota	Fractional Part	Surplus Seats	Final Apportionment
A	19,110	9.56	9	0.56	1	10
B	39,090	19.55	19	0.55		19
C	141,800	70.9	70	0.9	1	71
Total	200,000	100.01	98			100

b. The fraction for percent increase is the amount of increase divided by the original amount. The percent increase in the population of each state is determined as follows.

$$\text{State A: } \frac{19,302-19,110}{19,110} = \frac{192}{19,110} \approx 0.01005 = 1.005\%$$

$$\text{State B: } \frac{39,480-39,090}{39,090} = \frac{390}{39,090} \approx 0.00998 = 0.998\%$$

State A is increasing at a rate of 1.005%. This is faster than State B, which is increasing at a rate of 0.998%.

c. We use Hamilton's method to find the apportionment for each state with its new population. First we compute the standard divisor.

$$\text{Standard divisor} = \frac{\text{total population}}{\text{number of allocated items}} = \frac{200,582}{100} = 2005.82$$

Using this value, we show the apportionment in the following table.

State	New Population	Standard Quota	Lower Quota	Fractional Part	Surplus Seats	Final Apportionment
A	19,302	9.62	9	0.62		9
B	39,480	19.68	19	0.68	1	20
C	141,800	70.69	70	0.69	1	71
Total	200,582	99.99	98			100

The final apportionments are summarized in the following table.

State	Growth Rate	Original Apportionment	New Apportionment
A	1.005%	10	9
B	0.998%	19	20
C	0%	71	71

State A loses a seat to State B, even though the population of State A is increasing at a faster rate. This is an example of the population paradox.

3. **a.** We use Hamilton's method to find the apportionment for each school. First we compute the standard divisor.

$$\text{Standard divisor} = \frac{\text{total population}}{\text{number of allocated items}} = \frac{12,000}{100} = 120$$

Using this value, we show the apportionment in the following table.

School	Enrollment	Standard Quota	Lower Quota	Fractional Part	Surplus	Final Apportionment
East High	2574	21.45	21	0.45		21
West High	9426	78.55	78	0.55	1	79
Total	12,000	100	99			100

b. Again we use Hamilton's method.

$$\text{Standard divisor} = \frac{\text{total population}}{\text{number of allocated items}} = \frac{12,750}{106} = 120.28$$

Using this value, we show the apportionment in the following table

School	Enrollment	Standard Quota	Lower Quota	Fractional Part	Surplus	Final Apportionment
East High	2574	21.40	21	0.40	1	22
West High	9426	78.37	78	0.37		78
North High	750	6.24	6	0.24		6
Total	12,750	106.01	105			106

West High has lost a counselor to East High.

Concept and Vocabulary Check 13.4

1. Alabama
2. population
3. new-states
4. true

Exercise Set 13.4

1. **a.** The standard divisor is $\frac{1800}{30}$, or 60.

Course	Enrollment	Standard Quota	Lower Quota	Fractional Part	Surplus	Final Apportionment
College Algebra	978	16.30	16	0.30		16
Statistics	500	8.33	8	0.33		8
Liberal Arts Math	322	5.37	5	0.37	1	6
Total	1800	30	29			30

b. The standard divisor is $\frac{1800}{31}$, or 58.06.

Course	Enrollment	Standard Quota	Lower Quota	Fractional Part	Surplus	Final Apportionment
College Algebra	978	16.84	16	0.84	1	17
Statistics	500	8.61	8	0.61	1	9
Liberal Arts Math	322	5.55	5	0.55		5
Total	1800	31	29			31

Liberal Arts Math loses a teaching assistant when the total number of teaching assistants is raised from 30 to 31. This is an example of the Alabama paradox.

3. Standard divisor with 40 seats: $\frac{20{,}000}{40} = 500$. Use Hamilton's method.

State	Population	Standard Quota	Lower Quota	Fractional Part	Surplus	Final Apportionment
A	680	1.36	1	0.36	1	2
B	9150	18.30	18	0.30		18
C	10,170	20.34	20	0.34		20
Total	20,000	40	39			40

Standard divisor with 41 seats: $\frac{20{,}000}{41} = 487.8$. Use Hamilton's method.

State	Population	Standard Quota	Lower Quota	Fractional Part	Surplus	Final Apportionment
A	680	1.39	1	0.39		1
B	9150	18.76	18	0.76	1	19
C	10,170	20.85	20	0.85	1	21
Total	20,000	41	39			41

State A loses a seat when the total number of seats increases from 40 to 41.

5. a. Standard divisor: $\frac{3760}{24} = 156.7$. Use Hamilton's method.

State	Original Population	Standard Quota	Lower Quota	Fractional Part	Surplus	Final Apportionment
A	530	3.38	3	0.38	1	4
B	990	6.32	6	0.32		6
C	2240	14.30	14	0.30		14
Total	3760	24	23			24

b. Percent increase for state A: $\frac{680-530}{530} \approx 0.283 = 28.3\%$

Percent increase for state B: $\frac{1250-990}{990} \approx 0.263 = 26.3\%$

Percent increase for state C: $\frac{2570-2240}{2240} \approx 0.147 = 14.7\%$

c. Standard divisor: $\frac{4500}{24} = 187.5$. Use Hamilton's method.

State	New Population	Standard Quota	Lower Quota	Fractional Part	Surplus	Final Apportionment
A	680	3.63	3	0.63		3
B	1250	6.67	6	0.67	1	7
C	2570	13.71	13	0.71	1	14
Total	4500	24.01	22			24

A loses a seat while B gains, even though A has a faster increasing population. The population paradox does occur.

7. Original standard divisor: $\dfrac{8880}{40} = 222$

District	Original Population	Standard Quota	Lower Quota	Fractional Part	Surplus	Final Apportionment
A	1188	5.35	5	0.35		5
B	1424	6.41	6	0.41		6
C	2538	11.43	11	0.43	1	12
D	3730	16.80	16	0.80	1	17
Total	8880	39.99	38			40

New standard divisor: $\dfrac{9000}{40} = 225$

District	New Population	Standard Quota	Lower Quota	Fractional Part	Surplus	Final Apportionment
A	1188	5.28	5	0.28		5
B	1420	6.311	6	0.311	1	7
C	2544	11.307	11	0.307		11
D	3848	17.10	17	0.10		17
Total	9000	39.998	39			40

Percent increase by state:

A: 0% (no change) B: $\dfrac{1420-1424}{1424} \approx -0.0028 = -0.28\%$

C: $\dfrac{2544-2538}{2538} \approx 0.0024 = 0.24\%$ D: $\dfrac{3848-3730}{3730} \approx 0.032 = 3.2\%$

C loses a truck to B even though C increased in population faster than B. This shows the population paradox occurs.

9. a. Standard divisor: $\dfrac{10{,}000}{100} = 100$

Branch	Employees	Standard Quota	Lower Quota	Fractional Part	Surplus	Final Apportionment
A	1045	10.45	10	0.45		10
B	8955	89.55	89	0.55	1	90
Total	10,000	100	99			100

b. New standard divisor: $\frac{10,525}{105} = 100.238$

Branch	Employees	Standard Quota	Lower Quota	Fractional Part	Surplus	Final Apportionment
A	1045	10.43	10	0.43	1	11
B	8955	89.34	89	0.34		89
C	525	5.24	5	0.24		5
Total	10,525	105.01	104			105

Branch B loses a promotion when branch C is added. This means the new-states paradox has occurred.

11. a. Standard divisor: $\frac{9450 + 90,550}{100} = 1000$

State	Population	Standard Quota	Lower Quota	Fractional Part	Surplus	Final Apportionment
A	9450	9.45	9	0.45		9
B	90,550	90.55	90	0.55	1	91
Total	100,000	100	99			100

b. New standard divisor: $\frac{100,000 + 10,400}{110} = 1003.64$

State	Population	Standard Quota	Lower Quota	Fractional Part	Surplus	Final Apportionment
A	9450	9.42	9	0.42	1	10
B	90,550	90.22	90	0.22		90
C	10,400	10.36	10	0.36		10
Total	110,400	110	109			110

State B loses a seat when state C is added.

13. a.

State	Population	Modified Quota	Modified Lower Quota	Final Apportionment
A	99,000	6.39	6	6
B	214,000	13.81	13	13
C	487,000	31.42	31	31
Total	800,000		50	50

b.

State	Population	Modified Quota	Modified Lower Quota	Final Apportionment
A	99,000	6.39	6	6
B	214,000	13.81	13	13
C	487,000	31.42	31	37
D	116,000	7.48	7	7
Total	916,000		57	57

The new-states paradox does not occur. As long as the modified divisor, d, remains the same, adding a new state cannot change the number of seats held by existing states.

19. makes sense

21. does not make sense; Explanations will vary. Sample explanation: Mathematicians (Balinski and Young) have proved this to be impossible.

Chapter 13 Review Exercises

1.

Number of Votes	**4**	**3**	**3**	**2**
First Choice	A	B	C	C
Second Choice	B	D	B	B
Third Choice	C	C	D	A
Fourth Choice	D	A	A	D

2. $9+5+4+2+2+1=23$

3. 4

4. $9+5+2=16$

5. $9+5=14$

6. M receives 12 first-choice votes, compared to 10 for C and 2 for D, so M (Musical) is selected.

7.

Number of Votes	**10**	**8**	**4**	**2**
First Choice: 3 points	C: $10\times 3=30$	M: $8\times 3=24$	M: $4\times 3=12$	D: $2\times 3=6$
Second Choice: 2 points	D: $10\times 2=20$	C: $8\times 2=16$	D: $4\times 2=8$	M: $2\times 2=4$
Third Choice: 1 point	M: $10\times 1=10$	D: $8\times 1=8$	C: $4\times 1=4$	C: $2\times 1=2$

C gets $30+16+4+2=52$ points.
D gets $20+8+8+6=42$ points.
M gets $10+24+12+4=50$ points.

C (Comedy) gets the most points and is chosen.

8. There are 24 voters, so 13 votes are needed for a majority. None of the candidates has 13 first-place votes. D has the fewest first-place votes and is eliminated in the next round.

Number of Votes	**10**	**14**
First Choice	C	M
Second Choice	M	C

M (Musical) has 14 first-place votes, a majority, so a musical is selected.

9. There are 3 choices so we make $\frac{3(3-1)}{2}=3$ comparisons.

Comparison	**Vote Results**	**Conclusion**
C vs. D	18 voters prefer C to D. 6 voters prefer D to C.	C wins and gets 1 point.
C vs. M	10 voters prefer C to M. 14 voters prefer M to C.	M wins and gets 1 point.
D vs. M	12 voters prefer D to M. 12 voters prefer M to D.	D and M tie. Each gets $\frac{1}{2}$ point.

C gets 1 point, D gets $\frac{1}{2}$ point, and M gets $1\frac{1}{2}$ points. So M (Musical) wins, and is selected.

10. A receives 40 first-place votes, compared to 30 for B, 6 for C, and 2 for D. So A wins.

11.

Number of Votes	40	30	6	2
First Choice: 4 points	A: $40 \times 4 = 160$	B: $30 \times 4 = 120$	C: $6 \times 4 = 24$	D: $2 \times 4 = 8$
Second Choice: 3 points	B: $40 \times 3 = 120$	C: $30 \times 3 = 90$	D: $6 \times 3 = 18$	B: $2 \times 3 = 6$
Third Choice: 2 points	C: $40 \times 2 = 80$	D: $30 \times 2 = 60$	B: $6 \times 2 = 12$	C: $2 \times 2 = 4$
Fourth Choice: 1 point	D: $40 \times 1 = 40$	A: $30 \times 1 = 30$	A: $6 \times 1 = 6$	A: $2 \times 1 = 2$

A gets $160 + 30 + 6 + 2 = 198$ points.
B gets $120 + 120 + 12 + 6 = 258$ points.
C gets $80 + 90 + 24 + 4 = 198$ points.
D gets $40 + 60 + 18 + 8 = 126$ points.

B receives the most points, and wins.

12. There are 78 voters, so 40 first-place votes are needed for a majority. A has 40 first-place votes, and wins.

13. There are 4 candidates, so $\frac{4(4-1)}{2} = 6$ comparisons are needed.

Comparison	Vote Results	Conclusion
A vs. B	40 voters prefer A to B. 38 voters prefer B to A.	A wins and gets 1 point.
A vs. C	40 voters prefer A to C. 38 voters prefer C to A.	A wins and gets 1 point.
A vs. D	40 voters prefer A to D. 38 voters prefer D to A.	A wins and gets 1 point.
B vs. C	72 voters prefer B to C. 6 voters prefer C to B.	B wins and gets 1 point.
B vs. D	70 voters prefer B to D. 8 voters prefer D to B.	B wins and gets 1 point.
C vs. D	76 voters prefer C to D. 2 voters prefer D to C.	C wins and gets 1 point.

A gets 3 points, B gets 2 points, C gets 1 point, and D gets 0 points. So A wins.

14.

Number of Votes	1500	600	300
First Choice: 4 points	A: $1500 \times 4 = 6000$	B: $600 \times 4 = 2400$	C: $300 \times 4 = 1200$
Second Choice: 3 points	B: $1500 \times 3 = 4500$	D: $600 \times 3 = 1800$	B: $300 \times 3 = 900$
Third Choice: 2 points	C: $1500 \times 2 = 3000$	C: $600 \times 2 = 1200$	D: $300 \times 2 = 600$
Fourth Choice: 1 point	D: $1500 \times 1 = 1500$	A: $600 \times 1 = 600$	A: $300 \times 1 = 300$

A gets $6000 + 600 + 300 = 6900$ points.
B gets $4500 + 2400 + 900 = 7800$ points.
C gets $3000 + 1200 + 1200 = 5400$ points.
D gets $1500 + 1800 + 600 = 3900$ points.
B receives the most points, and wins.

15. A has a majority of first-place votes. In Exercise 14, B wins and so the majority criterion is not satisfied.

16. A is favored above all others using a head-to-head comparison. This is automatically true, since A has a majority of first-place votes. In Exercise 14, B wins and so the head-to-head criterion is not satisfied.

17. There are 2500 voters. 1251 first-place votes are needed for a majority. B has 1500 first-place votes, and is the winner.

18. B is favored above all others using a head-to-head comparison. This is automatically true, since B has a majority of first-place votes. In Exercise 17, B wins and so the head-to-head criterion is satisfied.

19. A receives 180 first-place votes, compared with 100 for B, 30 for C, and 40 for D. Therefore A wins.

20.

Number of Votes	**180**	**100**	**40**	**30**
First Choice: 4 points	A: $180 \times 4 = 720$	B: $100 \times 4 = 400$	D: $40 \times 4 = 160$	C: $30 \times 4 = 120$
Second Choice: 3 points	B: $180 \times 3 = 540$	D: $100 \times 3 = 300$	B: $40 \times 3 = 120$	B: $30 \times 3 = 90$
Third Choice: 2 points	C: $180 \times 2 = 360$	A: $100 \times 2 = 200$	C: $40 \times 2 = 80$	A: $30 \times 2 = 60$
Fourth Choice: 1 point	D: $180 \times 1 = 180$	C: $100 \times 1 = 100$	A: $40 \times 1 = 40$	D: $30 \times 1 = 30$

A gets $720 + 200 + 40 + 60 = 1020$ points.
B gets $540 + 400 + 120 + 90 = 1150$ points.
C gets $360 + 100 + 80 + 120 = 660$ points.
D gets $180 + 300 + 160 + 30 = 670$ points.

B gets the most points, and wins.

21. There are 350 voters. 176 first-place votes are needed for a majority. A has 180 votes, a majority, and wins.

22. There are 4 candidates, and therefore $\frac{4(4-1)}{2} = 6$ comparisons.

Comparison	**Vote Results**	**Conclusion**
A vs. B	180 voters prefer A to B. 170 voters prefer B to A.	A wins and gets 1 point.
A vs. C	280 voters prefer A to C. 70 voters prefer C to A.	A wins and gets 1 point.
A vs. D	210 voters prefer A to D. 140 voters prefer D to A.	A wins and gets 1 point.
B vs. C	320 voters prefer B to C. 30 voters prefer C to B.	B wins and gets 1 point.
B vs. D	310 voters prefer B to D. 40 voters prefer D to B.	B wins and gets 1 point.
C vs. D	210 voters prefer C to D. 140 voters prefer D to C.	C wins and gets 1 point.

A gets 3 points, B gets 2 points, C gets 1 point, and D gets 0 points. Therefore A wins.

23. A has a majority of first-place votes. Based on Exercises 19–22, only the Borda count method violates the majority criterion. B wins by the Borda count method.

24. There are 1450 voters. 726 first-place votes are needed for a majority. No candidate has a majority. A has the fewest first-place votes and is eliminated in the next round.

Number of Votes	**900**	**550**
First Choice	B	C
Second Choice	C	B

B has the majority of first-place votes, and wins.

There is a new preference table:

Number of Votes	700	400	350
First Choice	B	A	C
Second Choice	C	B	A
Third Choice	A	C	B

No candidate has a majority of first-place votes. C has the fewest first-place votes, and is eliminated in the next round.

Number of Votes	700	750
First Choice	B	A
Second Choice	A	B

A has a majority of first-place votes, and wins. This does not satisfy the monotonicity criterion, since the only change gave B more first-place votes, but after the change B lost the election.

26. A has 400 first-place votes, compared to 200 for B and 250 for C. Therefore A wins.

27.

Number of Votes	400	450
First Choice	A	C
Second Choice	C	A

C has the majority of first-place votes, and wins this election. The irrelevant alternatives criterion is not satisfied, because removing B changes the winner from A to C.

28.

Number of Votes	400	250	200
First Choice: 3 points	A: $400 \times 3 = 1200$	C: $250 \times 3 = 750$	B: $200 \times 3 = 600$
Second Choice: 2 points	B: $400 \times 2 = 800$	B: $250 \times 2 = 500$	C: $200 \times 2 = 400$
Third Choice: 1 point	C: $400 \times 1 = 400$	A: $250 \times 1 = 250$	A: $200 \times 1 = 200$

A gets $1200 + 250 + 200 = 1650$ points.
B gets $800 + 500 + 600 = 1900$ points.
C gets $400 + 750 + 400 = 1550$ points.

B gets the most points, and wins.

29.

Number of Votes	400	450
First Choice: 2 points	A: $400 \times 2 = 800$	B: $450 \times 2 = 900$
Second Choice: 1 point	B: $400 \times 1 = 400$	A: $450 \times 1 = 450$

A gets $800 + 450 = 1250$ points.
B gets $400 + 900 = 1300$ points.

B still gets the most points, and wins. The same thing happens if A drops out instead of C, and so the irrelevant alternatives criterion is satisfied.

30. $\dfrac{275+392+611+724}{40} = \dfrac{2002}{40} = 50.05$

31. With a standard divisor of 50.05:

Clinic	A	B	C	D
Average weekly patient load	275	392	611	724
Standard Quota	5.49	7.83	12.21	14.47

32. Using the results of Exercise 31:

Clinic	Standard Quota	Lower Quota	Upper Quota
A	5.49	5	6
B	7.83	7	8
C	12.21	12	13
D	14.47	14	15

33.

Clinic	Standard Quota	Lower Quota	Fractional Part	Surplus	Final Apportionment
A	5.49	5	0.49	1	6
B	7.83	7	0.83	1	8
C	12.21	12	0.21		12
D	14.47	14	0.47		14
Total	40	38			40

34.

Clinic	Average Weekly Patient Load	Modified Quota ($d = 48$)	Modified Lower Quota	Final Apportionment
A	275	5.73	5	5
B	392	8.17	8	8
C	611	12.73	12	12
D	724	15.08	15	15
Total	2002		40	40

35.

Clinic	Average Weekly Patient Load	Modified Quota ($d = 52$)	Modified Upper Quota	Final Apportionment
A	275	5.29	6	6
B	392	7.54	8	8
C	611	11.75	12	12
D	724	13.92	14	14
Total	2002		40	40

36.

Clinic	Average Weekly Patient Load	Modified Quota ($d = 49.95$)	Modified Rounded Quota	Final Apportionment
A	275	5.51	6	6
B	392	7.85	8	8
C	611	12.23	12	12
D	724	14.49	14	14
Total	2002		40	40

37. Standard divisor: $\frac{3320+10,060+15,020+19,600}{200}=\frac{48,000}{200}=240$

State	Population	Standard Quota	Lower Quota	Fractional Part	Surplus	Final Apportionment
A	3320	13.83	13	0.83	1	14
B	10,060	41.92	41	0.92	1	42
C	15,020	62.58	62	0.58		62
D	19,600	81.67	81	0.67	1	82
Total	48,000	200	197			200

38. Try modified divisor $d = 238$.

State	Population	Modified Quota	Modified Lower Quota	Final Apportionment
A	3320	13.95	13	13
B	10,060	42.27	42	42
C	15,020	63.11	63	63
D	19,600	82.35	82	82
Total	48,000		200	200

39. Try modified divisor $d = 242$.

State	Population	Modified Quota	Modified Upper Quota	Final Apportionment
A	3320	13.72	14	14
B	10,060	41.57	42	42
C	15,020	62.07	63	63
D	19,600	80.99	81	81
Total	48,000		200	200

40. Try modified divisor $d = 240.4$.

State	Population	Modified Quota	Modified Rounded Quota	Final Apportionment
A	3320	13.81	14	14
B	10,060	41.85	42	42
C	15,020	62.48	62	62
D	19,600	81.53	82	82
Total	48,000		200	200

41. a. Standard divisor: $\frac{7500}{150}=50$

School	Enrollment	Standard Quota	Lower Quota	Fractional Part	Surplus	Final Apportionment
A	370	7.4	7	0.4	1	8
B	3365	67.3	67	0.3		67
C	3765	75.3	75	0.3		75
Total	7500	150	149			150

b. Standard divisor: $\frac{7500}{151} = 49.67$

School	Enrollment	Standard Quota	Lower Quota	Fractional Part	Surplus	Final Apportionment
A	370	7.45	7	0.45		7
B	3365	67.75	67	0.75	1	68
C	3765	75.80	75	0.80	1	76
Total	7500	151	149			151

The Alabama paradox occurs. A loses a laptop when the overall number of laptops changes from 150 to 151.

42. a. Standard divisor: $\frac{200,000}{100} = 2000$

School	Original Population	Standard Quota	Lower Quota	Fractional Part	Surplus	Final Apportionment
A	143,796	71.90	71	0.90	1	72
B	41,090	20.55	20	0.55		20
C	15,114	7.56	7	0.56	1	8
Total	200,000	100.01	98			100

b. Percent increase of B: $\frac{41,420-41,090}{41,090} \approx 0.0080 = 0.8\%$

Percent increase of C: $\frac{15,304-15,114}{15,114} \approx 0.0126 \approx 1.3\%$

c. Standard divisor: $\frac{200,520}{100} = 2005.2$

School	New Population	Standard Quota	Lower Quota	Fractional Part	Surplus	Final Apportionment
A	143,796	71.71	71	0.71	1	72
B	41,420	20.66	20	0.66	1	21
C	15,304	7.63	7	0.63		7
Total	200,520	100	98			100

The population paradox occurs. C loses a seat to B, even though C is growing faster.

43. a. Standard divisor: $\frac{1650}{33} = 50$

Branch	Employees	Standard Quota	Lower Quota	Fractional Part	Surplus	Final Apportionment
A	372	7.44	7	0.44		7
B	1278	25.56	25	0.56	1	26
Total	1650	33	32			33

b. Standard divisor: $\frac{2005}{40} = 50.125$

Branch	Employees	Standard Quota	Lower Quota	Fractional Part	Surplus	Final Apportionment
A	372	7.42	7	0.42		7
B	1278	25.50	25	0.50	1	26
C	355	7.08	7	0.08		7
Total	2005	40	39			40

The new-states paradox does not occur. Neither branch A nor branch B loses any promotions.

44. false; Answers will vary.

Chapter 13 Test

1. $1200 + 900 + 900 + 600 = 3600$

2. 600

3. $900 + 600 = 1500$

4. $900 + 600 = 1500$

5. A received 1200 first-place votes, B received 1500, and C received 900. Therefore B wins.

6.

Number of Votes	1200	900	900	600
First Choice: 3 points	A: $1200 \times 3 = 3600$	C: $900 \times 3 = 2700$	B: $900 \times 3 = 2700$	B: $600 \times 3 = 1800$
Second Choice: 2 points	B: $1200 \times 2 = 2400$	A: $900 \times 2 = 1800$	C: $900 \times 2 = 1800$	A: $600 \times 2 = 1200$
Third Choice: 1 point	C: $1200 \times 1 = 1200$	B: $900 \times 1 = 900$	A: $900 \times 1 = 900$	C: $600 \times 1 = 600$

A gets $3600 + 1800 + 900 + 1200 = 7500$ points.
B gets $2400 + 900 + 2700 + 1800 = 7800$ points.
C gets $1200 + 2700 + 1800 + 600 = 6300$ points.

B receives the most points and is the winner.

7. There are 3600 voters. 1801 first-place votes are needed for a majority. No candidate has a majority. C receives the fewest first-place votes and is eliminated in the next round.

Number of Votes	2100	1500
First Choice	A	B
Second Choice	B	A

A receives the majority of first-place votes, and wins.

8. There are 3 candidates. The number of comparisons is $\frac{3(3-1)}{2}$, or 3.

Comparison	Vote Results	Conclusion
A vs. B	2100 voters prefer A to B. 1500 voters prefer B to A.	A wins and gets 1 point.
A vs. C	1800 voters prefer A to C. 1800 voters prefer C to A.	A and C tie. Each gets $\frac{1}{2}$ point.
B vs. C	2700 voters prefer B to C. 900 voters prefer C to B.	B wins and gets 1 point.

A gets $1\frac{1}{2}$ points, B gets 1 point, and C gets $\frac{1}{2}$ point. Therefore A wins.

9.

Number of Votes	240	160	60
First Choice: 4 points	A: $240 \times 4 = 960$	C: $160 \times 4 = 640$	D: $60 \times 4 = 240$
Second Choice: 3 points	B: $240 \times 3 = 720$	B: $160 \times 3 = 480$	A: $60 \times 3 = 180$
Third Choice: 2 points	C: $240 \times 2 = 480$	D: $160 \times 2 = 320$	C: $60 \times 2 = 120$
Fourth Choice: 1 point	D: $240 \times 1 = 240$	A: $160 \times 1 = 160$	B: $60 \times 1 = 60$

A gets $960 + 160 + 180 = 1300$ points.
B gets $720 + 480 + 60 = 1260$ points.
C gets $480 + 640 + 120 = 1240$ points.
D gets $240 + 320 + 240 = 800$ points.

A gets the most points, and wins.

10. A has the majority of first-place votes. Based on Exercise 9, the majority criterion is satisfied.

11. A has 1500 first-place votes, whereas B and C have 1000 each. Therefore A wins.

12. B is favored when compared to A, by 2000 votes to 1500. B is favored when compared to C, by 2500 votes to 1000. So B is favored in each head-to-head comparison. Based on Exercise 11, the head-to-head criterion is not satisfied, because A wins the election.

13. There are 210 voters. 106 votes are needed for a majority. No candidate has a majority. B receives the fewest first-place votes and is eliminated in the next round.

Number of Votes	130	80
First Choice	C	A
Second Choice	A	C

C receives a majority of votes, and wins.

14. New preference table:

Number of Votes	100	60	50
First Choice	C	B	A
Second Choice	A	C	B
Third Choice	B	A	C

No candidate has a majority. A has the fewest first-place votes and is eliminated in the next round.

Number of Votes	100	110
First Choice	C	B
Second Choice	B	C

B has the majority of first-place votes, and wins. The monotonicity criterion is not satisfied, because the only change gave more first-place votes to C, but C lost the second election.

15. B has 90 first-place votes, C has 75, and A has 45. Therefore B wins. If C drops out, there is a new preference table:

Number of Votes	90	120
First Choice	B	A
Second Choice	A	B

A has a majority of first-place votes, and wins. This changed outcome shows that the irrelevant alternatives criterion is not satisfied.

16. $\frac{119+165+216}{10} = \frac{500}{10} = 50$

17. A: $\frac{119}{50} = 2.38$ B: $\frac{165}{50} = 3.3$ C: $\frac{216}{50} = 4.32$

18. A: 2, 3; B: 3, 4; C: 4, 5

19.

Clinic	Average Weekly Patient Load	Standard Quota	Lower Quota	Fractional Part	Surplus	Final Apportionment
A	119	2.38	2	0.38	1	3
B	165	3.3	3	0.3		3
C	216	4.32	4	0.32		4
Total	500	10	9			10

20.

Clinic	Average Weekly Patient Load	Modified Quota ($d = 42$)	Modified Lower Quota	Final Apportionment
A	119	2.83	2	2
B	165	3.93	3	3
C	216	5.14	5	5
Total	500		10	10

21.

Clinic	Average Weekly Patient Load	Modified Quota ($d = 56$)	Modified Upper Quota	Final Apportionment
A	119	2.13	3	3
B	165	2.95	3	3
C	216	3.86	4	4
Total	500		10	10

22.

Clinic	Average Weekly Patient Load	Modified Quota ($d = 47.7$)	Modified Rounded Quota	Final Apportionment
A	119	2.49	2	2
B	165	3.46	3	3
C	216	4.52	5	5
Total	500		10	10

23. New standard divisor: $\frac{500}{11} = 45.45$

Clinic	Average Weekly Patient Load	Standard Quota	Lower Quota	Fractional Part	Surplus	Final Apportionment
A	119	2.62	2	0.62		2
B	165	3.63	3	0.63	1	4
C	216	4.75	4	0.75	1	5
Total	500	11	9			11

The Alabama paradox occurs. Clinic A loses one doctor when the total number of doctors is raised from 10 to 11.

24. New standard divisor: $\frac{500+110}{12} = \frac{610}{12} = 50.83$

Clinic	Average Weekly Patient Load	Standard Quota	Lower Quota	Fractional Part	Surplus	Final Apportionment
A	119	2.34	2	0.34	1	3
B	165	3.25	3	0.25		3
C	216	4.25	4	0.25		4
D	110	2.16	2	0.16		2
Total	610	12	11			12

The new-states paradox does not occur. No clinic loses doctors when a new clinic is added.

25. Answers will vary.

Chapter 14
Graph Theory

Check Points 14.1

1. Graphs (a) and (b) both have vertices *A, B, C, D,* and *E*. Also, both graphs have edges *AB, AC, BD, BE, CD, CE,* and *DE*.

   Because the two graphs have the same number of vertices connected to each other in the same way, they are the same.
   In fact, graph (b) is just graph (a) rotated clockwise and bent out of shape.

2. Draw points for the five land masses and label them *N, S, A, B,* and *C*.

   There is one bridge that connects North Metroville to Island A, so one edge is drawn connecting vertex *N* to vertex *A*. Similarly, one edge connects vertex *A* with vertex *B*, and one edge connects vertex *B* with vertex *C*. Since there are two bridges connecting Island C to South Metroville, two edges connect vertex *C* with vertex *S*.

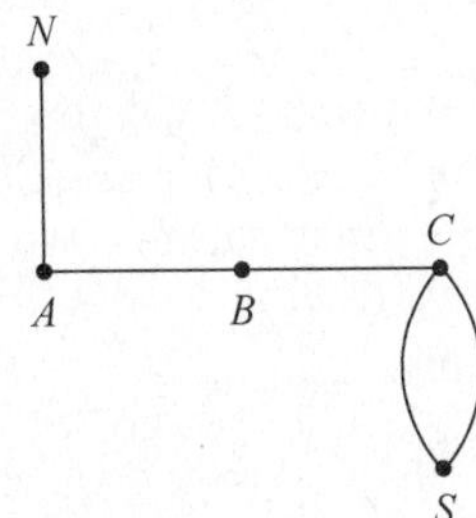

3. We use the abbreviations for the states to label the vertices: ID for Idaho, MT for Montana, WY for Wyoming, UT for Utah, and CO for Colorado. The precise placement of these vertices is not important.

   Whenever two states share a common border, we connect the respective vertices with an edge. For example, Idaho shares a common border with Montana, with Wyoming, and with Utah. Continuing in this manner, we obtain the following graph.

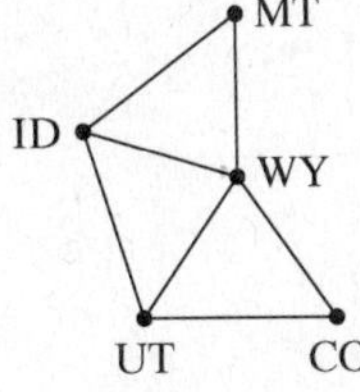

4. We use the letters in Figure 14.13 to label each vertex. Only one door connects the outside, *E*, with room *B*, so we draw one edge from vertex *E* to vertex *B*. Two doors connect the outside, *E*, to room *D*, so we draw two edges from *E* to *D*. Counting doors between the rooms, we complete the following graph.

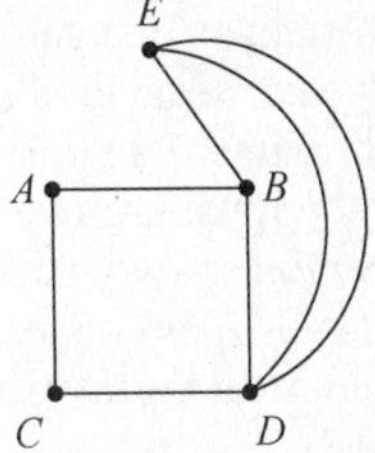

5. We label each of the corners and intersections with an upper-case letter and use points to represent the corners and street intersections. Now we are ready to draw the edges that represent the streets the security guard has to walk. Each street only needs to be walked once, so we draw one edge to represent each street. This results in the following graph.

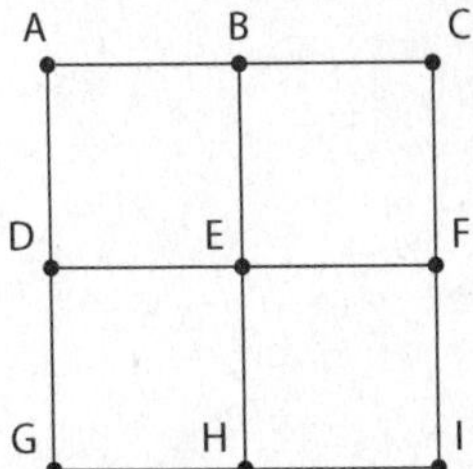

6. We systematically list which pairs of vertices are adjacent, working alphabetically. Thus, the adjacent vertices are *A* and *B*, *A* and *C*, *A* and *D*, *A* and *E*, *B* and *C*, and *E* and *E*.

Concept and Vocabulary Check 14.1

1. graph; vertices; edges; loop
2. equivalent
3. degree
4. adjacent; path; circuit
5. bridge
6. true

7. true

8. true

9. false

Exercise Set 14.1

1. There are six edges attached to the Pittsburgh vertex, so Pittsburgh plays six games during the week. One edge connects the Pittsburgh vertex to the St. Louis vertex, so one game is against St. Louis. One edge connects the Pittsburgh vertex to Chicago, so one game is against Chicago. Two edges connect the Pittsburgh vertex to the Philadelphia vertex, so two games are against Philadelphia. Two edges connect the Pittsburgh vertex to the Montreal vertex, so two games are against Montreal.

3. No. Montreal is farther north than New York but is drawn lower on the graph. However, the graph is not drawn incorrectly. Only the games between teams are important, and these are represented by the edges. Geographic position is not relevant.

5. Possible answers:

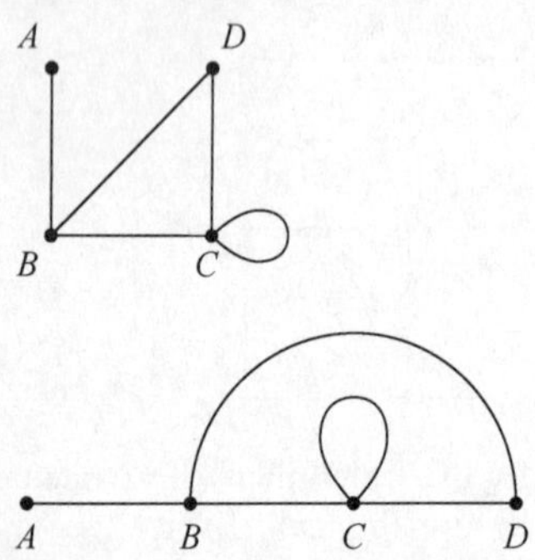

7. Both graphs have vertices A, B, C, and D and edges AB, AC, AD, and BD. The two graphs have the same number of vertices connected in the same way, so they are the same.

Possible answer:

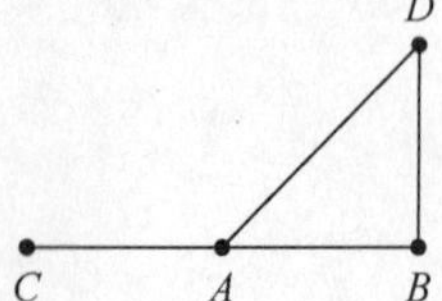

9. We label each student's vertex with the first letter of his or her name. An edge connecting two vertices represents a friendship prior to forming the homework group. The following graph results.

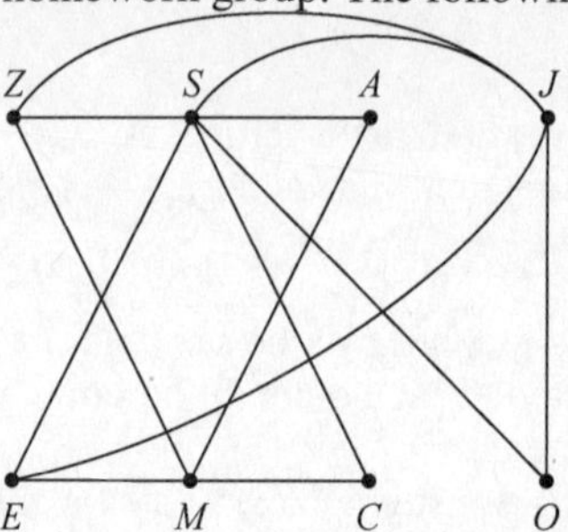

11. Label one vertex N, for North Gothamville. Label another S, for South Gothamville. Label the islands, from left to right, A, B, and C. Label three vertices accordingly. Use edges to represent bridges. The following graph results.

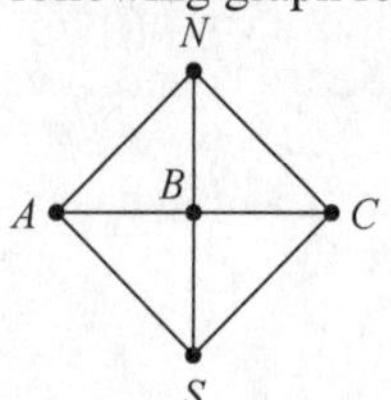

13. We use the abbreviations WA, OR, ID, MT, and WY to label the vertices representing Washington, Oregon, Idaho, Montana, and Wyoming. The following graph results.

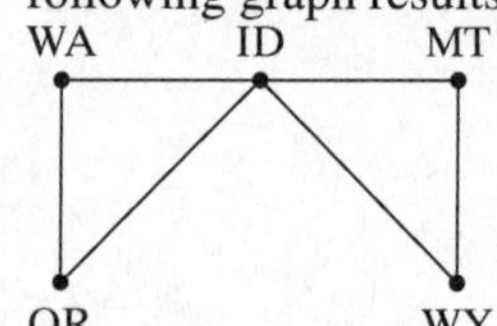

15.

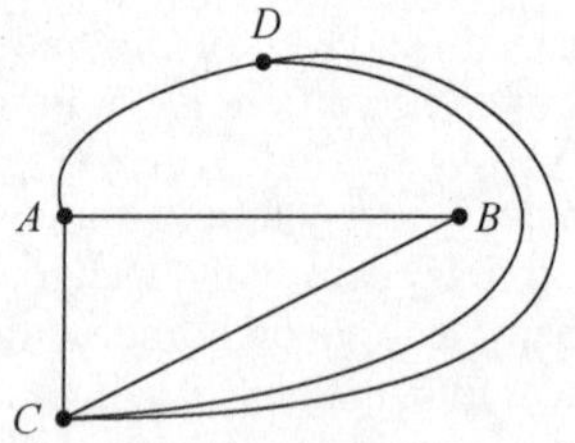

17.

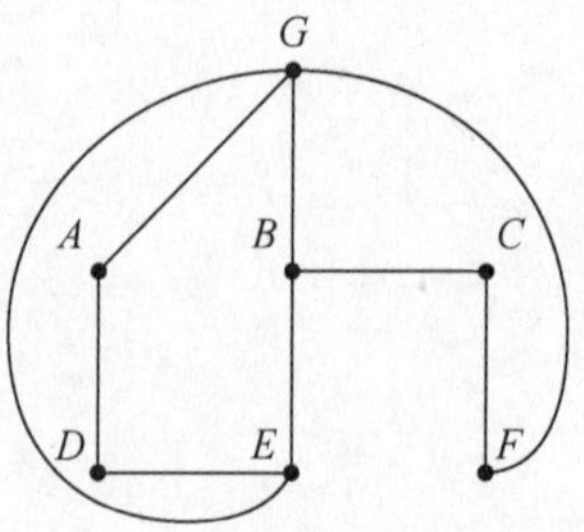

19.

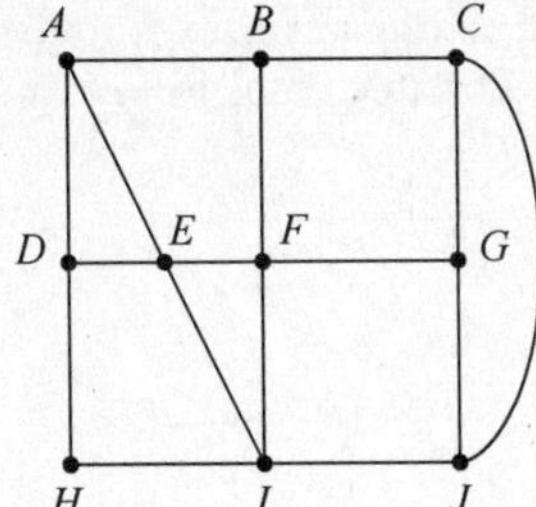

21.

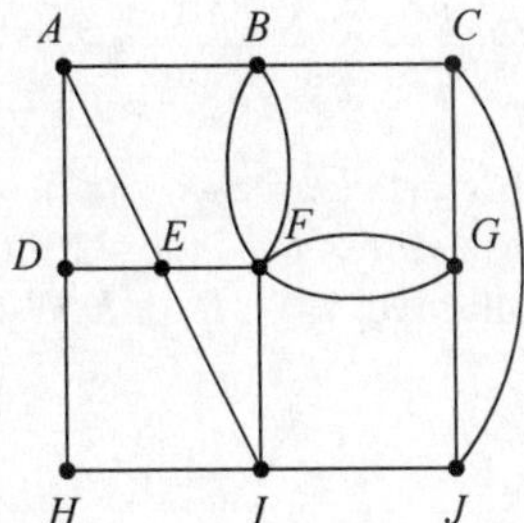

23. The degree of a vertex is the number of edges at that vertex. Thus, vertex *A* has degree 2, vertex *B* has degree 2, vertex *C* has degree 3, vertex *D* has degree 3, vertex *E* has degree 3, and vertex *F* has degree 1. (The loop at *E* counts for 2.)

25. Vertices *B* and *C* each have an edge connecting to *A*, so *B* and *C* are adjacent to *A*.

27. Starting at vertex *A*, we proceed to vertex *C*, then vertex *D*. This is one path from *A* to *D*. For a second path, start at vertex *A*, then proceed to vertex *B*, then *C*, then *D*.

29. The edges not included are the edge connecting *A* to *C*, and the edge connecting *D* to *F*.

31. While edge *CD* is included, the graph is connected. If we remove *CD*, the graph will be disconnected. Thus, *CD* is a bridge.

33. Edge *DF* is also a bridge. With it, the graph is connected. If *DF* is removed, vertex *F* stands alone, so the graph is disconnected.

35. Vertices *A, B, G, H,* and *I* each have two attached edges, which is an even number of edges. Thus *A, B, G, H,* and *I* are even vertices. Vertex *C* has five attached edges, vertex *E* has one, and vertices *D* and *F* have three. These are odd numbers of edges. Thus *C, E, D,* and *F* are odd vertices.

37. Vertex *F* has edges connecting to vertices *D, G,* and *I*. Thus *D, G,* and *I* are adjacent to *F*.

39. Begin at vertex *B*. Proceed to vertex *C*, then vertex *D*, then vertex *F*. This is one path from *B* to *F*. For a second path, begin at *B*, then proceed to *A*, then *C*, then *D*, then *F*.

41. Begin at vertex *G*. proceed to vertex *F*, then vertex *I*, then vertex *H*, then vertex *G*. This is a circuit. (The counterclockwise order also works.)

43. Begin at vertex *A*. Proceed to vertex *B*, then vertex *C*, then around the loop to *C* again, then vertex *D*, then vertex *F*, then vertex *G*, then vertex *H*, then vertex *I*.

45. *G, F, D, E, D* requires that edge *DE* be traversed twice. This is not allowed within a path.

47. *H, I, F, E* is not a path because no edge connects vertices *F* and *E*.

49. Possible answer:

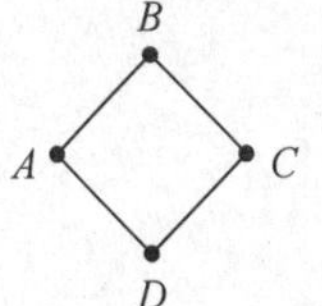

Each vertex has degree 2.

51. Possible answer:

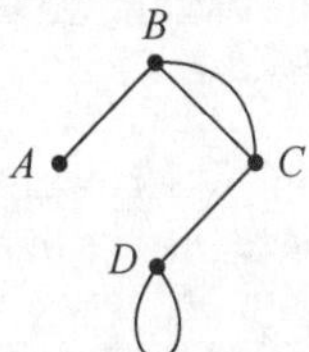

Vertex *A* has degree 1, and the rest have degree 3.

67. makes sense

69. does not make sense; Explanations will vary. Sample explanation: All circuits are paths.

71. Use vertices to represent the six members.

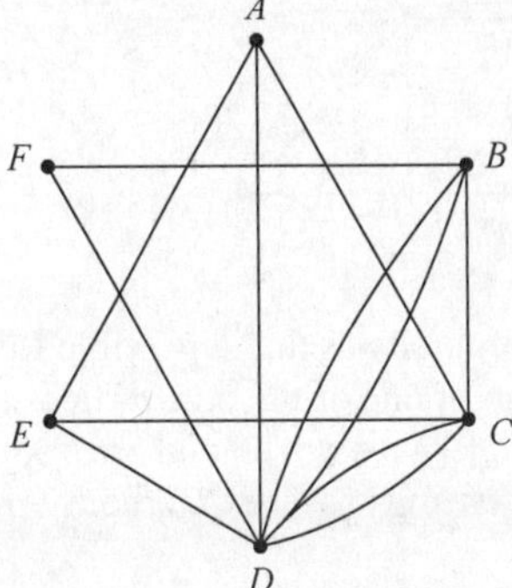

Check Points 14.2

1. We use trial and error to find one such path. The following figure shows a result.

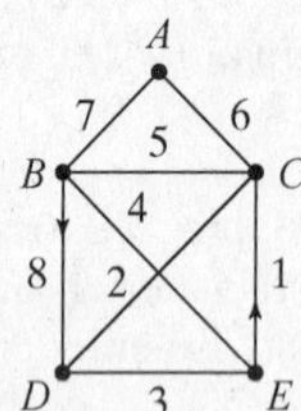

Using vertex letters to name the path, we write *E, C, D, E, B, C, A, B, D*.

2. We use trial and error to find an Euler circuit that starts at *G*. The following figure shows a result.

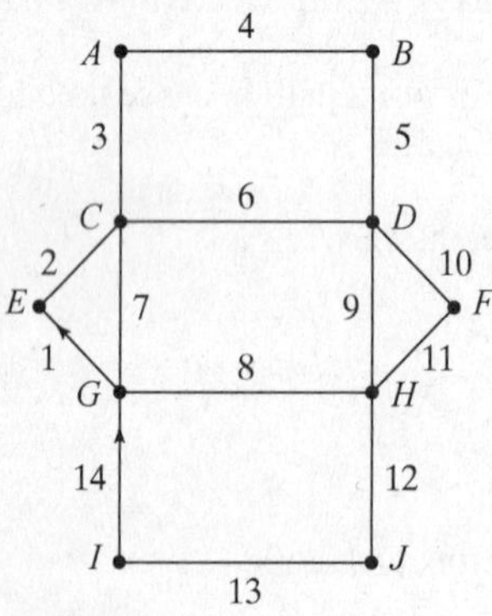

Using vertex letters to name the circuit, we write *G, E, C, A, B, D, C, G, H, D, F, H, J, I, G*.

3. a. A walk through every room and the outside, using each door exactly once, means that we are looking for an Euler path or Euler circuit on the graph in Figure 14.34(b). This graph has exactly two odd vertices, namely *B* and *E*. By Euler's theorem, the graph has at least one Euler path, but no Euler circuit. It is possible to walk through every room and the outside, using each door exactly once. It is not possible to begin and end the walk in the same place.

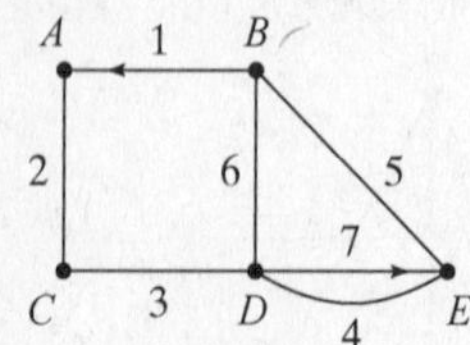

b. Euler's theorem tells us that a possible Euler path must start at one of the odd vertices and end at the other. We use trial and error to find such a path, starting at vertex *B* (room *B* in the floor plan), and ending at vertex *E* (outside in the floor plan) Possible paths follow.

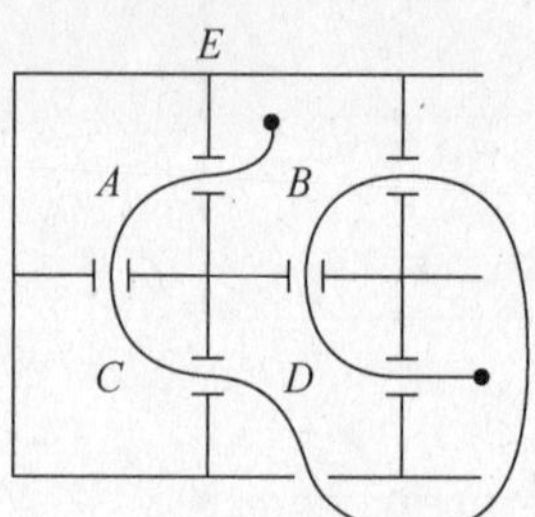

4. The graph has no odd vertices, so we can begin at any vertex. We choose vertex *C* as the starting point. From *C* we can travel to *A*, *B*, or *D*. We choose to travel to *D*.

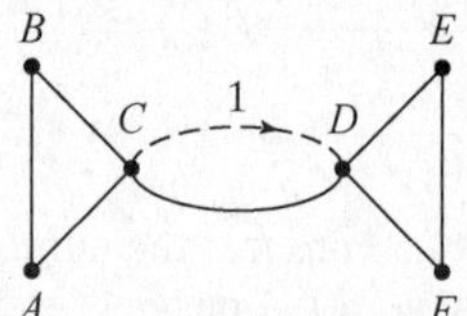

Now the remaining edge *CD* is a bridge, so we must travel to either *E* or *F*. We choose *F*.

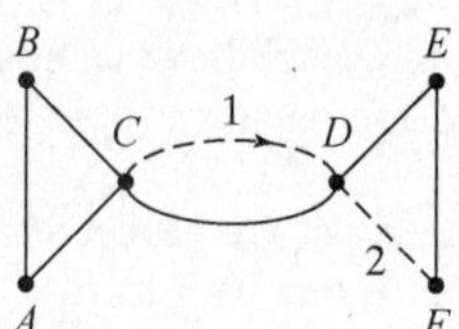

We have no choices for our next three steps, which are bridges. We must travel to *E*, then *D*, then *C*.

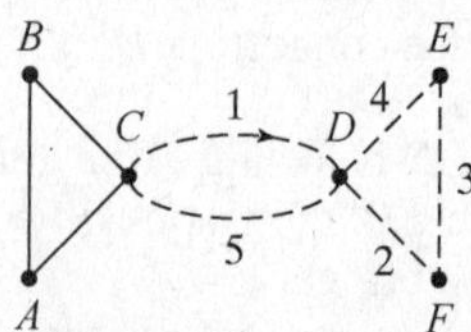

From *C*, we may travel to either *A* or *B*. We choose *B*. Then we must travel to *A*, then back to *C*.

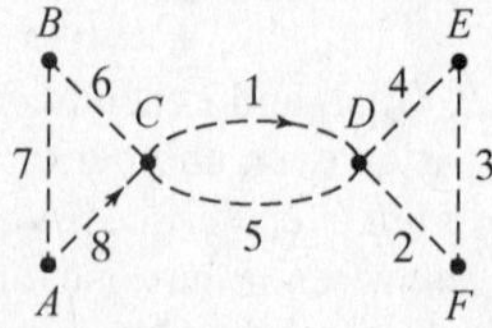

The above figure shows the completed Euler circuit. Written using the letters of the vertices, the path is *C, D, F, E, D, C, B, A, C*.

Concept and Vocabulary Check 14.2

1. Euler
2. Euler
3. two
4. no; any
5. odd
6. *E*; *E*; *D*
7. Fleury's; bridge
8. true
9. false
10. false

Exercise Set 14.2

1.

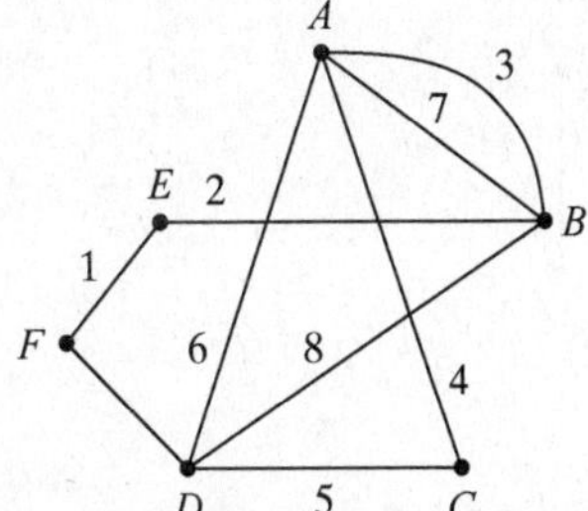

This path does not include edge *FD*, so it is neither an Euler path nor an Euler circuit.

3.

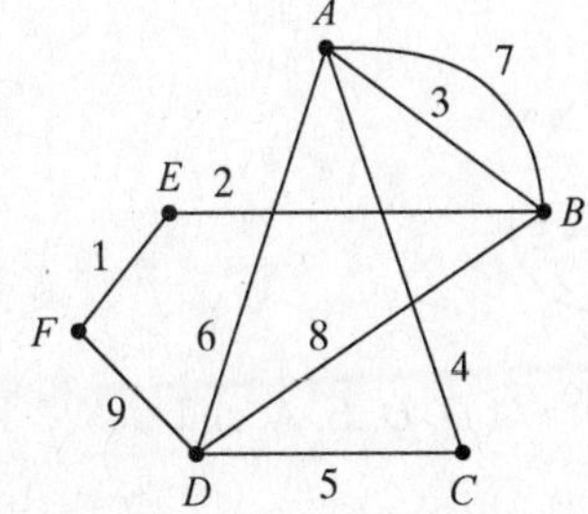

This path travels through each edge of the graph once, and only once. It begins and ends at *F*. Therefore, it is an Euler circuit.

5.

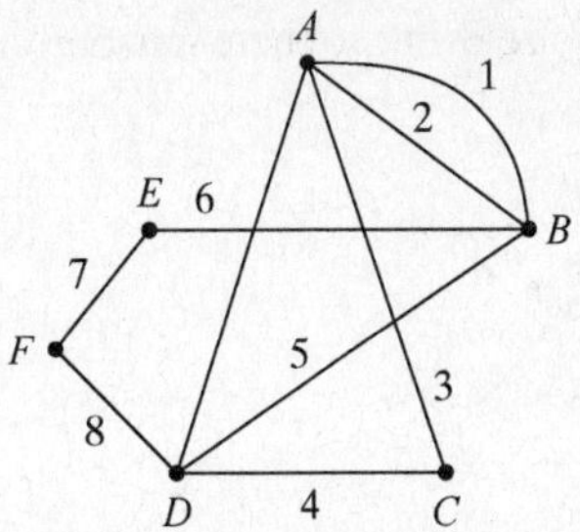

This path does not include edge *AD*, so it is neither an Euler path nor an Euler circuit.

7. **a.** There are exactly two odd vertices, namely *A* and *B*, so by Euler's theorem there is at least one Euler path.

   b.

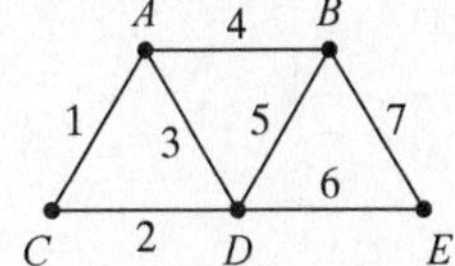

This path begins at *A* and ends at *B*.

9. **a.** There are no odd vertices, so by Euler's theorem, there is at least one Euler circuit.

   b.

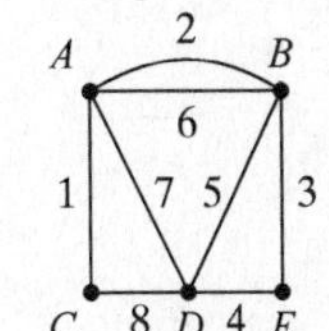

This circuit begins and ends at *C*.

11. There are more than two odd vertices, namely *B, D, G,* and *K*. Therefore by Euler's theorem, there are no Euler paths and no Euler circuits.

13. Since the graph has no odd vertices, it must have an Euler circuit, by Euler's theorem.

15. Since the graph has exactly two odd vertices, it has an Euler path, but no Euler circuit, by Euler's theorem.

17. Since the graph has more than two odd vertices, it has neither an Euler path nor an Euler circuit, by Euler's theorem.

19. a. All vertices are even, so there must be an Euler circuit.

b.

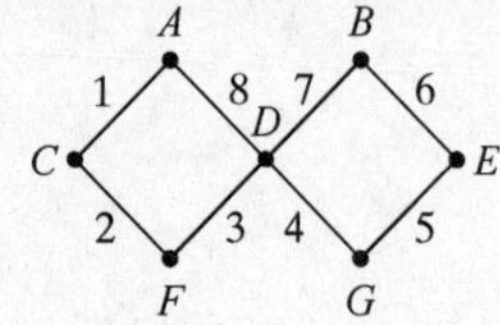

21. a. There are exactly two odd vertices, so there must be an Euler path.

b.

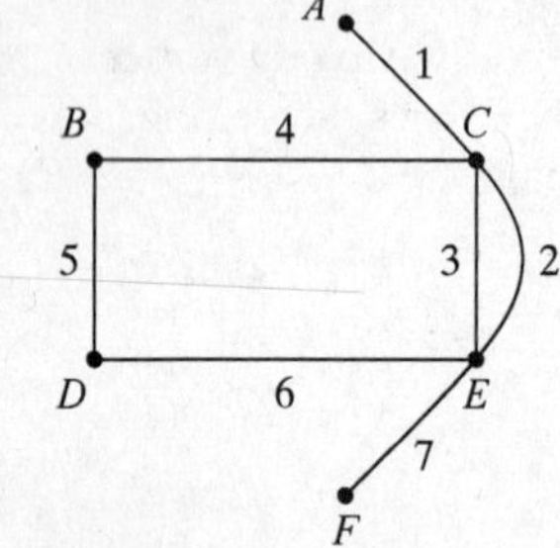

23. a. There are more than two odd vertices, so there is neither an Euler path nor an Euler circuit.

25. a. There are exactly two odd vertices, so there is an Euler path.

b.

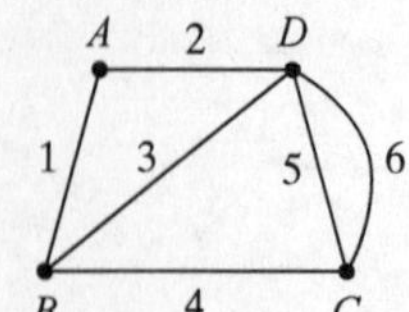

27. a. There are no odd vertices, so there is an Euler circuit.

b.

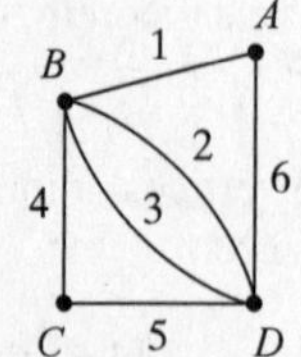

29. a. There are more than two odd vertices, so there is neither an Euler path nor an Euler circuit.

31. a. There are exactly two odd vertices, so there is an Euler path.

b.

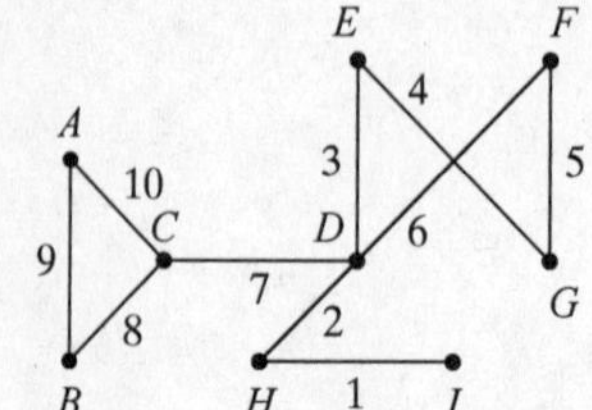

33. The two odd vertices in the graph are A and C. We start with A, so we must progress next to B. From B, we may travel to C, D, or E. We choose C.

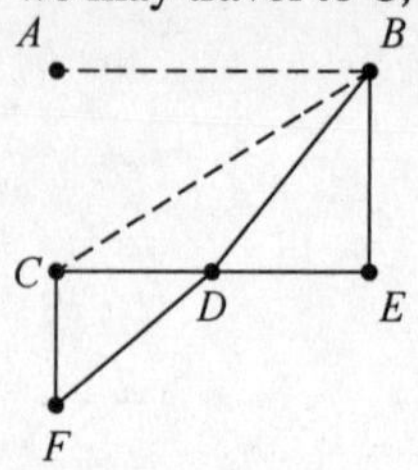

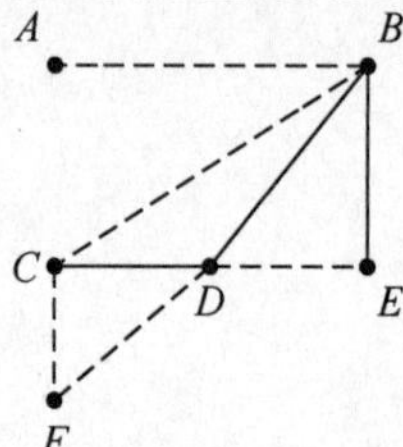

Next we travel to F, then D, then E.

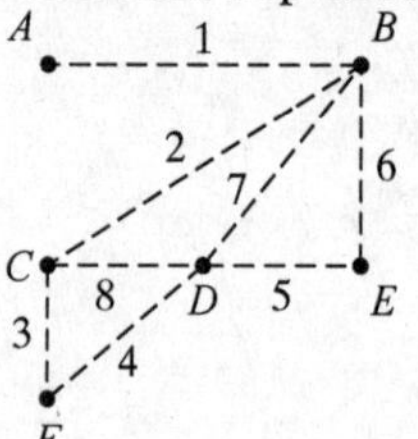

Finally we travel to B, then D, and last, to C. We label each step taken.

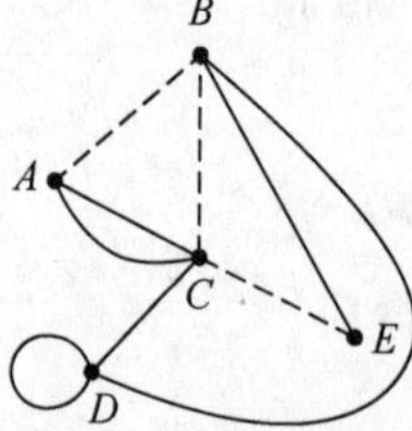

35. The two odd vertices in the graph are A and C. We start with A, then travel to B, C, and E.

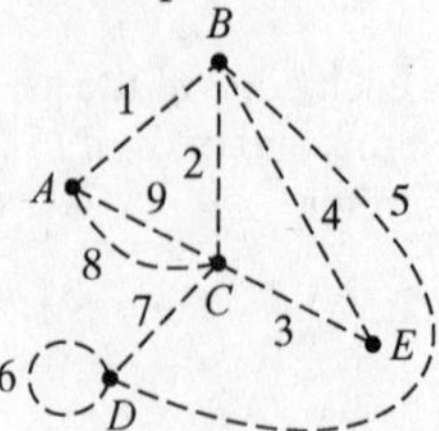

We continue on to B, D, D, C, A, and C. We label each step taken.

37. We begin with *A*, and travel to *D, H, G, F, E, B,* and *C.*

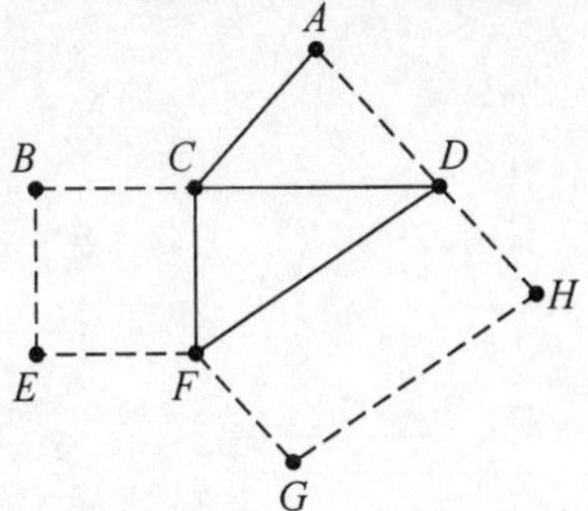

We continue on to *F, D, C,* and back to *A*. We label each step.

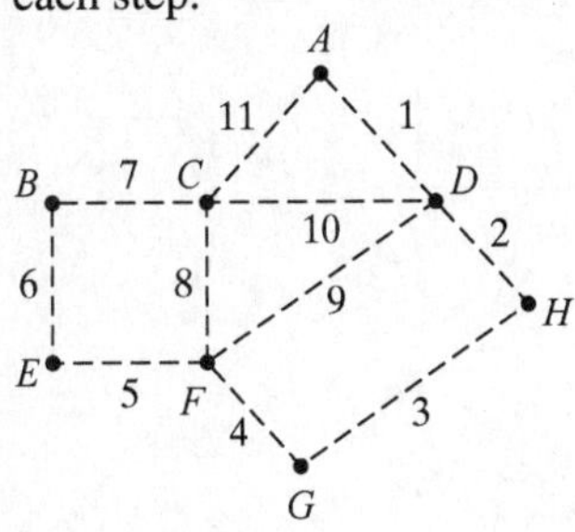

39. We begin with *A*, and travel to *C, G, K, H, I, L, J, F, B, E,* and *D.*

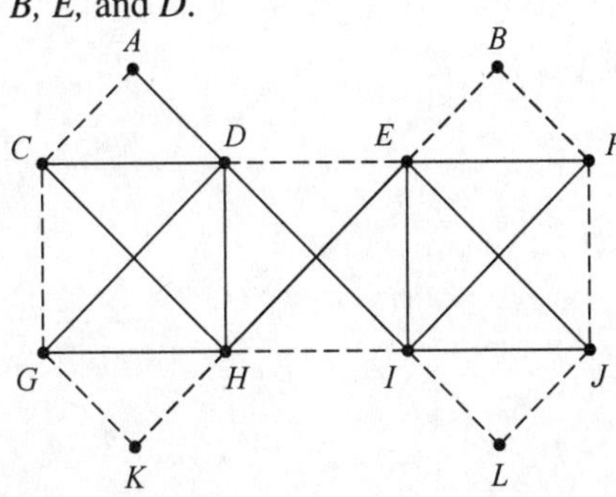

We continue on to *C, H, G, D, H, E, F, I, J, E, I, D,* and back to *A*. We label each step.

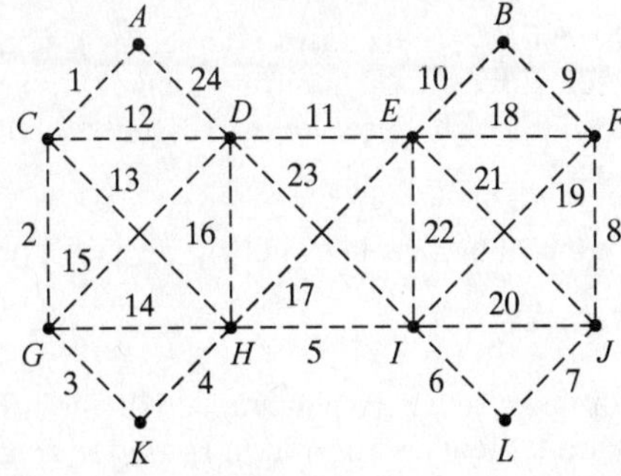

41. a. Remove *FG*.

b. Sample Euler circuit: *EC, CB, BD, DF, FA, AD, DG, GH, HC, CG, GB, BH, HE*

43. a. Remove *BA* and *FJ*.

b. Sample Euler circuit: *CA, AD, DI, IH, HG, GF, FC, CD, DE, EH, HJ, JG, GB, BC*

45. The graph that models the neighborhood has no odd vertices, so an Euler circuit exists with any vertex, including *B*, as the starting point.

47.

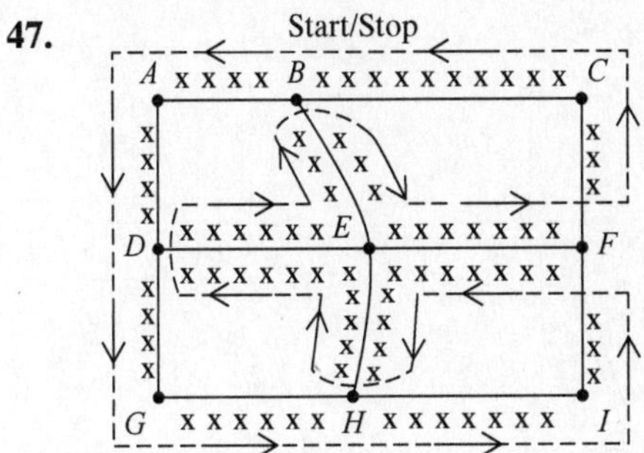

49. a.

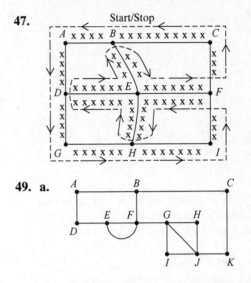

A B C
E F G H
D
I J K

b. There are exactly two odd vertices, namely *E* and *B*. Therefore the guard should begin at one of these vertices and end at the other.

51. a. Label the vertices *N* for North Bank, *S* for South Bank, and *A* and *B* for the two islands. Draw edges to represent bridges.

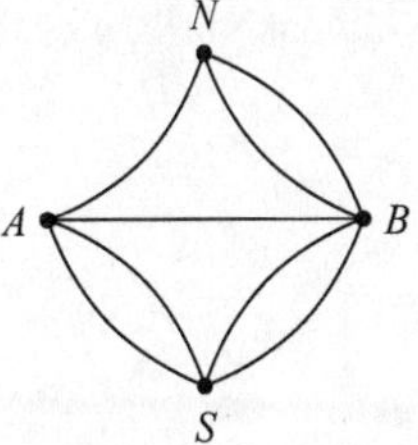

b. The graph has exactly two odd vertices, *N* and *B*, so residents can walk across all the bridges without crossing the same bridge twice.

c.

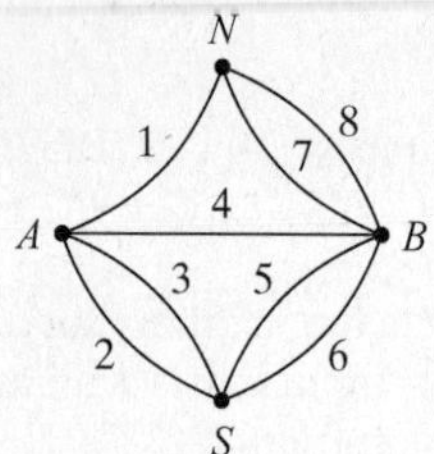

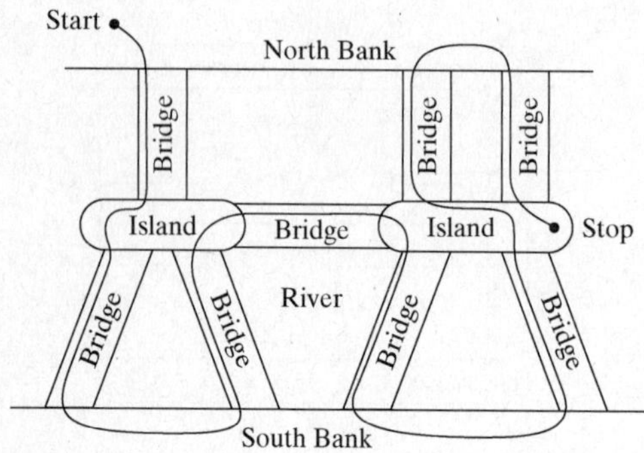

53. Use NJ to label the New Jersey vertex, M for Manhattan, SI for Staten Island, and LI for Long Island. Each edge represents a bridge.

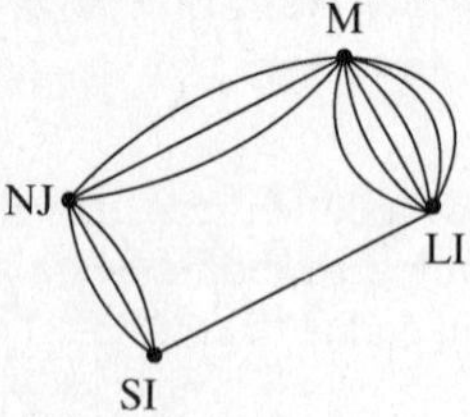

There are exactly two odd vertices, M and LI, so the graph has an Euler path. Therefore it is possible to visit each location, using each bridge or tunnel exactly once.

55. a.

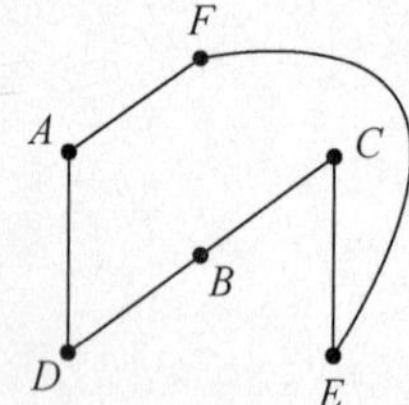

b. There are no odd vertices, so the graph has an Euler circuit. Therefore, it is possible to walk through each room and the outside, using each door exactly once.

c.

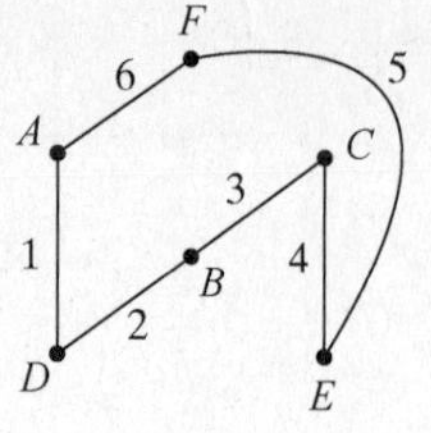

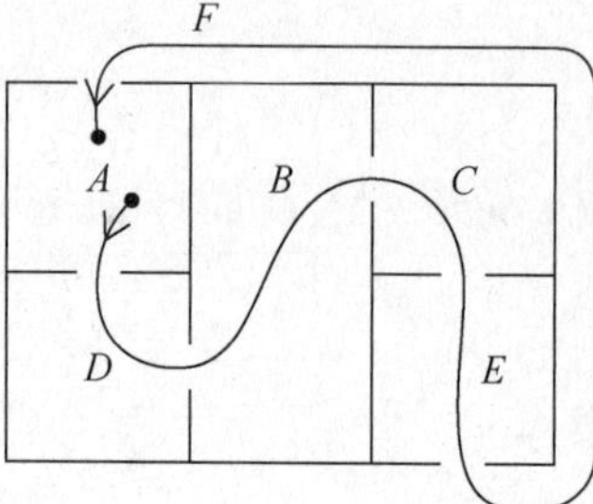

57.

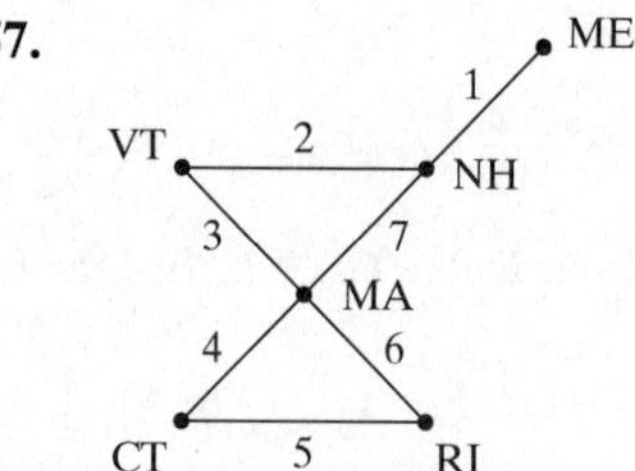

59. a.

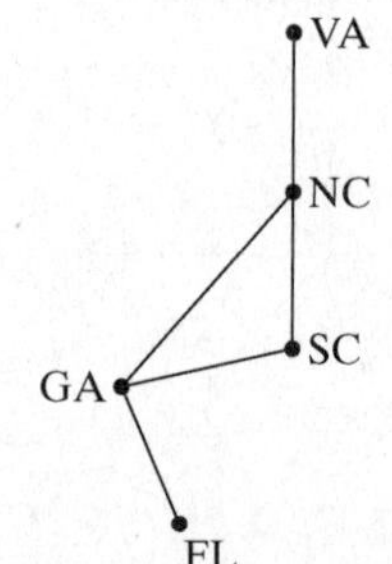

b. There are more than two odd vertices, so no Euler path exists. Therefore it is not possible to travel through these states, crossing each border exactly once.

d. For the same reason as in (b), this is not possible.

69. makes sense

71. does not make sense; Explanations will vary. Sample explanation: Fleury's Algorithm is used to find Euler paths or Euler circuits, not to determine if they exist.

Check Points 14.3

1. **a.** A Hamilton path must pass through each vertex exactly once. The graph has many Hamilton paths. An example of such a path is *E, C, D, G, B, A, F*.

   b. A Hamilton circuit must pass through every vertex exactly once and begin and end at the same vertex. The graph has many Hamilton circuits. An example of such a circuit is *E, C, D, G, B, F, A, E*.

2. In each case, we use the expression $(n-1)!$. For three vertices, substitute 3 for n in the expression. For six and ten vertices, substitute 6 and 10, respectively, for n.

   a. A complete graph with three vertices has $(3-1)! = 2! = 2\cdot 1 = 2$ Hamilton circuits.

   b. A complete graph with six vertices has $(6-1)! = 5! = 5\cdot 4\cdot 3\cdot 2\cdot 1 = 120$ Hamilton circuits.

   c. A complete graph with ten vertices has $(10-1)! = 9! = 9\cdot 8\cdot 7\cdot 6\cdot 5\cdot 4\cdot 3\cdot 2\cdot 1 = 362{,}880$ Hamilton circuits.

3. The trip described by the Hamilton circuit *A, C, B, D, A* involves the sum of four costs:

   \$124 + \$126 + \$155 + \$157 = \$562.

   Here, \$124 is the cost of the trip from *A* to *C*; \$126 is the cost from *C* to *B*; \$155 is the cost from *B* to *D*; and \$157 is the cost from *D* to *A*. The total cost of the trip is \$562.

4. The graph has four vertices. Thus, using $(n-1)!$, there are $(4-1)! = 3! = 6$ possible Hamilton circuits. The 6 possible Hamilton circuits and their costs are shown.

Hamilton Circuit	Sum of the Weights of the Edges	=	Total Cost
A, B, C, D, A	20 + 15 + 50 + 30	=	\$115
A, B, D, C, A	20 + 10 + 50 + 70	=	\$150
A, C, B, D, A	70 + 15 + 10 + 30	=	\$125
A, C, D, B, A	70 + 50 + 10 + 20	=	\$150
A, D, B, C, A	30 + 10 + 15 + 70	=	\$125
A, D, C, B, A	30 + 50 + 15 + 20	=	\$115

   The two Hamilton circuits having the lowest cost of \$115 are *A, B, C, D, A* and *A, D, C, B, A*.

5. The Nearest Neighbor method is carried out as follows:

   - Start at *A*.
   - Choose the edge with the smallest weight: 13. Move along this edge to *B*.
   - From *B*, choose the edge with the smallest weight that does not lead to *A*: 5. Move along this edge to *C*.
   - From *C*, choose the edge with the smallest weight that does not lead to a city already visited: 12. Move along this edge to *D*.
   - From *D*, the only choice is to fly to *E*, the only city not yet visited: 154.
   - From *E*, close the circuit and return home to *A*: 14.

   An approximate solution is the Hamilton circuit *A, B, C, D, E, A*. The total weight is $13 + 5 + 12 + 154 + 14 = 198$.

Concept and Vocabulary Check 14.3

1. Hamilton; Hamilton
2. complete; $(n-1)!$
3. weighted; weights; traveling; optimal
4. Brute Force
5. Nearest Neighbor; weight
6. false
7. false
8. false

Exercise Set 14.3

1. One such path is *A, G, C, F, E, D, B*.

3. One such circuit is *A, B, G, C, F, E, D, A*.

5. One such path is *A, F, G, E, C, B, D*.

7. One such circuit is *A, B, C, E, G, F, D, A*.

9. **a.** This graph is not complete. For example, no edge connects *A* and *B*. Therefore it may not have Hamilton circuits.

11. **a.** This graph is complete: there is an edge between each pair of vertices. Therefore it must have Hamilton circuits.

    b. There are 6 vertices, so the number of Hamilton circuits is $(6 - 1)! = 5! = 120$.

13. **a.** This graph is not complete. For example, no edge connects *G* and *F*. Therefore it may not have Hamilton circuits.

15. $(3 - 1)! = 2! = 2$

17. $(12 - 1)! = 11! = 39{,}916{,}800$

19. 11

21. $9 + 8 + 11 + 6 + 2 = 36$

23. $9 + 7 + 6 + 11 + 3 = 36$

25. $40 + 24 + 10 + 14 = 88$

27. $20 + 24 + 12 + 14 = 70$

29. $14 + 12 + 24 + 20 = 70$

31. On a complete graph with four vertices, there are 6 distinct Hamilton circuits. These are listed in Exercises 25–30. We have already computed the weight of each possible Hamilton circuit, as required by the Brute Force Method. The optimal solutions have the smallest weight, 70. They are *A, C, B, D, A*, and *A, D, B, C, A*.

33. Starting from *B*, the edge with smallest weight is *BD*, with weight 12. Therefore, proceed to *D*. From *D*, the edge having smallest weight and not leading back to *B* is *DC*, with weight 10. From *C*, our only choice is *CA*, with weight 20. From *A*, return to *B*. Edge *AB* has weight 40. The total weight of the Hamilton circuit is
$12 + 10 + 20 + 40 = 82$.

35. a. Add *AB*
Number of Hamilton circuits: $(4-1)! = 3! = 6$

b. Sample Hamilton circuit: *AD, DB, BC, CA*
Sample Hamilton circuit: *CA, AB, BD, DC*

c. Remove *CD*

d. Sample Euler circuit: *AC, CB, BD, DA*

37. a. Add *AB, AC, BC,* and *DE*
Number of Hamilton circuits: $(5-1)! = 4! = 24$

b. Sample Hamilton circuit: *AB, BC, CE, ED, DA*
Sample Hamilton circuit: *AB, BC, CD, DE, EA*

c. Remove *BD* and *BE*

d. Sample Euler circuit: *AE, EC, CD, DA*

39.

Hamilton Circuit	Sum of the Weights of the Edges	=	Total Weight
A, B, C, D, E, A	500 + 305 + 320 + 302 + 205	=	1632
A, B, C, E, D, A	500 + 305 + 165 + 302 + 185	=	1457
A, B, D, C, E, A	500 + 360 + 320 + 165 + 205	=	1550
A, B, D, E, C, A	500 + 360 + 302 + 165 + 200	=	1527
A, B, E, C, D, A	500 + 340 + 165 + 320 + 185	=	1510
A, B, E, D, C, A	500 + 340 + 302 + 320 + 200	=	1662
A, C, B, D, E, A	200 + 305 + 360 + 302 + 205	=	1372
A, C, B, E, D, A	200 + 305 + 340 + 302 + 185	=	1332
A, C, D, B, E, A	200 + 320 + 360 + 340 + 205	=	1425
A, C, E, B, D, A	200 + 165 + 340 + 360 + 185	=	1250
A, D, B, C, E, A	185 + 360 + 305 + 165 + 205	=	1220
A, D, C, B, E, A	185 + 320 + 305 + 340 + 205	=	1355

Using the Brute Force method, we compute the sum of the weights of the edges for each possible Hamilton circuit, as in the table above. The smallest weight sum is 1220, representing a total cost of $1220 for airfare. This results from the Hamilton circuit *A, D, B, C, E, A*. Thus, the sales director should fly to the cities in this order.

41.

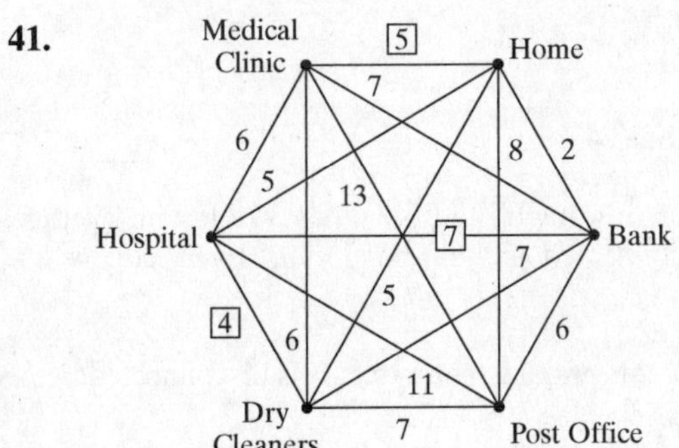

43. $2 + 6 + 7 + 4 + 6 + 5 = 30$

45. Label the vertices H for Home, B for Bank, P for Post Office, and M for Market.

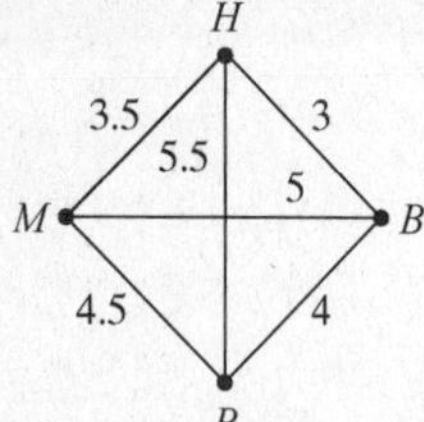

47. From Home, the closest errand is the Bank, 3 miles away. From the Bank, the closest remaining errand is the Post Office, 4 miles away. From the Post Office, the last remaining errand is the Market, 4.5 miles away. From the Market, Home is 3.5 miles away. The total distance for this Hamilton circuit is $3 + 4 + 4.5 + 3.5 = 15$ miles. This is the same route found in Exercise 46.

61. does not make sense; Explanations will vary. Sample explanation: Even the fastest existing super computer could not do that task in one evening.

63. makes sense

Check Points 14.4

1. The graph in Figure 14.51(c) is a tree. It is connected and has no circuits. There is only one path joining any two vertices. Every edge is a bridge; if removed, each edge would create a disconnected graph. Finally, the graph has 7 vertices and $7 - 1$, or 6, edges.

The graph in Figure 14.51(a) is not a tree because it is disconnected. There are 7 vertices and only 5 edges, not the 6 edges required for a tree.

The graph in Figure 14.51(b) is not a tree because it has a circuit, namely *A, B, C, D, A*. There are 7 vertices and 7 edges, not the 6 edges required for a tree.

2. A spanning tree must contain all six vertices shown in the connected graph in Figure 14.55. The spanning tree must have one edge less than it has vertices, so it must have five edges. The graph in Figure 14.55 has eight edges, so we must remove three edges. We elect to remove the edges of the circuit *C, D, E, C*. This leaves us the following spanning tree.

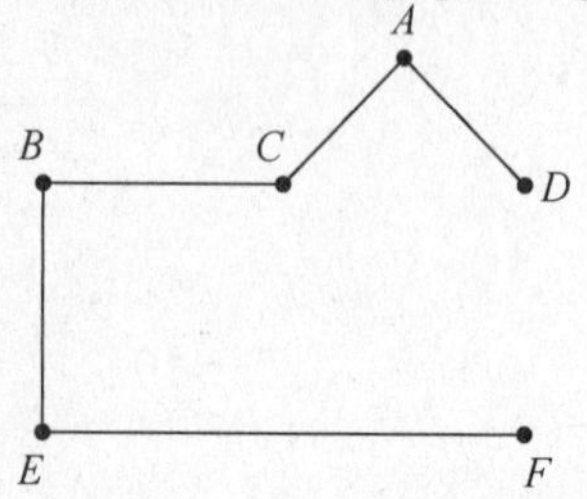

3. Step 1. Find the edge with the smallest weight. This is edge DE; mark it.

Step 2. Find the next-smallest edge in the graph. This is edge DC; mark it.

Step 3. Find the next-smallest edge in the graph that does not create a circuit. This is edge DA; mark it.

Step 4. Find the next-smallest edge in the graph that does not create a circuit. This is AB; mark it.

The resulting minimum spanning tree is complete. It contains all 5 vertices of the graph, and has $5 - 1$, or 4, edges. Its total weight is $12 + 14 + 21 + 22 = 69$. It is shown below.

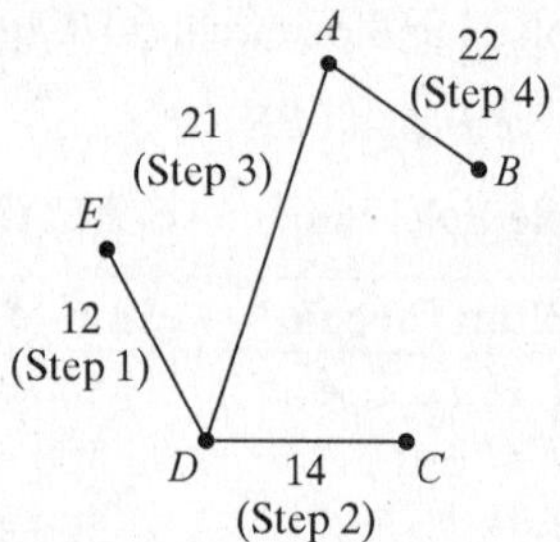

Concept and Vocabulary Check 14.4

1. tree; bridge; $n-1$

2. spanning

3. minimum spanning

4. Kruskal's; weight; circuits

5. false

6. true

Exercise Set 14.4

1. Yes, this graph is a tree. It has 3 edges on 4 vertices, is connected, and has no circuits. Every edge is a bridge.

3. No, this graph is not a tree. It is disconnected.

5. Yes, this graph is a tree. It has 3 edges on 4 vertices, is connected, and has no circuits. Every edge is a bridge.

7. No, this graph is not a tree. It has a circuit.

9. Yes, this graph is a tree. It has 6 edges on 7 vertices, is connected, and has no circuits. Every edge is a bridge.

11. i; If the graph contained any circuits, some points would have more than one path joining them.

13. ii; A tree with n vertices must have $n - 1$ edges.

15. iii

17.

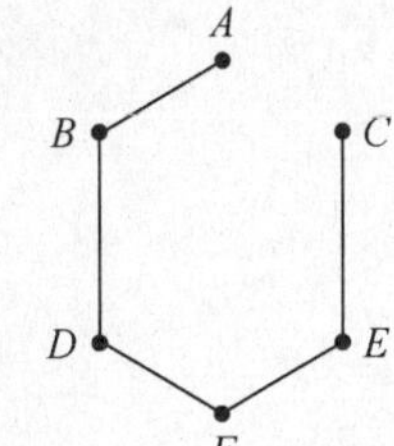

19.

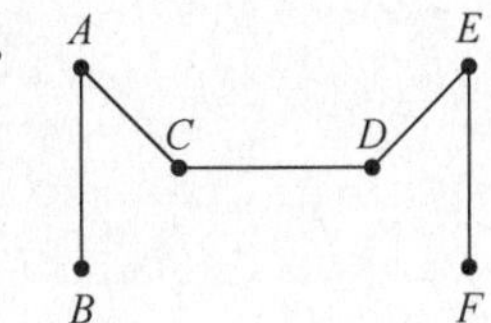

21.

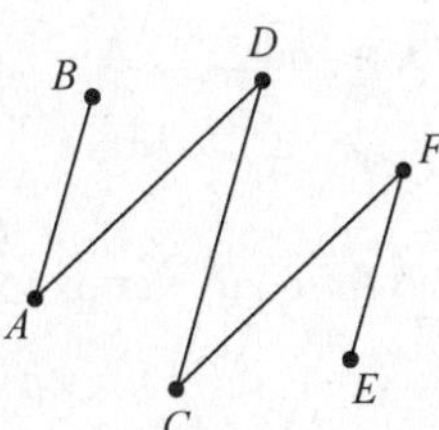

23. Kruskal's algorithm results in the following figure.

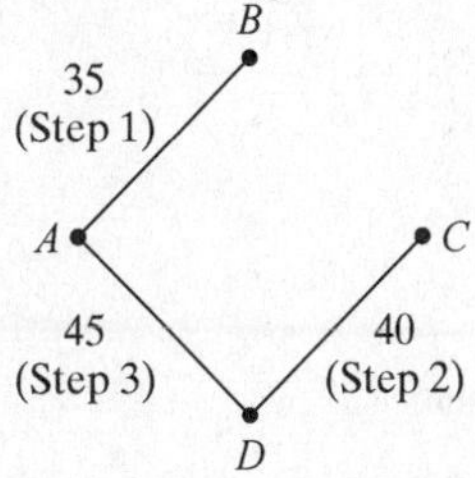

This minimum spanning tree has weight $35 + 40 + 45 = 120$.

25. Kruskal's algorithm results in the following figure.

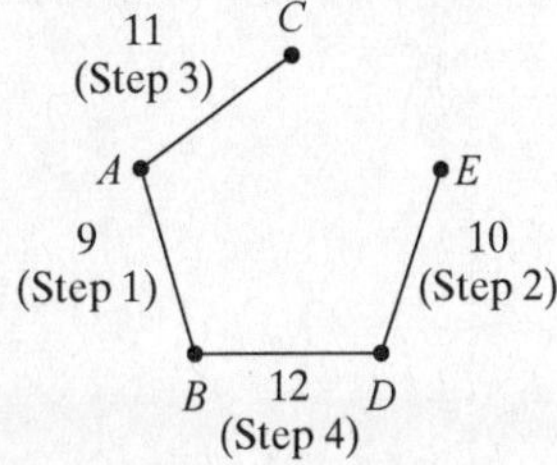

This minimum spanning tree has weight $9 + 10 + 11 + 12 = 42$.

27. Kruskal's algorithm results in the following figure.

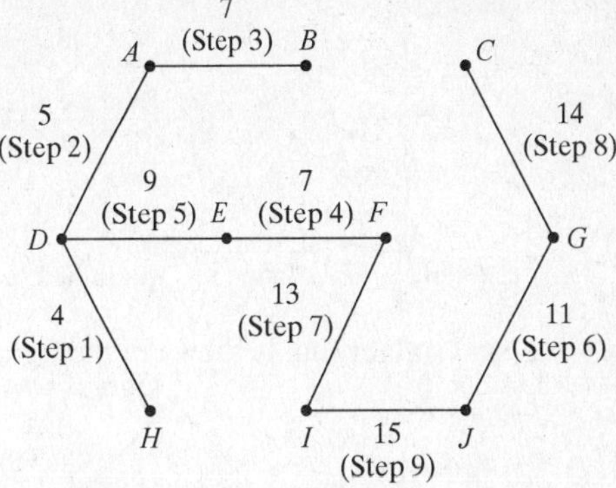

This minimum spanning tree has weight $4 + 5 + 7 + 7 + 9 + 11 + 13 + 14 + 15 = 85$.

29. Kruskal's algorithm results in the following figure.

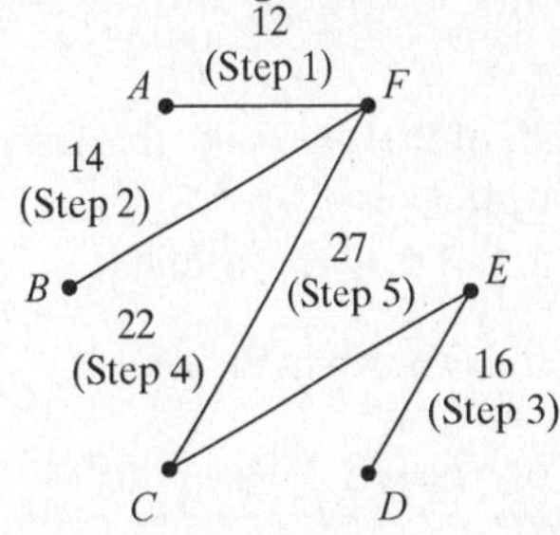

This minimum spanning tree has weight $12 + 14 + 16 + 22 + 27 = 91$.

31. Sample Spanning Tree: *AB*, *AC*, *CD*
Sample Spanning Tree: *AB*, *BC*, *CD*
Sample Spanning Tree: *AB*, *AD*, *CD*
Sample Spanning Tree: *AB*, *AD*, *BC*

33. Maximum Spanning Tree: *AE*, *BC*, *CD*, *CE*

Total weight is $\underbrace{15}_{AE} + \underbrace{14}_{BC} + \underbrace{18}_{CD} + \underbrace{17}_{CE} = 64$

35. Sample Maximum Spanning Tree: *AE*, *BC*, *BE*, *CF*, *DE*, *EH*, *FG*, *FJ*, *HI*
Total weight is

$$\underbrace{10}_{AE} + \underbrace{16}_{BC} + \underbrace{15}_{BE} + \underbrace{17}_{CF} + \underbrace{9}_{DE} + \underbrace{17}_{EH} + \underbrace{16}_{FG} + \underbrace{19}_{FJ} + \underbrace{22}_{HI} = 141$$

37.

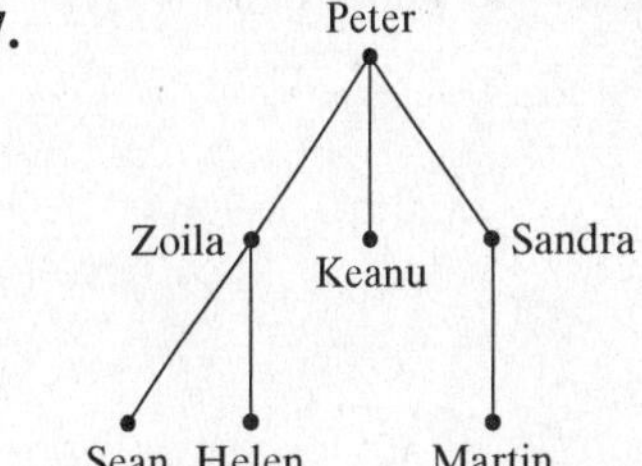

39. a.

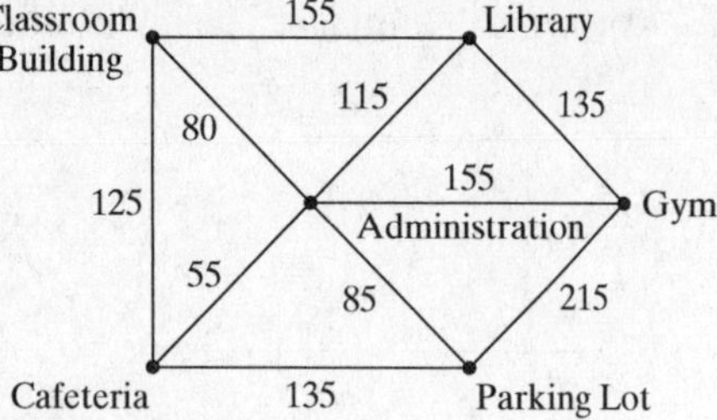

b. Kruskal's algorithm is shown in the figure.

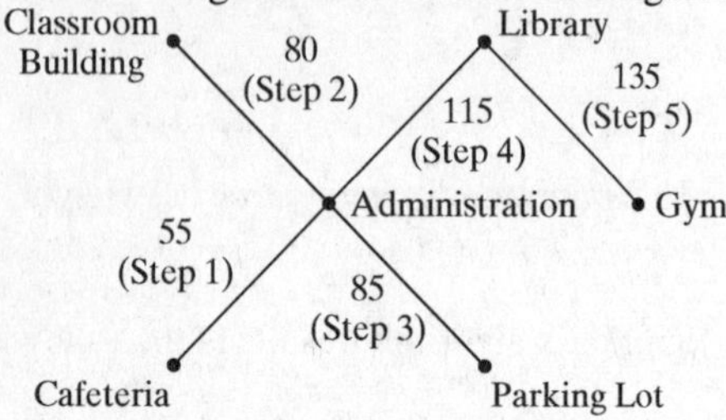

The total length of the sidewalks that need to be sheltered by awnings is
55 + 80 + 85 + 115 + 135 = 470 feet.

41. Kruskal's algorithm is shown in the figure.

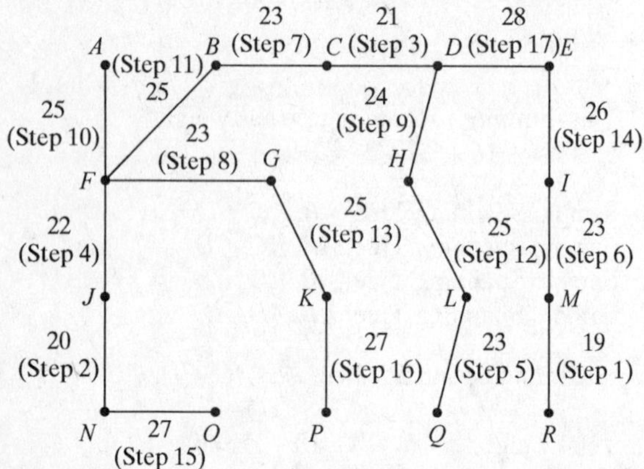

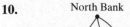

The smallest number of feet of underground pipes is
19 + 20 + 21 + 22 + 23 + 23 + 23 + 23 + 24 + 25 + 25 + 25 + 25 + 26 + 27 + 27 + 28 = 406 feet.

53. does not make sense; Explanations will vary. Sample explanation: You want a minimum *circuit*.

55. makes sense

Chapter 14 Review Exercises

1. Each graph has 5 vertices, *A, B, C, D,* and *E*. Each has one edge connecting *A* and *B*, one connecting *A* and *C*, one connecting *A* and *D*, one connecting *A* and *E*, and one connecting *B* and *C*. Both graphs have the same number of vertices, and these vertices are connected in the same ways. A third way to draw the same graph is

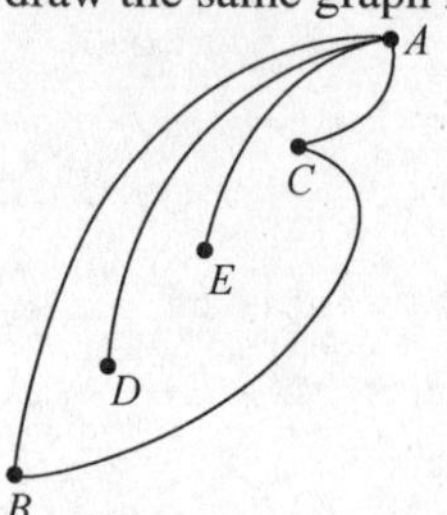

2. *A*: 5 (A loop adds degree 2.); *B*: 4; *C*: 5; *D*: 4; *E*: 2

3. Even: *B, D, E*; odd: *A, C*

4. *B, C,* and *E*

5. Possible answer: *E, D, B, A* and *E, C, A*

6. Possible answer: *E, D, C, E*

7. Yes. A path can be found from any vertex to any other vertex.

8. No. There is no edge which can be removed to leave a disconnected graph.

9. *AD, DE,* and *DF*

10.

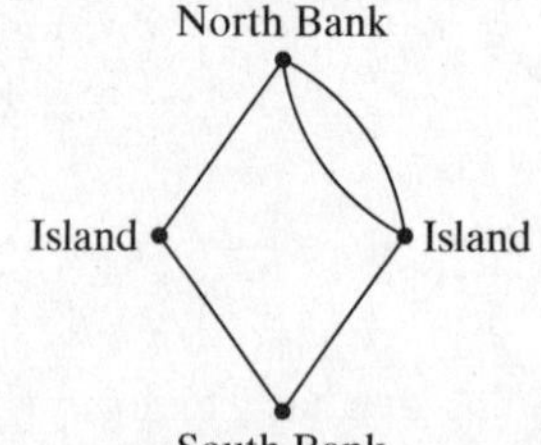

11. Use the states' abbreviations to label the vertices representing them.

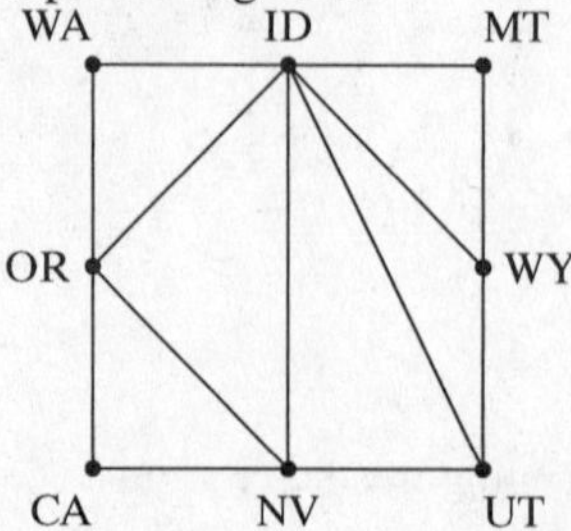

12.

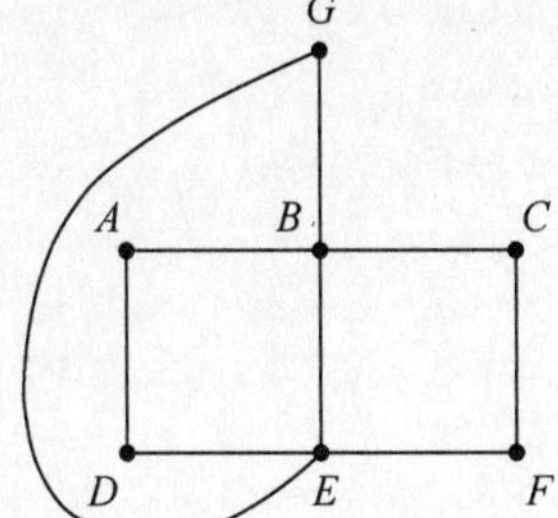

13. a. Neither. There are more than two odd vertices.

14. a. Euler circuit: there are no odd vertices.

b.

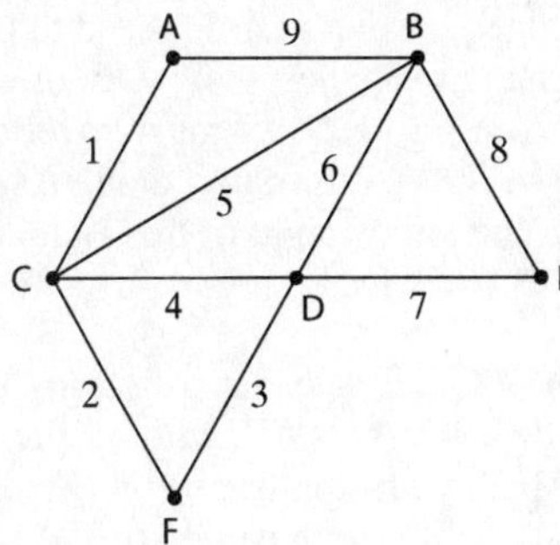

15. a. Euler path: there are exactly two odd vertices.

b.

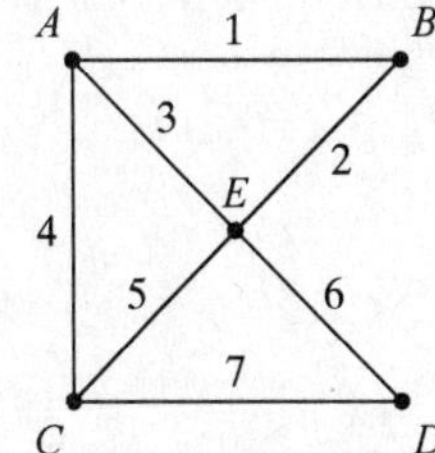

16. There are exactly two odd vertices, G and I. We start at G and continue to D, A, B, C, F, I, H, and E.

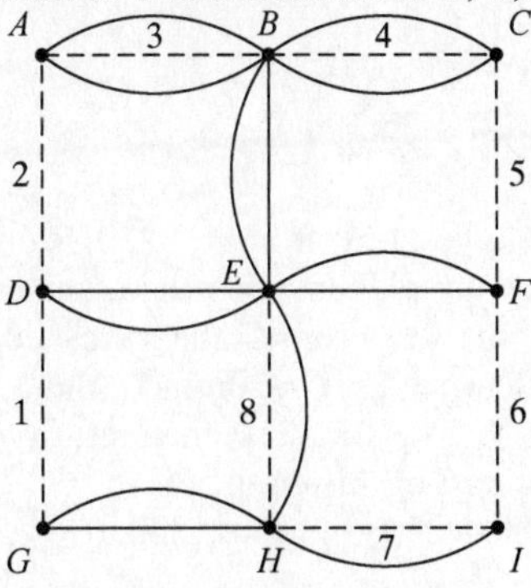

We continue erasing edges as we go, till we have completed an Euler path ending at I.

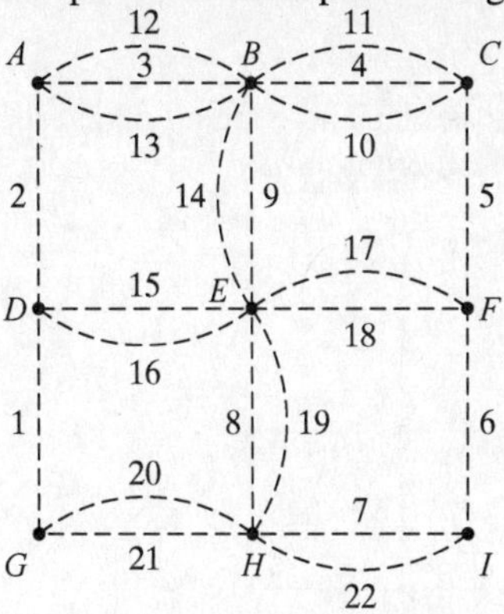

17. We may begin anywhere, since there are no odd vertices. We erase edges as we go, till we have the Euler circuit. We begin at A.

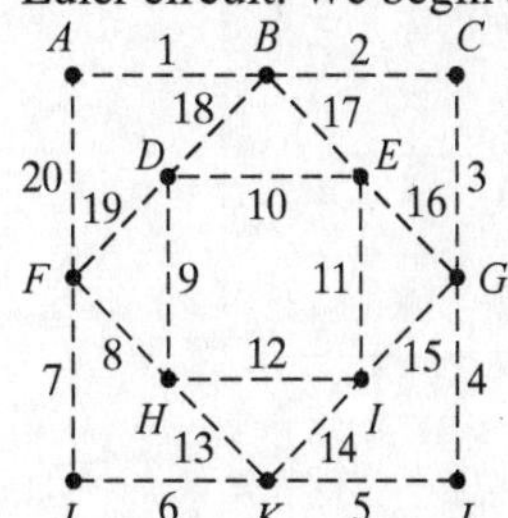

18. a. Yes, they would. The graph has exactly two odd vertices, so there is an Euler path.

b.

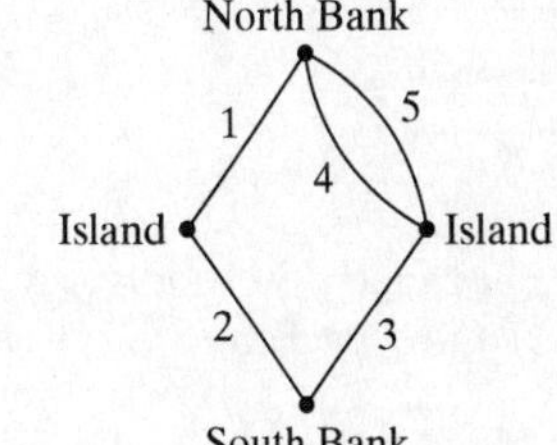

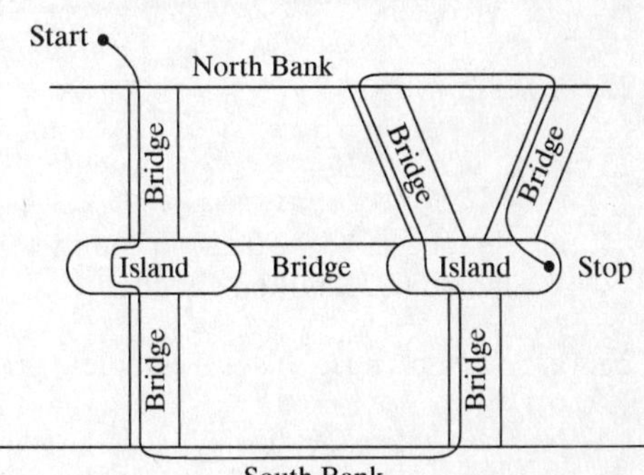

c. No; there is no such path. Since the graph has odd vertices, it does not have an Euler circuit.

19. Yes, it is possible. There are exactly two odd vertices, and therefore there is an Euler path (but no Euler circuit).

20. a. Yes it is possible. There are no odd vertices, so there is an Euler circuit.

b.

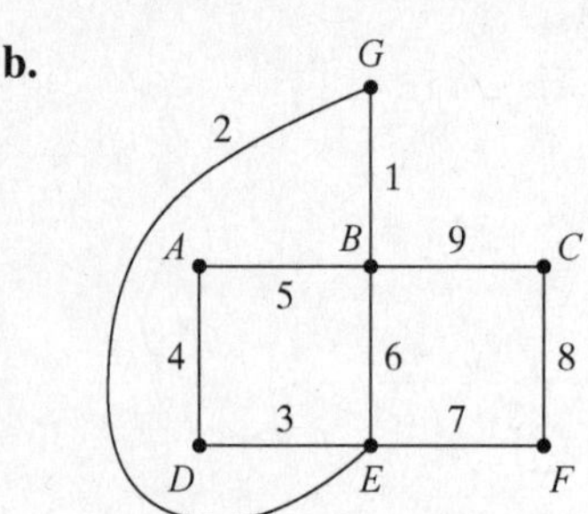

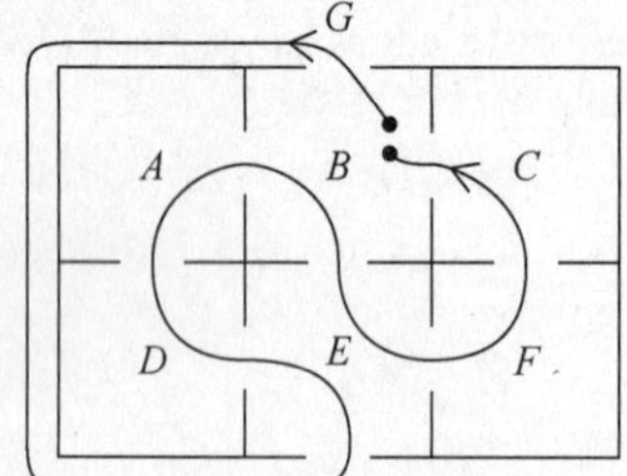

21. a.

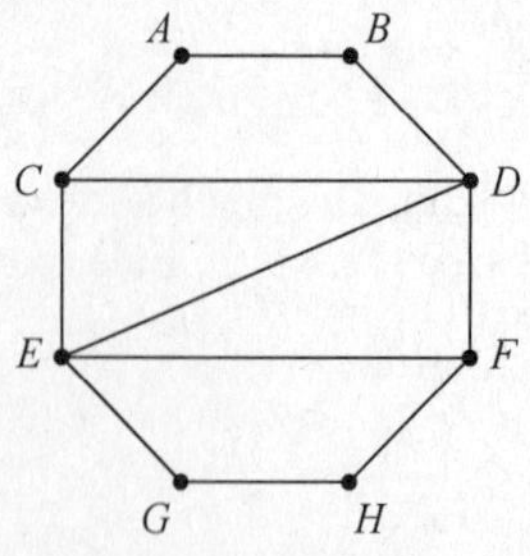

b. Yes. There are exactly two odd vertices *C* and *F*, so there is an Euler path.

c. The guard should begin at *C* and end at *F*, or vice versa.

22. *A, E, C, B, D, A*

23. *D, B, A, E, C, D*

24. a. No, because this is not a complete graph. It may not have Hamilton circuits.

25. a. Yes, because this is a complete graph.

b. $(4 - 1)! = 3! = 6$

26. a. No, because this is not a complete graph. It may not have Hamilton circuits.

27. a. Yes, because this is a complete graph.

b. $(5 - 1)! = 4! = 24$

28.

A, B, C, D, A:	$4 + 6 + 5 + 4$	=	19
A, B, D, C, A:	$4 + 7 + 5 + 2$	=	18
A, C, B, D, A:	$2 + 6 + 7 + 4$	=	19
A, C, D, B, A:	$2 + 5 + 7 + 4$	=	18
A, D, B, C, A:	$4 + 7 + 6 + 2$	=	19
A, D, C, B, A:	$4 + 5 + 6 + 4$	=	19

29. These are the only possible Hamilton circuits on a graph with 4 vertices. The lowest weight, 18, occurs on the circuits *A, B, D, C, A* and *A, C, D, B, A*. These are the optimal solutions.

30. Start with *A*. Then edge *AC* has the smallest weight, 2, of all edges starting at *A*. Proceed to *C*. From *C*, edge *CD* has the smallest weight, 5, of edges not returning to *A*. From *D*, we must travel *DB*, with weight 7, to *B*. We return to *A* along *BA*, with weight 4. The total weight of this Hamilton circuit is $2 + 5 + 7 + 4 = 18$.

31. Start with *A*. Of all paths leading from *A*, the path with smallest weight is *AB*, with weight 4. Proceed to *B*. The path with smallest weight leading from *B*, but not to *A*, is *BE*, with weight 6. The path with smallest weight leading from *E*, but not to *A* or *B*, is *ED*, with weight 4. From *D*, we proceed along *DC*, with weight 3, to *C*, the only remaining vertex. We then return to *A* along *CA*, with weight 7. The total weight is $4 + 6 + 4 + 3 + 7 = 24$.

32.

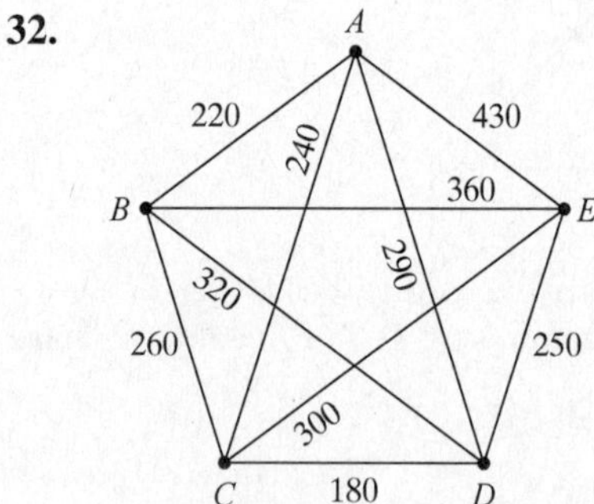

33. Start at *A*. The lowest cost from *A*, \$220, is on edge *AB*. From *B*, the lowest cost other than returning to *A* is \$260, on edge *BC*. From *C*, the lowest cost to a new city is \$180, on edge *CD*. From *D*, the salesman must fly to *E* for \$250, then return to *A* for \$430. The total cost of this circuit is $220 + 260 + 180 + 250 + 430 = \$1340$.

34. Yes. It is connected, has no circuits, has 6 edges on 7 vertices, and each edge is a bridge.

35. No. It has a circuit.

36. No. It is disconnected.

37.

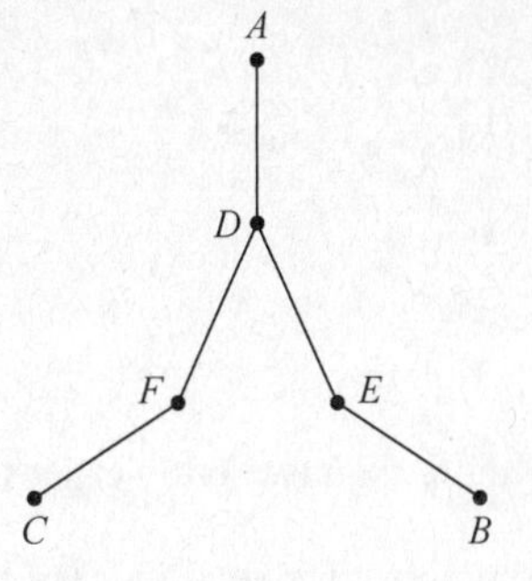

38.

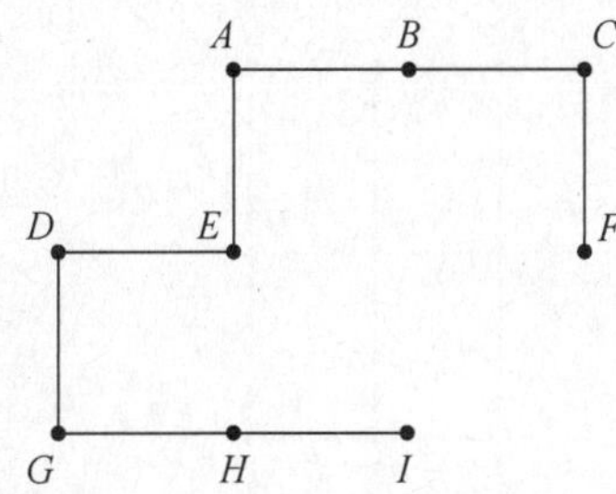

39. Kruskal's algorithm is demonstrated in the figure.

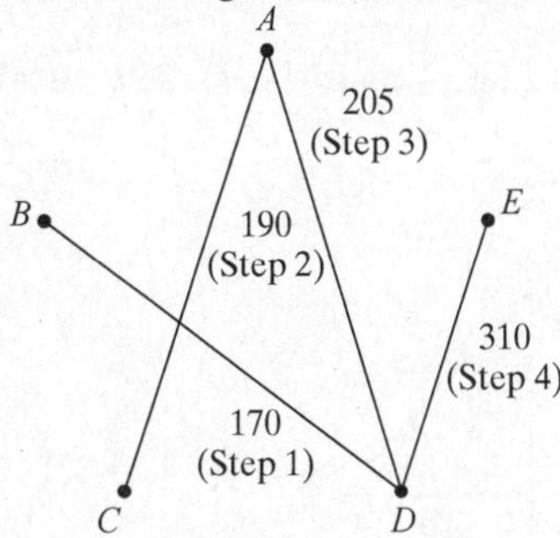

The total weight is
170 + 190 + 205 + 310 = 875.

40. Kruskal's algorithm is demonstrated in the figure.

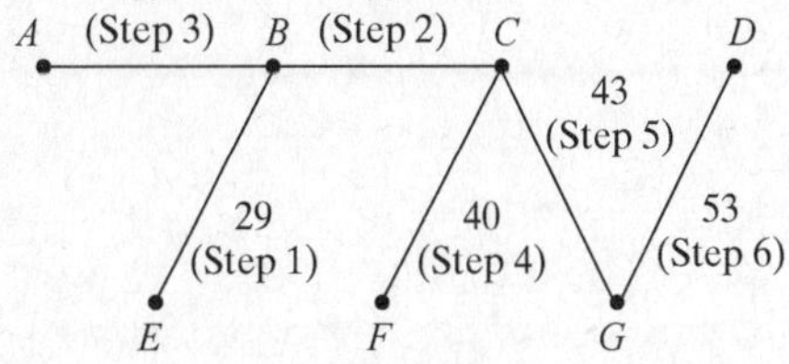

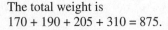

The total weight is
29 + 35 + 39 + 40 + 43 + 53 = 239.

41. The figure demonstrates Kruskal's algorithm and the layout of the cable system.

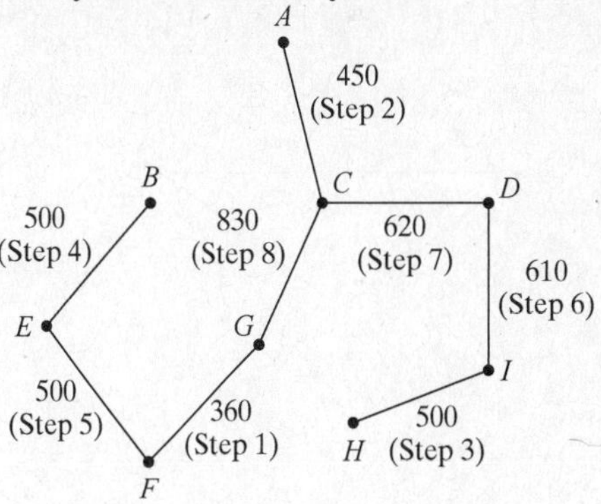

The smallest length of cable needed is
360 + 450 + 500 + 500 + 500 + 610 + 620 + 830 = 4370 miles.

Chapter 14 Test

1. *A*: 2; *B*: 2; *C*: 4; *D*: 3; *E*: 2; *F*: 1

2. *A, D, E* and *A, B, C, E*

3. *B, A, D, E, C, B*

4. *CF*

5.

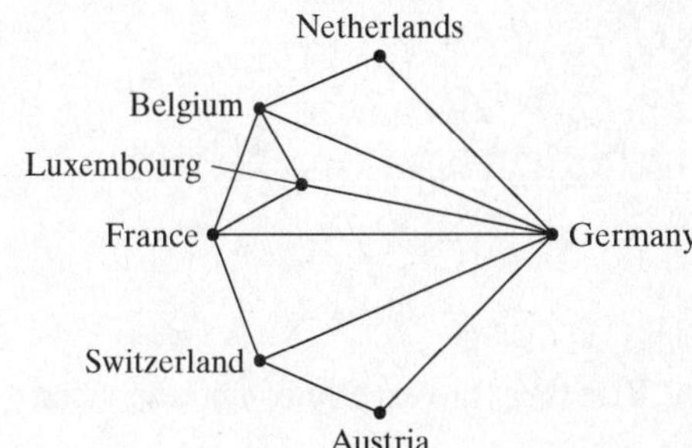

6. a. Euler path: there are exactly two odd vertices.

b.

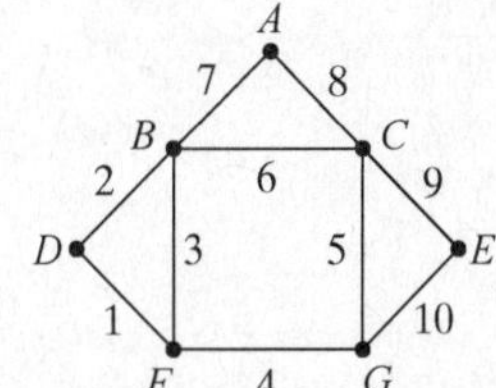

7. a. Neither: there are more than two odd vertices.

b. N/A

8. a. Euler circuit: there are no odd vertices.

b.

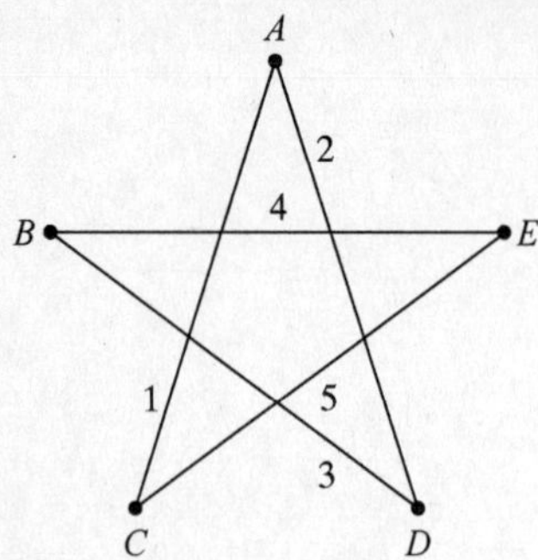

9. We begin at *A*, then proceed to *E, I, H*, and so on, erasing edges once they have been crossed. The result is shown in the figure.

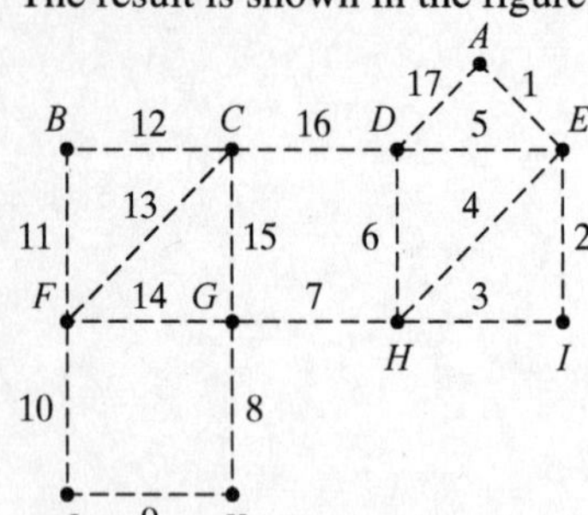

10. a.

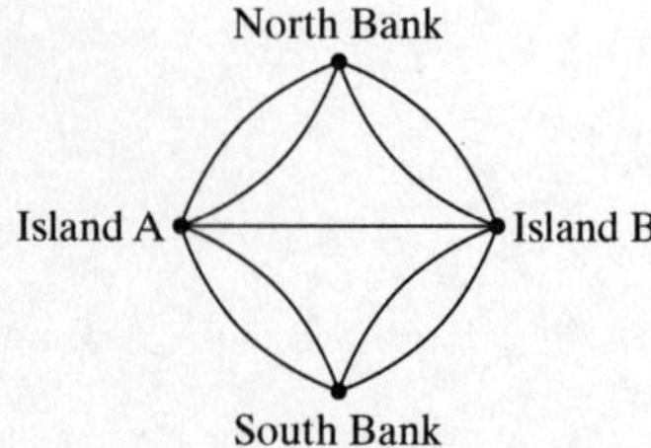

b. Yes: there are exactly two odd vertices.

c. It should begin at one of the islands, and end at the other island.

11. a.

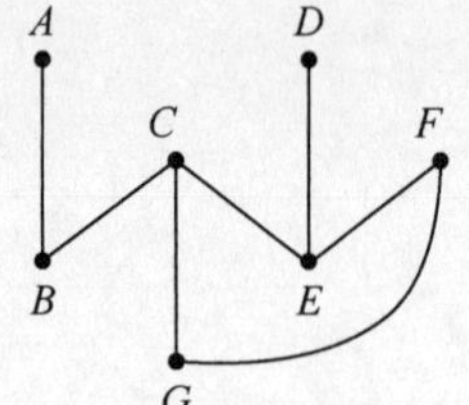

b. No: there are more than two odd vertices.

12. a. Let vertices represent intersections, and let edges represent streets.

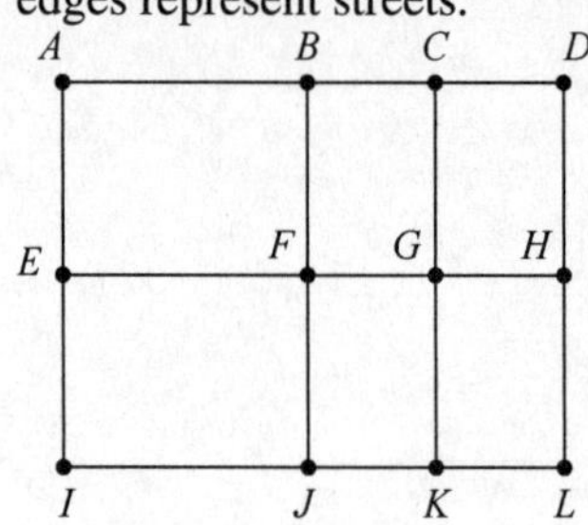

b. No: there are more than two odd vertices.

13. A, B, C, D, G, F, E, A and A, F, G, D, C, B, E, A.

14. $(5 - 1)! = 4! = 24$

15.

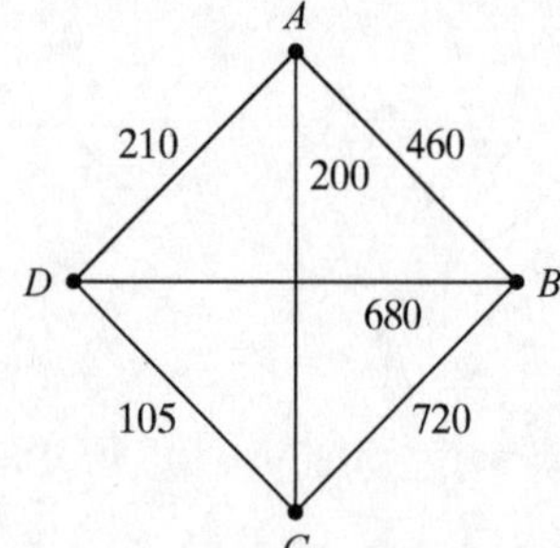

16.

Hamilton Circuit	Sum of the Weights of the Edges	=	Total Cost
A, B, C, D, A	460 + 720 + 105 + 210	=	$1495
A, B, D, C, A	460 + 680 + 105 + 200	=	$1445
A, C, B, D, A	200 + 720 + 680 + 210	=	$1810
A, C, D, B, A	200 + 105 + 680 + 460	=	$1445
A, D, B, C, A	210 + 680 + 720 + 200	=	$1810
A, D, C, B, A	210 + 105 + 720 + 460	=	$1495

The optimal route is *A, B, D, C, A* or *A, C, D, B, A*. The total cost for this route is $1445.

17. Starting from *A*, the edge with smallest weight is *AE*, with weight 5. Proceed to *E*. From *E*, the edge with smallest weight, and not leading back to *A*, is *ED*, with weight 8. From *D*, the edge with smallest weight, and to a new vertex, is *DC*, with weight 4. From *C*, only *B* remains. Edge *CB* has weight 5. Return to *A* by edge *BA*, with weight 11. The total weight of this Hamilton circuit is
$5 + 8 + 4 + 5 + 11 = 33$.

18. No; it has a circuit, namely *C, D, E, C*.

19.

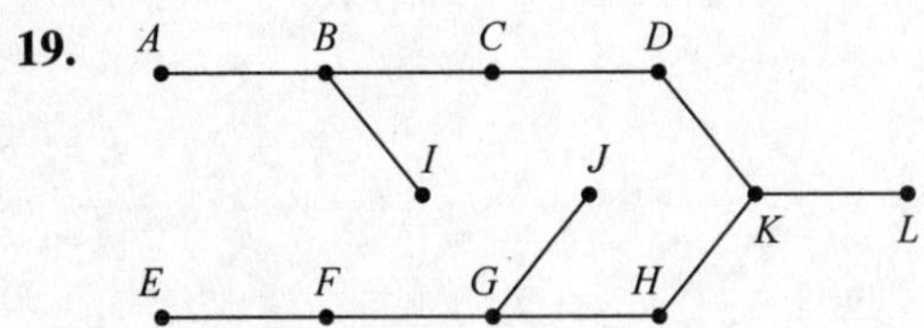

20. Kruskal's algorithm is shown in the figure.

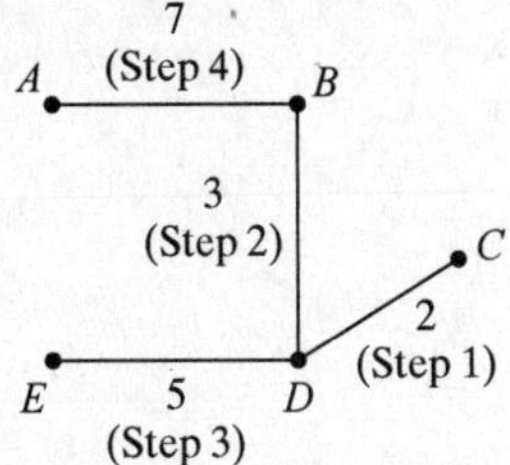

The total weight of the minimum spanning tree is $2 + 3 + 5 + 7 = 17$.